10-21-92 $375.00   (5 vols)

GREAT EVENTS
FROM
HISTORY II

GREAT EVENTS FROM HISTORY II

Human
Rights
Series

Volume 1
1900-1936

Edited by

FRANK N. MAGILL

SALEM PRESS

Pasadena, California   Englewood Cliffs, New Jersey

Library of Congress Cataloging-in-Publication Data
Great events from history II. Human rights series / edited by Frank N. Magill.
    p.   cm.
  Includes bibliographical references and index.
    1. Human rights—History—20th century—Chronol-
ogy. I. Magill, Frank Northen, 1907-

K3240.6.G74   1992
341.4'81'0904—dc20
ISBN 0-89356-643-8 (set)   92-12896
ISBN 0-89356-644-6 (volume 1)   CIP

PRINTED IN THE UNITED STATES OF AMERICA

PUBLISHER'S NOTE

Great Events from History II: Human Rights Series is the second set in the *Great Events from History II* series within the Magill family of reference books. This new series was inaugurated by *Great Events from History II: Science and Technology Series* (1991). The current volumes follow the format of the science and technology set, and, in addition, contain a geographical index to articles. This series joins the original, twelve-volume *Great Events from History: Ancient and Medieval* (three volumes, 1972), *Modern European* (three volumes, 1973), *American* (three volumes, 1975), and *Worldwide Twentieth Century* (three volumes, 1980). Combined, the volumes in the original *Great Events* series surveyed, in chronological order, major historical events throughout the world from 4000 B.C. to 1979.

The new series, *Great Events from History II* (GEFH II), will present entirely original articles, treating twentieth century events never before covered. The current five volumes of *Human Rights* address 462 topics in the history of human rights, both instances of human rights denial and human rights advances. GEFH II extends and supplements the original series by treating events by topic, rather than by geographical occurrence. Future volumes in GEFH II will concentrate on other major areas of contemporary culture.

Like the original *Great Events*, the articles in GEFH II are arranged chronologically by date of event, starting in 1900 with the Boxer Rebellion and ending in 1991 with market reforms in the restructured republics in the former Soviet Union. A broad range of human rights categories, twenty-seven in all, is addressed here. The categories, and the number of articles in each, are as follows: accused persons' rights (6), atrocities and war crimes (49), children's rights (10), civil rights (46), consumers' rights (11), disability rights (6), educational rights (6), gay persons' rights (7), health and medical rights (17), homeless people's rights (3), humanitarian relief (7), immigrants' rights (8), indigenous peoples' rights (28), international norms (4), nutrition (2), older persons' rights (2), peace movements and organizations (18), political freedom (51), prisoners' rights (14), racial and ethnic rights (45), refugee relief (9), religious freedom (5), reproductive freedom (10), revolutions and rebellions (30), voting rights (15), women's rights (24), and workers' rights (29). The categories overlap in content, covering as they do broad ranges of human experience. With that in mind, many articles are listed in the indexes under two separate categories.

The articles in this series run somewhat longer (2,500 words) than the entries in the original *Great Events* set, allowing more in-depth coverage of events that may have years of background and many areas of long-range significance. The format of these articles, while retaining the basic outline of the articles in the original series, has been somewhat revised to reflect the needs of the new subject orientation.

Each article still begins with the ready-reference listings: "Category of event" (describing the event under one or two of the areas listed above), "Time" (range of years, year, or, where applicable, specific date of event), and "Locale" (geographic location). Each article then gives a brief (two- or three-line) summary of the event and its significance. A list of "Principal Personages" who were key players in the event follows. The text begins with a "Summary of Event," a description of the event itself and background relevant to it. Here might be described the circumstances that led up to the event and backgrounds of the people involved. The "Impact of Event" section (which did not appear in the original *Great Events* series) devotes itself to an assessment of the immediate and long-range significance of the action, legislation, policy change, or other human rights development. Next, an annotated bibliography lists and describes between five and ten sources for further study, enabling the reader to choose among books and articles that will cast more light on the topic. These sources have been chosen for their relevance to the topic in question and for ease of availability. Finally, the "Cross-References" appearing at the end of each article lead the reader to other articles of interest which appear in the current five volumes.

In a reference work of this type, in which articles are arranged chronologically to provide a temporal perspective on the individual events, the editors thought it useful to add a complete chronological listing of all 462 articles at the end of each volume. In addition, several indexes were thought to be not only desirable but also necessary to provide maximum flexibility in retrieving information. At the end of volume 5, the reader will find five indexes: The "Alphabetical List of Events" indexes events alphabetically by article title; the "Key Word Index" cross-references events by several words per title; the "Category Index" lists all articles by human rights area (such as civil rights or political freedom); the "Geographical Index" separates articles by their country of occurrence, reflecting the international scope of the volumes; and finally, "Principal Personages" lists all key figures appearing in the corresponding subsection of each article, so that readers may find easily the events in which a particular person played a key role. In all five of these useful indexes, both the volume number and the page number appear following each index entry.

Great Events from History II: Human Rights Series, unlike the original *Great Events*, lists complete names of the academicians and scholars who wrote these articles, both at the end of the article, in a byline, and in a listing of contributors to be found in the front matter to volume 1. We wish to acknowledge the efforts of these specialists and thank them for making their expert knowledge accessible to the general reader.

CONTRIBUTING REVIEWERS

Patricia Alkema
Independent Scholar

G. Anandalingam
Independent Scholar

Robert B. Andersen
Bridgewater College

Frank W. Andritzky
Concordia University

Stanley Archer
Texas A&M University

Tom L. Auffenberg
Ouachita Baptist University

Abdulla K. Badsha
University of Wisconsin—Madison

James A. Baer
Northern Virginia Community College

Ann Marie B. Bahr
South Dakota State University

JoAnn Balingit
Independent Scholar

Geoffrey Bar-Lev
Independent Scholar

Iraj Bashiri
University of Minnesota

Erving E. Beauregard
University of Dayton

Patricia A. Behlar
Pittsburg State University

S. Carol Berg
College of Saint Benedict

Jack Bermingham
Pacific Lutheran University

John W. Biles
Southwestern University

Robert E. Biles
Sam Houston State University

Arthur Blaser
Chapman College

Jo-Ellen Lipman Boon
Independent Scholar

Gordon L. Bowen
Mary Baldwin College

Michael R. Bradley
Matlaw College

John Braeman
University of Nebraska—Lincoln

John A. Britton
Francis Marion College

William S. Brockington, Jr.
University of South Carolina at Aiken

Alan Brown
Livingston University

Kendall W. Brown
Brigham Young University

M. Leann Brown
University of Florida

Dallas L. Browne
Southern Illinois University at Edwardsville
York College of the City University of New York

Anthony R. Brunello
Eckerd College

Maurice P. Brungardt
Loyola University, New Orleans

David D. Buck
University of Wisconsin—Milwaukee

William H. Burnside
John Brown University

Laura M. Calkins
Oglethorpe University

Pamela Canal
Independent Scholar

Christopher J. Canfield
Independent Scholar

Byron D. Cannon
University of Utah

Sheila Carapico
University of Richmond

Frederick B. Chary
Indiana University Northwest

S. M. Chiu
Temple University

Peng-Khuan Chong
Plymouth State

Lawrence Clark III
Independent Scholar

B. Mawiyah Clayborne
Maharishi International University

Cynthia Price Cohen
Ralph Bunch Institute on the United Nations

Robert Cole
Utah State University

Robert O. Collins
University of California, Santa Barbara

Bernard A. Cook
Loyola University, New Orleans

David A. Crain
South Dakota State University

Nathaniel Davis
Harvey Mudd College

Roger P. Davis
University of Nebraska at Kearney

Bill Delaney
Independent Scholar

Connie de la Vega
University of San Francisco

Charles A. Desnoyers
La Salle University

Mustafah Dhada
University of Northern Colorado

Dixie Dean Dickinson
Tidewater Community College

Thomas I. Dickson
Auburn University

Jack Donnelly
University of North Carolina at Chapel Hill

John Dorman
Independent Scholar

David Leonard Downie
University of North Carolina at Chapel Hill

Daniel J. Doyle
Pennsylvania College of Technology

Jennifer Eastman
Mount Ida College

Craig M. Eckert
Eastern Illinois University

Christopher H. Efird
Sam Houston State University

David G. Egler
Western Illinois University

Robert P. Ellis
Worcester State College

Peter C. Engelman
New York University

Richard B. Finnegan
Stonehill College

Alan M. Fisher
California State University, Dominguez Hills

Nancy Elizabeth Fitch
Temple University
Lynchburg College in Virginia

Carol Franks
Portland State University

Richard A. Fredland
Indiana University-Purdue University at
Indianapolis

Larry N. George
California State University, Long Beach

Mitchel Gerber
Southeast Missouri State University

Hashim Gibrill
Clark Atlanta University

K. Fred Gillum
Colby College

Robert F. Gorman
Southwest Texas State University

Forest L. Grieves
University of Montana

Johnpeter Horst Grill
Mississippi State University

Jimmie F. Gross
Armstrong State College

Surendra K. Gupta
Pittsburg State University

CONTRIBUTING REVIEWERS

Nancy N. Haanstad
Weber State University

Cathy Moran Hajo
New York University

Celia Hall-Thur
Wenatchee Valley College

William Haltom
University of Puget Sound

Frances Vryling Harbour
George Mason University

Claude Hargrove
Fayetteville State University

Katy Jean Harriger
Wake Forest University

Fred R. van Hartesveldt
Fort Valley State College

Glenn Hastedt
James Madison University

Louis D. Hayes
University of Montana

Arthur W. Helweg
Western Michigan University

Michael F. Hembree
Florida State University

Mary A. Hendrickson
Wilson College

Mark Henkels
Western Oregon State College

Howard M. Hensel
Air War College

Gerald Horne
University of California, Santa Barbara

Ronald K. Huch
University of Papua, New Guinea

Mahmood Ibrahim
California State Polytechnic University, Pomona

Robert Jacobs
Central Washington University

Andrew Jamison
California State University, Northridge

Robert J. Janosik
Occidental College

Shakuntala Jayaswal
University of New Haven

Robert L. Jenkins
Mississippi State University

Philip Dwight Jones
Bradley University

Joseph S. Joseph
University of Cyprus

Richard C. Kagan
Hamline University

Edward Kannyo
Wells College

Paul W. Knoll
University of Southern California

Gregory C. Kozlowski
DePaul University

Sai Felicia Krishna-Hensel
Auburn University

P. R. Lannert
Independent Scholar

Caroline Godwin Larson
Independent Scholar

Eugene S. Larson
Los Angeles Pierce College

Michael M. Laskier
Spertus College of Judaica

Douglas A. Lea
Pennsylvania College of Technology
Pennsylvania State University
Kutztown University

Jean-Robert Leguey-Feilleux
Saint Louis University

Thomas T. Lewis
Mount Senario College

Roger D. Long
Eastern Michigan University

William C. Lowe
Mount Saint Clare College

Arthur L. Lowrie
University of South Florida

Dennis C. McAndrews
Attorney-at-Law

Lawrence J. McAndrews
St. Norbert College

Earlean M. McCarrick
University of Maryland

A. Kyle McClure
Independent Scholar

Arthur F. McClure
Central Missouri State University

Jennifer Cobb McClure
Independent Scholar

Judith H. McClure
Warrensburg R-VI School District

Scott McElwain
University of San Francisco

James Edward McGoldrick
Cedarville College

Paul Madden
Hardin-Simmons University

Cynthia Keppley Mahmood
University of Maine

Barry Mann
University of San Diego

Nancy E. Marion
University of Akron

Renée Marlin-Bennett
American University

Lyndon C. Marshall
College of Great Falls

Rubén O. Martinez
University of Colorado at Colorado Springs

Thomas David Matijasic
Prestonsburg Community College

Jonathan Mendilow
Rider College

Michael W. Messmer
Commonwealth University

Joan E. Meznar
University of South Carolina

Vidya Nadkarni
University of San Diego

Joseph L. Nogee
University of Houston

Cathal J. Nolan
University of British Columbia

Norma C. Noonan
Augsburg College

Robert C. Oberst
Nebraska Wesleyan University

Deepa Mary Ollapally
Swarthmore College

Kathleen K. O'Mara
State University of New York College at Oneonta

Ebere Onwudiwe
Central State University, Ohio

Kenneth O'Reilly
University of Alaska Anchorage

Judith A. Parsons
Sul Ross State University

Jerry A. Pattengale
Azusa Pacific College

D. G. Paz
Clemson University

Thomas R. Peake
King College

William A. Pelz
DePaul University

William E. Pemberton
University of Wisconsin—LaCrosse

Louis G. Perez
Illinois State University

Nis Petersen
Jersey City State College

Steven L. Piott
Clarion University of Pennsylvania

Marjorie J. Podolsky
Pennsylvania State University, Behrend College

Edna B. Quinn
Salisbury State University

Gregory P. Rabb
Jamestown Community College

Michael Rawson
Legal Aid Society of Alameda County

E. A. Reed
University of Texas at Austin

CONTRIBUTING REVIEWERS

Dennis Reinhartz
University of Texas at Arlington

John K. Roth
Claremont McKenna College

Frank Louis Rusciano
Rider College

Allen Safianow
Indiana University at Kokomo

Eve N. Sandberg
Oberlin College

Daniel C. Scavone
University of Southern Indiana

Thomas C. Schunk
University of Wisconsin—Oshkosh

Catherine V. Scott
Agnes Scott College

Asit Kumar Sen
Texas Southern University

L. B. Shriver
Independent Scholar

R. Baird Shuman
University of Illinois at Urbana-Champaign

Claudena M. Skran
Lawrence University

Christopher E. Smith
University of Akron

Harold L. Smith
University of Houston—Victoria

Ira Smolensky
Monmouth College

Richard B. Spence
University of Idaho

Taylor Stults
Muskingum College

Susan A. Stussy
Independent Scholar

J. K. Sweeney
South Dakota State University

Renée Taft
Council for the International Exchange of Scholars

Robert D. Talbott
University of Northern Iowa

Darryl C. Thomas
State University of New York at Binghamton

Jack Ray Thomas
Bowling Green State University

Stephen C. Thomas
University of Colorado at Denver

Randal J. Thompson-Dorman
U.S. Agency for International Development

Larry Thornton
Hanover College

H. Christian Thorup
Cuesta College

Glen E. Thurow
University of Dallas

Leslie V. Tischauser
Prairie State College

Evelyn Toft
Fort Hays State University

Howard Tolley, Jr.
University of Cincinnati

Mfanya Donald Tryman
Mississippi State University

Jiu-Hwa Lo Upshur
Eastern Michigan University

Indu Vohra
DePauw University

Laurie Voice
Sam Houston State University

Shirley Ann Wagner
Fitchburg State College

Thomas Jay Edward Walker
Pennsylvania College of Technology

Gregory J. Walters
Saint Mary's University

Frederick A. Wasser
Temple University

Donald V. Weatherman
Arkansas College

Martha Ellen Webb
Independent Scholar

Marcia J. Weiss
Point Park College

LIST OF EVENTS IN VOLUME I

LIST OF EVENTS IN VOLUME I

GREAT EVENTS
FROM
HISTORY II

THE BOXER REBELLION FAILS TO REMOVE FOREIGN CONTROL IN CHINA

Category of event: Revolutions and rebellions
Time: June-September, 1900
Locale: North China, especially Shantung and Chihli Provinces

The Boxer Rebellion marked the final attempt of the Chinese of the Ch'ing Dynasty to throw off the yoke of foreign imperialism

> *Principal personages:*
>   CHANG CHIH-TUNG (1837-1909), the governor-general of Hunan-Hupei, famous advocate of "self-strengthening" and ardent opponent of the Boxers
>   JUNG-LU (1836-1903), the principal adviser to Empress Dowager Tz'u-hsi
>   KUANG-HSÜ (1871-1908), the Chinese emperor imprisoned by his aunt Tz'u-hsi in the wake of the "One Hundred Days of Reform" of 1898
>   LI HUNG-CHANG (1823-1901), an influential Chinese official and a leading advocate of conciliation with foreign powers
>   TZ'U-HSI (1835-1908), China's Empress Dowager who, following the *coup d'état* of 1898, became sole ruler
>   COUNT ALFRED VON WALDERSEE (1832-1904), the commander of the international relief force sent to Beijing

Summary of Event

After the First Opium War (1839-1842) with Great Britain, China was continually subjected to foreign pressure. The Treaty of Nanking (1842), following the First Opium War, and the Tientsin Treaty (1858) and Peking Convention (1860), following the Second Opium War, allowed a system of foreign enclaves, the Treaty Ports, to be set up in dozens of Chinese cities. Foreign diplomats, not Chinese officials, controlled trade, administration, the collection of customs revenues, and the dispensing of justice in the Treaty Ports. By the late 1890's, this practice of extraterritoriality had been extended to cover all foreigners, and even Chinese subjects who had converted to Christianity were exempt from the power of Chinese courts.

Starting with the cession of Hong Kong to the British in 1842, the Ch'ing (Manchu) Dynasty had been forced to surrender territory and sovereignty as a result of war or threat. Russia exerted pressure in Manchuria and Central Asia; France seized control of Indochina in 1884; and a newly modernized Japan humiliated China in a war over influence in Korea in 1894-1895 and took Taiwan as a prize. In the wake of the Korean defeat, the older treaty powers redoubled their efforts, and new players, especially Germany, entered the race for concessions.

Despite persistent attempts at modernization, most notably the "self-strengthening movement" led by the officials Li Hung-chang and Chang Chih-tung, imperial armies and fleets routinely found themselves overmatched. Additionally, the great Taiping Rebellion (1850-1864) and the Nien and Muslim uprisings in the 1860's and 1870's—which by some estimates collectively took upward of thirty million lives—stretched resources to the limit and devastated much of the most productive land in the empire. By the late 1890's, secret societies and antiforeign militia had proliferated, particularly in the northern provinces of Chihli, Shantung, and Shensi, where Christian missionary activity and foreign encroachment had most recently become prominent.

In November, 1897, Germany, as part of a comprehensive program of naval expansion, had demanded and received a naval base and concession at Kiaochow Bay in Shantung. The methods by which the Germans consolidated their position, including punitive forays into the surrounding countryside and demands for the safety of their missionaries, increasingly inflamed the sensibilities of local groups and officials. Among the most prominent of these was an association of secret societies called the *I-ho ch'üan* (the Association of Righteousness and Harmony), most commonly known as the "Righteous and Harmonious Fists." As part of its ritual exercises, this group practiced the ancient Chinese art of *t'ai-chi ch'uan*, which included a form of shadow-boxing, prompting the foreign nickname of "Boxers."

The origin of the Boxers is obscure, but it is generally agreed that several of their constituent organizations had taken part in the White Lotus Rebellion of 1796-1804. Their beliefs may be characterized as nativist and fundamentalist: a blend of Taoist naturalism, Buddhist spirituality, Confucian ethics and politics, and a strong antiforeign bent. Previously, this had taken the form of anti-Ch'ing activities because the Manchus, who had founded the dynasty and still occupied the principal court positions, were ethnically distinct from the Han Chinese majority and were thus depicted in the Boxers' iconography as "foreign." Increasingly, however, the emphasis shifted to antimissionary activity, especially after the Germans extended their control over Shantung, the birthplace of Confucius, in 1898.

The Ch'ing government found itself in an increasingly untenable position. On one hand, it faced pressure from the Boxers and other hostile secret societies to protect the empire from foreign encroachment, while on the other, it had to recognize increasingly strident foreign demands to suppress antiforeign disorder. For a brief period in the summer of 1898, it seemed as if some of these issues would be resolved. Emperor Kuang-hsü, having recently attained his majority, now attempted, under the guidance of his adviser K'ang Yu-wei, an ambitious reform of Chinese governmental institutions along the lines of the Meiji Restoration in Japan. However, this "One Hundred Days of Reform" came to an abrupt end in September, 1898, when Kuang-hsü's aunt, the Empress Dowager Tz'u-hsi, prompted by her chief adviser, Jung-lu, and fearful of the consequences of extensive reform, staged a *coup d'état*. Kuang-hsü was placed under house arrest, K'ang Yu-wei barely fled with his life, and Tz'u-hsi ruled outright, swinging the dynasty toward a much more narrowly antiforeign position.

Encouraged by the tacit support of many local officials in North China, including the governor of Shantung, the Boxers staged increasingly provocative attacks on foreigners. By the summer of 1899, the major Boxer groups in Shantung, led by the Big Sword Society (*Ta-tao hui*), had taken as their slogan "*fu-Ch'ing, mieh-yang*" (support the Ch'ing, exterminate the foreigners) and with official support had now become the *I-ho t'uan*, or "Righteous and Harmonious Militia." The foreign powers, during the winter of 1899-1900, presented the Imperial Court with increasingly heated demands for suppression of the Boxers and threatened to send troops.

The Empress Dowager, impressed with the success of the militia in destroying foreign railroads and settlements, and fascinated by their claims of invulnerability to foreign bullets, called upon the army and people to defend the country from an anticipated invasion by the foreign powers. Emboldened by this outright imperial support, Boxer groups in Beijing, the metropolitan province of Chihli, and adjacent Shensi staged massive antiforeign demonstrations of their own. Hundreds of missionaries and thousands of Chinese converts were wounded and killed, often in deliberately gruesome fashion. A foreign relief force sent from Tientsin was turned back by Boxers and Chinese army units in early June. The German minister to China, Count Clemens von Ketteler, was shot down in the capital's streets. On June 21, 1900, the Ch'ing government declared war on all the treaty powers in China and commanded Boxer militia to besiege Beijing's foreign legation quarter.

The edict of June 21 directed Chinese officials throughout the empire to use their forces in conjunction with the Boxers to attack foreign strong points. With the exception of those in North China with close Boxer affiliations, however, provincial officials in the rest of the empire ignored, defied, or did their best to stall the implementation of the orders. Many of the army commanders, such as future Chinese president Yüan Shih-k'ai, maintained a considerable skepticism about the Boxers' combat abilities and did their best to stay aloof from the fighting. Disillusionment with the seemingly futile declaration of war and the leadership which implemented it, sympathy for the captive emperor and the expelled reformers, and the muted influence of more cosmopolitan Chinese officials all served to keep conditions in the capital chaotic and to blunt the force of the Boxers' siege of the legations.

By late July, a powerful international relief force of twenty thousand men, including Germans, Japanese, Americans, British, Russians, French, Austrians, and Italians, had been assembled in Tientsin under the command of Count Alfred von Waldersee. After two weeks of daily skirmishes and several intense fights, the allied forces fought their way to Beijing, entered the city through an unguarded sewer gate, and ended the siege of the legations on August 14. The court fled to Sian, most government forces surrendered quickly, and the Boxers, who had proven largely unreliable in battle, melted quickly into the North China countryside.

Incensed by the brutality meted out to foreigners and Chinese Christians at the hands of the Boxers, the allies launched continuous punitive expeditions into the suburbs of Beijing and Tientsin, burning, looting, and summarily executing suspected Boxers. International forces remained in occupation of the capital until September, 1901, and the Empress Dowager and her court did not return until the beginning of 1902.

The final peace treaty, the Boxer Protocols, accepted by the Chinese on January 16, 1901, was the most severe of the many "unequal treaties" imposed on China during the sixty years following the First Opium War. Among its provisions were allied demands for the execution, exile, degrading, and dismissal of officials charged with collaborating with the Boxers, the suspension of official examinations (based on classical texts of Confucianism) for five years in cities where Boxer activity had taken place, foreign occupation of the Beijing-Tientsin corridor, the erection of expiatory statues of von Ketteler and other "martyrs," and a crippling indemnity of $333 million. The indemnity, payable over thirty-nine years at four percent interest, required installments nearly matching the annual revenue of the empire.

Impact of Event

The immediate consequence of the Boxer Rebellion and Protocols was that the Ch'ing Dynasty effectively squandered its diminished legitimacy in the eyes of both the Chinese and the rest of the world while the roots of nationalism spread steadily, especially among Chinese communities abroad. While China avoided the fate of partition, the Manchu government appeared to be largely under the control of foreign powers. The weakness and lack of moral prestige of the central government contributed greatly to the trend toward regionalism which had been growing since mid-century. The most reactionary officials were purged, but people of ability, particularly those with modern or foreign training, tended to avoid taking their place in a government that had proven itself lacking in its hour of crisis. For the city dwellers in the ports and the peasants in the countryside, it appeared that nothing had been accomplished except an increase in foreign arrogance, Manchu ineptitude, and their own misery.

The empire was now in severe financial straits. The customs revenue (already under foreign control), internal transit taxes, and salt tax collectively proved inadequate to service the indemnity. The result was both a large increase in the tax burden of Chinese subjects and also the wholesale borrowing of money from Western banks to make the scheduled installments.

The Empress Dowager, fearful of reform in 1898, now reluctantly allowed many of the edicts of the "Hundred Days" to be implemented. The official examinations were abandoned in favor of more modern curricula. Army training was revamped to give an emphasis on modern weapons and tactics. A number of sinecure positions in the bureaucracy were eliminated. The most ambitious of the reforms was an alteration of the form of government itself. Chinese officials toured the West, studying various legislative systems. A plan for a constitutional monarchy was prepared, and in 1909 and 1910 elections were held for regional and national parliamentary bodies.

Already, however, the initiative had passed to a wide spectrum of reformers and revolutionaries for whom the Boxer Rebellion had proven conclusively that the Ch'ing had grown incapable of reform and too weak to rule. They ranged from the exiled K'ang Yu-wei, whose Constitutional Monarchist Party was soon superseded, to radical anarchist cells specializing in bombings and assassinations. Ultimately, the Revolutionary Alliance of Sun Yat-sen, encompassing a variety of republican, nationalist, reform, and secret society organizations, would mount the blow destined to topple this last Chinese dynasty on October 10, 1911. On February 12, 1912, the boy emperor P'u-i abdicated, ending millennia years of imperial rule.

Bibliography

Duiker, William J. *Cultures in Collision: The Boxer Rebellion.* San Rafael, Calif.: Presidio Press, 1978. A pioneering attempt to examine the cultural aspects of tradition and modernity as the background for the rise of the Boxers. English language references only.

Esherick, Joseph. *The Origins of the Boxer Uprising.* Berkeley: University of California Press, 1987. A major revisionist study based on extensive Chinese archival material and oral histories. Argues that the Boxers were never antidynastic, but instead that their opposition to Christianity grew out of the "social ecology" of the region. Scholarly yet readable. Numerous appendices and references.

Fleming, Peter. *The Siege at Peking.* London: Hart-Davis, 1959. Competent, solid, in the best tradition of English popular history. Extensive coverage of battle plans, tactics, and fortifications. Dated English language bibliography; no Chinese or Japanese sources.

O'Connor, Richard. *The Spirit Soldiers: A Historical Narrative of the Boxer Rebellion.* New York: Putnam, 1973. Gripping narrative history of the rebellion with an emphasis on explicating Chinese motives and activities. Strong ironic tone in treating the issues of imperialism and international cooperation. Efforts at deeper appreciation of Chinese conditions are undercut by a lack of Chinese sources.

Price, Eva Jane. *China Journal, 1889-1900: An American Missionary Family During the Boxer Rebellion.* New York: Scribner, 1989. A fine description of the strengths, shortcomings, and ultimate tragedy of the missionary enterprise in China as seen through the eyes of its practitioners. The letters and journal of the Prices, right up to the hour of their execution at the hands of a fraudulent military escort, reflect their deep love of the people, unflagging fortitude and good humor, and ultimate inability to comprehend fully the reasons for their fate.

Tan, Chester C. *The Boxer Catastrophe.* New York: W. W. Norton, 1971. Classic study, using extensive Chinese source material, of the diplomatic history of the rebellion. Tan's thesis that imperialism and Ch'ing ineptitude were the main causes of the movement has long been the standard interpretation. The volume is scholarly without being overly pedantic, and its great wealth of sources makes it highly useful to the expert as well as to the layperson.

Charles A. Desnoyers

Cross-References

Sun Yat-sen Overthrows the Ch'ing Dynasty (1911), p. 116; Students Demonstrate for Reform in China's May Fourth Movement (1919), p. 276; Japanese Troops Brutalize Chinese After the Capture of Nanjing (1937), p. 539; China Initiates a Genocide Policy Toward Tibetans (1950), p. 826; China Occupies Tibet (1950), p. 837; Mao Delivers His "Speech of One Hundred Flowers" (1956), p. 958; The Chinese Cultural Revolution Starts a Wave of Repression (1966), p. 1332; Demonstrators Gather in Tiananmen Square (1989), p. 2483.

THE PHILIPPINES ENDS ITS UPRISING
AGAINST THE UNITED STATES

Categories of event: Revolutions and rebellions; atrocities and war crimes
Time: 1902
Locale: The Philippines

Expansionism by the United States in the Philippines awakened feelings of ambivalence, selfishness, and altruism among the American people regarding treatment of Filipinos

Principal personages:
WILLIAM McKINLEY (1843-1901), the president of the United States from 1897 until his assassination early in 1901
THEODORE ROOSEVELT (1858-1919), the president of the United States (replacing McKinley) from 1901 to 1909, who continued McKinley's expansionist policy
ELIHU ROOT (1845-1937), the secretary of war from 1899 to 1904, chief engineer of the Philippine policy
EMILIO AGUINALDO (1869-1964), the leader of the struggle for Philippine independence, captured in 1901 and held in Manila as a prisoner of the U.S. Army
HENRY CABOT LODGE (1850-1924), a Republican senator from Massachusetts
GAMALIEL BRADFORD (1863-1932), the cofounder of the Anti-Imperialist League, who harshly criticized the imperialist policies of the United States
CORNELIUS GARDENER (1849-1921), a major in the U.S. Army who served as United States governor of Tayabas Province in the Philippines

Summary of Event

The Spanish-American War of 1898 led to a number of direct territorial annexations by the United States of America. In December, 1898, a peace treaty was signed between the United States and Spain which officially turned over to the United States the islands of Guam, Puerto Rico, and the Philippines. In the case of the latter, $20 million was paid by the United States to Spain. Even with this remuneration, the taking of the Philippines by America led to heated debates within the McKinley Administration: Should this group of islands be left to themselves, or should they receive "guidance" through suzerainty from the victorious American nation? In the end, the fate of the Philippines was left to President McKinley, who believed that the Filipinos were ignorant and childlike, and therefore unfit for self-government. McKinley chose to "educate, uplift, civilize, and Christianize" them by annexing the islands. Secretary of War Elihu Root was appointed official overseer of this process.

He organized and charged a newly created Philippine Commission to maintain the "happiness, peace, and prosperity of the people" and committed the United States government to the establishment of courts, municipal governments, a civil service, and schools.

Under a policy of "benevolent assimilation," Filipinos were to be integrated officially into Western culture as espoused and practiced by the United States. Implicit in this cultural ideal was the rhetoric of Social Darwinism: natural selection and survival of the fittest. For the most part, Americans viewed the Filipinos with a mixture of condescension and scorn, secure in the belief that Filipinos were incapable of managing their own affairs. Attitudes such as these began to manifest themselves in a blend of selfishness and altruism. Many believed that the acquisition of territory by the United States was always motivated by the highest ideals. On the other hand, the American articulation of expansionist policies in the Philippines, which promoted Social Darwinian principles, often resulted in racist notions such as the concept of the "white man's burden." This burden made the wearing of the mantle of expansionism a somewhat difficult task for many Americans. Consequently, the entire Philippine incursion was treated by the American people with a mixture of ambivalence, selfishness, and altruism. "Benevolent assimilation" began to be defined by those government officials who were implementing it, and American policy tended to confront public ambivalence with a good dose of patriotic selfishness. In the process, altruism was all but lost as "benevolent assimilation" was implemented more for American goals than for Philippine self-determination. American benevolence became a policy which thrived on the acquisition of territory for its own end. Any Philippine opposition to this policy was seen as the failure of the Filipino culture to grasp the ideas of progress, thereby justifying McKinley's assessment of Filipinos' unfitness for self-governance.

American policy in the Philippines was always justified as humanitarian by design, especially when compared to the decidedly inhumane policies of the previous Spanish rule. For their part, the Filipinos apparently did not see any difference between the two outside ruling powers. In 1899, under the leadership of Emilio Aguinaldo, the Philippine Insurrection began. Aguinaldo had originally proposed (for services rendered to the United States against the Spanish during the war) Philippine independence within a United States protectorate. His proposal was rejected immediately by the American government following the removal of Spanish suzerainty over the islands. Instead of negotiating with the insurgents and assisting the Filipino people in their struggle for self-determination, the United States elected to go to war with the *insurrectos*, using seventy thousand American troops to crush the indigenous independence movement. Any pretext of rescuing the Filipinos from latent Spanish oppressive rule was all but abandoned by the end of 1899. American ideals of peacefully "civilizing the uncivilized" were soon replaced with racist attitudes which were implemented savagely. The Filipinos, even without significant weaponry, soon managed to return such savagery. This was a short-lived response. The American military and economic power were, in the long run, too much for the *insurrectos,* and in 1902 the conflict came to an end.

Beginning in July of 1901, the Roosevelt Administration "elevated the application of extreme measures . . . into a policy that was official and acknowledged." Such measures were often brutal. Letters revealing to soldiers' loved ones the harshness and wickedness of the insurrection began to find their way into print shortly after the Roosevelt policy was put into effect. Writing in the Springfield, Massachusetts *Daily Republican* on April 9, 1902, publicist and historian Gamaliel Bradford described the savagery of the infamous "water cure" to his American readers: "placing a man on his back, forcing open his mouth and pouring into him a pail of water, till he swells up like a toad, and then squeezing it out again." An extract in the *New York Evening Post* of April 8, 1902, described the water cure in more vivid detail:

> If the tortures I've mentioned are hellish, the water cure is plain hell. The native is thrown upon the ground, and, while his legs and arms are pinned, his head is raised partially so as to make pouring in the water an easier matter. An attempt to keep the mouth closed is of no avail, a bamboo stick or a pinching of the nose will produce the same effect. . . . A gallon of water is much but it is followed by a second and a third . . . a fourth and even a fifth gallon. . . . By this time the body becomes an object frightful to contemplate.

Associated Press dispatches from Manila in the last week of January, 1902, noted without comment that General J. Franklin Bell, United States Army commander of the troublesome southern Luzon province of Batangas, had recently instituted new measures for the pacification of the Philippines. Veterans of this new campaign corroborated the resulting action by describing the herding of entire village populations into detention camps, where they would be under the surveillance and guard of American troops to "ensure the isolation of insurgent guerrillas." According to Colonel Arthur Wagner, the American Army officer in charge of isolating insurgent guerrillas in Batangas province, all civilians were to enter these camps with no belongings. Detention centers on average alllowed a twelve-foot by six-foot area for each inhabitant. A soldier under General Bell's command insisted that Bell's inhumanity exceeded that of the hated Spaniards: "They were content with 'concentrating' the miserable women and children left after the devastation of farms and villages, but General Bell marks the husbands and fathers and brothers as criminals to be hanged when caught."

The indigenous population was not the only victim during the insurrection. The environment also suffered greatly. The American Army, charged with the "extensive burning of barrios" so that the *insurrectos* could not find sanctuary, destroyed hundreds of thousands of acres of fertile land in their attempts to pacify the natives. Testifying before the Lodge Committee, which investigated wartime atrocities, Major Cornelius Gardener stated that environmental destruction on this scale was necessary if the Army was going to induce a famine. Apparently, the insurgents—including any village suspected of housing or of even being related to an *insurrecto*—could not be allowed to find food anywhere. This campaign of starvation was relatively successful. Gardener went on to report that one-third of the population had been killed by military slaughter, famine, or pestilence.

Impact of Event

It was the view of many Americans that the Philippine Insurrection had to be crushed. The United States had fought for the islands and had officially purchased them from Spain: Why give them up to an undeserving indigenous population? Furthermore, if the United States did not control the islands, then the Germans or the British would most certainly colonize them. Finally, the duty to extend Christianity and civilization was part of the American mission to tutor backward peoples. These reasons, along with a foreign policy elite who believed that America must prove its power through an aggressive policy abroad, help to explain why there was so little attention paid to the inhumanity of this mission. To gloss over or cover up any wartime atrocities would show America to be weak; any nation which was weak would not expand, and any nation that did not expand would perish. In the eyes of American policy engineers, this attitude provided sufficient justification for the use of extreme measures. "It is not civilized warfare, [because] we are not dealing with civilized people. The only thing that they know and fear is force, violence, and brutality, and we give it to them." These attitudes, fueled by Social Darwinian principles, were pervasive in American society at the turn of the twentieth century and were actualized abroad by American forces in the Philippines.

Many American troops looked at the Filipinos as being of one race and condition. Because they were dark-skinned, these soldiers labeled them "niggers," an extension of the contempt they had for African Americans back home. United States governmental proclamations complemented these feelings. By implying the inferiority of the Filipinos, many government edicts reflected the recently formalized Jim Crow codes of the South and the segregationist practices of the cities and unions of the North. The individual American soldier in the Philippines became an overseer, a master to an inferior race which needed discipline and training so as to be properly integrated into the Western ideal. The name given to this training was "benevolent assimiliation." The force to implement this assimilation was imperialism, bothersome to many Americans because it showed a powerful nation being driven by brute expansionism, camouflaged by a cultural atmosphere of altruism.

Bibliography

May, Glenn Anthony. *Social Engineering in the Philippines: The Aims, Execution, and Impact of American Colonial Policy, 1900-1913*. Westport, Conn.: Greenwood Press, 1980. A comparative history, the goal of which is to study the impact of one set of values upon another. Analyzes the values and goals of Americans who made Philippine policy and of Filipinos upon whom it was imposed. Challenges the widely held view of the United States as an essentially successful colonial power. Includes appendices, index, and bibliographical essay.
Miller, Stuart Creighton. *Benevolent Assimilation: The American Conquest of the*

Philippines, 1899-1903. New Haven, Conn.: Yale University Press, 1982. Explores American imperialism as an aberration or as part of a historical continuum, focusing specifically on the conquest of the Philippines. Creighton draws upon a wide range of views from generals, presidents, and soldiers to analyze the war itself and its challenge to America's sense of innocence. Contains a bibliography and an index.

Schirmer, Daniel B. *Republic or Empire: American Resistance to the Philippine War.* Cambridge, Mass.: Schenkman, 1972. A carefully researched study of the period in the late nineteenth and early twentieth centuries during which the United States conclusively turned to an imperial course. Deals especially with the American anti-imperialists who appeared in force during this era and gives attention to the Philippine War they so vigorously opposed. Extensive exemplification through primary sources makes this a valuable research source.

Storey, Moorfield, and Julian Codman. *Secretary Root's Record: "Marked Severities" in Philippine Warfare.* Boston: George H. Ells, 1902. A valuable primary source which documents the "actions and utterances" of President Roosevelt and Secretary Root during the Philippine-American War, as noted in the "Law and Facts Hearing." Reprints telegraphic circulares concerning American military tactics which traveled between the Philippines and Washington, D.C. Storey and Codman also provide some revealing commentary on this correspondence and on testimony from the hearing.

Storey, Moorfield, and Marcial P. Lichauco. *The Conquest of the Philippines by the United States, 1898-1925.* New York: G. P. Putnam's Sons, 1926. Supplements and comments upon *Secretary Root's Record.* Suggests that the American people were led, through false statements and suppression of the truth, to support the taking of the Philippines and to believe in the "American mission." The lack of an index makes this book cumbersome for research use.

Welch, Richard E., Jr. *Response to Imperialism: The United States and the Philippine-American War, 1899-1902.* Chapel Hill: University of North Carolina Press, 1979. Analyzes the response of various sectors of American society to imperialism and to the Philippine-American War. Responses are analyzed in a manner that reveals the strength of such social forces as racism and patriotism. Bibliography and index.

Thomas Jay Edward Walker
Cynthia Gwynne Yaudes

Cross-References

The Boxer Rebellion Fails to Remove Foreign Control in China (1900), p. 1; Legal Norms of Behavior in Warfare Formulated by the Hague Conference (1907), p. 92; U.S. Marines Are Sent to Nicaragua to Quell Unrest (1912), p. 137; Soldiers Massacre Indian Civilians in Amritsar (1919), p. 264; The Atlantic Charter Declares a Postwar Right of Self-Determination (1941), p. 584; Roosevelt Approves Internment of Japanese Americans (1942), p. 595; Marcos Declares Martial Law in the Philippines (1972), p. 1680; The United Nations Issues a Declaration Against Torture (1975), p. 1847; Indigenous Indians Become the Target of Guatemalan Death Squads (1978), p. 1972; Opposition Leader Benigno Aquino Is Assassinated (1983), p. 2198.

REFORMERS EXPOSE ATROCITIES AGAINST CONGOLESE LABORERS

Categories of event: Workers' rights and civil rights
Time: 1903
Locale: Belgian Congo

King Leopold II of Belgium colonized the Congo Basin and maximized his personal profits by terrorizing and committing unspeakable atrocities against the people of the Congo

Principal personages:

LEOPOLD II (1835-1909), the royal monarch of Belgium, whose reign over the Belgian Congo created one of the worst labor scandals in colonial history

SIR CHARLES DILKE (1843-1911), an author and radical member of the British Parliament committed to the welfare of Africans, who exposed Leopold's atrocities to the British Parliament

EDMOND D. MOREL (1873-1924), the chairman of the Congo Reform Association, which fought to end King Leopold's rule of the Belgian Congo

TIPPU TIB (1837-1905), an Arab-Swahili trader, merchant, and administrator in Central Africa whose empire in the Eastern Congo was absorbed by Leopold II

HENRY MORTON STANLEY (1841-1904), a journalist, soldier, explorer, and pioneer of Central Africa

Summary of Event

As Europe emerged from its Dark Ages, it struggled to break the Arab stranglehold on trade by developing sea routes to other continents. By the late 1400's, Portugal had pioneered sea routes along Africa's west and southern coasts. During explorations of Africa's coast, Europeans made contact with many African states that had achieved roughly equal levels of political development. Among these was the Congo kingdom.

Europe became wealthy as a result of a bloody and violent trade that developed in African slaves. Moral outrage and declining profits, however, curtailed the slave trade in the New World by the late 1800's. Europeans sought a new basis for their relationship with Africa and tried free trade. Africans proved so adept at pitting European rivals against each other that they nearly caused wars in Europe between rival commercial partners. To prevent competition from escalating out of control, fourteen world powers convened a conference in Berlin in 1884-1885. In essence, they carved up Africa among themselves. Belgium received the Congo and the right to monopolize internal and external trade and government.

King Leopold II of Belgium convinced the Berlin conference to grant him exclusive control over the Congo by declaring that the state he would establish in the Congo would be a neutral field for all commercial activity and that the natives would benefit from the blessings of justice and good government. He denounced material motives for acquiring the Congo. Great Britain, fearing French and Portuguese rivalry, preferred to support Leopold, who appeared to them as weak and no real threat. Germany also supported Leopold's claim as one means of taking the French government's mind off Rhine territory lost to Germany.

Immediately after his claims on the Congo were given international recognition, Leopold II began assembling a vast African army commanded by Belgian officers. Many "recruits" were forced into service against their will. Boys as young as eleven years of age were conscripted, trained, and used as porters and as the core of future regiments. Officers were paid bonuses for every conscript recruited, whether voluntarily or involuntarily. Ruthless force was applied to those who refused to go voluntarily.

Arab slave traders were initially used by Leopold II as high and mid-level administrators. The most famous of these Swahili-Arabs was Tippu Tib, who had helped Henry Morton Stanley pacify the Congo Basin Africans and had become the chief administrator of the Eastern provinces. Tib demanded a share of the ivory profits earned in his districts. This annoyed the ambitious and greedy Leopold II. He declared to Berlin conference members his abhorrence of slavery and opposition to Arab slave traders. Leopold ordered his armies to annihilate all Arabs operating in the Congo. This earned for him the praise of Europe and left him as the undisputed ruler of the Congo. Tippu Tib and other Swahili-Arabs who survived this war lived out the balance of their lives in exile on the island of Zanzibar, off the coast of Tanzania.

Leopold II then issued clandestine orders to remove all non-Belgian European merchants from his territory. This was accomplished in part through heavy taxation, which ruined many merchants and forced others to relocate. It became apparent that Leopold II had never intended to honor his promise of making the Congo a neutral commercial zone.

Leopold's next move was to order that all officers securing very low prices for ivory be paid big personal bonuses; officers buying ivory from natives at high prices were given either small bonuses or no bonus at all. This guaranteed that Leopold would acquire large quantities of cheap ivory. His officers imposed ivory quotas upon villages. If a village's quota was not met, the village chief, along with village women and children, was kidnapped and held until the ivory quota was met. Selected victims were killed to force compliance when kidnapping proved to be insufficient motivation.

The pneumatic rubber tire was growing in popularity, and there was a growing demand for rubber on world markets. Rubber vines and trees grew in abundance in the Congo. Seeing this opportunity, Leopold established rubber quotas for villages in addition to ivory quotas. Chiefs were told to force villagers to supply the quota demanded or suffer punishment. Noncompliance was considered an act of rebellion, and Leopold's soldiers declared war on rebellious villages. Armed with rifles, his soldiers easily overwhelmed villagers armed with spears, bows and arrows, swords, and clubs. For every bullet fired in a village raid, Belgian officers demanded that their African soldiers present them with one left hand as proof that a rebel had been eliminated. In the 1890's, white officers became suspicious of their African troops' loyalty. Subsequently, whites demanded that their African soldiers bring them both the right hand and genitals of males killed. This was deemed necessary to prevent soldiers from killing women and children and presenting their hands as evidence that they had crushed a rebellion. Women and children from rebellious villages, if captured, were enslaved and forced into both prostitution and involuntary collection of rubber.

Soldiers also forced villagers to supply all the fish, meat, vegetables, and fruit that they ate, regardless of season. Fish are abundant, for example, only during certain seasons of the year. A villager who could not catch the quota often had to travel far downriver and buy the balance at exorbitant prices. In extreme cases, to make such payments a son or daughter was sold into slavery.

Leopold II claimed that he eliminated slavery in the Congo when, in fact, he had merely introduced it in a new form and driven out potential Arab competitors. Africans were forced to go deeper and deeper into forests occupied by leopards, venomous snakes, and other threats. They often neglected to grow food for themselves to ensure that they met their excessive rubber quotas. The only escape from Leopold's tyrannical reign of terror was death or escape to another colonial territory.

On top of other demands, Leopold forced each village to repair specified sections of roads, railway tracks, and harbors. Most of his African subjects suffered from a chronic lack of sleep and poor nutrition. Sleeping sickness and malaria killed many in areas where these diseases had been rare before Belgian rule. Populations declined by more than 60 percent between 1890 and 1900. In many cases, whole villages migrated to neighboring colonies to escape Leopold's cruelties.

Missionaries reported these atrocities as early as 1892. Their reports were ignored until Leopold's soldiers began raiding villages in British colonies and capturing Africans. Those who survived often returned home missing their left ears, left hands, or left feet. British officials were outraged that such atrocities were committed against British subjects for Leopold II's personal gain. Sir Charles Dilke, a radical member of the British Parliament, introduced evidence of these atrocities into parliamentary debates in 1897, 1903, 1904, 1905, and 1906. This created public awareness of these atrocities in Europe. Leopold consistently denied that he ordered, condoned, or had knowledge of these horrors. He gagged the Roman Catholic church by assassinating irritating missionaries and declared that rival rubber merchants, jealous of his success, were using agitation against him to mask their own personal ambitions.

The fact remained that the Congo's forests and natural resources were being used not to benefit the Congo's inhabitants but to profit King Leopold II and his associates. Henry Richard Fox Bourne of the Aborigines Protection Society began writing extensively about the atrocities in the Congo. Edmond Morel, another reformer and convincing writer, also began publishing accounts of these atrocities as well as accusing Leopold of knowingly recruiting members of cannibal tribes from the Sudan into his army. Morel shocked Europe by reporting cases of reluctant rubber laborers being mutilated and eaten by Leopold's men. He claimed that white officers knew of these crimes and ignored them as long as ivory, rubber, and food quotas were met. He further claimed that Leopold invited European officials who were disenchanted with his policies to dine with him in Brussels, at his expense. They were offered a percentage of profits from their areas in return for covering up atrocities used to gain compliance with his labor demands. Many accepted his bribes and kept quiet, fearing that assassination was the alternative. Some who refused to cooperate later disappeared. Wild animals were alleged to be the cause of death.

In 1903, an outraged European public organized the Congo Reform Association in an effort to end Leopold's wanton abuse of power and public trust. European opinion noted that people should have the right to trade freely in the produce of their soil and to enjoy the fruits of their labor. Trade, free labor, and the right to possess private property were believed to be basic human rights and the essential basis of economics. Denial to the Congolese of their right to trade goods and labor was thought to strangle their development and reduce them to permanent slavery.

Leopold had thus violated Congolese rights by declaring that the state could appropriate all salable products of the land on which his citizens dwelt. In practice, he also appropriated their labor and gave them no judicial means to challenge these acts. Leopold thus destroyed a potentially mutually profitable relationship between whites and Africans throughout the Congo. Africans were reduced to tenants on Leopold's property rather than proud landowners.

Sir Charles Dilke, Sir Harry Johnston, Sir Edward Grey, Henry Fox Bourne, Edmond Morel, and the Congo Reform Association decided that Leopold's crimes against humanity were so heinous that his rule must be ended. From 1903 to 1908, they campaigned vigorously against Leopold. Public opinion in Belgium forced Leopold to resign, despite the fact that he surrendered the Congo to the Belgian public in a final failed ploy to maintain monopolistic control over commerce in the Congo. Defeated, humiliated, and broken, Leopold died in 1909, soon after handing over control of the Congo to a reform-minded Belgian government.

Impact of Event

An Italian official in Leopold's Congo government once noted that the black slave trade should have been labeled the white slave trade. Officials with a sense of decency came to the Congo filled with Belgian patriotism and human compassion, thinking that their mission was to uplift the natives. Such men were told, after reaching the Congo, to get rubber using the most barbaric and inhumane means conceivable. In this living hell, many perished from self-inflicted gunshots. Like the Africans, they too were victims of Leopold's system with its heartless, cruel policies. That system turned decent men into pitiful brutes, while Leopold and his associates in Belgium quietly pocketed the profits produced. Ultimately, Leopold was responsible for the anguish, suffering, and denial of rights of millions of Africans whom he had reduced to misery, poverty, and slavery. Leopold preferred to call this his "taxation scheme." No public accounts were produced to account for these taxes, and in fact, Leopold was their principal beneficiary.

Duplicity and deceit could not disguise Leopold's atrocities forever. Clean, healthy, prosperous, densely populated villages were reduced to ghost towns under his rule. The few malnourished, dirty, impoverished inhabitants who remained were those too sick, weak, or frightened to flee.

Denied their rights, whole regions fought back by rebelling. The wars of rebellion that occurred bear testimony to the resilience of the human spirit, even under appalling inhuman conditions. The rebellions also show that war and widespread bloodshed should be expected responses to attempts to deny people their fundamental human rights. The courage of the decent Africans and Europeans who stood up to and fought against Leopold's tyranny helped safeguard human rights for millions of people.

Acts establishing a new colonial charter for the Congo and transferring it to Belgian control, rather than Leopold's personal control, were passed in 1908. Forced labor was not outlawed under the new charter, and many of Leopold's administrators kept their positions. The efforts of Morel and other reformers, however, gradually dismantled Leopold's system. In June, 1913, the Congo Reform Association dissolved itself, having determined that the process of reform had gone far enough.

Bibliography

Anstey, Roger. *Britain and the Congo in the Nineteenth Century.* Oxford, England: Clarendon Press, 1962. Recounts Britain's rivalry for control of the Lower Congo and coast, followed by a period of collaboration with Leopold and consequent evolution of a policy to reform his government. Anstey explains why British plans to use Leopold as an instrument for their own exploitation of the Congo failed.

——————. *King Leopold's Legacy: The Congo Under Belgian Rule 1908-1960.* London: Oxford University Press, 1966. The Belgian government, Anstey argues, inherited a country whose tribal traditions and customary institutions had been badly damaged by King Leopold. It also inherited his forced labor system, with all of its abuses and atrocities. Anstey blames Leopold for the inadequate preparation of Africans to accept independence in 1960.

Doyle, A. Conan. *The Crime of the Congo.* New York: Doubleday, Page, 1909. Doyle's book accuses Leopold of committing the greatest crimes in human history up to 1904. A passionate and scathing indictment of the Congo Free State.

Keith, Arthur Berriedale. *The Belgian Congo and the Berlin Act.* New York: Clarendon Press, 1919. This book describes defects in the Berlin Act that were revealed by Leopold's abuse of power and privilege in the Congo. It suggests amendments to the act which would ensure that it delivered the benefits of civilization and freedom of trade to Africans under European tutelage.

Morel, Edmond D. *Edmond D. Morel's History of the Congo Reform Movement.* Edited by William Roger Louis and Jean Stengers. Oxford, England: Clarendon Press, 1968. A fascinating autobiographical account of Edmond Morel's life and his successful crusade against labor abuse and atrocities in Leopold's Belgian Congo. Provides the best contemporary record available of the Congo Reform Association and extensive supplementary material.

_____. *Red Rubber: The Story of the Rubber Slave Trade Flourishing on the Congo in the Year of France 1906.* New York: Negro Universities Press, 1906. A vivid record of Leopold's atrocities and a passionate plea to free humanity from them.

Slade, Ruth. *King Leopold's Congo: Aspects of the Development of Race Relations in the Congo Independent State.* London: Oxford University Press, 1962. Recounts the history of racial contact and the evolution of race relations in the Congo. Captures the debate in Belgium concerning whether Africans were capable of improvement and high culture.

Starr, Frederick. *The Truth About the Congo.* Chicago: Forbes, 1907. A collection of a series of *Chicago Tribune* newspaper articles written between January 20 and February 3, 1907, which exposed the American public to atrocities in the Congo.

Dallas L. Browne

Cross-References

The Belgian Government Annexes the Congo (1908), p. 103; The League of Nations Adopts the International Slavery Convention (1926), p. 436; Ethiopia Abolishes Slavery (1942), p. 607; The United Nations Amends Its International Slavery Convention (1953), p. 902; The United Nations Adopts the Abolition of Forced Labor Convention (1957), p. 985.

THE PANKHURSTS FOUND THE WOMEN'S SOCIAL AND POLITICAL UNION

Categories of event: Voting rights and women's rights
Time: October 10, 1903
Locale: Manchester, England

Through the use of civil disobedience and militant obstructionism, the WSPU introduced the issue of women's political rights into the mainstream of pre-World War I British politics

Principal personages:

EMMELINE PANKHURST (1858-1928), a leader of the women's suffrage movement in Great Britain; formed the Women's Social and Political Union (WSPU) in 1903

CHRISTABEL PANKHURST (1880-1958), Emmeline Pankhurst's daughter and cofounder of the WSPU

SYLVIA PANKHURST (1882-1960), Emmeline Pankhurst's daughter and a leader of the women's suffrage movement in Great Britain

MILLICENT GARRETT FAWCETT (1847-1929), a leader of the women's suffrage movement in Great Britain; president of the National Union of Women's Suffrage Societies (1897-1919)

H. H. ASQUITH (1852-1928), the leader of the Liberal Party and prime minister of Great Britain (1908-1916)

DAVID LLOYD GEORGE (1863-1945), the leader of the Liberal Party and prime minister of Great Britain (1916-1922)

REGINALD MCKENNA (1863-1943), the home secretary in the Liberal government in Great Britain (1911-1915)

Summary of Event

There are few examples of women being treated as equal to men in the history of humankind prior to the mid-nineteenth century. Inequality was the result of religious teachings, prejudice, and law. Women systematically were denied, solely on the basis of their gender, educational opportunity, meaningful employment, the right to vote, basic human rights, and a legal identity. This slowly began to change in Western societies as the result of the liberal ideas of the Enlightenment (during the eighteenth century) and as the result of the changes wrought by the Industrial Revolution (in the nineteenth century).

Great Britain was the first nation to experience an industrial revolution. Economic development led to demands by the emerging middle class for political change. The Reform Bill of 1832 extended suffrage to most middle-class males. Within one generation, the Liberal Party emerged, representing the middle class and heir to the

Enlightenment ideas of the rights of man. Reform bills in 1867 and 1884 extended
the right to vote to most adult males in Britain. Social legislation provided for a
basic public education, improved factory conditions, and solutions to some of the
social ills caused by industrialism.

Very little of the social legislation dealt with inequality based upon gender. In the
nineteenth century, British women were treated as inferior. Stereotypes and prejudices portrayed women as weak and incapable in most areas. Only after 1887 did
married women have the right to own property and to enter into contracts on an
equal basis with unmarried women. Most professions and occupations were closed
by statute to women. The only professions that were socially acceptable were those
of teacher, secretary, or homemaker. Industry, particularly the textile industry, employed women in large numbers but usually in nonskilled, low-paying jobs.

There were some who believed that the Enlightenment ideas of the "rights of
man" should apply to all people. *A Vindication of the Rights of Women* (1792) by
Mary Wollstonecraft and *On the Subjection of Women* (1869) by John Stuart Mill
were early statements on the need for, and the right of, woman suffrage. In the
1860's, small groups of educated, middle-class women began forming to discuss the
need for woman suffrage. The National Society for Women's Suffrage (1867), under
the leadership of Lydia Becker, and the Women's Franchise League (1889), under
the leadership of Richard and Emmeline Pankhurst, were the most important organizations advocating woman suffrage.

The National Union of Women's Suffrage Societies (NUWSS) was formed in 1897
under the leadership of Millicent Fawcett. This organization continued the policy of
working within the political system to achieve the vote for women. The Liberal
Party offered only nominal support for woman suffrage and made no serious attempt
to introduce legislation granting women the right to vote. The Conservative Party
was overtly hostile to the idea, and the House of Lords, with its right of veto, was
dominated by Conservatives.

With little to show from decades of working within the constitutional guidelines,
a more militant approach to the issue was proposed. The death of Richard Pankhurst
in 1898 temporarily forced Emmeline Pankhurst to abandon political activity and to
devote her efforts to providing a living for her family. Her daughter, Christabel, who
studied law but could not practice because of her gender, began working with the
North of England Society for Women's Suffrage, an organization primarily for working women.

To the great irritation of the Pankhursts, the Manchester branch of the Independent Labour Party (ILP) refused to admit women to a meeting hall which was named
for Richard Pankhurst. The ILP was the logical political home for the proposed
group, but Labour politicians were largely disinterested in woman suffrage as an
issue. The Pankhursts thus decided to form their own group, the Women's Social and
Political Union (WSPU). On October 10, 1903, the first meeting was held at the
Manchester home of Mrs. Pankhurst.

Little is known of the early meetings, as records of minutes, strategy, finances, and membership no longer exist. Two facts are clear: Men were excluded from membership, and the WSPU had a clear platform. In December, 1903, a WSPU pamphlet stated,

. . . for all purposes connected with, and having reference to, the right to vote at Parliamentary elections, words in the Representation of the People Act importing the masculine gender shall include women.

Simply translated, universal manhood suffrage should be understood to mean universal personhood suffrage. The statement of purpose by the WSPU was not new, but the group's method of attracting attention to the issue was.

Politics in Great Britain relied upon the constitutional method, that is, formal procedures which were to be followed in a prescribed manner. Earlier reform campaigns occasionally had resorted to nontraditional political tactics, such as propaganda campaigns, mass rallies and marches, demonstrations, and civil disobedience. The problem was always one of attracting the attention of the establishment and achieving a goal before the nontraditional tactics alienated that same establishment.

Prior to the WSPU, women's suffrage groups had not only followed the unwritten rules of political activism but had remained true to the stereotype of women. The Pankhursts observed that following the rules had achieved nothing. Over the next decade, the WSPU utilized every traditional and nontraditional tactic available. In addition to traditional speeches, rallies, and printed materials, WSPU suffragists made press headlines by heckling and taunting politicians wherever possible. In October, 1905, two women were ejected forcibly from a Manchester meeting hall and then arrested. The incident taught the WSPU that militancy attracted far more publicity than traditional tactics.

At first, militancy was subordinate to constitutional methods. Occasionally women suffragists were arrested, and hunger strikes were held to call attention to the movement. When force-feeding was used and several women were injured, the WSPU became more militant. In 1909, the first stone-throwing incidents occurred. This escalated by 1912 into even more violent acts such as the smashing of shop windows, arson, and vandalism of art works.

Government response to the militancy was predictable. Police raided WSPU headquarters and arrested suffragist leaders. Hunger strikes soon followed, and, in 1913, the government passed the Prisoners' Temporary Discharge for Ill-Health Act. The "Cat and Mouse Act," as it was quickly dubbed, allowed the government to release prisoners on hunger strike and rearrest them later. Also during this period, Emily Davison achieved martyrdom when she was killed after running in front of the king's horse at the 1913 Derby. The WSPU held a huge funeral procession through London to publicize her dedication.

Despite these efforts, the net result of the WSPU was to alienate potential supporters far more than to gain support for woman suffrage. Women's suffragists were considered by the government primarily to be an irritant and not a major problem. The outbreak of war in August, 1914, changed everything. Mrs. Pankhurst called an immediate halt to militancy, and the government released women suffragists from prison. Throughout World War I the WSPU, the NUWSS, and other women's suffrage organizations worked for the war effort. Traditional men's occupations were filled by women, thereby freeing men for the trenches. Largely because of the contributions by women to the war effort, a limited suffrage was granted to women in Great Britain in February, 1918. Voting equality was finally achieved with the Representation of the People Act of 1928.

Impact of Event

An exact impact of the WSPU is difficult to assess or quantify, but there are areas in which its significance can be seen. First, limited suffrage was granted to women in 1918, and suffrage equality was achieved in 1928. Second, WSPU civil disobedience and militant tactics became a permanent feature of British politics. Third, the stereotype of the submissive female was challenged. Finally, the culmination of the women's suffrage movement can be seen in the 1979 election of Margaret Thatcher as prime minister of Great Britain.

It cannot be proven that the Pankhursts and the WSPU were either crucial or essential to winning the vote for women. Indeed, it can be argued that their efforts actually were counterproductive. The WSPU overstepped the boundary of what was considered in that era to be acceptable political activist behavior. Their militant campaign alienated many potential supporters of woman suffrage in Great Britain. Moreover, it is probably accurate to state that women received the vote because of their war record between 1914 and 1918. The social changes brought about by the war resulted in political changes. It also can be argued that the efforts of the WSPU placed the issue squarely in the center of British politics, a place where it never had been before. Without such awareness, it is possible that woman suffrage would not have been granted in 1918.

Politics itself was changing, and the relatively placid constitutional system would never be the same. At the same time that women's suffragists were resorting to arson and window smashing, Ulster Protestants, with the assent of Conservative Party leadership, were arming and preparing for civil war. Radical labor unions in Great Britain, throughout Europe, and elsewhere advocated violence in strikes. In comparison to other, later movements, the militancy of the WSPU was quite tame. Indeed, a comparison could be drawn between the WSPU and the civil disobedience of either Mohandas Gandhi in India or Martin Luther King, Jr., in the American South. Marches, demonstrations, debates, sit-ins, and protests were characteristic of each of the movements, and each movement was concerned with basic human rights and human dignity.

Perhaps the greatest impact of the WSPU can be seen in the change in the image of women in Great Britain. WSPU suffragists, unlike their predecessors, were certainly not meek, submissive women. The hunger strikes, the demonstrations and scuffles, the rational speeches, and the intelligence of the leadership demonstrated that the suffragists could not be dismissed as a group of hysterical females. The

WSPU was well organized, determined, and efficient. That the members were will-ing to suffer imprisonment and even, in the case of Emily Davison, death, served to demonstrate that women were human beings who deserved equality.

It cannot be said that the WSPU, or the Representation of the People Act, or any other individual event or act brought about equality for women in Great Britain. Margaret Thatcher, however, served as prime minister of Great Britain from 1979 to 1990, a period of service longer than that of any other prime minister since the eighteenth century. That she could even vote can be traced to the determination of the woman suffragists of the WSPU.

Bibliography

Barker, Dudley. "Mrs. Emmeline Pankhurst." In *Prominent Edwardians.* New York: Atheneum, 1969. One of four biographical sketches presented to illustrate the age, which was one of glitter and of unrest. A brief introduction to the topic.

Dangerfield, George. *The Strange Death of Liberal England.* New York: Capricorn Books, 1961. A significant, albeit dated, book. Studies various political crises in Great Britain in the five years preceding World War I. Unsympathetic to women's issues and harsh in judgment of the Pankhursts. No footnotes.

Holton, Sandra Stanley. *Feminism and Democracy: Women's Suffrage and Reform Politics in Britain, 1900-1918.* New York: Cambridge University Press, 1986. Pro-vides an overview of the women's suffrage movement in Great Britain. Primary focus is on the differences among the political groups within the suffragist move-ment.

Hume, Leslie Parker. *The National Union of Women's Suffrage Societies, 1897-1914.* New York: Garland, 1982. Studies the impact of the NUWSS, which coordinated the activities of a coalition of nonmilitant women's suffrage organizations. Con-cludes that the conciliatory attitude of the NUWSS countered the negative effects of the WSPU's militancy. Has an excellent bibliography and is well documented.

Mitchell, David. *The Fighting Pankhursts: A Study in Tenacity.* London: Jonathan Cape, 1967. Briefly surveys the WSPU years, then offers a portrait of the Pank-hurst children following the achievement of woman suffrage in Great Britain. Useful for understanding the motivations of the Pankhursts.

Pankhurst, Emmeline. *My Own Story.* 1914. Reprint. New York: Kraus Reprint, 1971. Written at the beginning of World War I. Praises the militant wing of the women's suffrage movement. Must be read carefully because of its omissions and rational-izations.

Pankhurst, Sylvia. *The Life of Emmeline Pankhurst: The Suffragette Struggle for Women's Citizenship.* 1935. Reprint. New York: Kraus Reprint, 1969. This work and her *The Suffragette Movement* (1931) reflect not only the devotion of a daugh-ter to her mother but also the dedication of a suffragist to the cause of women's rights. Must be read carefully because of its subjectivity.

Rosen, Andrew. *Rise Up, Women! The Militant Campaign of the Women's Social and Political Union, 1903-1914.* London: Routledge & Kegan Paul, 1974. Utilizes numerous primary sources and is a scholarly overview of the WSPU. Well documented.

Rover, Constance. *Women's Suffrage and Party Politics in Britain, 1866-1914.* London: Routledge & Kegan Paul, 1967. Considered to be the best overview of the lengthy struggle for suffrage by women in Great Britain. Primarily a political analysis, and certainly not a paean to the personalities involved. Has an excellent bibliography, is well documented, and includes numerous useful appendices.

Wright, Almroth E. *The Unexpurgated Case Against Woman Suffrage.* London: Constable, 1913. This virulent attack on the women's suffrage movement conveys the resentment and antipathy faced by women suffragists. Useful for understanding the fear and prejudice of the era.

William S. Brockington, Jr.

Cross-References

The British Labour Party Is Formed (1906), p. 58; Women's Institutes Are Founded in Great Britain (1915), p. 167; Parliament Grants Suffrage to British Women (1918), p. 247; Gandhi Leads a Noncooperation Movement (1920), p. 315; The Nineteenth Amendment Gives American Women the Right to Vote (1920), p. 339; The Minimum Age for Female British Voters Is Lowered (1928), p. 442; The SCLC Forms to Link Civil Rights Groups (1957), p. 974; Thatcher Becomes Great Britain's First Female Prime Minister (1979), p. 2024.

PANAMA DECLARES INDEPENDENCE FROM COLOMBIA

Category of event: Revolutions and rebellions
Time: November 3, 1903
Locale: Panama City, Republic of Panama

Maneuverings surrounding the construction of the Panama Canal sparked a revolution in Panama

Principal personages:

MANUEL AMADOR GUERRERO (1833-1909), the first president of Panama and a leader of the independence movement

PHILIPPE JEAN BUNAU-VARILLA (1859-1940), a French engineer who worked to persuade the United States government to select the Panama route for a canal

THEODORE ROOSEVELT (1858-1919), the twenty-sixth president of the United States (1901-1909); supported the canal and the Panama route

JOHN HAY (1830-1905), the U.S. secretary of state under Theodore Roosevelt; supported the independence of Panama and negotiated the canal treaty

Summary of Event

When other parts of the Spanish Empire declared independence, Panama, a part of the Spanish viceroyalty of Nueva Granada, remained loyal to the crown. Economic reasons, however, caused many Panamanians to reconsider their loyalty before Ferdinand VII allowed free trade in 1813. Panama prospered until free trade was repealed. The repeal resulted in a resurgence of patriotic fervor that caused Spain to appoint governors who were determined to retain the isthmus at any cost. Violations of civil and political rights occurred with regularity. The patriots' cause benefited from the dissatisfaction created by the governors' use of censorship, arbitrary arrests, and persecution of suspects.

In October, 1821, Colonel José de Fábrega became the first native-born isthmian to serve as governor. The patriots guessed correctly that Fábrega would be reluctant to shed the blood of his fellow countrymen. On November 27, 1821, shortly after an uprising began in the interior towns, the citizens of Panama City invaded the main plaza and demanded a meeting of the *cabildo* (council) to decide the future of the isthmus. The next day the *cabildo* met, declared independence from Spain, and accepted union with Colombia.

The union with Colombia led to much civil unrest. Political instability in Colombia, opposition to the dictatorship of Colombian ruler Simon Bolívar, and the breakup of the extensive republic of Gran Colombia in 1830 gave the isthmus opportunities to express its desire for autonomy or independence. Unsuccessful rebellions occurred in 1827, 1830, 1831, and 1832. Both political and economic factors played a part in the uprisings. Panamanians could not accept the arbitrary exercise of power by officials from other areas and wanted free trade, free ports, and free transit.

Panamanians responded to civil war in Colombia by proclaiming the Free State of Panama in November, 1840. External threats from England and Colombia, however, forced the Free State to sign a treaty of reincorporation after only thirteen months.

Various projects for canals, roads, and railroads across Panama's narrow isthmus had been proposed since early in the colonial period. Panamanians would have welcomed such projects and partially blamed Colombia's government for lack of progress. Colombia, however, thought the interest that France and England expressed in such projects was a threat to its control of the isthmus and signed the Bidlack Treaty of 1846 with the United States to guarantee the neutrality of the isthmus and Colombian sovereignty. Panama regarded the treaty as an attempt by the United States to increase its influence and power in the area. Nevertheless, a half-century and many North American military interventions later, Panama turned to the United States for assistance in achieving independence and constructing a canal.

The French, undeterred by the Bidlack Treaty, pursued their plans for a railroad across the isthmus but were unable to find financing. The settlement of Oregon in 1848 made people in the United States aware of the problem of transit. William H. Aspinwall, a U.S. citizen, organized the Pacific Mail Steamship Company and planned a transisthmian railroad. His efforts led to the organization of the Panama Railroad Company, which completed the railway on January 27, 1855.

From the time of the completion of the railroad until the country's independence, Panama experienced international, national, and local problems. Liberal-conservative disputes involving civil disturbances in Colombia, the withdrawal of local self-government by Bogotá, and economic and racial problems on the isthmus resulted in forty different administrations, fifty riots, five attempts at secession, and thirteen major interventions by the United States. By the end of the nineteenth century, Colombia had pushed Panama into independence by refusing to consider the desires of the area, failing to provide security for property and persons, denying Panamanians the vote, conducting illegal arrests and detention, and imposing censorship and arbitrary and excessive taxation.

A small group of Panamanians became convinced that Panama could never expect any permanent, satisfactory political arrangement or economic progress as long as Panama remained under the control of Colombia. The failure of two French canal companies between 1879 and 1898 convinced them that independence under the protection of the United States was the only answer. The United States had a definite interest in a canal and, after the failure of the New French Canal Company, had assumed the right to build it in Panama.

In the first months of 1903, a group of influential Panamanians began meeting secretly to plan an insurrection. Captain James R. Beers, the port captain working for the railroad company, was leaving for a vacation in the United States, and he was asked to ascertain the feelings of the railroad officials in New York. It was hoped that Beers could obtain promises of support and aid, perhaps even from the U.S. government. The answers Beers brought back were so encouraging that the insurrectionists sent Manuel Amador Guerrero, the railroad medical officer, to New York to make further inquiries.

Just as a discouraged Amador Guerrero was preparing to leave New York, Philippe Bunau-Varilla, the head of the New French Canal Company, arrived. Bunau-Varilla, believing that the United States was the only nation that could complete the canal, was determined to vindicate France and salvage his own reputation. He took control. After a series of "accidental" meetings with high U.S. government officials, including Secretary of State John Hay and President Theodore Roosevelt, he was able to assure Amador Guerrero that the United States would permit a revolution to succeed and would recognize the new republic.

Bunau-Varilla supplied Amador Guerrero with money, a declaration of independence, military plans, and a national flag. When Amador Guerrero returned to Panama, he found his fellow revolutionaries unhappy with Bunau-Varilla, timid, and unwilling to continue. Resolute action by Amador Guerrero and his wife saved the revolution. Amador Guerrero arranged for the commander of the Colombian forces in Panama to aid the movement in return for a generous financial arrangement for himself and his men.

The revolution started on November 3, 1903, after the U.S. warship *Nashville* docked in Colón. The U.S. military presence prevented the Colombian troops in Colón from suppressing the revolt. The officials of the Panama Railroad, who were citizens of the United States, also contributed to the success of the revolt by arranging to keep all rail cars in Panama City, making it impossible to transport Colombian troops across the isthmus.

The municipal council of Panama City declared Panama's independence the same day and called a public meeting for the next afternoon. The meeting selected a *junta* of three men as a provisional government. The *junta* provided for a constitutional convention and for presidential elections, in which Amador Guerrero was chosen as the first president.

Panama was forced to pay a price for the assistance of Bunau-Varilla and the United States. As a condition of his support, Bunau-Varilla demanded appointment as Panamanian minister to the United States. He was replaced one month later by a Panamanian, but in that month he negotiated a canal treaty with the United States that was similar to one Colombia had rejected. The few new provisions in the treaty made it more favorable to the United States. Bunau-Varilla pointed out to the two Panamanian diplomats sent to help negotiate the treaty that any delay in accepting the treaty could lead to withdrawal of U.S. protection and to new negotiations for a canal treaty with Colombia. U.S. protection was essential for the preservation of Panamanian independence. The arguments were not lost on the diplomats nor upon the Panamanian *junta*. The treaty was accepted by the *junta* and by virtually every town council in the new republic.

Impact of Event

When Panama became independent in 1903, the new government accepted the canal treaty with the United States, giving the United States a physical presence in the new nation and an interest that led to limitations on political action by the government of Panama. The average Panamanian citizen did not gain political power either. A small group of elite families controlled the republic until the end of the 1960's, when the commander of the national guard seized control of the country. The United States accepted two new canal treaties in 1978 under which the Panamanian government, but not the individual citizen, gained politically.

Observation of civil rights was not characteristic of the colonial period or of Colombian rule. Censorship, arbitrary arrests and imprisonment, exile, illegal taxation, and physical abuse were commonly used against political opponents and the poor. Independence improved the abusive conditions but did not eliminate them. The political patterns of electoral fraud, political violence, arbitrary decisions, suppression and abuse of opponents, and use of political control for economic benefit characteristic of the previous periods continued to be the norm. The masses that had only rarely participated in the political process remained passive. The poor were given no economic consideration by the elite factions who dominated Panama.

The construction of the railroad in the 1850's and the later construction of the canal depended heavily upon the recruitment of black laborers from the English-speaking Caribbean. Many blacks remained in Panama and congregated in their own sections of Panama City and Colón. They continued to speak English and to attend Protestant churches, and their racial and cultural differences from other Panamanians made them a conspicuous minority.

Economic development did come with the construction and operation of the canal, but the more technical and higher-paying jobs were given to U.S. citizens during the first forty years of the canal's operation. Panamanians reacted negatively to the political and economic influence of the United States, and nationalism increased. When U.S. interventions aroused Panamanian anger, the blacks became an easy target for protests; the United States was not so easily attacked. Blacks also competed with the "native" Panamanians for jobs. The administration of the canal used the division between the blacks and other Panamanians to maintain an adequate and docile labor supply.

The growth of Panamanian nationalism was given an added impetus by U.S. cultural influence. The cultural influences on everyday life were pervasive and readily apparent to the average citizen. The canal remained closely tied to the independence of Panama and to the lives of the Panamanians.

Bibliography

Bishop, Joseph Bucklin. *Theodore Roosevelt and His Time Shown in His Own Letters.* 2 vols. New York: Charles Scribner's Sons, 1920. The author was secretary of the canal commission. This is a favorable picture of Roosevelt. It includes interesting and useful insights about the canal and Roosevelt's participation.

Bunau-Varilla, Philippe. *Panama: The Creation, Destruction, and Resurrection.* London: Constable, 1913. A self-serving account of events. It vindicates the author and France. There is no bibliography, but some of the author's letters are included.

McCullogh, David. *The Path Between the Seas: The Creation of the Panama Canal, 1870-1914.* New York: Simon & Schuster, 1977. A detailed account of events surrounding the creation of the canal and a brief summary of the pre-1903 period. Has an extensive bibliography.

Millander, G. A. *The United States in Panamanian Politics: The Intriguing Formative Years.* Danville, Ill.: Interstate Printers, 1971. This is a good, brief explanation of the 1903 revolution. It has an extensive annotated bibliography.

Niemeier, Jean Gilbreath. *The Panama Story.* Portland, Ore.: Metropolitan Press, 1968. This work was written from articles in the *Panama Star and Herald.* The newspaper articles are quoted extensively.

Perez-Venero, Alex. *Before the Five Frontiers: Panama from 1821-1903.* New York: AMS Press, 1978. Contains a good history of nineteenth century Panama but does not include the 1903 revolution. Has an extensive bibliography.

Robert D. Talbott

Cross-References

The Philippines Ends Its Uprising Against the United States (1902), p. 7; U.S. Marines Are Sent to Nicaragua to Quell Unrest (1912), p. 137; El Salvador's Military Massacres Civilians in *La Matanza* (1932), p. 464; The Atlantic Charter Declares a Postwar Right of Self-Determination (1941), p. 584; Indigenous Indians Become the Target of Guatemalan Death Squads (1978), p. 1972; Somoza Is Forced Out of Power in Nicaragua (1979), p. 2035; Presidential Candidates Are Killed in Colombian Violence (1989), p. 2465; Sandinistas Are Defeated in Nicaraguan Elections (1990), p. 2564.

INTERNATIONAL AGREEMENT ATTACKS
THE WHITE SLAVE TRADE

Categories of event: Civil rights and women's rights
Time: May 18, 1904
Locale: Paris, France

Ratification of the Agreement for the Suppression of the White Slave Traffic marked the first coordinated international effort to attack involuntary prostitution

Principal personages:

WILLIAM ALEXANDER COOTE (1842-1919), the secretary of the National Vigilance Association for the Suppression of the White Slave Traffic, located in the United Kingdom

WILLIAM THOMAS STEAD (1849-1912), an innovative British journalist, editor of the *Pall Mall Gazette*, and crusader against white slavery

JOSEPHINE BUTLER (1828-1906), the secretary of the British and Continental Federation for the Abolishment of Government Regulation of Prostitution, a longtime antiwhite slavery activist

Summary of Event

Involuntary prostitution, which came to be known as white slavery in the late nineteenth century, is an enduring phenomenon in human history. The late nineteenth and early twentieth centuries saw an increasing assault on this aspect of human society. The 1904 Paris Conference on the White Slave Trade was the first internationally coordinated governmental attempt to suppress the traffic.

During the early and mid-nineteenth century, many nations took measures to regulate the practice of prostitution. The two major motives for this were the desire to keep a practice regarded as immoral, but unsuppressible, under control and the wish to prevent the spread of venereal disease. Typically, prostitutes were required to dwell in certain districts of the city, to register, and to submit to periodic medical examinations. They commonly lived in licensed brothels. Prostitution was monitored by special police, often plainclothes officers, who were frequently corrupt. The system usually failed to regulate all the prostitutes, and as time passed, resistance to the system grew from several quarters.

While some women entered prostitution because of poverty and a lack of employment opportunities for women, others entered because of the sexual mores of the period. Many middle- and upper-class women felt ruined after being seduced and believed that they could not return to their families. This drove them into prostitution to survive. Others were tricked, trapped, or kidnapped into prostitution. A fear of venereal disease led to a high demand for virginal prostitutes. To meet this demand, the pimps, procurers, and brothel keepers used a variety of methods to entice or trap young women into a life of prostitution. Some women were ensnared by offers of marriage or a job in a household. Another method involved placing job offers at employment agencies that found work abroad for women. Once they arrived at their place of work, women discovered that they had been deceived, but it was usually too late. Sometimes the women were forced to purchase various items, such as clothing, and then were forced to stay in the brothel to "work off" the resulting debts.

Often the methods involved transport of the women between nations (or states in the United States), because this made it more difficult for the women to escape. This transportation became known as the white slave trade or traffic. In the nineteenth century, it was fairly widespread. Because of the corruption of its morals police, Belgium was a center for this traffic. The king of Belgium himself reportedly spent more than £1,800 a year importing British girls from British procuresses.

In the second half of the nineteenth century, the American and European public become more aware of this traffic, and an assault on the regulation of prostitution and on the white slave trade began. One early leader of this movement was Josephine Butler, an upper-class British woman who became involved in social work with prostitutes in the mid-1860's. She played a major part in the fight to repeal the Contagious Diseases Act, which was at the core of Britain's regulation system. While upholding the goal of marriage, she held that the talents of many women unable to find husbands were being wasted by society. She argued that since the structure of industrialized society prevented them from gaining employment, they were forced into prostitution to survive. They should not be punished, she said, while their clients went untouched. Her efforts led to the foundation in 1875 of the British and Continental Federation for the Abolishment of Government Regulation of Prostitution. Soon afterward, she became involved in the battle against child and involuntary prostitution.

At the instigation of her publisher, Alfred Dyer, she wrote a pamphlet, *A Letter to the Mothers of England*, assailing the white slave traffic between England and Belgium, which she blamed on Belgium's corrupt regulatory system and the inadequacy of British law protecting young women. (The age of consent in Britain at the time was thirteen years.) The resulting investigation led to the conviction of many agents of the Belgian morals police but few lasting results.

In 1885, the editor of the *Pall Mall Gazette*, William Thomas Stead, entered the fight against white slavery. The early efforts of Butler and others led him to investigate the problem. With the help of Butler and the Salvation Army, he formed a secret investigation committee. The inquiry culminated when Stead, with the aid of a reformed procuress, Rebecca Jarret, staged a procuration to demonstrate that it was quite possible to carry off young girls to the Continent for immoral purposes without being caught or prevented from doing so. Beginning on July 6, 1885, he published a six-part series revealing the results of his investigations in the *Pall Mall Gazette* under the title "The Maiden Tribute of Modern Babylon." Stead himself was arrested because of legal complications arising from the demonstration procuration he had arranged, and his series produced a massive public outcry that led to the passage of a bill raising the age of consent to sixteen years. Stead also helped found the British National Vigilance Association, which became important under William Alexander Coote in moving the battle against white slavery to the international level.

After several years of effort as the secretary of the British National Vigilance Association, Coote became frustrated with the meagerness of the results achieved by the organization acting alone. His success increased after 1898, when he was inspired to found cooperating vigilance associations in all of the nations plagued by the white slave trade. Because the trade was international, cooperation between nations would be required to destroy it. His efforts led to the calling of the International Congress on the White Slave Traffic in 1899 in London and to the foundation of vigilance associations in many nations. These organizations and his continuing work led the French government in turn to invite sixteen nations to send delegates to Paris on July 25, 1902, to formulate an international agreement to fight the white slave trade.

Thirty-six delegates represented the sixteen nations at the conference. After five days' deliberation, a nine-article agreement was hammered out. Thirteen nations (Belgium, Denmark, France, Germany, Great Britain, Holland, Italy, Norway, Portugal, Russia, Spain, Sweden, and Switzerland) ratified the agreement on May 18, 1904. Austria-Hungary, Brazil, and the United States later ratified the agreement.

The Agreement for the Suppression of the White Slave Traffic called for a variety of measures to be taken. Five of its articles detailed concrete action to be carried out by the signatory nations. Article 1 provided for the establishment of national authorities that would coordinate information regarding the white slave trade. Article 2 arranged the keeping of watch over railway stations, ports, and similar locations for the purpose of intercepting white slave traffickers and preventing procuration in these sites. Article 3 provided for investigations to discover the place of origin of foreign prostitutes in the signatory nations (to aid in their eventual repatriation) and for governmental assistance in repatriation. Article 4 dealt with funding repatriation. Article 6 concerned the supervision of agencies that sought to provide employment abroad for women. The agreement thus provided the first international framework for the battle against white slavery.

The Agreement for the Suppression of the White Slave Traffic was the culmination of many years of effort by activists. It was, however, only the beginning of the international assault on the trade. These efforts had not yet ceased in 1991.

Impact of Event

The Agreement for the Suppression of the White Slave Traffic led to additional international conventions, congresses, and agreements. A conference in Spain in 1910 produced an agreement which held that it was a criminal act to procure women under twenty years old under any conditions, and that for women twenty or older, procuration was illegal if fraud or violence was involved. After its founding, the League of Nations entered the battle, raising the age of consent to twenty-one and in 1921 organizing a system for monitoring international employment agencies. Experts were appointed to investigate the traffic. Further agreements were made in the years to follow, including the amendment of the 1904 agreement by the United Nations in 1949.

These international agreements often proved difficult to enforce, as they depended on the willingness and capability of the signatory nations to carry them out. To some extent, private organizations took up some of the work and duties set forth in the agreements. Groups such as the International Catholic Associations for Railway Station Work, Les Amies de la Jeune Fille, and various National Vigilance Associations did their part to ensure that the agreements were carried out.

During the first fifteen years of the twentieth century, public awareness of the existence of white slavery mounted. In the United States, this led to a veritable white slavery panic. Numerous books were published, and several laws were passed, such as the 1910 Mann Act, which made it a crime to transport a woman across a state line "for immoral purposes." The United States also proclaimed its adherence to the 1904 agreement. The public hysteria produced a reaction which sought either to deny the existence of the white slave trade or to show its occurrence to be less common than reformers claimed.

The traffic in women did decline as the twentieth century progressed. The decrease in licensed prostitution and the end of regulatory systems helped to bring about a change in the recruiting systems of prostitution, which in turn contributed to a reduction in the traffic in women. The actual enforcement of the agreements also helped, to a lesser extent, to bring about a decline in the white slave traffic.

Another important factor in the decline of the white slave traffic has been the increasing liberation of women in the twentieth century. Women are better educated and more liberated in the field of sexual mores. Better education has left them less vulnerable to the tricks of white slave traffickers, and freer sexual mores have helped to create a decline in the demand for prostitutes and an increase in the proportion of prostitutes who choose their profession voluntarily. Economic necessity and inducements remain important factors in recruitment, but deception, coercion, and international transportation have declined in importance.

Although involuntary prostitution has long been a part of human society, the twentieth century witnessed its significant decline. With the abolition of the regulation system, the international cooperation arising from the agreement of 1904 and the treaties that followed it, and the increasing liberation of women, white slavery has ceased to be a matter of great public concern and has decreased markedly in occurrence.

Bibliography

Bell, Ernest A., et al. *Fighting the Traffic in Young Girls*. Chicago: L. H. Walter, 1911. A typical example of the antiwhite slavery propaganda by reformers in the United States during the early twentieth century. It includes a chapter by William A. Coote discussing the 1904 agreement, one of its most useful features for a contemporary reader. No reference features.

Bullough, Vern L., and Bonnie L. Bullough. *The History of Prostitution.* New Hyde Park, N.Y.: University Books, 1964. Discusses the history of prostitution from its origins to the early 1960's. At the time of its writing, few serious histories of prostitution had been done. It is not as thorough as their later work. Includes bibliography, endnotes, and index.

_____. *Women and Prostitution: A Social History.* Buffalo, N.Y.: Prometheus Books, 1987. Discusses the history of prostitution from its origins to the mid-1980's. It argues the importance of the sexual double standard in the persistence of prostitution. It contains an excellent chapter on the history of the movements against government regulation of prostitution and white slavery. Includes a bibliography, endnotes, and an index.

Decker, John F. *Prostitution: Regulation and Control.* Littleton, Colo.: Fred B. Rothman, 1979. A study of the various methods used through history to regulate or control prostitution. It provides a primarily legal rather than historical perspective. Includes an index and a large bibliography.

Grittner, Frederick K. *White Slavery: Myth, Ideology, and American Law.* New York: Garland, 1990. This work ably discusses the perception of white slavery by the American public from the nineteenth century to 1985. The author shows how and why perception of the existence of white slavery grew in the early twentieth century and culminated in the white slavery panic of 1909-1914, the focus of his work. He then traces the aftermath of the panic. Includes index and bibliography.

Niemoeller, Adolph Fredrick. *Sexual Slavery in America.* New York: The Panurge Press, 1935. Surveys the many forms of sexual slavery which have existed since ancient times, with primary emphasis on their occurrence in the United States. The author devotes an entire chapter to the structure and history of white slavery and the movements against it in the nineteenth and twentieth centuries. Also includes the texts of several relevant laws and treaties, including the text of the 1904 agreement. Includes footnotes but no other reference features.

United Nations. *International Agreement for the Suppression of the White Slave Traffic, Signed at Paris on 18 May 1904, Amended by the Protocol Signed at Lake Success, New York, 4 May 1949.* Lake Success, N.Y.: United Nations Publications, 1950. This is the actual text of the agreement signed in 1904 in Paris as modified after the creation of the United Nations. It also lists those who actually signed the treaty in 1904. The changes from the 1904 text are slight. No reference features, but none are needed for the five pages of text.

John W. Biles
Robert E. Biles

Cross-References

The Bern Conference Prohibits Night Work for Women (1906), p. 75; The Saint-Germain-en-Laye Convention Attempts to Curtail Slavery (1919), p. 287; The League of Nations Adopts the International Slavery Convention (1926), p. 436; The International League for Human Rights Is Founded (1942), p. 590; The United Nations Adopts the Universal Declaration of Human Rights (1948), p. 789; The Geneva Convention Establishes Norms of Conduct in Warfare (1949), p. 808; The U.N. Convention on the Political Rights of Women Is Approved (1952), p. 885; The United Nations Amends Its International Slavery Convention (1953), p. 902; The United Nations Issues a Declaration on Equality for Women (1967), p. 1391; A U.N. Convention Condemns Discrimination Against Women (1979), p. 2057.

SUPREME COURT DISALLOWS A
MAXIMUM HOURS LAW FOR BAKERS

Category of event: Workers' rights
Time: April 17, 1905
Locale: United States Supreme Court, Washington, D.C.

In Lochner v. New York, *the Supreme Court held unconstitutional a maximum-hours law for bakers, thus casting doubt on the constitutionality of other labor laws*

> *Principal personages:*
> RUFUS PECKHAM (1838-1909), an associate justice of the Supreme Court and author of the majority opinion in the *Lochner* case
> JOHN MARSHALL HARLAN (1833-1911), an associate justice of the Supreme Court and dissenter in the *Lochner* case
> OLIVER WENDELL HOLMES (1841-1935), an associate justice of the Supreme Court and dissenter in the *Lochner* case
> LOUIS D. BRANDEIS (1856-1941), a reform-minded lawyer who was later appointed to the Supreme Court

Summary of Event

Labor had been seeking a shorter workday and workweek since early in the nineteenth century. Even before mid-century, workers in the building trades had been generally successful in obtaining a sixty-hour workweek; however, they were not typical of nineteenth century workers. By the end of the century, many other industries and occupations had achieved a ten-hour day and a sixty-hour week. Cigar makers had, in fact, gotten their workweek below fifty hours in some states, but there were still many less fortunate workers in other occupations. It was necessary for them tc work eleven- to thirteen-hour days and sixty-five or more hours per week.

Bakers were among the most disadvantaged of workers in late nineteenth century New York. They routinely worked from eleven to thirteen hours a day, seven days a week. They worked for a master baker, who was someone who owned an oven but was often not much better off than they were. Not only did bakers work long hours, they worked in what were frequently unsanitary conditions. Bakeshops, as they were called, typically were located in the basements of tenement houses, many of which were infested with vermin. It was not uncommon for there to be a leaky sewer pipe running through the area where bread was being made. Unwittingly, many consumers of their product were also affected by the unsanitary conditions in which the bakers toiled.

Eventually, the political processes in the state of New York worked to the advantage of the bakers. Diverse political forces, especially social reformers and politicians hoping to reap political support in future elections from grateful laborers, were instrumental in the passage of the Bakeshop Act of 1895. The New York State legislature passed the act unanimously. Although labor leaders generally supported the bill, organized labor had not yet become a strong political force and was not primarily responsible for the law's passage. Similarly, labor did not play a major role in the adoption of social welfare programs in a number of European nations in the late nineteenth and early twentieth centuries. The programs had been promoted by bureaucrats and politicians.

The New York law set the number of hours that bakers could be required or permitted to work at ten per day and sixty per week. It also included various sanitary regulations and provisions for state inspections. Violation of the act constituted a misdemeanor. When a bakeshop owner in Utica, New York, was prosecuted for violating the hours provisions of the act, he unsuccessfully challenged the legislation in New York courts. Failing there, he appealed to the United States Supreme Court, arguing that the legislation was unconstitutional because the state legislature had exceeded its authority. A closely divided Supreme Court held the hours provisions of the Bakeshop Act unconstitutional.

The majority of the Court held the maximum hours provisions to be in violation of the due process clause of the Fourteenth Amendment to the Constitution. This amendment had been added to the Constitution in the post-Civil War years for the purpose of protecting the recently freed slaves. In the late nineteenth and early twentieth centuries, however, the vagueness of some of its language permitted the Supreme Court to use it to protect business from regulatory laws enacted by state legislatures. Such was the case in *Lochner v. New York*; in fact, it was the first time that the Court did this with a law which had been upheld by the highest court in the state of its origin.

Justice Rufus W. Peckham wrote the majority opinion. To him, the language of the New York statute was the equivalent of saying that the employee was prohibited from contracting or agreeing to work for more than ten hours per day. He perceived this as interfering with the right of contract between employer and employee, which he believed to be protected by the due process clause of the Fourteenth Amendment. In focusing specifically on bakers, he noted that no one had ever contended that they were less intelligent than other workers or less able to take care of themselves without the protecting arm of the state. In order to complete his argument, Justice Peckham had to overcome the fact that the Court had previously upheld as a valid exercise of a state's police power a law enacted by the state of Utah limiting workers in underground mines to an eight-hour day. He managed this by defining the police power of a state as the power of a state to protect the safety, health, morals, and general welfare of the public, none of which he believed to be accomplished by the New York law. It was a law that protected bakers, not the public, and baking, unlike mining, was not in his view a dangerous occupation which warranted state protection. Nor did the wholesomeness of bread depend upon how many hours the baker worked.

What if a law such as this were to be upheld? Justice Peckham did what judges frequently do when striking down legislation. He produced a parade of horrors by suggesting extreme cases of state intervention in people's lives. Peckham suggested that there would be no limit to what government could do. He offered the vision of doctors, lawyers, and other professional people being prohibited from tiring their brains and athletes being prohibited from exercising too much, both of which might impair the fighting ability of the nation.

Justice John Marshall Harlan wrote a dissenting opinion in which two of his brethren joined. He acknowledged the existence of a liberty of contract but also noted that it was a matter of settled law that this right was not absolute. He suggested that the New York maximum hours law then before the Court might have been the product of the state legislature's recognition that employees in baking establishments did not negotiate with their employers from a position of equality and thus were compelled to agree to work long hours. It was a question of relative power, not a question of the intelligence of bakers. In an attempt to show the reasonableness of the New York legislation, Justice Harlan cited several health reports related to bakers. The reports showed that their average age was lower than that of other types of workers. When epidemics struck, bakers were among the first to die because their health had already been so damaged by the conditions under which they worked. Although Justice Harlan considered the legislation reasonable, the majority was not convinced. Neither was Harlan convinced that baking was a safe occupation.

Justice Oliver Wendell Holmes, a jurist who became well known for his dissenting opinions, also registered disagreement with the majority. His dissent, however, was quite different from that of Justice Harlan. Holmes objected that the justices constituting the majority had read their preferences for *laissez faire* economics into the Fourteenth Amendment. He denied, however, that any particular economic theory had been written into the Constitution. In a democratic system, Justice Holmes believed, popularly elected legislatures were the proper instruments for making policy and courts should be very hesitant to substitute their judgments for those of the people's elected representatives. He did not suggest that the Supreme Court lacked the power to hold legislation unconstitutional but rather that the power was properly used only when it was perfectly clear to any reasonable person that the Constitution had been violated. In the view of Justice Holmes, that could not be said of the New York maximum hours law. His view did not prevail.

Impact of Event

The immediate impact of *Lochner v. New York* was that New York bakers continued to work long hours under dismal working conditions. They were subjected to intense heat, their eyes and lungs were affected by constant exposure to flour dust, and they worked at night, which often interfered with proper sleep. The impact of the *Lochner* case, however, extended beyond bakers.

Since "liberty of contract" had been read into the Fourteenth Amendment, it meant that *Lochner v. New York* had cast a constitutional shadow over minimum wage and maximum hours legislation being considered in other states. Efforts to improve the conditions of working people did not come to an abrupt halt because of the *Lochner* decision, but reformers had to draft their legislation in such a way as to distinguish it from the New York law which had been held unconstitutional.

Even before the *Lochner* decision had been handed down, the state of Oregon had established a ten-hour day for women working in factories and laundries. Like the New York Bakeshop Act, it had been violated and challenged. Progressive attorney Louis D. Brandeis was retained to defend the law's constitutionality before the Supreme Court. Brandeis noted that the Court had earlier disallowed the New York law because the justices had not been convinced that it was a health or safety measure. He concluded that it was his job to convince them, without challenging their underlying theory, that the Oregon law was, in fact, health legislation. To do this, he produced a new kind of legal brief, one which flooded the justices with hundreds of pages of medical and economic data as well as similar laws enacted in other states and foreign countries, and which came to be called a "Brandeis brief." Throughout, he emphasized the childbearing functions of women and the effect that mothers' overwork would have on their children. His strategy was successful, and the Court upheld the Oregon law.

Following *Lochner v. New York* and *Muller v. Oregon*, the case sustaining maximum hours for women, social reform policies in the United States took on a distinct maternalist orientation. Such policies were strongly supported and lobbied for by women's clubs well before women obtained suffrage. The members were not working-class women. They were, for the most part, married middle-class women.

Although protective legislation for women workers stood a better chance of withstanding constitutional challenge than similar legislation benefiting all workers, the Supreme Court was not consistent. In 1917, it upheld a state maximum hours law for all factory workers without ever mentioning *Lochner*, but in 1923 relied upon *Lochner* as precedent in striking down congressional legislation providing a minimum wage for women and children in the District of Columbia. *Lochner v. New York* continued to have a blighting effect on legislation to improve the conditions of American labor until it was finally overruled in 1937.

Bibliography

Commons, John R., ed. *History of Labor in the United States, 1896-1932.* Vol. 3 in *History of Labor in the United States.* New York: Macmillan, 1935. This is a pioneering work of American labor history. Volume 3, containing Don D. Lescohier's "Working Conditions" and Elizabeth Brandeis' "Labor Legislation," is particularly helpful for placing *Lochner v. New York* in context. Thoroughly documented, with extensive bibliography and index.

Kens, Paul. *Judicial Power and Reform Politics: The Anatomy of Lochner v. New York.* Lawrence: University Press of Kansas, 1990. This volume is an excellent study of all aspects of the case. It is particularly useful for its description of conditions in turn-of-the-century bakeshops in New York and the politics of the Bakeshop Act. Includes bibliography and index.

Lerner, Max. "The Supreme Court and American Capitalism." In *Essays in Consti-tutional Law*, edited by Robert G. McCloskey. New York: Alfred A. Knopf, 1957. Originally published in 1933, an interpretation of the Supreme Court as the insti-tution which links the nation's supreme law and its economic system of capitalism. Not quite a theory of economic determinism, it fit the *Lochner* era well and ex-plained the views of justices Holmes and Harlan, as well as Peckham, but would not accommodate an activist, rights-oriented Court such as existed in the 1960's.

Skocpol, Theda, and Gretchen Ritter. "Gender and the Origins of Modern Social Policies in Britain and the United States." *Studies in American Political Develop-ment* 5 (Spring, 1991): 36-93. This long, well-documented article explains how differing governmental structures and class structures led to paternalistic social policies in Great Britain and maternalistic social policies in the United States in the early twentieth century. In relation to the United States, it offers an interesting discussion of the role of women's clubs.

Strum, Philippa. *Louis D. Brandeis: Justice for the People.* New York: Schocken, 1984. This biography of the Progressive lawyer and later Supreme Court justice is generally useful but particularly so for one chapter, "The Brandeis Brief." In-cludes bibliography and index.

United States Supreme Court. *"Lochner v. New York." United States Reports* 198 (1905): 45. The case itself is the best source of information on the views of Su-preme Court justices. It is relatively brief and within the grasp of readers without a legal background.

_____. *"Muller v. Oregon." United States Reports* 208 (1908): 412. This is the case regarding maximum hours for women. It too is worth reading.

Patricia A. Behlar

Cross-References

Massachusetts Adopts the First Minimum-Wage Law in the United States (1912), p. 126; Ford Offers a Five-Dollar, Eight-Hour Workday (1914), p. 143; Brandeis Be-comes the First Jewish Member of the Supreme Court (1916), p. 172; The Interna-tional Labour Organisation Is Established (1919), p. 281; Steel Workers Go on Strike to Demand Improved Working Conditions (1919), p. 293; The Wagner Act Requires Employers to Accept Collective Bargaining (1935), p. 508; Social Security Act Es-tablishes Benefits for Nonworking People (1935), p. 514; The Congress of Industrial Organizations Is Formed (1938), p. 545; Autoworkers Negotiate a Contract with a Cost-of-Living Provision (1948), p. 766; Chávez Forms Farm Workers' Union and Leads Grape Pickers' Strike (1962), p. 1161; Chávez Is Jailed for Organizing an Ille-gal Lettuce Boycott (1970), p. 1567.

BLACK LEADERS CALL FOR EQUAL RIGHTS AT THE NIAGARA FALLS CONFERENCE

Categories of event: Civil rights; racial and ethnic rights
Time: August 1-7, 1905
Locale: Fort Erie, New York

The Niagara Movement, which was founded by W. E. B. Du Bois and William Monroe Trotter, attempted to elevate the position of blacks in America at the beginning of the twentieth century

Principal personages:
W. E. B. DU BOIS (1868-1963), the leading black opponent of racism during the first half of the twentieth century
ANDREW CARNEGIE (1835-1919), a leading steel manufacturer and philanthropist
THEODORE ROOSEVELT (1858-1919), the twenty-sixth president of the United States (1901-1909)
WILLIAM HOWARD TAFT (1857-1930), the twenty-seventh president of the United States (1909-1913)
WILLIAM MONROE TROTTER (1872-1934), the editor of *The Guardian*
BOOKER T. WASHINGTON (1856-1915), an influential black leader and founder of the Tuskegee Institute

Summary of Event

The Niagara Movement was formed largely as a response to the indifference to the plight of blacks in America. Despite the promises of the Civil War and Reconstruction, lynching and mob violence went unchecked throughout the South during the Jim Crow period (1881-1914). Outbreaks of rioting were also common in the North at this time. By the turn of the century, interracial violence had become a national problem.

In the first two decades of the twentieth century, America's three most important spokesmen for the rights of blacks were Booker T. Washington, W. E. B. Du Bois, and William Monroe Trotter. Washington, who was an adviser to Theodore Roosevelt and a friend to white millionaires, counseled accommodation by blacks. Washington drew sharp attacks from Du Bois, editor of *The Crisis,* and Trotter, editor of *The Guardian,* for his insistence that blacks settle for a vocational education instead of striving for higher education.

The philosophical division between Washington's supporters, the Bookerites, and his detractors, the anti-Bookerites, became even more apparent after a Boston riot. Trotter arranged to confront Washington at a public meeting to be held in the Columbus Avenue African Methodist Episcopal Zion Church. When Washington was introduced to the two thousand people in attendance, a riot ensued in which one person was stabbed and Trotter himself was arrested. As a result of the exaggerated coverage given to the event in the newspapers, the anti-Bookerites received considerable support. Trotter had become, in effect, a martyr for the radical left.

In 1903, the need for a militant and unified organization became evident to Washington. In February, Washington informed Du Bois of his plan to unite all black spokesmen. With the financial assistance of Washington's friend Andrew Carnegie, Washington arranged for the conference to be held at Carnegie Hall in New York during the first week of January. Invitations were sent to twenty-eight blacks, only eight of whom were anti-Bookerites. Monroe Trotter was not invited. News of the meeting was kept secret from the public.

Essentially, the conference of 1903 set the groundwork for a more permanent organization. The Bookerites and the anti-Bookerites at the meeting arrived at a compromise position. They also agreed to appoint a permanent Committee of Twelve at a later date. Although the conference gave the appearance of harmony, this façade was shattered later by comments made in the press by Washington and Du Bois.

Du Bois became disillusioned with the Committee of Twelve when, in July, 1904, it adopted a more conservative platform than had been agreed on in January and appointed Washington as its chairman. After resigning from the Committee of Twelve in March, 1905, Du Bois, with the urging of Monroe Trotter, set about to form a more radical organization. Trotter suggested forming a "strategy board" that would become a national anti-Washington organization. After resolving that no expenses were to be paid by any white benefactors, Du Bois and Trotter met with F. L. McGhee of St. Paul and C. E. Bentley of Chicago to plan a meeting to be held that summer in western New York. Invitations were mailed to black leaders in seventeen states.

During the first week of August, 1905, twenty-nine black men from all over the country gathered at Fort Erie, New York, and christened their organization the Niagara Movement. Having learned their lesson from the Committee of Twelve, the men organized an executive system of overlapping jurisdictions to prevent domination by any one member. Du Bois was elected general secretary, and George Jackson, a lawyer from Cincinnati, was elected general treasurer. Both men worked in conjunction with an executive committee made up of the chairmen and each state's local chapter. Work was divided among special committees, the most important of which, the Press and Public Opinion Committee, was headed by Monroe Trotter. The state committees were assigned the roles of securing just legislation for blacks and of carrying out educational and propaganda functions.

The "Declaration of Principles," which had been drafted by Du Bois and Trotter, was a radical document that was the foundation for a radical organization. In blunt language, the document accused the white race of "ravishing and degrading" the black race and pleaded for the cooperation of all men of all races. It also demanded that whites grant suffrage, equal civil rights, equal economic opportunities, and equal opportunities for an education to all blacks. Du Bois and Trotter had hoped that their fledgling organization would confront Booker T. Washington and his white supporters.

The Tuskegee Machine, led by Washington, opposed the Niagara Movement from the outset. Washington's supporters infiltrated the Niagara Movement and tried to isolate it. Although Washington almost entirely agreed with the Declaration of Principles, he did not agree with the founders' plan for achieving their goals: the political emphasis, agitation, the lack of attention to economic development, and the demand for an immediate end to all racial discrimination.

In spite of the harassment from Tuskegee, the Niagara Movement made considerable progress during its first year. In December, 1906, Du Bois reported to the group's 170 members in thirty-four states that more than one thousand pamphlets had been distributed. State chapters across the country had worked in conjunction with local protest groups in such major cities as New York and Philadelphia and in the District of Columbia. Members had also demonstrated against a segregated exposition in Jamestown, Virginia, and had protested an amendment to the Hepburn railroad-rate bill that legalized segregated passenger seating in trains. When the Niagara Movement convened in Harper's Ferry in August, 1906, for its second annual conference, the only serious problem seemed to be the lack of funds.

Problems, however, had already begun to surface in the months preceding the meeting, and they continued throughout the year. Early in 1906, Du Bois had angered Trotter by forming a women's auxiliary of the movement. In the fall, a serious breach developed between Trotter and Clement Morgan, the state secretary of the Massachusetts branch. Trotter objected vehemently when Morgan accepted the Republican Party's nomination for a seat in the legislature, thereby violating the movement's rule forbidding members to hold office. In a show of protest, Trotter resigned from the Committee on Arrangements.

Trotter's final break from the Niagara Movement came in the fall of 1906, as plans for another meeting took shape. Trotter proposed that Du Bois be replaced as general secretary, and that the head of the Massachusetts branch should be elected, not appointed. After Du Bois and Morgan rejected Trotter's proposals, Trotter formally withdrew his membership from the Niagara Movement in 1908.

Trotter's departure was the beginning of the end for the Niagara Movement. Du Bois admitted that his inexperience as a political leader was an obvious factor in the organization's decline. Encouraged by the rift between the founders of the movement, the Tuskegee Machine escalated its attacks against Du Bois in black newspapers. The lack of a formal national headquarters and a regular paid staff also contributed to the movement's decline. After Trotter's resignation, the group held two more meetings, neither of which had a large attendance. In 1910, the Niagara Movement ceased operations altogether when Du Bois encouraged its members to join the National Association for the Advancement of Colored People (NAACP).

Impact of Event

Before the Niagara Movement disbanded, this relatively small organization had a significant impact on American politics. Ever since its founding in 1905, the Niagara Movement had denounced President Theodore Roosevelt for his well-publicized views that blacks were racially inferior. The Niagara Movement's opposition to President Roosevelt had reached its peak when soldiers from the all-black Twenty-fifth Infantry regiment had been accused of running rampant through the streets of Brownsville, Texas, killing one man and wounding two others. Roosevelt himself had denounced the soldiers and encouraged his chosen successor, William Howard Taft, to do the same during the campaign of 1908. In the summer of 1907, the Niagara Movement, meeting in Boston, set the theme for the coming presidential election by calling on the five hundred thousand black voters of the North to use their votes to defeat Taft. As a gesture of gratitude, the Niagara Movement supported Senator Joseph Benson Foraker's bid for the Republican nomination because he had dissented from the majority report by the Committee on Military Affairs on the Brownsville incident. Even though Foraker did not win the nomination, the movement's supporters had built up enough political momentum both during and after the election of 1908 to help Woodrow Wilson win the election of 1912.

Although the Niagara Movement ceased to exist after the formation of the NAACP in 1910, it had a definite effect on the formation of the fledgling organization. The majority of the black founders, including Du Bois and Trotter, came to the NAACP from the Niagara Movement and became the dominant black constituency within the organization. The memory of the financial problems that had plagued the Niagara Movement convinced many of these former members of the need to secure support from liberal whites. The Niagara Movement also served as a catalytic force in the shift of the consensus of black thought from the Bookerite doctrine to the protest tradition that was first endorsed by the movement and later adopted by the NAACP. Finally, many of the goals of the Niagara Movement, particularly the emphasis on higher education, material advancement, and voting rights, were adopted by the NAACP. Although it can be said that the Niagara Movement was too radical for its time, the NAACP was undoubtedly an organization whose time had come.

The Niagara Movement's most important legacy, though, was the awareness it fostered among whites of the seriousness of the plight of blacks in America. For the first time in the twentieth century, whites were told, in strong language, by blacks themselves that blacks were not inferior beings and that they were entitled to all the rights enjoyed by other Americans. By employing such effective methods as editorializing in black newspapers and organizing local demonstrations, the Niagara Movement prepared the way for the national protest movements of the 1960's.

Bibliography

Blaustein, Albert P., and Robert Zangrando, eds. *Civil Rights and the American Negro.* New York: Trident Press, 1968. This episodic account of the Civil Rights movement asserts that the Niagara Movement was a natural response to the injustices of the Jim Crow period. The only chapter that even mentions the Niagara Movement provides merely a one-page summary toward the end.

Fox, Stephen R. *The Guardian of Boston: William Monroe Trotter.* New York: Atheneum, 1970. Chapter 3 provides the most comprehensive account of the Niagara Movement available. Although the emphasis is on Trotter, the author gives attention to the roles played by Washington and Du Bois. The author also provides a lengthy explanation for the demise of the movement.

Logan, Rayford W., ed. *W. E. B. Du Bois: A Profile.* New York: Hill & Wang, 1971. The Niagara Movement is discussed at length in William H. Ferris' article "The Emerging Leader—A Contemporary View." Written before the demise of the movement, the article paints a deceptively harmonious and optimistic picture of its inner workings.

Marable, Manning. *W. E. B. Du Bois: Black Radical Democrat.* Boston: Twayne, 1986. Manning demonstrates how the Niagara Movement evolved into the NAACP. He also places the movement within the context of the American political scene.

Morris, Aldon D. *Origins of the Civil Rights Movement.* New York: Free Press, 1984. Morris stresses the militant side of the Niagara Movement. He also illustrates the similarity between the goals of the movement and the goals of the NAACP.

Rampersad, Arnold. *The Art and Imagination of W. E. B. Du Bois.* Cambridge, Mass.: Harvard University Press, 1976. In Chapter 5, entitled "The Mantle and the Prophet," Rampersad gives a philosophical overview of the similarities between the tenets of the movement and Du Bois's own personal position as it was stated in his writings. The absence of much factual material regarding the movement itself would make this inappropriate for someone who is interested in the history of the group.

Tuttle, William M., ed. *W. E. B. Du Bois.* Englewood Cliffs, N.J.: Prentice-Hall, 1973. In the article entitled "Radicals and Conservatives," Kelly Miller's biases color his description of the Niagara Movement as the product of Du Bois's "poetic mind." Miller, however, does offer an interesting explanation of the significance of the cities chosen by the founders as the sites for their meetings.

Alan Brown

Cross-References

The Ku Klux Klan Spreads Terror in the South (1920's), p. 298; The Congress of Racial Equality Forms (1942), p. 601; CORE Stages a Sit-in in Chicago to Protest Segregation (1943), p. 618; Race Riots Erupt in Detroit and Harlem (1943), p. 635; CORE Stages the "Journey of Reconciliation" (1947), p. 718; *Brown v. Board of Education* Ends Public School Segregation (1954), p. 913; Parks Is Arrested for Refusing to Sit in the Back of the Bus (1955), p. 947; The SCLC Forms to Link Civil Rights Groups (1957), p. 974; Eisenhower Sends Troops to Little Rock, Arkansas (1957), p. 1003; The Council of Federated Organizations Registers Blacks to Vote (1962), p. 1149; The Black Panther Party Is Organized (1966), p. 1348.

UPTON SINCLAIR PUBLISHES *THE JUNGLE*

Categories of event: Workers' rights and consumers' rights
Time: 1906
Locale: Chicago, Illinois

Sinclair's novel about labor exploitation and unsanitary conditions in the meat-packing industry shocked the American public and expedited governmental reforms

Principal personages:
  UPTON SINCLAIR (1878-1968), an idealistic author who advocated socialism
  THEODORE ROOSEVELT (1858-1919), the twenty-sixth president of the United States (1901-1909), known as the "trust buster"
  JONATHAN OGDEN ARMOUR (1863-1927), the head of Armour & Co., one of the giant meat-packing firms at the time of publication of *The Jungle*
  HARVEY WILEY (1844-1930), the chief chemist of the U.S. Department of Agriculture from 1883 to 1912, a crusader for federal controls of food additives

Summary of Event

In the early years of the twentieth century, the combination of laissez-faire capitalism and the Industrial Revolution was creating monopolistic industries in America and generating huge fortunes for those who controlled them. These captains of industry sincerely believed that mass production would benefit humanity by making consumer goods cheap and abundant. They believed that business competition was a good thing because it stimulated innovation and efficiency. Their aim was to get the maximum production from the minimum investment in labor and raw material. Social Darwinism was exactly the theory that appealed to their needs. This is a theory that the struggle for existence improves the human species because the stronger thrive while the weaker perish. The extrapolation from Charles Darwin's theories regarding the evolution of plant and animal life seemed to justify driving workers to the limits of human endurance, encouraging unrestricted immigration to swell the labor pool, and using corporate profits to control federal, state, and local governments and make it virtually impossible for workers to put up any organized resistance.

Big business interests also controlled public opinion through the newspapers and magazines. Many of these publications were owned outright by powerful capitalists; most others were dependent on advertising revenue derived from business interests and did not dare to offend them. The attitude of the money barons of the period is succinctly expressed in the motion picture *Citizen Kane* (1941). The fictional protagonist Charles Foster Kane, owner of vast financial interests including a chain of newspapers, says, "The public will think what I tell them to think."

Mechanization and mass-production methods tended to replace skilled labor and resulted in a tremendous demand for unskilled workers who could be taught to do repetitive tasks. Employers hired efficiency experts to study their operations and break down the entire production process into the simplest possible components. The essence of the system was that the worker was not free to move around the factory but had the product conveyed to him or her by mechanical apparatus. The great comedian and movie producer Charlie Chaplin satirized this dehumanizing procedure in his classic film *Modern Times* (1936), a work modeled after Sinclair's *The Jungle.*

The general public tended to believe in the system because it seemed to represent progress: It was producing an abundance of cheap goods that seemed to be raising everyone's standard of living. An example was Henry Ford's mass-produced Model T Ford, which was making it possible for the average American to own an automobile, a wonderful machine that opened up the world for recreation and exploration, and formerly had been a symbol of upper-class status. The newly developing art form of advertising presented only the positive aspects of modern industrial production and ignored what went on behind the scenes.

The demand for labor attracted illiterate, impoverished immigrants from all over Europe. They came to America with the dream of attaining a quality of life that was unthinkable in their native countries. Most of them were absorbed by the factory system, where they found themselves working even harder than they had in their homelands. They tried to organize, but there were many problems: religious differences, a variety of languages, competition from the influx of immigrant workers, and political corruption. Employers often had politicians and police on their side. Strikes were broken up by "goons" (hired thugs) and "scabs" (strikebreakers), aided and abetted by the police. Labor organizers were jailed on trumped-up charges. Worst of all, the flood of immigration created such relentless competition for jobs that workers were deprived of bargaining power. This naturally created a considerable amount of hostility among the various ethnic groups, making it difficult for workers to organize effectively.

Inspired by his discovery of socialism, the idealistic young author Upton Sinclair selected the meat-packing industry as an example of capitalistic exploitation of human labor. He spent two months investigating working and living conditions in and around the Chicago packing houses and presented his findings in the form of a novel, focusing on the career of a single immigrant laborer named Jurgis Rudkus. What happens to Jurgis is intended to symbolize what happens to working people generally under laissez-faire capitalism.

Jurgis begins his working career as a powerful young man full of optimism and ambition. He and his young wife believe in the American dream of acquiring their own home and living a comfortable life through hard work, honesty, and thrift. Jurgis is gradually broken down by the excruciating work in the slaughterhouse. He also becomes disgusted by greed and corruption which destroy human lives and result in incredibly filthy handling of meat. Diseased animals and putrefying meat are regularly sold to the American public and exported all over the world. The buildings are infested with rats, which often get mixed in with the sausage meat. Sinclair piles one horrible detail on top of another. His most memorable example combines big business' exploitation of labor and its disregard for the consumer in the pursuit of profit: Some workers, exhausted by the long hours and speeded-up tempo dictated by the merciless machinery of mass production, actually fall into cooking vats and become part of the product that is sold to the public as "pure leaf lard."

Jurgis works hard and continues to cling to the American dream until he injures himself on the job. After recuperating for two months, he finds that he has been replaced by younger, stronger men and can only get a job in a fertilizer plant, where he works under the most appalling conditions. His career continues on a downhill course. He becomes addicted to drinking, is thrown in jail, is blacklisted, drifts from one temporary job to another, and becomes a strong-arm robber and a strikebreaker. His wife, son, and father all die tragically. Finally, all alone and in despair, Jurgis happens to attend a meeting where he hears a brilliant socialist speak on the evils of capitalism. Jurgis' whole life is turned around by the realization that he is not really alone but shares the same problems as millions of other workers. Socialism becomes a substitute for religious faith. Sinclair hoped that his prescription would be accepted by the masses.

Sinclair had started his literary career as a hack writer of fiction for young people. This experience taught him how to write in simple language. *The Jungle* became famous because it was easy to read and easy to understand. Almost immediately, other writers began to publish novels exposing other branches of American business. The exposé novel has continued to be a popular genre of fiction.

Impact of Event

The most immediate effect of *The Jungle* was that it expedited the passage of the Pure Food and Drug Act of 1906, which prohibited shipment of adulterated foods and drugs in interstate commerce and required honest labeling. The Meat Inspection Act was passed in the same year. Enforcement of these acts led to the creation in 1930 of the Food and Drug Administration, an agency which gradually acquired more and more supervisory control over production and sale of consumer goods. This legislation helped to establish a precedent for further government control of business operations.

Government control of business had a strong, usually positive, effect on consumer rights. The nation's health was better, and consumers felt less anxious about what they were eating and feeding their children. It would be hard to imagine living in a civilized society without such safeguards. This, however, was not the effect Sinclair had tried to achieve. In his autobiography, he wrote: "I aimed at the public's heart, and by accident I hit it in the stomach." The public was much more concerned about the food it ate than about the plight of the workers who produced it. What people remembered about the book was "rats in the sausage."

The history of *The Jungle* symbolizes the main problem of socialism as a solution to the world's problems. Human nature is arguably more selfish than cooperative. It is impossible to get an entire population to work hard for an ideal: People want tangible personal rewards, and these are the things that capitalism has provided more effectively than has socialism. The unrest in the Soviet Union, China, and Eastern Europe in the early 1990's demonstrated that socialistic dictatorships may start off with idealistic principles but are forced to resort to guns and concentration camps to motivate their constituents to produce. Sinclair himself lost his zest for socialism in his old age and changed his credo to "social justice." As applied to big business, this might be translated into the modern term of "corporate social responsibility."

In the long run, *The Jungle* was most important in the influence it had on other artists. The book was a bestseller in America and Great Britain and made Upton Sinclair famous. He went on to write influential propagandistic fiction and nonfiction for sixty years. His works have been translated into forty-seven languages in thirty-nine countries. He showed how complex economic and political ideas could be effectively presented in dramatic form and appeal directly to the masses.

In Sinclair's model, a viewpoint character is broken by an oppressive system and finally comes to realize the need for political action. The reader identifies with the viewpoint character and thereby shares in that character's conversion to an ideology. Variations of *The Jungle* have appeared throughout the world because it proved to be such a valuable propaganda tool. Because Sinclair's model can be used just as effectively to arouse public anger against socialistic bureaucracy as against capitalistic megalopoly, novelists in the Soviet Union, China, and Eastern Europe have attacked the evils of socialism with the same tool that Sinclair forged to promote it. In *Mammonart* (1925), a nonfiction work, Sinclair's thesis is that all art is propaganda, that it cannot help but be propaganda, and that modern artists should not feel squeamish about using their work as propaganda to agitate for the betterment of mankind.

The most important effect of *The Jungle* and its many imitations was that they undermined the popular belief that the ambitious individual can find happiness and financial success through hard work and thrift—the so-called "American dream." Instead, these works helped to promote a mass consciousness of the need for joint action to effect improvement in human affairs.

Bibliography

Agee, James. "A Mother's Tale." In *Fifty Best American Short Stories, 1915-1965*, edited by Martha Foley. Boston: Houghton Mifflin, 1965. This intriguing and highly unusual short story describes the whole process of raising and butchering cattle from the point of view of an animal who managed to escape from the slaughterhouse.

Asch, Peter. *Consumer Safety Regulation.* New York: Oxford University Press, 1988. Asch, an economist concerned with regulation, analyzes the major arguments advanced for consumer protection laws. Many, though not all, of the economic arguments for regulation are weak. He argues that consumer protection laws often

have perverse consequences. The right to safety, however, must also be considered. The effect of Sinclair's *The Jungle* in promoting disclosure laws is discussed.

Bellamy, Edward. *Looking Backward: 2000-1887*. 1887. Reprint. Boston: Houghton
Mifflin, 1917. Originally published in 1887, this early science-fiction novel had a
profound impact on Upton Sinclair and many other intellectuals of his generation.
Like Sinclair's novels, it uses a fictional form to present a socialist message.

Gould, Lewis L., ed. *The Progressive Era*. Syracuse, N.Y.: Syracuse University Press,
1974. This collection of eight essays by prominent historians covers both domestic
and international affairs and provides portraits of most of the important personalities of the era. The extensive notes for each chapter offer a wealth of source
material for further study.

Kazin, Alfred. *On Native Grounds: An Interpretation of Modern American Prose
Literature*. New York: Reynal & Hitchcock, 1942. Written by a distinguished liter-
ary critic, this book is a classic in its field. Chapter 4, entitled "Progressivism:
The Superman and the Muckrake," is especially pertinent to the study of Upton
Sinclair and the period in which he wrote *The Jungle*.

Mookerjee, R. N. *Art for Social Justice: The Major Novels of Upton Sinclair*. Metuchen, N.J.: Scarecrow Press, 1988. Although this is a small book of only 151
pages, it contains an intelligent overview of Sinclair's career with many direct
quotations, comprehensive footnoting, and a valuable bibliography. A full chapter
is devoted to *The Jungle*.

Pridgen, Dee. *Consumer Protection and the Law*. New York: Clark Boardman, 1990.
Pridgen, formerly a member of the attorneys' staff of the Federal Trade Commission, gives a comprehensive account of the history and present status of laws for
the protection of the consumer. She covers relevant court decisions and offers a
history of the Federal Trade Commission and other regulatory agencies. She is
quite sympathetic to consumer protection. Topics include seller misrepresentation, buyer's justifiable reliance, and the doctrine of *caveat emptor*.

Sinclair, Upton. *The Autobiography of Upton Sinclair*. New York: Harcourt, Brace &
World, 1962. Published only a few years before the author's death, this book provides the best introduction to his philosophy and his unique personality. The book
contains a great deal of firsthand information about Sinclair's most important
novel, *The Jungle,* and describes the many famous people he came to know during
his lifetime.

Steinbeck, John. *The Grapes of Wrath*. New York: Viking Press, 1939. This famous
novel by a Nobel Prize-winning author is an excellent example of the kind of
literature that was directly inspired by Upton Sinclair's *The Jungle*. Steinbeck
chronicles the plight of Tom Joad and his family during the Great Depression of
the 1930's and gives a detailed account of the hardships endured by itinerant agricultural workers in California.

Trilling, Lionel. *The Middle of the Journey*. New York: Viking Press, 1947. This
important novel by a distinguished American teacher and author dramatizes the

loss of faith in socialism among American intellectuals as a result of growing public awareness of the evils of the socialist system as established in Soviet Russia. Like *The Jungle,* it presents complex theoretical ideas in an easy-to-read fictional format.

Bill Delaney

Cross-References

Supreme Court Disallows a Maximum Hours Law for Bakers (1905), p. 36; The Pure Food and Drug Act and Meat Inspection Act Become Law (1906), p. 64; Ford Offers a Five-Dollar, Eight-Hour Workday (1914), p. 143; Congress Prohibits Immigration of Illiterates over Age Sixteen (1917), p. 231; The International Labour Organisation Is Established (1919), p. 281; Steel Workers Go on Strike to Demand Improved Working Conditions (1919), p. 293; The Immigration Act of 1921 Imposes a National Quota System (1921), p. 350; A U.S. Immigration Act Imposes Quotas Based on National Origins (1924), p. 383; Social Security Act Establishes Benefits for Nonworking People (1935), p. 514; Consumers Union of the United States Emerges (1936), p. 527; The International Organization of Consumers Unions Is Founded (1960), p. 1062; Chávez Forms Farm Workers' Union and Leads Grape Pickers' Strike (1962), p. 1161; Nader Publishes *Unsafe at Any Speed* (1965), p. 1267; Congress Passes the Occupational Safety and Health Act (1970), p. 1585.

THE IRANIAN CONSTITUTION BARS
NON-MUSLIMS FROM CABINET POSITIONS

Category of event: Religious freedom
Time: 1906-1907
Locale: Iran

The constitution of Iran guaranteed individual religious freedom but denied non-Muslims access to high government office

Principal personages:

MOZAFFAR OD-DIN SHAH (1853-1907), the Iranian ruler who signed the first portion of the constitution when near death

MOHAMMAD ALI SHAH (1872-1925), Mozaffar's successor, who was bitterly opposed to the constitutional movement

MIRZA MALKAM KHAN (1833-1908), a onetime Iranian royal minister who was typical of the liberal constitutionalists

SHEIKH FAZLULLAH NURI (1841-1910), a staunch advocate of establishing a government on Islamic principles who was typical of the religious scholars (*ulama*) who joined the constitutional movement

SAYYID JAMAL OD-DIN AL-AFGHANI (1838-1897), a leading Pan-Islamicist who pioneered the alliance between the liberals and the *ulama* that made the Iranian revolution of 1905-1907 possible

Summary of Event

In the second half of the nineteenth century, Iran became increasingly enmeshed in international politics. The Russian empire was expanding to the southeast, while that of the British in India was moving toward the northwest. Iran was the unwilling buffer between those two imperial giants.

Iran's population at that period was approaching ten million people. More than a third of that number, however, were nomadic or seminomadic tribesmen. The rest of the country's inhabitants were scattered over the countryside in villages and hamlets. Under the Safavid dynasty (ca. 1500-1727), Iran had been a major force in the Middle East, but the fall of the Safavid empire was followed by seventy years of civil war and political chaos. The Qajar dynasty, which claimed the throne in 1796, never enjoyed the prestige of the Safavids. The Qajars exerted real authority only in their capital, Teheran, and in a few other cities. To govern the rest of the country, the Qajars depended on an intricate series of alliances with tribal chiefs and local landlords.

The weakness of the Qajar government meant that the dynasty was comparatively poor. Their extortionate policies were much resented, but the Qajars were never able to gain sufficient wealth to sustain their imperial pretensions. This made them an easy mark for European entrepreneurs eager to gain a commercial advantage in exchange for a comparatively small contribution to the royal purse. In this way, Europeans began to exert more control over Iran's economy. Iran's merchant class (the *bazaaris*) was especially hurt by the influx of relatively cheap European goods. Old patterns of production and distribution were disrupted.

Europe's influence was further emphasized in March, 1890, when the Qajar king granted the British a monopoly over the production, processing, and sale of tobacco in Iran. Iranians were avid smokers and the crop was widely grown. Farmers, petty manufacturers, and shopkeepers all faced the prospect of losing control over this valuable cash crop.

All classes of Iranian society began to protest the granting of the tobacco concession. A few individuals who had been educated in Europe or in Iran's few European-style schools led the way by complaining that the Qajars were selling out to British imperialists. They carried on their protest through pamphlets and newspapers printed in England or Russia and smuggled into Iran.

At the same time, the religious scholars (*ulama*) also began to involve themselves in the controversy. The *ulama*, educated in the Islamic religious sciences, far outnumbered those trained in modern schools. Also, the *ulama* of the Imami branch of Shī'ism, which the Safavid emperors made the majority sect in Iran, enjoyed a particularly close relationship with the masses, especially the merchants. Many scholars came from mercantile families and found their most devoted followers in that group. Although they were contemptuous of the Qajars, they did not trust those educated in European schools. To the *ulama*, the liberals seemed to be as bad as the imperialists.

As the tobacco controversy heated up, some of the liberals approached Sayyid Jamal od-Din al-Afghani, who was on an extended visit to Iran. Al-Afghani convinced the liberals that they had to express their opposition to the Qajars in Islamic terms. Only then would the *ulama* and the *bazaaris* join them. The liberals followed his advice, and al-Afghani began writing to the scholars arguing that they and the liberals both wanted the same Islamic reforms. Religious scholars had greater access to the masses than did the liberals. Many of them were preachers in mosques, and soon their sermons were filled with attacks on the Qajars. The protest grew so strong that the king was forced to withdraw the tobacco concession. He expelled al-Afghani for his participation in the controversy. Al-Afghani's work in bringing the liberals and religious scholars together, however, set the stage for more serious political change.

Throughout his reign, Mozaffar od-Din Shah dragged Iran further into foreign debt. Mozaffar was a sickly man, and his doctors talked him into making several trips to famous European spas. In order to finance those expeditions, Mozaffar floated a number of large loans from the Russians. Scattered protests continued.

The Iranian revolution began in December of 1905. The governor of Teheran had several prominent merchants publicly beaten for refusing to cooperate with his economic policies. In protest, a crowd of *bazaaris* and *ulama* went to the Royal Mosque. In turn, a government minister hired a mob to drive them out. Several merchants and scholars were roughed up. The throng then proceeded to a shrine outside the city, where they claimed religious sanctuary. They issued a number of demands to the king, but these were not specifically formulated. Mozaffar fired the governor of Teheran, and revolutionary fervor abated temporarily.

By the end of the summer of 1906, protests had reached dramatic proportions. Several thousand prominent citizens left Teheran for the city of Qom, a famous religious center. Another fourteen or fifteen thousand people took refuge on the grounds of the British embassy. Life in Teheran came to a standstill. This time the protestors demanded an elected parliament (*majlis*). The king was forced to concede. The first *majlis* met in October of 1906, and one of its committees set about drafting a constitution, known as the Fundamental Law. In the throes of his final illness, Mozaffar signed the document in December of 1906. The Fundamental Law was a fairly brief document, much of it patterned on the constitution of Belgium. Unlike Great Britain, Belgium was not a threat to Iran, so the framers of the law thought it would not inspire much opposition.

In October, 1907, a much larger document, "The Supplementary Fundamental Law," was reluctantly approved by the new king, Mohammad Ali Shah. This second portion of the constitution reflected some of the tensions that had emerged between the liberals and the religious scholars. After the initial success of the constitutional revolution, some of the *ulama* began to suspect that they and the modernizers did not mean quite the same thing when speaking of Islam. One of the prominent scholars, Sheikh Fazlullah Nuri, said, "What is the use of a constitution cooked in a British stew pot?" The question of the rights of religious minorities was a case in point.

Although the Safavids had made Imami Shī'ism the dominant sect in Iran, large numbers of the Sunni sect (the majority in the Muslim world outside of Iran) remained. Sunnism was particularly strong among the tribal groups. No one considered banning Sunni participation in government, because their minority status made it unlikely that any Sunnis would find their way to high office. Christians of several sects, Jews, and Zoroastrians also lived in Iran, mostly in the cities. During the nineteenth century, European missionary and benevolent organizations began working with the Jewish and Christian groups. They built schools and hospitals that generally improved the social and economic position of the minorities. That development, however, raised the suspicion that Jews and Christians were agents of European imperialists.

In the *majlis*, religious minorities had reserved seats. Their representatives were supposed to take care of the needs of their communities. The liberal constitutionalists wanted to ensure absolute equality among all Iranians, but the *ulama* opposed that measure on several grounds. Having non-Muslims ruling over Muslims was to them a doctrinal and practical impossibility; moreover, they suspected Jews and Christians of having imperialist sympathies. As a compromise, the liberals conceded the principle that only Muslims could hold high government office and agreed to ban any missionary attempts to convert Muslims. Since the missionaries had never been successful in attracting converts from Islam, this did not amount to a serious denial of rights. The constitution did, however, guarantee personal religious freedom. Jews and Christians continued to practice their faiths without government interference. The constitution's ban on non-Muslims in the cabinet did not rouse any significant opposition among the religious minorities, perhaps because these groups had never had much influence in any of Iran's previous governments. Indeed, the prevalence of monarchy meant that even Muslim Iranians had not had much say in the way they were governed. The revolution of 1905 and the constitution were attempts to give ordinary Iranians some influence on the policies of the state.

Impact of Event

Iran's constitutional experiment ultimately failed. Mohammad Ali Shah was driven into exile in 1909. He had tried twice to overthrow the parliament and on the second attempt succeeded, but after his ouster a coalition of landlords even more reactionary than the king took control in Teheran. A few constitutionalists, including the prominent religious scholar Sheikh Fazlullah Nuri, held out in Tabriz, but eventually the Russians took the city and turned them over to the government. Many, like Nuri, were given the briefest of trials and hanged.

During World War I, Iran was occupied by British and Russian troops. Although the latter withdrew following the 1917 Russian Revolution, Great Britain retained a considerable amount of influence after the war. The British were not interested in reinstating the constitution. Their policy focused on keeping Iran stable so that the British could control Iran's expanding oil industry.

Iran never had a strong military tradition. Before the late nineteenth century, kings had relied on tribal levies when they needed an armed force. In 1879, a Cossack Brigade was established. The troopers were Iranians and the officers were Russians. Their primary duty was to protect the king. In 1917, the Russian officers withdrew, and their Iranian subordinates succeeded them as the unit's commanders. One of these, Reza Khan, staged a military coup in 1921. Although Reza was anti-British, he accepted British help in taking over the government. In 1928, Reza declared himself Shahan Shah (king of kings) and founded the Pahlavi dynasty. He and his son, Mohammad Reza, were to be its only monarchs. Throughout the rule of the Pahlavis, the constitution of 1906-1907 was, in theory, the law of the land, but the Pahlavis observed it only when it served their political purposes.

When the revolution of 1978-1979 began, an alliance of Western-educated liberals and religious scholars emerged, similar to that formed in 1890. Both sides looked back to the tobacco protest and the constitutional movement for heroic models. The names of Sayyid Jamal od-Din al-Afghani and Fazlullah Nuri were invoked constantly. Although the new constitution of the Islamic Republic of Iran was built more thoroughly on Islamic principles than that of 1906-1907, it still guaranteed religious toleration for Jews, Christians, and Zoroastrians. Like the earlier document, the new constitution did not allow religious minorities to hold high government office.

The revolutionaries of 1978-1979 were also fearful of foreign interference. They looked upon the Shah Mohammad Reza as a puppet of the British and Americans. They believed that both Great Britain and the United States would attempt to crush them. Once again, Jews and Christians in Iran were suspected of harboring anti-revolutionary sentiments. In the years after 1980, however, that suspicion diminished. Many Jews and Christians fought in the war with Iraq. Those who died were given "martyr" status alongside that accorded Iranian Muslims killed in the war.

In many ways, the Iranian revolution of 1978-1979 was a continuation of the one that began in 1905. It resolved some of the tensions between liberals and *ulama* in favor of the latter. The *ulama* still appeared to command the loyalty of the Iranian masses as well as that of the *bazaaris*.

Bibliography

Arjomand, Saïd Amir, ed. *Authority and Political Culture in Shī'ism*. Albany: State University of New York Press, 1988. This is a collection of articles covering every aspect of Shī'ism's relationship to politics. Some concern the sixteenth and seventeenth centuries, which were crucial in the formation of Iranian Shī'ism. Also contains translations of texts, including two tracts on the 1906-1907 constitution.
_____. *The Turban for the Crown: The Islamic Revolution in Iran*. Oxford, England: Oxford University Press, 1988. This work will help Americans understand the role that religious scholars have played in Iranian politics. Between religious scholars and ordinary Iranians there exists a very delicate relationship. Although the *ulama* appear to be the leaders, they can only maintain that role by heeding the demands of their followers.
Keddie, Nikki. *Iran: Religion, Politics, and Society*. Totowa, N.J.: Frank Cass, 1980. Keddie is one of the most prominent among a comparatively small number of Euro-American scholars who really seem to understand Iranian history. In part, this is a result of Keddie's extensive use of Persian sources. This collection of some of her shorter articles covers a number of aspects of the 1905 revolution and its aftermath.
_____, ed. *Religion and Politics in Iran*. New Haven, Conn.: Yale University Press, 1983. An outstanding collection of essays by some of the best European and American scholars of Iran. Several of them present divergent accounts of the role of the *ulama* that constitute an informative debate on that subject.
_____. *Roots of Revolution: An Interpretive History of Modern Iran*. New Haven, Conn.: Yale University Press, 1981. This work is a genuine tour de force. Keddie manages to make sense of Iran's history from the nineteenth century through the revolution of 1978-1979. She covers the period between the tobacco protest and the revolution very well.
Nashat, Guity. *The Origins of Modern Reform in Iran, 1870-1880*. Urbana: University of Illinois Press, 1982. Although the works of Keddie and Arjomand cited in this bibliography cover the backgrounds of the *ulama*, Nashat's book pays attention to the liberal constitutionalists, giving them due credit for their contribution to modern Iran.

Wilber, Donald N. *Iran Past and Present.* Princeton, N.J.: Princeton University Press, 1981. Although some of Wilber's views now appear dated, this book remains a handy single-volume introduction to the long and complex history of Iran. Places the first constitution of Iran in the context of the many events that led to it and that have flowed from it.

Gregory C. Kozlowski

Cross-References
The Muslim League Attempts to Protect Minority Interests in India (1906), p. 87; The Pahlavi Shahs Attempt to Modernize Iran (1925), p. 406; Khomeini Uses Executions to Establish a New Order in Iran (1979), p. 2013; Iranian Revolutionaries Hold Americans Hostage (1979), p. 2045; The United Nations Votes to Protect Freedoms of Religion and Belief (1981), p. 2146.

THE BRITISH LABOUR PARTY IS FORMED

Category of event: Workers' rights
Time: February 12, 1906
Locale: London, England

The formation of the Labour Party, with its trade unionist and socialist principles, created a voice for the lower classes in a leading industrial and capitalist society

Principal personages:
KEIR HARDIE (1856-1915), the first leader of the Labour Party and the primary driving force behind trade unionist and socialist political action
RAMSAY MACDONALD (1866-1937), the first Labour prime minister, elected in 1924
JOHN BURNS (1858-1943), the first working-class person to become a cabinet minister
BEN TILLETT (1860-1943), the founder of the London dockworkers' union
HENRY MAYERS HYNDMAN (1842-1921), the leader of the Socialist Democratic Federation

Summary of Event

The lower classes of any society rarely, if ever, have the opportunity for direct access to the primary decisionmaking bodies, let alone the chance to obtain control in a collective manner of the reins of government. The creation of the Labour Party in 1906 was one of the first significant steps with direct, purposeful links to working-class objectives for political action and leadership in any industrial country to that time. That this should have occurred in Great Britain, the country of origin of both capitalism and modern industrialism, is all the more significant.

The Labour Party evolved out of a series of attempts by workers, socialists, and trade unionists to play a direct role in the British parliamentary system. Class privilege was at the heart of the British political tradition. Attempts to change the electoral system dated to the Reform Act of 1832. Efforts such as Chartism during the 1830's and 1840's failed to gain the vote for workers or to make Parliament more accessible to persons of the lower classes. Although the Reform Acts of 1867 and 1884 extended the ballot to males, first in the industrial and then in the agricultural sector, a supporting role was still the only means by which the newly enfranchised, but still largely powerless, workers could attempt to affect political outcomes. By the end of the nineteenth century, an informal coalition had been formed between labor groups and the Liberal Party to such an extent that candidates with dual support were referred to as Lib-Labs.

The rapid industrialization of Great Britain had created serious problems that society either ignored or only slowly addressed. Various groups claimed to possess the needed solutions and used these plans as a means of attracting followers. Trade unionists and socialists were two of the more significant camps out of which a variety of organizations emanated in the nineteenth century. The Labour Party would finally emerge from the efforts of these groups. At times these bodies worked independently, and at other times they formed coalitions. All played varying roles in heightening awareness of the issues and attempting to draw members into supporting class-based political issues and organizations. Principal among these were the Trades Union Congress (TUC), Social Democratic Federation (SDF), Fabian Socialists, and the Independent Labour Party (ILP).

One of the primary groups from which Labour emerged was the Trades Union Congress (TUC), formed in 1868 partially as an outgrowth of the extension of the vote to male workers the previous year. The TUC was particularly concerned with working conditions and compensation for work-related illness, disability, and unemployment. As a federation of unions, the TUC concentrated on union issues more than political candidates. Some of its members were more politically active. Keir Hardie, one of the first trade unionist representatives elected to Parliament, was a leader within the TUC. Hardie, with roots in Scottish trade unions and socialist ideology, would more than any other individual influence the progression of events that led to the formation of the Labour Party.

The ability of the lower classes to address grievances or to seek gains was limited and worsening. A number of labor-management conflicts had widened the gulf between the two. These confrontations heightened trade unionist and socialist leaders' awareness of their lack of political power. One major success by labor, the London Dock Strike of 1889, heightened expectations of what might be achieved. Broad-based support, widespread publicity, and effective leadership from such figures as John Burns and Ben Tillett demonstrated what was possible. Both Burns and Tillett emerged as leaders in the TUC as a consequence.

The drive toward political independence began a few years later, with the creation of the Independent Labour Party (ILP) in January, 1893. Spearheaded by Keir Hardie, representatives of the SDF, Fabians, various trade unions, and other organizations convened to establish a mechanism for more direct support of candidates who would be independent of other parties and directly committed to trade unionism and socialism. This new organization—yet another coalition—was a major step toward the eventual creation of the Labour Party. The formation of the group, while intensifying collective efforts and heightening public awareness of a common agenda, was on a relatively small scale and without major public fanfare. The group lacked a cause that would ignite the public's imagination and create sufficient support for the autonomous political faction.

That event occurred in 1900. Railroad workers that year struck the Taff Vale Railway Company. The company sued and won damages for lost revenue. The Taff Vale court decision, upheld by the House of Lords in 1901, presented a fundamental threat to workers' ability to act collectively in labor-management disputes. The drive to reverse this decision was the essential galvanizing force that forged the coalition of various labor and socialist elements which previously had worked in splintered fashion on separate trade-specific or ideologically divergent programs.

Coalition building was difficult given the idiosyncrasies of some of the leaders of the various organizations. The debate over the best strategy and the question of whether to include socialists in the aims of labor had long kept the major players in the trade unionist and socialist camps from coalescing for action. The socialists were split among various groups, with the likes of the SDF, led by Henry Mayers Hyndman, on the more radical end of the spectrum contrasted with the middle-class-supported Fabian Socialists. The Fabians, with Beatrice and Sidney Webb and George Bernard Shaw among their leaders, called for gradual, evolutionary political introduction of socialist policies and programs.

A more direct step, with concrete measures for supporting independent candidates, had been taken on February 27, 1900. Keir Hardie organized the creation of the Labour Representation Committee (LRC), supported by the TUC, the ILP, Fabians, and the SDF. (The SDF would drop out shortly thereafter.) To many historians, the establishment of the LRC was the pivotal step in creating the Labour Party. The events of 1906 were but a culmination of the decisions to act made in 1900. The LRC went beyond the efforts of any of the separate organizations that established it and extended previous efforts at political action. The sole purpose of the LRC was to achieve political victories in parliamentary elections for candidates tied to labor. The composition of this new body guaranteed that both trade unionism and socialist principles would be fused in the solutions offered to the nation by candidates identified with the LRC. Trade unions were initially slow to respond to the new organization, which initially only provided endorsements and encouragement of candidates directly identified as labor candidates. The subsequent uproar over the Taff Vale case contributed to the rapid rise in popularity of the LRC, which had 847,000 members by 1903. Ramsay MacDonald, who later would become the first Labour prime minister, served as the first secretary of this new political coalition. In 1903, the LRC established a political fund. In a firm stand for independence, it demanded that LRC candidates should not be affiliated with other political parties.

The final step of political autonomy came with the election of January, 1906. In the midst of an overwhelming victory by the Liberals, twenty-nine out of fifty candidates sponsored by the LRC were elected to Parliament. Of these, only three were opposed by Liberals. A sufficient number of Labour candidates were elected to form a new parliamentary Labour Party caucus. On February 12, the newly elected representatives met and selected officers, including Keir Hardie as the first chair. Three days later, the slate and the decision to call itself the Labour Party were carried by the conference of the LRC. This name change was the end of one era and the beginning of a new phase of a Labour opposition party, voicing lower-class, trade unionist, and socialist aspirations in Parliament. The Labour Party would gain control of the government several times during the twentieth century.

Impact of Event

The decision to form the LRC in 1900, the election victory in January, 1906, and the final, formal establishment of what is now known as the Labour Party demonstrated the growing social divisions in British society and the commitment of an increasing segment of the electorate from the lower and middle classes to support an agenda tied to implementing some of the demands of Labour's constituency. The electoral successes in 1906 are significant as demonstration that social and labor issues could not be ignored easily. Legislation was passed during the next few years that rectified some of labor's pressing concerns and began to implement what would later be called the British welfare state.

The efforts at political activism which dated from the 1830's were finally realized. One significant difference from the Chartist agenda was the inclusion of socialist representatives and principles in the Labour Party. The supporters of candidates identified with Labour rose from more than 300,000 in 1906 to 500,000 in 1910 and 4.5 million in 1922. Labour would achieve control of Parliament for the first time in 1924, with Ramsay MacDonald as prime minister. Labour would become a major force in British politics after World War II and continue to hold significant power until the 1970's.

Among the immediate consequences was the reversal of the implications of the Taff Vale case by passage of the Trade Disputes Act of 1906. Unions gained some rights, although the challenges, both legislative and otherwise, to actions taken during collective bargaining were not fully removed. The coalition backing Labour began to broaden significantly when the miners voted in 1908 to affiliate with the Labour Party.

The Workmen's Compensation Act (1906) nearly doubled those covered, from seven to thirteen million, by expanding the list of diseases included under the legislation. In 1908, Parliament established an eight-hour day for miners and provided state-supported pensions for some workers. Female workers were targeted in 1909 by the establishment of a minimum wage for certain sweatshop-type employment.

In addition to pension and workers' compensation provisions, some elements of a broadening state responsibility for society, but especially the lower classes, began to be enacted. These measures demonstrated socialist concerns that extended beyond union or work activities. Primary among these early acts were those that required medical inspection of school children (1907) and enabled, although did not mandate, school food programs. A Housing and Town Planning Act (1909) targeted urban slums. These legislative actions, although important, still required the support of the Liberal Party, which was in control of the government. The Labour electoral achievements of 1906 spurred others to be more attentive to a large segment of society that had gone too long without a platform in the national government. Other pieces of the Labour demands would begin to emerge in subsequent years. The successes of 1906 were encouraging to Labour's supporters; however, these gains did not resolve the ideological and class conflict inherent in a modern industrial society.

Bibliography

Cole, G. D. H., and Raymond Postgate. *The British People, 1746-1946.* New York: Barnes & Noble, 1961. A pioneering classic in working-class history. Provides extensive information on social, labor, and political history from 1746 to 1946.

Hinton, James. *Labour and Socialism.* Amherst: University of Massachusetts Press, 1983. Examines the relationship between trade unionism and the range of working-class interests and distinguishes the nature of London politics and unionism from other regions. Covers the period from 1867 to 1974 in a tone critical of failures of Labour.

Howell, David. *British Workers and the Independent Labour Party: 1888-1906.* Manchester, England: Manchester University Press, 1983. The most comprehensive study on one of the key forerunners of the Labour Party. Analysis of the significance of the ILP forms concluding chapters of this major work.

McBriar, A. M. *Fabian Socialism and English Politics, 1884-1918.* Cambridge, England: Cambridge University Press, 1962. Extensive study of the Fabian Socialists, with concluding chapters on Fabian influence on the origins of the Labour Party. Useful to gain a more complete picture of the issues and forces from which Labour emerged.

McKibbin, Ross. *The Evolution of the Labour Party, 1910-1924.* London: Oxford University Press, 1974. Examines early successes of the party in the context of local and parliamentary politics and traces the rise of Labour along with the decline of the Liberals. Claims that socialism was not vital to Labour's popularity.

Martin, Ross. *TUC: The Growth of a Pressure Group, 1868-1976.* Oxford, England: Clarendon Press, 1980. A broad overview of the Trades Union Congress, which was one of the key players in setting the agenda that Labour adopted.

Pelling, Henry. *The Origins of the Labour Party, 1880-1900.* London: Clarendon Press, 1965. The classic study on the topic. Focuses primarily on the Independent Labour Party, establishing a general evolution of Labour rather than raising critical questions or providing social-class analysis.

_____. *A Short History of the Labour Party.* London: Macmillan, 1961. Covers the period from 1906 forward. Includes an annotated bibliography.

Reid, Fred. *Keir Hardie.* London: Croom Helm, 1978. A brief analysis of the first labor and socialist representative elected to Parliament. Raises critical questions as to Hardie's real attitude toward the working class.

Daniel J. Doyle

Cross-References

The Pankhursts Found the Women's Social and Political Union (1903), p. 19; Supreme Court Disallows a Maximum Hours Law for Bakers (1905), p. 36; The International Labour Organisation Is Established (1919), p. 281; Steel Workers Go on Strike to Demand Improved Working Conditions (1919), p. 293; Great Britain Passes Acts to Provide Unemployment Benefits (1920), p. 321; British Workers Go on General Strike (1926), p. 429; The Wagner Act Requires Employers to Accept Collective Bargaining (1935), p. 508; The International Labour Organisation Wins the Nobel Peace Prize (1969), p. 1509; Solidarity Leads Striking Polish Workers (1980), p. 2112; Solidarity Regains Legal Status in Poland (1989), p. 2477.

THE PURE FOOD AND DRUG ACT AND MEAT INSPECTION ACT BECOME LAW

Categories of event: Consumers' rights; health and medical rights
Time: June 30, 1906
Locale: Washington, D.C.

With the support of President Theodore Roosevelt and a diverse consumer movement, Congress finally passed two watershed laws that provided Americans with some protection in the purchase of food and drugs

Principal personages:

THEODORE ROOSEVELT (1858-1919), the moderately progressive president whose "square deal" tried to promote general welfare

HARVEY WASHINGTON WILEY (1844-1930), the chief chemist of the Department of Agriculture, a crusader for federal regulation of food and drugs

UPTON SINCLAIR (1878-1968), a reformer and writer whose novel *The Jungle* (1906) exposed conditions in the meat-packing industry

ALBERT J. BEVERIDGE (1862-1927), a historian and Republican senator from Indiana, author of the meat inspection amendment

SAMUEL HOPKINS ADAMS (1871-1958), a writer whose articles in *Collier's Weekly* attracted attention to the false claims of patent medicines

Summary of Event

In the United States during the last quarter of the nineteenth century, food processing was becoming highly industrialized, with dubious chemicals used to preserve food and to improve its taste. At the same time, urbanization and the modernization of transportation were resulting in impersonal national markets without the personal contact between consumer and producer that was common in an earlier age. In response to these new conditions, an emerging consumer movement called for the federal government to regulate the purity and quality of food and drugs sold in interstate commerce.

Senator Algernon Paddock in 1879 introduced the first comprehensive bill to regulate food and drugs on a national scale. The Paddock bill passed the Senate but failed in a House committee, blocked by a powerful coalition of states-rights Democrats and "Old Guard" Republicans who were committed to protecting vested interests and the status quo. By 1906, some 160 food and drug bills had been introduced into Congress, and eight limited laws were passed, mostly dealing with imports and exports. Consumer advocates were somewhat more successful with state legislatures, with about half the states adopting some regulations. Standards of enforcement, however, varied greatly from state to state.

The most energetic and influential crusader for federal regulation was Harvey Wiley, the chief chemist for the Department of Agriculture from 1883 to 1912. Wiley emphasized the need for accurate labeling of all dangerous chemicals. His most famous project was the so-called poison-squad experiments, which lasted from 1902 to 1907. A dozen young men volunteered to act as test subjects for experiments on the effects of borax and other food preservatives. The results gave quantitative evidence of the negative effects of many preservatives. After this project, journalists often referred to Wiley as "Old Borax."

Early in the twentieth century, reformers known as "progressives" placed a high value on the issue of consumer rights, and they looked to the expansion of the federal government as a means of improving the general welfare. By that time, moreover, medical and chemical scientists had achieved impressive accomplishments, resulting in a widespread appreciation for the role of modern science. Thus, conditions were increasingly favorable for a resurrection of the Paddock bill.

The public was shocked in 1901 when twenty children died from the effects of inoculation against diphtheria. The following year, Congress passed and President Theodore Roosevelt signed into law the Biologics Control Act, which required makers of vaccines and antitoxins to have a federal license. Manufacturers lobbied in favor of the law in an effort to restore public confidence and eliminate unfair competition. With public opinion sympathetic to more general legislation, Senator William Hepburn of Iowa and Representative Henry Hansbrough of North Dakota introduced a bill to regulate all food and drugs sold in interstate commerce. The Hepburn-Hansbrough bill passed in the House, but in the Senate the Old Guard, led by Senator Nelson Aldrich of Rhode Island, was able to prevent the measure from being reported out of committee.

Reforming journalists, called "muckrakers" by Roosevelt, were determined that the issue not be allowed to die. Numerous articles describing horrors in food and drugs appeared in such magazines as *McClure's* and *The Ladies' Home Journal*; especially influential was Samuel Hopkins Adams' series entitled "The Great American Fraud," published in *Collier's Weekly* from October, 1905, to February, 1906. Adams' well-researched articles concentrated on unscrupulous nostrums that were either ineffective or dangerous, such as cure-all medicines that contained cocaine and other addictive substances. The series was published in book form by the American Medical Association, creating a sensation among the reading public.

By that time, Roosevelt was convinced of the "righteousness" and popular appeal of food and drug legislation, and he recommended such a law to Congress in his State of the Union Address of December 5, 1905. The day after the president's speech, Senator Weldon Heyburn of Idaho and Representative James Mann of Illinois introduced versions of the Hepburn-Hansbrough bill into Congress. Recognizing a change in public opinion, Senator Aldrich decided to allow a vote on the Senate floor, and the bill was passed on February 21, 1906, by a vote of sixty-three to four. In the House, however, there were long hearings, with organized opposition from whiskey distillers and food processors. Speaker of the House Joseph Cannon, a leader of the Old Guard, kept the bill from being placed on the House calendar. By early March, the bill appeared to be dead.

By coincidence, however, Upton Sinclair's muckraking book, *The Jungle*, appeared for sale on February 16. Having investigated the Chicago packing houses, Sinclair hoped to arouse sympathy for the conditions of the workers and promote the cause of socialism, but in the process he also included graphic descriptions of the filth and poisons that were put into canned meats. Sinclair was disappointed that the public read *The Jungle* as an appeal for food legislation, lamenting, "I aimed at the public's heart, and by accident I hit it in the stomach."

The progressive senator from Indiana, Albert Beveridge, read the book, and, recognizing its value in promoting food legislation, he sent a copy to the president. Although Roosevelt reacted negatively to Sinclair's "ridiculous socialistic cant," he was horrified at the book's descriptions of the packing houses, and he instructed the secretary of agriculture to investigate the matter. He also appointed Charles Neill, a commissioner of the Department of Labor, and James Reynolds, a lawyer and settlement-house leader, to visit Chicago and determine if Sinclair had described the packing houses accurately. In May, the two-man commission reported that *The Jungle* did not misrepresent the deplorable conditions of the industry.

Informed of the Neill-Reynolds report, Senator Beveridge met with Department of Agriculture officials and formulated a bill that would require federal inspectors to enforce sanitary standards in packing establishments and approve of the quality of meat and its additives before it could be sold in interstate commerce. On May 25, Beveridge presented the bill as an amendment to the agricultural appropriation bill, and the bill passed the Senate without a dissenting vote. In the House, however, the Beveridge bill faced strong opposition, and it had to get through the Agriculture Committee, which was chaired by Representative James Wadsworth of New York, a stock raiser himself. When Wadsworth introduced amendments that weakened the bill, Roosevelt released the Neill-Reynolds report to the press. After a public outcry, members of the House worked out a compromise that charged the government rather than the industry for the costs of inspection and put limits on the judicial review of federal inspectors. With the approval of Speaker Cannon, the compromise bill passed the House on June 19. After Beveridge and other progressives reluctantly accepted the compromises, the conference version of the bill was approved quickly by both chambers. On June 30, President Roosevelt signed the measure into law.

Meanwhile, the public support in favor of the Beveridge bill had put irresistible pressure on the House to vote on the pure food and drug bill, and on June 20 Speaker Cannon finally allowed the bill to be reported out of the Rules Committee. Three days later, it was approved by a vote of 241 to 17 and then went to a Conference Committee, where it was strengthened. The resulting "Wiley law" forbade the sale or transportation of adulterated or fraudulently labeled foods or drugs within interstate commerce. Like the meat inspection law, it was ready for Roosevelt's signature on June 30, 1906.

Impact of Event

Historians emphasize that the issue of food and drug regulation became more relevant with the modernization process. When society had been predominantly rural, with local markets, consumers tended to have face-to-face acquaintance with their sources of food. In contrast, the large-scale preservation of foodstuffs to be sold on a national market made it impossible for individuals to have personal knowledge of consumer products.

The combination of the Pure Food and Drug Act and the Meat Inspection Act greatly extended the power of the federal government to regulate goods in interstate commerce, and concomitantly the two laws represented a decline in the idea that state governments alone could exercise police powers in the public interest. At the time, a number of states-rights proponents, using a strict interpretation of the Tenth Amendment, questioned the constitutionality of the laws, but in *Hipolite Egg Company v. United States* (1911), the Supreme Court ruled that the laws were permissible under the authority of Congress to tax and regulate commerce.

In the short term, progressives were often disappointed that enforcement was not more rigorous. Because the Pure Food and Drug Act had been cast in broad language, federal regulators had to conduct long, complex proceedings to establish standards for chemical preservatives, whiskey, and other items. Harvey Wiley was among those who wanted more energetic enforcement. Within a year after passage of the law, he and President Roosevelt strongly disagreed about whether saccharin was injurious to health. Wiley was even more dissatisfied with the policies of President William Howard Taft, and during the election of 1912, Wiley, although long a Republican, publicly resigned in protest, supporting the candidacy of Woodrow Wilson.

Since 1906, there have been many debates about the specifics of food and drug regulation, but there has never been any serious suggestion that the two laws should be repealed. It was probably inevitable that the early enforcement of the laws would be rather weak, but during the course of the twentieth century the trend has been toward greater control. In 1938, Congress made a number of significant changes in the Federal Food, Drug, and Cosmetic Act, with additional requirements passed in 1958, 1962, and 1965.

The 1906 legislation was an important landmark in the movement toward consumers' rights in the United States. Framers of the two laws rejected the extreme ideologies of socialism and laissez-faire, and they believed that government could provide adequate protection from harmful merchandise without destroying the benefits of the competitive marketplace. The Meat Inspection Act was based on the premise that the government had the responsibility of protecting consumers from harmful products unfit for human consumption, while the Pure Food and Drug Act emphasized that consumers had the right to make informed judgments based on the accurate labeling of a product's contents. Contrary to some fears at the time, the laws did not lead to a government takeover of the food and drug industries, and businesspeople quickly learned how to prosper within a regulated environment. In general, the two laws of 1906 have been examples of the constructive effects of moderate governmental intervention.

Bibliography

Anderson, Oscar. *The Health of a Nation: Harvey Wiley and the Fight for Pure Food.* Chicago: University of Chicago Press, 1958. The standard biographical account of the chief chemist of the Department of Agriculture, with an emphasis on his campaign for the Pure Food and Drug Act. This is a scholarly book based on original sources, a work that succeeds in revealing Wiley's personality and ideas.

Braeman, John. *Albert J. Beveridge: American Nationalist.* Chicago: University of Chicago Press, 1971. An excellent study of the life and career of the progressive senator who wrote and sponsored the meat inspection amendment. Pages 102-111 are devoted to the legislation. Braeman emphasizes the diversity within the progressive movement.

Crunden, Robert. *Ministers of Reform: The Progressives' Achievement in American Civilization, 1889-1920.* New York: Basic Books, 1982. One of the best and most interesting treatments of the progressive movement, concentrating on the civic religion and the moral indignation within the movement's culture. Chapter 6 is devoted specifically to the muckrakers and the passage of the 1906 legislation, with anecdotes and colorful material about the people involved.

Gould, Louis. *The Presidency of Theodore Roosevelt.* Lawrence: University Press of Kansas, 1991. A scholarly and balanced treatment of the policies and ideas of Roosevelt while he was president. There is a useful account of Roosevelt's role in both the passage and the early administration of the 1906 laws, with an analysis of the various interpretations of the progressive movement.

Harris, Leon. *Upton Sinclair: American Rebel.* New York: Thomas Y. Crowell, 1971. A standard biography that contains a fascinating account of the writing of *The Jungle* and Sinclair's efforts on behalf of the Meat Inspection Act. Harris includes a helpful account of Sinclair's ideology and his correspondence with President Roosevelt.

Sullivan, Mark. "The Crusade for Pure Food." In *America Finding Herself.* Vol. 2 in *Our Times.* New York: Charles Scribner's Sons, 1927. A lively and interesting account of the personalities and controversies that led to the 1906 laws. As a journalist and major editor of the period, Sullivan was able to consult with individuals such as Sinclair, Wiley, and Adams.

Young, James Harvey. *Pure Food: Securing the Federal Food and Drugs Act of 1906.* Princeton, N.J.: Princeton University Press, 1989. The most scholarly book available about the thirty-year struggle that led to the passage of the law, with a great deal of material about the various people involved in the struggle. Advanced students of the field will find that the footnotes have very useful discussions of primary sources and historiography.

Thomas T. Lewis

Cross-References

Supreme Court Disallows a Maximum Hours Law for Bakers (1905), p. 36; Upton

Sinclair Publishes *The Jungle* (1906), p. 46; Consumers Union of the United States Emerges (1936), p. 527; The World Health Organization Proclaims Health as a Basic Right (1946), p. 678; The International Organization of Consumers Unions Is Founded (1960), p. 1062; Congress Passes the Occupational Safety and Health Act (1970), p. 1585; WHO Sets a Goal of Health for All by the Year 2000 (1977), p. 1893; An International Health Conference Adopts the Declaration of Alma-Ata (1978), p. 1998; The U.N. Principles of Medical Ethics Include Prevention of Torture (1982), p. 2169.

FINLAND GRANTS WOMAN SUFFRAGE

Categories of event: Voting rights and women's rights
Time: July 20, 1906
Locale: Helsinki, Finland

Finland's franchise law of 1906, which made the small country the first European state to grant suffrage to women, was part of a reform effort by the Swede-Finn leaders

Principal personages:
> NICHOLAS II (1868-1918), the czar of Russia from 1894 to 1917 whose Russification efforts in Finland led to the 1906 crisis
> NIKOLAI BOBRIKOV (1839-1904), the Russian governor general of Finland from 1898 to 1904 who was given dictatorial powers in 1903
> JOHAN VILHELM SNELLMAN (1806-1881), the leading Finnish spokesperson for cultural nationalism emphasizing the Finnish language
> SERGEY YULYEVICH WITTE (1849-1915), the Russian minister of finance (1892-1903) and premier during the 1905 revolution; urged reforms in Russia and Finland
> BARONESS ALEXANDRA GRIPENBERG (1856-1911), the leader of the Finnish Women's Association in the 1880's

Summary of Event

It was against the background of increased Russification that Finnish nationalism developed dramatically after 1890 and led to the 1906 reforms that brought voting rights to women and several other liberating changes. Russia had acquired control of Finland in 1809 after a century of rivalry with Sweden for control of the country. From 1809 until the 1917 Russian revolution, Finland remained under Russian control. Russification of Finnish culture characterized the entire period but intensified in the late nineteenth century under Czar Alexander III (1881-1894) and his successor Nicholas II (1894-1917). Russia's efforts to impose its own language and culture stimulated interest in the Finnish and Swedish languages as a focus of resistance to Russification and otherwise stimulated national solidarity to preserve Finnish cultural identity and autonomy. With this came heightened interest in constitutional reform, broadening the rights of citizens, including women, in order to achieve the necessary unity to withstand pressures from Russia.

Throughout the century of Russian hegemony, Finland remained largely autonomous politically and managed to enter the industrial age with vigor. The rise of factories and enlargement of trade brought into the Finnish work force increasing numbers of women who, in turn, sought better educational opportunities and certain social reforms that would protect their property and personal rights. They found sympathy among some national reform leaders who saw democracy as an essential prerequisite for national independence, since it would link divergent groups in a common front.

Language played a key role in the development of Finnish nationalism. One branch of the national movement promoted the Swedish language as the quintessential feature of Finland's identity. Swedish was, and is, spoken by about 7.5 percent of Finland's population. Known as the Swede-Finn or Svecoman Movement, this element of Finnish nationalism was fostered notably by Axel Olof Freudenthal, a professor of language and literature at the University of Helsinki. The son of a Swede who had migrated to Finland in 1798, Freudenthal promoted language-related nationalism until his retirement in 1904, arguing that Swedish culture was superior to Finnish. An even more influential cultural nationalism known as the Fennoman Movement saw Finnish language and literature as the mark of Finland's identity. Its roots lay in the eighteenth century work of Professor Henrik Gabriel Porthan of the University of Turku (later moved to Helsinki). In the nineteenth century, its leading proponent was Johan Wilhelm Snellman. Both of these language-related national movements were important to the development of Finnish nationalism in the period of militant Russification and thus contributed to the setting of the 1906 constitutional reforms.

The 1905 revolution in Russia interrupted Russification, as Nicholas II's government was forced to make major concessions. After months of strikes, premier Sergey Witte urged the czar to issue the October Manifesto that promised civil liberties and an elected legislative body, the Duma. Although the Duma would be increasingly restricted in later years, it was a significant innovation. As these events unfolded in Russia, the crisis spread into Finland in a new wave of labor unrest and popular resistance known as the Great Strike. All social classes were involved, heightening the sense of unified resistance. This united front depended ultimately on maintaining a solid coalition of various groups. Common to most of the resisting parties was the belief that the Finnish Diet should be transformed into a highly democratic legislature based on broad popular support. Before the end of 1905, the Four Estates that comprised the Diet drew up a constitutional model that would extend the vote to all citizens, both male and female, over the age of twenty-four.

By early 1906, Nicholas II was ready to reverse at least temporarily the Russification policy and to urge the Finns to replace their outmoded legislative system with a more democratic unicameral parliament elected by universal suffrage. The fact that the czar was not so much interested in establishing democracy as in mitigating unrest did not detract from the importance of the constitutional reforms that included not only a broader franchise but also a genuine legislative role for the new unicameral parliament, the Eduskunta.

That women were included in the larger electorate was a result both of the reformers' need for mass support and of women's own efforts to improve their condition. With increased industrialization of the economy after 1860, women had entered the work force in larger numbers and were developing means to express their needs related to family life, property, and education. In 1884, they founded the Finnish Women's Association, which provided a labor exchange, educational programs, and lobbying in behalf of women's interests. One of its principal goals was greater access by women, including those in the poorer segments of the working class, to university education. Women had been admitted on a restricted basis as early as 1871, but by the 1890's held some instructorships not only in the university but also in certain normal schools. The Women's Association also established international visibility as its principal leader, the Baroness Alexandra Gripenberg, attended the 1888 Women's Congress in Washington, D.C., that founded the International Council of Women. Several other women's advocacy organizations developed in Finland, especially during the decade preceding World War I.

Although Finnish women had become significant to the work force and broader social life of Finland by 1906, enfranchisement was crucial to their further development. The fact that there was little resistance to enfranchising women in 1906 was a result of their importance in the economy and as part of the consensus supporting democratization. The greatest degree of sympathy for women's rights came from the Finnish Social Democratic Party, known before 1903 as the Finnish Labour Party. Its reform program of 1906 included the vote for women as well as equal pay for equal work. Two generations of steady advocacy by women's rights groups had prepared the way for political equality. Without the right to vote, women's gains since 1860 had remained limited. Admission to university education and professorships, divorce and parental rights, economic assistance and other needs had depended upon educating the public and lobbying legislatures. Inclusion in the 1906 franchise opened the door to direct involvement by women in the political process upon which further reforms depended.

Impact of Event

The most immediate effect of the 1906 reforms was the increased presence of women in the political process. Nineteen women, mostly supporters of the Social Democrats' program calling for extensive social reform, were elected in 1907 to the Eduskunta. The Social Democrats won approximately 40 percent of the legislative seats in 1907 and proceeded to advocate a wide range of reforms, many of them pertinent to the needs of women. Renewed Russification after 1908 limited the actual results, but Russian rule was entering its last decade. After the Russian Revolution of 1917, Finland won its independence. Thereafter, women continued to be a significant part of Finnish political life, eventually accounting for about one-third of the lawmakers. Women served in the Finnish military during World War I and beyond in a special women's auxiliary organization known as the Lotta Svard. They were ready to do their share in both politics and defense.

The 1906 enfranchisement was inspirational to Finnish women and those of other countries. In a sense, Finnish women were in a privileged position by being the first European women to gain the vote. At the same time, they faced new challenges. They entered vigorously into reform efforts, especially after Finland declared independence in 1917 and established itself as a republic. The reforms most desired by women after enfranchisement included enhancing their role in coeducational schools and universities, greater access to civil service jobs and the judicial bench, rights of legal guardianship in divorce cases and for unmarried mothers, and several goals related to economic security. Eventually, progress was made on all these fronts. A law of 1924 required that either the principal or assistant principal in coeducational schools be a woman, and in the period from 1922 to 1936 a series of laws provided for equal status for children born out of wedlock. By 1927, full professorships were opened to women, and in the same year women were permitted to become judges and to enter diplomatic and consular service on an equal basis with men. Finnish women also became as well educated as the country's men and eventually slightly outnumbered men in higher education. Their legislative role contributed to the establishment of an extensive welfare program, including provisions for women's and children's rights and equal rights with men in determining children's citizenship.

By the 1980's, Finland was widely recognized as one of the best places for women to live and work. A Population Crisis Committee report of 1988 cited Finland as second only to Sweden and slightly ahead of the United States. The major criteria were economic and legal conditions, health, and educational opportunities. This exemplary status resulted from a number of factors, among them the fact that early in the twentieth century constitutional reforms that accompanied heightening nationalism brought women into the voting public several years, and in some cases decades, before women in most other countries.

Bibliography

Jackson, J. Hampden. *Finland.* New York: Macmillan, 1940. This older study of Finland is still valuable for demonstrating the balance among social classes and the sexes in Finland. Finnish resistance to Russification by the regime of Nicholas II is given clear treatment, providing the reader with perspective on the sweeping reforms of 1906 that included the enfranchisement of women. The detail and analysis compensate to some degree for the lack of elaborate documentation. Contains selected notes and index.

Jutikkala, Eino. *A History of Finland.* New York: Praeger, 1962. A highly analytical history that provides strong coverage of continuity and discontinuity in Finnish society. Jutikkala's study is one of the most essential for understanding that country's modern development. Several chapters focus on the modernization of Finland, particularly its quest for freedom and identity in the period of Russian domination. The acquisition of the franchise by women is set in the context of that struggle. Jutikkala shows that it was motivated less by ideology than by the necessity for compromise to prevent political retrogression. The work, however, lacks documentation. Includes an index.

Lundin, C. Leonard. "Finland." In *Russification in the Baltic Provinces and Finland, 1855-1914*, edited by Edward C. Thaden. Princeton, N.J.: Princeton University Press, 1971. A compact summary of Russia's policy, especially during the reigns of Alexander III and Nicholas II, of imposing Russian culture in the Baltic region. It was against this background that the constitutional changes that included universal suffrage were enacted.

Millett, Kate. *Sexual Politics.* New York: Ballantine, 1978. This widely read study of the politics of the male-female relationship examines psychological, historical, political, and other aspects. Millett develops a theory of sexual politics that focuses on power-structured relationships that have developed within the patriarchal civilizations that have prevailed historically. Includes a useful historical survey of the sexual revolution and analyzes its political and social impact. This section provides valuable information on women's suffrage movements in Europe and the United States. Contains notes, bibliography, and index.

Senkkonen, Sirkka, and Elina Haavio-Mannila. "The Impact of the Women's Movement and Legislative Activity of Women MPs on Social Development." In *Women, Power, and Political Systems,* edited by Margherita Rendel. New York: St. Martin's Press, 1981. This analysis shows the longer-range results of women's political and social liberation in Finland, demonstrating progress accompanied by continuing problems. Women account for about one-third of Finland's parliamentary representatives and have a significant presence in business and education.

Wuorinen, John Henry. *A History of Finland.* New York: Columbia University Press, 1971. This general history, with an unusual grasp of the underlying social and economic driving forces of Finland's modernization, provides valuable information on the status and impact of women. Wuorinen shows that the emancipation of women rested on more than two generations of concerted efforts. In the middle and late nineteenth century, women were admitted to higher education and to the medical profession. Inheritance laws were modernized, and in other respects women moved forward politically and socially. These events and the attainment of the franchise are treated systematically. Contains selected notes and documents, select bibliography, and index.

Thomas R. Peake

Cross-References

The Pankhursts Found the Women's Social and Political Union (1903), p. 19; Women's Institutes Are Founded in Great Britain (1915), p. 167; Parliament Grants Suffrage to British Women (1918), p. 247; The League of Women Voters Is Founded (1920), p. 333; The Nineteenth Amendment Gives American Women the Right to Vote (1920), p. 339; The Minimum Age for Female British Voters Is Lowered (1928), p. 442; French Women Get the Vote (1944), p. 646; The U.N. Convention on the Political Rights of Women Is Approved (1952), p. 885; Women in Switzerland Are Granted the Right to Vote (1971), p. 1605.

THE BERN CONFERENCE PROHIBITS NIGHT WORK FOR WOMEN

Categories of event: Women's rights and workers' rights
Time: September 19, 1906
Locale: Bern, Switzerland

For the first time in European history, nations agreed collectively to advance an international standard for labor forbidding the employment of women at night

Principal personages:

EMILE FREY (1845-1917), a Swiss political leader; the presiding officer of the Bern Conference in 1906

WILLIAM II (1859-1941), the emperor of Germany who called the first international labor conference at Berlin in 1890

SIDNEY WEBB (1859-1947), a British Fabian Socialist and supporter of the British Labour Party who advocated economic and social reform

BEATRICE WEBB (1858-1943), Sidney's wife, also a Fabian Socialist and holder of similar views

MILLICENT GARRETT FAWCETT (1847-1929), a British suffragist and leader of the National Union of Women's Suffrage Societies

MARY MACARTHUR (1880-1921), a British labor organizer and reformer

ISHABEL M. GODRON, THE COUNTESS OF ABERDEEN (1857-1939), a British feminist and advocate of labor reforms for women

FLORENCE KELLEY (1859-1932), a socialist, the foremost American advocate of prohibition of night work for women

Summary of Event

The gathering of representatives of fourteen European nations in Bern, Switzerland, in September of 1906 and their agreement to act in concert to ban night work for women marked not only the culmination of labor reformers' efforts to protect female workers and advance their welfare but also the establishment as operative the principle of international agreement and action in the field of industrial reform and workers' rights. Although this international convention was the first of its kind, and partly for that reason was limited in its scope, it set the standard for increasingly rigorous international labor legislation in the twentieth century. After World War I, the Treaty of Versailles took up where the Bern Convention left off. The League of Nations, through its International Labour Office, committed itself to the advancement of international standards for economic and social democracy and continued to reaffirm that night work for women and children had no legitimate place in modern industrial society. Ironically, even until 1930, the leading industrial nation in the world, the United States, continued to defy this principle.

The Bern Conference of 1906 and the night work treaty it forged was the culmination of a movement that had been active in Europe for more than a generation. This international agreement was the product of prolonged public-spirited efforts exerted by feminists, labor reformers, Social Democrats, and Marxian socialists. These groups were the first to respond to the physical and economic abuses of the factory system, especially as these assaulted the welfare of women and children.

In the nineteenth century, women who worked at night were unusually burdened and threatened—by the generally unhealthy conditions in the factory, by the night-work hours that rarely provided for breaks or rest periods, and by the accumulated fatigue that came from their responsibilities as mothers and wives during the day in addition to the "unnatural" hours of night employment. The result was, too often, neglect of family, ill health, high accident rates at home and on the job, and high morbidity.

The English were the first to legislate on behalf of female and child workers, directing themselves particularly to the grueling and unhealthy conditions in mining and addressing both the length of and specific hours worked. The increasingly popular sentiment was to "protect" women and children from "hard" labor, as found in the mines, from excessively long hours, and from "unnatural" and potentially immoral employment outside the home at night. In the English Factory Act of 1844, children under the age of thirteen were limited to six and one-half hours of work per day, and women were limited to twelve, with a provision prohibiting work between 8:30 P.M. and 5:30 A.M. The 1847 Ten Hours Act reduced the workday for women in textile mills to ten hours and continued to stipulate the specific hours of the workday, which were to be between 6:00 A.M. and 6:00 P.M.

The pioneering efforts to prohibit night work for women in England were taken up by the Swiss at mid-century. The Swiss Confederation was advanced in social legislation compared to most European nations. The confederation in 1877 adopted a law, first enacted in 1864 by the single canton of Glarus, that prohibited night work for all workers. Although employers made repeated efforts to repeal or amend this act, the political consensus upheld the prohibition of night work. By the end of the nineteenth century, several other European nations had legislated some form of night-work prohibition for women: Austria and Russia in 1885, The Netherlands in 1889, Germany in 1891, and France in 1892. At the same time, support for this reform began to affect communities outside Europe. New Zealand prohibited night work for women in 1881, and Massachusetts was the first in the United States to endorse the principle, in 1890.

The growing political consensus opposed to night work for women in the nineteenth century was generated by diverse individuals and groups. Although European feminists such as Millicent Garrett Fawcett, leader of the National Union of Women's Suffrage Societies, supported and advanced protective labor legislation for women and children, they were primarily concerned with political, and not economic or social, rights for women. Middle-class political feminists tended to oppose night work on moral grounds, seeing it as a major threat to healthy family life and often equating it, at least rhetorically, with prostitution.

The strongest proponents for night-work reform were labor unionists and those of the political left, particularly the broad range of European socialists, including Fabians and Labour Party members in England such as Sidney and Beatrice Webb, Social Democrats in England, France, and Germany, and Marxian socialists. Female socialists in particular were often divided on the issue of protectionism, with some feminist socialists arguing that true equality for women should eschew protective legislation. Despite the divisions within the socialist ranks, these reformers generally agreed on the need to protect all citizens from the destructive effects of industrial capitalism and consequently advanced night-work reforms as but one part of the new economic and social order to be wrought by socialism. The increasing political pressure from the left resulted in the movement from unilateral, national legislation to the consideration of a multinational or international agreement on labor standards.

In 1890, the emperor of Germany, William II, became an unexpected advocate of this kind of social and economic reform, calling for international cooperation and a conference on labor in Berlin. The emperor's sudden leadership in the arena of labor reform at this time was a defensive response to the growing strength of the socialist movement in Germany and across Europe, as well as to the threat of strikes in the Ruhr. His purpose was to moderate if not undermine the political influence of the working-class movement. The calling of the Berlin Conference successfully marshaled official and diplomatic support for cooperative labor reform that European nations had previously been reluctant to give.

The Swiss, in particular, and their Federal Council president, Emile Frey, had repeatedly issued calls for international treaties for the uniform regulation of labor during the previous two decades but had consistently met with official indifference. In the process of organizing their own conference in 1889, the Swiss acknowledged the superior ability of German leadership to effect commonly held objectives and quickly supported the emperor. The Berlin Conference brought representatives of the major European powers together to consider the needs of workers, the first time that such a meeting had occurred.

The agenda for the Berlin Conference was too broad, diverse, and ambitious to be effective. The conference proved disappointing to many reformers because it did not result in any binding agreement among the fourteen participating nations. It did, however, establish the goal of setting international labor standards and set Europe on the road to international action and treaty making. The conference's recommendation against night work for women resulted in France, Germany, and Italy legislating against the practice. More important, the conference made clear the need for an international instrument to effect both research and action on the front of labor reform.

By 1900, the International Association for Labor Legislation had been established, and its creation, the International Labour Office, directed its efforts to the specific problem of night work. In 1903, it requested the Swiss Federal Council to initiate an international conference. Organizers had learned the lessons of Berlin, and the proposed conference was to focus on only two of the most grievous abuses in industry: night work and the use of white phosphorus in the match industry. Memoranda on the two issues were sent to the fourteen European governments in the spring of 1904, and in September of 1906, in Bern, the first international labor treaty and the first article of the International Labor Code were endorsed by Germany, Austria, Hungary, Belgium, Denmark, Spain, France, Great Britain, Italy, Luxembourg, The Netherlands, Portugal, Sweden, and Switzerland.

The Bern Convention of 1906 forbade the use of white phosphorus in the match industry and night work for women. With regard to the latter, the treaty made clear that the major European nations would no longer tolerate the pernicious and debilitating effects of night work on women. It forbade the practice without distinction of age and required that the night's rest should have a minimum duration of eleven consecutive hours, to include the hours from 10:00 P.M. to 5:00 A.M. The prohibition was to apply to all industrial undertakings employing more than ten workers, except those that employed only members of the proprietor's family. Exceptions were allowed, in particular, those resulting from "force majeure" (events beyond control) or those in which night work was necessary to prevent losses, as when certain materials deteriorated quickly. Although the terms of the convention required ratification by the participating parties no later than December 31, 1908, the date was later extended to January 14, 1910. By January of 1912, all parties had ratified the agreement, and it came duly into force. For female industrial workers, it marked the beginning of a European economic community that recognized and protected their rights to earn a living without the major risks of ill health and neglect of family responsibilities.

Impact of Event

The Bern Convention acted as a stimulus to ever-increasing rigor among the European nations in protecting women from employment at night. States that traditionally had been reluctant to embrace such reforms, for example, Belgium and Spain, passed appropriate legislation, while those nations that had already passed night-work laws made it a point of pride to advance beyond the requirements of the convention. The treaty also extended night-work reforms beyond the continent, as it came to be applied to European colonies, possessions, and protectorates. The standard set by the signatories influenced nonparticipating nations as well. Bosnia, Herzegovina, Serbia, and Greece had legislated against night work for women by 1912, and the beginnings of protective legislation in industry were advanced in Japan, India, and Argentina. By 1914, the success of the Bern Conference had encouraged the scheduling of a second meeting, but this meeting was canceled as a result of the outbreak of World War I.

The war constituted a serious setback to the accomplishments of Bern. As a "force majeure," it abrogated previous reforms, and under emergency war powers most labor legislation throughout Europe was disregarded. Hours were lengthened; and overtime and night shifts became common. Even England, after almost a century of disuse, revived the practice of night work for women. Moved by patriotic ardor, labor, at least at the beginning of the conflict, acquiesced in its loss of protective standards. By the last years of the war, however, it became apparent to both workers and policymakers that increased production was ultimately counterproductive, as it resulted in diminished returns. By 1916, several European nations had moved to restore the provisions of labor legislation operative before the war.

The principles and agreements of the Bern Convention were reaffirmed at war's end. The Treaty of Versailles devoted a special chapter to labor, committed the signatories to the principles of social justice, and created an agency within the League of Nations, the International Labour Office, to direct and enforce labor standards protecting workers in industry. At a conference held in Washington, D.C., in 1919, delegates took up the issues of protective legislation at the point where Bern had left off and went beyond the earlier provisions in prohibiting night work for women in all public and private industrial undertakings. In addition, the process of ratification and enforcement was quickened. The new convention was implemented on June 21, 1921. The experience of the war and the almost universal commitment to international cooperation in the quest for peace and social justice made the acceptance and implementation of this second night-work convention more rapid than that of the first.

By 1928, thirty-six countries had abolished night work for women in industry or had taken steps toward its prohibition. These included all the European nations with the exception of three (Monaco, Albania, and Turkey), India, Japan, several European dependencies in Africa, the British Dominions, and nine countries in Central and South America. Because the United States did not ratify the Versailles Treaty and embrace the League of Nations, it became the most significant exception to the collective and universal condemnation of night work for women. On the eve of the Great Depression, only one-third of the United States had any legislation prohibiting night work, and where such laws had been passed, they proved to be limited and ineffective. Ultimately, the Depression itself forced state and federal lawmakers to address the rights and needs of all workers, including women, and prohibit night work for women under the auspices of New Deal labor legislation.

Bibliography

Anderson, Bonnie S., and Judith P. Zinsser. "Women of the Cities" and "Traditions Rejected." In *A History of Her Own: Women in Europe*. Vol. 2. New York: Harper & Row, 1988. These volumes constitute a thorough and comprehensive history of women in Europe. Although the works cited do not make specific mention of the Bern Convention, they offer an excellent treatment of the social and political circumstances bearing on working women and the forces that propelled labor reform during the period.

Boxer, Marilyn, and Jean H. Quataert, eds. *Socialist Women: European Socialist Feminism in the Nineteenth and Early Twentieth Centuries.* New York: Elsevier North-Holland, 1978. An interesting but uneven collection of essays which discuss various aspects of socialist feminism during the period when socialism was gaining strength throughout Europe. This volume is particularly helpful in exploring the conflicts among women, who were often torn between their commitment to socialism and to feminism, and the diverse approaches to protective legislation for working women.

Kelley, Florence. *Modern Industry in Relation to the Family, Health, Education, and Morality*. New York: Longmans, Green, 1914. An excellent example of the works produced by social and labor reformers at the time of the Bern Conference. As an American socialist with ties to European reformers, Kelley's polemic is indicative of those who condemned industrial capitalism as antiwomen and antifamily.

Lewenhak, Sheila. *Women and Trade Unions: An Outline History of Women in the British Trade Union Movement*. New York: St. Martin's Press, 1977. Given the role of Great Britain in advancing the first protective legislation for women and the political role that unionism played in this effort, this volume offers an excellent overview of women's organizations and objectives.

Thoennessen, Werner. *The Emancipation of Women: The Rise and Decline of the Woman's Movement in German Social Democracy, 1863-1933*. Glasgow: Pluto Press, 1976. An interesting and informative national study of the women's movement in Germany, especially the various programs for labor reform. Insight into the role of William II as a social reformer. Some mention of international efforts to address the most grievous abuses in industry.

Tilly, Louise A., and Joan W. Scott. *Women, Work, and Family*. New York: Holt, Rinehart and Winston, 1978. An excellent, factual, and analytical presentation of the impact of industrialism in Europe on women and the family. Although the emphasis is not on labor reform itself and the Bern Convention is not discussed, this is a fine overview of both the causes and effects of the rise in employment among women.

Nancy A. White

Cross-References

Supreme Court Disallows a Maximum Hours Law for Bakers (1905), p. 36; The British Labour Party is Formed (1906), p. 58; Ford Offers a Five-Dollar, Eight-Hour Workday (1914), p. 143; The League of Nations Is Established (1919), p. 270; The International Labour Organisation Is Established (1919), p. 281; The International League for Human Rights Is Founded (1942), p. 590.

JAPAN PROTESTS SEGREGATION OF JAPANESE IN CALIFORNIA SCHOOLS

Categories of event: Racial and ethnic rights; educational rights
Time: October 25, 1906
Locale: San Francisco, California

Japan protested the San Francisco Board of Education's decision to segregate Japanese from other students in city schools

Principal personages:

SHUZO AOKI (1844-1914), the Japanese ambassador who protested the segregation

THEODORE ROOSEVELT (1858-1919), the president of the United States during the crisis

ELIHU ROOT (1845-1937), the secretary of state under Roosevelt

KINMOCHI SAIONJI (1849-1940), the prime minister of Japan at the time of the crisis

EUGENE SCHMITZ (1864-1928), the mayor of San Francisco whose anti-Japanese rhetoric helped to precipitate the crisis

Summary of Event

On October 11, 1906, scarcely six months after Japan had magnanimously donated more than $246,000 in aid (exceeding the combined donations of the rest of the world) to help alleviate the suffering caused by the San Francisco earthquake, the San Francisco Board of Education repaid Japan's kindness by voting to segregate Japanese children from "white" children in its schools.

The Japanese government was at first stunned by this blatant expression of racial bigotry. The Japanese hoped that cooler and wiser heads would prevail in California and that the order would be quickly rescinded. After waiting for two weeks, Japanese Prime Minister Kinmochi Saionji instructed his ambassador, Shuzo Aoki, to deliver a note of protest into the hands of American Secretary of State Elihu Root on October 25, in which the government of the United States was reminded that Japanese citizens were guaranteed equal rights by treaty and that the "equal right of education is one of the highest and most valuable rights. . . ." Saionji went on to say that even if the "oriental schools" provided for Asian children were to be equal to other schools, the segregation of Japanese children "constitutes an act of discrimination carrying with it a stigma and odium which it is impossible to overlook."

The Japanese government cautioned its citizens against any anti-American retribution in Japan and counseled the Japanese in San Francisco to bear the insults and discrimination "with equanimity and dignity." Japanese newspapers, although outraged at this blatant racial insult, generally suggested that the wisest course for Japan to take was to appeal to the American sense of honor and fair play.

President Theodore Roosevelt was both embarrassed and outraged at the San Francisco action and promised Aoki and the Japanese government that the matter soon would be resolved. As was his wont, Roosevelt began a propaganda campaign in the press to try to marshal national pressure against San Francisco and to give the Japanese the impression that he was actively engaged in resolving the issue. Much to his horror, several southern congressmen sprang to the defense of their fellow racists in California. They interpreted the issue as being one of states' rights and reminded Roosevelt that the recent *Plessy v. Ferguson* (1896) Supreme Court ruling allowed the individual states to maintain "separate but equal" public education facilities.

For its part, the San Francisco School Board was somewhat at a loss to understand the extent and importance of the international crisis that it had caused. One must remember that for nearly thirty years Chinese had been excluded as immigrants to the United States and those Chinese who happened to be residents of California had been denied virtually all political and civil rights as a matter of course. Native-American, African-American, Mexican, Chinese, Korean, "Hindoo," and other children routinely had been segregated from "white" children. Why now this sudden uproar?

The anti-Japanese bigotry was the result of a series of unfortunate coincidences. First, Japanese immigration to California previously had been but a minor irritant compared to the problems posed by the influx of Chinese laborers in the 1870's and 1880's. Fewer than ten thousand Japanese had come to California before 1900, and perhaps only half of them remained as residents. California labor contractors, however, discovered the industrious Japanese laboring in Hawaiian cane fields after the Hawaiian Revolution of 1894. Thousands were lured to California by these contractors and found ready employment in the developing agricultural sector. As their numbers increased, so did their economic influence at nearly every level. By 1905, organized labor in California had mounted a campaign against Japanese immigration based on the fact that Japanese undercut American workers by working longer hours for less money.

Second, the 1906 earthquake had contributed to the general malaise and sense of anomie in San Francisco in much the same irrational way that citizens of Tokyo would turn against helpless innocent Koreans in the earthquake of 1923. "White" San Franciscans who lost their homes in the earthquake quite irrationally were outraged that a handful of Japanese had survived with their homes and businesses intact. Even worse, a few enterprising Japanese set up thriving cheap restaurants that catered to the workers involved in the urban recovery. In the eyes of the bigots, then, the Japanese seemed to be prospering at the expense of the suffering "whites."

Third, the San Francisco *Chronicle*, perhaps in an attempt to out-sensationalize William Randolph Hearst's *Herald*, chose that time to mount an irresponsibly provocative campaign against Japanese immigration. It published unsubstantiated and patently absurd charges that Japanese were spying on American coastal defenses for Japan and that they were acquiring huge tracts of land in the Central Valley, not only for its rich farmland but also for strategic military purposes. Without question the worst fear that they dredged up was the horror of racial miscegenation. They claimed that hundreds, perhaps thousands, of adult Japanese men were routinely placed side-by-side with young, innocent "white maidens" in the city's schools. Actually, some twenty-three Japanese males, none older than sixteen years of age, were dispersed throughout the city schools, placed temporarily in lower grades until their English language skills improved. The lascivious innuendo was greater than truth.

In response, during the late summer of 1906, a Japanese Exclusion League blossomed, ironically led by four recent European immigrants to the city. Pickets in front of Japanese restaurants handed out printed boxes of matches that read, "White people, patronize your own race." Gangs of thugs assaulted lone Japanese in the streets and threw stones at the windows of Japanese residents. Petitions were circulated urging the exclusion of Japanese immigrants.

A final factor in the bigotry directed against the Japanese was the rabidly racist campaign of the mayor of the city. Eugene Schmitz was facing an imminent indictment for bribery and corruption by a reformist movement and hoped to use the growing anti-Japanese hysteria to gain political support. Schmitz joined the Japanese Exclusion League in a series of outdoor public meetings. Before long, this unprincipled political opportunist had further inflamed the already irrational bigots. The result was that the school board yielded to the demands of the rabble and voted to establish a separate school for all "orientals," including the Japanese. After a few months, the more responsible citizens of the city managed to bolster enough support to force another vote in the school board, but not before many Japanese children were denied the right to an education in their neighborhood schools and not before many Japanese adults were assaulted, threatened, and coerced to pay "protection money" by the local police.

Roosevelt met several times with city and state leaders and reached a tacit agreement that the school segregation crisis could be resolved if some agreement could be reached to further restrict the immigration of Japanese laborers. Ambassador Aoki was receptive to Roosevelt's invitation to discuss the issue but reminded him that Japan already restricted the number of passports granted to persons wishing to immigrate to the United States. He suggested that it would be better if the United States would restrict immigration from Hawaii and Mexico, since apparently most Japanese who came to California arrived from those countries. After months of discussion, Roosevelt and the Japanese arrived at what has been called the Gentlemen's Agreement, which severely limited the number of Japanese immigrants.

For the time being, ninety-three Japanese children returned to their neighborhood schools and San Francisco and California settled down to await nervously the next wave of xenophobic hysteria. Unfortunately, they did not have long to wait.

Impact of Event

The effect of the San Francisco school segregation incident was most directly felt by the ninety-three children who had their education interrupted for a year. To have required them to travel, in some cases, across the whole city to the "oriental school" was at least inconvenient and in some cases dangerous. The greatest impact was the denial of their human and civil rights. To be singled out for discrimination on the basis of race was, and always will be, a demeaning insult. The only thing that ameliorated and stopped the discrimination was the fact that Japan, by 1906, had become a powerful military world power. Japan could not be insulted with impunity. Unfortunately, the children of Chinese, Korean, Filipino, Mexican, Native American, African-American, and other "nonwhite" origins did not have a strong and proud nation to enforce their rights. Those unfortunate students were forced to endure the insult and degradation of "separate but equal" schools.

Regrettably, the Japanese Exclusion League did not simply evaporate with the hysteria. Like the irrational xenophobia that fed the crisis, the League continued on, nurtured by the fear and hatred of ignorant and bigoted people. It was to surface again in 1913, when the California legislature passed an Alien Land Act which denied landowning to people (such as the Japanese) who could not become citizens. It would flourish again in 1921 and 1924, when the United States Congress passed immigration acts favoring immigrants from northern and western Europe and restricting the number of Japanese immigrants to less than one hundred per year. One might argue that the racial bigotry evident in the San Francisco school segregation crisis of 1906 was precisely the same virulent strain of xenophobia that would sanction the incarceration of loyal Americans of Japanese ancestry in 1942.

Curiously, within the so-called Gentlemen's Agreement that resolved the school segregation crisis was the basis for a somewhat different but perhaps more dangerous problem. That agreement allowed for those Japanese already resident in the United States to bring their families to join them. The citizens of California were startled to discover that Japanese residents in California used this rule to bring their parents and sometimes women whom they had married "by proxy" to live with them. The children born to Japanese in the United States were natural-born citizens. The state of California could deny the political and civil rights of aliens but could not do so to their citizen children with the same impunity. Therefore, the Gentlemen's Agreement was but a puny bandage over the cancer of racial bigotry. It covered an unsightly wound, but the problem continued to eat at the American body politic.

It can be argued also that the San Francisco school segregation crisis of 1906 helped to breed a resentment and self-fulfilling paranoia in Japan. Japan bitterly resented the insult perpetrated against its citizens. This anger and resentment, along with the latent American suspicions bred by racial bigotry, would contribute to much of the malice that would lead the two nations into a senseless and horrible war a generation later.

Bibliography

Bailey, Thomas A. *Theodore Roosevelt and the Japanese-American Crisis: An Account of the International Complications Arising from the Race Problem on the Pacific Coast.* Stanford, Calif.: Stanford University Press, 1934. Solid but somewhat dated. Integrates the crisis into the greater history of Japanese-American foreign relations. Places Roosevelt squarely in the imbroglio. Indexed, but the bibliography is dated.

Boddy, E. Manchester. *Japanese in America.* Los Angeles, Calif.: E. M. Boddy, 1921. A curious short monograph written to counter the arguments of the Japanese Exclusion League. It examines and refutes each argument with California and federal census and immigration statistics. Still valuable for its glimpse of the visceral quality of the debate. No index or bibliography, but contains a list (with addresses) of the California Japanese residents' associations.

Daniels, Roger. *The Politics of Prejudice: The Anti-Japanese Movement in California and the Struggle for Japanese Exclusion.* Berkeley: University of California Press, 1974. Masterful treatment of the politics of racial bigotry. Together with Penrose, depicts the leaders of the "nativist" movement in California with chilling clarity. Valuable bibliography of primary sources.

Gulick, Sidney L. *The American-Japanese Problem: A Study of the Racial Relations of the East and West.* New York: Charles Scribner's Sons, 1914. Despite being dated, it is an interesting attempt by Christian ministers to refute the arguments of the Japanese Exclusion League. Forms the basis of the work by Boddy. Gulick had been a missionary to Asia.

Iriye, Akira. *Pacific Estrangement: Japanese and American Expansion, 1897-1911.* Cambridge, Mass.: Harvard University Press, 1972. A brilliantly written examination of the mutual animosities between two imperialist states. Masterful incorporation of recent scholarship in both languages. Chapters 5 and 6, "Confrontation: The Japanese View" and "Confrontation: The American View," are excellent. Source notation and bibliography in both languages is impressive.

Neu, Charles E. *An Uncertain Friendship: Theodore Roosevelt and Japan, 1906-1909.* Cambridge, Mass.: Harvard University Press, 1967. A solid revisionist interpretation. Uses Roosevelt's extensive personal correspondence to portray him as a shrewd politician whose own racial prejudices made him more sympathetic to the Japanese Exclusion League bigots than to the Japanese. Good use of primary documents. Solid bibliography.

Penrose, Eldon R. *California Nativism: Organized Opposition to the Japanese, 1890-1913.* San Francisco: R. and E. Research Associates, 1973. Despite an annoying lack of organization, this is a surprisingly sophisticated examination of the exclusionist movement. Uses newspapers and correspondence of the principal participants to examine the politics of the movement and the background of its leaders. No index, but appendices include the various anti-Asian exclusion acts.

Louis G. Perez

Cross-References

The Immigration Act of 1921 Imposes a National Quota System (1921), p. 350; A U.S. Immigration Act Imposes Quotas Based on National Origins (1924), p. 383;

Roosevelt Approves Internment of Japanese Americans (1942), p. 595; *Brown v. Board of Education* Ends Public School Segregation (1954), p. 913; Meredith's Enrollment Integrates the University of Mississippi (1962), p. 1167; Congress Formally Apologizes to Japanese Internees (1988), p. 2392.

THE MUSLIM LEAGUE ATTEMPTS TO
PROTECT MINORITY INTERESTS IN INDIA

Category of event: Racial and ethnic rights
Time: December 30, 1906
Locale: Dacca, India

The All-India Muslim League was established in 1906 to promote the political, educational, social, and economic interests of India's minority Muslim community

Principal personages:

AGA KHAN III, SIR MOHAMMAD SHAH (1877-1957), the leader of the 1906 Simla delegation and a founder and first president of the All-India Muslim League

LORD GILBERT JOHN MINTO (1845-1914), the viceroy of India who received the Muslim delegation at Simla

NAWAB MOHSIN UL-MULK, SAYYID MAHDI ALI (1837-1907), a founding member of the Muslim League

KHWAJA SALIM ULLAH, a Muslim who called the organizational meeting of the All-India Muslim League

MAULANA MUHAMMAD ALI, the principal architect of the Muslim League's constitution

Summary of Event

On December 30, 1906, a meeting of delegates to the Muhammadan Educational Conference (MEC) gathered to establish the Muslim All-India Confederacy. The site of the formation of what would be known thereafter as the All-India Muslim League was Dacca, the capital of the newly formed, predominantly Muslim province established by the 1905 partition of Bengal. Delegates to the MEC, more than three thousand from all of India, answered a call by Khwaja Salim Ullah to discuss establishing a political organization that would safeguard Muslim social, economic, and political interests from what was considered unfair competition and influence by majority Hindus in British India. Muslim leaders perceived encroaching disenfranchisement from European-ruled India.

Thus was born an association conceived because of the perception of a duality of interests and goals between British India's two main communities, Hindus and Muslims. The league would later facilitate not only Indian independence but also the partition of the subcontinent into two sovereign countries, India and Pakistan. That partition would have its origins in the communal and political diversity of Indian Hindus and Indian Muslims during the period from 1857 to 1947, a period known as the nationalist era.

Muslim separatism and the "two-nations" principle derived from the idea that

Indian Muslims were culturally and politically distinct from India's Hindus. Indian Muslims, however, comprised many ethnic groups, reflecting the nations of the subcontinent's invaders. They were Arabs, Turks, Afghans, and Persians as well as indigenous South Asians who were converts from Hinduism. These ethnic groups constituted a syncretic Indian Islam influenced by varying cultural traditions; India's Muslims did not, therefore, constitute a monolithic group except in terms of their communal differences with the Hindu majority.

After 1857, cultural and religious nationalism became especially important to Indians, especially Muslims. Hindus had tended to adapt better to their invaders, stressing their distinctiveness as a community less than Muslims did and assimilating more easily. With the political advent of the East India Company, Muslims and several martial ethnic groups such as the Rajputs, Sikhs, and Marathas found themselves jockeying for position to fill the political void left by faltering Moghul imperial rule. Several of these groups vied with one another and with the British and the French in an attempt to fill that void. After the Indian mutiny of 1857, the British made tangible what had been true since the Battle of Plassey in 1757 and formally established the British Raj. The events of 1857 reflected badly, justifiably or not, on the Muslims, since they were perceived as having the most to gain by disrupting British rule in northern India. For a brief time after the conflict, however, since both Hindus and Muslims had been involved, there was a sense of Indian nationalism; for some it meant simply "anti-British." Indian nationalism was cemented when Queen Victoria of England became Empress of India and India was proclaimed the "jewel" in the British Crown.

When the British officially announced their political hegemony, Indian nationalism became interlocked with culture, religion, and politics, most noticeably between Hindus and Muslims. With the government in the hands of foreigners who needed indigenous bureaucrats and administrators to operate it, there was keen competition for economic and political representation and influence. Muslims, shouldering a greater part of the burden in 1857 and having been defeated by the British in governance of India, fell behind more progressive Hindus who eagerly sought positions within the British Raj. Hindus also adapted more readily to the British educational system, and educated Hindus were the first chosen when opportunities for Western education and government and military employment were opened to Indians. If this were not enough, the influence of the British extended even to social matters, affecting the lives of the indigenous governed in terms of religious and cultural practices and even language usage. This trampling on social traditions had led directly to the conflict of 1857.

Accompanying Hindu participation in the British Raj was a Hindu renaissance reviving the symbols, myths, heroes, and history of ancient Hindu rule in India. Such organizations as the Brahma Samāj and the Āryā Samāj suggested to non-Hindus that Indian nationalism reflected only the interests of the majority. Muslim revival and reassessment was one response to this.

The nineteenth century Muslim community was reflected by two main schools of thought, the Aligarh and Deoband movements. Both looked toward Islamic revitalization, but the Aligarh movement, founded by Sir Sayeed Ahmad Khan, was progressive, looking toward Western traditions and science to uplift the Muslim community rather than the orthodox revival desired by the Deoband movement. In 1875, Sayeed Khan founded the Muhammadan Anglo-Oriental College at Aligarh. Unlike some other Muslims, he saw British India not as a *Dar al-harb*, a country of the enemy, but as *Dar al-Islam*, a country of peace. Within the latter, Khan believed Muslims and Islam could flourish and prove loyal to the goverment.

In 1867, Maulana Muhammad Qasim Nanawtawi founded the Deoband movement. Members of this group had been very active during 1857. Education was seen by both Sayeed Khan and Maulana Nanawtawi as paramount to cultural revival and survival under British rule. Whereas Khan more than accommodated Western learning, Maulana Nanawtawi did not. His curricula reflected more orthodox Muslim learning and focused on Islamic distinctiveness. It did not reflect an interest in equipping its students for participation in a government believed to be hostile to Muslims.

Further straining communal harmony was the birth in 1885 of an institution instrumental in bringing about Indian independence from British rule in 1947—the Indian National Congress. With it came the beginnings of a political separation that would evolve into partition of the subcontinent. Although Muslims were members and officials of the Congress, many were concerned that it did not adequately reflect their interests and would work only to the advantage of its predominantly Hindu membership. Sayeed Khan was very much against the Congress, in part because he wanted to foster better relations between Muslim subjects and British officialdom. He saw the Congress as antigovernment and as a vehicle only for protest and "agitational" politics. To this end, he established the Joint Committee of The Friends of India, opposing the Congress's goals and objectives. All these political machinations, as well as the 1905 partition of Bengal, which created a new province in which Muslims increased their representations on legislative bodies, led to the deputation to Simla of thirty-six influential Muslims to see Lord Gilbert John Minto, the viceroy of India, on October 1, 1906. The delegation, led by Aga Khan III, included Muslim landowners, lawyers, nobles, and merchants addressing the viceroy on "communal interests of diverse Indian communities." The delegation advised the government that the relative numerical strength of a community should not be an issue for the government but instead the "political importance and value" of each community should be considered. In detailing the distinctiveness of Indian Islam, the delegation built upon the recent partition of Bengal, which would have worked in Muslims' political favor had Hindu protests not nullified it in 1911.

Two months after the delegation, Nawab Waqar-ul-Mulk explained the difference between the newly formed Muslim League and the Congress. The league did not seek to emulate the agitational politics of the Congress but to submit any demands to the government with due respect. The league stressed a [Muslim] national duty to be loyal to the British rule, to defend the British Empire, and to give the enemy (Hindus) a fight in doing so.

Impact of Event

The establishment of the All-India Muslim League provided Indian Muslims with a national political and communal voice different from the usual regional cultural and educational organizations, which were not as effective in political lobbying. The league, however, largely represented the interests of prosperous and influential Muslims wanting equal input into the governance of India along with influential Indian Hindus. With the Indian National Congress, it was a major negotiating factor in the bid for *svaraj* (self-government), a Congress goal announced in 1906, and later in the bid for independence and, finally, in the establishment of Pakistan.

The league was in place to protest the nullification of the partition of Bengal in 1911, which depleted Bengali Muslim representation on legislative and advisory boards and councils. The league's purpose was also to harness and focus the political and economic interests of subcontinent Muslims. It was not, however, a grass-roots movement, as the Congress became under the guidance of Mahatma Gandhi and Jawaharlal Nehru. Its impact on the lives of average Muslims was thus negligible until 1947, when the partition of India led to mass migrations of Hindus and Muslims and to a painful and often deadly refugee problem. The league, however, provided a regional voice on world problems affecting the status of Muslims, particularly the fall of the Ottoman Empire and the resultant Indian Khilafat movement. The league and its leaders became symbols of Pan-Islamism.

As a political voice of Muslim leadership, the Muslim League was necessary to the passage of the Minto-Morley Reforms under the Indian Councils Acts of 1909, which provided the foundation for a set of constitutional safeguards for Muslims and other groups. These safeguards included separate electorates and proportional representation, instruments to strengthen the political influence of Muslims on government. The league also addressed nationalist inclinations, especially as it became clear that gradual self-government would eventually lead to political independence from Great Britain. It would be the Muslim League and its leader, former congress member Mohammed Ali Jinnah, that would usher in the Islamic state of Pakistan with Jinnah as *Qaid-i-Azam* (supreme leader) of the new country. It is safe to say that without the political machinations of both there would be no Pakistan. It was Jinnah, as president of the league, who articulated most effectively the two-nation policy that finally convinced the British that there would have to be a division of the subcontinent upon their leave-taking. In August, 1947, Pakistan became a reality— the embodiment of minority rights politics in India.

Bibliography

Ahmad, Aziz. *Studies in Islamic Culture in the Indian Environment.* Oxford, England: Clarendon Press, 1964. This excellent study looks at Indian Islam in a regional way, highlighting its evolution and development in a non-Muslim environment. Aziz sees this as the "long story of divided coexistence of Hindus and Muslims in India, leading to divided existence as India and Pakistan in the twentieth century."

Faruqi, Ziya-ul-Hasan. *The Deoband School and the Demand for Pakistan.* New York: Asia Publishing, 1963. A rare monograph on the Deoband school, which like the better-known Aligarh movement contributed to the sense of separatism among prosperous Muslims during the Indian nationalist era (1857-1947). Includes a helpful glossary of terms and religious and political movements.

Gopal, Ram. *Indian Muslims: A Political History, 1858-1947.* New York: Asia Publishing, 1959. Starts with the military conflict of 1857 at Meerut and the events that transpired as a result of it. Gopal concludes that the separatism between Hindus and Muslims was not communally based but the result of divide-and-conquer strategies by the British Raj.

Hamid, Abdul. *Muslim Separatism in India.* London: Oxford University Press, 1971. Very important and balanced monograph on the history of the Muslim separatist movement that would eventually lead to the partition of India.

Mujeeb, M. *The Indian Muslims.* London: Allen & Unwin, 1967. A cultural, social, and religious encyclopedic study of Indian Muslims that gives a comprehensive look at this community up to 1960. A nice review for the specialist.

Rajput, A. B. *Muslim League: Yesterday and Today.* Lahore, Pakistan: Muhammad Ashraf, 1948. Important and rare monograph on the history of the All-India Muslim League. Very light on the history of its inception but strong on personalities and the last twenty years of British India. A definite polemic but very useful.

Wolpert, Stanley. *India.* Englewood Cliffs, N.J.: Prentice-Hall, 1965. Much more interesting treatment of the history of India and the interactions between its two major communities than the recent revised edition. A must-read, comprehensive treatment introducing the communal dynamics of the Indian subcontinent from medieval times.

Nancy Elizabeth Fitch

Cross-References

Gandhi Leads a Noncooperation Movement (1920), p. 315; Gandhi Leads the Salt March (1930), p. 447; India Signs the Delhi Pact (1931), p. 459; The Poona Pact Grants Representation to India's Untouchables (1932), p. 469; India Gains Independence (1947), p. 731; The Indian Government Bans Discrimination Against Untouchables (1948), p. 743; Sikhs in Punjab Revolt (1984), p. 2215; Indira Gandhi Is Assassinated (1984), p. 2232.

LEGAL NORMS OF BEHAVIOR IN WARFARE FORMULATED BY THE HAGUE CONFERENCE

Categories of event: Atrocities and war crimes; international norms
Time: October 18, 1907
Locale: The Hague, The Netherlands

The Second Hague Peace Conference of 1907 revised and expanded the rules developed during the 1899 conference to mitigate suffering and protect the rights of persons in international war

> *Principal personages:*
> THEODORE ROOSEVELT (1858-1919), the president of the United States (1901-1909) who took the initiative to reconvene the Hague Conference
> NICHOLAS II (1868-1918), the sovereign of Russia who convened the First Hague Peace Conference
> WILHELMINA (1880-1962), the sovereign of The Netherlands who sent the invitations to attend the Second Conference at The Hague

Summary of Event

In the second half of the nineteenth century, advances in technology were rapidly making the use of force more destructive. There was a growing need to limit what states were allowed to do in the course of armed conflict; the laws and customs of war had to be revised and expanded. A number of international agreements began to do that. For example, the 1864 Geneva Convention sought to improve the condition of wounded soldiers in the field, and the 1874 Brussels Declaration attempted to codify the norms of land warfare.

As the nineteenth century drew to a close, the expansionist drive of the great powers made the outbreak of war more likely. It became more urgent to codify the standards of civilized warfare. The initiative came from Czar Nicholas II, who invited all nations maintaining diplomatic relations with the Russian government to meet for the purpose of seeking the most effective means of preserving peace, limiting armaments, and regulating the conduct of war. The Hague was selected as the site for this conference. At the request of Russia, the Dutch monarch issued the invitations. Twenty-six governments participated in the First Hague Peace Conference from May 18 to July 29, 1899.

That first conference failed to provide new approaches to peace or to limit armaments. It did produce, among other things, new rules of international law to protect both combatants and noncombatants from the effects of war and provided the foundation for the 1907 Hague Conference. This second conference, in fact, had been expected to meet sooner. The 1899 negotiations were seen as useful, and an early reconvening was supported by the diplomats involved. More urgent problems intervened, as Russia found itself at war with Japan, and plans for the next conference were set aside. The Interparliamentary Union (an organization of representatives of parliaments of sovereign states working for international cooperation) decided in 1904 to urge U.S. President Theodore Roosevelt to convene the Second Hague Conference. He accepted and immediately sounded out the governments represented at the first conference. All responded positively. The termination of the Russo-Japanese War, however, led the Czar to resume the initiative. It was on his invitation that the queen of The Netherlands convoked the Second Hague Peace Conference.

This time, forty-four nations participated in the proceedings, from June 15 to October 18, 1907. Once again, the participants failed to devise effective ways of preserving peace or controlling armaments. They did, however, draft an unprecedented number of agreements setting limits to the conduct of hostilities, safeguarding human rights, and reducing the brutality and destructiveness of war. The most important of these was Convention IV, a revision and expansion of one of the conventions written in 1899. It provided the most comprehensive set of rules to that date for military operations on land. The regulations, as they were called in the convention, were of considerable significance for the protection of human rights. On a personal level, many of the rules promised to protect individuals in a variety of ways. The regulations stated that prisoners of war must be humanely treated. Specific rules established, often in very detailed manner, the extent of their protection, for example, the kind of work they could be ordered to do and their compensation for it. The sick and wounded must be treated according to the Geneva Convention, revised in 1906. Some of the means and methods of combat were also regulated. For example, it was forbidden to use poisoned weapons or to kill soldiers who had laid down their weapons. A belligerent occupying enemy territory was allowed to exercise its authority but with a number of restrictions. For example, the occupant must respect the rights of the people living there, their private property, and their religious practices. Pillage was forbidden. The states that were party to this convention agreed that they would issue instructions to their armed forces ensuring compliance with these regulations.

Other conventions specified that hostilities between states must not begin without prior and explicit warning. They prohibited the use of armed force for the purpose of recovering contract debts owed by a government unless the debtor state refused or failed to reply to an offer of arbitration, or failed to comply with the result of the arbitral proceedings. This was a small step in the attempt to restrict the sovereign right of states to use armed force, a goal that eventually was achieved on a much larger scale by the League of Nations, the 1928 Pact of Paris (the Kellogg-Briand Pact), and the United Nations.

Another 1907 Hague convention specified the rights and duties of neutral states, essentially protecting them from the destruction of war in return for their concerted efforts not to be of assistance to any of the belligerents. Some of the rules protected specific human rights. If, for example, some of the armed forces of a belligerent entered the territory of a neutral power, the latter was obligated to intern them for the duration of the war and provide the food, clothing, and relief required by humanity. After the war, the neutral power would be entitled to compensation for the internment expenses incurred.

The last eight conventions written at The Hague regulated naval warfare. They included provisions ensuring the security of maritime trade against the sudden outbreak of war and, to this end, protected against seizure of merchant vessels belonging to one of the belligerents found in an enemy port at the beginning of a war. Other provisions distinguished merchant ships converted into warships, protected the freedom of sea lanes in times of war, and ensured the safety of vessels not involved in the conflict by forbidding the laying of unanchored contact mines, which are indiscriminate.

The Hague regulations developed for land warfare were made applicable to naval bombardment. This was meant to protect the population of undefended ports, towns, or villages and to preserve buildings used for artistic, scientific, or charitable purposes and otherwise reduce the destructiveness and harshness of war.

Some provisions developed in 1899 were meant to adapt to maritime warfare the principles of the Geneva Convention for the protection of sick and wounded personnel. These were revised and expanded in 1907, specifying the conditions under which hospital ships and medical personnel could carry out their humanitarian mission.

The conventions further elaborated the rules of capture in naval warfare, exempting from capture postal cargoes and vessels used exclusively for fishing along the coast, or those employed in local trade or engaged in religious, scientific, or philanthropic activities. The conventions set up an International Prize Court to ensure greater justice in the capture of merchant ships or their cargo.

Finally, rules were made to protect the rights of neutral powers in naval war. The kinds of activities belligerent ships could engage in while in neutral ports were specified, for example, as was the length of time belligerent ships could stay in neutral ports.

The rules and regulations written in 1907 were significant, but the nations represented at The Hague were aware that further development was needed. The Second Hague Peace Conference had failed to create institutions to preserve international peace and reduce armaments. The delegates were convinced, however, that their efforts had been useful and that this work should continue. They agreed, therefore, that a Third Peace Conference should be held in about eight years. This lack of urgency was astounding in light of growing international tensions and an increasing risk of war. By 1915, the scheduled date of the third conference, World War I was under way. The third conference never met.

Impact of Event

The 1907 conference substantially clarified and expanded the laws and customs of war. It showed a concern for curbing the brutality of armed conflict and reducing the suffering of both combatants and noncombatants. It is true that rapid technological developments would soon make war infinitely more devastating and that human suffering would reach unprecedented heights. The humanitarian rules of behavior would nevertheless save millions of human beings from inhumane treatment.

The legal norms of behavior, although far from evenly or generally applied, were sufficiently respected that large numbers of prisoners were taken and cared for. Wounded were attended to, medical facilities were, more often than not, given some protection, and some restraint was shown in the conduct of military operations. Undeniably, what was needed was a better way of preserving international peace, but human rights would have been infinitely more imperiled without the rules developed at The Hague. It must be remembered that a small step was taken to limit the sovereign right of states to go to war, in this case a prohibition to do so for the collection of international debts under some conditions. The League of Nations, the 1928 Kellogg-Briand Pact, and the United Nations would go much further than that. A new philosophy on the lawful use of force was emerging.

Humanitarian agencies, particularly the International Red Cross, have played an important role in the application of legal norms of behavior in war. Relentless visits or inspections (in the battlefield, in military hospitals, and in prisoner-of-war camps) by their representatives enabled them to document violations and to apply pressure for better observance of the law. Exposure occasionally led to public outcries and sanctions (for example, the war crimes trials following World War II). It would be an error to believe that most armies or most governments are anxious to violate the law. Every war finds leaders, commanders in the field, and lesser combatants who refuse to surrender to inhumanity. The norms of behavior found in the law of war, such as the Hague rules, give them an instrument to justify their restraint.

The Hague rules were tied to a particular period of history and its values and priorities. War rapidly changed and technology created drastically new problems in the conduct of warfare. International society changed just as much, requiring the law to be revised periodically, particularly under the sponsorship of the International Red Cross and the United Nations. A number of the rules written in 1907, however, remain a part of today's law of war.

The 1907 conference showed that large-scale codification was feasible. It demonstrated a widely shared conviction that, difficult as the task may be, nations could develop legal restraints. It was important to affirm or reaffirm standards of humane conduct. This did not solve the problem of war, but as efforts are made to find alternatives to armed violence, it remains important to attempt to protect basic human rights, even (or perhaps especially) in wartime.

Bibliography

Bailey, Sydney D. *Prohibitions and Restraints in War.* London: Oxford University Press for the Royal Institute of International Affairs, 1972. An interesting study presenting diverse sources of restraint in the conduct of war. The author examines the norms of Christian ethics and those of international law, then turns to the work of the International Red Cross for the development of a body of humanitarian law. He also examines the work of the United Nations in protecting human rights in armed conflicts and finally considers the norms arising from arms control and disarmament agreements.

Best, Geoffrey. *Humanity in Warfare.* New York: Columbia University Press, 1980. Reviews the history of the principles and rules of war and the influence of specific periods on their evolution. A serious, thoughtful book trying to approach this difficult subject with objectivity. Very helpful in understanding the role of restraints in war. Provides a useful chronological guide to the formulation of the law of war and a substantial bibliography.

Detter Delupis, Ingrid. *The Law of War.* Cambridge, England: Cambridge University Press, 1987. Gives a succinct presentation of the law of war including its special characteristics and the place of the Hague rules in the modern system. Provides a clear overview of the present norms of this body of law and explains their evolution and application. Includes an extensive bibliography.

Oppenheim, L. *International Law.* 7th ed. Vol. 2 in *Disputes, War, and Neutrality*, edited by H. Lauterpacht. London: Longmans, Green, 1948-1952. Presents the Hague law in the context of the evolution of the law of war. Discusses the application of specific rules developed at The Hague and their subsequent revision and expansion. Provides a useful and sufficiently compact review of the war crimes trials. A record of the ratifications of the Hague conventions is found in the appendix.

Pictet, Jean. *Development and Principles of International Humanitarian Law.* Dordrecht, The Netherlands: Nijhoff, 1985. A short, basic text discussing the nature and character of humanitarian law and its basic principles. Reviews its history and the main conventions articulating its rules. Presents the main problems in contemporary application in wartime. Includes a good bibliography and a list of recent armed conflicts.

Rosenblad, Esbjörn. *International Humanitarian Law of Armed Conflict.* Geneva: Henry Dunant Institute, 1979. An excellent statement of the practical need for a continuing development of humanitarian law applicable in wartime. Reviews the contemporary problems involved and the various efforts to overcome them. Provides a useful context for the study of the Hague rules. Includes an extensive bibliography.

Scott, James Brown. *The Hague Peace Conferences of 1899 and 1907.* Baltimore, Md.: The Johns Hopkins University Press, 1909. This is the most basic work on the Hague conferences. Volume 1 gives an excellent account of the two conferences and an extensive discussion of the conventions negotiated there. Volume 2 provides the full text of all documents as well as diplomatic materials concerning the two conferences. Extremely useful.

Walzer, Michael. *Just and Unjust Wars.* New York: Basic Books, 1977. A remarkably interesting and insightful study of restraints in war, both moral and legal, demonstrating their relevance and applications even in the bitter armed conflicts of recent history. The author also discusses the limitations of restraints. Provides many historical examples and case studies.

Jean-Robert Leguey-Feilleux

Cross-References

Germany First Uses Lethal Chemical Weapons on the Western Front (1915), p. 161; Japanese Troops Brutalize Chinese After the Capture of Nanjing (1937), p. 539; Nazi War Criminals Are Tried in Nuremberg (1945), p. 667; The United Nations Adopts a Convention on the Crime of Genocide (1948), p. 783; The Geneva Convention Establishes Norms of Conduct in Warfare (1949), p. 808; Eichmann Is Tried for War Crimes (1961), p. 1108; The Statute of Limitations Is Ruled Not Applicable to War Crimes (1968), p. 1457; Lieutenant Calley Is Court-Martialed for the Massacre at My Lai (1970), p. 1555; The United Nations Issues a Declaration Against Torture (1975), p. 1847; Barbie Faces Charges for Nazi War Crimes (1983), p. 2193.

THE YOUNG TURK MOVEMENT STAGES A CONSTITUTIONAL COUP IN TURKEY

Category of event: Revolutions and rebellions
Time: July 24, 1908
Locale: Istanbul, Turkey

After more than five hundred years of rule under despotic sultans, a group called the "Young Turks" declared the Ottoman Empire to be a constitutionally limited multinational monarchy

Principal personages:

AHMED RIZA (1859-1930), a propagandist for the Committee of Union and Progress (CUP); edited its newspaper from exile abroad

ENVER PASHA (1881?-1922), the head of the military branch of the CUP; virtual dictator of the Ottoman government between 1913 and 1918

ZIYA GÖKALP (1876-1924), the best-known interpreter of Turkish nationalism during and after World War I, a liberal literary and cultural figure.

ABDUL-HAMID II (1842-1918), the most autocratic and, eventually, the most hated Ottoman sultan, overthrown by the Young Turks

MIDHAT PASHA (1822-1883), the head of the Young Ottoman movement of the late 1860's; associated with the first Ottoman constitution of 1876

Summary of Event

Although autocratic rule had for centuries been a mark of sultanic government in the Ottoman Empire, the last quarter of the nineteenth century probably stood out as the most despotic period of modern times. Experiences earlier in the century, first Napoleon I's occupation of Sultan Selim III's Egyptian province (between 1798 and 1802), then loss of Greece following local insurrection and European intervention (in the 1820's), and nearly complete separation of several Eastern Mediterranean provinces (Egypt and Greater Syria) in the 1830's had forced a number of important changes during the period known as the *Tanzimat*, between 1839 and 1876. Many imperial reforms involving new legal codes, tax laws, and some moves toward local administration by councils were announced as aiming at better government for Ottoman subjects of all nationalities. The fact that the Ottoman sultanate ruled peoples of different nationalities and religious backgrounds complicated *Tanzimat* aims considerably. The main ethnic nationalities were Turks and Arabs, but there were also Kurds, Balkan Slavs, and Armenians. The first two minority groupings were Muslims, while the latter two were Christian. In addition, the so-called Arab provinces contained populations that, while ethnically more or less homogenous, were divided into distinct religious communities, or *millets*. This was the case of Egypt, with a significant Coptic Christian minority, and especially Syria, with different Christian religious minorities (Maronites, Greek Orthodox, and Catholics). In addition, Jews existed as a separate *millet* in almost all provinces.

Internal multinationalism and multisectarianism definitely complicated Ottoman reform efforts during the *Tanzimat*, but one must also add foreign interventionism to these factors. A number of foreign-imposed treaties or conventions, not only political and military but also commercial in nature, caused defenders of the legitimate sovereignty of the Ottoman Empire to despair. Among these "agreements" were the London Convention of 1841, regaining Ottoman rule in Egypt and Syria but laying down limiting restrictions in a number of areas, the Treaty of Paris, ending the Crimean War in 1856 but initiating a new series of indirect control factors (especially in the form of foreign loans), and the international Congress of Berlin in 1878, which would become very important for the group that would become the Committee of Union and Progress.

This latter agreement came at a very critical time, just after the closing of the *Tanzimat* period in 1876. Ostensibly the reason for ending the *Tanzimat* had been the adoption of a formal Ottoman constitution in 1876. This was done at the bidding of a group of liberal reform thinkers called the "Young Ottomans," led by a former provincial governor, Midhat Pasha. At that time, the newly installed sultan, Abdul-Hamid II, rose to the Ottoman throne only after promising to respect the Young Ottoman constitution. Empirewide elections were to be held for the first all-Ottoman Parliament, which would have the responsibility of representing all subgroupings, whether ethnic or sectarian, on the basis of a single "national" electoral law. One could argue that the very short-lived experiment barely scratched the surface in terms of representational democracy. What seems to have occurred was an elitist-oriented process of selection of representatives to serve in the Istanbul Parliament; individual prestige and influence, more than actual dedication to representing the political aspirations of a wider constituency, characterized the parliamentary qualifications of various provincial leaders at this time.

It was the reaction of the empire's age-old enemy, Czarist Russia, that caused the first Ottoman Parliament, and with it the nascent principles of representative government in the Ottoman Empire, to founder. In 1877, Russia launched a military campaign against Abdul-Hamid. Russia claimed that, whatever the value of the new representative basis for government in Istanbul, the Turks were mistreating their Bulgarian subjects (Slavic "cousins" to the Russians). Ostensibly to stop the Russians from benefitting from their aggression, an all-European Congress at Berlin intervened in 1878 to "correct" the terms reached by war. Soon after the Congress of Berlin's benevolent "corrections," which provided for an international administrative responsibility for a symbolically restored Bulgaria, Cyprus fell under British control and Bosnia and Herzegovina (later parts of Yugoslavia) under Austrian. Several years later, Tunisia was occupied by France (1881) and Egypt by Britain (1882).

Such blatant foreign interventionism gave the sultan an excuse to suspend both the 1876 constitution and the parliament. In Abdul-Hamid's mind, such conditions of menace against the Ottoman throne would never end. In fact, even when the Young Turk successors to the Young Ottomans succeeded in restoring the 1876 constitution, their presumed devotion to maintaining the integrity of the empire would be seriously hampered, between 1908 and 1914, by interventionist and exploitative pressures that were not at all dissimilar to those used by Abdul-Hamid to rid himself of the first Ottoman constitution.

When the Committee of Union and Progress (CUP), or Young Turks, emerged in the early 1890's, no one could predict the future impact of bitter realities originating either inside the empire or among its foreign neighbors. Originally formed by students of mixed national origins studying in Istanbul, the CUP gradually attracted a wide variety of supporters among groups disgruntled with the effects of the sultan's absolutist rule. Ottoman writers in exile, notably Ahmed Riza, published articles devoted to analysis of parliamentary government in Europe, principles of the free press, respect for individual rights and property, and other potential reforms.

Political causes taken up by the CUP, however, came from other sources. One such source was the eminent essayist devoted to a reflourishing of "true" Islamic values in Ottoman society, Ziya Gökalp. Although Gökalp inspired CUP members with lofty idealism in the period before the 1908 coup, the strained circumstances that followed reestablishment of the 1876 constitution would eventually cause him to alter the universalist orientation of his writings in favor of a clearer Turkish ethnic (or Pan-Turkish) bias. This latter feature in Gökalp's profile was also reflected in the contribution of perhaps the most important wing of the Young Turk movement, composed of revolutionary cells in the Ottoman military. In fact, it was this link with the military that made it possible for the theoretical aims of the Young Turks to be realized through definitive action.

In July, 1908, disgruntled elements of the Ottoman army supporting the Young Turk movement carried out the coup that compelled Sultan Abdul-Hamid to restore the constitution of 1876 and to prepare for empirewide elections to an Ottoman Parliament. The moment this happened, various individuals and groups within the empire braced for the effects constitutional government might have on their respective interests. Unlike the brief constitutional experience of 1876-1877, the Young Turk constitution enjoyed several specific foci of support within the wider ranks of Ottoman society. At the same time, however, it faced some equally specific internal sources of opposition.

Impact of Event

The Young Turk coup of July 24, 1908, was generally greeted as a stroke for freedom of expression and democratic representation. Side effects, however, indicated troubles yet to come. Almost immediately after the coup, politically interested "foreign" groups took advantage of transitional confusion to declare obvious advantages for themselves at the expense of the new Istanbul regime. Austria-Hungary annexed the provinces of Bosnia and Herzegovina (under their protection since 1878), and Bulgaria (under international administrative supervision since 1878) declared itself independent from any further Ottoman control. Armenian separatists also hoped for an opportunity to declare their independence and boycott any Armenian participation in the all-Ottoman Parliament.

Despite these events, the Young Turk regime moved quickly to restore parliamentary government in the Ottoman Empire. By the time parliamentary representatives were elected, however, signs of conservative resistance to the new government had emerged. A countercoup was attempted in 1909. Although the anti-Young Turk movement did not go very far in 1909, one might suppose that its supporters would have preferred to maintain the separate communal spheres, or *millets*, for Jews, Christians, and other non-Islamic religious groupings. Such convictions ran counter to the spirit of civic universalism that Young Turk supporters hoped to establish in Ottoman representative government.

Successful reversal of the coup attempt of 1909 depended on loyal military support, something that foreshadowed the movement toward stricter central control. By 1910, a number of prominent political leaders both from the capital and from the provinces had gained a forum for expressing views on the future of constitutionalism in the Ottoman Empire. Paramount among the former were the so-called centralists, under the leadership of Ahmed Riza, and their political opponents, the decentralists, who had been inspired by the contributions of Ottoman Prince Sabaheddin to the Young Turk movement as early as 1900.

CUP leaders soon realized that diverse options for charting the future of the empire were causing splits within their own ranks. Emergence of a so-called Liberal Union within the movement threatened to prepare the way for a second party that could and did contest votes in the parliament. Pressures to control divergent political views mounted. These were given convenient justification when, in 1911, Italian forces invaded Tripoli, necessitating rapid moves toward a wartime budget and conscription. In the rush of events connected with the conflict, excuses could be made, especially by the centralist wing of the CUP, for the restriction of political activity. Soon, the Liberal Union found its members being silenced and the results of important elections altered at their expense. The CUP was finally forced out of office in July, 1912, when the army showed hostility to the government. The Liberal Union took over briefly.

In the interim between the 1912 Balkan War and a second round in 1913, the Young Turk leader and military chief Enver Pasha carried out what amounted to an executive coup in January, 1913. Many political opponents were removed, extraordinary powers were granted to the executive branch to prepare to defeat the Balkan enemies, and a campaign of Pan-Turkism was adopted to bolster Turkish (but not necessarily other imperial subject nationalities') morale. It was this policy of Pan-Turkism, combined with the strongarm internal political and police tactics adopted by the 1913-1918 "triumvirate" leaders (Enver Pasha, Mehmet Talaat Pasha, and Ahmed Djemal Pasha), that turned the last stage of the Young Turk regime into a veritable military dictatorship. Seen in this light, the Ottoman pact with the Central Powers (Austria-Hungary and Germany) in World War I—a fateful alliance that led to the destruction of the Ottoman Empire in 1918—can be called a reflection of the eventual alignment of the military wing of the Young Turk movement with anti-democratic forces for whom constitutions were just so much paper.

Bibliography

Ahmad, Feroz. *The Young Turks: The Committee of Union and Progress in Turkish Politics, 1908-1914.* Oxford, England: Clarendon Press, 1969. Ahmad's brief but detailed study of the period of actual Young Turk government, not planned revolution, is considered scholarly and authoritative.

Lewis, Bernard. *The Emergence of Modern Turkey.* New York: Oxford University Press, 1961. A broad textbook covering the traditional government of the Ottoman Empire. Lewis provides key chapters on the *Tanzimat* period, the 1876 and 1908 constitutions, and the aftermath of the Young Turk period.

Mardin, Serif. *Genesis of Young Ottoman Thought.* Princeton, N.J.: Princeton University Press, 1962. Primarily a study of intellectual trends and figures associated with the making of the 1876 constitution, this book provides necessary background on the factors influencing the Young Turks by the 1890's.

Ramsaur, Ernest E. *The Young Turks.* Princeton, N.J.: Princeton University Press, 1957. The earliest detailed study of the Young Turks, emphasizing the events and influences that occurred between the 1876 constitution and its restoration by the Young Turk coup in 1908.

Shaw, Stanford J., and Ezel Kural. *History of the Ottoman Empire and Modern Turkey.* Vol. 2. New York: Cambridge University Press, 1977. Shaw's text covers much more time than Lewis' but does not contain as much specific information on the Young Turks. The accuracy of some factual information in this book has been questioned by some reviewers.

Byron D. Cannon

Cross-References

The Iranian Constitution Bars Non-Muslims from Cabinet Positions (1906), p. 52; The Muslim League Attempts to Protect Minority Interests in India (1906), p. 87; Sun Yat-sen Overthrows the Ch'ing Dynasty (1911), p. 116; Armenians Suffer Genocide During World War I (1915), p. 150; Greek and Turkish Inhabitants of Cyprus Clash over Political Rights (1963), p. 1218; A United Nations Peace Force Is Deployed in Cyprus (1964), p. 1236.

THE BELGIAN GOVERNMENT ANNEXES THE CONGO

Category of event: Indigenous peoples' rights
Time: November 1, 1908
Locale: Brussels, Belgium

As a consequence of the international outcry over the treatment of Africans under the rule of King Leopold II, the Belgian government assumed control of the Congo and initiated reforms

Principal personages:

LEOPOLD II (1835-1909), the Belgian king (1865-1909) and founder of the Congo Independent State

EDMOND DENE MOREL, GEORGE E. P. A. MOREL-DE-VILLE (1873-1924), a British journalist and indefatigable campaigner for reform in the Congo

SIR EDWARD GREY (1862-1933), a Liberal politician and foreign secretary of the United Kingdom (1905-1916)

JULES RENKIN (1862-1934), the first minister for colonies of Belgium (1908-1918); introduced the first serious reforms in the Congo

Summary of Event

The Congo Independent State (also called the Congo Free State) was unique among European imperial ventures in Africa. Although resembling a European colony, technically the Congo State was a sovereign country, recognized as such since 1885 by most of the major powers. Its ruler was King Leopold II of Belgium, but there was no constitutional connection between Belgium and the Congo State until 1908. The state was run largely as Leopold's private business concern.

From the start of his African venture in the 1870's, Leopold had portrayed his motives in acquiring the Congo watershed as humanitarian. He intended to suppress the slave trade and to bring commerce, prosperity, and "civilization" to the Africans. He adhered to the 1885 Berlin General Act, which included a pledge to "watch over the preservation of the native tribes and to care for the improvement of their moral and material well-being." Although the Congo State did take measures to end the slave trade, Leopold in fact exhibited little concern for the rights of Africans in the Congo.

The rule of the Congo Independent State was imposed and maintained, where necessary, by military force. All land which was deemed unoccupied was confiscated by the state. Taxation, especially in the early years, was left to the discretion of local officials and could assume various forms. A considerable amount was collected in the form of export commodities (ivory, groundnuts, and especially wild rubber). Women were required to provide cassava bread for the state's workers and soldiers. Residents also had to provide government stations with meat and fish. Taxes were also payable in labor for the government: cutting wood for the river steamers, transporting officials in canoes, acting as porters on expeditions, and laboring on various public projects. These impositions were spread unevenly, with villages located near government stations bearing the heaviest burdens. Payment of taxes in currency was prohibited in most cases, a policy often criticized as retarding the development of a money economy in the territory. Taxes were enforced with collective punishments, detentions, and corporal punishment. Such policies were not atypical of the early years of European rule in Africa, but the Congo State came under criticism for being much harsher and more exploitative than other colonies in Africa.

It was the state's financial weakness which led to the increasingly brutal treatment of the Africans. As an independent state, Leopold's Congo had no metropolitan power to support it financially, and those who had invested money, including Leopold, sought to profit quickly. Leopold, beginning in the early 1890's, made concessions of vast territories to various private firms in order to exploit the Congo's resources. The most notorious of these firms were the *Société anversoise du Commerce du Congo* (known as Anversoise), the Anglo-Belgian India Rubber and Exploring Company (Abir), and the *Compagnie du Kasai* (created in 1901). The state held a large proportion, usually half, of the stock in these companies, and state officials sat on their governing boards. Company agents were often hired by the state and had few restrictions on their powers. Most of the territory not parceled out in concessions was assigned to the so-called "private domain," which was to be exploited directly by the state.

In the 1890's, wild rubber replaced ivory as the main focus of economic activity, and it was in the rubber industry that the worst abuses of the Africans occurred. Neither the state nor the concession firms were strongly capitalized, and they relied on crude extraction in order to turn a profit. Local officials were given goals to meet; they in turn set the quota of wild rubber each village was required to produce and received a commission on the amount gathered. In addition, private competition was excluded, in order to keep the purchase price of rubber low. European officials often used African assistants, commonly known as *capitas*, to enforce the quotas. Missionaries reported that the taking of hostages (especially women), whipping, and mutilation (especially the amputation of hands) were not uncommon methods of enforcing the quotas. The practice of mutilation was said to derive from the requirement that (African) soldiers had to account for each bullet used by bringing back the hand of the victim.

Over time, such reports of atrocities, mostly provided by Protestant missionaries, led to criticism of the Congo State in the outside world. The publication, which Leopold tried to block, in 1904 of an investigation by the British consul Roger Casement created an uproar in Britain and led Edmond Dene Morel to found the Congo Reform Association (CRA). Morel's campaign soon spread to other countries and was particularly strong in the United States. In the face of increasing international condemnation and prodded by the British Foreign Office, Leopold convened an independent commission of inquiry to look into Casement's charges. The commission failed to find any evidence of mutilation or murder by European officials and attributed the cases of mutilation to an "inveterate native custom" of taking a trophy from the dead or those believed dead. On several issues, such as the use of labor taxes, the commission approved of the government's policies while criticizing aspects of their implementation. Nevertheless, the resulting report, released in 1905, substantiated most of Casement's findings. It found abuses in the tax system, unauthorized military expeditions by the concession companies, and improper supervision over the companies. Leopold set up a further commission to recommend proper reforms.

Soon after the report of the commission of inquiry, Sir Edward Grey, a known critic of Leopold's Congo, became foreign secretary of Great Britain. By 1906, the Hearst newspapers in the United States had taken up the campaign against Leopold. A reform movement also appeared in Belgium itself, drawing on the growing strength of the Socialist party in the Belgian parliament. Even the Catholic party, hitherto Leopold's main supporter in Belgium, began to distance itself from his policies.

Belgian public opinion had always been somewhat ambivalent toward Leopold's imperial ambitions, and many Belgians saw little reason for the government to become involved in them. The idea of annexing the Congo had been raised twice previously, in 1895 and 1901, but the parliament had voted against it, primarily because the king was opposed. By 1906, the strength of international opinion left little alternative to Belgian annexation. The reform measures introduced by Leopold in that year, including the termination of the Abir and Anversoise concessions, were deemed inadequate by Morel and the CRA, who argued that no true reforms could be expected so long as Leopold controlled the Congo. In November, Grey told a delegation of reformers that he favored a Belgian annexation of the Congo. In December, the Belgian parliament debated the Congo issue and voted to examine the question of annexation.

After months of difficult negotiations with Leopold, the treaty which transferred the Congo to Belgium and the acts establishing a new colonial charter were passed by the Belgian Chambers in August and September, 1908. The annexation came into force on November 1, although it was not announced in the Congo until November 16. The annexation did not satisfy Morel. The king retained limited powers in the new Belgian Congo. Existing concessions remained, although the administrative powers of the companies were curtailed. Forced labor was not outlawed under the new colonial law, and most of Leopold's officials continued in their jobs. Morel and the CRA convinced the British and American governments to withhold recognition of the annexation until the system had been completely reformed and the rights of Africans protected.

Impact of Event

On paper, the Belgian annexation did little to change the situation in the Congo. The Leopoldian system, however, was gradually dismantled, because of continued pressure by Morel and the efforts of Jules Renkin, the new minister of colonies.

Renkin introduced his reform program in October of 1909. Free trade was to be introduced area by area over three years, and the importation of consumer goods for Africans would be encouraged. At the same time, payment of taxes in currency was to be introduced, and taxation in the form of provisions was abolished. Morel was still unimpressed and held his most dramatic rally ever, with the Archbishop of Canterbury on the dais, in November. Although Morel held out for strong guarantees for African property rights, world interest in the Congo soon flagged. Leopold's death in December, 1909, left the reformers without a convenient target. Leopold's successor, Albert I, favored a humane policy in Africa and had even visited the colony himself, something Leopold had never done. Renkin was granted the authority in 1912 to remove officials who were known to be corrupt or had misbehaved under the old regime. That same year, the old governor, Baron Théophile Wahis, a staunch supporter of Leopold, was also replaced. Renkin also established a training academy for colonial officials, with certain courses emphasizing ethics and toleration for local customs. In June, 1913, the Congo Reform Association dissolved itself, having determined that its job was done. The United States and Great Britain granted recognition to the Belgian Congo.

Underlying many of the improvements in the Congo after 1908 was a shift in the focus of commercial exploitation from forest products to mining and plantations. The wild rubber industry was on the decline after 1907, largely as the result of destructive methods of tapping the trees. Elephant herds were being exterminated. Copper, cobalt, and diamonds were to replace rubber and ivory at the top of the list of exports. The big mining concerns, notably the *Union Miniére du Haut Katanga*, came to realize that they needed a steady, experienced work force and could not rely on forced labor or seasonal levies. In the 1920's, they adopted a more benevolent policy toward their workers, providing housing, health care, food, and education for them and their families. The crude exploitation of the red rubber era became a thing of the past, to be replaced by a more subtle, and more profitable, approach.

Gradually, the Belgian Congo came to resemble other European colonies in Africa, which is to say that it was paternalistic. Africans still had few legal rights, faced open discrimination, and had no voice in government, but outright brutalization was curbed. Forced labor remained but was more closely regulated. In later decades, the government required Africans to grow specific crops. The government did encourage mission schools through subsidies, producing in the long run a relatively high literacy rate, but discouraged advanced education for Africans. When independence suddenly came in 1960, the tensions implicit in this more humane, paternalistic colonial system would find their outlet in a bloody civil war.

Bibliography

Anstey, Roger. *King Leopold's Legacy: The Congo Under Belgian Rule, 1908-1960*. London: Oxford University Press, 1966. An excellent companion volume to Ruth Slade's book. Particularly useful for its emphasis on social trends in addition to economic and political developments. The author's reliance mainly on published sources is something of a weakness. Index and bibliography.

Brausch, Georges. *Belgian Administration in the Congo.* 1961. Reprint. New York: Greenwood Press, 1986. A concise work, written by a former Belgian administrator. Although his concern is mainly to defend Belgium's record in the Congo, the author provides useful information about changes in policy, particularly after World War II. Brief bibliography, no index.

Cookey, S. J. S. *Britain and the Congo Question, 1885-1913.* New York: Humanities Press, 1968. A detailed account of British diplomacy regarding the Congo. Well documented, using both Belgian and British archival materials. Includes a solid account of the reform campaign and the political debates on the issue. The book is not concerned with events in the Congo except as they affected relations between Britain and Belgium. Bibliography and index.

Gann, Lewis H., and Peter Duignan. *The Rules of Belgian Africa, 1884-1914.* Princeton, N.J.: Princeton University Press, 1979. As the title indicates, this work is concerned mainly with the backgrounds, motivations, and experiences of colonial officials. It is also strong in its discussions of economics and of changing colonial policies, but it is not on the whole concerned with the African perspective. Includes a critical examination of some of the accusations against the Congo Independent State. Index and good bibliography.

Martelli, George. *Leopold to Lumumba: A History of the Belgian Congo, 1877-1960.* London: Chapman & Hall, 1962. A well-written book, at times dramatic and at times polemical in defense of the European record in Africa. It is strongest on the Congo Independent State, particularly its founding, but its discussion of the Belgian period is superficial. Index, map, no references, no bibliography.

Morel, Edmond Dene. *E. D. Morel's History of the Congo Reform Movement.* Edited by W. Roger Louis and Jean Stengers. Oxford, England: Clarendon Press, 1968. Morel's own history of his campaign up to 1904 provides an interesting insight into the personality of Leopold's nemesis. The editors have added chapters carrying the story to 1913, as well as a series of critical discussions of several of Morel's more controversial claims.

Slade, Ruth. *King Leopold's Congo: Aspects of the Development of Race Relations in the Congo Independent State.* London: Oxford University Press, 1962. This book is the standard history in English of the Congo Independent State. The subtitle is somewhat misleading, as race relations are not the main focus of the work, which is a political and diplomatic history. Indexed, with bibliography and a useful map.

T. K. Welliver

Cross-References

Reformers Expose Atrocities Against Congolese Laborers (1903), p. 13; The International Labour Organisation Is Established (1919), p. 281; Advisory Councils Give Botswana Natives Limited Representation (1920), p. 304; The League of Nations Adopts the International Slavery Convention (1926), p. 436; The Atlantic Char-

STUDENTS CHALLENGE CORPORAL PUNISHMENT IN BRITISH SCHOOLS

Categories of event: Children's rights and educational rights
Time: September 4-15, 1911
Locale: Great Britain

British schoolchildren demanded an end to corporal punishment in a wave of school strikes in 1911, but Parliament did not abolish it until 1986

Principal personages:
SIR ROBERT MORANT (1863-1920), a civil servant who was private secretary to Sir John Gorst and permanent secretary to the Board of Education (1899-1911)
SIR ROBERT BLAIR (1859-1935), the education officer of the London County Council, in charge of state-supported elementary and secondary schools in greater London
STEWART HEADLAM (1847-1924), a member of the London County Council (1907-1924), a leading champion of high-quality education for the working class
SIR JOHN GORST (1835-1916), the minister in charge of the Education Department (1895-1902)

Summary of Event

School discipline through corporal punishment is as old as organized schools in the Western world. Egyptian papyri and Mesopotamian clay tablets tell of masters beating their students to get them to learn. In the Middle Ages, children were viewed as miniature adults, and physical punishment was justified by biblical authority. Beating, caning, birching—by whatever name, corporal punishment was the standard teaching method.

In the mid-seventeenth century, however, the ideas of the Czech pastor and educator Jan Comenius began to spread in England. Comenius questioned the utility of corporal punishment, argued that teaching should appeal to the senses and the intellect rather than require rote memorization aided by the birch, and contended that education should be humane. English educational reformers took up Comenius' ideas. At the end of the century, the educator and diarist John Aubrey proposed the creation of academies in which students would be trained to learn for the sake of learning. In his schools, there would be "no such thing as the turning up of bare buttocks for pedants to exercise their cruel lusts" with whips and canes. Such ideas, however, were minority ones throughout the seventeenth, eighteenth, and nineteenth centuries. Corporal punishment remained the norm in English schools.

Most English children, however, did not attend state-supported schools until after

1870. Before then, if children went to school at all, they went either to elementary schools sponsored by religious groups (most commonly operated by the Church of England, but there were also schools operated by the Wesleyan Methodist church and the Roman Catholic church) or to private schools operated as profit-making ventures. The role of the state's Education Department was limited to inspecting those religious schools that received state matching funds and to supporting the training of teachers. Discipline in the religious schools was enforced with the birch. In the private-venture schools, in contrast, masters were less ready to cane, largely because the parents of working-class children often resented such discipline. This was not always true, of course. Sometimes children who were beaten at school got a second beating at home; sometimes parents used the schoolmaster as a public flagellator.

English elementary education was transformed by the Education Act of 1870, which permitted the creation of elected boards of education with the power to fund elementary schools by levying a local property tax. Board schools, as they were called, grew in number between 1870 and 1914, and more and more children received their education in them. Because the board schools relied on corporal punishment, more and more children experienced the birch.

Not all parents approved of corporal punishment, however, and from time to time they brought charges of assault against schoolmasters or even assaulted the master. The courts usually backed up the schoolmaster in such cases unless the beating were especially brutal or the magistrate had especially vivid memories of his own beatings. In one such case, the magistrate decided that the cane used to administer the beating was not strong enough and presented the master with a stronger weapon. Occasionally, priests of the Church of England caned children who attended the services of rival churches.

Public attitudes toward corporal punishment, not only in the schools but also in other areas of British life, changed in the latter part of the nineteenth century. Public executions, long a staple of the British scene, were abolished in 1868. After a long debate, flogging in the British army was ended in 1881. Corporal punishment in the schools remained a hot topic for argument. Humanitarians basically followed the line laid down by Comenius two hundred years earlier. They maintained that the practice was indecent, brutalizing, and counterproductive to the learning process. Supporters of corporal punishment thought that the practice was normal. They argued that God had ordained the rod as the appropriate way to train children. They also believed that corporal punishment instilled discipline and character. By the 1880's, however, the arguments in favor of corporal punishment had begun to seem old-fashioned.

Working-class radical and labor organizations were in the forefront of opposition to corporal punishment in the schools. As labor candidates began to be elected to school boards, they campaigned for the abolition, or at least the limitation, of corporal punishment. Many of the school board members sponsored by the Independent Labour Party after its organization in 1893 took a vocal role in opposition. At the turn of the century, opponents of corporal punishment organized the Society for the Reform of School Discipline, a national pressure group that collected statistics, produced literature in an effort to mold public opinion, and lobbied Members of Parliament and educational administrators to end corporal punishment.

The Education Department's policy on corporal punishment reflected the attitudinal change. Education inspectors had long complained about instances of excessively harsh discipline. In the 1880's, the department began formalizing specific recommendations for the inspectors. The recommendations were that only the headmaster should cane, not student teachers or members of the school's board of managers, that caning should be used only as a last resort, and that a written record of each caning should be kept. These regulations were dropped in the 1890's, but in 1901 a new set of regulations was introduced by Sir John Gorst, who oversaw the Education Department. Gorst's regulations, which probably were drafted by Sir Robert Morant, the department's chief civil servant, established the principles that corporal punishment was to be forbidden in kindergartens and in girls' schools, and that in boys' schools it was not to be used as an ordinary method of punishment. The regulations, however, left the implementation of the principles to the judgment of each school's headmaster and board of managers. In practice, then, caning continued to be a common method of punishment.

What the children thought about corporal punishment is unclear. Reminiscences of school life come mostly from the middle and upper classes and sometimes look back at the birch with nostalgia. It is much more likely that children hated the birch. This was revealed in October, 1889, when a number of short-lived schoolboys' strikes closed a number of schools in London, Leeds, Liverpool, and Northampton. Inspired by the successful strikes of London gas workers and dockers that summer, the boys demanded a shorter school day, free meals, and the abolition of school fees, corporal punishment, and homework. The strike was put down easily enough, but it was the forerunner of the London school strike of 1911.

The years 1910 and 1911 in Britain were tense with respect to labor relations. The economy was prospering, and corporations were earning large profits. Workers, however, were dissatisfied with their lot. Despite the high level of corporate profits, the workers' weekly wages did not increase. Slow but steady inflation during the preceding fifteen years had eroded the purchasing power of the pound, so workers actually had seen their economic position worsen. Finally, workers' political aspirations, expressed in the Labour Party, were frustrated because Parliament was dominated by the Liberal and Conservative parties. Labour thus was unable to achieve its main political goal, the legislative reversal of two court decisions, the *Taff Vale* case and the *Osbourne* judgment, which limited the legal activities of trade unions.

These factors led to numerous strikes, walkouts, demonstrations, and even riots in 1910 and 1911. Complicating matters was the general upswing in violence, both in words and in deeds, which characterized the period. Tensions over the constitutional role of the House of Lords, the relationship of Ireland to Britain, and the rise of the militant women's suffrage movement created an atmosphere that fostered violence as a means of solving problems.

The school strike of 1911 occurred within this context of violence. It started in Llanelly, South Wales, on Monday, September 4, when pupils walked out of the Bigyn Council Boys' School to protest caning. Newspapers treated this as a school-boy lark or dismissed it as a prank, but on Friday, September 8, several schools in Liverpool were struck. The Liverpool boys demanded the abolition of both the cane and school fees, an extra half day of holiday per week, and pay of a penny a week for monitors.

Over the weekend, word of the strikes spread through what can only be called a children's grapevine, and Monday, September 11, saw the strike spread across the nation. Children at six schools in the East London working-class districts of Shore-ditch and Islington went out. The next day, the movement spread in London, and to schools in Hull, Sheffield, Bradford, and Grimsby, all industrial towns in the North of England. On Wednesday, schools in the Battersea neighborhood of South London went out, as did schools in Leeds and Birkenhead in the North, Coventry and Not-tingham in the Midlands, Colchester in the Southeast, Greenock in Scotland, and Dublin. Thursday saw strikes at Newcastle, Middlesborough, and Blackburn in the North, Stoke-on-Trent, Burton-on-Trent, and Birmingham in the Midlands, and the seaport of Southampton. The week ended with walkouts in Sunderland, Lancaster, and Cardiff in Wales.

The response of the authorities was to use both the police and the cane to break the strikes. Sir Robert Blair, the Education Officer of the London County Council, denied that any strikes were happening, secure in the knowledge that police consta-bles had been sent to each school where a strike was in progress. Stewart Headlam, an Anglican priest who had become a Labour Party socialist and who was the mem-ber of the London County Council most active in promoting education, was furious about the strike. "They should be whipped," he angrily declared. Headlam's pro-gressive educational ideas did not include abandoning the cane. The London County Council's Education Committee under Blair's leadership reasserted its right to beat students. The schoolchild revolt against the cane had been put down.

Impact of Event

These strikes had much in common. First, they were ephemeral, rarely lasting for longer than a day. Second, the student strikers' goals were similar, as they all wanted abolition of the cane and of school fees. Third, most of the strikes took place in industrial areas that were the scenes of strikes by adult workers. Fourth, the chil-dren, some of whom undoubtedly came from union families, clearly were adapting the methods of industrial action that they saw being used around them. The children formed strike committees, exhorted their fellow students with violent rhetoric, and organized marches with banners like those of the labor unions. Some striking chil-dren threw stones at the children who chose to go to school, thereby emulating their parents even in intimidating strikebreakers.

Historians cannot identify the children involved in the strike, or even who their leaders were. Newspapers and other observers were so dismissive that they did not bother even to record the names of the strike leaders. Thus it is impossible to know who participated or how that participation may have affected children's later lives.

The school strike probably was bound to fail. Much larger strikes, put on by powerful unions and involving the suspension of economically important labor such as transport and mining, failed. How could a strike by schoolchildren hope to succeed?

After World War II, progressive educators began to reexamine methods of discipline and came to reject corporal punishment as an appropriate, or even an effective, method. Two important studies of the British educational system commissioned by the government, the Newsom Report of 1963 and the Plowden Report of 1967, recommended the abolition of corporal punishment. Responding to these reports, some local education authorities ended corporal punishment in their districts. The government, however, declined to make any general rules, and the teachers' unions opposed abolition despite their socialist ideology, fearing that they could not keep discipline in their classrooms without the rod.

Some teachers rejected the birch, however, and formed the Society of Teachers Opposed to Physical Punishment (STOPP) in the early 1970's. This society campaigned for abolition throughout the decade. Partly as a result of STOPP's efforts, about 20 percent of schools in Britain had abandoned the cane by 1980. STOPP's biggest victory came in 1981, when the Lancashire Education Authority became the largest school district to abandon the cane.

Matters came to a head in the following year, when the European Court of Human Rights, an agency of the European Common Market to which Britain belonged, ruled that pupils could not be punished physically if their parents objected. This decision sparked a political row. On one hand, the National Union of Teachers voted to work for abolition, and Labour-controlled local education authorities began to abolish. On the other hand, many members of the Conservative Party argued that caning was a grand British tradition and that it was wrong for a Common Market institution, the European Court of Human Rights, to interfere with an internal British matter. This, they said, was an example of how Britain had lost its sovereignty by joining the Common Market.

After three years of debate, the government of Prime Minister Margaret Thatcher proposed a compromise. Its measure, the Education (Corporal Punishment) Bill, would have required schools to compile a register of pupils whose parents did not mind their being caned. The idea of dividing schoolchildren into beatables and unbeatables was called silly, and the House of Lords killed the bill. In the following year, 1986, another Education Bill had an amendment abolishing corporal punishment attached to it in the House of Lords. The House of Commons accepted the amendment by the narrow margin of one vote (231 in favor, 230 against) on July 22, 1986. The law, which took effect in September, 1987, applied to children in state schools or to those whose fees in private schools were paid by the state, so children in the private sector who paid their own fees remained canable.

Bibliography

Armytage, W. H. G. *Four Hundred Years of English Education.* Cambridge, England: Cambridge University Press, 1964. A standard, clearly written survey of the development of elementary and secondary education in England since the 1560's. Focuses on the effects of the Industrial Revolution, the movement toward universal education, and the growth of the state educational system in the late nineteenth and early twentieth centuries, from the political point of view.

Dangerfield, George. *The Strange Death of Liberal England.* New York: Capricorn Books, 1961. Originally written in 1935, this entertaining, well-written, and brilliantly conceived work remains indispensable for understanding the period from 1906 to 1914. It weaves together the stories of how the power of the House of Lords was reduced, how the Tory Party supported rebellion in Northern Ireland, and how the labor and suffragette movements became increasingly militant. Full of vivid character sketches.

Ensor, R. C. K. *England, 1870-1914.* Vol. 14 in *The Oxford History of England*, edited by Sir George Clark. Oxford, England: Clarendon Press, 1960. A standard reference source for the political, social, economic, and diplomatic history of the period. Includes an index and bibliography.

Gardner, Phil. *The Lost Elementary Schools of Victorian England: The People's Education.* Dover, N.H.: Croom Helm, 1984. Focusing on private-venture schools, this book draws a comprehensive picture of what the education of most working-class children was like in the nineteenth century. Carries the story up through the end of the 1920's.

Hurt, J. S. *Elementary Schooling and the Working Classes, 1860-1918.* London: Routledge & Kegan Paul, 1979. A clearly written study of what elementary schools were like between the introduction of state-funded board schools and compulsory education in the 1870's and the end of World War I. An excellent account.

Lawson, John, and Harold Silver. *A Social History of Education in England.* London: Methuen, 1973. A sprightly written, well-illustrated, and fascinating survey of the history of English education in its social context from Anglo-Saxon times to the 1970's. The book connects the extent of educational provision with changes in population, the development of the class structure, the growth of literacy, and changes in the social roles of women and children.

Lowndes, G. A. *The Silent Social Revolution: An Account of the Expansion of Public Education in England and Wales, 1895-1965.* 2d ed. London: Oxford University Press, 1969. A useful survey of teachers, what they taught, and the schools they taught in.

Simon, Brian. *Education and the Labour Movement, 1870-1920.* London: Lawrence & Wishart, 1965. A survey of the policies concerning education held by trades unions, radical political groupings, and the Labour Party, written from a socialist perspective.

D. G. Paz

Cross-References

The American Civil Liberties Union Is Founded (1920), p. 327; Supreme Court Rules That States Cannot Compel Flag Salutes (1943), p. 629; The United Nations Children's Fund Is Established (1946), p. 689; Spanish Becomes the Language of Instruction in Puerto Rico (1949), p. 801; The United Nations Adopts the Declaration of the Rights of the Child (1959), p. 1038; Congress Enacts the Bilingual Education Act (1968), p. 1402; Congress Passes the Child Abuse Prevention and Treatment Act (1974), p. 1752; The United Nations Adopts the Convention on the Rights of the Child (1989), p. 2529.

SUN YAT-SEN OVERTHROWS THE CH'ING DYNASTY

Category of event: Revolutions and rebellions
Time: October 10, 1911
Locale: Wuchang, People's Republic of China

The Revolution of 1911, led by Sun Yat-sen, ended the two-thousand-year-old monarchy in China and introduced the ideas of democracy, independence, and social and economic justice to the Chinese people

Principal personages:
SUN YAT-SEN (1866-1925), the leader of the Revolution of 1911, elected provisional president of the new Republic
K'ANG YU-WEI (1858-1927), the famous scholar, advocate of constitutional monarchy, and rival of Sun Yat-sen
LIANG CHI-CHAO (1873-1929), the disciple of K'ang Yu-wei, a prolific writer and editor
HUANG HSING (1874-1916), the revolutionary leader with a reputation second only to Sun Yat-sen, minister of war in the new Republic
YUAN SHIH-KAI (1859-1916), the first president of the Republic; attempted to restore the monarchy in 1915

Summary of Event

In the nineteenth century, China was faced with a series of unprecedented problems—bureaucratic incompetence, widespread corruption, rebellions, and natural calamities which contributed to the precipitous decline of the once-robust ruling Manchu (or Ch'ing) dynasty. At the same time, as never before, China was threatened from the outside. Beginning with the Opium War (1839-1842), she suffered a string of military defeats at the hands of the Western powers. The Treaty of Nanking that ended the Opium War, and similar subsequent treaties, imposed on China numerous debilitating conditions which in effect relegated her to near-colonial status by the end of the century.

The combination of these circumstances helped revive the dormant anti-Manchu sentiment among the Chinese (the Chinese regarded the Manchus as alien conquerors), as manifest in the Taiping Rebellion (1850-1864) which came close to toppling the dynasty. The eventual suppression of the Taipings, aided by the Western powers, who saw the rebels as a threat to their own interests, afforded the dynasty a respite in which feeble attempts were made to resuscitate dynastic fortunes in the 1870's and 1880's. Without the will and resolve on the part of its leaders to make fundamental institutional changes, the reform movement was short-lived and ineffectual. By 1895, when Japan handily defeated China in a struggle over Korea, it was clear that China's decline could be arrested only by revolution to overthrow the monarchical system and replace it with a republican government attuned to the interests of its citizens.

One of the first advocates of revolution was Sun Yat-sen. Born to a well-to-do peasant family in a village near Canton on November 12, 1866, Sun was sent at the age of thirteen to Honolulu, where his older brother had a small business. He was enrolled in the Iolani School, operated by Anglican missionaries, and then at Oahu College, graduating in 1883. Concerned that he might be too susceptible to Christian influence, his brother sent him back to his native village. Soon, however, he was "banished" to nearby Hong Kong following an incident in which he was found desecrating village deities. After enrolling for a brief period at Queen's College, a government high school, he was admitted to the newly founded medical college in Hong Kong, graduating in 1894. He began his medical practice in Macao, a Portuguese colony west of Hong Kong, but was soon drawn to revolutionary activities.

During this time, like many of his contemporaries, Sun was a reformist. In the summer of 1894, for example, he journeyed north in order to petition Li Hung-chang, the preeminent leader of the reform movement, to plead for educational and economic reforms. Only after he failed to elicit a positive response did he become convinced that revolution was the only recourse. Consequently, in the fall of that year, he returned to Honolulu where, with the help of his brother, he founded his first revolutionary organization, the Hsing Chung Hui (Revive China Society), with about one hundred members. A branch was set up in Hong Kong the following year. Sun and his supporters launched an uprising in Canton in March, 1895, with arms smuggled from Hong Kong. It was a disaster, with several dozen rebels killed and Sun himself fleeing to Japan.

Sun cut off his queue (a symbol of submission to Manchu rule), donned Western clothes, and sailed for the United States to seek financial support from the Chinese communities there. The Chinese business community was generally sympathetic to K'ang Yu-wei and his disciple, Liang Chi-chao, who had formed the "Protect-the-Emperor" Society to promote constitutional monarchism. K'ang, a former imperial adviser instrumental in the ill-fated reforms of 1898, was a traditional scholar of national reputation, while Liang was a prolific and effective writer widely respected for his progressive political views. Together, they vigorously advocated the institution of a constitutional monarchy along the lines of Meiji Japan. Until 1905, they enjoyed the support of the majority of the Chinese business communities in the United States and the thousands of Chinese students in Japan. By contrast, Sun's support came mainly from the poorer Chinese overseas, missionaries, Chinese Christians, and members of the secret societies, all on the fringes of Chinese society.

In the fall of 1896, Sun was in London. On October 11, he was kidnapped by the Chinese legation and held captive for almost two weeks. He would have been shipped back to China and been executed for his revolutionary activities had not the British government intervened for his release. This event, publicized by the British newspapers, propelled Sun into the international limelight. Returning to Japan almost two years later, he gradually won the support of the Chinese students and of some well-known Japanese politicians. It was through these Japanese politicians that he finally came to an agreement with Huang Hsing to form a broad revolutionary coalition by bringing together all revolutionary groups under an umbrella organization, the T'ung Meng Hui (Revolutionary Alliance) on August 20, 1905. Huang, a native of Hunan province, had led an abortive uprising in 1900 and had sought refuge in Japan. He was influential among the large contingent of students from that province. The new alliance made Sun its chair and adopted his ideas as the program for the revolution. Branches of the alliance sprouted in China, claiming many well-known literary figures as its members and many revolutionary organizations as its allies. The pace of the revolution accelerated.

Between 1905 and the fall of 1911, Sun had launched at least half a dozen uprisings in the south. After these failures, the T'ung Meng Hui leaders shifted their focus to the central provinces. Their opportunity came early in 1911, when the government announced the nationalization of railway construction which had been financed through private investment. As the projected railways were in Szechwan, Hunan, and Hupeh provinces, opposition of bondholders there was most vehement. In Szechwan, it became an insurrection. The government was compelled to transfer some of the troops from Wuchang, an important political center in Hupeh, to quell the mounting riots there. Sensing the vulnerable government position at Wuchang, the revolutionary leaders, many of whom were officers in the New Army units, decided to act by late October. In the evening of October 9, however, a bomb exploded accidentally at revolutionary headquarters in the neighboring city of Hankow. Police raids led to the arrest of some thirty conspirators and seizure of documents containing the names of others. On the morning of October 10, units of the New Army, heavily infiltrated by the revolutionaries, attacked government offices and quickly seized control of Wuchang. In rapid succession, fifteen provinces seceded from the central government. The Revolutionary Government was established in Nanking in early December and elected Sun provisional president on December 29, upon his return from the United States.

Meanwhile, in desperation the Ch'ing government turned to the only man who had the power to deal with the revolutionaries, Yuan Shih-kai, the creator of the New Army, who had betrayed the reformers of 1898. Yuan had been retired in 1908. In early November, 1911, he was invested with full powers to control the imperial administration and command the army and navy. With his superior forces, he scored some quick victories and convinced the revolutionaries that he had to be appeased. After weeks of secret negotiations, an agreement was reached in which Sun agreed to resign as provisional president in favor of Yuan if the latter could arrange the abdication of P'u-i, the last emperor, and pledge his support to the Republic. Yuan, using threats and tactful persuasion, wrenched an abdication decree from the court on February 12, 1912. He was elected provisional president two days later. The 268-year-old Ch'ing Dynasty came to an end barely four months after the uprising in Wuchang.

Impact of Event

The Revolution of 1911 was an epochal event in Chinese history. Not only did it overthrow the two-thousand-year-old monarchy, but it also destroyed the ideological system that perpetuated it. The inauguration of the Republic was an irrevocable break with the past.

Sun Yat-sen has been revered by many Chinese as the "Father of the Republic" and his ideas enshrined as an infallible guide for national reconstruction by his followers in the Kuomintang (Nationalist Party). Outside China, the revolution was a source of inspiration for nationalist movements in Korea, Indochina, and Indonesia.

The objectives of the Revolution of 1911, as originally conceived by Sun Yat-sen, remained unfulfilled. His ideas on democracy were largely borrowed from the West and introduced to a society with a different ethos and tradition. They were understood by very few of his compatriots and were not shared even by most of his colleagues in the Revolutionary Alliance who, after all, hailed from different backgrounds and whose interest in the revolution did not go beyond the overthrow of the monarchy. The traditional political order was destroyed, but the traditional social elite remained ensconced throughout the country, presaging the rise of regional militarism in the following decades. Sun had envisaged a period of political tutelage following the overthrow of the dynasty, a period in which all social ills such as opium smoking, foot binding, and bureaucratic abuses would be eradicated and local self-government by popular elections under a provisional constitution would be instituted. Then, in no more than six years, a permanent constitution would be adopted, creating a truly democratic government based on the separation of powers. The political turmoil in the following decades prevented this part of Sun's program from being put into practice. Perhaps the most important idea of Sun was his third Principle of the People—"people's livelihood," or socialism, which aimed at the regulation of capital and equalization of land ownership.

The decade preceding the fall of the monarchy was marked by widespread and spontaneous popular movements against imperialism, arbitrary taxation, and bureaucratic corruption. Although the Revolutionary Alliance and its successors failed to provide any direct organizational and intellectual leadership to harness these forces to serve the wider revolution, the Revolution of 1911 nevertheless gave these movements new impetus. The disintegrational process set in motion by the fall of the monarchy enabled revolutionary ideas to penetrate all strata of Chinese society. The May Fourth Movement (a protest on May 4, 1919, against the unfair treatment of China at the Versailles Peace Conference that eventually became a cultural revolution) was in large measure the convergence of these forces, which paved the way for the rise not only of radical political ideologies but also new patterns of social behavior and cultural values.

Bibliography

Fairbank, John King. *The Great Chinese Revolution, 1800-1985.* New York: Harper & Row, 1986. This is an interpretive analysis of modern Chinese history by an acknowledged authority.

Franke, Wolfgang. *A Century of Chinese Revolution, 1851-1949.* Columbia: University of South Carolina Press, 1970. An excellent account by a German Sinologist with a good introduction and adequate bibliography.

Hsu, Immanuel C. Y. *The Rise of Modern China.* New York: Oxford University Press, 1990. A comprehensive history of modern China with a detailed account of the Revolution of 1911. Good bibliography and full documentation.

Schiffrin, Harold Z. *Sun Yat-sen and the Origins of the Chinese Revolution.* Berkeley: University of California Press, 1970. Currently the latest in scholarship on Sun Yat-sen as a revolutionary leader before 1905.

Sharman, Lyon. *Sun Yat-sen: His Life and Its Meaning.* Reprint. Stanford, Calif.: Stanford University Press, 1968. This is a reprint of an old volume by an American writer, daughter of a missionary in China. It criticizes the Sun Yat-sen cult that emerged after his death.

Wright, Mary C., ed. *China in Revolution: The First Phase.* New Haven, Conn.: Yale University Press, 1968. A volume of essays on different facets of the revolutionary movement in modern China. Authors are leading scholars in their fields. Excellent introduction.

S. M. Chiu

Cross-References

The Boxer Rebellion Fails to Remove Foreign Control in China (1900), p. 1; Lenin and the Communists Impose the "Red Terror" (1917), 218; Lenin Leads the Russian Revolution (1917), p. 225; Students Demonstrate for Reform in China's May Fourth Movement (1919), p. 276; Ho Chi Minh Organizes the Viet Minh (1941), p. 573; The Nationalist Vietnamese Fight Against French Control of Indochina (1946), p. 683; China Initiates a Genocide Policy Toward Tibetans (1950), p. 826; China Occupies Tibet (1950), p. 837; Mao's Great Leap Forward Causes Famine and Social Dislocation (1958), p. 1015; The Chinese Cultural Revolution Starts a Wave of Repression (1966), p. 1332.

INTELLECTUALS FORM THE SOCIETY OF AMERICAN INDIANS

Category of event: Indigenous peoples' rights
Time: October 12, 1911
Locale: Columbus, Ohio

The Society of American Indians, although short-lived, served notice that the future of the indigenous population of the United States was no longer solely in the hands of white Americans

Principal personages:

CHARLES EASTMAN (1858-1939), the most prominent founding member of the society

ARTHUR C. PARKER (1881-1955), an anthropologist and Seneca Indian, the most important person in the organization, growth, and development of the society

CARLOS MONTEZUMA (1867-1923), the "fiery Apache" leader of the radical wing of the society, a physician who was uprooted from the reservation and educated in the "white man's" schools

HENRY ROE CLOUD (1886-1950), a Winnebago Indian, Yale graduate, and youngest leader of the Society of American Indians

FAYETTE A. MCKENZIE (1872-1957), an Ohio State University sociologist who, while not an Indian, assisted in the formation of the organization and guided its development

Summary of Event

Historically, American Indians have reacted to the European penetration of North America both through traditional tribal responses and by attempting to establish a larger Indian cultural identity. Initially, it was mostly tribal responses that dictated how American Indians confronted and negotiated with the conquering Europeans. Over the years, the decimation of many Indian societies as a result of disease, alcohol, and war took shape. Survivors were relegated to culturally alien reservations.

During the Progressive Era of the early 1900's, a number of nationally organized indigenous movements appeared. Led by an emerging educated Indian middle class, these organizations stressed the need for a common Indian identity and the inclusion of Indian culture in the larger United States society. By participating in these new associations, group members hoped not only to forge a sharper sense of identity for themselves but in the process to address basic problems facing Native Americans. The first and perhaps most noteworthy of these new organizations was the Society of American Indians, founded in 1911 as the American Indian Association. Its ideological mission was to call to the attention of white America the viewpoint that the

Indian race was a vital part of a progressive and democratic society.

Arthur C. Parker, a Seneca Indian, anthropologist, author, and lecturer, Dr. Charles Eastman, a respected biographer of Indian life, and Dr. Carlos Montezuma, an Apache physician and radical leader for Indian recognition, helped to organize the American Indian Association in 1911. Founded as a forum for intellectuals to pursue an exploration of varying viewpoints within a pan-Indian framework, the organization quickly outgrew its original intent. In order to create a more distinct Indian character, the group reorganized in 1912 as a more pronounced Indian movement. Renamed the Society of American Indians (SAI), it quickly went about setting itself apart from other "progressive" white-run reform organizations. To secure access to political recognition, Washington, D.C., was selected as the SAI headquarters. The nation's capital became the center of activity for the society's executive committee, which was charged with the responsibility for writing a provisional constitution. The document which was produced included the following organizational objectives: promoting the advancement of Indian freedom through enlightenment; providing an open forum for discussion of the welfare of the Indian race; promoting citizenship and obtaining the rights thereof; opposing any movement opposed to the Indian race; and respecting the honor of the Indian race for the good of the United States.

The organizational structure of the SAI had three categories of membership: active, Indian associate, and associate. The first two categories were open to members of the indigenous culture only. Actives were members of Indian populations within the geographical boundaries of the United States, and Indian associates included all indigenous natives living in Canada and Latin America. Both active and Indian associate members could hold office and vote, but the latter could vote only on tribal matters pertaining to their own tribe. The third category, associate member, consisted of all non-Indian-blood individuals who had an interest in Indian affairs.

With Washington, D.C., as its base and with an organizational structure that allowed for Indian as well as non-Indian support, the SAI appeared ready to engage in activities benefiting the much-maligned and previously intellectually ignored indigenous population. Arthur C. Parker, editor of the society's journal (*Quarterly Journal*, 1913-1915, *American Indian Magazine*, 1915-1920), took on the task of forging a national Indian identity. Using pan-Indianism as the central theme in all issues, the journal soon found an audience in both white and Indian intellectual and political circles. The publication, in addition to printing conference proceedings and the society's political views, addressed key issues currently affecting reservation politics. As such, the journal helped to secure entrance into intellectual circles previously not reachable. The journal also served to set the stage for future conference agendas, addressing immediate as well as traditional concerns of the indigenous culture. It became an important source for conference debates and added a degree of intellectual integrity to the cause of the Indian.

The choice of Columbus Day, 1912, for the opening of the first SAI conference (in Columbus, Ohio) was purposeful. It was as if the experiences of Native Americans during the previous centuries of European rule were to be vindicated. From this point forward, red and white people, according to conference goals, would interact on a plane appropriate to ensuring the growth of all society from the vantage point of each group's best qualities. Attempting to present American Indians as intelligent and possessing "civilized" political, economic, and social capacities on a par with white Americans, agendas encouraged discussion aimed at eliciting support for current indigenous industrial, educational, legal, and political undertakings.

Identifying these concerns from a viewpoint that Indians were as capable as agriculturalists, mechanics, homemakers, and educators as were white people, the conference not only attempted to serve the needs of the indigenous population but also attempted to articulate an Indian self-consciousness in the process. Calling attention to low standards of education found on the reservations and the denial to Indians of political and legal access and redress in the entire cultural process helped to rally support for the SAI. Conference memoranda continued to incorporate an identification of a lack of specific governmental programs as a central cause for the low standard of living for many indigenous Americans living on reservations. To this extent, much of the conference was directed toward confronting current Indian social problems which sprang, in part, from the creation and perpetuation of pejorative stereotyping of Indians by whites. To correct any misrepresentation of the Indian race, the conference adopted a two-point program calling for the integration of American Indians into mainstream society but without the removal of Indian individuality. The first conference, at least, ended in a certain degree of unity.

Although there was unanimity at the first conference, the same cannot be said for the conferences that followed. Political factionalism emerged as the organization evolved. This was largely a result of the inability of leaders to find a common ground from which the SAI could spread the idea that Indian culture and tradition were integral to the white historical experience in America and that the Indian contribution to American development was more than a side show hawking wares, war dances, and ancient ceremonies. Fueled by internal disagreements over goals and aspirations and confronted by outside political antagonists who saw government policy as a way of continuing the differences between Indians and whites in civil authority, the organization declined into a factionalism that blurred the unity of purpose. By the time of the 1923 Chicago conference, the organizational leadership was badly divided over a variety of issues. Tourism and the desire to cash in on curiosity about American Indians had replaced previous goals. By the end of the 1923 conference, most of the basis for unity of purpose had crumbled. The organization, reeling in ineffectiveness, could not withstand the encroaching power of anti-Indian white political groups.

In retrospect, it appears that from the very beginning the organization had within itself the seeds for its own destruction. As time went on, an ever-increasing emphasis on addressing age-old tribal grievances encouraged a separatism that subverted an inclusive pan-Indian vision. The SAI leadership was itself a reflection of this pattern. Within the national leadership, factionalism mirrored traditional tribal animosities, defeating in the end the quest for a pan-Indian ideal. The organization's dissolution into a show-time event, a spectacle, signaled the reality of its formal demise.

Impact of Event

The SAI disbanded soon after the 1923 conference without fully achieving any of its goals for improving the immediate condition of Native Americans. The stated goals of the Indian progressives, although noble, were unwisely planned and rarely realized. Nevertheless, certain noteworthy consequences did result from the efforts of the short-lived organization. The elevation of reservation problems to the national political arena is a case in point. The organization made progress toward providing services to a constituency which had been prevented from gaining any access to the national political agenda. Initially, at least, low-cost legal assistance, education, and medical services were provided to many of the tribes represented in the organizational leadership structure. In some areas then, the SAI showed a commitment to the progressive social reform ideals of the period.

These accomplishments paled in comparison to the factionalism that helped to defeat the original purpose of the organization. In many instances, petty infighting among tribal bureaucrats impaired the effectiveness of the organization, leading instead to the society's downfall. The leadership had divided over such mainstream political issues as the abolition of the Bureau of Indian Affairs and the condemnation by whites of the continuance of ceremonial practices such as the use of peyote in religious ritual. The role of non-Indians in the reform efforts of the group also contributed to the SAI's demise. Bothered by internal divisiveness and frustrated by external realities such as the denial of citizenship (which ironically was granted in 1924) to indigenous Americans, many associate members lost the willingness to act in consort with other members as a united political pressure group. Individual interests soon challenged a weakly constructed structure of political unity. The idea of community easily collapsed in the process.

Even so, the rise of the Society of American Indians helped to signal an end to an era when white reformers discussed the Indians' future in isolation. To be sure, there would continue to be those who thought they knew what was best for Native American groups. Future generations of indigenous Americans supporting the ideals of pan-Indianism sprang from the efforts of the SAI, giving Native Americans more voice in their own future.

Bibliography

Hagan, William T. *American Indians.* Chicago: University of Chicago Press, 1961. The general reader should seek out significant overall histories of the American Indian that also may include information on the SAI. This book is a good place to start. It is an excellent overview of the relationship between whites and American Indians from colonial times to the New Deal and a bit after. Chronology, bibliography, and index.

Hertzberg, Hazel W. *The Search for an American Indian Identity: Modern Pan-*

Indian Movements. Syracuse, N.Y.: Syracuse University Press, 1971. Explores the question of the relation of Native Americans to the rest of United States society through identifying, analyzing, and comparing the basic varieties of pan-Indianism and tracing their historical development. Focuses on the period between 1900 and 1930 (the formative years of the pan-Indian movement in the United States) by outlining the forces that produced this movement and its responses to the encroachment of white society. Includes index and bibliography.

Hoxie, Frederick, ed. *Indians in American History: An Introduction.* Arlington Heights, Ill.: Harlan Davidson, 1988. Contains chronologically arranged essays by thirteen authors who speak from a variety of disciplines and perspectives, providing an introduction to the Indian side of United States history. Draws attention to the depth and complexity of the American Indian experience. Further reading suggestions following each chapter make the book useful for research. Indexed.

Iverson, Peter, ed. *The Plains Indians of the Twentieth Century.* Norman: University of Oklahoma Press, 1985. A collection of eleven articles that address issues as diverse as water rights and religious heritage. An initial capsule history by the editor provides a historical context for these discussions. The book as a whole emphasizes Indians' ability to adapt to penetration from the outside while maintaining their identity. Indexed.

Kelly, Lawrence C. *The Assault on Assimilation: John Collier and the Origins of Indian Policy Reform.* Albuquerque: University of New Mexico Press, 1983. A biography of one of the major reformers of Indian policy in twentieth century America. Collier fought the white power establishment that believed it knew what was best for the indigenous population. Kelly brings to light Collier's support of the maintenance of traditional Indian culture through a somewhat complex program of economic development and legal protection. Bibliography and index.

Wilson, Raymond. *Ohiyesa: Charles Eastman, Santee Sioux.* Urbana: University of Illinois Press, 1982. A biography of a key individual involved in the Society of American Indians. This book gives the essential details of Charles Eastman's life. Bibliography and index.

Thomas Jay Edward Walker
Cynthia Gwynne Yaudes

Cross-References

The American Civil Liberties Union Is Founded (1920), p. 327; The Indian Reorganization Act Offers Autonomy to American Indians (1934), p. 497; U.S. Government Encourages Native Americans to Settle in Cities (1950's), p. 820; Congress Passes the Civil Rights Act (1964), p. 1251; The Inter-American Court of Human Rights Is Established (1969), p. 1503; Congress Ratifies the National Council on Indian Opportunity (1970), p. 1537; Congress Passes the Equal Employment Opportunity Act (1972), p. 1650; Native Americans Occupy Wounded Knee (1973), p. 1709; A World Conference Condemns Racial Discrimination (1978), p. 1993.

MASSACHUSETTS ADOPTS THE FIRST MINIMUM-WAGE LAW IN THE UNITED STATES

Category of event: Workers' rights
Time: 1912
Locale: Massachusetts

For the first time in the United States, employers' obligation to provide a minimum "living wage" was established in law

> *Principal personages:*
> EUGENE N. FOSS (1858-1939), the governor of Massachusetts
> SAMUEL GOMPERS (1850-1924), the president of the American Federation of Labor
> THEODORE ROOSEVELT (1858-1919), the twenty-sixth president of the United States, convinced by the effort in Massachusetts and elsewhere to put a minimum-wage plank into his 1912 platform

Summary of Event

The idea of a minimum wage was gaining increasing support throughout the industrialized world by the late nineteenth century. Among English-speaking nations, New Zealand and Australia led the way; both passed minimum-wage legislation in the 1890's. In 1910, Great Britain followed the example of its offshoots and adopted a law patterned after the Australian legislation.

The United States lagged far behind these nations in promoting a minimum wage. In fact, both the National Association of Manufacturers (NAM) and the American Federation of Labor (AFL) opposed minimum-wage laws, albeit for completely different reasons. The NAM argued that all such legislation was a violation of the free market and would hurt the economy, while the AFL feared that government intervention to set wages would lead working people into a situation of growing state control.

Not all businesses or AFL unions opposed minimum wages. Some progressively minded businesspeople realized that their employees needed wages that would support a minimum standard of living if they were to be productive. They supported the minimum-wage proposals in the hope that the laws would force their more brutal competitors to raise wage levels.

The union movement was likewise split. In California and New York, AFL-organized labor opposed the legislation as unwarranted government paternalism that would only weaken unions and hurt working people. In Washington State, on the other hand, the leaders of organized labor worked with advocates of minimum-wage laws to get the reform passed. Splits took place even within single states, as in New York, where the Brooklyn Central Labor Union pushed for the minimum wage in spite of AFL opposition.

Despite the lack of unified labor support and the opposition of much of the business world, the Women's Trade Union League began to make minimum-wage legislation, along with the eight-hour day, key demands beginning in 1909. In Massachusetts, a campaign for a minimum wage for female workers was organized in 1910 by the local branches of labor and reform organizations as well as the Women's Trade Union League. The lot of the working women of that time was expressed tersely in the words of Violet Pike in her *New World Lessons for Old World Peoples* (1912):

> I go to work at eight o'clock.
> I work until six o'clock.
> I have only one-half hour for lunch.
> I work overtime in the busy season.
> I do not get extra pay for overtime work.
> I earn eight dollars a week in the busy season.
> I earn three or four dollars a week in the slow season.
> I have no work at all for three months.
> I pay for my needles and thread.
> I pay for my electric power.
> My trade is a bad trade.

Numerous government reports, including the studies made by the New York Factory Investigating Commission, proved that the vast majority of women were not working for "pin money." Women worked for the same reason that men worked: to support their households. Of course, many young women married in hopes of escaping the factory. The evidence suggests that a large number of these women soon returned to industrial labor, as their husbands' wages alone were insufficient to support a family.

Not only were female workers subjected to wretched working conditions and even lower pay than their male counterparts, they also were less often able to fight successfully against this situation. Unionization levels for the United States' eight million female workers remained fairly constant and low from 1900 to 1910, with gains being made only in certain textile factories, where less than 5 percent of female workers were unionized.

Although the lot of the male worker was not significantly better, many labor activists and reformers believed that more public sympathy could be gained if a campaign began with a focus on the "fairer sex." In addition, the opposition of the AFL, which was the major labor affiliation of male union members, made a campaign for a universal minimum-wage law more difficult. Although not seen as a cure-all, the enactment of a minimum wage was thought of as a way to establish the principle that workers had the right to a living wage.

In order to rally public support for their position, minimum-wage supporters pressured the Massachusetts legislature to establish a commission to investigate women's wages in relation to the cost of living. In the spring of 1911, a newly created commission studied wages in laundries, candy factories, and retail stores. After extensive evidence was collected, the commission concluded that many workers could not meet even their most basic human needs on the low wages paid by their employers. As a result, four out of five commission members recommended passage of a minimum-wage law to the Massachusetts legislature. Even the fifth commission member agreed with the others in broad outline, although he had differences on specific provisions in the report.

The legislation drafted was based largely on existing minimum-wage laws in the industrial world, particularly New Zealand and Australia. The proposed Massachusetts statute varied from the Australian Victoria Act of 1896 in that the former applied only to women and minors. Thus, critics noted that the human rights of male workers were completely ignored by the Commonwealth of Massachusetts, although the Australian and New Zealand laws and the English Trade Boards Act of 1909 applied to workers of both sexes.

In spite of the moderate nature of the proposed reform, representatives of the Massachusetts manufacturers, particularly those in the textile industry, opposed the bill vigorously. Their argument was that the increased labor costs the law would impose would make Massachusetts uncompetitive with other regions and nations. Thus, the labor rights gained would be an illusion, since they quickly would be replaced by unemployment.

The employers' logic was quickly rejected by most workers, who easily contrasted their poverty with the profits of those for whom they labored. It appeared that a bitter struggle was to take place. The struggle was avoided when the lone dissenting member of the original investigating commission came forth with a compromise proposal. This proposal changed the proposed minimum-wage law from establishing legal wage rates based solely on human needs to considering the financial situation of the industry. In the words of the legislation, "the financial condition of the occupation and the probable effect thereon of any increase in the minimum wages paid" had to be taken into account.

Of even greater immediate significance, the new proposal changed original mandatory enforcement to a scheme whereby a commission would investigate employers for failing to pay minimum wages but could "punish" employers only by publishing the offending firms' names in the newspapers. As the miserable living conditions of workers were largely already known, critics charged that this was of little value. In addition, it was noted that much of Massachusetts' production was shipped outside the state, where consumers would remain unaware of the specific wage levels of a given manufacturer.

Since labor candidates had made an excellent showing in the last state elections in Massachusetts, legislators were eager to have something prolabor to show the voters. Still, they did not wish to offend the business community. The new nonmandatory minimum-wage law suggestion was thus immediately supported by large numbers of state legislators.

This blunted reform legislation was acceptable to, or at least tolerated by, the manufacturers, since it was expected to have little practical effect on their businesses. On the other hand, the reformers who had campaigned for a minimum-wage law believed that it was better to accept this compromise and at least establish the principle of a minimum wage in law than to have no law at all. Thus, the first minimum-wage statute was entered onto the books in Massachusetts in 1912.

Impact of Event

Although the Massachusetts law remained largely in unchanged, and ineffective, form until 1933, it set a new principle that was to have a great impact on American society. In the year it was passed, the Massachusetts minimum-wage law was influential in persuading Theodore Roosevelt and the Progressive Party to add minimum wages for women and children as a plank in their 1912 presidential platform.

In 1913, the year following the enactment of the Massachusetts law, eight other states throughout the country passed minimum-wage laws. Did these new laws actually help the workers they were designed to benefit? The answer to this question is not an easy one. The evidence suggests that the effectiveness of the laws varied widely from state to state.

In many states, the minimum wage was set so low as to have no practical impact. Only in those states where the minimum was set high and strictly enforced, such as California, did there appear to be any clear benefit for the workers. Ironically, Massachusetts, with its nonmandatory legislation, saw more than half the women in some industries receiving less than the officially established minimum wage.

Many labor organizations, including the American Federation of Labor (AFL), opposed the minimum-wage laws out of fear that they might become maximum-wage laws. Further, they thought the principle of promoting the notion of a "living wage" not valuable enough to offset the danger that the government increasingly would step in and regulate industrial relations to the benefit of employers and to the detriment of labor.

All the same, the passage of the first minimum-wage law in Massachusetts was seen by many as the beginning of a new attitude in the United States. No longer were people content to allow wages to be determined completely by market forces. The concept of a minimum standard of living to which workers were entitled started to gain acceptance.

The nineteenth century notion of property rights as sacred and above all other considerations in society was challenged by the idea of a living wage as a human right. In addition, the concept of government legislation to protect the rights of workers was further enhanced by the minimum-wage law's being upheld by the Supreme Judicial Court of Massachusetts in 1918. Many later labor reforms that recognized the human rights of employees were influenced by the principles put forth in Massachusetts.

Bibliography

Brandeis, Elizabeth. "Labor Legislation." In *History of Labor in the United States, 1896-1932*, edited by John R. Commons et al. Vol. 3. New York: Macmillan, 1935.

This work is obviously dated but remains unsurpassed for wealth of detail, clear presentation, and readable text. Its documentation is extremely complete and based mainly on primary sources. Contains a bibliography and complete index.

Douglas, Dorothy W. "American Minimum Wage Laws at Work." *American Economic Review* 9 (Spring, 1919): 701-738. A useful contemporary survey of different state laws that places the Massachusetts statute in the context of its time. It allows the reader to see the relative effectiveness of minimum-wage laws on the books in the United States by the end of World War I.

Foner, Philip S. *The AFL in the Progressive Era, 1900-1913.* Vol. 5 in *History of the Labor Movement in the United States.* New York: International Publishers, 1979. Focusing on the role of the largest U.S. trade union federation, this work provides the reader with a heavily documented account of the American labor movement in the years before World War I. Includes detailed reference notes and index.

_____. *On the Eve of America's Entrance into World War I, 1915-1916.* Vol. 6 in *History of the Labor Movement in the United States.* New York: International Publishers, 1982. Dealing with various topics, such as the Women's Trade Union League and the struggle for the eight-hour day, this volume challenges key parts of the earlier interpretation of labor history and does so in a very interesting and readable manner. Includes detailed references and index.

Stein, Emanuel. "Wage Laws." In *Labor Cases and Materials: Readings on the Relation of Government to Labor,* edited by Carl Raushenbush and Emanuel Stein. New York: F. S. Crofts, 1946. Focused on the legal aspects of labor legislation, this work is helpful for those who want to study the legal history of minimum-wage laws. Not recommended for the average reader, this work fills a need for those who wish to examine the legal, as opposed to social and political, development of minimum-wage legislation.

William A. Pelz

Cross-References

Supreme Court Disallows a Maximum Hours Law for Bakers (1905), p. 36; The British Labour Party Is Formed (1906), p. 58; The Bern Conference Prohibits Night Work for Women (1906), p. 75; Ford Offers a Five-Dollar, Eight-Hour Workday (1914), p. 143; The International Labour Organisation Is Established (1919), p. 281; Great Britain Passes Acts to Provide Unemployment Benefits (1920), p. 321; The Wagner Act Requires Employers to Accept Collective Bargaining (1935), p. 508; The Congress of Industrial Organizations Is Formed (1938), p. 545; Autoworkers Negotiate a Contract with a Cost-of-Living Provision (1948), p. 766; Chávez Forms Farm Workers' Union and Leads Grape Pickers' Strike (1962), p. 1161; Chávez Is Jailed for Organizing an Illegal Lettuce Boycott (1970), p. 1567; Congress Passes the Equal Employment Opportunity Act (1972), p. 1650.

THE CHILDREN'S BUREAU IS FOUNDED

Category of event: Children's rights
Time: April 9, 1912
Locale: Washington, D.C.

The establishment of the Children's Bureau marked the first time the U.S. government accepted responsibility for the basic rights and welfare of its youngest citizens

Principal personages:

JANE ADDAMS (1860-1935), the founder of Hull House in Chicago, an advocate of child labor laws

FLORENCE KELLEY (1859-1932), a social worker connected with Hull House and the Henry Street settlement

JULIA LATHROP (1858-1932), the first head of the Children's Bureau

BENJAMIN BARR LINDSEY (1869-1943), an international authority on juvenile delinquency, one of the first juvenile court judges

EDGAR GARDNER MURPHY (1869-1913), an Episcopalian minister, founder of the first children's labor organization

JOHN SPARGO (1876-1966), the author of *The Bitter Cry of the Children* (1906)

LILLIAN D. WALD (1867-1940), a pioneer in public health nursing who originated the idea of a national children's bureau

Summary of Event

At the beginning of the twentieth century, the sentimental portrait of carefree, rosy-cheeked children protected within the bosom of the loving family was a myth of the popular imagination. The reality of the lives of many American children was much harsher. One in twenty children died before the age of five; probably half of these deaths were preventable. At least two million children were working long hours in mines and factories, often under appalling conditions. Arrangements for the care of orphaned, neglected, or delinquent children were inadequate or nonexistent. The death or desertion of the family wage-earner, usually the male head of household, spelled tragedy for mothers without insurance, widows' benefits, or government support. They often had to work outside the home, leaving a child as young as eight or nine to care for even younger children.

In the late eighteenth and early nineteenth centuries, the political movement called Progressivism was gaining followers among middle-class Americans. This optimistic movement, with its faith in the power of democracy, demanded reforms of the abuses of unrestrained industrialism and urban political corruption. In the traditional American belief in rugged individualism, the plight of the poor was considered the result of their own shiftlessness. Social activists from settlement houses in Boston, New York, and Chicago, however, recognized poverty as a widespread social problem that could not be solved by private charity. These reformers began to work for legislation for better housing, fair labor policies, and the rights of women.

These issues were closely tied to the problem of child labor. Some states had laws protecting the rights of children on the books, but they were seldom enforced. Americans had strong feelings about the sacredness of family life and a fear of government interference in private matters. The reformers appealed to the rising spirit of Progressivism, arguing that social problems could be better solved through legislation than charity. Focusing on the inhumanity of the lives of poor children, the reformers argued that strong, healthy children were the hope for a democratic society, and that improving children's lives was an investment in the future.

American children had always worked on family farms and as apprentices learning a trade, and this work was considered beneficial as training for responsible adulthood. Clearly, however, the child who worked under dangerous conditions without adequate food or rest was exhausted and debilitated—not benefited—by this labor. While industrialists continued to argue for the benefits of work for the child, reformers accused them of exploiting children as a cheap source of labor and an alternative to investing in machinery.

In 1906, John Spargo published *The Bitter Cry of the Children*, which aroused national indignation with its graphic description of the horrors of the lives of poor children. Breaker boys, some as young as nine or ten, worked in the mines, crouched for ten-hour shifts picking slate from coal chutes, breathing clouds of coal dust. Accidents such as crushed hands and cut fingers were common. All too often boys were pulled into machinery and mangled to death. Others worked underground in mud on fourteen-hour shifts as mule drivers. Conditions in other industries were equally terrible. Working children were often exposed to toxic substances. Some were poisoned when their bodies absorbed dyes in textile mills or phosphorus used in making matches. Others inhaled varnish used in furniture manufacturing or naphtha fumes from rubber-making. Some children were shipped from state to state, following seasonal work in agriculture or canning, and denied an opportunity for an education.

Even before Spargo's book raised public consciousness about the lives of children, some communities had begun to institute health measures to save young lives from the ravages of rickets, pneumonia, measles, tuberculosis, and malnutrition. Boston, Massachusetts, began a program of preventive medicine in 1894, providing prenatal care for mothers and medical exams for schoolchildren. In 1897, the city of Rochester, New York, cut the death rate of infants and children in half by pasteurizing the milk supply. In 1908, New York City created the Divison of Child Hygiene, recognizing the need for special attention to the health of children.

The public attitude toward the treatment of delinquent children was changing, too, largely because of the work of Judge Benjamin Barr Lindsey. Lindsey, one of the first to treat young offenders as victims of their environment, was horrified by their abuse by the police. He believed that children could not be saved by a criminal law based on fear and vengeance, but rather needed kindness and patient understanding. His work in the early years of the twentieth century revolutionized the field of juvenile law.

This growing public attention to the needs of children, combined with the efforts of social workers to regulate child labor, led to the founding of the Children's Bureau. The earliest organized attempt to pass a child labor law was initiated by Edgar Gardner Murphy, an Episcopalian minister appalled by the treatment of children in southern textile mills. Murphy founded the Alabama Child Labor Committee in 1901. Although the group succeeded in passing a state law for a minimum working age, the mill owners were powerful enough to keep the law from being enforced. In 1904, Murphy founded the National Child Labor Committee to work for local and state legislation. Social activists such as Jane Addams, Florence Kelley, and Lillian Wald, however, believed that a federal government agency for the protection of children was the only way to overcome industry's organized opposition to legislation.

In 1893, Kelley and Addams, both associated with Hull House in Chicago, were instrumental in the passage of the Illinois Factory Act regulating minimum age and hours for working children. The Illinois Supreme Court, however, declared the law unconstitutional. Not until 1903 did Illinois pass an effective child labor law.

In 1906, the National Child Labor Committee introduced a bill in Congress asking for the establishment of a children's agency in the federal government. This, and the efforts of social activists, resulted in President Theodore Roosevelt calling the White House Conference on the Care of Dependent Children in 1909. This conference, with representatives from charitable organizations in all the states and from the juvenile courts attending, passed a resolution for the establishment of the Children's Bureau.

Congress finally passed the law establishing the Children's Bureau as an agency in the Department of Commerce and Labor in 1912. President William Howard Taft signed the bill into law. The Bureau had no power to enact or enforce legislation. Its duties were to

> investigate and report . . . upon all matters pertaining to the welfare of children and . . . especially [to] investigate the questions of infant mortality, the birth rate, orphanages, juvenile courts, desertion, dangerous occupations, accidents and diseases of children, employment, and legislation affecting children.

Named as the first head of the bureau was Julia C. Lathrop, of the Illinois State Board of Charities, an associate of Jane Addams with a long record of activism in the field of mental health and the juvenile courts. Lathrop was the first woman appointed as chief of a federal agency and the highest paid woman in government service at that time.

Impact of Event

Even with the interests of children consolidated in one federal agency, legislative progress was slow and painstaking. The states feared federal intrusion into their traditional rights, and families and churches felt threatened by the idea of the government taking over their duties.

From 1912 to 1921, the bureau investigated and reported on infant and child mortality rates, community care for neglected and delinquent children, aid to families, and child labor. Lathrop sent a plan for public health services for mothers and children to Congress in 1917. Her plan included maternity care, preventive medical care, and health services for rural children. As a result of Lathrop's efforts, Congress in 1921 passed the Sheppard-Towner Act, the first federal grant to states funding maternal and infant care. Lathrop also asked women to write to her about their families and sent them free booklets, often with a personal note of encouragement. Two Children's Bureau pamphlets, *Prenatal Care* and *Infant Care*, became the most frequently requested government documents of all time.

Attempts to regulate child labor were less successful at first. In 1916, Congress adopted the recommendation of the National Child Labor Committee prohibiting interstate shipment of products made in factories by children under the age of fourteen (sixteen in mines) and limitation of the workday to eight hours. In 1918, the Supreme Court, citing states' rights, declared the law unconstitutional. The next attempt to regulate child labor was a proposed constitutional amendment giving Congress the right to regulate workers under the age of eighteen. Organized interests of agriculture and industry succeeded in defeating this amendment with a scare campaign, threatening that this legislation would allow government control of family life. Not until 1938 did Congress pass the Fair Labor Standards Act, which set a minimum wage for all workers, allowed a maximum workweek of forty-four hours, and prohibited interstate shipment of goods produced by children under the age of sixteen.

One of the most important results of the Children's Bureau advocacy for children was passage of the Social Security Act in 1935. Families benefited by the provisions for old-age insurance, employment compensation, and public health. More directly, this legislation gave the bureau administrative responsibility for three programs: maternal and child health services, medical care for crippled children, and child welfare services.

As government agencies were reorganized, the Children's Bureau came under several different jurisdictions. In 1980, the bureau became an agency in the Department of Health and Human Services. Once the laws against child labor were passed, the bureau turned its attention to urgent problems as they arose. Some issues of concern have included child abuse, racism, day care, foster care and adoption, and mental retardation. The Children's Bureau, in keeping with its original purpose, has successfully convinced the public that the basic rights and welfare of children are indeed the business of government.

Bibliography

Bradbury, Dorothy E. *The Children's Bureau and Juvenile Delinquency.* Washington, D.C.: Government Printing Office, 1960. An overview of specific actions of the bureau in the field of juvenile delinquency throughout its history, as well as a list of government publications on this subject.

Bremner, Robert H. "The Home and the Child." In *From the Depths: The Discovery of Poverty in the United States.* New York: New York University Press, 1956. Traces the development of social reform in the late nineteenth and early twentieth centuries and shows how the social reform movements led to legislation in housing, child labor, women's issues, and safety in the workplace.

Davis, Allen F. "Working Women and Children." In *Spearheads for Reform: The Social Settlements and the Progressive Movement, 1890-1914.* New York: Oxford University Press, 1967. A detailed history of contributions to social reform by activists in the settlement house movement in Chicago, Boston, and New York. Biographical information about major figures such as Jane Addams and Florence Kelley, documented by private correspondence and contemporary newspaper articles.

Faulkner, Harold U. "Children's Rights." In *The Quest for Social Justice, 1898-1914.* New York: Macmillan, 1931. Reprint. Chicago: Quadrangle Books, 1971. A useful historical overview of the Progressive Era, describing the development of new awareness by the public of the injustices of the Industrial Revolution. Details the growth of social consciousness in organized labor, economic and political demands by women, and the rights of children.

Green, Frederick C. "Six Decades of Action for Children." *Children Today* 6 (March/April, 1972): 2-6. A history of the evolution of the original Children's Bureau from its beginning as a service of the Department of Labor and Commerce to its current status in the Department of Health and Human Services. Describes the bureau's changing concerns and influence on legislation to improve the lives of children.

Lindsey, Benjamin B. "The Origin of the Juvenile Court." In *1905-1915: The Progressive Era.* Vol. 13 in *The Annals of America.* Chicago: Encyclopaedia Britannica, 1968. Lindsey recounts his success in counseling young offenders, showing how his philosophy of personal attention turns boys away from a life of crime.

Reece, Carolyn. "The Children's Bureau 75th Anniversary: The Commitment Continues." *Children Today* 16 (September/October, 1987): 4-9. Notable for its poignant quotations from letters written by mothers to Julia Lathrop asking for medical help in childbirth and the care of infants. Also contains a chart listing organizational changes and legislation passed as a result of action of the Children's Bureau.

Spargo, John. *The Bitter Cry of the Children.* 1906. Reprint. Chicago: Quadrangle Books, 1968. One of the most influential books of its time, widely read by the general public. A passionate yet factual account of the lives of children who are neglected, starved, exhausted, and abused. Discusses nutrition, education, and child labor. Quoted in the *Congressional Record* to support legislation for children's rights.

Tobey, James A. *The Children's Bureau: Its History, Activities, and Organization.* Baltimore, Md.: The Johns Hopkins University Press, 1925. A government monograph, one of a series, detailing the history, function, activities, and organization of the Children's Bureau. Facts and statistics for activities of the agency in its early years.

Marjorie J. Podolsky

Cross-References

Supreme Court Disallows a Maximum Hours Law for Bakers (1905), p. 36; The Pure Food and Drug Act and Meat Inspection Act Become Law (1906), p. 64; The Bern Conference Prohibits Night Work for Women (1906), p. 75; Massachusetts Adopts the First Minimum-Wage Law in the United States (1912), p. 126; Sanger Opens the First Birth-Control Clinic in the United States (1916), p. 184; Social Security Act Establishes Benefits for Nonworking People (1935), p. 514; The First Food Stamp Program Begins in Rochester, New York (1939), p. 555; The United Nations Adopts the Declaration of the Rights of the Child (1959), p. 1038; The Equal Pay Act Becomes Law (1963), p. 1172; Head Start Is Established (1965), p. 1284; Congress Passes the Child Abuse Prevention and Treatment Act (1974), p. 1752; Congress Enacts the Education for All Handicapped Children Act (1975), p. 1780; The United Nations Adopts the Convention on the Rights of the Child (1989), p. 2529.

U.S. MARINES ARE SENT TO NICARAGUA TO QUELL UNREST

Category of event: Political freedom
Time: August 3, 1912
Locale: Nicaragua

The presence of U.S. Marines in Nicaragua hindered national self-determination, sustained a government remote from the people, and reinforced conditions leading to social revolution

Principal personages:

JOSÉ SANTOS ZELAYA (1845-1919), the nationalist dictator of Nicaragua (1893-1909) who troubled the United States

JUAN J. ESTRADA (1871-1947), a Nicaraguan general and figurehead leader of the 1909 revolt that overthrew Zelaya

ADOLFO DÍAZ (1874-1964), the conservative president of Nicaragua (1913-1917 and 1926-1928) who, as provisional president in 1912, asked the United States to send in Marines

AUGUSTO CÉSAR SANDINO (1895-1934), the legendary Nicaraguan guerrilla leader whom the U.S. Marines could never catch

ANASTASIO SOMOZA GARCÍA (1896-1956), the longtime dictator of Nicaragua (1936-1956) who had Sandino assassinated

LUIS SOMOZA DEBAYLE (1922-1967), the oldest son of Somoza García; became president (1956-1963) upon his father's assassination

ANASTASIO SOMOZA DEBAYLE (1925-1980), the other son of Somoza García, who as head of the national guard and as dictator (1967-1979) was probably the most brutal of the Somoza rulers

Summary of Event

Nicaragua's history in the nineteenth century was a violent struggle among many political actors, and human rights abuse was the norm. Although never systematically documented by scholars, election fraud, political corruption, intimidation, abuse of civilians, wanton destruction and confiscation of property, exile, execution, and murder were common.

This disorder and violation of human rights diminished toward the end of the century as power began to coalesce around the dictatorship of the liberal José Santos Zelaya. In spite of arbitrary rule, his government did expand education, augment state power, professionalize the armed forces, and stimulate trade and commerce. Disorder returned and human rights violations escalated after Zelaya resigned in 1909. His enemies had launched a revolution on Nicaragua's Atlantic coast that succeeded because they had United States protection at a critical juncture. The United States had its own complaints against Zelaya. His stout defense of Nicaraguan sovereignty had led the United States to locate the transisthmian canal in Panama rather than Nicaragua in 1903 even though the latter had been the U.S. government's first choice.

Unfortunately, the canal problem was not resolved once Panama won the prize. Zelaya, like many Nicaraguans, resented losing and entertained visions of having a second canal built by another world power. He voiced his fury publicly in nationalistic outbursts in which he pushed for a canal agreement with the new naval powers of Germany and Japan. Such actions aroused U.S. concerns over Nicaragua's strategic location as a place either to build a second canal or to interfere with the one in Panama. In light of the Monroe Doctrine and the Roosevelt Corollary, which presumed to exclude Old World powers from the Western Hemisphere, it was unlikely that the United States would allow a second canal to be built. Thus, when the opportunity arose, the United States helped to end Zelaya's rule.

The revolution against Zelaya, led by conservatives and joined by Zelaya's governor and general on the Atlantic coast, Juan J. Estrada, broke out in the Atlantic port of Bluefields on October 10, 1909. Zelaya's forces caught two United States soldiers of fortune laying mines in the San Juan River. Summarily tried, condemned, and promptly executed by a firing squad on November 19, 1909, they shared a fate common to losers on either side. Even though the soldiers had received commissions as officers in the revolutionary movement, and as a result had forfeited any rights as American citizens, the United States quickly broke diplomatic relations over the incident. Trying to salvage his regime but not his position, Zelaya resigned on December 1, 1909, and went into exile. Internationally, U.S. nonrecognition gave belligerency status to the revolutionaries and allowed them to import arms legally. In addition, the United States sent gunboats to the area as early as May and landed Marines after the revolution started and again in 1910, ostensibly to protect American lives and property. By declaring Bluefields a neutral zone, the United States effectively prevented Nicaraguan government forces from shelling the revolutionaries. The latter's control of the port guaranteed them a sufficient flow of customs revenues and armament to force the liberals to acknowledge defeat. The United States had already refused to recognize the Nicaraguan congress' choice to replace Zelaya, the distinguished liberal jurist Dr. José Madriz, and insisted, contrary to fact, that the conservatives represented the will of the Nicaraguan people. This decision fatally flawed U.S. policy, since the liberals were a majority and could be expected to win fair elections and to dispute conservative rule. Conservative control could only be achieved with U.S. intervention, a continued U.S. presence, and enough conservative muscle to intimidate liberals. In such a context, armed struggle and further human rights abuse were inevitable. Additionally, the United States repeatedly violated the principle of national self-determination as a political and human right. Finally, U.S. actions delayed the creation of the Nicaraguan nation and set in motion events that led to decades of human rights abuse.

The U.S. backed Estrada as provisional president in 1910 and helped him put together a bipartisan government that included liberals. The Marines left, however, and the coalition unraveled and collapsed. Disorder grew. Estrada resigned in May, 1911, in favor of the vice president, conservative Adolfo Díaz. The liberal revolt, led by Benjamín Zeledón, was not long in coming. President Díaz requested United States intervention, officially to protect North American lives and property but really to preserve Díaz in the presidency. The landing of U.S. Marines on August 3, 1912, brought in more than twenty-seven hundred soldiers, who occupied the main railroad and principal cities. Conservative forces quickly hunted down the liberals and publicly paraded Zeledón's body. The Marines were to occupy Nicaragua almost continuously from 1912 until 1933. Up until 1925, one hundred Marines were enough to indicate whom the United States supported and to keep the peace. The U.S. presence and preferences, however, continued to undermine Nicaraguan independence and self-determination.

The U.S. was not evenhanded and showed favoritism toward Nicaraguan conservatives and American bankers, whose avarice quickly discredited the participants. The disorder following Zelaya's downfall in 1909 brought financial chaos to Nicaragua. A growing list of unpaid debts to various foreign creditors raised the specter, at least in U.S. eyes, of European intervention. Through its Nicaraguan agents, the United States arranged to put Nicaragua's financial house in some order, since loans from New York bankers satisfied European creditors and removed reasons for European intervention. The price, however, was high and mortgaged the country's future customs duties and rail and steamship revenues. The agents who collected these monies were nominated by U.S. bankers and represented their interests. These bankers set up the National Bank of Nicaragua, whose board of directors met not in Nicaragua but in New York City. Profit-making possibilities were many. Heavily discounted loans were bought up and then paid off at full value. The proposed Knox-Castillo Agreement of 1911 was an initial attempt to raise these unsavory practices to the level of a treaty between the two countries but was never ratified by the U.S. Senate. The latter roundly criticized President William Howard Taft's proudly trumpeted "Dollar Diplomacy" as unprincipled.

Nevertheless, President Woodrow Wilson approved much of the same policy for inclusion in the Bryan-Chamorro treaty (signed in 1914, ratified in 1916), which gave the United States a monopoly over any canal constructed through Nicaragua for only three million dollars, which passed directly to those U.S. banks holding Nicaraguan debts. After finishing the Panama Canal in 1914, the United States was not going to engineer a second one in Nicaragua; the overriding purpose of the treaty was to prevent any other world power from possessing an isthmian canal. Diplomatic historians have long argued about the relative weight of strategic, economic, and moral concerns in the conduct of United States foreign policy. The ostensible reason for sending U.S. Marines to Nicaragua in 1912 was to protect American lives and property. The real reason, however, was the strategic importance the United States attached to the Panama Canal. For Nicaragua, the U.S. presence led to a political stalemate, and without a thorough restructuring of the locus of power, human rights violations continued to be a significant problem.

Impact of Event

It is little wonder that the loss of the canal, the presence of U.S. soldiers, the financial misdealings, U.S. support for the unpopular conservatives, and the growing disorder eventually produced a profound reaction in Nicaragua. The United States sensed this, wanted out, and withdrew the Marines in 1925. They trained the Nicaraguan National Guard as a replacement and supported a conservative-liberal coalition government. None of these actions, however, put Nicaragua on a course of self-determination and independence. The conservatives undermined the bipartisan government, and by May, 1925, there was another full-scale liberal rebellion. The Marines were sent in again in 1926. By February, 1927, there were fifty-four hundred U.S. Marines and eleven destroyers and cruisers in Nicaraguan cities and ports. U.S. officials finally decided that if they switched sides and supported the liberals, which they did in the May 12, 1927, Espino Negro Pact, they might be able to extricate themselves from the Nicaraguan morass. All liberal generals except one, the legendary August César Sandino, signed the Espino Negro Pact and agreed to accept the outcome of a U.S.-administered election in 1928, which everyone knew the liberals would win. Sandino's refusal to participate in the pact sprang from his belief that the others had sold out to the Americans. He demanded that the United States leave Nicaragua immediately and let it solve its own problems without U.S. tutelage. The United States supported the National Guard's efforts to hunt Sandino down, but his classic guerrilla warfare tactics kept the National Guard at bay and increasingly made life difficult for the Americans and the Nicaraguan government. For six years, the United States had two thousand soldiers fighting Sandino and lending support and training to the National Guard. There were significant human rights violations on both sides. A U.S.-backed and -directed scorched-earth policy and forced removal and resettlement of villagers were intended to deny support to Sandino. Manned air strikes, orchestrated by the United States, decimated Sandinista-controlled pueblos and killed many civilians, including women and children. Nevertheless, Sandino and his movement endured. Finally, the United States decided to cut its losses. It withdrew the Marines in January, 1933, without having been able to neutralize Sandino. Its parting mistake, however, was to install Anastasio Somoza García as head of the National Guard. Somoza had ingratiated himself with U.S. embassy personnel and had won the appointment based on his contacts and facility in English.

The National Guard had been trained to eliminate Sandino, which it had failed to do. Somoza won its allegiance by successfully planning and carrying out the assassination of Sandino on February 23, 1934, after Sandino left a meeting with Nicaraguan president Juan Bautista Sacasa. Somoza's control of the National Guard led to President Sacasa's ouster and his own selection as president in 1936. The National Guard became his personal vehicle and enabled him to stay in power and accumulate more than sixty million dollars by 1944. Until his assassination in 1956, Somoza ruled Nicaragua as a dictator. His network of informants and spies was extensive and identified opponents who were targeted for beatings, torture, illegal imprisonment, and murder. He passed power on to his two sons, who continued to rule and amass incredible wealth. All three maintained close ties with the United States. The U.S. government flew Somoza to the Panama Canal Zone in 1956 in an unsuccessful attempt to prevent his assassination. Luis Somoza Debayle graduated from Louisiana State University, and his brother, Anastasio Somoza Debayle, attended the U.S. Military Academy at West Point. Both continued and further refined the system of political repression developed by their father. In 1961, the Sandinista Front of National Liberation (FSLN), named in honor of Sandino, was founded and began an eighteen-year guerrilla struggle against the Somozas. The movement came to fruition when the last of the Somozas went into exile and the Sandinistas took power on July 19, 1979.

Bibliography

Booth, John A. *The End and the Beginning: The Nicaraguan Revolution.* 2d ed. Boulder, Colo.: Westview Press, 1985. First-rate survey of twentieth century Nicaraguan politics. Covers the Zelaya period, U.S. intervention, and Sandino well but concentrates on the Somoza era and the Sandinista revolution. Extensive references and index.

Denny, Harold Norman. *Dollars for Bullets: The Story of American Rule in Nicaragua.* New York: Dial Press, 1929. Highly critical of U.S. intervention in Nicaragua. Castigates U.S. bankers for their excessive greed. A good read but sadly dated and strident in tone. References and index.

Dunkerley, James. *Power in the Isthmus. A Political History of Modern Central America.* London: Verso, 1988. A formidable and massive survey of Central American politics. The scope, analytical framework, empirical detail, and cerebral reflection make this a necessary reference work, although some will find the analysis too highbrow and esoteric for their tastes. Excessively long sentences will be a burden to others. Much consideration given to class conflict and the mechanisms of elite control. The latter three-fourths of the book is given over to the period after 1950. Earlier chapters achieve a better synthesis and higher standard of excellence. Abundant references and index.

Hill, Roscoe R. *Fiscal Intervention in Nicaragua.* New York: Paul Maisel, 1933. A standard work on the unsavory details of United States financial involvement in Nicaragua. Told from the U.S. bankers' point of view. Somewhat dated. Readers will be in need of a fresh approach to understand the larger ramifications of the intriguing relationship between U.S. politicians and their bankers.

Macaulay, Neill. *The Sandino Affair.* Chicago: Quadrangle Books, 1967. Fascinating account of one of the pivotal figures in Nicaraguan history. Captures Sandino's charisma, the dynamics of the guerrilla movement, and the reasons it succeeded against the U.S. Marines. Excellent sources, bibliography, and index.

Millett, Richard. *Guardians of the Dynasty.* New York: Orbis Books, 1977. History of the Nicaraguan National Guard and its symbiotic relationship with the Somozas. Looks forward to the day when both would disappear. References and index.

Stansifer, Charles. "José Santos Zelaya: A New Look at Nicaragua's Liberal Dictatorship." *Revista Interamericana* 7 (Fall, 1977): 468-485. A revisionist account convincingly presented that maintains that Zelaya has been wrongly depicted as a bloodthirsty tyrant when in fact he was a nationalist who did much for the national development of Nicaragua. Limited coverage. References but no index.

Stimson, Henry L. *American Policy in Nicaragua.* New York: Charles Scribner's Sons, 1927. A carefully crafted defense of U.S. policy in Nicaragua by one of the chief American participants, who was later to be secretary of state. Stimson orchestrated the 1927 Espino Negro Pact that got all the liberal generals except for Sandino to agree to a U.S.-sponsored election putting the liberals back in power. No index or sources.

Woodward, Ralph Lee, Jr. *Central America: A Nation Divided.* 2d ed. New York: Oxford University Press, 1985. Excellent history of Central America, with Nicaragua covered in detail and put in the larger context of Central American and hemispheric politics. Judicious and fair. Exceptional balance among political, economic, and social forces. Good index and a penetrating bibliographic essay of fifty-three pages.

Maurice P. Brungardt

Cross-References

The Boxer Rebellion Fails to Remove Foreign Control in China (1900), p. 1; The Philippines Ends Its Uprising Against the United States (1902), p. 7; Panama Declares Independence from Colombia (1903), p. 25; El Salvador's Military Massacres Civilians in *La Matanza* (1932), p. 464; Castro Takes Power in Cuba (1959), p. 1026; Brazil Begins a Period of Intense Repression (1968), p. 1468; Marcos Declares Martial Law in the Philippines (1972), p. 1680; An Oppressive Military Rule Comes to Democratic Uruguay (1973), p. 1715; Allende Is Overthrown in a Chilean Military Coup (1973), p. 1725; The Argentine Military Conducts a "Dirty War" Against Leftists (1976), p. 1864; Indigenous Indians Become the Target of Guatemalan Death Squads (1978), p. 1972; Somoza Is Forced Out of Power in Nicaragua (1979), p. 2035; Argentine Leaders Are Convicted of Human Rights Violations (1985), p. 2280.

FORD OFFERS A FIVE-DOLLAR, EIGHT-HOUR WORKDAY

Category of event: Workers' rights
Time: January, 1914
Locale: Detroit, Michigan

Henry Ford pioneered the assembly line method of automobile manufacturing, raised worker productivity, and shared profits with his workers through higher wages and benefits and shorter working hours

Principal personages:

HENRY FORD (1863-1947), an inventor and industrialist who constantly pursued efficiency, waste reduction, lower consumer prices, and mass production

HARRY BENNETT (1892-1979), the chief of security at Ford Motor Company, who took a hard antiunion and antiworker stand

ALEXANDER MALCOMSON (1865-1923), the first vice president of Ford Motor Company and its first major investor

Summary of Event

In 1864, modern steel production began with the open-hearth process. Detroit's location along the Great Lakes offered it a role in this new industry, and many foundries sprang up. In 1865, the first short stretch of pipeline carried oil along the Allegheny River. Cheap oil, steel, and transportation set the stage for Henry Ford to revolutionize the automobile industry.

Henry Ford's idol was inventor Thomas Edison, whose methods produced the telephone, the phonograph, incandescent electric lamps, and film for movie cameras. Ford's imitation of Edison's "tinkering" eventually led to the creation of the Model T. Ford believed that it was his duty to make better products and better people by promoting gifted employees. For him, science alone could free people from drudgery and increase the productivity of labor. Science could also find better and cheaper methods of making goods and better ways to carry those goods from the manufacturer to the consumer.

Henry Ford grew up on a farm and believed that there was too much needless work and duplication of effort. As a young man, he spent several years in Detroit learning mechanics. He later returned to his farm, where he spent his spare time with the idea of building an internal combustion engine. His first invention was a steam-operated tractor, and by April, 1893, he had completed work on his first car.

Other automobile inventors saw cars as a fad and a luxury. By contrast, Henry Ford dreamed of mass producing inexpensive cars. Consequently, few bankers or investors of his era were willing to finance his company. They considered him an eccentric, but Ford was ahead of his time. One man, Alexander Malcomson, had faith in Ford's dream. He put up $25,000 of his own money to finance Ford and convinced others to invest. He became the first vice president of Ford Motor Company.

Henry Ford, like most businesspeople of his time, was influenced by Frederick W. Taylor's time and motion studies. If workers bumped into each other when assembling cars, Ford reorganized their movement and the timing of their work. If they spent time walking over to a storage area to retrieve parts, Ford moved the storage area closer to the worker. He created assembly lines in his factories to bring parts to selected groups of workers for assembly. Soon whole cars moved along conveyor belts to worker groups, each specializing in one of five thousand jobs that could be learned easily and sequenced so that cars could be assembled rapidly. Since each worker produced much more per hour, profits skyrocketed. At the same time, Ford used some of these cost savings to reduce the price of his cars. Every time that he reduced his prices, his market grew and his profits increased. In little more than ten years, Ford had become one of America's first billionaires. He financed most of this growth and expansion with corporate profits and savings.

When Ford began making cars, it took more than a day and a half to make each car. By introducing and perfecting the use of the assembly line, he eventually was able to produce one car every twenty-nine seconds. With each incremental increase in efficiency, his profits soared. As early as 1905, he began sharing profits with his workers. In 1913, Ford was able to pay workers a total of ten million dollars over and above their salaries. He tied profit sharing to employee efficiency and saw workers and management as partners in production.

In 1914, Henry Ford was well known in and around Detroit and the Midwest, but neither he nor his cars were known nationwide. On January 5, 1914, Ford Motors released a statement nationwide announcing the introduction of the five-dollar, eight-hour workday, beginning on January 12. Most of the fourteen thousand workers at Ford's Highland Park plant worked nine hours a day at $2.34 a day before the change. By January 14, 1914, Ford was the best-known man in America, and workers across the United States saw him as a hero. He became a national celebrity, and people around the world avidly began to discuss Henry Ford, his assembly techniques, and his wage policies. Some observers consider his announcement one of the greatest publicity stunts in history.

Ford did not automatically grant every employee the pay raise and hours reduction following his announcement; employees had to qualify. Ford established a sociological department, headed by Dean Samuel Marquis, an Episcopalian minister. To certify that an applicant was worthy of the bonus, this department only accepted applications from men over twenty-two years of age who had worked for the company for a minimum of six months. Dean Marquis and his sociologists could exclude a worker from benefits for gambling, drinking, having a dirty house, eating unhealthy foods, or having bad saving habits. Men with stable marriages and loving families were preferred over bachelors. Men who rented out rooms to boarders who were strangers were denied bonuses, because Ford believed that boardinghouses encouraged immorality. Men who cared for aged parents were entitled to early bonus packages because they were considered virtuous. Many workers claimed that Henry Ford was too paternalistic; Ford's response was to ignore many violations of his sociological department's regulations. Almost 90 percent of those who applied for bonuses eventually received them.

Why did Ford raise wages so dramatically? Ford claimed that he wanted to lift workers out of poverty. The surplus value of his workers' labor had made him rich, and he saw them as partners in his own progress. Thus, they were entitled to share the benefits of the wealth that they helped created. He also believed that the U.S. economy would grow faster if workers could afford to buy the products that they made. Raising salaries made it possible for workers to buy Fords, expanding the market for his products. Ford claimed that higher wages would make workers pay more attention to their work and improve the quality of the cars produced. If Ford's customers were happy with their cars, they would continue to use Ford cars and encourage others to buy them. Raising wages improved quality control by encouraging each worker to monitor the quality of each product that passed his work station; as workers now shared profits and profits depended on quality.

Henry Ford understood business. He estimated that the five-dollar day would add ten million dollars to his annual payroll. Some experts claim that he had no choice, that he was forced to raise wages to attract labor in a market that was short of workers. Immediately following the announcement of the five-dollar day, huge lines of workers formed outside his plants. His chief of security, Harry Bennett, turned fire hoses on crowds of job seekers in subzero weather, but this did not stop them from coming. They merely changed into dry clothing and returned, insisting on jobs. More than ten thousand workers thronged Ford's plants in Highland Park for weeks, hoping to participate in the five-dollar-a-day workers' heaven that Ford had created. If this announcement was designed to attract labor, it worked extremely well and gave Ford his pick of the best labor available.

Other labor analysts claim that Ford's problem was not a shortage of labor but high turnover rates. In 1913, Ford Motors hired 50,448 workers, yet its average labor force was 13,623. Ford Motors thus had a turnover rate of 370 percent. Vacancies could have been a real problem if Ford had had trouble filling them, but it never did. More than 40 percent of the jobs in its plants took only one or two days to learn and were designed to be taught rapidly to unskilled laborers. Another 36 percent of the jobs took one week or less to learn. Under these circumstances, it is unlikely that Ford created the five-dollar day to reduce labor turnover, although turnover did decline dramatically.

Still other observers argue that Ford had to pay higher wages to get workers to work harder. As machines drove men to their breaking point, workers resented being treated like machines and would seize every opportunity to shirk work or remain idle. Ford's high wages gave them an incentive to work hard—they knew that they could not earn such high wages elsewhere, so to hold on to lucrative jobs, they would drive themselves to the limit voluntarily. The trouble with this theory is that Ford's laborers worked on automated assembly lines where machines dictated the pace of work. Ford's time and motion studies had determined precisely how fast men could work and machine speed was set accordingly.

If this is true, then why announce a five-dollar day? Ford's profits hit $13 million by 1912, $27 million in 1913, and $32 million in 1914. Some experts argue that Ford was vulnerable to work stoppages. The opportunity costs of work stoppages were very high because Ford's assembly techniques created huge profits from labor, even though the Model T, the main Ford product, sold for less than $600. For example, it is estimated that a one-week shutdown of Ford's plants in 1913 would have cost the company at least $542,000 in lost earnings. Similar shutdowns would have cost less than $184,000 in the much more diversified General Motors plants and less than $43,000 for Studebaker, another competitor. Ford's competition would have been delighted to see Ford rapidly lose profits and perhaps its share of the market.

In short, Ford's labor force was the source of its prosperity as well as its weak spot. Many Ford workers had recently immigrated to America in hopes of finding a better life for themselves and their children. Life in Detroit's crowded low-income neighborhoods made them very vulnerable to appeals by labor unions, such as the International Workers of the World (the "Wobblies"), who were very active in Detroit. They urged workers to organize and seize control of factories from the managers and owners. In the spring of 1913, they had successfully shut down Studebaker for a short time. Fear of a similar shutdown and plant takeover may have motivated Henry Ford to announce his famous five-dollar day.

Fear of industrial unrest permeated the minds of automobile executives throughout late 1913 and early 1914. Ford Motor Company executives were no exception. Charles Sorensen, head of production at the Highland Park plant, said in one interview that he was ordered to pay workers wages of five dollars a day in order to stifle the IWW and other unions. This, Sorensen claimed, was Ford's means of taking away from the unions their greatest source of appeal—the desire for material gain and benefits. Ford simply co-opted the unions' strategy by not only offering workers high wages before the union could demand them but by offering wages higher than any union organizer would have the nerve to demand.

Impact of Event

Other automobile companies did not follow Ford's lead for many years. Nevertheless, the results of the five-dollar day for Ford were clear. The labor force became much more stable, total production costs declined, and workers volunteered many cost-cutting ideas to management, whom they saw as partners rather than as adversaries. Laborers feared losing jobs that paid so much above the industry average, and there is little evidence of labor unrest. Ford claimed that the five-dollar day reflected the growing productive power of his labor force. As they demonstrated to him that they were capable of creating more wealth, he was willing to offer them ever larger amounts from profits.

The five-dollar day was part of a larger change in life-style. Ford checked workers' personal hygiene and the cleanliness of their homes, encouraged savings habits, and rewarded stable, wholesome family life. These actions were not motivated solely by greed or the desire to reduce the number of workers who could share profits; Ford attempted to create a better world.

Ford not only raised workers' wages but also built hospitals for workers. He once ordered his plant managers to hire older workers when it was brought to his attention that they were underrepresented in his work force. Ford ordered his plant managers to conduct complete studies of every job in his factories to determine which could be performed by the blind and the crippled. He ordered that these jobs be allocated to handicapped workers because he believed they could earn the same wages as others if given a fair chance. Ford also routinely hired ex-convicts, because he sincerely believed that reform was possible, and that given the chance to earn a good living under acceptable circumstances, most ex-criminals would abandon a life of crime. He hired teachers, at his own expense, to teach his workers proper English and the fundamentals of good citizenship in a democracy.

Ford's declaration of the five-dollar workday gave workers greater bargaining power, even though employers attempted to resist this trend. Collective bargaining did not come to Ford Motors until after Ford's death, when Henry Ford II and his group of "whiz kid" advisers recognized labor unions. Henry Ford's pay increase helped avoid unionization in his plants. By raising the absolute material standards of many blue-collar workers, however, he also forced American society to place a higher value on such work. The five-dollar day made many of these workers middle-class by virtue of their income. Many aspired to improve their children's education and offer them better opportunities in life. Higher wages made it easier for factory workers to achieve these goals, as well as to buy better homes in more expensive neighborhoods. In these settings, their children played with children from middle-class, well-educated families and began to acquire the values, attitudes, and taste of the middle class before acquiring the traditional middle-class educational credentials and jobs.

The five-dollar day made workers aware of the fact that they were worth more because they could produce more with the help of machines. Consequently, the modernization of industry became less difficult. Workers began to associate better standards of living and benefits with the increased output of labor that machines made possible, rather than feeling alienated from machines. Perhaps this explains why Ford's workers often designed new machines for their plants: Every effort to improve the efficiency and productivity of workers in the Ford plants would be rewarded. Ford frequently promoted such workers and widely publicized the promotions. The five-dollar day was a turning point in history, for it publicly recognized and rewarded labor's increasing value and the right of workers to share the profits that their labor created. This eliminated some of the hostility to industrialization and allowed it to proceed more smoothly.

Bibliography

Bennett, Harry. *We Never Called Him Henry.* New York. Fawcett Publications, 1951. Many blame the brutal treatment of some Ford employees on the heavy-handed tactics of Harry Bennett. In this book, Bennett argues that at all times he was acting under direct orders from Henry Ford. A bitter book that is critical of Henry Ford and portrays Ford as an industrial dictator.

Brough, James. *The Ford Dynasty: An American Story.* Garden City, N.Y.: Doubleday, 1977. A wonderfully imaginative book full of narrative and dialogue woven around accurate historical details. Brings the history of Henry Ford, his family, his friends, and his company to life for the reader. This book is entertaining as well as informative.

Collier, Peter, and David Horowitz. *The Fords: An American Epic.* New York: Summit Books, 1987. Details the rise of the Ford dynasty over three generations and the conflicts that almost tore this great family apart. Portrays Henry Ford as generous and optimistic, yet intolerant, cranky, and bitter. Edsel Ford is seen as a doomed prince dominated by a doting father. Henry Ford II is seen as the avenger who saved the company and avenged his father, Edsel. This book reads like a movie script.

Ford, Henry, with Samuel Crowther. *My Life and Work.* Garden City, N.Y.: Doubleday, Page & Co., 1926. Henry Ford's authorized autobiography. It is full of pithy sayings that capture his philosophy of life and business. His view of the five-dollar day is that it was the best business decision he ever made. A great source for Henry Ford's view of the origin and growth of Ford Motors.

Lacey, Robert. *Ford: The Men and the Machines.* Boston: Little, Brown, 1986. A rich account of the public accomplishments and private tragedies of four generations of the Ford family. Portrays Henry Ford as a complicated man, at once a pacifist and a war profiteer; a champion of minority rights and an anti-Semite; a dedicated family man who supported a wife, mistress, and illegitimate son; a loving father who bullied and hounded the son that he loved into an early grave. Use of the Freedom of Information Act allows Lacey to offer fresh insight on the family's ties to J. Edgar Hoover and others. Riveting details hold the reader's interest.

Nevins, Allan. *Ford: The Times, the Man, the Company.* New York. Charles Scribner's Sons, 1954. Most historians consider this the standard reference work on Henry Ford. It is still among the most exhaustively researched works available on Henry Ford.

Sinclair, Upton. *The Flivver King: A Story of Ford-America.* Detroit: United Automobile Workers of America, 1937. A very imaginative and entertaining pocket novel about several generations of a family that works for Henry Ford. Sinclair portrays Ford as a man who began with idealistic purpose but was corrupted by money, power, and greed. The last half of the novel depicts Henry Ford as an industrial tyrant who mercilessly drives his men by using machines to establish a ruthless pace of work. Sinclair claims that Ford reduced men to automatons who worked so hard that they did not have the energy to enjoy family or friends after work. For Sinclair, the five-dollar day did little to soften the dehumanization of the worker.

Sward, Keith. *The Legend of Henry Ford.* New York: Holt, Rinehart and Company, 1948. A must for the serious scholar. Sward's book is balanced, even-handed, and meticulously researched. Sward explores and explodes many myths, such as the notion that Henry Ford always put profits before principle. He demonstrates that although Ford was a great businessman, he was also principled.

Dallas L. Browne

Cross-References
Supreme Court Disallows a Maximum Hours Law for Bakers (1905), p. 36; Upton Sinclair Publishes *The Jungle* (1906), p. 46; Massachusetts Adopts the First Minimum-Wage Law in the United States (1912), p. 126; Steel Workers Go on Strike to Demand Improved Working Conditions (1919), p. 293; The Wagner Act Requires Employers to Accept Collective Bargaining (1935), p. 508; The Congress of Industrial Organizations Is Formed (1938), p. 545; Autoworkers Negotiate a Contract with a Cost-of-Living Provision (1948), p. 766.

ARMENIANS SUFFER GENOCIDE DURING WORLD WAR I

Category of event: Atrocities and war crimes
Time: 1915 to the early 1920's
Locale: Armenia and Turkey

The genocide of nearly one million Armenians by the Ottoman Empire was a carefully orchestrated plan by that government and its officials to provide a final solution to the Armenian question

> *Principal personages:*
> MEHMET TALAAT PASHA (1872-1921), a member of the Young Turk triumvirate that ruled the Ottoman Empire from 1913 to 1918
> ENVER PASHA (1881?-1922), another Young Turk triumvir
> AHMED DJEMAL PASHA (1872-1922), the third triumvir
> ABDUL-HAMID II (1842-1918), one of the last sultans of the decaying Ottoman Empire; the Young Turks staged a revolution that pared him of all real power
> HENRY MORGENTHAU (1856-1946), the United States ambassador to Turkey during the Armenian genocide

Summary of Event

Several factors contributed to the massacre of close to one million Armenians in Turkey during World War I. The Ottoman Empire was in rapid decline in the latter half of the nineteenth century. European powers, notably the United Kingdom, France, Russia, and (after 1871) Germany gradually severed various parts of the once-great empire. The Treaty of San Stefano ended the Russo-Turkish War of 1877-1878 at Turkey's expense. The genesis of the war was the massacres carried out by Turkish troops in Bulgaria in 1876. As a result of the Treaty of San Stefano, the Ottomans lost territory to Russia. The imperial Russian government acted as the protector of Christians within the Muslim Ottoman Empire, and Russia pressured the Ottoman government to allow Christian Armenians to have administrative autonomy in eastern Turkey. A second treaty, the Treaty of Berlin (1878), signed by the Ottoman Empire and Russia, essentially modified the San Stefano stipulations by allowing the Ottoman government to agree only to treat the Armenians fairly. The modification eliminated the earlier treaty's insistence on better treatment of the Armenians as a condition for the withdrawal of Russian troops from eastern Turkey. Nevertheless, the Armenians were confident that Russian policy and national interest would effectively guarantee their safety from any attempts by the Turks to massacre their people.

Sultan Abdul-Hamid II carried out a large-scale massacre of Turkish Armenians between 1894 and 1896. The sultan justified his actions by accusing the Armenian mountaineers of the Sassoun district with rebelling against government authority.

He claimed that the Armenians' refusal to pay customary protection tribute to Kurdish chieftains was sufficient grounds for military action. In the end, although the totals are estimates, between 200,000 and 250,000 Armenians were killed by Turks and Kurds (the latter are also an ethnic minority, but are Muslims). International protests and Russian threats averted a greater loss of Armenian lives. This event, together with the discontent of national minorities within the Ottoman Empire, especially in the Black Sea area, eroded the power of the sultanate. Turkey was perceived by the great powers as the "sick man" of Europe.

In Salonika, Turkish army officers loyal to the Committee of Union and Progress (the "Young Turks") were embracing a new revolutionary ideology and a program of action that would capsize Abdul-Hamid II's regime and, they hoped, restore the empire to its former grandeur. On July 23, 1908, Abdul-Hamid II was overthrown. The Young Turks, however, were not able to consolidate power until January 26, 1913, when Enver Pasha and Mehmet Talaat Pasha took control of the Ottoman Empire. They were joined later by Ahmed Djemal Pasha. These three constituted the dictatorial triumvirate that was responsible both for Turkey's entry into World War I on the side of the Central Powers and for the genocide of nearly one million Armenians.

These men espoused a new ideology known as "Pan-Turkism." This ideology was shaped by the intellectual Ziya Gökalp, who was a close friend of Mehmet Talaat Pasha and a member of the Central Council of the Committee of Union and Progress. Mehmet Talaat Pasha was a forceful advocate for extermination of the Armenian people as part of an effort to "Turkify" Turkey.

The triumvirate planned the extermination of the Armenians before the outbreak of World War I. The genocide was discussed by members of the Central Council in 1913 at a series of secret meetings. A chief aim of the Young Turks was the reunification of Ottoman Turkey with Turkish Caucasia (which was part of Russia) and Central Asia, but the Armenians were an obstacle to their Pan-Turkish empire. The Armenians were accordingly scheduled for elimination. It is unclear if the triumvirs really believed that the Armenians might pose a threat to Turkey by fighting on the side of Russia in the event of war. From 1913 onward, the officials of the *junta* at Constantinople informed governors and police chiefs of their planned genocide of the Armenians. The exact time would be determined by events.

After Germany invaded France on August 2, 1914, the Turkish government moved swiftly to join the war on the side of Germany. Ottoman troops crossed the Egyptian border and had a minor clash with British forces, and the United Kingdom declared war in response. The war served as a pretext for the planned genocide, and the triumvirs were poised to strike at the Armenians. The Dashnak Party, an Armenian political party, called on its members and all Turkish Armenians to be loyal to Turkey in the event that war broke out between Russia and Turkey. Nearly one-quarter million Armenians were inducted into the Ottoman armed forces. During January, 1915, Turkish forces led by Enver Pasha suffered a major defeat by Russia at Sarikamish, on the Russian border. The *junta* was convinced that military defeat by the

Russians was imminent and feared that revolution might break out among their sub-jugated nationalities. The Turkish triumvirate made the crucial decision to extermi-nate the Armenians in order to deflect attention from their failure on the battlefield and to implement their ideology of "Turkey for the Turks."

Melvanzrade Rifat, a member of the Central Council, recorded a telling discus-sion at a council meeting to the effect that, since Turkey was at war, the time was opportune to exterminate the Armenians while the European powers were preoc-cupied with their own struggles. Rifat noted the council's decision that even though the projected massacre might create some difficulty and public objections, it would be an accomplished fact and thus closed forever before the Europeans could react. Another member of the Central Council did not mince words, stating that an easy technique to exterminate the Armenians would be to send Armenians troops to the front to fight the Russians. The Armenians who were engaged with the Russians would then face fire from special forces in their rear sent there by the government for that purpose; they would be trapped and annihilated.

The massacres began on April 24, 1915, when the leaders of the Armenian com-munity in Constantinople were seized by the authorities and executed. This date is still commemorated as the beginning of the Armenian genocide, which would con-tinue in spurts, after 1915, until the early 1920's. Armenian military units were dis-armed by the Ottoman government. They were systematically starved, beaten, and finally shot. Squads of fifty or one hundred Armenian troops were sent into the countryside, allegedly to work on roads and other projects, and shot by Turkish troops. Two thousand Armenian soldiers were sent out from Kharput in July, 1915, and murdered in the countryside; their bodies were piled in caves. Many thousands of Armenians were murdered in this fashion.

The Ottoman government, to save ammunition, decided to carry out mass depor-tation of Armenians, claiming that they posed a national security threat near the Russian border, where Russian forces were penetrating eastern Turkey. Many of the deportations, however, occurred far from the front. The deportation of many thou-sands was done during the summer months of 1915. Few of the deportees reached their destination in the Syrian wilderness. In Angora (modern Ankara), the *vali* (governor) refused to deport Armenians. He was replaced by the Young Turks with a governor more eager to do the bidding of the Central Council. This reliable party man carried out the wishes of the *junta*. Most of the Armenian inhabitants of An-gora were moved at night to an area called Asi Yozgad, where Turkish tanners and butchers murdered the defenseless Armenians and threw their bodies into a river from a bridge. The sight and stench of the many bodies in the river compelled the authorities to close the bridge during the hours of daylight. The triumvirs did not keep count of the dead. According to an American relief worker, Stanley Kerr, of eighty-six thousand Armenians once living in the city of Sivas, only fifteen hundred remained in 1918. Fifteen thousand Armenians were killed in Bitlis, in the adjacent district, in a single day in 1915.

Kurds were used by Turkish officials to murder Armenians. The Ottoman government recruited Kurds and ordered them to kill Armenians, especially the males, children, and old women; young women were often spared. Kurds tossed bodies of Armenians into ravines, cisterns, and caves. Mehmet Talaat Pasha, after making himself grand vizier, boasted to the American ambassador, Henry Morgenthau, that he had done in three months what Abdul-Hamid II had failed to do in thirty years. Morgenthau protested the massacres. Talaat replied, "The massacres! What of them? They merely amused me."

The massacres were repeatedly denied by Turkish and German officials as inventions of the newspapers. When the fact of the massacres was established, both the *junta* and its German allies dismissed them as a national security necessity. The United States protested and, along with the United Kingdom, made it clear that Turkish officials would be held personally responsible for the atrocities in the Armenian provinces of Turkey. Otherwise, nothing further could be done until the end of the war.

A Turkish military tribunal tried the triumvirs in absentia for complicity in mass murder of the Armenians. Their sentences were carried out in various ways: Mehmet Talaat Pasha was killed by Armenian exiles in 1921; Ahmed Djemal Pasha was assassinated on July 21, 1922, in Soviet Georgia, also by Armenian exiles; and Enver Pasha was killed in action in the Bukhara region on August 4, 1922, leading an attack against Soviet troops.

Impact of Event

The calculated murder of the Armenians generated world outrage. Unfortunately, that outrage took the form of parades, speeches, fund-raising for the hapless survivors, and protests from several foreign offices in a futile attempt to stop the genocide. These efforts provided no meaningful punitive or ameliorative effects.

What effect did the Armenian genocide have on the survivors? Did it teach the world, especially the great powers, to take extra care to prevent such atrocities in the future? The answers are easy enough, at least at first glance. The governments of the United States, England, and France reacted incredulously to the mounting evidence of the mass extermination of a people. Gargantuan evil seems beyond imagining, although history is replete with pogroms and genocide. In August, 1939, Adolf Hitler, in discussing his planned murder of the Polish people, asked his advisers, "Who still talks nowadays of the extermination of the Armenians?" Hitler understood how quickly that slaughter was forgotten by the world. Who would be concerned about the Poles or the Jews in the midst of a world war?

The establishment of the League of Nations after World War I was an important development and perhaps did prevent many atrocities. The League of Nations was clearly concerned about human rights and had some limited success against the slave trade. Its several conventions on the rights of people to be free from compulsory labor and state torture were giant steps that laid at least a foundation for respect of human rights. The Armenian genocide did not inspire all these efforts, but it did galvanize much contemporary interest in mass atrocities.

The world forgot the Armenian genocide too quickly. In part, such forgetfulness was connected with the enormous slaughter on the battlefields of Europe and Africa; another several hundred thousand deaths did not seem to matter. They did matter. Killing armed soldiers was not the same thing as murdering defenseless civilians.

Humanity surely learned something from the Armenian genocide. It was not, however, a sufficiently learned lesson.

Bibliography

Gökalp, Ziya. *The Principles of Turkism.* New York: Columbia University Press, 1959. Discusses Turkish nationalism and the need for Turks to rediscover their soul. The author glorified the warlike Turks' history and praised Turkish leaders such as Attila, Genghis Khan, Timur, and Babur. Gökalp's theories were not racist or imperialistic, but in the hands of the Young Turks they were misapplied and used as a rallying cry for racial and religious purity.

Hartunian, Abraham. *Neither to Laugh Nor to Weep: A Memoir of the Armenian Genocide.* Boston: Beacon Press, 1968. A detailed and sympathetic treatment of how a people was murdered. Interesting for its graphic descriptions of torture, drowning, and other nightmarish ways to exterminate people.

Kinross, Patrick Balfour. "The Last of the Sultans." In *The Ottoman Centuries: The Rise and Fall of the Empire.* New York: William Morrow, 1977. A thorough account of the personal foibles of Abdul-Hamid II: He was paranoid, surrounding himself with thousands of spies, agents provocateurs, secret police, and a fortified residence. It is no wonder that the Ottoman Empire was the "sick man" of two continents.

Kloian, Richard. *The Armenian Genocide: News Accounts from the American Press, 1915-1922.* Richmond, Calif.: ACC Books, 1985. This work, a voluminous collection of contemporary news accounts of the genocide, tells a poignant but credible story of the first holocaust of the twentieth century. The author comments on numerous specific atrocities that prove that there was a holocaust. Turkish revisionism is forever debunked by this interestingly designed and executed account of the Armenian genocide.

Lang, David M. *The Armenians: A People in Exile.* Winchester, Mass.: Allen & Unwin, 1981. Describes successive genocides against the Armenians by Ottoman rulers. The focus is on the years from 1894 to 1918. A balanced account by any criterion.

Morgenthau, Henry. *Ambassador Morgenthau's Story.* Garden City, N.Y.: Doubleday, 1918. An eyewitness account by the United States ambassador on the scene. The book is thorough and vivid, replete with quotations from Turkish officials who initiated and managed the massacre of thousands of Armenians. This book proves that the extermination was a well-developed state policy of the ruling triumvirate.

Claude Hargrove

Cross-References

El Salvador's Military Massacres Civilians in *La Matanza* (1932), p. 464; Nazi Concentration Camps Go into Operation (1933), p. 491; The Sudanese Civil War Erupts (1955), p. 941; The Iraqi Government Promotes Genocide of Kurds (1960's), p. 1050; Indonesia's Government Retaliates Against a Failed Communist Coup (1965), p. 1305; Conflicts in Pakistan Lead to the Secession of Bangladesh (1971), p. 1611; Burundi's Government Commits Genocide of the Bahutu Majority (1972), p. 1668; Khmer Rouge Take Over Cambodia (1975), p. 1791; East Timor Declares Independence but Is Annexed by Indonesia (1975), p. 1835; Palestinian Civilians are Massacred in West Beirut (1982), p. 2164; Hunger Becomes a Weapon in the Sudanese Civil War (1988), p. 2354.

THE DEFENSE OF INDIA ACT IMPEDES
THE FREEDOM STRUGGLE

Categories of event: Indigenous peoples' rights and political freedom
Time: March, 1915
Locale: India

The Defense of India Act enabled the British government to wield extraordinary powers, bypassing existing laws to suppress dissent in India during World War I

Principal personages:
ANNIE BESANT (1847-1933), a British theosophist and active leader in India's independence movement
MAHATMA GANDHI (1869-1948), a Hindu nationalist leader and social reformer
BAL GANGADHAR TILAK (1864-1920), a leading Indian journalist and politician
JOHN MORLEY (1838-1923), the secretary of state for India, a man of moderate views
MOTILAL NEHRU (1861-1931), a successful Indian lawyer, president of the All-India Congress in 1928
JAWAHARLAL NEHRU (1889-1964), the leader in India's independence movement and first prime minister of India (1947-1964)
REGINALD DYER (1864-1927), a British general who ordered the attack on Jallianwallah Bagh

Summary of Event

The redeployment of Indian and British troops to locations in Europe and Africa during World War I sharply reduced the number of units available for maintaining control and suppressing dissent in India. This provided a timely opportunity for the revolutionary groups already active in India to accelerate the pace of their activities. At the same time, an opportunistic coalition between wartime enemies of Britain and the revolutionaries became feasible. Germany and Turkey, for example, were anxious to divert Britain's attention from the war effort. They attempted to contribute to the undermining of colonial authority by providing a measure of support for the revolutionaries, who were willing to accept help from foreign sources. Finally, revolutionary groups based in San Francisco (Ghadr Movement), Berlin (Indian Independence Committee), Kabul (Provisional Government of India), Geneva, and Paris (Madame Bhikhaji Cama's circle) continued actively to support their fellow Indians.

A series of repressive measures were adopted by the British to cope with the complex situation. Initially, there was some reluctance to take this path, since a large proportion of the revolutionaries were highly educated Indians trained to believe in the rule of law and civil liberties. This belief had sustained them in their manner of conducting the struggle for independence. Nevertheless, their activities continued to trouble the British authorities.

The first signs of a British crackdown had appeared several years earlier, when the nationalist slogan Bande Mataram (which can be translated as Victory to the Motherland) was banned. Likewise, the Indian Criminal Law Amendment Act of 1913 had identified conspiracy as an independent criminal offense. This had resulted in the trial and sentencing of several people whose actions were subject to the definitions of this new code. A demonstrably repressive attitude came to characterize Indo-British relations despite the conciliatory efforts of liberal British leaders such as John Morley, secretary of state for India.

The Defense of India Act was therefore the logical outgrowth of a period of increasingly stringent controls that preceded its adoption. Modeled along the lines of the Defense of the Realm Act which prevailed in wartime Britain, the Defense of India Act was far more extensive in its provisions. It was presented as a wartime measure ostensibly designed to protect British military interests and thus to promote war objectives. In fact, its mandate went far beyond the protection of purely military interests, since its provisions endowed the government with extraordinary powers to supersede the existing legal system. These included the appointment of special tribunals to hold summary trials. Provincial authorities could convene these tribunals, giving them extensive powers and jurisdiction over a wide range of activities.

The new laws were loosely interpreted and applied arbitrarily and with varying levels of intensity in different regions of the country. Thus, publications banned in one province could be found in another. Individuals used the mandate of the Defense of India Act for suppression of civil liberties but did so to different degrees. The principal clauses of the act authorized the government to empower any civil or military authority to deny individuals the right to enter or reside in designated areas on the basis of mere suspicion that they might be acting in a manner prejudicial to the government's or the public's interests. Authorities could enter and search buildings and also seize property of individuals if they believed that it was being used for purposes that were contrary to the rules of the Defense of India Act. The power of the press to comment on such events was curbed through censorship rules, thereby enabling the authorities to intern citizens without trial. Those who were brought to trial were often arrested and convicted on the basis of flimsy evidence. Individuals were sentenced to imprisonment of ten or more years, even to transportation for life, and in several cases the death penalty was imposed. Confessions of an accused person or parties known to him or her were often cited as the principal evidence.

The manner in which confessions were obtained was a matter of great concern even to the judges involved at the time. In his commentary on this issue, Justice Straight, a British judge, expressed his belief that the police spent an extraordinary amount of their time and energy in extracting confessions. What was even more curious was the large number of apparently voluntary confessions that were retracted. This is further confirmed by statements of prisoners regarding the poor conditions prevailing in detention centers and the brutality of the police.

The effective suspension of civil rights and liberty in India resulted in the "carte blanche" approach adopted by the government during this period. This was further encouraged by the seeming acquiescence of "moderate" Indian politicians to this measure. As a result, a series of highly publicized trials were held throughout the country, many in Bengal and Punjab. The most extensive were the Lahore Conspiracy Trials, a series of three trials that heard evidence of a conspiracy for a general uprising against the British authorities. The elaborate plan involving revolutionaries from abroad, as well as from several regions of the country, hoped to overpower the war-weakened garrisons, disrupt communications, release political detainees, and assemble in Lahore to carry out the rest of their goals. Unfortunately, a police informer who had infiltrated the ranks of the conspirators alerted the authorities. A large proportion of the several hundred revolutionaries who were tried were convicted of serious crimes punishable by death. Of the thirty-eight death sentences handed out, eighteen were later commuted to transportation for life. Fifty-eight people were given varying periods of imprisonment and an equal number were given life sentences and transported. Characterized as a conspiracy to wage war against the King Emperor, this elaborate attempt to achieve freedom from colonialism was effectively prevented.

The struggle for freedom was not entirely centered on uprisings of this nature. Simultaneously, Annie Besant, head of the Theosophical Movement in India, launched the "Home Rule" campaign. She publicized her ideas through two publications that she controlled, *New India* and *Commonweal*. Congress was initially reluctant to endorse the idea, but eventually, Bal Gangadhar Tilak became active in the establishment of a Home Rule League which came into being on April 28, 1916. In August, the government moved against Mrs. Besant's publications and demanded exorbitant securities. Upon rejection of her appeal by the Madras High Court and the Privy Council, she sold her two presses. The censorship provisions of the 1915 Act, in combination with the restrictions of the 1910 Press Act, had strengthened the government's power to suppress free speech. The response to Mrs. Besant's continuing efforts to make speeches in support of the Home Rule League was to ban her entry into various cities. Eventually, she was interned in order to secure her silence. This action was condemned both in India and overseas. Indignation swept a number of moderates into supporting the Home Rule campaign, including Motilal Nehru, a prominent lawyer and father of independent India's first prime minister, Jawaharlal Nehru.

Impact of Event

World War I had a tremendous impact on the freedom struggle in India by diverting Britain's attention away from the need for political reforms in the country. Consequently, the leaders of the freedom struggle believed that they had to look elsewhere for support, since the British appeared preoccupied with their own wartime concerns. The German government even went as far as signing a written agreement with an Indian committee promising to insist on Indian freedom in the event of a German victory. Indian sympathies were often with Turkey and Germany, despite the fact that Indian soldiers were fighting their armies and contributing in other ways to the British war effort.

The war provided the opportunity for British authorities to adopt special regulations and laws which quickly were used to suppress a wide variety of activities that had little or no direct relation to military concerns. The new powers assumed during this time were wide-ranging and absolute. The efficacy of these powers in eradicating dissent showed the authorities how much they had come to depend on these special provisions. Consequently, when the wartime measures lapsed, there was a move to extend or enact similar laws. An inquiry committee, the Rowlatt Commission, was appointed to study the matter. The committee recommended that trial by jury should continue to be used as a means of controlling seditious activities. The continued suspension of existing laws and the continuation of extraordinary powers at the level of provincial government were also endorsed. This was predictably unpopular and was not received well among the Indian intellectuals and professionals who had been hoping for some signs of understanding of their desire for self-government. The Rowlatt Bills, as they were known, came into law on March 17, 1919, over the objections and boycott of the Indian members of the Legislative Council.

From the perspective of the nationalists, this measure was another example of the intransigence of imperial domination. Mohandas Karamchand (known as Mahatma, or "Great Soul") Gandhi called for the start of a civil disobedience movement on April 6, 1919. A series of violent public reactions, including lootings, murder, and mass meetings, followed. In the Punjab, the order banning public meetings of more than four persons was disregarded by a peaceful crowd of five thousand, leading to the notorious massacre at Jallianwalla Bagh, in the city of Amritsar, on April 13, 1919. The British General Reginald Dyer was tried for his part in this atrocity and relieved of his command. Tensions between the government and the people were heightened considerably by this event.

There is reason to conclude that some of the precipitating incidents leading to the full-fledged launching of the Indian independence movement were, in part, a result of the climate of tension and mistrust created by the application of the Defense of India Act. Not only did the provisions of this act bypass the existing code of law, it revealed to the Indian intelligentsia the fragility of reason and the growing reliance over time of the British on authoritarian measures to maintain control over the population. The bond of trust and sense of fair play were undermined, leading to the creation of a rift between the colonial government and the leadership of the freedom struggle. The leadership turned to the masses, mobilizing them to express their sense of injustice and thus accelerating the momentum of the independence movement.

Bibliography

Brown, Judith M. *Modern India: The Origins of an Asian Democracy.* Delhi: Oxford

University Press, 1985. The author suggests the presence of a strand of continuity in the tradition of repression first introduced by the British and then coopted by the nationalists. One of the most competent analyses of a complex relationship between the governing and the governed.

Dodwell, H. H., ed. *The Indian Empire, 1858-1918.* Vol. 6 in *The Cambridge History of India.* Cambridge, England: Cambridge University Press, 1932. A standard reference for this period, reflecting largely a British perspective on events. Not as detailed as some of the other sources for this period.

Masani, Rustom Pestonji. *Britain in India: An Account of British Rule in the Indian Sub-continent.* Oxford, England: Oxford University Press, 1960. An excellent analysis of British rule in India with special emphasis on identifying sources of change.

Majumdar, R. C., ed. *The History and Culture of the Indian People.* Vol. 11 in *Struggle for Freedom.* Bombay: Bharatiya Vidya Bhavan, 1978. The most detailed source for the history of the freedom struggle from the Indian perspective. It is particularly informative on the location and origin of the various groups that shared the common goal of political freedom.

Nehru, Jawaharlal. *Nehru: The First Sixty Years.* Vol. 1. New York: John Day, 1965. A compilation of Nehru's writings, speeches, press conferences, and other documents that provides an invaluable perspective on the independence movement from within.

Sarkar, Sumit. *Modern India, 1885-1947.* Delhi: Macmillan, 1983. This is a detailed account of the emergence of a modern nation from a left-of-center viewpoint. The specialist would be well advised to read this scholarly work that includes information not easily available in other sources.

Sai Felicia Krishna-Hensel

Cross-References

The Muslim League Attempts to Protect Minority Interests in India (1906), p. 87; Soldiers Massacre Indian Civilians in Amritsar (1919), p. 264; Gandhi Leads a Noncooperation Movement (1920), p. 315; Women's Rights in India Undergo a Decade of Change (1925), p. 401; Gandhi Leads the Salt March (1930), p. 447; The Statute of Westminster Creates the Commonwealth (1931), p. 453; India Signs the Delhi Pact (1931), p. 459; The Poona Pact Grants Representation to India's Untouchables (1932), p. 469; India Gains Independence (1947), p. 731; The Indian Government Bans Discrimination Against Untouchables (1948), p. 743; The Indian Parliament Approves Women's Rights Legislation (1955), p. 924.

GERMANY FIRST USES LETHAL CHEMICAL WEAPONS ON THE WESTERN FRONT

Category of event: Atrocities and war crimes
Time: April 22, 1915
Locale: Ypres, Belgium

By initiating lethal chemical warfare in World War I, Germany broke an important legal, moral, and psychological barrier protecting soldiers and civilians

Principal personages:
ERICH VON FALKENHAYN (1861-1922), the commander in chief of the German forces (1914-1916)
FRITZ HABER (1868-1934), the director of the Kaiser Wilhelm Institute for Physical Chemistry and Electrochemistry; supervised the German chemical weapons effort
DUKE ALBRECHT VON WÜRTTEMBERG (1865-1935), commander of the German Fourth Army (1914-1917)

Summary of Event

The initial decision to use lethal chemical weapons at Ypres in April, 1915, was the product of disappointed expectations, frustration, and blood. At the start of World War I in August, 1914, each side expected a relatively easy victory by Christmas. Instead, the war escalated to a scale never before seen. More than 800,000 men were killed, wounded, or captured in the early battles of First Marne, First Ypres, Masurian Lakes, and Tannenberg. This figure does not include casualties from smaller skirmishes and naval encounters or those who simply fell ill in the unhealthy conditions of trench warfare. Nor were most of these casualties the expected lot of hardened professionals: Most soldiers had been civilians or, at most, in national part-time militias only a few months before. Far from being over by Christmas, in early 1915 the war had no end in sight. The war was to drag on for almost four more years and would be fought by nearly a whole generation of young men of draft age.

For their part, the Germans had expected to sweep through Belgium and then to encircle and overwhelm the French army. This so-called Schlieffen Plan, however, failed to work as expected. The French, Belgian, and British forces were able to halt and even push back the invaders. By mid-October, 1914, the Western Front had crystallized into an essentially static line extending some four hundred miles, from the North Sea to Switzerland. The main tactics applied by both sides consisted of attrition and siege, punctuated by deadly but more or less futile attempts to push through the opposing forces.

Both sides sought ways to break out of the stalemate. Chemical warfare, poison gas in particular, seemed to some a possible solution to the impasse. This was not a decision to be made lightly, however. Although there are accounts of limited uses of poisonous gases in the Middle Ages and even in the wars between Athens and Sparta (431-403 B.C.), no modern army had ever used them. Indeed, when British government officials considered the possibility during the Crimean War (1855), they rejected the idea out of hand on the grounds that the effects were so terrible that "no honorable combatant" could take advantage of them. This sense was behind the international Hague Declaration of 1899 which explicitly prohibited "the use of projectiles the object of which is the diffusion of asphyxiating or deleterious gases." In the same vein, the 1874 Brussels Declaration Concerning the Laws and Customs of War, as well as regulations annexed to the Hague Conventions of 1899 and 1907, recognized a principle dating back at least to Roman times forbidding the use of "poison or poisoned weapons."

The decision to use lethal chemical weapons was highly controversial in military circles. Nevertheless, General Erich von Falkenhayn, commander-in-chief of the German forces after the initial German failures, asked for volunteers among the commanders of his armies to try out the technology developed and overseen by Dr. Fritz Haber. With the exception of Duke Albrecht von Württemberg, commander of the Fourth Army, no one was willing to use this untested and distasteful new technology.

April 22, 1915, was a beautiful spring day near the Belgian town of Ypres. The afternoon, a Thursday, was dry and sunny with a pleasant breeze blowing off the German trenches. Even the war seemed relatively quiet. Not long after the heavy shelling began again at 5:00 P.M., two almost invisible greenish yellow clouds rose into the air near the outlying village of Langemark. The clouds merged and crept in the direction of the Forty-Fifth Algerian Division and the French Eighty-Seventh Division, by a twist of wind only skirting the Canadian First Division to the east. At first, no one among the Allies understood what was happening.

As the chlorine gas filled the trenches, it became clear that something lethal was in the air. Men and animals started gasping, choking, and crying out in pain. Within a few minutes, hundreds fell to the ground, dying. Most of those who could do so fled in blind panic, thus forcing even more of the poisonous gas into their lungs. A few had the presence of mind to wet handkerchiefs and hold them to their faces to provide some protection as they ran.

Chaos reigned all the way back to Ypres along a four-mile gap, where only a few minutes before there had been a seemingly immovable front. Men totally divorced from military discipline choked the roads. Frightened horses without drivers dragged heavy guns. Coughing, choking, purple-faced soldiers told wild tales to anyone they met.

The Germans were not able to exploit the hole they had just put in the Allied line, nor could they profit from subsequent uses of chemical weapons in the battle. By the end of the Second Battle of Ypres on May 27, all they had accomplished was a flattening of the Allied line.

The Germans later claimed that only two hundred of their casualties at the five-week Second Battle of Ypres came from chemical weapons. The Allies said that fifteen thousand of the fifty-nine thousand casualties they suffered were a result of chemical weapons, including five thousand deaths. Although historians doubt the figures on both sides, the results of the first use of modern, lethal chemical weapons at Ypres make it clear that chemical warfare, even against untrained and unprotected opponents, is both terrifying and deadly but is no guarantee of military victory. This is significant in light of later claims that military necessity morally justifies the use of chemical warfare.

The Germans argued that their initial use of chlorine was not a violation of the regulations annexed to the 1899 Hague Declaration, since the gas escaped from canisters and was not part of a projectile. The French, who may have used tear gas in hand grenades beginning in the winter of 1915, responded to the chlorine clouds by putting tear gas in artillery shells during the fall of 1915. They claimed that their actions were not improper because the chemicals involved were not lethal. By the time the two technologies were combined, it was possible for a cynic to say that each side was merely retaliating against the violation of the other. No one mentioned Article 23(a) of the regulations annexed to the Hague Conventions of 1899 and 1907 prohibiting the use of "poison or poisoned weapons."

Impact of Event

Chemical weapons took a terrible human toll over the next three and one-half years. Of the approximately fifteen million casualties suffered in World War I, more than one million soldiers were hospitalized or killed because of exposure to chlorine, phosgene and its relatives, or mustard gas. Moreover, the airborne nature of chemical weapons allows them to spread beyond the immediate battlefield. This makes them relatively uncontrollable area weapons, prone to harming civilians who happen to be in the wrong place at the wrong time. More than two thousand total civilian casualties can be documented from industrial accidents and attacks by the Germans that individually led to twenty or more French or Belgian casualties. Use of chemical weapons also contributed to the erosion taking place in the concept of insulating civilians from military activities. As General Peyton March, chief of staff for the United States Army, wrote later, "War is cruel at best, but the use of an instrument of death, which, once launched, cannot be controlled, and which may decimate noncombatants—women and children—reduces civilization to savagery."

After the war, proponents argued that chemical weapons were actually more humane than conventional high explosives. They based their claim on the assertion that the weapons are highly effective militarily, yet kill a smaller proportion of those who are disabled by them than do more conventional weapons. Both sides in World War I had some tactical successes using chemical weapons, but, for the war as a whole, as at Ypres, the weapons did not produce overall victory. As to their humanity, all three of the main lethal chemicals used in World War I involve very significant suffering, both physical and psychological. Victims of phosgene or chlorine end up black in the face, spitting blood, and drowning in their own bodily fluids. An unprotected victim of mustard gas will suffer blisters on every inch of the body the aerosol droplets touch, internal or external. Long-term respiratory damage for survivors was common. Conventional weapons may or may not be physically less unpleasant as sources of wounds and death, but they are often perceived as producing less horrifying kinds of injury.

The fact that chemical weapons have not been militarily decisive, while they have inflicted considerable physical and emotional pain, suggests that they may cause unnecessary suffering. This is one of the criteria recognized in international law, including the Hague Conventions of 1899 and 1907, for protecting soldiers' human rights. Chemical weapons substantially increased the suffering of a generation of young men without being crucial to the final result. They certainly killed substantial numbers of civilians needlessly.

The experience with chemical weapons from 1915 to 1918 strengthened the international conviction that chemical warfare ought to be forbidden explicitly under international law. That conviction took the form of a prohibition on the use in war of asphyxiating, poisonous, or other gases, and of bacterial methods of warfare, written into the Geneva Protocol of 1925. As of 1991, there were 129 parties to this treaty. Formal reservations of the right to retaliate convert the protocol into a no-first-use pact, but, as such, the moral and legal tradition against first use in war has proven remarkably sturdy. The only unambiguous first users of chemical weapons since World War I are Italy in Ethiopia in 1935-1936, Japan against China from 1937 to 1945, Egypt against Yemen in 1963-1967, and Iraq against Iran from 1984 to 1988 and against its own Kurdish citizens in 1988. Evidence in all but a handful of other cases is highly questionable.

Chemical weapons continue to be a concern in international politics. Their utilization in the Iran-Iraq war, and especially against Kurdish civilians, has heightened fears that a legal ban on first use is not sufficient to stop a power with a chemical arsenal. Use against the Kurds also emphasizes the particular suitability of chemical weapons for use against unprotected civilians. Thus, negotiations under the auspices of the Conference on Disarmament attempted to ban development, production, possession, and transfer of chemical weapons. Important strides have been made toward a new chemical weapons convention. Although success may still prove elusive, a worldwide distaste for chemical arsenals and the desire to limit proliferation may lead to an even wider prohibition against the use of chemical weapons.

Bibliography

Brown, Frederick J. *Chemical Warfare: A Study in Restraints.* Princeton, N.J.: Princeton University Press, 1968. An account of the history of the use of chemical weapons and attempts (mainly failed in Brown's view) to restrain use by legal measures. Also discusses the "humanity" of chemical warfare. Although one may well disagree with Brown's conclusions, the book contains important material about chemical warfare and chemical arms control that is difficult to find elsewhere.

Fotion, Nicholas G., and Gerard Elfstrom. "Weapons of War." In *Military Ethics: Guidelines for Peace and War.* Boston: Routledge & Kegan Paul, 1986. An interesting and persuasive utilitarian argument for why use of some kinds of weapons, including chemical and biological weapons, ought to be morally condemned, while use of others is permissible. Distinguishes between first use and retaliation. Conclusions are very different from those of Richard Krikus, cited below.

Haber, L. F. *The Poisonous Cloud: Chemical Warfare in the First World War.* New York: Oxford University Press, 1986. A painstaking and thorough account of the origins, development, organization, use, and effects of chemical weapons in World War I. Written by the son of chemist Fritz Haber, who presided over the German chemical weapons program. One especially thoughtful chapter deals with the psychological effects of chemical weapons. Some of the conclusions are controversial, but this book should not be missed by anyone interested in the history of chemical warfare.

Hart, Liddell. *History of the First World War.* London: Cassell, 1970. Originally published in 1930 under the title *The Real War, 1914-1918*, this book provides a readable and detailed account of World War I that manages to capture not only successes and failures of strategy on the grand level but a good deal of the flavor of what it was like to live through the events chronicled. Provides a good background for understanding chemical warfare in the context of World War I.

Krikus, Richard J. "On the Morality of Chemical/Biological War." In *War, Morality, and the Military Profession*, edited by Malham Wakin. 2d ed. Boulder, Colo.: Westview Press, 1986. Argues that, in terms of their effects on soldiers and civilians, chemical and biological weapons are no more morally improper than are conventional weapons. Argues that the traditional condemnation is a historical artifact. A useful contrast to Fotion and Elfstrom, cited above. His argument is not entirely persuasive, but his conclusions are shared by many.

Spiers, Edward M. *Chemical Warfare.* Chicago: University of Illinois Press, 1986. A useful account of the modern history of chemical warfare and chemical arms control, now somewhat dated by the fact that it was written before the 1988 chemical weapons offensives by Iraq.

Stockholm International Peace Research Institute. *The Rise of CB Weapons.* Vol. 1 in *The Problem of Chemical and Biological Warfare.* New York: Humanities Press, 1971-1975. Part of a series which constitutes the definitive account of chemical and biological weapons before the 1970's. This volume provides an overview and covers the history of chemical weapons and warfare from 1914 to 1970. It also evaluates more than two hundred alleged uses. Other volumes deal with technology, international law, and arms control negotiations. Unsympathetic to use or possession of chemical weapons, SIPRI still manages to be both comprehensive and carefully objective in its approach.

Frances Vryling Harbour

Cross-References

Legal Norms of Behavior in Warfare Formulated by the Hague Conference (1907),

p. 92; Nations Agree to Rules on Biological Weapons (1972), p. 1662; The United Nations Issues a Declaration Against Torture (1975), p. 1847; Soviets Invade Afghanistan (1979), p. 2062; Iraq's Government Uses Poison Gas Against Kurdish Villagers (1988), p. 2397.

WOMEN'S INSTITUTES ARE FOUNDED IN GREAT BRITAIN

Category of event: Women's rights
Time: September 11, 1915
Locale: Llanfair, Wales

Although known primarily for their focus on home economics, the Women's Institutes exerted a fundamental influence on British society by empowering the lives of rural women and addressing a variety of social and health issues

Principal personages:

MARGARET WATT (1868-1948), the catalyst for the creation of the Women's Institutes in Great Britain

ADELAIDE HUNTER HOODLESS (1857-1910), the founder of the Women's Institutes movement in Canada

LADY GERTRUDE DENMAN (1884-1954), the first chairperson (1917-1946) of the National Federation of Women's Institutes in Great Britain

Summary of Event

The history of the women's movement in both Great Britain and the United States usually begins with the suffragettes. The suffragettes' singular focus on acquiring the vote and the general limitation of participation in the suffrage movement to middle-class women from towns and cities means that limiting a study of women's rights to the suffrage issue presents an incomplete picture of the emerging women's movement, which sought a full and equal role for women in a modern society. Studies of society generally ignore rural women. The process of modernization largely entails the incorporation of traditional society into new ways of living, usually through migration from rural to urban areas. Even at the beginning of the twentieth century, a significant number of women lived on farms or in small villages.

Conditions in rural Great Britain throughout the nineteenth century deteriorated as the industrialization of society occurred. The population shift to urban centers left a vacuum behind. Food imports further contributed to the depression of the countryside. Village life ceased to be the heart of British culture as the urban centers increased their dominance. With these changes, the lives of rural women became even more isolated from larger social and political contexts.

In Great Britain at the beginning of the twentieth century, rural women were consumed by work and had little time or opportunity for social networks beyond the family. The rapid transformation of urban society generally had bypassed the rural communities. Women in the countryside were isolated. The contrast between rural and urban life caused some to seek changes in the agricultural regions. Economic and health conditions were of particular interest.

Some government leaders had recognized the flagging rural conditions and responded in 1889 with the creation of the Board of Agriculture. Attention increasingly focused on education for the agricultural regions. In 1901, the Agricultural Organization Society (AOS) was formed to create a coalition of farmers and other rural interests. As the AOS searched for models of reform, its attention was drawn to Canadian efforts to promote agrarian development through rural adult education. Women's Institutes, begun in Canada in 1897, were one of the useful strategies noted.

The first Women's Institute was established on February 19, 1897, at Stoney Creek, Ontario, by Adelaide Hunter Hoodless. A lack of knowledge of basic hygiene had contributed to the death of one of Hoodless' children. Her ensuing desire to learn and promote family-care practices motivated her to form an organization to promote education in child care and other health practices related to the home. Domestic matters, rather than the general well-being of the rural community or agricultural development, were the exclusive concern of this first institute. The movement spread in Canada, but it never caught on there to the extent that it did in Great Britain. The British need for such programs was greater, caused in part by the relative agricultural prosperity of Canada resulting from the export of grain to Europe. Thus, the formation on September 11, 1915, of the Women's Institute at Llanfair, Wales, was especially significant given the degree of change the British movement promoted, the growth and prominence of the movement in Great Britain, and the subsequent spread of the organization from Great Britain to many other countries.

Much of the initial drive to form the Women's Institutes in Great Britain came from Margaret Watts, a Canadian who had moved to Great Britain in 1913 following the death of her husband. She had been active in spreading the Women's Institutes in Canada. After she gave a speech on her Canadian experiences with the Women's Institutes, the AOS hired her as part of a small group directed to organize rural women with the specific objective of establishing Women's Institutes in Great Britain. North Wales was suggested as a starting point, given the region's need for cross-cultural collaboration (between English- and Welsh-speaking groups as well as among different religious congregations). In addition, some attempts had been made in the area to bring women into participation with men in attempts at economic growth; women, however, had been reluctant to speak their minds openly in these mixed groups.

The first meeting of the Women's Institutes at Llanfair offered little to suggest the impact that the organization would make in the daily lives of rural women. The small charter group was led by individuals whose position in society suggested connections with the rural elite and by local officials interested in promoting the venture. The idea for establishing this institute was promoted by the head of the AOS and by a local landowner, Colonel R. Stapleton-Cotton, who was engaged in aspects of rural economic development. The meeting was held in the cottage of Mrs. W. E. Jones, who became the institute's vice president and treasurer. Her husband was the agent for the Marquis of Anglesey, the principal landowner in that region of Wales. Mrs. R. Stapleton-Cotton became the institute's first president. Margaret Watt was not directly involved in establishing the group; however, she arrived a few days later to support the new endeavor and to instill some of the organizational characteristics gained from her Canadian experiences. She moved quickly to promote the creation of similar groups elsewhere. Although the initiative for starting the Llanfair Women's Institute had come in part from several men and had official backing, rural women controlled the agenda and destiny of the group. That control was the essential and lasting significance of the group's formation.

In the beginning, the movement was tied to a program first promoted by the AOS and the Board of Agriculture. World War I, which had begun just a year earlier, heightened the perceived need for rural groups of any complexion to promote improved production and quality of foodstuffs. Indeed, the promotion of the Women's Institutes was connected directly to concern over potential food shortages caused by the reduction in the work force because of the war. As a result, domestic production of foodstuffs such as jam was associated with the Women's Institutes from the start.

The institutes appealed to a culture with a strong tradition of self-help organizations such as the "friendly societies." Great Britain was the place of origin for the cooperative movement as well. In fact, Margaret Watt first came to the notice of agrarian reformers on the basis of a speech she had made to a cooperative society gathering in London. The mutual-benefit nature of the Women's Institutes on ostensibly safe topics of home and hearth and the growing popularity of scientific management in the form of home economics also contributed to the popularity of the British Women's Institutes.

Growth was rapid, with more than one hundred Women's Institutes formed by 1917. The AOS found itself overwhelmed by the response and yielded direction and support for organizing the spread of the institutes to the Board of Agriculture. This government agency supported the movement in the early years through monetary grants and provision of staff.

Of considerable importance was the role played by the social elite as leaders of the body, especially at the regional and national levels. Social privilege was important in working with the government for legislative actions, a strategy that became part of the Women's Institutes' agenda. This linkage with government did advance the direct role of women in political action, albeit by those of the upper class.

Leaders of the movement, especially Lady Gertrude Denman, its first national chairperson, sought to cut the formal ties with the Board of Agriculture to assure the movement a greater degree of autonomy. The rules of the Women's Institutes called for nonsectarian and nonpolitical activity. The latter restriction, however, suggested the maintenance of the status quo and thereby the fundamentally conservative nature of the movement. These surface qualities were essential to the institutes' acceptance by the general populace in the rural communities.

Impact of Event

The growth of the movement in Great Britain and the eventual use of the Women's Institutes as a model for rural women's development projects in many other countries testified to the responsive chord struck by the first institute. The most significant influence of the Women's Institutes was the general empowerment of women to take control of aspects of their daily lives and to experience the consequences of working together for local, regional, or even national goals. The Women's Institutes brought women to a level of broad political action unprecedented to that point. Networks for women were created across social class lines, although much of the group's real power was in the hands of the upper-class leaders.

The actions that the national and some local groups undertook were of varying importance. Primary among the goals was the promotion of education for rural women, with a focus on home economics. Special emphasis was given to hygiene and nutrition. Through these means, the quality of life of many rural families was improved.

Only gradually did an awareness of larger social issues emerge, yet from the start, the Women's Institutes had a profound effect on the role of rural women. This influence stemmed from two factors. Some local groups included women who were also interested in such other issues as suffrage or the attainment of a more active role for women in society. The nature of the organization, as a basically conservative group, meant that its support for various issues of concern was harder for politicians to reject. In the group's earliest years, the direct connection with the Board of Agriculture was a two-way street; potential government control of the movement was matched by opportunities for direct input by the Women's Institutes to government officials. For an organization that comprised women only, this access was a unique situation. Even after the formal ties were severed, the conservative nature of the organization, the relatively safe reform agendas it adopted, and its broad social-class membership provided opportunities for effective lobbying for change. Some of the issues that the Women's Institutes lobbied directly for in the organizations' first fifteen years included removing the exemption of women from jury duty, maintaining women on the rural constabulary, providing adult education for women, promoting health issues (including public education on venereal disease), and establishing access to emerging communication technology, with the goal of at least one telephone in every village.

For many women, the Women's Institutes were the first experience with any form of public action. Some members eventually would pursue active political lives, especially on the local level. The Women's Institutes were a vital mechanism for bringing rural women into direct participation in public affairs and into elected office.

Bibliography

Dudgeon, Piers, ed. *Village Voices.* London: Sidgwick & Jackson, 1989. Includes discussion of the broader accomplishments of the Women's Institutes in social reform. Personal recollections and photographs abound as the movement is set in both personal and historical contexts. The absence of a bibliography is indicative of the testimonial nature of this study.

Goodenough, Simon. *Jam and Jerusalem.* Glasgow: Collins, 1977. Stresses the accomplishments of the movement, giving a public-relations tone to the writing. Lists of numerous resolutions adopted by the national conferences focus on the

Women's Institutes' principal areas of interest and accomplishments, including social reform. The first book on the topic to emphasize the broader consequences of the Women's Institutes. No bibliography. Photographs included.

Huxley, Gervas. *Lady Denman, G.B.E.* London: Chatto & Windus, 1961. An admiring biography of the first president of the National Federation of Women's Institutes that includes chapters on her role in the early years. Places her personal life, as a woman of privilege in an unhappy marriage, in perspective of her very public role. No bibliography, some photographs.

Jenkins, Inez. *The History of the Women's Institutes Movement of England and Wales.* Oxford: Oxford University Press, 1953. The first substantive history of the movement, written in an admiring tone by an insider. Provides more detail on the movement's origins than any other source. Includes a brief bibliography.

McCall, Cicely. *Women's Institutes.* London: William Collins, 1943. A chatty account of the movement with particular emphasis on the organization's role in aiding children evacuated from the cities during World War II. Illustrated with drawings and paintings. No bibliography.

Daniel J. Doyle

Cross-References

The Pankhursts Found the Women's Social and Political Union (1903), p. 19; Finland Grants Women Suffrage (1906), p. 70; Parliament Grants Suffrage to British Women (1918), p. 247; The League of Women Voters Is Founded (1920), p. 333; The Nineteenth Amendment Gives American Women the Right to Vote (1920), p. 339; The Minimum Age for Female British Voters Is Lowered (1928), p. 442; The World Health Organization Proclaims Health as a Basic Right (1946), p. 678; The U.N. Convention on the Political Rights of Women Is Approved (1952), p. 885; The United Nations Issues a Declaration on Equality for Women (1967), p. 1391; A U.N. Declaration on Hunger and Malnutrition Is Adopted (1974), p. 1775; The World Conference on Women Sets an International Agenda (1975), p. 1796; A U.N. Convention Condemns Discrimination Against Women (1979), p. 2057.

BRANDEIS BECOMES THE FIRST
JEWISH MEMBER OF THE SUPREME COURT

Category of event: Racial and ethnic rights
Time: 1916
Locale: Washington, D.C.

President Woodrow Wilson's nomination of Louis Brandeis to the Supreme Court broke the corporate lawyers' attack on Jewish lawyers and legitimized new approaches to the law

Principal personages:

LOUIS D. BRANDEIS (1856-1941), a leader of the Progressive movement and an active Zionist, an associate justice of the U.S. Supreme Court from 1916 to 1939

WOODROW WILSON (1856-1924), the twenty-eighth president of the United States, who nominated Brandeis to the Supreme Court

WILLIAM HOWARD TAFT (1857-1930), the twenty-seventh president of the United States and the chief justice of the United States from 1921 to 1930

A. LAWRENCE LOWELL (1856-1943), the president of Harvard University and president of the American Bar Association; organized Boston lawyers against Brandeis

THOMAS J. WALSH (1859-1933), a Democratic senator and pro-Brandeis advocate on the Senate Judiciary Committee

HENRY CABOT LODGE (1850-1924), a Republican senator from Massachusetts who organized corporations, lawyers, Republican politicians, and the elite of Boston to oppose Brandeis

ROBERT M. LA FOLLETTE (1855-1925), a senator from Wisconsin who was decisive in President Wilson's decision to nominate Brandeis

CHARLES ELIOT (1834-1926), a president of Harvard University who dramatically endorsed Brandeis

Summary of Event

On January 28, 1916, President Woodrow Wilson nominated Louis Dembitz Brandeis to the Supreme Court of the United States. Prior to the nomination, he conferred privately only with Senator Robert M. La Follette, the leader of the Progressive Party. The suddenness of the announcement and the secrecy of the decision to appoint a Jew caused a political sensation. For more than four months, the longest period in the history of Supreme Court nominations, the Senate Judiciary Committee heard heated and complicated testimony. The committee's final report of 1,316 pages revealed that the issues involved radical threats to the American legal system. Brandeis' confirmation on June 1 and appointment on June 5 signaled reform in the

United States' economic, political, and social systems. The appointment broke a taboo that kept Jews from serving on the Supreme Court and in high positions in government and education.

Louis Brandeis was born on November 13, 1856, in Louisville, Kentucky, to Adolph and Frederika Dembitz Brandeis. His parents had come to the United States from Austria after the 1848 Prussian Revolution. After finishing high school, he traveled in Germany for three years. In 1875, he entered Harvard Law School, where he was graduated with highest honors.

In 1879, he established a law practice in Boston that grew into a profitable business. He also became known as the "people's lawyer" because of his *pro bono* advocacy in cases involving the public interest—municipal railway monopolization, life insurance practices, public land conservation, and maximum-day labor laws for women and children. He joined with the Progressive movement in its attack on corporate size and the exploitation of the working class and the consumer. For Brandeis, the sacred concept of "protection of property" had to be balanced with concepts of equity and social justice. He promoted an active view of government that made it a regulator of industry and a force for economic and social opportunity, and he became a close adviser to La Follette and Wilson.

Brandeis became famous for reforming legal arguments in the 1908 Supreme Court case of *Muller v. Oregon.* The state of Oregon was challenged for its statute restricting women to ten hours of labor per day. The employer, Muller, argued that the Fourteenth Amendment protected his "life, liberty and property." Without using any constitutional precedents, Brandeis amassed more than one hundred pages of sociological and economic data to prove that excessive hours of toil were a threat to a woman's constitution. Brandeis won his case. Subsequently, he used similar arguments to protect child labor. Brandeis advocated that the law must promote social justice even if there is no legal precedent. This type of sociological and idealistic rather than strictly legal argument became known as the "Brandeis brief."

Reared as a nonreligious German Jew in Kentucky and Boston, Brandeis did not directly feel the virulent anti-Semitism that arose in the United States in the early twentieth century. A massive riot and a lynching demonstrated the violent aspect of this prejudice against Russian and Polish Orthodox Jews. Hundreds of Jews were injured when the largest anti-Semitic police riot in American history erupted on New York City's Lower East Side in July, 1902. In Atlanta, Georgia, Leo M. Frank, the president of the local chapter of the Jewish organization B'nai B'rith, was dragged from his jail cell by an anti-Semitic mob and lynched in August, 1915, just six months before Brandeis' nomination.

The anti-Semitism evident at Brandeis' Senate hearings was subtle. Neither the Boston Brahmins nor the Wall Street lawyers would openly admit their motives. Brandeis' nomination was seen as a slap in the face of the conservative Anglo-Saxon male elite who ruled America's corporations, law firms, and government offices. Brandeis was an outsider who denied the legitimacy of the legal system that supported unfettered capitalism. Since Brandeis' intellect, knowledge of the law, and judicial accomplishments were unimpeachable, the Senate hearings focused on the nature of his character.

The attack on Brandeis' nomination was led by the Boston and Wall Street legal elite: Henry Cabot Lodge, senator from Massachusetts; A. Lawrence Lowell, a corporate lawyer, a former president of the American Bar Association, and the president of Harvard University; and William Howard Taft. Lodge questioned Brandeis' fitness to serve: "For the first time in our history a man has been nominated to the Supreme Court with a view to attracting to the President a group of voters on racial grounds. Converting the United States into a Government by foreign groups is to me the most fatal thing that can happen to our Government. . . ." The lawyers made the vague charge that Brandeis lacked the "judicial temperament and capacity" to be a proper judge and that he did not have "the confidence of the people." When repeatedly asked by friends or colleagues to give details as to why Brandeis was personally unfit to be a judge, neither Lodge nor Lowell offered any. Taft believed that Brandeis and other Jewish lawyers would interpret the Constitution to uphold anticorporate social and economic reforms. Senator Thomas Walsh, Brandeis' leading defender on the Senate Judiciary Committee, recognized that the attack dealt with Brandeis' religion and radicalness. "No doubt much of the hostility toward Mr. Brandeis had its origin in the senseless racial prejudice," he said. "The real crime for which this man is guilty is that he has exposed the inequities of men in high places in our financial system."

Throughout the four months of debate, it became clear to many that the charges against Brandeis were spurious and were coming from a group of men in Boston and Wall Street. In fact, this group had hired a lobbyist, Austen Fox, to stall the proceedings. A surge of support from Harvard rallied Charles W. Eliot, president emeritus of Harvard, to Brandeis' defense. His testimonial praised Brandeis' "gentleness, courage . . . altruism and public spirit." President Wilson waited until the end of the hearings to endorse his candidate. He was aware that his attempt to nominate Brandeis in 1912 for the position of United States attorney general had been thwarted because of anti-Semitism and opposition from the legal and corporate elite. In 1915, the prestigious Cosmos Club of Washington, D.C., initially refused Brandeis' membership application because he did not "belong." Only Wilson's direct intervention broke the religious ban, and Brandeis was allowed entry. Wilson avoided a religious defense of Brandeis' appointment and argued that it was necessary to promote the social, economic, and political values of his "New Freedom" and of Progressivism. Rallying the country to his platform through the Brandeis appointment may, indeed, have given Wilson the edge in winning the presidential race of 1916.

Brandeis remained publicly quiet. During the hearings he wrote to his brother that "eighteen centuries of Jewish persecution must have enured me to [these] hardships." After his confirmation, he privately analyzed the campaign against him. He blamed large corporations for being morally "abnormal and lawless" and blamed "men like A. Lawrence Lowell who had been blinded by privilege." He held special scorn for those who had abstained from comment.

On the Court, Justice Brandeis became famous for his advocacy of social justice. For Jews, he was a hero, and he was a voice of commitment to Jewish and Western values until he retired from the Court in 1939.

Impact of Event

The appointment of Louis Brandeis to the Supreme Court did not end anti-Semitism. In fact, it made Brandeis acutely aware of his Judaic background. To many conservatives, the Supreme Court was the bastion of tradition and order. In 1916, the Court consisted of eight Christian judges, all native-born, seven of whom were of Anglo-Saxon heritage. Brandeis was an outsider—a Jew and a radical who sought to change the law. The Court itself harbored a renowned anti-Semite, Associate Justice James Clark McReynolds. After Brandeis' appointment, McReynolds refused to speak to him for three years and would not sit next to him for an annual Supreme Court picture. Neither would he accept a Jew as a law clerk. McReynolds staunchly opposed the nomination of any more Jews to the Court.

Brandeis' professional success helped to encourage other Jews to seek legal and educational careers. The politics of Progressivism tolerated these aspirations. According to Frederick Rudolph, during the early twentieth century, Jews in the United States possessed "an intellectual tradition that was altogether foreign to the style of the raw materialistic country to which they emigrated." It was this tradition that made them good allies with the social and economic reformers. Brandeis mentored many able lawyers by offering them positions as his law clerks. He generously endowed many Jewish and educational charities, thus giving many Jews and scholars an opportunity to become successful.

The Jewish challenge to the professions created a backlash. Throughout the college and university systems of the United States, quotas were instituted to limit Jews from attaining the education necessary to join the white-collar professions of law, medicine, academia, and science. For example, in the 1920's, A. Lawrence Lowell, still president of Harvard, announced that he would limit Jewish admissions to Harvard by no longer selecting the freshman class on the basis of scholarship alone. The admissions policy would instead be based on an applicant's "character and fitness and the promise of the greatest usefulness in the future as a result of a Harvard education." Consequently, Harvard reduced its Jewish enrollment from 25 percent to less than 15 percent.

Brandeis' eloquence on the bench and his growing involvement with Zionism made him a role model for many Jews. His strong advocacy for the disadvantaged was compared to the moral indignation of the great Jewish prophet Isaiah. As an American Zionist, he played an active part in drafting the Balfour Declaration, which set up a homeland for Jews. His ascension to the Supreme Court highlighted and furthered the contribution of Jews to American government and society.

Bibliography

Abraham, Henry J. *Justices and Presidents: A Political History of Appointments to the Supreme Court.* 2d ed. New York: Oxford University Press, 1985. Includes analyses of the relationship between Wilson and Brandeis and of William Howard Taft's opposition to Brandeis and Benjamin Cardozo. Most helpful are the appendices, which rate the justices. Brandeis is considered, along with his Jewish colleagues Felix Frankfurter and Benjamin Cardozo, to be among the top twelve in the history of the Court. Taft is "near great," and McReynolds is a "failure."

Auerbach, Jerold S. *Rabbis and Lawyers: The Journey from Torah to Constitution.* Bloomington: Indiana University Press, 1990. A brilliant analysis of the Jewish role in American legal thought. The chapter on Brandeis argues that his sense of legal advocacy was derived from two sources: the prophetic pronouncements of the Torah and the laws of the U.S. Constitution. His creativity derived from his being an outsider to both traditions. An excellent discussion of Brandeis' Zionistic views in terms of his commitment to American values.

_____. *Unequal Justice: Lawyers and Social Change in Modern America.* New York: Oxford University Press, 1976. A history of the American Bar Association's early twentieth century struggle to restrict blacks from membership and to prevent Jews from obtaining judicial appointments.

Burt, Robert A. *Two Jewish Justices: Outcasts in the Promised Land.* Berkeley: University of California Press, 1988. A comparative study of Louis Brandeis and Felix Frankfurter. Burt concludes that Brandeis' Jewish experience provided him with a sense of mission to save the outcast.

Gerber, David A. ed. *Anti-Semitism in American History.* Urbana: University of Illinois, 1986. Provides excellent background reading on the anti-Semitism of the nineteenth and twentieth centuries.

McWilliams, Carey. *A Mask for Privilege: Anti-Semitism in America.* Boston: Little, Brown, 1948. The classic study on the nature of anti-Semitism in the United States. A stinging attack on how the privileged groups used anti-Semitism to protect "their attempted monopoly of social, economic, and political power." McWilliams' critique can be applied to the Boston Brahmins and Wall Street lawyers who opposed Brandeis.

Mason, Alpheus T. *Brandeis: A Free Man's Life.* New York: Viking Press, 1946. The best detailed biography of Louis D. Brandeis. Excellent on Brandeis' legal cases and his nomination. Does not adequately deal with his Jewishness and Zionism. Based on voluminous primary sources.

Todd, A. L. *Justice on Trial: The Case of Louis D. Brandeis.* New York: McGraw-Hill, 1964. A well-documented record of the Senate Judiciary hearings on the Brandeis nomination. Todd concentrates more on the political nature of the struggle than on the anti-Semitism. He provides thorough background on the personalities and the arguments.

Richard C. Kagan

Cross-References

"Palmer Raids" Lead to Arrests and Deportations of Immigrants (1919), p. 258;

The Immigration Act of 1921 Imposes a National Quota System (1921), p. 350; A U.S. Immigration Act Imposes Quotas Based on National Origins (1924), p. 383; HUAC Begins Investigating Suspected Communists (1938), p. 550; Israel Is Created as a Homeland for Jews (1948), p. 761; Marshall Becomes the First Black Supreme Court Justice (1967), p. 1381; O'Connor Becomes the First Female Supreme Court Justice (1981), p. 2141.

THE EASTER REBELLION FAILS TO WIN
IRISH INDEPENDENCE

Category of event: Revolutions and rebellions
Time: April 24-30, 1916
Locale: Dublin, Ireland

Although the Easter Rebellion failed to establish Ireland's independence from Great Britain, it helped persuade the Irish people that they must ultimately seek freedom from British rule

Principal personages:

PATRICK PEARSE (1879-1916), an Irish poet and teacher, commander in chief of the republican forces in the rebellion

EOIN MACNEILL (1867-1945), an Irish scholar and chief of staff of the Irish Volunteers, who tried to stop the rebellion

SIR ROGER CASEMENT (1864-1916), an Irish revolutionary who persuaded the German government to provide arms for the rebellion

JAMES CONNOLLY (1868-1916), an Irish socialist, leader of the Citizen Army, and military commander of the republican forces in Dublin

THOMAS CLARKE (1857-1916), an early organizer of the Irish Republican Brotherhood (IRB) and a leader of the rebellion

SEAN MACDERMOTT (1884-1916), a political organizer, journalist, member of the military council of the IRB, and leader in the rebellion

Summary of Event

The 1916 Easter Rebellion was led by men who saw the history of Ireland since the Middle Ages as little more than a fight for freedom from English oppression. They believed that the English had dispossessed the Irish of their ownership of the land and turned them into powerless tenant farmers subject to the whims and cruelty of absentee English landlords; that England had imposed a Protestant state structure upon a fundamentally Roman Catholic people; and that the English had systematically attempted to destroy what nationalists called the Irish nation, politically, economically, and culturally. The research of Irish, British, and American historians, especially research late in the twentieth century, has demonstrated that these views were inaccurate. The rebels of 1916, however, were not historians: They were men of action, committed to an emotional crusade.

England was first drawn into affairs in Ireland in 1170, when an Irish chieftain invited an English earl and his men to help him defeat other Irish chieftains. The English were so successful that many more were soon seeking their fortunes in Ireland, intermarrying with the native nobility, and adopting Irish law and customs. Eventually, they rebelled against the authority of their nominal sovereigns, the kings of England. In 1534, King Henry VIII was so vexed by the Anglo-Irish nobles that he demanded that all lands in Ireland be surrendered to the Crown, which would regrant them to loyal vassals. This policy was enforced by his daughter, Queen Elizabeth I.

At about the same time, the land issue became associated with religious conflict between England and Ireland. Henry VIII had brought the Reformation to England by breaking with the Roman Catholic church and creating his own Church of England, with himself as its head. While England thus accepted Protestantism, Ireland remained staunchly Catholic. After a rebellion led by the Catholic nobility of Ulster (a province in northeastern Ireland), Elizabeth's successor, James I, decided that the only way to curb Catholic power was to confiscate the lands owned by the Ulster nobles. These were then sold or rented to Protestant landlords.

The dispossession of Catholic landowners continued and expanded over the next century, so that by 1700 they owned less than 12 percent of the land and largely had been replaced by a Protestant "Ascendancy" class. Most Irish Catholics were reduced to the status of poor tenant farmers, barely surviving on the estates of Protestant landlords. In the 1640's, and again in 1689, Catholic nobles and their followers unsuccessfully revolted against Protestant rule. After the revolt of 1689, the English passed a series of penal laws which deprived Roman Catholics in Ireland of all political rights, as well as the right to buy land. While the Roman Catholic church itself was not banned, all of its activities were tightly restricted. The penal laws cemented the Irish belief that Britain was determined both to enslave the Irish politically and to destroy their religion.

At the beginning of the nineteenth century, Ireland was allowed to elect members to the British Parliament. When Irish Catholics were given full political rights in 1829, they voted for candidates who supported some sort of autonomy, or "home rule," for their country. In 1886, the Irish members in Parliament introduced the first home rule bill, but it failed because the Liberal prime minister, William Gladstone, could not persuade all of the members of his party to support it. After an election in 1910, however, the Irish members held the balance of power between the Liberals and opposition Conservatives, who were almost evenly split. In return for Irish support of a revolutionary program of social spending, the Liberals promised to pass a home rule bill, which became law in 1914 but was suspended because World War I had recently begun.

Many Irish nationalists, however, were unsatisfied by home rule, under which Ireland would still be part of the British Empire. They demanded that Ireland become an independent republic. The most extreme of these nationalists were members of a secret society called the Irish Republican Brotherhood (IRB). With the start of World War I, the IRB saw an opportunity, while Britain was occupied with trying to defeat Germany, to free Ireland through an armed insurrection. The organization which they hoped would carry out the revolution was the Irish Volunteers, a paramilitary group which had been created early in 1914, ostensibly for the purpose of ensuring that the British carried out the promises of home rule. In fact, the Volunteers had been infiltrated from their inception by members of the IRB, who planned to manipulate the Volunteers for their own purpose.

The situation was soon complicated by the fact that the leadership of the Volunteers encouraged members of the organization to join the British Army, in hopes of demonstrating that Ireland had earned the right to home rule. Although thousands answered the call, a minority of about 13,000 (out of 180,000), refused to consider serving the nation they viewed as an oppressor, and now seceded from the Volunteers. They were led by a professor of early Irish history, Eoin MacNeill. MacNeill disapproved of any cooperation with the war effort, but he was neither a member of the IRB nor aware that the secret society was actually taking over his organization.

The real leaders had already begun to plan an armed uprising. The most prominent among them was Patrick Pearse, a poet and schoolmaster who was obsessed with the need for a "blood sacrifice" in order for Ireland truly to become a nation. Others included Tom Clarke, an old revolutionary from the nineteenth century; James Connolly, a socialist trade union organizer and leader of a tiny "Citizens' Army" of republican socialists; Sir Roger Casement, a former member of the British Consular Service who was already negotiating with the Germans for a shipment of arms; and Sean MacDermott, a violent young nationalist from Ulster. These and other members of the military council of the IRB decided upon Easter, 1916, as the date to begin their rebellion.

What followed was a fiasco. In order for the IRB to issue orders to the Volunteers to begin maneuvers on Easter Monday, April 24, MacNeill finally had to be informed of what was occurring. He was outraged and countermanded the orders. In the last few days before Easter weekend, he was persuaded to change his mind. He then learned that a German ship bringing arms had been intercepted by the British Navy, following the arrest of Sir Roger Casement, and he realized that the rebellion was doomed. Pearse and the others went ahead anyway, and many of the Volunteers, who really had no idea of what was going on, received several sets of confusing, contradictory orders. The result was that when the rebellion began in Dublin, only about one thousand Volunteers showed up. Even though their numbers gradually grew through the week, the rebels never had more than about eighteen hundred men with which to fight twenty-five hundred British troops and more than nine thousand members of the Royal Irish Constabulary (police). In addition, the British soon brought thousands of reinforcements into Dublin.

The overall plan of the rising was to seize the General Post Office (GPO) building in central Dublin, which would be used as the rebel headquarters, and a number of other strategic points in the city. Once the GPO had been taken, on Monday morning, Pearse appeared in front of the building to read a proclamation declaring independence and the creation of an Irish republic. Most of the people of Dublin, however, remained unaware of the rebellion until sporadic firing began around Dublin Castle, the home of the British administration. A rebel attack was quickly beaten off by British guards. British forces in the city, now alerted to the situation, began counterattacking.

Over the next five days, several battles occurred, a few with heavy casualties on both sides. The British brought up artillery to bombard the GPO, and the center of Dublin was badly damaged. The superior numbers and equipment of the British troops gradually squeezed all of the rebel positions in a tightening stranglehold until, on the following Saturday evening, April 29, Pearse agreed to surrender. The word spread to other rebel posts and, by Sunday morning, the Easter Rebellion was over.

Impact of Event

The immediate impact of the Easter Rebellion was minimal: It was seen at the time as a total failure. Certainly, it did not establish an independent Irish republic, the primary goal. Within a few days after the surrender, nearly every important member of the IRB had been rounded up and was in jail, on his way to a court-martial for treason. Rank and file members of the Volunteers who had participated in the rising were disarmed and sent home. The British administration did not even declare martial law, and life in Dublin went on much as it had before the rebellion.

Nor did the rising at first have much effect on attitudes in Ireland. Most people outside Dublin had not even been aware that a rebellion was occurring until it was over: They read about it in the newspapers. In the capital itself, the insurrection had elicited little support from the populace. The first reaction to the takeover of the General Post Office was widespread looting in downtown department stores. Rebels marching to join the fighting were often jeered at; onlookers yelled that, if the Volunteers wanted to fight someone, they should join the army and fight the Germans. When British reinforcements arrived in Dublin, on Wednesday, April 26, dozens of Irish women greeted them with tea and cakes. The general disgust at the rising was revealed as captured rebels were marched off to jail: Many Dubliners loudly suggested that they should be shot.

That is precisely what happened. Three days after the surrender, the executions started. Within two weeks, hasty courts-martial of the leaders of the rebellion were followed by seventy-seven death sentences. Many were convicted on weak or even irrelevant evidence, without any clear reason. Although ultimately only fifteen executions were carried out, these were extremely shocking to many of the Irish people, who now began to reassess their views. Most remained supporters of home rule and the peaceful evolution of Irish freedom, but sympathy for the heroism of the doomed rebels was developing. As Patrick Pearse had predicted, they had made the blood sacrifice necessary for the Irish people to realize their own nationhood. While World War I dragged on and home rule remained suspended, an increasing number of the Irish questioned whether the British would ever give them their independence.

In the meantime, many of the remaining leaders of the rising were given reprieves by the British government, and they immediately began reorganizing the IRB and the Volunteers, this time to fight political, rather than military, battles. The new goal was to defeat the British in Parliament by replacing the Irish supporters of home rule with republicans. In election propaganda, the republicans constantly portrayed the executed leaders of the Easter Rebellion as patriots who had been murdered for their heroic service to Ireland's freedom.

The British themselves inadvertently aided this effort in 1917 by threatening to impose conscription on Ireland, as had been done in Great Britain. Although the threat was never carried out, all shades of nationalist opinion greatly resented it. A turning point had been reached, as indicated by the elections of 1918, shortly after the Armistice was signed. Avowed republicans overwhelmingly defeated home rulers in three-fourths of all Irish parliamentary constituencies. Rather than going to London, however, the new Irish members met together in Dublin, calling themselves the "Dail Eireann," which was Gaelic for "Irish Parliament." In January, 1919, they declared Ireland an independent republic. By then, they had widespread support throughout the country. Ireland was finally on the road to real independence.

Bibliography

Caulfield, Malachy. *The Easter Rebellion.* New York: Holt, Rinehart and Winston, 1963. An extremely well-written and entertaining account of the rebellion. Caulfield depicts the rising in a highly dramatic, moment-by-moment style, attempting to see into the minds of the participants on all sides. Although he portrays the republicans as heroes, his point of view is generally balanced.

Fitzgerald, Redmond. *Cry Blood, Cry Erin.* New York: C. N. Potter, 1966. A colorful discussion of the Irish nationalist movement from the early nineteenth century to the end of the Irish civil war in 1923. Written from a nationalist perspective by an Irishman obviously sympathetic to the republicans. The main virtue of this work is its outstanding series of illustrations, especially many clearly reproduced photographs from the period 1914-1923.

Kee, Robert. *Ireland: A History.* London: Weidenfeld & Nicolson, 1980. This is probably the best introduction to Irish history, particularly to the centuries-long conflict between Ireland and Britain, for the general reader. Kee debunks many of the myths of Irish history and also shows how they influenced future events, effectively connecting past and present.

McHugh, Roger, ed. *Dublin 1916: An Illustrated Anthology.* New York: D. Elliot, 1980. A very unusual compilation of diary entries, autobiographical accounts by participants, contemporary newspaper stories, interviews, essays, poetry, and historical articles related to the rising. McHugh attempts not only to retell the story of the rebellion but also to put the mind of the reader in the midst of its milieu by going beyond more traditional historical methods. Also includes excellent illustrations.

Martin, F. X., ed. *Leaders and Men of the Easter Rising: Dublin 1916.* Ithaca, N.Y.: Cornell University Press, 1967. Includes nineteen articles by prominent Irish historians sketching both individuals and issues on all sides of the Easter Rebellion. Especially helpful are an essay on Augustine Birrell and the British administration, as well as a chapter on the part played by the Anglo-Irish Ascendancy class. Each chapter includes a short bibliography.

Nowlan, Kevin B., ed. *The Making of 1916: Studies in the History of the Rising.* Dublin, Ireland: Stationery Office, 1969. A collection of articles commissioned by the Irish government to commemorate the fiftieth anniversary of the rebellion. Surprisingly objective, despite its sponsor. Several of the essays provide useful background material, and two unusual chapters explain the influence of the Gaelic cultural movement on the nationalist movement.

O'Broin, Leon. *Dublin Castle and the 1916 Rising.* New York: New York University Press, 1971. The only full-length discussion of the response of the British administration in Dublin to the rising. Although scholarly in intent, it is nevertheless very readable by a general audience. O'Broin's experience as secretary of the Irish Department of Posts and Telegraphs is reflected in his ability to present the rebellion from the viewpoint of the government bureaucracy.

Thomas C. Schunk

Cross-References

The Paris Peace Conference Includes Protection for Minorities (1919), p. 252; Ireland Is Granted Home Rule and Northern Ireland Is Created (1920), p. 309; The Statute of Westminster Creates the Commonwealth (1931), p. 453; British Troops Restore Order in Northern Ireland (1969), p. 1485; The Emergency Provisions (Northern Ireland) Act Is Passed (1973), p. 1720; An IRA Prisoner Dies in an English Prison After a Hunger Strike (1976), p. 1870; Two Founders of Peace People Win the Nobel Peace Prize (1977), p. 1932.

SANGER OPENS THE FIRST BIRTH-CONTROL CLINIC IN THE UNITED STATES

Category of event: Reproductive freedom
Time: October 16, 1916
Locale: Brooklyn, New York

The first birth-control clinic, opened by Margaret Sanger, publicized the need for safe and available contraception and ignited a movement to secure reproductive freedom for all women

Principal personages:
MARGARET SANGER (1879-1966), the American leader in the birth-control movement
ETHEL BYRNE (1883-1955), a nurse and the sister of Margaret Sanger, whose hunger strike in 1917 attracted nationwide attention
FANIA MINDELL, an interpreter and birth-control advocate from Chicago who helped organize and open the Brownsville clinic
JONAH J. GOLDSTEIN (1886-1967), the attorney who represented Margaret Sanger, Ethel Byrne, and Fania Mindell following their arrests at the Brownsville clinic
FREDERICK E. CRANE (1869-1947), a New York State Court of Appeals justice
ANTHONY COMSTOCK (1844-1915), the American morals crusader who lobbied for a series of antiobscenity laws

Summary of Event

By 1850, state and federal legislation had outlawed most forms of contraception in the United States. The "Comstock Law," passed in 1873 and named for the antivice crusader Anthony Comstock, labeled contraception "obscene" and banned the circulation of contraceptive information through the mails. Although government antagonism did not deter middle- and upper-class families from voluntarily reducing their birth rates—by acquiring contraceptive knowledge through sympathetic doctors or deceptive mail-order firms—legal restrictions and moral inhibitions prevented most poor and uneducated women from using birth control, although many women resorted to crude, ineffective, and often dangerous practices. Attempts to distribute birth control proved largely unsuccessful until Margaret Sanger began her pioneering crusade in 1916 by opening the first birth-control clinic in the United States, a revolutionary event that initiated a social movement dedicated to legalizing contraception and liberating sexuality.

Margaret Sanger first took an interest in sex education and birth control in the early 1910's as a young nurse in New York City, where she accompanied doctors to the tenement districts of New York's Lower East Side. There she met women who suffered from exhaustion, venereal disease, and the consequences of self-induced abortions—women who pleaded to know the "secrets" to controlling their fertility that were denied them by their churches and government.

Sanger's experiences as a nurse persuaded her to seek a means of educating women about their bodies. Encouraged and advised by friends from New York's intellectual salons and radical political circles, including such vocal advocates of birth control as Emma Goldman, Elizabeth Gurley Flynn, and Bill Haywood, Sanger left nursing to devote herself to helping women acquire safe and effective contraception, not only to prevent unwanted pregnancies but also to give women the choice of greater sexual freedom.

Over the next four years, Sanger published articles and pamphlets on sexual hygiene and contraceptive techniques, using information she had gathered during trips abroad to France, England, and Holland and assimilated under the tutelage of the English sex psychologist Havelock Ellis. In 1914, Sanger's most controversial publication, an extremist newspaper called *The Women Rebel*, prompted postal authorities to indict Sanger for violating obscenity laws. Her trial was eventually dismissed, but the publicity generated by her arrest and the subsequent arrest and imprisonment of her husband, William Sanger, for distributing a birth-control pamphlet created a legion of new supporters.

From April to July of 1916, Sanger toured the country, drumming up support for her controversial cause. She met vocal and stubborn resistance, but audiences overwhelmingly supported the notion of legalized birth control and Sanger's demand for women's sexual emancipation. The tour convinced Sanger of the need for affordable, accessible clinics. Upon her return to New York in October, Sanger moved quickly to capitalize on the publicity generated by her speaking appearances. She vowed to extend the fight for legalized birth control into a direct-action campaign—the opening of a clinic.

In early October of 1916, Sanger, with her sister Ethel Byrne, a nurse, and Fania Mindell, an interpreter from Chicago, rented a small storefront apartment in Brownsville, a working-class Jewish and Italian neighborhood in Brooklyn. The three women canvassed the dingy grid of tenements and circulated flyers printed in English, Italian, and Yiddish that advertised the clinic and offered information on birth prevention from trained nurses.

On October 16, Sanger, Byrne, and Mindell opened the doors of a makeshift birth-control clinic modelled after state-run clinics in Holland that Sanger had observed in 1915. On the first day alone, more than one hundred women obtained contraceptive advice. For ten cents, each woman received one of Sanger's sexual hygiene pamphlets and instruction on the proper use of contraceptives. The clinic also distributed suppositories and condoms.

Sanger and her coworkers kept careful records on each new client and listened to emotional accounts of difficult pregnancies, neglected children, and illegal abortions. One woman told Sanger, "When I was married, the priest told us to have lots of children, and we listened to him. I had fifteen. Six are living. Nine baby funerals in our house."

More than four hundred women came to the clinic before an undercover police-woman and vice-squad officers arrived on the tenth day and placed Sanger, Byrne, and Mindell under arrest for distributing contraceptive devices. After a night in prison and arraignment in court, Sanger reopened the clinic but was arrested a second time on November 14 and charged with maintaining a public nuisance. Sanger opened the clinic for a third time on November 16, but police forced the clinic land-lord to evict his tenants, and the clinic closed its doors permanently.

The arrests of Sanger, Byrne, and Mindell and their ensuing trials thrust the issue of birth control onto the front pages of the nation's newspapers, giving the cause its greatest publicity to date. Ethel Byrne came to trial first on January 4, 1917. She entered a courtroom filled with socially prominent women from New York, organized by Gertrude Minturn Pinchot as the "Committee of One Hundred," a group that financed much of the early work of the birth-control movement. Byrne's attorney, Jonah J. Goldstein, argued that the New York state law that made it a misdemeanor for anyone to distribute contraception—except for doctors in cases of venereal disease—opposed the best interests and well-being of the people. The court, however, refused to hear any medical testimony in support of Goldstein's claims; they sentenced Byrne to thirty days in Blackwell's Island prison.

Byrne immediately went on a hunger strike, following the example of English suffragettes. The publicity tactic succeeded, and the press ran daily reports of Byrne's weakened condition. After 185 hours without food or water, Byrne was forcibly fed, prompting Sanger and the Committee of One Hundred to protest to legislators and state officials and to call for Byrne's release at a giant rally for birth control at Carnegie Hall on January 26. Several days later, Sanger and Pinchot convinced Governor Charles Seymour Whitman to release Byrne before her condition proved fatal.

Sanger's trial began on January 29 before a courtroom crowded with fifty women who had visited the Brownsville clinic. Several of them testified for the prosecution, stating that they had received contraceptive information from Sanger. While these witnesses incriminated Sanger, their accounts of infant deaths, miscarriages, and severe poverty substantiated the need for birth-control clinics to many throughout the country who followed the case. After several days of testimony, the court offered Sanger a suspended sentence if she promised to uphold the law. She refused and was sentenced to thirty days in prison. Meanwhile, the court convicted Fania Mindell of distributing obscene material and fined her fifty dollars.

Sanger served her time in prison without incident and appealed her conviction. Her case journeyed through the courts for nearly a year before Judge Frederick E. Crane of the New York Court of Appeals sustained Sanger's conviction on January 8, 1918. Crane's liberal interpretation of the law, however, enabled physicians to prescribe contraception for general health reasons, rather than exclusively for venereal disease, making the law non-gender-specific, since only men had previously received birth control for the prevention of disease. Crane's decision also provided a degree of legal protection for future clinics that employed a certified physician. The new interpretation of the law was a small victory for the birth-control movement but an emphatic first step in overturning a series of state and federal legal restrictions denying women the right to control their fertility.

Impact of Event

The Brownsville clinic provided a rallying point and a cause célèbre for the early organizers of the birth-control movement. Supporters of the first clinic went on to form, in 1921, the American Birth Control League, a powerful lobby group for legislative change, and in 1923, the Birth Control Clinical Research Bureau, the prototype for a chain of doctor-staffed birth-control clinics that opened across the country in the 1920's. Moreover, the publicity generated by the Brownsville clinic brought the issue of birth control into the nation's living rooms, churches, and schools, and led to a more open discussion of sexuality, gender roles, and family planning.

In fact, the opening of the first clinic and the emergence of a viable national movement marked a momentous shift in the sexual attitudes of middle-class America. The very idea of available birth control challenged traditional beliefs about marriage and family. The substantial support for legalized, accessible contraception among the middle classes signaled a general approval of sex for pleasure and a growing acceptance of female sexual expression within the marriage bond. As birth control became more widely used in the 1920's, more women had the option of choosing careers and endeavors outside the home and found greater autonomy in both their public and private lives.

The effectiveness of the Brownsville clinic in increasing the nation's awareness of birth control did not, however, immediately increase the availability of contraception for the poor. Rather, the legal consequences of the Brownsville case—giving doctors the only legal authority to dispense contraceptives—excluded poor women from increased contraceptive availability, since few could afford medical care. Even in the 1920's, few working-class women had access to safe and reliable contraceptives; withdrawal and rhythm were still the most popular methods of birth control.

Furthermore, the increased dependence on doctors for birth control initiated an alliance with the medical profession that shifted the impetus of the birth-control movement from women's rights to medical advocacy, leaving women with a diminished role in controlling the means of contraception. At the same time, Sanger turned increasingly to the guidance and financial support of the socially prominent and wealthy, who were generally more concerned with reducing birth rates than with empowering women to achieve equality through the control of their own bodies. Not until the 1960's and the rise of the women's movement was birth control redefined as a reproductive rights issue rather than primarily a medical one.

The Brownsville clinic laid the foundation for the future work of the birth-control movement and the personal crusade of Margaret Sanger. Sanger followed the same tactics she used in Brownsville—direct action, agitation, publicity, and education— to challenge further obscenity laws in the 1920's and 1930's and to solidify a network of clinics and sympathetic physicians so that a majority of Americans had access to birth control by World War II. Sanger's crusade for safe, available, and effective birth control culminated in the 1950's, when she organized the international birth-control movement and arranged financial support for the development of the birth-control pill. The activist, reformer, writer, and mother of three died in 1966 at the age of eighty-seven, having devoted her life to family planning, sexual enlightenment, and reproductive autonomy for all women.

Bibliography

D'Emilio, John, and Estelle B. Freedman. *Intimate Matters: A History of Sexuality in America.* New York: Harper & Row, 1988. A scholarly interpretation of the history of sexuality that includes two chapters on Sanger and a short account of the Brownsville clinic. The authors' analyses of contraceptive techniques, devices, and availability make this a valuable resource to the student of reproductive freedom and the birth-control movement.

Gordon, Linda. *Woman's Body, Woman's Right: A Social History of Birth Control in America.* New York: Penguin Books, 1977. A thorough social history of women's sexuality, feminism, and birth control. Gordon argues persuasively that the birth-control movement coalesced around women united by their shared experience, but that Sanger, in particular, impeded women's progress toward achieving reproductive self-determination by courting elites and the medical establishment. Gordon's account of the Brownsville clinic is short but insightful. Includes an index and reference notes.

Kennedy, David M. *Birth Control in America: The Career of Margaret Sanger.* New Haven, Conn.: Yale University Press, 1970. A useful social history of the formative years of the birth-control movement but a flawed biographical study of Sanger's career, filled with unsupported criticisms of Sanger's leadership abilities. Kennedy overlooks Sanger's skills as a publicist and minimizes several of her major achievements, including the opening of the Brownsville clinic. Includes an index and select bibliography.

Reed, James. *From Private Vice to Public Virtue: The Birth Control Movement and American Society Since 1830.* New York: Basic Books, 1978. A resourceful history of birth control with a biographical focus on four major figures (Sanger, Robert Dickinson, Clarence Gamble, and Gregory Pincus). Reed's recognition of Sanger's organizational and public relations skills corrects many distortions in Kennedy's earlier treatment. Includes a short summary of the Brownsville clinic, a bibliographic essay, and an extensive index.

Sanger, Margaret. *My Fight for Birth Control.* New York: Farrar & Rinehart, 1931. Sanger's first autobiography, which includes an extended but sometimes inaccurate account of the Brownsville clinic and subsequent trials. The book is largely a work of propaganda but offers insight into Sanger's social and political vision. Illustrations, but no reference features.

_____. *Margaret Sanger: An Autobiography.* New York: W. W. Norton, 1938.

Sanger's second and more polished autobiography condenses the account of the Brownsville clinic in *My Fight for Birth Control* but provides a better context for the event. It tells how Sanger wished to be perceived. Includes an index.

Peter C. Engelman

Cross-References

The Nineteenth Amendment Gives American Women the Right to Vote (1920), p. 339; Sanger Organizes Conferences on Birth Control (1921), p. 356; The National Council of Churches Supports Birth Control (1961), p. 1096; The Supreme Court Rules That State Laws Cannot Ban Contraceptives (1965), p. 1290; The National Organization for Women Forms to Protect Women's Rights (1966), p. 1327; *Roe v. Wade* Expands Reproductive Choice for American Women (1973), p. 1703; Prolife Groups Challenge Abortion Laws (1989), p. 2443; The National Organization for Women Sponsors an Abortion Rights Rally (1989), p. 2489.

RANKIN BECOMES THE FIRST WOMAN
ELECTED TO CONGRESS

Category of event: Women's rights
Time: November 7, 1916
Locale: Montana

Jeannette Rankin became the first woman elected to the United States House of Representatives in 1916, four years before the Nineteenth Amendment extended suffrage to all women in the United States

> *Principal personages:*
> JEANNETTE RANKIN (1880-1973), the first woman elected to the United States Congress
> CARRIE CHAPMAN CATT (1859-1947), the president of the National American Woman Suffrage Association
> HATTIE W. CARAWAY (1878-1950), the first woman elected to the United States Senate, filled out the term of her deceased husband and was reelected to two terms of her own
> ELIZABETH CADY STANTON (1815-1902), an early feminist who was one of the first to realize the importance of women serving in legislative bodies

Summary of Event

Jeannette Rankin's 1916 election to the United States House of Representatives was a landmark occasion. Only a few women had ever held public office in the United States, none on the national level. Officeholding was almost always conditional upon suffrage (voting). Because women could not vote in most of the United States until the twentieth century, they rarely held public office.

The American colonies, and later the United States, based their legal system on English common law. Under common law, a married woman could not own property (even property which she brought into the marriage) and had no legal identity separate from her husband's. During the colonial period, voting and officeholding usually were restricted to property owners and hence closed to married women. There were a few instances of unmarried women (spinsters or widows) as property owners voting in the colonial period, and at least one woman tried to serve in a colonial legislature. On January 21, 1648, Margaret Brent, a landowner who would have been entitled to a vote in the assembly if she had been a man, tried unsuccessfully to be seated in the Maryland House of Burgesses. She demanded two votes in the assembly, one as the executrix for the estate of the deceased governor and one for herself as a freeholder.

After the American Revolution, qualifications for voting and holding office gradually were relaxed. Nothing in the Articles of Confederation or the Constitution specifically prohibited women from voting or holding office. These decisions were left to the states. For a brief time after the Revolution, some women voted in a few states. As the states drew up constitutions, most specifically restricted suffrage to males over the age of twenty-one and began to eliminate property qualifications for voting and holding office. Soon, all adult white males were eligible to vote in all states, while no woman could vote anywhere.

Women in the United States were more concerned in those years with their economic and legal status than with their political status. The rights to vote and to hold public office were so far outside their experience that most did not even realize that they could demand them. Women's concerns focused on economic and social issues, such as protection from abusive husbands, the right to initiate divorce proceedings, and control over their earnings, their property, and their children. Many were encouraged when New York became the first state to pass a married woman's property act (1849) and was emulated by several other states. Women still had to contend with many laws that were not in their best interests.

There were a few women who realized that the only way they could influence legislation and get rid of discriminatory laws was by voting for and serving as members of legislative bodies. One of these was Elizabeth Cady Stanton, who, with Lucretia Mott and three other women, called the Women's Rights Convention held at Seneca Falls, New York, on July 19 and 20, 1848. It adopted the "Declaration of Sentiments and Resolutions," modeled upon the Declaration of Independence, which cited women's grievances against men, including the denial of suffrage to women and their resulting lack of representation in legislative bodies. The ninth resolution, calling for woman suffrage, was considered so radical that it passed by a narrow margin only after heated debate and was the only one not passed unanimously.

Although some women in eastern states organized for the right to vote after the Seneca Falls convention, the first gains for woman suffrage and officeholding came in the West. In 1869, the Wyoming Territorial Legislature passed the first woman suffrage bill in the United States. In February, 1870, Esther Morris of South Pass City, Wyoming, became justice of the peace. She was nominated for the legislature in 1873 but withdrew before the election. Wyoming continued woman suffrage when it became a state in 1890 and was joined by Colorado (1893), Idaho (1896), and Utah (1896). Utah also allowed woman suffrage as a territory, 1870-1887.

It was during the suffrage campaign in Washington State that Jeannette Rankin began her involvement in political activity as a means of improving conditions for women and children. Like many reformers of the Progressive Era, she discovered the plight of the poor during visits to several cities. At the time, she was a restless young woman from Missoula, Montana, searching for her place in life. She attended the New York School of Philanthropy, where she learned from many of the country's leading social activists. She was graduated in 1909 and worked briefly as a social worker, becoming so frustrated by laws which handicapped rather than helped women and children that she left social work. She enrolled at the University of Washington and worked for the woman suffrage movement there. Her role in the Washington suffrage victory (1910) was small, but she perceived woman suffrage as the way to change laws unfair to women and children.

On February 2, 1911, she spoke to the Montana legislature on behalf of a woman suffrage bill and asked that it be submitted to the voters in a referendum. It was narrowly defeated. Rankin had, however, inspired many Montana women, who offered their assistance in a future suffrage campaign. She also attracted attention from suffragists outside Montana who invited her to join their campaigns. Her experience working in suffrage campaigns in New York, California, Ohio, Florida, and Michigan led to her appointment as a field secretary for the National American Woman Suffrage Association (NAWSA) in 1913.

When the Montana legislature called a woman suffrage referendum in 1914, Rankin resigned from NAWSA and returned to Montana to lead the campaign for suffrage. As president of the Montana Equal Suffrage State Central Committee, she traveled throughout the state. While building a network to support suffrage, she also laid the foundation for her later campaign for public office. She focused on ways women voters could improve conditions relating to the home and children's welfare.

On July 11, 1916, Rankin announced that she would be a candidate for one of Montana's two at-large seats in the United States House of Representatives. Although most of her ideas leaned toward those of the Progressive Party, she filed as a Republican candidate. One of eight candidates (and the only woman), she campaigned widely throughout the state, with her brother, Wellington Rankin, serving as her campaign manager. She accused the federal government of caring more about hogs than children and contended that Congress needed a woman to look after the interests of children. She was not the only woman running for Congress in 1916: There were unsuccessful female candidates in California, Colorado, and Washington.

As first, it looked as though Rankin had lost. She prepared to concede the election to the other Republican candidate, George Farr. The votes from the rural areas of eastern Montana changed the balance in Rankin's favor. Two days after the election, Jeannette Rankin was declared the winner, the first woman ever elected to Congress. Her election was especially surprising given that the Democratic presidential candidate, Woodrow Wilson, carried Montana.

Impact of Event

Jeannette Rankin's election to the United States House of Representatives had significant impact on the political activities of women in the United States. It encouraged woman suffrage and served notice that elective public office was open to women.

The most immediate impact was on woman suffrage. Rankin's election encouraged all factions of suffragists. Such leaders as Carrie Chapman Catt of the NAWSA and Alice Paul of the National Woman's Party united temporarily in honoring Rankin before her swearing-in at the emergency session of Congress on April 2, 1917. When Rankin voted against the United States' entry into World War I on April 6,

1917, Catt reacted angrily, believing that Rankin's vote hurt the suffrage movement. Thereafter, the relationship between them was uneasy, with Catt supporting Rankin's male opponent in the 1918 Senate race. Nevertheless, Rankin cosponsored the proposed woman suffrage amendment to the U.S. Constitution and opened the debate in the House of Representatives on January 10, 1918. She was not, however, in the Congress which finally passed the Nineteenth Amendment in 1919 and had little role in the final campaign for it in Congress or in the ratification campaign that culminated in victory in August, 1920.

Rankin's election signified that elective public office, and especially membership in the United States Congress, was no longer restricted to men. She decided not to seek reelection to the House in 1918. Redistricting placed her in a congressional district where she had little support, and her vote on the war was very unpopular in Montana. She instead ran unsuccessfully for the Senate. Soon, however, there were women Congressional candidates, and a few of them were elected. Between Jeannette Rankin's first election to Congress in 1917 and her second on November 5, 1940, twenty-five women were elected to the House and one, Hattie Caraway of Arkansas, was elected to the Senate. (The first woman Senator, however, was Rebecca Latimer Felton of Georgia, who was appointed to fill a vacancy from October 2, 1922, to November 22, 1922.) The number of women serving in each Congress remained small, far below the percentage of women in the United States population. It was not until the 1982 election that the total number of women ever elected to the United States House of Representatives reached one hundred.

Women also made slow gains in other elective offices. Two women were elected as state governors in 1924. Nellie Tayloe Ross of Wyoming was elected to complete her deceased husband's term but was defeated for reelection in 1926. Miriam A. Ferguson of Texas was elected to complete the term of her impeached husband, James. She lost bids for reelection before winning another term in 1932. Not until 1974, when Ella Grasso was elected as governor of Connecticut, was a woman elected whose husband had not previously held the office. Since the 1970's, women have been elected to public office in the United States in greater numbers, especially on the state and local levels.

Bibliography

Chamberlin, Hope. *A Minority of Members: Women in the U.S. Congress.* New York: Praeger, 1973. This is a collection of brief personal and political biographies of the eighty-five women who served in the U.S. Congress between 1917 and 1972, with a postscript on the effects of the 1972 election. Good information on Rankin's elections and activities in Congress. Chart of women members of Congress 1917-1973. Some photographs. Index. Contains no references.

Flexner, Eleanor. *Century of Struggle: The Woman's Rights Movement in the United States.* New York: Atheneum, 1968. This standard account of the women's rights movement is sound, if occasionally out of date because of new research. It has little information on Jeannette Rankin's election but is useful in placing it in the context of the women's rights and suffrage movements. Contains some illustrations, complete endnotes, and index.

Gertzog, Irwin N. *Congressional Women: Their Recruitment, Treatment, and Behavior.* New York: Praeger, 1984. This volume in the *Women and Politics* series contains little information about Rankin's elections or specific activities in Congress. It is useful in examining the overall effects of that election on later generations of women in the House of Representatives. Contains tables, appendices, and index. Complete list of references.

Giles, Kevin S. *Flight of the Dove: The Story of Jeannette Rankin.* Beaverton, Oreg.: Lochsa Experience, 1980. Biography focusing on Rankin as a dissident and feminist. It is useful for insights on her character and family relationships and for information about her elections to Congress (1916 and 1940). Extensive material on her antiwar activities. Contains a list of references and some photographs. No index.

Harper, Ida Husted. *History of Woman Suffrage, 1900-1920.* 1922. Reprint. New York: Arno, 1969. Fifth volume in the National American Woman Suffrage Association's official account of the suffrage movement. Contains limited information about Rankin's activities as a suffrage worker, her election, and her sponsorship of the suffrage amendment. Coverage reflects the cool relationship between Rankin and the NAWSA leadership. Some references in body of text, index, and appendices.

McGinty, Brian. "Jeannette Rankin: First Woman in Congress." *American History Illustrated* 23 (May, 1988): 32-33. Brief article focusing on Rankin's congressional career. Also contains brief biographical information and some references to her antiwar activities. Written for a popular audience. No references. One photograph.

The National American Woman Suffrage Association. *Victory: How Women Won It, A Centennial Exposition, 1840-1940.* New York: H. W. Wilson, 1940. Uncritical brief account of the achievement of woman suffrage. Reflects the NAWSA's position but gives little information on Rankin. Useful chart of woman suffrage in states and territories in appendix. Brief list of references. No index.

Wilson, Joan Hoff. " 'Peace Is a Woman's Job . . .': Jeannette Rankin and American Foreign Policy: The Origins of Her Pacifism." *Montana: The Magazine of Western History* 30 (January, 1980): 28-41. First of two parts. Deals primarily with Rankin's antiwar attitudes and actions. Brief but good biographical information and an analysis of the influences on her character. Some mention of her congressional campaign. Good analysis of biographical sources. Some photographs.

Woloch, Nancy. *Women and the American Experience.* New York: Alfred A. Knopf, 1984. General history of women in the United States. Chapters on feminism and suffrage and on the twentieth century help place Rankin's election in context. References, photographs, tables, and index.

Judith A. Parsons

Cross-References

The Pankhursts Found the Women's Social and Political Union (1903), p. 19; Finland Grants Woman Suffrage (1906), p. 70; Parliament Grants Suffrage to British Women (1918), p. 247; The Nineteenth Amendment Gives American Women the Right to Vote (1920), p. 339; Women's Rights in India Undergo a Decade of Change (1925), p. 401; Nellie Tayloe Ross of Wyoming Becomes the First Female Governor (1925), p. 412; The Minimum Age for Female British Voters Is Lowered (1928), p. 442; Franklin D. Roosevelt Appoints Perkins as Secretary of Labor (1933), p. 486; French Women Get the Vote (1944), p. 646; The U.N. Convention on the Political Rights of Women Is Approved (1952), p. 885; Women in Switzerland Are Granted the Right to Vote (1971), p. 1605; Thatcher Becomes Great Britain's First Female Prime Minister (1979), p. 2024; Benazir Bhutto Becomes the First Woman Elected to Lead a Muslim Country (1988), p. 2403.

THE MEXICAN CONSTITUTION ESTABLISHES
AN ADVANCED LABOR CODE

Category of event: Workers' rights
Time: 1917
Locale: Querétaro, Mexico

Article 123 of the Constitution of 1917 set the legal basis for unionization and other workers' rights that placed Mexico at the international forefront of labor activism

> *Principal personages:*
> FRANCISCO J. MÚGICA (1884-1954), a revolutionary politician and leading radical spokesman at the Constitutional Convention of 1917
> PASTOR ROUAIX (1874-1950), an engineer who entered revolutionary politics, the main author of Article 123
> VENUSTIANO CARRANZA (1859-1920), the president of Mexico (1915-1920)
> PORFIRIO DÍAZ (1830-1915), a political and military leader who became dictator in the late 1800's, forced to resign by the revolution in 1911
> LUIS MORONES (1890-1964), a labor organizer who used Article 123 to help build a powerful union in the 1920's
> VICENTE LOMBARDO TOLEDANO (1894-1968), a radical labor leader of the 1930's

Summary of Event

The difference between the violent repression of the 1906 miners' strike in Cananea, Sonora, in northwestern Mexico and the ultimately triumphant strike of oil workers in and around the Caribbean port of Tampico in the late 1930's is measured by more than time and distance. In the intervening three decades of revolutionary change, an obscure but determined group of political activists from across the nation gathered in the small, provincial city of Querétaro to write a constitution that contained one of the world's most advanced labor codes of its day. Article 123 of that constitution established the legal bases for unionization, strikes, and improved conditions for workers. Mexican labor unions' growth in membership and influence in the period between the strikes in Cananea and Tampico was directly related to Article 123.

The labor violence at Cananea was typical of the unrest in the last years of the dictatorship of Porfirio Díaz. Late nineteenth century railroad construction and foreign investment had stimulated an economic boom which, in spite of prominent pockets of prosperity, had also brought with it onerous working conditions in mines and factories. The laborer in a mine, a textile mill, or a brewery generally worked a seven-day week for ten or more hours a day. Pay was so low that workers had inadequate diets and lived in unsanitary housing. Foreign observers of the condition of these workers often dismissed the Mexican lower class as passive and practically helpless, a misconception soon discredited by the revolution.

Worker assertiveness began to emerge in 1906. The American-owned Cananea Consolidated Copper Company's low wages for Mexican workers and inflated prices at its company stores sparked a confrontation with miners in Sonora. During five days of one-sided fighting, at least thirty workers and their family members perished. The strike ended in failure, but labor unrest spread to other areas.

Francisco Madero led the overthrow of Díaz in 1911, but his short-lived government never went beyond a limited program of political reform centered on elections and greater voter participation. The urgent demands of workers and peasants for social and economic change became more strident as the feebleness of the Madero policies became apparent. Madero's government was overthrown in 1913 by a recalcitrant military faction, and Madero was shot while allegedly attempting to escape. By then, workers were active in several revolutionary movements. In particular, a group called the House of the World's Worker promoted anarchist solutions for workers' problems.

By 1916, the regime of Venustiano Carranza had emerged from the chaos of the revolution with substantial support from anarchist labor unions, which supplied six "Red Battalions" of armed workers for the crucial fighting in 1915. Carranza saw that the adoption of a constitution would add legitimacy to his government and open a forum for the discussion of social and economic issues that had arisen in the revolution. His government organized the October, 1916, elections for a special congress to draw up a new constitution. After years of political disorder, only 20 to 30 percent of the eligible voters participated in the elections, and apparently no labor union or workers' party offered a labor candidate. Although the elected delegates were mostly middle class (more than one-half were college-educated professionals), the years of labor unrest gave them a decided awareness of the concerns of workers.

The radical leader Francisco J. Múgica had considerable influence in writing the constitution. The son of a provincial schoolteacher, Múgica saw the impact of poverty throughout Mexico during his decade of peripatetic revolutionary activity after 1906. One of the first to join in efforts to overthrow Díaz, Múgica was determined to mold the constitution into a legal device for sweeping social and economic reform, including betterment of the working class.

The primary author of Article 123 was a Carranza loyalist whose ideology was somewhat more moderate than the radicalism of Múgica. Pastor Rouaix, a forty-two-year-old engineer, was typical of the mixture of middle- and lower-class influences in the convention. The son of a mestizo construction worker, Rouaix was a quiet, conscientious student who surpassed his humble origins when he earned an engineering degree and became a successful surveyor. His rise in politics was rapid. Between 1913 and 1917, he was governor of Durango and headed Carranza's Ministry of Development. Throughout his political career, he revealed a consistent sense of social conscience that derived from his youth, when he had seen exploitative merchants and landowners practicing their wiles on unwitting workers and peasants.

Even though he was not a gifted orator, Rouaix was the guiding force behind the drafting of Article 123. He and a handful of colleagues wrote the original draft in a series of meetings during the first two weeks of January, 1917. He relied on the work of several staff members from the Ministry of Development who had assembled studies on labor conditions in Mexico and labor legislation in other nations. The Rouaix group's concern about the plight of workers in Mexico led it to move far beyond existing labor law to give the national government the central role in the amelioration of these conditions.

With Múgica's powerful presence behind the proposed Article 123, Rouaix and his colleagues enjoyed a surprisingly easy victory when their proposal reached the floor of the constitutional convention. The discussion of Article 123 took place during the evening of January 23. The previous successes of Múgica and the radicals apparently had established the tenor of the debate. By 10:15 P.M., the delegates, weary from earlier sessions and impressed by the left's enthusiasm, voted their approval.

The final version was a ringing endorsement of the cause of the working people and, in particular, the organization of labor unions. As a part of the document, called the Constitution of 1917, Article 123 established a maximum eight-hour workday, abolished debt peonage, and recognized the strike as a legitimate tool in labor-management relations. Article 123 also created government standards to benefit the health and safety of workers and required the states to pass minimum wage laws and other regulations to benefit workers. These changes did not go into effect immediately, of course, because the new constitutional provisions required additional national and state legislation, the formation of government agencies to oversee enforcement, and time for workers to form unions to initiate their own actions. Even though these reforms were more abstract than real, the course of Mexican labor history had clearly taken a profoundly different direction.

Carranza signed the constitution into effect on January 31, 1917, some nine months before the outbreak of the Bolshevik Revolution in Russia. Mexico's new labor code was based on the acceptance of private property and free enterprise, so it was not as extreme as the system-shattering program of the Bolsheviks. This comparison is misleading, because it takes the Mexican Constitution out of its context. The Mexican environment was one in which large estates and corporations (often owned in part or wholly by United States, British, or French investors) dominated the commercially active sectors of the economy. The Constitution of 1917, through its labor code (and other radical sections such as Article 27, restricting the rights of property ownership), threatened to disrupt established patterns of business operations in order to improve the lives of workers. In that sense, Article 123 was a radical part of a revolutionary document.

Impact of Event

The Carranza government did not immediately enforce Article 123, but the presence of this new labor code was a large stimulus to the growth of labor unions. The anarchist unions quickly joined forces in the Regional Confederation of Mexican Workers (CROM), headed by the ambitious Luis Morones. Morones established CROM in 1918, and in ten years claimed, with exaggeration, that it had nearly two million members. Adept at politics as well as union organization, Morones was minister of industry in the cabinet of President Plutarco Elías Calles (1924-1928) and used his executive authority to extend the application of Article 123 to the benefit of CROM. Working conditions and wages improved, but not for everyone. Unions outside CROM saw few improvements and usually lost influence and members to Morones. Wages rose significantly for some sectors of CROM as a result of a series of government-settled labor disputes that favored workers over management. Most Mexican workers, however, were left out of these improvements. New migrants to the cities from rural areas found limited opportunities for employment, and the available nonunion jobs carried low salaries. Article 123 remained an unfulfilled promise for Mexican workers except for the fortunate groups within the ranks of CROM.

Morones suffered severe defeats in the political struggles of the late 1920's, defeats which were exacerbated by his flamboyant corruption. CROM splintered into factions, one of which—the Confederation of Mexican Workers (CTM)—emerged under the leadership of Vicente Lombardo Toledano in the 1930's. Lombardo, a lean-figured, sharp-tongued, free-willed Marxist, collaborated with President Lázaro Cárdenas (1934-1940) to propel the CTM to a position of power in national politics. The reform of federal labor laws in 1931 had broadened even further the impact of Article 123 and furnished Lombardo and Cárdenas with an even stronger tool in their dealings with labor. More important, more than two decades of labor activism finally had produced a movement that could not be denied. Lombardo, a close ally of Cárdenas, sponsored a variety of programs among workers, including sports and recreational events as well as mass meetings and educational conferences. Workers were not content with their higher prestige in the Depression decade, however, and demanded concrete improvements in wages and working conditions. They initiated a wave of disruptive strikes in the mid-1930's. Cárdenas and Lombardo supported them on these issues, and soon members of the CTM made impressive gains. For example, electrical and textile workers, streetcar operators, and miners struck for and received substantial wage increases. The ten-hour day and other oppressive working conditions of the Díaz years became the exception rather than the rule, at least in areas under the dominion of the CTM, which soon had well in excess of one million members. These material improvements in the lives of workers were more broadly based than the changes of the 1920's, but nonunion laborers again received only spillover from these benefits.

The most dramatic evidence of the increased power of organized labor under Article 123 came in the 1938 confrontation between Mexico's oil workers' union (allied with the CTM) and United States and British petroleum companies. In an assertion of spontaneous union activism, Mexican oil workers around Tampico used strikes to demand improved wages and working conditions in the oil fields. The oil companies refused to grant these demands and defied not only the unions but also Mexican law and, by implication, Article 123. President Cárdenas responded decisively. On

March 18, 1938, he signed a decree which nationalized the oil properties of the defiant companies, thereby placing the Mexican government in charge of the bulk of the petroleum industry. The working-class population of Mexico City engaged in a massive demonstration of support for the nationalization. On March 22, an estimated crowd of 200,000 people, led by the CTM and the oil workers' union, celebrated what many present hailed as Mexico's economic declaration of independence. Article 123 and union activism contributed to this assertion of nationalism, which had repercussions throughout Latin America and other Third World regions for years to come. During the Cárdenas presidency, Mexican workers made significant gains both in material terms and in terms of their sense of involvement in national life.

Article 123 triggered two decades of labor unionization and union activism in Mexico, but by the 1940's, the initial impetus for reform declined. The CTM was a large and powerful organization, but as it became enmeshed in politics, the thrust of worker initiatives collapsed under the weight of union and government bureaucracy. CTM leaders continued to have decisive influence in national life, but they often seemed more concerned about elite politics than about the needs of ordinary workers. The history of Article 123 remained, however, a symbol and an example of the legitimization of unionization and the empowerment of the working class.

Bibliography

Anderson, Rodney D. *Outcasts in Their Own Land: Mexican Industrial Workers, 1906-1911.* De Kalb: Northern Illinois University Press, 1976. A careful study of working conditions in mines and factories and the consequent labor unrest that contributed to the coming of the revolution and the writing of Article 123.

Ashby, Joe C. *Organized Labor and the Mexican Revolution Under Lázaro Cárdenas.* Chapel Hill: University of North Carolina Press, 1967. A detailed study of labor activism in the 1930's, including the oil workers' strike and the expropriation of the property of United States and British oil companies. Reveals the ramifications of Article 123 under Cárdenas.

Hart, John M. *Anarchism and the Mexican Working Class, 1860-1931.* Austin: University of Texas Press, 1987. An analysis of the rise and decline of anarchist groups in the Mexican labor movement. Mexican anarchists insisted that the future lay with a vision of a decentralized industrial society, but their movement was lost in the political machinations and military repression of the mid-1910's.

_____. *Revolutionary Mexico. The Coming and Process of the Mexican Revolution.* Berkeley: University of California Press, 1987. An interpretive history from the Díaz era to 1924 that provides an extensive discussion of the causes of labor unrest (Chapter 2), the struggle and defeat of an autonomous labor movement (Chapter 9), and the triumph of the central government over worker and peasant movements (Chapter 10). Hart includes essays that compare the Mexican revolution with revolutions in Iran, China, and Russia (Chapters 7 and 11).

Knight, Alan. *The Mexican Revolution.* 2 vols. Cambridge, England: Cambridge University Press, 1986. A massive survey and analysis that focuses on events from

1910 to 1920. The author's commentary on the political, economic, and social issues of the revolution extends over a much broader chronological framework. Although Knight attributes limited importance to the Constitution of 1917, his text provides a thorough examination of the revolutionary setting in which it was written and the ups and downs of the labor movement throughout the decade.

Meyer, Michael C., and William L. Sherman. *The Course of Mexican History.* New York: Oxford University Press, 1990. A readable introductory text that combines clear style with a command of the full sweep of Mexican history from the Maya to the modern age. Chapters 32-34 give an overview of the events surrounding the emergence of the Constitution of 1917 and the labor movement within the context of the revolution.

Niemeyer, Eberhardt Victor. *Revolution at Querétaro: The Mexican Constitutional Convention of 1916-1917.* Austin: University of Texas Press, 1974. The most extensive study in English of politics, ideologies, and personalities that produced the Constitution of 1917. Chapter 4 covers the origins and content of Article 123. Niemeyer includes useful biographical sketches of the main authors of the constitution.

Richmond, Douglas W. *Venustiano Carranza's Nationalist Struggle, 1893-1920.* Lincoln: University of Nebraska Press, 1983. A full account of the rise and demise of Carranza. Richmond argues that Carranza was not a radical but a nationalist whose main goal was the restriction of United States economic power in Mexico. He accepted Article 123 but did little for its immediate implementation.

Ruiz, Ramón Eduardo. *Labor and the Ambivalent Revolutionaries: Mexico, 1911-1923.* Baltimore, Md.: The Johns Hopkins University Press, 1976. A succinct discussion of the relationship of revolutionary leaders such as Madero and Carranza with organized labor. Ruiz generalizes that leaders offered labor the promise of meaningful reform through Article 123 but had actually accomplished very little as of 1923.

John A. Britton

Cross-References

Supreme Court Disallows a Maximum Hours Law for Bakers (1905), p. 36; The British Labour Party Is Formed (1906), p. 58; Massachusetts Adopts the First Minimum-Wage Law in the United States (1912), p. 126; Lenin and the Communists Impose the "Red Terror" (1917), p. 218; Lenin Leads the Russian Revolution (1917), p. 225; The International Labour Organisation Is Established (1919), p. 281; Steel Workers Go on Strike to Demand Improved Working Conditions (1919), p. 293; The Wagner Act Requires Employers to Accept Collective Bargaining (1935), p. 508; The Congress of Industrial Organizations Is Formed (1938), p. 545; Perón Creates a Populist Political Alliance in Argentina (1946), p. 673; Castro Takes Power in Cuba (1959), p. 1026.

BOLSHEVIKS DENY ALL RIGHTS TO THE RUSSIAN ORTHODOX CHURCH

Category of event: Religious freedom
Time: 1917-1918
Locale: Russia

In 1918, the new Bolshevik government began confiscating church property, forbidding religious instruction in schools, and taking civil rights away from priests

Principal personages:
> TIKHON, VASILY BELAVIN (1865-1925), the first Russian patriarch of the Orthodox church since the time of Peter the Great; led the church against the Bolsheviks from 1918 to 1923
> VLADIMIR ILICH LENIN (1870-1924), the architect of the October, 1917, Bolshevik Revolution
> GEORGY Y. LVOV (1861-1925), the titular head of the provisional government from March until July, 1917

Summary of Event

The Bolshevik Revolution of October, 1917, meant serious trouble for the Russian Orthodox church. Church authorities for centuries had closely associated themselves with the Russian monarchy. The Russian church had evolved from the Greek Orthodox church, which followed the doctrine of caesaropapism; that is, the head of the state was also the head of the church. In the tenth century, Kievan Grand Prince Vladimir made Orthodox Christianity the official religion of Russia.

For a period in the seventeenth century, during the "Time of Troubles," the head of the church (the patriarch) emerged as a more important political leader than the Russian emperor, but Peter the Great reestablished the power of the emperor over the church in the eighteenth century. Peter created the Holy Synod to replace the patriarch as head of the church. Synod members were selected by the emperor. Despite the protests of many radical priests in the nineteenth century, state control of the church remained intact into the twentieth century.

At the time of the 1917 revolutions, the Russian Orthodox church was still a powerful institution. It continued to receive political and financial benefits from the government of Czar Nicholas II through 1916. Nevertheless, when the February revolution of 1917 overthrew the czar, the Holy Synod offered Nicholas II only perfunctory support. Although some Orthodox priests, particularly in the rural areas, remained loyal and even refused to admit that the czar had abdicated, there were many in the clergy who not only backed the February revolutionaries but also wished to see the order of Russian society completely overturned. The lower clergy in the church long had been associated with radical reform activity. It was not unusual for radical priests to take the lead in anticzarist organizations.

The Holy Synod attempted to work positively with the provisional government established after Nicholas II's abdication, but it was not long before conservative members of the synod began to resent the government's attempt to advance the cause of church reform. Georgy Lvov, titular head of the provisional government in March, 1917, on several occasions tried to circumvent the Holy Synod to achieve reforms he believed to be necessary. Lvov had hoped that an all-Russian church council (*sobor*) that he had helped to plan for the autumn of 1917 would adopt reform measures, but he soon realized that the *sobor* would be restrained by the ultraconservative synod. Lvov's intended reforms were far from sweeping, but clergy at all levels were alarmed that he wanted to reduce the role of the church in education.

Throughout the summer and early autumn of 1917, the church and the provisional government experienced numerous changes in leadership. In these circumstances, it was very difficult to reach an understanding as to what position and role the church would have in the new regime. By the end of July, 1917, uncertainty about the future drew liberal and conservative clergy together in defense of the church. There was grave concern that the church was on the verge of losing its privileged place in Russian society. This reality led the church's hierarchy to ally itself more firmly with conservative political interests. The church, therefore, continued to support Russia's participation in World War I at a time when the army was in shambles, large numbers of people were without food, and industry was at a standstill. Those who argued for dramatic social reform (especially the Bolshevik Party) were accused by the church of disloyalty to the country. Even reform-minded priests tended to support the war effort.

The provisional government, shaky and under attack from the left and the right since May, collapsed in September, 1917, and the Bolshevik Party seized control of the government in mid-October. Before the October Revolution, Orthodox church officials had condemned the Bolsheviks as traitors and haters of Christ. The organizers of the Bolshevik Revolution, Vladimir Ilich Lenin and Leon Trotsky, accepted the view of Karl Marx that religious belief made people fatalistic about their circumstances and sapped their will to accomplish needed change.

While the Bolsheviks were attempting to consolidate their authority in the days just after the revolution, the church *sobor* was in session. The *sobor*, a gathering of representatives from all ranks of the clergy, was swift in its condemnation of the Bolshevik takeover. Conservative leaders in the *sobor* believed that the time had come for the church, in a twentieth century Time of Troubles, to choose one person to guide the future of the institution. They prepared to reestablish the office of the patriarch, a position abolished by Peter the Great in the eighteenth century. Traditionally, the patriarch was not only the highest church official but also a national leader with great influence in government. This is what conservatives in the *sobor* desperately wanted in 1917. Although some clergy objected to the plan, the *sobor* selected Tikhon (Vasily Belavin), formerly archbishop of Vilna. His name was drawn from an urn that contained the names of three nominees who had received sufficient votes from the *sobor*. Tikhon lacked outstanding characteristics of leadership, but, with the Bolsheviks in power, it really mattered very little. Church officials clearly deceived themselves if they thought any person holding the title of patriarch could have any impact on the Bolsheviks.

Lenin's first act against the church came on December 4, 1917, when he ordered the nationalization of all land in Russia. As the church was the single biggest land-owner in Russia, this was a serious blow to its finances. In succeeding weeks, the Bolshevik government closed church schools and seminaries, made marriage a civil ceremony, and placed records of births, marriages, and deaths in government hands. On January 23, 1918, Russia was made a secular state by government decree. This meant that all religious observances would disappear from state functions and that the government would make no further payments to the church. During the course of 1918 and beyond, recalcitrant priests and monks were arrested and imprisoned or killed. When the great civil war began in March, 1918, the assault on the church, which sided with the opponents of the Bolsheviks, intensified. It is important to point out, however, that Lenin recognized the significant place that religion held in the lives of many Russian citizens. He did not try to prevent private religious wor-ship, nor did he arrest Patriarch Tikhon or disband the *sobor.* Throughout 1918 and into the early 1920's, the patriarch and the *sobor* continued to berate the Bolshevik Party. (The Bolsheviks officially changed the name of their party to "Communist" in February, 1918.) The patriarch, for example, contended that the revolution was part of an international Jewish-Masonic conspiracy. The czar had been cast out so that Russian Christians could be made slaves of the Jews. The *sobor,* meanwhile, encouraged Russian believers to resist the separation of the church from the state.

It was not until 1922 that Lenin brought charges against Patriarch Tikhon and had him arrested. Tikhon was later released when he agreed to end his protests against the Communist government. By that time, it was clear that all hopes of displacing the Communist regime were gone.

Impact of Event

The denial of church rights by the Bolsheviks put an end to the privileged rela-tionship the Orthodox church long had held with the government of Russia. For centuries, the church and the emperors had reinforced and protected each other psy-chologically and financially. Suddenly, the church and its followers needed to fight for survival. Orthodox followers benefited from the New Economic Policy (NEP) imposed by Lenin in 1921. The NEP provided for slowing down the march toward a fully Communist state. The government backed away from an aggressive assault on religious belief. It was not until Joseph Stalin came to power, after a brief power struggle following Lenin's death in 1924, that a major effort was made to eradicate all religious worship in the Soviet Union (which was officially formed in 1922). Even Stalin, however, was forced to relax his efforts in the burst of patriotism that accom-panied the Soviet Union's participation in World War II.

During the 1920's and 1930's, many church officials and priests left Russia to pursue their faith in other European locales. Wherever they migrated, they found other Russians who had fled from the country before the Bolsheviks could secure the borders. Large numbers of émigrés, including many from the Russian intelligentsia, found their way to France, Belgium, Czechoslovakia, Germany, and Bulgaria. Even among those who had become disillusioned with the practices of the Orthodox church, there was never doubt that the church still existed in exile. For those who were not fortunate enough to escape, it would be necessary to carry out religious observances in secrecy during the times of the most severe repression. There was no way that Christian followers who remained in Russia could match the government's massive funding of atheist organizations and publications that were intended to denigrate religious belief, yet scholars are unanimous in suggesting that there was never much chance that the Communist government would succeed in eliminating religious belief or the longing of Russian believers for the return of their church.

The greatest impacts of the early Bolshevik attack on the Orthodox church were to reduce its political significance, to deplete its financial resources, to create an aging and vastly diminished clergy, and to discourage young people from following the religion of their parents. It was not until the emergence of Mikhail Gorbachev as the Soviet leader in 1985 that circumstances improved for the church as an institution. Gorbachev, although an atheist, showed little opposition to religious ceremonies. In the spirit of *glasnost* (openness) and *perestroika* (restructuring), he joined in the celebration of one thousand years of Russian Orthodox Christianity in 1989. Subsequent events in 1990-1991, principally the crumbling of the central power of the Soviet state, brought about a major revival of church activities. In some of the Soviet republics, it seemed likely that the Orthodox church again would have a major political, as well as spiritual, role.

Bibliography

Conquest, Robert. *Religion in the USSR*. New York: Praeger, 1968. A brief and readable account of religion in the Soviet Union from World War I through the time of Nikita Khrushchev. Conquest describes the Bolshevik tactics of suppression and the ultimate failure of those tactics to eradicate religious belief. The author follows a chronological approach. There are notes and an extensive bibliography.

Curtiss, John Shelton. *The Russian Church and the Soviet State, 1917-1950*. Boston: Little, Brown, 1953. This is the best work on the Orthodox church and the Bolsheviks from 1917 to 1928. Curtiss writes well, and his study is notably unbiased. The book is suitable for the general reader as well as the serious scholar. Highly recommended. Index, notes, and bibliography.

Freeze, Gregory L. *The Parish Clergy in Nineteenth Century Russia: Crisis, Reform, Counter-Reform*. Princeton, N.J.: Princeton University Press, 1983. Although not an easy book to digest, the reader who perseveres will be richly rewarded. The author delves into the serious problems that burdened the church in the nineteenth century, problems that had not disappeared at the time of the Bolshevik Revolution. Superb notes, glossary, bibliography, and index.

Kolarz, Walter. *Religion in the Soviet Union.* New York: St. Martin's Press, 1961. Using a wealth of sources, the author describes in detail the fate of religion under Soviet rule. He contends that Communist ideology could not fulfill the spiritual needs of the people. Therefore, efforts to wipe out religious belief had to fail. Index and extensive notes.

Zernov, Nicolas. *The Russian Religious Renaissance of the Twentieth Century.* New York: Harper & Row, 1963. A somewhat biased but nevertheless interesting account of the Russian church in exile after 1917. The author discusses the religious ferment that occurred among those who fled Russia after the Bolsheviks came to power. Especially interesting is his discussion of the legacy of the Russian intelligentsia. Appendix and index.

Ronald K. Huch

Cross-References

Lenin and the Communists Impose the "Red Terror" (1917), p. 218; Lenin Leads the Russian Revolution (1917), p. 225; Stalin Reduces the Russian Orthodox Church to Virtual Extinction (1939), p. 561; Soviet Jews Demand Cultural and Religious Rights (1963), p. 1177; Gorbachev Initiates a Policy of *Glasnost* (1985), p. 2249.

THE BALTIC STATES FIGHT FOR INDEPENDENCE

Category of event: Revolutions and rebellions
Time: 1917-1920
Locale: Northeastern Europe

*Estonia, Latvia, and Lithuania established themselves as independent states be-
tween 1917 and 1920, overcoming diverse opposition*

> *Principal personages:*
> KONSTANTIN PÄTS (1874-1956), the first head of state of the Estonian Re-
> public (1918)
> ANTANAS SMETONA (1874-1944), the first Lithuanian head of state (1918)
> and later dictator (1926)
> KARLIS ULMANIS (1877-1942), the Latvian head of state (1918) and later
> dictator (1934)
> JOHAN LAIDONER (1877-1953), the commander of the Estonian Army (1918-
> 1920)
> PETERIS (P. I.) STUCHKA (1865-1932), a Latvian Bolshevik and head of
> the Latvian Soviet government (1919)
> RÜDIGER VON DER GOLTZ (1865-1946), the commander of German forces
> in the Baltic
> PRINCE P. R. BERMONT-AVALOV (1884-1973), the nominal head of the "West
> Russian" army and government (1919)

Summary of Event

The revolutionary ferment that gripped the Russian Empire in 1917 gave birth to
sweeping changes in that Empire's Baltic provinces. By 1920, Estonia, Latvia, and
Lithuania had emerged as independent republics after a long and difficult struggle
against Soviet, White Russian, and German forces.

The Baltic peoples share a common geography and, accordingly, rather similar
historical experiences. Beginning in the late Middle Ages, the eastern Baltic was a
bone of contention among Nordic (Danes, Swedes, and Teutonic Knights) and Slavic
(Poles and Russians) powers. The Baltic peoples, who were neither Nordic nor Slavic,
retained their cultural identities through centuries of shifting foreign domination,
but their cultures also were shaped and differentiated by these outside influences.
The Estonians, like the kindred Finns, were strongly influenced by Scandinavia and
adopted the Lutheran faith. The Lithuanians, long under Polish influence, were Roman Catholic. The Latvians, subjected to the most diverse set of rulers, were a
mixture of Lutheran, Catholic, and Orthodox.

The Russian Empire cemented its rule in the Baltic region during the eighteenth
century, but local authority was entrusted to the hands of the aristocracy, most of
which was of German origin. Much of the native population was reduced to serf-

dom. In the 1860's, serfdom was abolished, but the period from 1881 to 1905 witnessed efforts by the czarist government to "Russianize" the Baltic. The attacks on native language and culture, however, provoked resentment and unified people in defense of their heritage. Increased education and economic development bred a native intelligentsia that would supply the first generation of national leaders.

The worst abuses of the czarist regime were curbed after the 1905 revolution, but the Baltics remained bound to Russia. No "Latvia" or "Lithuania" existed. The former was divided among the duchies of Kurland (Courland) and Livonia (Livland) and part of the province of Vitebsk, while Lithuanians were split among the provinces of Kowno (Kaunas), Vilna (Vilnius), and Suwalki. The "Estonia" (Estland) shown on Russian maps represented only the northern half of the future state.

All things considered, the situation did not bode well for the creation of independent national states. With the exception of the Lithuanians, who had a powerful state in the fourteenth and fifteenth centuries, the Baltic peoples had no experience with self-rule, and none had any acquaintance with a democratic state. National ideas would prove stronger than these obstacles.

The first to demand autonomy were the Estonians. The fall of the Romanov Monarchy in February, 1917, ushered in a Russian Provisional Government committed to democratic reform, including limited self-determination for non-Russians. In April, 1917, thousands of Estonians demonstrated in Petrograd (Leningrad), demanding autonomy. The Provisional Government granted this, and in July extended the limited autonomy to Livonia and Kurland, the chief Latvian areas. The action of the Provisional Government, however, granted rights only to specific provinces, not to peoples.

The Latvians and Lithuanians faced a different situation. Since 1915, Lithuania and the Latvian region up to the Dvina (Daugava) river had been under German occupation. The Germans planned to unite the Baltic provinces with Germany through a personal union under Kaiser Wilhelm II. In September, 1917, a Lithuanian State Council appeared in Vilnius, led by Antanas Smetona. In December, it declared independence from Russia as a constitutional monarchy but was forced to accept accommodation with Germany.

The same fate befell the Estonian and Latvian lands in early 1918. In February, the Germans occupied the entire Baltic region and sponsored councils, composed mostly of ethnic Germans, who at once proclaimed independence from Russia and union with Germany. Only with the surrender of Germany in November were authentic national councils able to act freely. That month, the Estonian Republic formed under the leadership of Konstantin Päts, an independent and united Latvia formed under Karlis Ulmanis, and the Lithuanian Council renounced its union with Germany and proclaimed a republic.

A new threat faced the Baltics from the east. V. I. Lenin's Soviet regime denounced the new states as "bourgeois" regimes that oppressed the rights of the peasants and workers. The Bolsheviks formed Soviet-style countergovernments and launched the Red Army on a mission of "liberation." Soviet troops quickly overran most of the region, but only in Riga, where there was a large working-class element, did the Bolsheviks achieve any real control, under the leadership of Peteris Stuchka. Stuchka, however, proposed not an independent Soviet Latvia but one joined to Russia in fraternal socialist union.

In January, the Estonians conducted a remarkable national rally, and with some help from the Finns and British, expelled the Red forces. In the south, the Lithuanian government stopped the Reds and clung to power in Kaunas. Soviet Latvia fell in May, but into German hands.

In early 1919, General Count Rüdiger von der Goltz organized thousands of discharged German soldiers into a volunteer force to "fight Bolshevism." His real aim was to restore German power in the Baltic, and to this end he set up a puppet regime in Riga. Von der Goltz's troops were beaten in June by a mixed Estonian-Latvian force, and Ulmanis was restored to power. Von der Goltz tried again in October when, allied with the White Russian Prince P. R. Bermont-Avalov, he made another attack on Riga. Realizing that their national existence was at stake, the Latvians repelled him, and the German-Russian force was disbanded.

The Estonians faced a similar problem with White Russians under General N. N. Iudenich. Iudenich demanded Estonia's help in his war against the Soviets but refused to recognize its independence. Estonian commander Johan Laidoner refused to join the Russians in their march on Petrograd. Iudenich's venture failed, and his end paved the way for negotiations between the Soviets and the Estonians. Exhausted by civil war and preparing for a new war with Poland, the Bolsheviks wanted peace on their Baltic flank. The Soviet-Estonian treaty of February, 1920, included recognition of Estonia's complete independence. Soviet Russia signed similar agreements with Lithuania (July) and Latvia (August).

Although the Baltic states had secured de facto independence, they still lacked formal recognition from the Western powers and the League of Nations. These finally granted recognition to Estonia and Latvia in 1921 and to Lithuania in 1922.

Impact of Event

During their history, the Baltic peoples had often been passed from the hand of one conqueror to the next. This could have happened again in 1918-1919 were it not for the collective desires and actions of these populations. The regimes of Päts, Ulmanis, and Smetona may not have been especially democratic or representative, but they did represent independence, whereas the Soviet and pro-German options offered only continued subjugation to a larger state. Independence was the only means for the Baltic nations to retain control of their destinies. Deprived of large-scale foreign support (Allied aid, mostly British, was limited and sporadic), the Baltic governments ultimately survived on the strength of popular nationalism. A case in point is the Estonian army. It grew from a mere six thousand troops in January, 1919, to more than seventy thousand by June, representing a substantial effort by a population of under one million. The Latvian army showed a similar effort. Coercion alone cannot explain this response. The wars of independence exacted a huge toll in misery from the populations, who often saw their homes invaded and plundered repeatedly. Support for independence, often tenuous at first, grew swiftly and held firm. The independence of the Baltic states, therefore, is a lasting example of what a people can accomplish when united behind a national idea.

It also demonstrates some of the limitations and pitfalls in such ideas. Independence alone did not bring prosperity, reconcile social tensions, or balance a budget. The economic and political lives of these new republics were plagued with problems and crises. The prominent role of the military in the founding of the states led to a strong influence on politics, and in the end all dissolved into military or semimilitary dictatorships. This, in part, contributed to the ease with which all three were forcibly reincorporated into the Soviet Union in 1940.

The national ideas, however, have not disappeared. During the late 1980's, new governments in the Soviet-ruled Baltic states again demanded autonomy or independence, with its foundation and inspiration in the struggle of 1917-1920.

Bibliography

Bilmanis, Alfred. *A History of Latvia.* Princeton, N.J.: Princeton University Press, 1951. Strongly nationalist viewpoint, but a useful general resource on Latvia with emphasis on the modern period. Not useful for developments past 1940. Index and bibliography.

Hiden, John. *The Baltic States and Weimar Ostpolitik.* Cambridge, England: Cambridge University Press, 1987. Scholarly and informative work on German-Baltic relations in the 1920's. The first portion deals with the von der Goltz episode. This work is appropriate for the reader desiring more detail on this aspect. Bibliography and index.

Jackson, J. Hampden. *Estonia.* London: Allen & Unwin, 1941. Somewhat dated and biased, but still a useful general history with a contemporary view of the independence period. Small bibliography, index.

Page, Stanley W. *The Formation of the Baltic States.* New York: Howard Fertig, 1970. Excellent survey of the independence struggles and their aftermath. A basic work on the topic. Bibliography and index.

Rauch, Georg von. *The Baltic States: The Years of Independence, 1917-1940.* London: C. Hurst, 1974. Useful, brief survey of the independence period, with emphasis on politics. Originally published in German. Bibliography and index.

Raun, Toivo. *Estonia and the Estonians.* Stanford, Calif.: Hoover Institution Press, 1987. Perhaps the best overall work on Estonia. Comprehensive history with good treatment of modern period. Extensive bibliography, index.

Senn, Alfred Erich. *The Emergence of Modern Lithuania.* New York: Columbia University Press, 1959. Excellent history of the independence period and Lithuanian politics. Extensive bibliography, index.

Tarulis, Albert N. *American-Baltic Relations, 1918-1922: The Struggle over Recognition.* Washington, D.C.: Catholic University Press, 1965. Examines the national and international issues involved in the American and Western recognition of the

Baltics, with an emphasis on Lithuania. Bibliography and index.

Vardys, V. Stanley, and Romuald J. Misiunas, eds. *The Baltic States in Peace and War, 1917-1945.* University Park: Pennsylvania State University Press, 1978. A collection of thirteen essays dealing with diverse aspects of the independence period. Presumes a general knowledge of the topic. Part 1 covers 1917-1920. Notes, bibliographies, and index.

Richard B. Spence

Cross-References

Finland Gains Independence from the Soviet Union (1917), p. 212; Lenin and the Communists Impose the "Red Terror" (1917), p. 218; Lenin Leads the Russian Revolution (1917), p. 225; Germans Revolt and Form Socialist Government (1918), p. 241; The Paris Peace Conference Includes Protection for Minorities (1919), p. 252; The League of Nations Is Established (1919), p. 270; Ireland Is Granted Home Rule and Northern Ireland Is Created (1920), p. 309; The Atlantic Charter Declares a Postwar Right of Self-Determination (1941), p. 584; Soviets Take Control of Eastern Europe (1943), p. 612; Lithuania Declares Its Independence from the Soviet Union (1990), p. 2577.

FINLAND GAINS INDEPENDENCE FROM
THE SOVIET UNION

Categories of event: Political freedom and indigenous peoples' rights
Time: 1917-1920
Locale: Helsinki, Finland

After being under Swedish and Russian rule for more than seven centuries, Finland declared its independence on December 6, 1917, and eventually gained Soviet recognition in the Treaty of Tartu (October 14, 1920)

Principal personages:

NIKOLAI BOBRIKOV (1839-1904), the Russian general who served as the governor-general in Finland (1898-1904); proponent of "Russification"

ADOLF IVAR ARWIDSSON (1791-1858), a Finnish patriot active in the nationalist movement; exiled to Sweden in 1822

EINO RUDOLF HOLSTI (1881-1945), the minister to Britain (1918-1919) and Finnish foreign minister (1919-1922)

ELIAS LÖNNROT (1802-1884), a physician who collected the tales of the "Kalevala" and published the first authoritative version in 1835

CARL GUSTAF MANNERHEIM (1867-1951), a Finnish general and politician; led "White" forces in the 1918 Civil War

NICHOLAS II (1868-1918), the Russian czar (1894-1917) who authorized "Russification" of Finland prior to independence

JUHO KUSTI PAASIKIVI (1870-1956), a Finnish politician who negotiated the Treaty of Tartu

JOHAN VILHELM SNELLMAN (1806-1881), a cultural figure who promoted the use of Finnish language as equal to Swedish and Russian

KAARLO JUHO STÅHLBERG (1865-1952), the president of the Finnish Diet (1914); elected as the first president of the Finnish Republic (served 1919-1925)

PEHR EVIND SVINHUFVUD (1861-1944), a member of the Finnish legislature (1907-1914); exiled to Siberia (1914-1917); served as prime minister (1917-1918) and president of Finland (1931-1937)

Summary of Event

"Swedes we are not, Russians we can never be; let us therefore be Finns." Thus wrote Adolf Ivar Arwidsson, in an apt characterization of the Finnish sense of self-identity. The challenge was especially daunting, as the small Finnish population had to endure six centuries of Swedish domination followed by another century of Russian rule.

The story of the striving for national independence is a lengthy one. Swedish control over Finnish territory began in the twelfth century and steadily expanded.

Because of Finland's isolated location, a degree of regional self-rule became possible, but the Finns were still a subject population. Finland's geographic location unfortunately placed it in the middle of competition between the empires of Sweden and Russia. Under Peter the Great, the Russian Empire expanded to the northwest toward the Gulf of Finland. Extended warfare continued between the two nations, especially in the Great Northern War (1700-1721). Russian forces invaded the Swedish Empire in 1808, and Sweden ceded Finland to Russia in the peace treaty of 1809.

Shifting masters did not initially reduce existing Finnish rights. Czar Alexander I promised to continue Finnish institutions and legal practices. A governor-general served as the czar's personal representative in the Finnish city of Helsinki. Gradually, however, Finnish autonomy and institutions eroded or vanished. Despite Finland's transfer to Russia, substantial Swedish influence continued. Swedish was the primary language of the duchy's social elite, as well as being used in local government, education, law, commerce, and culture. Finns were widely perceived as rustic, illiterate, and incapable of leadership or importance.

This perception began to change in the 1820's and 1830's, with the emergence of a Finnish cultural and national consciousness. Adolf Arwidsson was banished from Finland for his views. Several individuals began collecting the national epic, the "Kalevala," comparing oral variations to recreate the story, which represents an ancient literary and cultural manifestation of early traditions and Finnish mythology. Elias Lönnrot is the most famous of those who compared the versions of the Kalevala and developed a coherent written story. Johan Vilhelm Snellman advocated the use of Finnish, a language with no clear connections with Swedish or Russian, as it was the daily tongue of the ordinary people. Relations between the Russians and Finns improved in the 1860's, during the reign of Czar Alexander II (1855-1881). Expanded use of the Finnish language was authorized by an 1863 decree. The Russian monarchy permitted the creation of a Finnish parliament (or diet) in 1863. By 1878, Finnish military units were authorized. These were positive changes that enhanced the sense of national identity.

This improved atmosphere deteriorated in the 1890's, with the imposition of policies representing "Russification" of the Finnish Grand Duchy. These events coincided with the assignment of General Nikolai Bobrikov as governor-general. Finnish army units were merged with the Russian army and placed under Russian officers. The term of military service was extended, and a new conscription law was imposed in 1901. Many youths evaded this unpopular draft. Russian became a compulsory language in Finnish schools, and Russians dominated the Finnish civil service. A decree of Czar Nicholas II (1899) confirmed the primacy of Russian laws over Finnish laws. The Finnish Diet continued but with reduced powers and influence.

These infringements on Finnish liberties led to widespread resistance. More than 500,000 signatures were obtained (out of a population of less than three million) protesting Russification. A delegation of five hundred traveled to St. Petersburg to present the petition personally to the Czar, but he refused to see them. Finnish nationalism grew and was reinforced by Jean Sibelius' famous composition, "Finlandia." First performed in 1900, the piece became an example of musical nationalism. Russian authorities occasionally banned its performance because of its anti-Russian effect on Finnish audiences.

As Russification policies continued, various factions considered their responses. The "Compliants" argued that accommodation with Russian authorities and policies might retain a degree of autonomy. The "Constitutionalists" looked to the historic rights of the Finns and demanded that the Russians honor those principles and institutions. The "Activists" opposed past, present, and future Russification and called on Finns to strive for national independence, advocating the use of force if necessary to achieve that goal.

A new unicameral legislature was created in 1907, with two hundred elected members. A revised suffrage law gave the vote to people twenty-four years of age or older, including women, making Finland a prominent example of voting democracy. The granting of suffrage to women was the first such example in modern Europe. This reform increased the number of voters from 126,000 to nearly 1.3 million. Twenty-five women won seats in the 1907 Diet elections. A second assembly was elected in 1910, but the authorities quickly dissolved it. A third assembly was elected in 1910 but was also dissolved before the end of the year. These conditions greatly increased Finnish antagonism to Russian influence and authority.

Finland's chance to declare independence came in the chaotic period of World War I and the Russian Revolution, as Russian military defeats and Russia's deteriorating internal situation weakened that country. With the overthrow of the Russian monarchy in March, 1917, events moved rapidly. Pehr Evind Svinhufvud provided executive leadership as the head of government following his return in 1917 from exile in Siberia. The Bolshevik seizure of power in Petrograd (formerly St. Petersburg) gave the Finnish independence movement the confidence to declare independence on December 6, 1917. On December 31, 1917, the new Soviet government responded favorably. National unity appeared to be a reality. In fact, the next several years brought more trauma to the Finns before complete independence was confirmed in the fall of 1920. In early 1918, Finland became embroiled in a civil war between diverse parties and ideologies attempting to determine the shape and values of the new state. Violent conflict pitted Finnish "Reds" and "Whites." Carl Gustaf Mannerheim, a later president of the republic, commanded the "White" forces in this conflict.

By the civil war's end in May, 1918, the pro-socialist and pro-Bolshevik "Red" movement had been defeated decisively at a cost of approximately twenty-four thousand dead on both sides. This critical period also included a short-lived German intervention in the last year of World War I. Only afterward could the Finns create the institutions of an independent state. A new constitution was written, elections took place, and in July, 1919, Kaarlo Juho Ståhlberg became the first president of the Finnish Republic. Foreign Minister Eino Rudolf Holsti successfully gained the support of the Paris Peace Conference for this new infant republic.

Problems with the Soviet government between 1918 and 1920 had to be resolved.

Boundary disputes and other controversies slowed the process, but negotiations in the summer and fall of 1920 culminated in the October 14, 1920, Treaty of Tartu by which the Soviet Union guaranteed Finnish independence. The same year, Finland entered the League of Nations as a full member.

Impact of Event

Achieving national independence permitted the Finns to develop their national institutions and to adapt them as conditions required. Finland's freedom as a sovereign nation in the twentieth century illustrates a fundamentally democratic outlook and the ability to adjust to its dominant Soviet neighbor. The political system, based on the July, 1919, constitution, is a republic with a national parliament elected by universal suffrage on the basis of proportional representation. The minimum voting age as of 1991 was eighteen. A variety of political parties offers voters a wide spectrum of ideologies and proposed agendas. Cabinets usually have been formed by coalition, as one party rarely wins a majority of parliamentary seats. This situation encourages compromise in reaching a consensus or formal decision. Executive power is placed in an elected president. Civil rights are guaranteed and protected by the state, and the vitality of Finnish democracy is promoted by this democratic system.

The major challenges to Finland's independence and foreign policy came from its neighbor, the Soviet Union. Although the 1920 Treaty of Tartu appeared to resolve major issues and guarantee independence, the years since 1920 have seen major confrontations and even several wars between the two nations. Disputes over the Karelian area led to severe problems in the early 1920's. Relations seriously deteriorated in the late 1930's, culminating in the Soviet invasion of Finland in November, 1939. This Winter War (fall, 1939-spring, 1940) was an uneven contest between the large Soviet and small Finnish populations. Finland surrendered in March, 1940. Following the German invasion of the Soviet Union in June, 1941, Finland and the Soviet Union became combatants again in what is known as the Continuation War (summer, 1941-fall, 1944). Finnish defeat in this war resulted in shifts of territory and the imposition of reparations to be paid to the Soviet Union.

Since its location creates potential dangers, as history clearly shows, Finland adopted a policy of strict neutrality in the post-World War II years. This policy is especially identified with President Paasikivi (1946-1956), who helped negotiate the Treaty of Tartu in 1920 with the Soviet Union. Finland had not joined, by 1991, either the North Atlantic Treaty Organization or the Warsaw Pact. This policy of "Finlandization" has been viewed as a model for other small nations in similar circumstances, adjacent to large and powerful neighbors. Finland became a member of the United Nations in 1955 and joined the European Free Trade Association as an associate member.

From its beginnings as a free nation, and especially since 1945, Finland has been very successful in continuing its national development and providing the opportunities for the enhancement of the rights of its citizens. Progressive leadership and policies are widely admired for the social, economic, and political benefits provided for this hardy population. Today, Finland serves as a successful example of a working democracy in which its citizens find security and opportunity, built on a heritage of which they can be proud.

Bibliography

American University. *Finland: A Country Study.* Washington, D.C.: Government Printing Office, 1983. Useful reference guide for modern Finland. Includes historical background, but the main focus is on recent domestic institutions and conditions. Gives a balanced overview of the nation since independence.

Jackson, John Hampden. *Finland.* New York: Macmillan, 1940. Although dated, it is a broad survey of Finnish history. The effort to achieve independence is a major theme. Good coverage of the domestic scene for the early twentieth century. Explains Finland's problems with its Soviet neighbor.

Jagerskiold, Stig Axel Fridolf. *Mannerheim, Marshal of Finland.* Minneapolis: University of Minnesota Press, 1986. Biography of the famous military and political figure, based on extensive work in the Mannerheim archives. An abridged version of an eight-volume biography. Excellent coverage of independence and post-independence periods.

Jutikkala, Eino, and Kauko Pirinen. *A History of Finland.* New York: Dorset Press, 1988. Readable account of Finnish history with ample coverage of the earlier period of Swedish and Russian control. A clear narrative of the independence movement and further development of the nation after World War I. Includes material on the Winter War and the Continuation War. Brief treatment of events after 1944.

Kirby, D. G., ed. *Finland and Russia, 1808-1920: From Autonomy to Independence— A Selection of Documents.* London: Macmillan, 1975. Important documentary publication contains 152 primary sources. Includes government texts, newspaper accounts and editorial opinions, and treaties and agreements. From the School of Slavonic and East European Studies, University of London.

Mannerheim, Carl Gustaf. *Memoirs.* New York: E. P. Dutton, 1954. The marshal's autobiography in English, written in his retirement and published after his death. Contains vital periods of his life and leadership, but is sometimes selective in choice and interpretation of events. Virtually all English-language secondary sources use this memoir as a key source.

Mead, William Richard. *Finland.* London: Benn, 1968. Solid account of Finnish history, including the Swedish and Russian periods as well as the years since independence. Thorough research based on extensive sources. Tends to focus more on political issues than on social or cultural life. Useful survey of the independence issue.

Rintala, Marvin. *Four Finns: Political Profiles.* Berkeley: University of California Press, 1969. Brief readable account of four major figures in Finnish history in the twentieth century: Mannerheim, Paasikivi, Ståhlberg, and Väinö Tanner. Places them in the context of political and national issues and problems in which each played a central part as active participants in the independence movement.

Smith, C. Jay. *Finland and the Russian Revolution, 1917-1922.* Atlanta: University of Georgia Press, 1958. Detailed account of the relationship between Finland and Russia in this critical period. Includes political, diplomatic, and military aspects as well as Russification policies from the 1890's.

Warner, Oliver. *Marshal Mannerheim and the Finns.* Helsinki: Otava Publishing, 1967. Very adequate biography of Mannerheim and his leadership in crucial periods of twentieth century Finnish history. Based on interviews and relevant documentary archival materials. A sympathetic portrayal of Finland and the famous general.

Wuorinen, John H. *A History of Finland.* New York: Columbia University Press, 1965. Useful general history by a noted scholar of Finnish history. Similar to the Jutikkala and Pirinen account. Helpful for understanding the land and its people. Has major focus on political issues but blends social and cultural aspects as well.

Taylor Stults

Cross-References

Finland Grants Woman Suffrage (1906), p. 70; Bolsheviks Deny All Rights to the Russian Orthodox Church (1917), p. 202; The Baltic States Fight for Independence (1917), p. 207; Lenin and the Communists Impose the "Red Terror" (1917), p. 218; Lenin Leads the Russian Revolution (1917), p. 225; Soviets Take Control of Eastern Europe (1943), p. 612; The Brezhnev Doctrine Bans Acts of Independence in Soviet Satellites (1968), p. 1408; Soviets Invade Afghanistan (1979), p. 2062; Soviet Troops Leave Afghanistan (1989), p. 2449; Soviet Troops Withdraw from Czechoslovakia (1990), p. 2570; Lithuania Declares Its Independence from the Soviet Union (1990), p. 2577.

LENIN AND THE COMMUNISTS IMPOSE THE "RED TERROR"

Category of event: Atrocities and war crimes
Time: 1917-1924
Locale: Postrevolutionary Russia

The Bolsheviks under Vladimir Ilich Lenin seized power in Russia and proceeded to eliminate opposition by ruthless repression and violation of fundamental human rights

Principal personages:
> VLADIMIR ILICH LENIN (1870-1924), the leader of the Communists who seized ruling authority
> LEON TROTSKY (1879-1940), the Marxist whom Stalin defeated in the struggle to succeed Lenin
> JOSEPH STALIN (1879-1953), the ruthless dictator who made the Soviet Union a world power

Summary of Event

Russia entered World War I allied with Britain and France against the Central Powers, of which Germany and Austria were the chief members. Although Russians fought bravely, the country's poorly developed industries could not meet the needs of the armed forces or the civilians. Decades of protest against autocratic rule had divided Russia at a time when conduct of the war demanded national unity. The war brought defeat and the end of czarist rule. Nicholas II abdicated in March, 1917, amid revolution.

The abdication left Russia without a legal government. Nicholas named Prince Georgy Lvov as prime minister. Lvov became leader of a committee from the Duma, Russia's ineffectual parliament. That committee formed a provisional government that was largely under the influence of liberals who wanted a constitutional republic. More radical factions desired sweeping social and economic, as well as political, changes and therefore viewed the provisional government with malice.

Among the dissidents, two Marxist movements, the Mensheviks and the Bolsheviks (Communists), competed for power with other factions. The government's decision to continue the war gave the Bolsheviks a major propaganda advantage. They demanded immediate peace. Lvov and Aleksandr Kerensky, the minister of war, tried to revitalize military efforts, but discipline in the army was extremely poor, and mass desertions occurred. Lvov resigned in July, 1917, and Kerensky became prime minister while German armies advanced and the provisional government languished in confusion.

In the midst of this disarray, Vladimir Ilich Lenin, leader of the Bolsheviks, returned to Russia after three years spent in exile for revolutionary activities. He called for the overthrow of the government as a prelude to peace and a radical restructuring of society. Soon the populace of Petrograd became an uncontrollable mob demanding peace, and the Bolsheviks grew rapidly. Kerensky's frantic effort to find support failed as military units defied his orders. On November 6, 1917, Communists seized control of the capital and arrested ministers of the provisional government. A Military Revolutionary Committee, under Leon Trotsky, had gained support of the garrison in Petrograd. Armed force brought the Communists to power.

At the time of their victory, the Communists were still only one of several revolutionary groups in the capital. Ever since the unsuccessful uprising of 1905, Soviets (revolutionary councils) had provided leadership for various socialist factions in the country. The Petrograd Soviet of Workers' and Soldiers' Deputies was the most important such body in 1917. Socialist Revolutionaries, Mensheviks, and Bolsheviks all had blocs of support within it, as they did within Soviets elsewhere. A Congress of Soviets convened as the Communists seized power in Petrograd. Most Mensheviks and Socialist Revolutionaries denounced the Bolsheviks' action and left the congress to protest it. This lack of action left Lenin's party in control.

Lenin demanded "all power to the soviets" and total authority for the Communist Party. The congress declared the immediate creation of a socialist society and instituted a Council of Peoples' Commissars to lead the new regime. Lenin was chairman, Trotsky foreign commissar, and Joseph Stalin commissar of nationalities.

The transition to dictatorship did not proceed smoothly. Most government officials were hostile and went on strike as soon as commissars appeared to take charge. The state bank refused to give money to the new rulers. The Communists responded with brutal coercion.

Once the Congress of Soviets had disbanded, the Communist Party cemented its control over a one-party state. Against some opposition within his own Central Committee, Lenin made peace with the Germans on terms humiliating and costly to Russia, but the imminence of a German conquest had left no alternative. When Socialist Revolutionary protests became violent and a dissident wounded Lenin, his regime imposed a reign of terror executed by the Extraordinary Commission for Combating Counterrevolution and Sabotage (Cheka), the Communist secret police.

Among the victims of the terror were former officials of the provisional government who, upon release from jail, denounced Bolshevik tyranny and demanded free elections to choose a constituent assembly. The Cheka incarcerated them at Kronstadt Naval Base. Lenin ordered the abolition of hostile local councils and city governments.

Immediately after the Communist coup, Lenin had promised parliamentary elections, but he feared that the outcome might be detrimental to his party. Trotsky persuaded him to hold the elections rather than risk a severe reaction for reneging on the promise. The results confirmed Lenin's fears. Of the 703 deputies chosen, only 168 were Communists. The Socialist Revolutionaries had a clear majority. The people had spoken; Lenin decided to silence them.

The Communists arrested more opposition leaders to intimidate the assembly into declaring a vote of confidence in Lenin's government. When that body met, it nevertheless elected Socialist Revolutionary leader Viktor Chernov its president rather than accept dictation from the Communists. When the deputies recessed, the Communists would not allow them to reconvene. They shot those who protested. The duly elected assembly was no more, and the Communists had full control of the government.

By this time the plight of the imperial family was precarious. Nicholas, Czarina Aleksandra, and their five children were under house arrest at Ekaterinburg, Siberia. In July, 1918, local Soviet leaders executed all of them. Even the family dog died in a volley of gunfire.

Despite its control of the central government, the position of the Communist Party was not secure across Russia. It needed a large, disciplined military force to impose its directives and to fight opposition groups in various parts of the country. Trotsky proceeded to construct the Red Army. Military training became compulsory for urban workers and peasants. People deemed incurably anti-Communist became conscripted laborers. Capital punishment awaited deserters. Trotsky coerced former officers of the czar's army to serve his regime; reprisals awaited their families if they refused. Political commissars watched such officers and indoctrinated the troops.

To feed the Red Army, the government forced peasants to deliver to the state all but the minimum needed for their own subsistence. Peasants often resisted and suffered execution for doing so. In factories, managers worked under the supervision of Communist Party agents.

Sporadic uprisings against the regime were unsuccessful. Organized military forces gathered around commanders of the old imperial army and navy, and civil war raged until 1921. Despite Western and Japanese interventions, the Communists won. Foreign assistance to the anti-Communists was insufficient but just enough to allow the Bolsheviks to claim they were defending Russia against outside aggressors.

The empire of the czars had been a multiethnic state in which Russians dominated other peoples. Resentment led to secessions, beginning in 1917, as the war effort disintegrated. Finland, the Ukraine, Latvia, Lithuania, and Estonia declared independence. The Communists lacked the means to prevent the loss of the Baltic states, but they did reclaim a large sector of the Ukraine, which they made a Soviet republic despite Lenin's avowed subscription to the principle of self-determination of peoples. In Central Asia, the Red Army, aided by Communist subversives, imposed its rule without regard to the wishes of the peoples involved. When the Union of Soviet Socialist Republics came into being in 1922, its constitution affirmed the right of constituent republics to secede, but rulers in the Kremlin had no intention of allowing secession. Despite losses of territory, the Russian empire remained intact, with Lenin in control.

Not only did the Communists impose their rule upon the non-Russians of their country, but they also dealt severely with all dissidents within Russia itself. In March, 1921, sailors at Kronstadt supported striking workers in Petrograd. Trotsky led the

Red Army in conquering the naval base. Many of the sailors who surrendered were shot, and many more went to prison camps.

The strength of the Kronstadt rebellion, in addition to continuing unrest in general, convinced Lenin to compromise Communist ideology in order to save his regime. From 1921 until his death in 1924, he followed a New Economic Policy (NEP), a temporary retreat from state socialism. The government allowed small businesses and factories to operate in private hands, and it obtained foreign investments to aid the economy. Although many problems remained, the NEP did bring stability that aided Lenin's government.

The achievement of relative stability gave Lenin an opportunity to eliminate his opponents in a systematic way. Frightened Socialist Revolutionaries, Mensheviks, and others fled into exile. Many who remained spent years in prison and went into exile afterward. By the end of 1922, organized opposition no longer existed within the country.

In addition to dealing with opposition parties, Lenin had to face contention within the Communist Party, where abject surrender to the Germans and the NEP contradictions of Marxism had aroused criticism. Some Bolsheviks, including Trotsky, became alarmed at the growth of bureaucracy as a power base for dictatorship. A workers' opposition protested the trend toward despotism and joined Trotskyites in complaining about the NEP. At the same Party Congress that adopted the NEP, Lenin denounced deviations from this program and vowed to stop them. He purged Party membership from 730,000 to 530,000. The secret police arrested troublesome Party members.

Although Lenin was dictator, he claimed that the Soviet government operated on the principle of democratic centralism, which allowed free discussion at all levels until a Party Congress established policy. This freedom was, however, entirely theoretical. The Political Bureau of the Central Committee (Politburo) ran the party, and its members sat on the Council of Peoples' Commissars and controlled the state.

In July, 1918, a Congress of Soviets adopted a constitution with a Declaration of Rights of Toiling and Exploited People. It soon became clear, however, that this was not a guarantee of rights but an expression of aspirations for the future. This remained the case in the constitution of 1923, of which Joseph Stalin was the chief author. Despite proclamations about human rights in official documents, the peoples of the Soviet Union were subjects more than citizens, as policies toward education, religion, and the Jews indicated.

Impact of Event

In the early days of Bolshevik rule, schools became chaotic, as revolutionary fanatics introduced an anarchic concept of freedom. The state eventually imposed discipline and made schools instruments of propaganda. Attendance was compulsory, and teaching had to conform to Communist ideology. Children learned to spy on their parents, and the Young Communist League (Komsomol) became a training ground for future Party members.

Since communism was militantly atheistic, Lenin's regime attacked Russia's churches. The Orthodox church ceased to be the state religion, and the government seized its properties, including schools. A decree in 1921 forbade teaching religion to young people. When church leaders demanded freedom of religion under the constitution, the Communists responded with terror. They murdered the metropolitan of Kiev and executed twenty-eight bishops and 6,775 priests. Despite mass demonstrations in support of the church, repression cowed most ecclesiastical leaders into submission. Bishops asked their people to accept the authority of the government and promised to refrain from political pronouncements and activities. In return, the regime allowed the church to continue its strictly ceremonial and sacramental ministries.

Lenin believed public interest in religion would disappear as Marxist ideology prevailed through state-controlled education. Although individual clergy members and members of various sects continued to defy the government and paid a high price for their disobedience, the Orthodox hierarchy remained subservient. Some bishops became tools of propaganda by telling the world that the Soviets respected freedom of religion.

In contrast with its animosity toward Christians, the regime appeared at first favorably disposed toward Jews. Among thirty-one members of the first Communist Party Central Committee, five were Jews. War Commissar Trotsky was a Jew, as was Grigory Zinoviev, director of the Comintern, the agency to promote revolutions worldwide. Jews obtained positions even in the Cheka.

Since Jews were welcome in the Communist Party, many believed that a new day of freedom and opportunity had dawned for Soviet Semites. Others regarded the disproportionate number of Jews in the Red leadership as evidence that Communism was an international Jewish conspiracy, and some Gentiles distrusted Jews because of their prominence in the Cheka.

When Lenin came to power, he recognized the Jews as a minority entitled to self-determination, but since the Jews were dispersed across the country, that recognition was meaningless. Stalin said that all minorities would eventually be submerged into a single socialist culture, a prospect acceptable to Jews who had become Communists. Jews who remained religious, however, were often victims of persecution.

Communist leaders showed special hatred of Zionism, the belief that world Jewry should repossess Palestine, its historic homeland. Jewish Communists induced their government to outlaw Zionist organizations as counterrevolutionary. Soon the state ordered all Jewish social bodies to disband, and confiscation of Jewish schools and synagogues followed. Jews in so-called bourgeois occupations—clergymen, landlords, businesspeople, and moneylenders—suffered the same discriminations imposed upon their gentile counterparts.

Writing prophetically in the nineteenth century, novelist Fyodor Dostoevski had predicted that, when it came, the Russian revolution would begin with the promise of great freedom but lead to a cruel despotism. The rule of authoritarian czars gave way to that of totalitarian Soviets. A revolution many expected to produce a free and just society led to perhaps the most rigorous police state in history. Atrocities that began under Lenin reached huge proportions under Stalin, whose purges of the Communist Party and imposition of collective farming brought death to at least ten million people.

Bibliography

Balabanoff, Angelica. *Impressions of Lenin.* Translated by Isotta Cesari. Ann Arbor: University of Michigan Press, 1964. The author of this highly critical appraisal of Lenin knew him well and participated as a leading figure in radical movements in several countries. She shows how Lenin manipulated people to make them his accomplices and betrayed Marxism in order to acquire personal dictatorship.

Mailloux, Kenneth F., and Heloise P. Mailloux. *Lenin: The Exile Returns.* Princeton, N.J.: Auerbach Publications, 1971. This is a vivid account of how Lenin and his Bolshevik supporters seized power from the confused provisional government and then rendered other revolutionary factions impotent by the tactic of dividing and conquering. It shows that Lenin never maintained a sincere commitment to democracy either within the Communist Party or for the Soviet Union.

Pipes, Richard. *Formation of the Soviet Union: Communism and Nationalism, 1917-1923.* Rev. ed. Cambridge, Mass.: Harvard University Press, 1980. This comprehensive history is the work of one of the leading authorities on the Soviet Union. It is especially valuable for coverage of the Bolsheviks' policy toward non-Russian nationalities. It shows how the Communists derived great advantages from the civil war.

Steeves, Paul D. *Keeping the Faiths: Religion and Ideology in the Soviet Union.* New York: Holmes & Meier, 1989. This is a survey of religious history from Christian beginnings in the ninth century to the date of publication. It covers Christianity, Judaism, and Islam and relates the fortunes of each under czars and Soviets. It is especially useful for its coverage of non-Orthodox churches and sects.

Wolfe, Bertram. *Three Who Made a Revolution.* New York: Dell Books, 1964. Perhaps the best history of the Bolshevik Revolution, this penetrating biographical study of Lenin, Trotsky, and Stalin is a masterpiece of research and writing. The author was acquainted with several original Bolsheviks and lived for a time in Moscow. No student of the Russian Revolution can afford to ignore this work.

James Edward McGoldrick

Cross-References

Bolsheviks Deny All Rights to the Russian Orthodox Church (1917), p. 202; The Baltic States Fight for Independence (1917), p. 207; Finland Gains Independence from the Soviet Union (1917), p. 212; Lenin Leads the Russian Revolution (1917), p. 225; Stalin Begins Purging Political Opponents (1934), p. 503; Stalin Reduces the Russian Orthodox Church to Virtual Extinction (1939), p. 561; Soviets Take Control of Eastern Europe (1943), p. 612; Khrushchev Implies That Stalinist Excesses Will

LENIN LEADS THE RUSSIAN REVOLUTION

Category of event: Revolutions and rebellions
Time: March-November, 1917
Locale: Russia

The deprivations and turmoil caused by World War I made revolution almost inevitable in Russia, the only country in Europe without any form of representative government

Principal personages:
>VLADIMIR ILICH LENIN (1870-1924), the leader of the revolutionary Bolshevik party who would become the first Communist leader of Russia
>LEON TROTSKY (1879-1940), Lenin's collaborator and the creator of the Red Army
>NICHOLAS II (1868-1918), the deposed ruler of Russia and the last czar
>ALEXANDRA (1872-1918), the German wife of Nicholas II
>PRINCE ALEKSANDR F. KERENSKY (1881-1970), the war commissar of the provisional government and prime minister of Russia

Summary of Event

Prior to 1900, Imperial Russia was largely a land of illiterate peasants controlled by the wealthy nobility. Life in the countryside was much like that of the feudal period of Central Europe in the sixteenth century. On the large estates and in the cities, the aristocracy lived rich, wasteful lives. The beginning of the twentieth century saw a slow, subtle change in the conditions of the Russian people.

Industrialization came to Russia near the beginning of the twentieth century, later than in the rest of Europe. In each country, industrialization had created changes in class structures; this had forced changes in governmental policies, usually in the form of creation of representative governments. In Russia, modernization in the industrial sense created an urban working class that was politically unrepresented and economically exploited.

This new working class was a forced, artificial creation of the czar and had not evolved slowly, as it had elsewhere. There had not been an artisan or guild community on which to draw, and one had to be created. Peasants were forced from the land into the cities to fill the positions created by new factories and service organizations. The Russian worker was an illiterate, violent protester, given to revolutionary types of protest and rebellion that by its nature bordered on anarchy, rather than the conservative union member who evolved in other countries.

A revolution in 1905 led Czar Nicholas II to promise reform. The distrust that many workers held for him and his government, however, caused secret revolutionary societies to emerge. It was during this time that several new types of leaders emerged. These men were professional revolutionists. Scholars as well as trained Marxists, they believed in the need to unite the world under socialism and that the violent overthrow of nations was the way to accomplish this. After the revolution in 1905, many new converts to revolutionary socialism developed in Russia.

One of these revolutionary leaders was Vladimir Ilich Ulyanov, more commonly known by his revolutionary pen name, Lenin. He became the head of an arm of the Russian Social Democratic Party, the Bolsheviks. The Bolsheviks (which can be translated as "those of the majority") gained their name at the Congress of Brussels in 1903. The opponents of Lenin's party, the Mensheviks (or minority party), were also present at the congress. Together, the parties planned changes in the Russian government. The Mensheviks favored strengthening the weak parliamentary arm of government, the Duma. The Bolsheviks, under the leadership of Lenin, called for revolutionary overthrow of the government.

In 1914, with the beginning of World War I, the talk of revolution died down. When the Austrian government declared war on Russia, the people rallied to the needs of the country and to their czar. The revolutionaries, with the exception of the Bolsheviks, vowed to put aside their demands for the duration. Brave and patriotic peasants, under the guidance of often inferior generals and with outdated, often defective, weapons and materials, were at first decidedly effective. They advanced deep into Austrian territory. Germany changed the outcome, however, by coming to the assistance of Austria. Under the pressures of war, the Russian government began to fail miserably. Not only were the weapons inferior but ammunition was in short supply. Transportation was inadequate and at times nonexistent.

Between fourteen and fifteen million men were mobilized for the army. One-third to one-half of all peasant households were left without their primary workers. The fuel shortage caused by the war affected agricultural production and delivery. The threat of invasion, the disruption of all services, and the food shortages that grew with each year of the war left the countryside in a state of deprivation and panic.

The attitudes of the czar's court seemed to fuel resentment among the people of Russia. Czarina Alexandra was German. She and many of the court advisers and families were often heard to make pro-German comments even as Russians died on the battlefields opposing German armies. Trains were given over to support the war effort, but the strain was more than they could deal with adequately. Rumors began to circulate that speeding troop trains often shunted other trains onto side tracks, where they stayed for days or forever in Russia's vast wastelands. Rumors stated that the trains shunted aside were often hospital trains and that the wounded were being left to die. Food from central Russia being sent into the cities was left to spoil in other trains.

The early part of 1917 saw a series of more than thirteen hundred strikes by more than six hundred thousand workers. On March 8, 1917, a spontaneous riot that lasted for three days broke out in the capital city of Petrograd because of bread and coal shortages. On March 10, reserve army troops were sent in to quell the riots, but the troops mutinied and joined the rioters. By March 12, a revolution had occurred.

Czar Nicholas II abdicated on March 15, and the Duma established a provisional government the same day.

Immediately, the Petrograd Soviet of Workers' and Soldiers' Deputies established a shadow government that rivaled the provisional government of Russia and forced a partnership on all decisions. The initial revolution had only taken days, but the question remained as to what form of government would be established and which political group would control it.

In the outlying areas of Russia, transportation and communication being so poor, many of the peasants did not know for years that a revolution had taken place. In other areas, chaos and terror reigned. The land-hungry peasants of Russia saw the revolution as an opportunity to acquire the land for which they had always yearned. Mass murder and torture were not unusual tactics. Some land changed hands several times. The food shortages that were crippling the cities worsened as peasants turned to rebellion instead of farming.

By June, 1917, the outlying areas of Russia were also suffering from growing ethnic and nationalistic movements. In areas such as Georgia and the Caucasus, where Muslims and non-Russian ethnic groups had always suffered as second-class citizens under the Russian nobility, movements to separate from the Russian government grew. There were rumors of appeals by some to Germany and Austria for citizenship in return for aid and assistance in overthrowing their Russian masters.

July 16-18, 1917, saw the Bolsheviks make their early and abortive attempts to take over the government. The provisional government had failed to accomplish the two major demands of the revolutionaries, the end of the war and land reform. Bolsheviks, soldiers, sailors, and mobs of civilians attempted to take Petrograd, against Lenin's advice. Lenin knew that the time was not right and that the Bolsheviks were not organized enough to pull off a coup, so he joined forces with the popular Trotsky to gain strength. The coup attempt failed, and Lenin and several other leaders fled to Finland to escape execution.

Lenin began to call for a second revolution, one of the proletariat, or workers. He stated that the original revolution had been one of the bourgeois or middle class and that it obviously was going to maintain the status quo of exploiting the workers. A trained Marxist, Lenin knew that Russia was not really ready for a proletariat revolution. Karl Marx had outlined a plan for revolution that required a secure and effective capitalist economy to ensure the success of a socialist revolution. Active, violent revolution was not a necessary ingredient in Marx's plan, but successful economics was. Russia did not have any of the necessary ingredients: The economy was not based on capitalism, it was not successful, and it did not possess an established, organized labor class. Lenin was determined to push through a revolution that would attain the ends he believed would lead Russia and, by her example, the rest of the world, into a Marxist socialistic utopia.

Lenin's attempt came on November 7, 1917. Trotsky helped to organize a Red Army, highly trained and provided with military technology as advanced as Trotsky could obtain. The Bolsheviks took control of the provisional government, but the revolution was not over. From November 7, 1917, until December, 1920, Russia would be in civil war. It took three years for Lenin and Trotsky to pull the country together under the leadership of the socialists.

Impact of Event

The Russian people, particularly the peasants, had never known freedom. They were ripe for any political idea that promised them a measure of input and self-determination. The revolutionary groups in Russia made these promises; Bolshevism offered the most. Tired of working the land that they could never own, going hungry while their masters ate unsparingly of the food they had produced, the peasants were the most exploited class. They would, however, continue to be exploited under the new regime of Communism. The land for which the peasants fought was taken from them and managed by the state.

To Lenin, the peasants were a great body of uneducated, unthinking, animalistic creatures, much like the farm animals they raised. The proletariat, or urban labor class, was the group that was to be freed, trained, and utilized to create the new society that Russia was to become, and would set an example for the rest of the workers of the world.

Many socialists in other countries of Europe staged small uprisings in sympathy with the Russian Revolution. The country most affected was Germany. At one point there was fear that its government was in danger of being overthrown, but nationalism prevailed. The industralized nations of Europe had evolved a sense of self and identity lacking in Russia, an unindustrialized, feudalistic society. Lenin did not understand the impact that nationalism would have on the socialists of Europe. They were in most cases Germans, Italians, and Frenchmen first, and socialists second.

Undaunted by the failure of the rest of Europe to follow the lead that Russia had set, Lenin continued to consolidate his power and to reform Russia into the Communist state that he was sure would eventually be emulated by the rest of Europe and then the world.

In 1920, when the civil war in Russia finally ended, Lenin began an era of forced collectivization of land and dictatorial control of peasant labor. Peasants would continue to be hungry as they toiled in their fields in an effort to produce the food needed in war-torn and devastated Russian cities.

The urban labor force was regimented into labor battalions. Its dream of worker-owned factories ended with takeovers by the government. This was followed by a reign of terror ordered by Lenin to remove any dissent or opposition to the government. Minorities were killed when any discussion of nationalistic movements reached governmental agencies. Religious affiliation was outlawed, as Lenin perceived it as a source of antigovernment agitation.

Lenin died in 1924. After a brief power struggle, Joseph Stalin, not Trotsky, took control. Trotsky remained head of the Red Army but was eventually discredited by Stalin, who saw him as a possible threat to his own power.

The Russian Revolution impacted all the world as countries lined up to join with or to fight against the Communists. The history of the twentieth century has been that of opposition to communism or, as in the case of China and much of Latin America, the adoption of communism and the fighting and plotting against the foes of communism.

Bibliography

Adams, Arthur E., ed. *The Russian Revolution and the Bolshevik Victory: Why and How.* Boston: D. C. Heath, 1960. A collection of essays, mostly by Russian writers, that shed light on the causes and the personalities of the Russian Revolution.

Brown, Anthony Cave. *On a Field of Red.* New York: G. P. Putnam's Sons, 1981. Contains information on Russian history from 1917 to 1939 and goes into great depth concerning the revolution itself and its impact on Russia's development. There is very little consideration given to earlier Russian history as an explanation for the conditions of the country or government. Has an excellent map showing the placement and areas of intervention of the British, German, Austrian, Japanese, and American troops after 1918. A complete index is included.

Crankshaw, Edward. *The Shadow of the Winter Palace: Russia's Drift to Revolution, 1825-1917.* New York: Viking Press, 1976. Deals with the Czarist government's attitudes and concerns. Some mention of Rasputin and the personalities of the court officials. A complete index and notes on sources are provided. No illustrations, but a few maps are included.

Hughes, H. Stuart, and James Wilkinson. *Contemporary Europe: A History.* 6th ed. Englewood Cliffs, N.J.: Prentice-Hall, 1987. An overview of European history from 1914 through the 1980's. Deals with the effects of the Russian Revolution on the rest of Europe. This is a good reference for the impact and the political decisions made by European leaders in their dealings with the Russian governments. Excellent illustrations and maps as well as a complete index.

Lindeman, Albert S. *A History of European Socialism.* New Haven, Conn.: Yale University Press, 1983. This book is not a look at the Russian Revolution except as an outcome of the socialistic movement itself. Invaluable to an understanding of the political movements engendered by the Industrial Revolution in Europe. A reading guide, complete bibliography, and index are provided.

Riasanovsky, Nicholas V. *A History of Russia.* 4th ed. New York: Oxford University Press, 1984. A broad overview of Russian history from its beginnings through 1945. Complete index, maps, pictures, and a reading list in English.

Celia Hall-Thur

Cross-References

Bolsheviks Deny All Rights to the Russian Orthodox Church (1917), p. 202; The Baltic States Fight for Independence (1917), p. 207; Lenin and the Communists Impose the "Red Terror" (1917), p. 218; Stalin Begins Purging Political Opponents

CONGRESS PROHIBITS IMMIGRATION OF ILLITERATES OVER AGE SIXTEEN

Category of event: Immigrants' rights
Time: May 1, 1917
Locale: Washington, D.C.

The U.S. Congress, in an effort to exclude as immigrants those of ethnic origin considered incompatible with the racial stock of the country's founders, required literacy as a condition of admission

Principal personages:

HENRY CABOT LODGE (1850-1924), a United States senator from Massachusetts and advocate of the literacy test

GROVER CLEVELAND (1837-1908), the twenty-second and twenty-fourth president of the United States

WILLIAM HOWARD TAFT (1857-1930), the twenty-seventh president of the United States

WOODROW WILSON (1856-1924), the twenty-eighth president of the United States

Summary of Event

In the late nineteenth century, the U.S. government for the first time began to accept the responsibility for restricting immigration. As long as there had been no question that people were welcome to enter and to become citizens of the United States—as had been the case since the American Revolution—each state was at liberty to regulate the flow of foreign nationals within its borders. After 1830, however, because of a large increase in the numbers of immigrants, especially from Catholic Ireland, where famine had motivated huge numbers to emigrate, a somewhat different public attitude emerged.

It became a matter of public anxiety, especially in the eastern United States, not only that the increased immigration was likely to create an oversupply of labor (a major concern of labor unions) but also that there were many entering the country who were deemed undesirable. Many people came to believe that laws should be made and enforced that would restrict the numbers and the kinds of people who would be allowed to enter the United States. In their party platforms, politicians of the period included promises to enact laws restricting immigration of criminals, paupers, and contract laborers—largely unskilled workers who were promised free transportation to America contingent upon repayment once admission was obtained and wages were earned. Others vowed themselves in favor of preventing the United States from becoming a place where European countries could conveniently rid themselves of their poor and of their criminal elements and stated their preference for what they would consider to be worthy and industrious Europeans—to the particular exclusion of laborers from China.

Beginning in 1875, numerous acts dealing with the problem of immigration were passed by Congress. Effective enforcement, however, was the problem with the earliest provisions for exclusion. Many began to believe that large numbers of those who were not wanted could be refused admission by virtue of the fact that they would be unlikely to pass a simple literacy test. A senator from Massachusetts, Henry Cabot Lodge, was an early and influential advocate of a literacy test. In one of his congressional speeches, Senator Lodge proposed to exclude from admission any individual who could neither read nor write. (Literacy in any language was to be qualifying; knowledge of English was not to be required.)

It was believed, according to the senator, that the test would prevent immigration of many Italians, Russians, Poles, Hungarians, Greeks, and Asians, and that it would cause the exclusion of fewer of those who were English-speaking or who were Germans, Scandinavians, or French. Lodge insisted, in his argument, that the latter were more closely kin, racially, to those who had founded and developed the United States, and that therefore they would be more readily appreciated. (The senator made allowance for the Irish, even though he saw them as being of different racial stock, because they spoke English and had been associated with the English peoples for many centuries.) He further argued that the northern European immigrants were the ones most likely to move on to the West and South, where population was needed, whereas the southern Europeans—those intended to be excluded by the test—tended to stay in the crowded cities of the North and East, creating slums and placing a disproportionate financial burden on local charitable institutions. He categorized as also unlikely to pass the test those who intended only temporary stays—those who came to earn money that would not be used to further the country's development but whose purpose was to work and live in the poorest of conditions until their savings were adequate to return and to make life better for a family in their country of origin.

In 1896, a Senate bill that included provision for the literacy test was sponsored by Lodge. The same bill was introduced in the House of Representatives. Congress passed the bill, but it was vetoed by President Grover Cleveland. The House was able to override the veto, but the Senate took no action.

In his veto message, President Cleveland indicated his extreme displeasure with the intent of the bill, reminding Congress of the fact that many of the country's best citizens had been immigrants who may have been deemed inferior. His opinion of the literacy test was that it would be no true measure of the quality of an applicant for admission, and that illiteracy should not be used as a pretext for exclusion when the real reasons were obviously different.

The controversy over the literacy test went on for approximately twenty-five years. Meanwhile, the idea became more popular. In 1907, the Joint Commission on Immigration was funded by Congress and charged to investigate U.S. immigration policy. In 1911, the commission released its forty-one-volume report. The literacy test was adopted as a provision of the Comprehensive Immigration Act of 1917—which was based primarily on recommendations of the commission—but only after similar attempts had been vetoed by President William Howard Taft in 1913 and by President Woodrow Wilson in 1915. Wilson twice vetoed the act of 1917 as well, only to have Congress pass it over his objections after his second veto.

President Wilson argued, in his first veto message to Congress, that the literacy test was an unprincipled departure from the nation's policy toward immigrants. He expressed concern that the literacy test, rather than being a test of character or of fitness to immigrate, was instead a penalty for not having had the opportunity for education and would exclude those who sought that very opportunity in order to better their circumstances.

The 1917 act provided that all persons seeking admission who were over sixteen years of age and who were physically capable of reading were to be tested. Those who were unable to read a few dozen words in some language or dialect were to be excluded from admission as immigrants. There were numerous exceptions, and in many cases illiteracy could be overlooked. Those seeking escape from religious persecution were excepted, as were those formerly admitted who had resided in the United States for five years and who had then departed but had returned within six months. Illiterate relatives of those passing the test were admissible if otherwise qualified.

Impact of Event

The main objective of the literacy test—to exclude those of certain ethnic origins or traditions—failed to reduce immigration in general and from the countries of southern and eastern Europe in particular. Other provisions had effectively discouraged emigrant Asians from choosing the United States as their intended destination. Instead, immigration increased in the four fiscal years that followed enactment of the 1917 law; 1,487,000 applicants were admitted in that period. Of that number, only 6,142 aliens (less than 0.5 percent) were deported for having failed the literacy test. Most of these were from Mexico, French Canada, or Italy.

Case studies of aliens who were unable to pass the literacy test indicate that humane attempts were made by immigration authorities to ensure that the 1917 law was not cruelly enforced. Admission for a limited period could be granted, under bond, for those who otherwise qualified but who were unable to pass the test. Applicants were given a chance to take classes in reading and writing a language of their choice, and more than one opportunity to pass the literacy test could be granted for those who appeared capable of sustaining themselves. Canadian immigration often was the alternative for those whose cases could justify no further extensions of time in which to pass the test and for whom deportation was no longer avoidable.

The racist attitudes of leaders such as Lodge were to dominate U.S. immigration policies until much later in the twentieth century, after the United States had participated in two world wars and after there had been refutation of earlier studies that attributed superior intellect and character to the northern European stock. The fact that the Spanish had colonized the Southwest considerably before northern Europeans began populating the Eastern seaboard seems not to have been considered.

Bibliography

Abbott, Edith. *Immigration: Select Documents and Case Records.* New York: Arno Press, 1969. Contains extracts of immigration acts and relevant court decisions as well as social case histories from the files of Illinois immigration officials. Indexed.

Fairchild, H. P. "The Literacy Test and Its Making." *Quarterly Journal of Economics* 31 (1916): 447-456. Describes the events preceding and the attitudes surrounding Congress' several attempts to require a literacy test. According to the author, President Cleveland changed his mind after his veto of the 1896 bill and stated that, had he been better informed, he would have signed it into law.

Orth, Samuel Peter. "The Guarded Door." In *Our Foreigners: A Chronicle of Americans in the Making.* New Haven, Conn.: Yale University Press, 1920. Published shortly after the enactment of the 1917 law requiring the literacy test, when not a great deal had been written about the subject, this book provides insight into the language and thinking of the period. Even though a small book, it contains an index and an annotated bibliography that groups immigrant subject material according to race or country of origin. The cited chapter provides background to the act of 1917.

Schwartz, Abba P. "Immigration." In *The Open Society.* New York: William Morrow, 1968. The author was appointed in 1962 by President John F. Kennedy to be an assistant secretary of state in charge of immigration, refugee, and travel control policies. This chapter traces the immigration laws through the period of reform in the 1960's. The book is indexed and provides chapter-by-chapter sources.

United States Immigration Commission. *Reports of the Immigration Commission.* 41 vols. Washington, D.C.: Government Printing Office, 1911. The report of the congressional commission's investigation of U.S. immigration policy.

P. R. Lannert

Cross-References

Japan Protests Segregation of Japanese in California Schools (1906), p. 81; "Palmer Raids" Lead to Arrests and Deportations of Immigrants (1919), p. 258; The Immigration Act of 1921 Imposes a National Quota System (1921), p. 350; Nansen Wins the Nobel Peace Prize (1922), p. 361; Congress Establishes a Border Patrol (1924), p. 377; A U.S. Immigration Act Imposes Quotas Based on National Origins (1924), p. 383.

THE BALFOUR DECLARATION SUPPORTS A JEWISH HOMELAND IN PALESTINE

Categories of event: Political freedom and religious freedom
Time: November 2, 1917
Locale: London, England

The British government, in a letter sent to Lionel Walter Rothschild, announced its support for the establishment of a Jewish home in Palestine

Principal personages:

ARTHUR BALFOUR (1848-1930), the British foreign secretary, supporter of Jewish aspirations for a homeland

CHAIM WEIZMANN (1874-1952), a scientist and Zionist leader, the first president of the state of Israel

LIONEL WALTER ROTHSCHILD (1868-1937), the president of the British Zionist Federation, who received the letter that came to be known as the Balfour Declaration

EDWIN MONTAGU (1879-1924), the only Jew in Great Britain's cabinet, opposed the declaration

Summary of Event

The story of the Balfour Declaration's role in Zionism, the Jewish independence movement, began two thousand years ago with the loss of Jewish independence. After the Roman conquest of ancient Israel in 63 B.C.E. (before common era—the same as "before Christ" in the Christian form of notation) and the unsuccessful Jewish revolts in the century that followed, most of the surviving Jews were expelled from their land. So began the exile of the Jewish people and the loss of their political rights.

The Jews' desire for the reestablishment of political independence is a relatively new phenomenon, but religious attachment of Jews to Israel had never abated. Jews trickled back to Palestine throughout the Middle Ages and the Renaissance for reasons of piety, often combined with necessity. The Spanish Inquisition, for example, sent a wave of Jews back to their ancient home.

Not until the American and French revolutions did Jews come to be considered citizens in their adopted lands, and then only in countries experimenting with new freedoms. With the rise of nationalism and the refinement of civil rights in the West, Jewish nationalism became problematic. How could a Jew be loyal to France while maintaining the centuries-old belief that the sojourn in foreign lands was temporary and would be followed by a return to Palestine?

For some, the answer came from the imperfect realization of citizenship. Prejudice and persecution continued despite legal equality. Pogroms in Eastern Europe emphasized the frailty of Jewish rights, and early Zionists such as Leo Pinsker and Theodor Herzl argued that Jewish life would continue to be endangered unless Jews lived in a Jewish land. The rise of nationalism in nineteenth century Europe inspired Jews to change religious sentiments about Zion into political reality. In 1897, the first World Zionist Congress was held. Participants and their supporters urged the return of Jews to Palestine, and about twenty-five thousand Jews emigrated between 1902 and 1903.

Britain recognized an opportunity in Zionist aspirations. Around the turn of the century, Britain entertained the notion of using the Jewish desire for a homeland as a tool of British imperial policy. The Zionist movement rejected offers of settling Jews in British East Africa, Cyprus, and the Sinai.

During World War I, Jews resided in countries at war with each other. The Jews of Palestine were in a particularly precarious position because of persecution by the Ottomans. Some Jews in Palestine wanted to join the Turkish army in opposition to czarist Russia; others, including those deported by the Ottomans, supported the British. The Zionists' aim was to choose the side that was most likely to help Jews achieve independence in Palestine.

The British government's interests were in winning the war and in maintaining control over the Holy Land after the war. Getting the support of the populace in an area controlled by the Ottomans was an important part of its strategy. The British did this by making promises to both the Arabs and the Jews. Raw calculations of power were not the only motivations for this policy, however. The British government was influenced as well by the romantic or religious pro-Zionist ideals of some of its members. Arthur Balfour was among those who came to have an emotional attachment to the idea of a Jewish national home. His Christian upbringing led him to believe in a special role for the Jew in the Holy Land. Similar views were held by Prime Minister Lloyd George. On the practical side, British leaders hoped this policy would win support for the British war effort from Jews all over the world.

The connection between British war interests and Jewish interests in a national home was actively pursued by Zionist leader and scientist Chaim Weizmann, a Russian Jew who had emigrated to England in 1904. Weizmann had done a great service to the British by developing a synthetic substitute for a key component in an essential explosive. The chemist became friends with many prominent British leaders, and he used his personal warmth and persuasiveness to convey the message of Zionism to them.

One member of the British cabinet strongly opposed British support for a Jewish homeland. Edwin Montagu was secretary of state for India and the only Jew in the cabinet. He represented the tension within the Jewish community over loyalty to one's country versus loyalty to Zion. Montagu believed that a Jewish national home would lead people to question the loyalty of British Jews and would create problems with India's Muslim population.

The government, however, came to the decision that support for Zionist aspirations would be to Great Britain's advantage. Government representatives and Zionist leaders negotiated the text of the Balfour Declaration. The Zionists wanted the government to support Palestine as the Jewish homeland. The government, sensitive to the Arab population that might also serve as a bulwark against the Ottoman Turks, chose a milder phrase supporting a Jewish homeland in Palestine.

The Balfour Declaration was a letter dated November 2, 1917, from Arthur Balfour, the British foreign secretary, to Lionel Walter Rothschild, the president of the British Zionist Federation. It read, in part,

> His Majesty's Government view with favour the establishment in Palestine of a national home for the Jewish people, and will use their best endeavours to facilitate the achievement of this object, it being clearly understood that nothing shall be done which may prejudice the civil and religious rights of existing non-Jewish communities in Palestine, or the rights and political status enjoyed by Jews in any other country.

This simple communiqué brought widespread rejoicing in Jewish communities. Britain had hoped that in the Allied countries the Balfour Declaration would mobilize Jews to deepen the commitment of their governments to the Allied cause. In the Central Powers, it was hoped that British support for a Jewish homeland would end Jews' support of their own governments. The strategy was partially successful. The Jews had no influence in the newly formed Soviet Union, but in England, the United States, and to a lesser degree France, most Jews rededicated themselves to supporting the Allied war effort. Most German Jews were not swayed to the British and Zionist causes, but in Palestine, the vast majority of Jewish inhabitants gave their allegiance to the Allies. After the war, further support for the declaration came from the Jews of many other countries. At the end of the war, the Western governments included the text of the Balfour Declaration in the document granting Great Britain control of Palestine.

Zionists read the declaration in the most inclusive of terms, assuming that the British were committed to unlimited immigration of Jews to Palestine. In 1922, these hopes were reined in because the Arabs feared that Jews were taking over their land. The Churchill White Paper limited Jewish settlement to the area of Palestine west of the Jordan. To the Arabs, the Balfour Declaration was not sufficient to guarantee Arab rights. To the Zionists, the Churchill White Paper's restrictions were a necessary evil.

Violence continued intermittently between Jews and Arabs. By 1939, the severity of the situation prompted the British government to, in effect, rescind its support for a Jewish national home in Palestine. The White Paper of May, 1939, stated that Great Britain would create a state of Palestine, one that was neither exclusively Arab nor exclusively Jewish, within ten years. More important, the White Paper announced the prohibition of the sale of land to Jews and the elimination in five years of all Jewish immigration to Palestine.

In essence, the White Paper of 1939 repudiated the Balfour Declaration on the eve of the Nazi Holocaust. The new British policy restricting Jewish immigration to Palestine had the effect of contributing to the death of many Jews who could not find asylum from the horrors of Hitler's Europe.

The Zionists continued their planning for a Jewish national home. In 1942, they decided to advocate an independent Jewish state. In 1947, the new United Nations voted to partition Palestine into Jewish and Arab states. In 1948, Zionist leaders announced the independence of Israel.

Impact of Event

The Balfour Declaration affected two groups of people, Jews and Arabs. Neither group enjoyed the rights that sovereignty conferred upon people, and both groups suffered persecution.

For the Arabs of Palestine, the Balfour Declaration came to symbolize British abandonment of Arab independence goals. At first, there was no Arab consensus about whether Zionism was good or bad for Arabs. Many Arab leaders initially ignored Zionism, and some saw common Jewish and Arab interests. The British had promised independence to Arabs, and Weizmann and the Hashemite representative, Emir Feisal, held some cordial discussions of joint aims. When the Zionists failed to work independently of the British to oppose French control of Syria, talks broke down. Other Arab leaders had, from the beginning, argued that Jewish independence was inimical to Arab nationalist aims. Cooperation for independence between Arabs and Zionists ended in 1919. As a result of the Balfour Declaration and increased immigration of Jews to Palestine, antagonism increased. Instead of complementing each other, the two independence movements began to view themselves in opposition. Violence between the communities in Palestine spread and intensified.

For the Jews, the Balfour Declaration gave Zionism the official recognition and support of a great power. Before the Balfour Declaration, Zionism met resistance from those Jews who wanted to enjoy their newly granted citizenship in modern countries. They wanted to be Jewish—to have the right to believe and worship as Jews—but they wanted to be citizens of modern states, with all the political freedoms that these countries afforded. They did not want their loyalty to be questioned.

Zionists, however, pushed for the Balfour Declaration because they correctly believed that official recognition of Zionist aims by a world power would provide an imprimatur of legitimacy to their movement. Not only would this recognition convince the nations of the world that a Jewish homeland was both right and possible, but it would also convince Jews that a Jewish national home in Palestine was desirable.

The tangible effects of the declaration included the founding of the Hebrew University in Jerusalem and a resurgence of interest in emigration to Palestine. After the declaration, more Jews settled in Palestine. Prior to World War I, there were an estimated eighty-five thousand Jews in Palestine. Many died from the war or from the famine that came with it, and the Jewish population declined to fifty-five thousand. British documents recorded authorized immigration to Palestine of more than five thousand in 1920. The highest level of immigration prior to the release of the White Paper of 1939 came in 1935, when more than sixty thousand Jews moved to Palestine.

The Balfour Declaration was a seminal document that helped transform Jewish aspirations. Despite the serious problems afflicting the state of Israel, it has remained a Jewish national home. The 1991 airlift of Ethiopian Jews to Israel is reminiscent of the airlifts of Jews from Yemen, Aden, and Iraq after the War of Independence.

Although the Balfour Declaration did not explicitly support the establishment of an independent Jewish state, the prospect of a Jewish national home recognized by the Western powers vitalized the movement. In this way, the Balfour Declaration helped make the creation of the Jewish state possible.

Bibliography

Dugdale, Blanche E. C. *Arthur James Balfour: First Earl of Balfour, K.G., O.M., F.R.S., 1906-1930.* London: Hutchinson, 1936. The second volume of a biography written by Lord Balfour's niece. The chapter on Balfour and Jewry reveals the complexity of the foreign minister's attachment to Zionist principles. Discusses how important Zionism was to Balfour the man as well as to Balfour the foreign minister.

Khalidi, Walid, ed. *From Haven to Conquest: Readings in Zionism and the Palestine Problem Until 1948.* Beirut, Lebanon: The Institute for Palestine Studies, 1971. Articles and excerpts from Zionist, neutral, and anti-Zionist sources make the anti-Zionist case. Quality is uneven. The excerpt by J.M.N. Jeffries on the Balfour Declaration is too vitriolic to contribute to sober analysis. Other selections, including Edwin Montagu's memorandum opposing the issuance of the Balfour Declaration and Frank E. Manuel's analysis of the role of American Justice Louis D. Brandeis in the formulation of the Balfour Declaration, are more useful.

Khouri, Fred J. *The Arab-Israeli Dilemma.* Syracuse, N.Y.: Syracuse University Press, 1985. By an American-born political scientist. The work maintains an objective tone, and the historical details closely match those recorded in Howard M. Sachar's volume. Khouri's book focuses on the relationship between the state of Israel and its Arab neighbors after 1948.

O'Brien, Conor Cruise. *The Siege: The Saga of Israel and Zionism.* New York: Simon & Schuster, 1986. Written by an Irishman who has been a diplomat, academic, and journalist. Extremely engaging and empathetic account. Accepts the legitimacy of the existence of a Jewish state but attempts to give voice to all sides' opinions. Includes extensive bibliography and extremely helpful chronological table and glossary.

Sachar, Howard M. *A History of Israel: From the Rise of Zionism to Our Time.* New York: Alfred A. Knopf, 1979. A comprehensive and detailed work, free of jargon. The text is difficult to penetrate because the author conveys so much information. The author's pro-Zionist beliefs are apparent, but the history is balanced. Devotes an entire chapter to the Balfour Declaration. Carefully interprets the roles of power politics and moral concerns in the formulation of British policy.

Weizmann, Chaim. *Trial and Error: The Autobiography of Chaim Weizmann.* New York: Harper and Brothers, 1949. Weizmann was preeminent among Zionist leaders in his push for official British recognition of Jewish aims in Palestine. His memoirs, while not unassuming, provide a readable account of the interplay of personalities behind the modern history of Zionism and the Jewish state.

Renée Marlin-Bennett

Cross-References

Brandeis Becomes the First Jewish Member of the Supreme Court (1916), p. 172; Hitler Writes *Mein Kampf* (1924), p. 389; Nazi Concentration Camps Go into Operation (1933), p. 491; Palestinian Refugees Flee to Neighboring Arab Countries (1948), p. 749; Israel Is Created as a Homeland for Jews (1948), p. 761; The United Nations Creates an Agency to Aid Palestinian Refugees (1949), p. 814; Israel Enacts the Law of Return, Granting Citizenship to Immigrants (1950), p. 832; Eichmann Is Tried for War Crimes (1961), p. 1108; Arab Terrorists Murder Eleven Israeli Olympic Athletes in Munich (1972), p. 1685; Barbie Faces Charges for Nazi War Crimes (1983), p. 2193; The Palestinian *Intifada* Begins (1987), p. 2331; Israel Convicts Demjanjuk of Nazi War Crimes (1988), p. 2370.

GERMANS REVOLT AND
FORM SOCIALIST GOVERNMENT

Category of event: Revolutions and rebellions
Time: 1918-1919
Locale: Germany

The German Revolution marked a defeat for autocratic monarchy and a victory for responsible government

Principal personages:

FRIEDRICH EBERT (1871-1925), the leader of the German Social Democrats who succeeded Prince Maximilian von Baden as chancellor

PRINCE MAXIMILIAN VON BADEN (1867-1929), the last chancellor of the Kaiserreich

PHILIPP SCHEIDEMANN (1865-1939), the chancellor when Ebert was made president

KARL LIEBKNECHT (1871-1919), a stirring "Spartacist" orator

ROSA LUXEMBURG (1871-1919), a gifted "Spartacist" writer and leader

WOODROW WILSON (1856-1924), the U.S. president who pressured Germans to abandon the Kaiser

PAUL VON HINDENBURG (1847-1934), the popular German chief of staff, later elected president

ERICH LUDENDORFF (1865-1937), the quartermaster general who called on democrats and socialists to take the blame for defeat

WILHELM GRÖNER (1867-1937), the successor to Ludendorff

Summary of Event

The German Revolution of 1918-1919 was a direct result of German defeat in World War I. As of 1914, only a handful of German liberals were also "Republicans." The Social Democrats (SPD) were revisionist Marxists, too old and conservative to promote revolution, and German society was too prosperous and complacent to demand radical change.

Four years of war, blockade, rationing, casualties, and shortages greatly reduced German national morale. The failure to end the war victoriously was a factor in the German industrial strike of January, 1918, the first major sign of popular antiwar sentiments. The strike was called off on February 3 as Germany prepared for the 1918 drive to take Paris. When this gamble failed, Germany's chance for victory was gone. Her allies (Bulgaria, Turkey, and Austria-Hungary) began to capitulate or collapse, and her outnumbered soldiers on the Western Front began to surrender. Her enemies (Britain, France, the United States, and Italy) advanced with increasing confidence, divided on some territorial issues but united in their war aim of demanding the removal of the Kaiser, whom they blamed for the war itself.

In September of 1918, the High Command—Field Marshal Paul von Hindenburg and Quartermaster-General Erich Ludendorff—insisted that the Kaiser's new chancellor, Prince Maximilian von Baden, seek an immediate armistice from the Allies and also form a broader coalition government, including the Centrists, Progressives, and Socialists, whom Ludendorff blamed for his military defeat. The armistice notes between Prince Max and United States President Woodrow Wilson clearly pressured Prince Max into making the October 28 reforms by which the Kaiser's veto power in the Bundesrat, his personal control of the chancellor, and his personal command of the army were all ceded to the popularly elected Reichstag. On paper, the Kaiser had become only a figurehead. Wilson, however, persistently declined to make any binding commitment to Kaiser Wilhelm, who headed the Allied list of German war criminals to be tried. The German people began to view their kaiser as an obstacle in the armistice negotiations.

Decisive events were set in motion when the German navy's October 28 order for a quixotic "last battle" against the British caused a seamen's mutiny beginning on October 29. This unplanned incident sparked a flame of revolt that spread through northern and western German cities, with demonstrators calling for peace, bread, and the kaiser's abdication. As the authority of the Kaiserreich crumbled, the Berlin Socialist leaders, who had planned to seize power after the armistice signing at Compiègne on November 11, were forced to advance this action by two days.

Saturday, November 9, became the day of the German Revolution. Berlin's workers staged marches shouting for the kaiser to step down. In the chancellery, Prince Max and a changing group of political leaders agreed that the time for abdication had come. They telephoned their views to the General Staff Headquarters at Spa, where the kaiser listened to Hindenburg, Wilhelm Gröner (Ludendorff's replacement), and other generals emphatically telling him that he no longer had the support of the troops and must abdicate.

At noon, as the demonstrators converged on the chancellery, Prince Max had the Wolff Telegraph Agency announce that the Kaiser had resolved to renounce the throne, although in fact Wilhelm fled to Holland on November 10 before signing any abdication. Meanwhile, Prince Max invited Friedrich Ebert to become chancellor. Ebert was the leader of the Social Democrats (SPD), the largest single party in the adjourned Reichstag. With this peaceful if dubiously legal step, the German party leaders combined legitimacy with revolution.

Ebert's immediate task was to calm the crowds in Berlin, where fifteen people had been killed, as a first step toward establishing national control and order. Near day's end he received a telephone call from General Gröner, promising the support of Hindenburg and the army. The most potent force on the German right appeared to accept the revolution.

Late the following afternoon, some three thousand socialists, workers, and soldiers met at the Berlin Circus Busch to establish a new revolutionary government. Amid speeches calling for socialist unity, three SPD members, including Ebert and Philipp Scheidemann, were chosen as commissars, as were three leaders of the Independent Socialists, or USDP. A small band of antiwar radicals, calling themselves Spartacists after the leader of a Roman slave revolt, were excluded from any substantive role. The Spartacist leaders, Karl Liebknecht and Rosa Luxemburg, declined any honorary posts. Constitutional questions were left to a later national Assembly, and social and human rights issues to a future Reich Congress of Workers and Soldiers.

The "bloody days" of the revolution in December and January stemmed from Berlin police power disputes between paramilitary leaders. After the Marstall Incident of December 23-24, the Independent Socialists resigned as commissars and became active opponents of the bourgeois-socialist coalition. The Spartacists, again excluded from power at the December 16-18 Reich Congress of Councils, turned to the desperate expedient of depending on the prestige and financial support of a foreign source, Russian communism, represented in Germany by Lenin's agent, Karl Radek. The German Community Party, or KPD, was launched in Berlin on January 1, 1919. In hopes of gaining broader support, the new party joined the Berlin police dispute in January. At the Sunday, January 5, mass demonstration in the Siegesallee, the USDP, KPD, and Shop Stewards proclaimed Ebert's overthrow, the establishment of a revolutionary government, and a general strike for January 6. Seriously threatened, Ebert's government fought back, resorting to right wing Freikorps volunteers to suppress the uprising. On January 15, Liebknecht and Luxemburg were apprehended, brought to Freikorps headquarters at the Hotel Eden, openly clubbed into insensibility, and subsequently shot. The SPD coalition government began to depend increasingly on aggressive Freikorps elements of a reviving right wing.

In the National Assembly elections of January 19, the SPD polled 37.9 percent and the Independents 7.6 percent, a 45.5 percent total that was socialism's best showing in the Weimar era but not a mandate for socialization. The Assembly elected Ebert as provisional president and Philipp Scheidemann as chancellor. Sporadic civil strife in Germany continued from January through May, with twelve hundred or more killed in Berlin in March.

The Second Reich Congress of Workers' and Soldiers' Councils met from April 8-14 to discuss economic and social goals for the projected councils which were to be part of the new government. These sessions were the most extensive discussions of citizen's rights and socialization plans by a major forum during the revolution. Some of their ideas were referred to in the new constitution, but not always in enforceable form.

After the June 28 signing of the Treaty of Versailles, the Weimar National Assembly voted approval (262-75) of the new constitution, which went into effect on August 14, 1919. The national government returned from Weimar to Berlin. The Weimar constitution, drafted by a committee under Professor Hugo Preuss, made Germany a people's state republic governed by parliamentary democracy. Proportional representation in the Reichstag gave voting status to small minority parties, making it difficult for any one party to gain a majority, and coalition governments were the norm in the Weimar period. Suffrage for men and women at age twenty was universal. Article 48 of the constitution gave the president extensive emergency powers which were significant in the decline and fall of the republic from 1930 to 1933.

The fifty-seven clauses devoted to individual and group rights were hailed as advanced and groundbreaking. Some of these, however, were only the philosophical slogans of different political parties: "all Germans are equal before the law," "motherhood has a claim to the protection and care of the state," "war veterans shall receive special consideration," "the right of private property is guaranteed," "freedom of contract prevails," and "labor is under the special protection of the Commonwealth." Some of these ideas were sorted into practical gains by the Reichstag or by the National Economic Council, but the councils often became tools of business interests. The constitution's economic promises were hard to achieve, even before the Wall Street crash in 1929.

In the spring of 1920, the army's "Kapp Putsch" in Berlin and subsequent national elections showed a distinct ultraconservative trend. The most dangerous threats to the Weimar Republic came from the Nationalist right, fatally consolidated in 1933 by Adolf Hitler's Nazi movement.

Impact of Event

The German Revolution and the Weimar Republic had more of a lasting impact on the German people than upon their neighbors, who hoped that defeat in World War I had shown Germany the folly of aggressive nationalism and militarism. Later, after the Nazi takeover of 1933, the German Revolution and Republic were widely blamed for failing to prevent this calamity. In fact, the Weimar era did make some progress in human rights. Ending the arbitrary monarchy of the Hohenzollerns and the legal titles of hereditary nobility were steps in democratization, as were suffrage and equal rights for women and the end of Prussia's property-based three-class suffrage system. The regulation of working conditions, especially for children, was a real reform, as were improvements in health, both in conjunction with the League of Nations. In the field of civil liberties, the Weimar constitution balanced individual and group rights in search of a German sense of community, with state intervention permissible only by authority of law.

Certainly, there were misadventures and mistakes. In Germany as elsewhere, direct government provisions proved disappointing. The most significant use of the referendum was in the 1929 Nazi-Nationalist propaganda attack on the Young Plan of war reparations financing. More frequently criticized was the failure to develop a revolutionary armed force similar to the Red Army which Trotsky created in Russia. Some of the critics overlook the extent of political confusion and revulsion against war which dominated post-Armistice Germany.

Less easy to comprehend is the republic's failure to reform and purge the judiciary, the civil service, and the educational system. Conservative judges were notoriously lenient to right wing extremists, while higher education in the humanities and sciences was overwhelmingly limited to upper-class and upper-middle-class students. The "workers' republic" treated the working class as inferiors, while right-

and left-wing intellectuals derided and ridiculed the institutions and leaders of the republic.

The division of the left was a problem for the revolution. No single party had a majority in the Reichstag, and the Social Democratic leaders of 1918 were already known as revisionists and reformers rather than Marxist radicals. If Ebert and his colleagues were guilty of betraying the revolution and stabbing the revolution in the back, as some accused, they did it in plain sight and with the support of the voters. It was the minority extremists who perpetuated the division, while blaming it on the majority.

In broad terms, the German Revolution of 1918 and the Weimar Republic were the products of defeat and were burdened by the Treaty of Versailles, the Ruhr occupation, the inflation of 1923, and mass unemployment following the Wall Street crash of 1929. In spite of all this, after the Nazi era and the devastation which Germany brought upon itself in World War II, the West German people in 1949 resurrected a republican government much like the Weimar regime of 1919.

Bibliography

Coper, Rudolf. *Failure of a Revolution*. London: Cambridge University Press, 1955. This is a short and readable account, decidedly pro-Spartacist in interpretation. The book includes an index and bibliography but no systematic documentation of the author's sources.

Eyck, Eric. *A History of the Weimar Republic*. Vol. 1. Cambridge, Mass.: Harvard University Press, 1962. This standard general history of the period supplies a German perspective. The coverage of the 1918 revolution is brief. Includes notes, an index, and an extensive bibliography.

Haffner, Sebastian. *Failure of a Revolution*. Translated by George Rapp. London: André Deutsch, 1973. Ludendorff and Ebert are the chief villains in this brief and entertaining but superficial and even fanciful account. Index of persons only. No documentation or bibliography.

Halperin, S. William. *Germany Tried Democracy*. New York: Thomas Y. Crowell, 1946. A well-written survey of the years 1918 to 1933, this book presents the interpretation that the Weimar Republic "was sabotaged by friend and foe alike." No documentation, but has an index and extensive bibliography.

Lutz, R. H. *The Fall of the German Empire*. 2 vols. Berkeley: University of California Press, 1932. These volumes contain a selection of documents and articles from Lutz's twelve-volume work, *Causes of the German Collapse in 1918* (University of California Press, 1934). Includes an index and a chronology of events but no bibliography.

Pinson, Koppel. *Modern Germany*. New York: Macmillan, 1954. This college textbook contains two factually detailed narrative chapters on the German collapse and revolution in 1918-1919. Includes notes, bibliography, and index.

Rosenberg, Arthur. *The Birth of the German Republic*. Translated by Ian F. D. Morrow. New York: Oxford University Press, 1931. A classic account by a USDP-KPD participant and scholar. The author's political viewpoint does color his interpretation, but the narrative gives a valuable sense of the period.

Ryder, A. J. *The German Revolution of 1918*. New York: Cambridge University Press, 1967. This work is broadly based and scholarly. Updates some of the earlier research. Perhaps the most useful single volume on the subject. Includes notes, index, and bibliography.

Scheidemann, Philipp. *The Making of New Germany*. Translated by J. E. Mitchell. 2 vols. New York: D. Appleton, 1929. These memoirs give the author's impressions of the events of November 9 and 10, of which he was a witness and participant.

Waldman, Eric. *The Spartacist Uprising of 1919 and the Crisis of the German Socialist Movement*. Milwaukee: Marquette University Press, 1958. A brief, clear, readable, and critically well-balanced analysis of crucial factors within the Spartacist movement. Includes notes, bibliography, and index.

K. Fred Gillum

Cross-References

Lenin and the Communists Impose the "Red Terror" (1917), p. 218; Lenin Leads the Russian Revolution (1917), p. 225; The Paris Peace Conference Includes Protection for Minorities (1919), p. 252; The League of Nations Is Established (1919), p. 270; The International Labour Organisation Is Established (1919), p. 281; Hitler Writes *Mein Kampf* (1924), p. 389; Mussolini Seizes Dictatorial Powers in Italy (1925), p. 395; Germany Attempts to Restructure the Versailles Treaty (1925), p. 423; Hitler Uses Reichstag Fire to Suspend Civil and Political Liberties (1933), p. 480.

PARLIAMENT GRANTS SUFFRAGE TO BRITISH WOMEN

Categories of event: Voting rights and women's rights
Time: February 6, 1918
Locale: London, England

The grant of the vote to women age thirty and over marked the removal of a significant symbol of women's subordinate status in Great Britain

Principal personages:

DAME MILLICENT (GARRETT) FAWCETT (1847-1929), the president of the National Union of Women's Suffrage Societies, the largest women's suffrage organization

DAVID LLOYD GEORGE (1863-1945), the prime minister in 1918

CHRISTABEL PANKHURST (1880-1958), a daughter of Emmeline Pankhurst and a prominent leader of the Women's Social and Political Union

EMMELINE PANKHURST (1858-1928), the leader of the Women's Social and Political Union, a militant suffrage organization

SYLVIA PANKHURST (1882-1960), a daughter of Emmeline Pankhurst and leader of the East London Federation of Suffragettes

RACHEL (RAY) STRACHEY (1887-1940), an influential leader of the National Union of Women's Suffrage Societies

Summary of Event

The granting, in 1918, of the vote to British women age thirty and over marked the culmination of a struggle for a basic women's right that had been in progress for nearly half a century. The vote was a symbol of the political power that women lacked. Enfranchisement of women was seen as a means of overthrowing male tyranny in all aspects of life.

In late nineteenth century Britain, women were still denied opportunities in many areas. Although a few women's colleges had been established, higher education existed almost entirely to benefit men. Women who wished to be considered respectable were discouraged from seeking paid employment. Those who persisted discovered that jobs were segregated by sex, with higher paying positions reserved for men. Until the 1880's, a married woman did not even have the legal right to own property; her property became her husband's when she married.

The discrimination was justified by the "separate spheres" doctrine. It was claimed that men and women were designed by nature to perform different roles, and women were best suited to be wives and mothers. It was impossible for all women to marry since women outnumbered men, but those who remained single were viewed as incomplete persons for not having experienced marriage and motherhood. These restrictions were bitterly resented by women who did not believe that their destiny should be determined by their sex.

The organized campaign for woman suffrage began in 1866, when Parliament considered extending the franchise to several million more men. Barbara Bodichon, Emily Davies, Elizabeth Garrett, and others collected almost fifteen hundred signatures on a petition requesting that the vote also be extended to women. When the government introduced a franchise bill the following year, John Stuart Mill, speaking for women, proposed an amendment that would have added woman suffrage to the measure. After Parliament rejected the amendment, women formed several suffrage societies. In 1897, these societies joined forces and formed the National Union of Women's Suffrage Societies (NUWSS), the organization that directed the suffrage campaign until the vote was granted.

Opponents of woman suffrage believed that women's nature made them unsuited for participation in political life. It was claimed that women were too emotional to evaluate the issues rationally. Others maintained that women lacked sufficient knowledge of public matters. Their expertise, it was argued, was in household and family matters and had no relevance to the political issues voters had to resolve. Also, voting was often carried out in pubs or other places where alcohol was being consumed; the coarse language and brawling which often broke out was considered an inappropriate environment for ladies. Finally, because many believed women to have a higher moral nature than men, it was feared that if women had the vote they would support reforms, such as temperance legislation, which men believed to be detrimental to their interests.

During their first thirty years of organized struggle, women made little progress in gaining the vote in national elections. Woman suffrage drew its main political support from members of the Liberal Party, but that party refused to proceed with legislation because its leaders believed that most women would vote Conservative. Women were thought to be especially susceptible to the influence of the Church of England, and the church's active members tended to be Conservatives. Although the Conservative Party therefore might have gained the most from woman suffrage, it refused to sponsor legislation because its members tended to believe that a woman's place was in the home.

Despite the barriers they encountered, women made substantial gains. Many who opposed granting women the vote in national elections accepted women voting in local elections. Local government often involved education, health, and welfare, which were issues perceived as being an extension of women's domestic role. By 1900, women had gained the right to vote in many municipal and county elections and for school boards. Their responsible participation in local elections was important in undermining Conservative resistance to women voting in national elections.

Emmeline Pankhurst and her daughters Christabel and Sylvia formed the Women's Social and Political Union in 1903. This marked the beginning of a new stage in the suffrage campaign. The union deliberately sought confrontation to force politicians to deal with the suffrage issue. The union gained, through its flamboyant tactics, much more publicity than had the NUWSS. On the other hand, its use of unlawful acts, such as setting fire to post boxes, hampered efforts to obtain suffrage legislation by making it difficult for the government to grant the vote without appearing to be giving in to violence.

World War I created conditions that helped to achieve woman suffrage. Most suffragists were loyal supporters of the government's war policy and concentrated their energies on Britain's war effort. The suffrage groups stopped campaigning for the vote, thereby giving the government the opportunity to enact reform without appearing to be giving in to pressure. The war also forced the government to consider franchise reform in order to allow men in the armed forces to vote.

Once the process of reforming the franchise was under way, it was difficult not to include some measure of woman suffrage. Conservatives who had doubts about the principle of woman suffrage were persuaded that it was wiser to include a modest women's franchise clause in the bill than to risk the revival of agitation for a more radical measure after the war.

Millicent Fawcett, president of the NUWSS, agreed to accept a limited proposal in return for a pledge that some measure of woman suffrage would definitely be included in the bill. Fawcett suggested that setting a higher eligibility age for women than for men would be the least objectionable means of restricting the number of female voters. She recommended that the age of thirty be adopted. The committee drafting the bill accepted her proposal.

The bill was thus a modest measure deliberately limited to make it acceptable to all parties. This helped the women's suffrage clause to pass the House of Commons easily in June, 1917, by a vote of 385 to 55. The Representation of the People Act, which became law on February 6, 1918, was an important step toward ending the subordinate position of British women in public life, but in order to gain acceptance from the all-male legislature it had been carefully worded to minimize the degree of change it would bring. It extended the vote only to a carefully restricted group of women—those age thirty or older who themselves were qualified to vote in local elections or were married to men qualified to vote in local elections. The women's elation at having gained the principle of woman suffrage was thus dampened by an awareness that the campaign would have to continue in order for them to achieve equal suffrage rights.

Impact of Event

The 1918 Representation of the People Act established the principle of woman suffrage, thus opening the door to the establishment of full and equal suffrage in 1928. The act was followed by a series of changes in law and policy which removed many restrictions on women's opportunities. Measures were passed allowing women to be elected to the House of Commons, to be members of juries, to enter professions previously closed to them, and to receive degrees from the University of Oxford.

Under the Representation of the People Act, almost 8.5 million women gained the vote. Women constituted 39.6 percent of the electorate in the first general election in which they could vote, held in December, 1918. Candidates for election were very conscious of the new female voters and made special efforts to appeal to them. The three major parties added proposals to their election platforms designed to attract female voters. The women who had campaigned for woman suffrage were disappointed, however, by this first experiment with a female electorate. Seventeen women sought seats in the House of Commons in that first election, but only one was elected. The election resulted in a substantial increase in votes for the Conservative Party, and it is believed that the Conservatives benefited more from the new female voters than did the other parties.

When it had become clear in 1918 that Parliament would enact woman suffrage, many women shared Ray Strachey's excitement that women now had the power to bring about sweeping changes in their lives. Strachey expected equal pay and equal employment opportunities to follow the vote, but she overestimated the impact of the franchise. While important as a symbol of women's acceptance as active citizens, suffrage did not bring a dramatic change in their lives. Instead of voting as a group for reforms specifically affecting women, female voters were drawn into existing political parties and adopted the political views of those parties. Furthermore, the women age thirty or older who had the vote were more likely to be married and not in paid employment, and thus did not always have the same outlook on issues as younger women, who were more often single and working to support themselves.

Bibliography

Holton, Sandra. *Feminism and Democracy: Women's Suffrage and Reform Politics in Britain, 1900-1918*. Cambridge, England: Cambridge University Press, 1986. Shows that while the Women's Social and Political Union may have been the most militant in terms of tactics, it is misleading to view it as the most radical group. The democratic suffragists within the NUWSS were more radical because they urged adult suffrage and sought to link the Labour Party with the women's suffrage movement.

Hume, Leslie Parker. *The National Union of Women's Suffrage Societies, 1897-1914*. New York: Garland, 1982. The most important study of the main women's suffrage organization. Provides much information not available in other sources. Stresses the shift in the NUWSS focus from women's right to equality to the notion that women needed the vote to protect their interests as wives and mothers. Bibliography and index.

Kent, Susan. *Sex and Suffrage in Britain, 1860-1914*. Princeton, N.J.: Princeton University Press, 1987. Demonstrates that the women's suffrage movement was not the single-issue campaign claimed by previous writers. Shows that suffrage was sought as part of a broad attack on the subordination of women. Less useful on the politics of reform than other studies. Includes an index and a bibliography.

Mackenzie, Midge, ed. *Shoulder to Shoulder*. New York: Alfred A. Knopf, 1975. The companion volume to the television series of the same name. Concerned only with the Women's Social and Political Union's contribution to the suffrage campaign. Especially valuable for the numerous pictures documenting the activities of the suffragettes. Also reproduces selections from suffragette letters and other writings to provide an account in the participants' own words. Index and brief bibliography.

Romero, Patricia W. *E. Sylvia Pankhurst: Portrait of a Radical.* New Haven, Conn.: Yale University Press, 1987. Excellent biography of one of the leading suffragettes. Very readable. Very frank about some of the less attractive aspects of Pankhurst's personality. Contains new information on her private life. Useful on the East London Federation of Suffragettes. Index and extensive endnotes but no bibliography.

Rosen, Andrew. *Rise Up, Women! The Militant Campaign of the Women's Social and Political Union, 1903-1914.* London: Routledge & Kegan Paul, 1974. The most thorough account of the WSPU. Makes extensive use of the unpublished records of the WSPU. Critical of WSPU tactics, but not an unsympathetic study. Index, bibliography, and a few photographs.

Smith, Harold L., ed. *British Feminism in the Twentieth Century.* Amherst: University of Massachusetts Press, 1990. An account of the broader feminist movement of which the suffrage campaign was an important part. Includes a chapter on Emmeline Pankhurst's ideas showing how Romanticism shaped her views on how to bring about political change. Has an index and a brief bibliography.

Harold L. Smith

Cross-References

The Pankhursts Found the Women's Social and Political Union (1903), p. 19; Women's Institutes Are Founded in Great Britain (1915), p. 167; The Nineteenth Amendment Gives American Women the Right to Vote (1920), p. 339; Women's Rights in India Undergo a Decade of Change (1925), p. 401; The Minimum Age for Female British Voters Is Lowered (1928), p. 442; French Women Get the Vote (1944), p. 646; The U.N. Convention on the Political Rights of Women Is Approved (1952), p. 885; The United Nations Issues a Declaration on Equality for Women (1967), p. 1391; Women in Switzerland Are Granted the Right to Vote (1971), p. 1605; Thatcher Becomes Great Britain's First Female Prime Minister (1979), p. 2024; A U.N. Convention Condemns Discrimination Against Women (1979), p. 2057.

THE PARIS PEACE CONFERENCE INCLUDES PROTECTION FOR MINORITIES

Categories of event: Peace movements and organizations; racial and ethnic rights
Time: 1919
Locale: Paris, France

The Paris Peace Conference attempted to make the protection of the civil rights of ethnic, religious, and linguistic minorities a matter of international concern

Principal personages:
WOODROW WILSON (1856-1924), the president of the United States (1913-1921)
ROBERT LANSING (1864-1928), the secretary of state under Wilson
EDWARD M. HOUSE (1858-1938), the special presidential emissary at Paris
DAVID LLOYD GEORGE (1863-1945), the prime minister of Great Britain
GEORGES CLEMENCEAU (1841-1929), the premier of France

Summary of Event

Before World War I, full and equal civil rights were denied to minorities, or subject nationalities, within the multinational empires of Germany, Austria-Hungary, Russia, and Ottoman Turkey. Ethnic, religious, and linguistic minorities such as the Finns, Czechs, Poles, Lithuanians, Latvians, Estonians, Serbs, Croats, Slovenes, Greeks, Romanians, Bulgarians, Ukrainians, and Jews suffered varying degrees of discriminatory treatment under alien, imperial rule in Central and Eastern Europe. The empires refused full political rights to minorities with regard to such activities as voting and holding public office. Economic rights to property ownership and to engage in certain professions were restricted. Freedom of religious worship was limited in many regions for minorities. Linguistic traditions were threatened by the imposition of official languages in imperial governmental and educational institutions.

By 1918, all four multinational empires had collapsed. Military defeat and the exhaustion and deprivations suffered during World War I produced revolutions which overthrew the imperial governments of Germany, Austria-Hungary, Russia, and Turkey. The victorious Allied and Associated Powers met in Paris in 1919 to create a peace settlement which was meant to make the Great War "the war to end all wars." Part of this settlement involved the redrawing of the map of Central and Eastern Europe to restructure these regions geographically.

It was U.S. president Woodrow Wilson's insistence on the Fourteen Points concerning the concepts of equality, liberty, and justice for all peoples and nationalities that added a new dimension to the territorial reconstruction of Europe at the Paris Peace Conference. Wilson's stress on the principle of "national self-determination," which emphasized the right of all national groupings to determine their own destinies, made even more complex the redrawing of the map of postwar Europe. Self-determination, as a practical policy, was virtually impossible to implement. In Central and Eastern Europe, in particular, ethnic, religious, and linguistic groupings were so intermixed that nothing short of massive population removals and transfers would have allowed each nationality to have its own separate state. Not only would such a policy have been impracticable, not to mention inhumane, but the multitude of new states this policy would have created would each have been too small and weak to have any real chance of survival in political, economic, or military terms.

Consequently, the practical redrawing of frontiers made necessary the existence of large minority populations in the newly created and reorganized states of Central and Eastern Europe. The reorganized state of Poland contained not only some twenty-seven million Poles but also one million Germans, three to five million Ukrainians, and two to three million Jews. The new state of Czechoslovakia counted among its total population of fourteen million citizens some three million Germans, one-half million Magyars, and one-half million Ruthenians. The new state of Yugoslavia counted, in addition to its main Serbian, Croatian, and Slovenian populations, one-half million Germans, one-half million Magyars, one-half million Albanians, and six hundred thousand Macedonians, out of a total population of twelve million.

Wilson's principle of national self-determination was significant for the minority populations in postwar Central and Eastern Europe because they regarded it as a concept which, by extension, could be applied to minority civil rights. The minorities in the newly created and reorganized states considered themselves to be nationalities, just as Poles, Czechs, and Serbians, among others, had considered themselves subject nationalities within the pre-1918 multinational empires. For this reason, representatives of the minority populations pressed the leading statesmen at the Paris Peace Conference to regard the protection of minority civil rights as an important feature of the peace settlement.

It was in the interest of such countries as the United States, Great Britain, and France to consider the wishes of minorities not only for obvious ethical reasons but also in an attempt to ensure long-term stability and peace in the newly reconstructed regions of Europe. The growing resistance and opposition of the subject nationalities before World War I had produced internal instability which weakened the Austro-Hungarian, Ottoman, and Russian empires. Balkan nationalism in Southeastern Europe had contributed to the outbreak of the general war in Europe in 1914.

Precedents were not lacking for the Paris Peace Conference to impose special minority-rights obligations on newly created and reorganized states. In 1878, the Congress of Berlin had elaborated provisions on religious freedom and political equality to be embodied in the public law of the new principality of Bulgaria and had imposed similar guarantees as a condition of its recognition of the independence of the states of Montenegro, Serbia, and Romania. The congress also included in the Treaty of Berlin specific clauses for the protection of religious liberties in the Balkan territories that remained within the Ottoman Empire. Consequently, Wilson and his chief advisers, Secretary of State Robert Lansing and Special Presidential Emissary

Colonel Edward M. House, set out to persuade other leaders at Paris, such as British prime minister David Lloyd George and French premier Georges Clemenceau, to join the United States in pursuing measures to protect minorities in the newly created and reorganized states of Central and Eastern Europe. Wilson's insistence on this policy resulted in the establishment of the Committee on New States and the Protection of Minorities at the Peace Conference.

The committee devised a series of minorities treaties by which each newly created, or reorganized, state pledged itself to grant fair and equal treatment to the minority populations within its frontiers and agreed that the execution of its pledges should be treated as a matter of international concern. Four of the defeated powers, Austria, Hungary, Bulgaria, and Turkey, had to make similar agreements as part of the separate peace treaties they signed with the Allied and Associated Powers at Paris. At a later date, Germany also had to pledge itself to protect minority rights, but only with regard to the province of Upper Silesia. The United States, Great Britain, France, and Italy were afraid that imposing further minority protection obligations on a still powerful Germany might help to legitimize future efforts by Berlin to champion the cause of German minority populations in Central and Eastern Europe, causing destabilization in that reconstructed region. By the mid-1920's, the defeated powers and the new states of Poland, Czechoslovakia, Romania, Yugoslavia, Greece, Albania, Lithuania, Latvia, Estonia, and Finland, as well as Iraq, had pledged themselves to the protection of minority civil rights.

The undertaking of formal pledges to protect minority rights became a prerequisite for the above states to enter the League of Nations, the organ created by the Paris Peace Conference to regulate international affairs. The principle of minority protection was not incorporated into the wording of the covenant that established the league because it was believed that this might be too contentious an issue for many prospective member states. The drafters of the covenant wanted to avoid the impression that the League of Nations would continually pursue policies that might be regarded as unduly interfering in the domestic affairs of individual states. The league did take upon itself the role of ultimate guarantor of minority civil rights. Minority populations in the defeated and new states of Central and Eastern Europe were given the right to petition the league over grievances. The League Council had the power to appoint special "Committees of Three," to which each minority petition was submitted. Between 1921 and 1929, 150 such committees were appointed. Theoretically, the league had not only moral but also more practical means of persuasion, such as economic sanctions, to pressure signatories of the minorities treaties and clauses to live up to their pledged obligations. By incorporating such powers into the functions of the League of Nations, the Paris Peace Conference attempted to make the protection of the civil rights of minority populations a concern of the international community.

Impact of Event

For all of its efforts, the work of the Paris Peace Conference proved to be largely ineffectual in protecting the civil rights of minorities in Central and Eastern Europe in the interwar period. Despite its theoretical powers, the League of Nations could do little more than exert moral pressure concerning minority rights, relying on the unwillingness of governments to be recognized, in the League's Assembly, as having failed to carry out their treaty obligations. Finding enough support for stronger sanctions proved to be extremely difficult.

The minorities themselves urged the league often to establish an independent and permanent minorities commission, with the same functions and powers as the mandates commission, which oversaw the rights of native populations in league-mandated territories outside Europe. The powers of the league with regard to European minorities were based on formal treaties. Nothing could be added to the minorities treaties without the consent of the signatories, and the signatories were utterly opposed to the creation of a permanent commission. They believed that a minorities commission would represent an unacceptable source of interference in their domestic affairs by the League of Nations and the international community. As it was, the hostility and lack of cooperation of the signatory states toward the temporary, ad hoc "Committees of Three" frustrated league attempts to deal effectively with minority grievances.

Even more infuriating to the signatory states was the fact that the other countries that entered the League of Nations chose not to pledge themselves formally to the protection of minority rights. The victorious Allied and Associated Powers and the nonbelligerent countries joining the league were afraid that such a pledge might obligate them to admit the claims of such racial, religious, and linguistic minorities as the African-American populations of the United States, the Irish in Great Britain, the Flemings in Belgium, the Bretons in France, the Basques in Spain, and the Chinese in the Japanese-controlled Shantung Peninsula. The principles of national self-determination and, by extension, the protection of minority civil rights appeared to be acceptable to the victorious and nonbelligerent powers at Paris and in the league only if they could be imposed on the defeated countries and the small, newly created states of Europe, too weak to oppose such impositions. The real purpose of the minority rights provisions of the Paris peace settlement was not to protect particular groups but to give stability to the political and territorial postwar settlement in Central and Eastern Europe.

The precedent set at Paris in establishing the protection of minority civil rights as a matter of international concern had some significance. Although the successor organization to the League of Nations, the United Nations, did not include minority protection in its founding charter, the United Nations and the international community have taken an increasing interest in minority rights since 1945, as an aspect of the growing world concern for human rights issues.

Bibliography

Bailey, Thomas. *Woodrow Wilson and the Lost Peace.* Chicago: Quadrangle Books, 1944. Critical interpretation of the United States' role in the failures of the Paris

Peace Conference. Condemns Wilson for his inability to translate ideals, such as the principle of self-determination, into reality. Argues that America must, in the post-World War II world, avoid its interwar policy of isolationism to make the peace last. Index and excellent bibliography.

Birdsall, Paul. *Versailles Twenty Years After.* Hamden, Conn.: Archon Books, 1962. Well-written and highly critical analysis of the Paris Peace Conference, written just before America's entry into World War II. Birdsall condemns the inadequacies and harshness of the peace settlement, along with American isolationism, as the reasons for the breakdown of stability and peace in Europe. Index and bibliography.

Hudson, Manley. "The Protection of Minorities and Natives in Transferred Territories." In *What Really Happened at Paris: The Story of the Peace Conference, 1918-1919 by American Delegates,* edited by Edward M. House and Charles Seymour. New York: Charles Scribner's Sons, 1921. Detailed account by an American delegate of the minorities question and Wilson's central role in its settlement. A somewhat uncritical analysis, but interesting to the general reader nevertheless.

Lederer, Ivo, ed. *The Versailles Settlement: Was It Foredoomed to Failure?* Boston: D. C. Heath, 1960. The best collection available of short essays, articles, and excerpts concerning the Paris Peace Conference. Both historians and statesmen contributed. The general reader interested in the minority rights issue will find the last four articles the most useful. Includes suggestions for further reading.

Macartney, C. A. "League of Nations' Protection of Minority Rights." In *The International Protection of Human Rights*, edited by Evan Luard. New York: Praeger, 1967. Intelligent and critical analysis of the background of the league's efforts to protect minorities. Provides detailed information concerning the minority treaties and the resistance the league faced from the treaty states and their friends in attempting to implement this policy. Bibliography and index.

Marks, Sally. *The Illusion of Peace: International Relations in Europe, 1918-1933.* New York: St. Martin's Press, 1976. The best analysis of pre-Nazi, interwar, international relations in Europe. Particularly critical of the Paris Peace Conference and the weaknesses of the League of Nations. Places the minorities issue in this context. Easily accessible to the general reader, with a good index and bibliography.

Mayer, Arno. *Political Origins of the New Diplomacy, 1917-1918.* New Haven, Conn.: Yale University Press, 1959.

_____. *Politics and Diplomacy of Peacemaking: Containment and Counterrevolution at Versailles, 1918-1919.* New York: Alfred A. Knopf, 1967. Still the best examinations of the ideas and interests that influenced and determined the Paris peace settlement. The minorities issue is thoroughly analyzed. Extensive index and bibliography provided in both books.

Nicolson, Harold. *Peacemaking 1919.* New York: Grosset & Dunlap, 1965. Written by one of the most important members of the British delegation, this remains the best personal account of the Paris Peace Conference. The issues, personalities, and day-to-day events at Paris are well summarized. Nicolson's personal diaries are included. Index.

Walters, F. P. *A History of the League of Nations.* 2 vols. London: Oxford University Press, 1952. A useful supplement to Sally Marks' *The Illusion of Peace.* Provides a detailed and sympathetic study of the league and its interwar activities. Gives a thorough account of the league's dealings with the minorities issue. Excellent index and bibliography.

Douglas A. Lea

Cross-References

The Baltic States Fight for Independence (1917), p. 207; Finland Gains Independence from the Soviet Union (1917), p. 212; The Balfour Declaration Supports a Jewish Homeland in Palestine (1917), p. 235; The League of Nations is Established (1919), p. 270; Ireland Is Granted Home Rule and Northern Ireland Is Created (1920), p. 309; Germany Attempts to Restructure the Versailles Treaty (1925), p. 423; The Atlantic Charter Declares a Postwar Right of Self-Determination (1941), p. 584; The United Nations Adopts Its Charter (1945), p. 657; Israel Is Created as a Homeland for Jews (1948), p. 761; A Hungarian Uprising Is Quelled by Soviet Military Forces (1956), p. 969; Soviet Jews Demand Cultural and Religious Rights (1963), p. 1177; The United Nations Votes to Protect Freedoms of Religion and Belief (1981), p. 2146; Soviet Troops Withdraw from Czechoslovakia (1990), p. 2570; Lithuania Declares Its Independence from the Soviet Union (1990), p. 2577.

"PALMER RAIDS" LEAD TO ARRESTS AND DEPORTATIONS OF IMMIGRANTS

Category of event: Immigrants' rights
Time: 1919-1920
Locale: The United States

The Palmer raids, fueled by antiradical and anti-immigrant sentiments, were the most spectacular anticivil rights excesses of the Red Scare of 1919-1920

Principal personages:

A. MITCHELL PALMER (1872-1936), the attorney general who created a new division of the Bureau of Investigation for the war against radicalism

J. EDGAR HOOVER (1895-1972), the head of the Justice Department throughout 1919

EDWARD Y. CLARKE, a member of the Southern Publicity Association who, in 1920, was given the task of organizing, managing, and increasing the membership of the Ku Klux Klan

WILLIAM D. HAYWOOD (1869-1928), the dynamic leader of the class-conscious, revolutionary Industrial Workers of the World

EMMA GOLDMAN (1869-1940), a Russian-American anarchist who was deported from the United States to Russia at the height of the Red Scare

ALEXANDER BERKMAN (1870-1936), a Russian-American anarchist and editor of the *Blast*, deported to Russia with his lover Emma Goldman

Summary of Event

In an attempt to rid the nation of radicalism, in 1919 United States Attorney General A. Mitchell Palmer ordered various police units of the government to raid the homes and headquarters of suspected radicals and aliens. The raids and the arrests that followed were directed against those, usually foreign-born, who were accused of radicalism. This offense covered everything from parliamentary socialism to Bolshevism, encompassing "radical feminism," anarchism, and labor militancy as well. In the immediate postwar period, American resistance to anything foreign stemmed from rumors and formal pronouncements of a great radical foreign conspiracy aimed at overthrowing the American way of life. Many Americans, encouraged by political rhetoric and official pronouncements, were convinced that a communist revolution was imminent and that a reaffirmation of traditional American values, coupled with a good dose of law and order, was the only thing that would make America safe for Americans.

In several respects, Palmer's antiradical crusade continued the espionage and sedition prosecutions of the war years. The Overman Committee investigating German espionage during World War I, for example, simply switched to hunting communists and socialists after the war. The most spectacular excesses of the "Red Scare" ended by 1921, but it is arguably more accurate to say that the scare became part of the political climate in the United States for many years to come. Antiradicalism, for example, played a significant role in the political agitation for immigrant restriction and antiforeign sentiments that followed the raids.

In 1919, the U.S. government and organizations purporting to defend "Americanism" responded to any activity that was perceived to be radical: strikes were busted (1919 steel and coal strikes, for example); newspapers called for government action against all radicalism, perceived or real; duly elected legislators were denied their seats in the New York State Assembly; and the National Security League, whose main weapon was "organized patriotism," successfully lobbied Congress to pass laws authorizing the deportation of aliens and other "irreconcilable radicals." The American Legion, advocating the Americanization of United States society, declared that radicals were mostly from non-English speaking groups. Individual state legislatures, among them those of Idaho and Oregon, came close to passing laws forbidding any publication not written in English. In short, "It was an era of lawless and disorderly defense of law and order, of unconstitutional defense of the Constitution, of suspicion and civil conflict—in a very literal sense, a reign of terror," according to historian Frederick Allen.

Public reaction to radicalism so affected Palmer that he ordered the Justice Department's Bureau of Investigation (the predecessor of the Federal Bureau of Investigation) to infiltrate and investigate all radical groups. Following the implementation of this program, the bureau's head, J. Edgar Hoover, reported back to Palmer that revolution was imminent. Palmer then organized a federal dragnet aimed at stepping up the raids and arrests. On January 2, 1920, federal agents arrested more than six thousand people, most without proper warrant, incarcerating them in jails and detention centers for weeks and even months without granting rights to legal counsel or bail. Of those arrested, 516 were eventually deported, including the feminist, anarchist, and militant labor organizer Emma Goldman and fellow anarchist and labor organizer Alexander Berkman.

The intolerance expressed in the Palmer raids took many forms. Some advocated book censorship and others inflicted agony on "hyphenated Americans," including African Americans, who were arguably the chief victims of the Palmer raids and their aftermath. As African Americans moved to the North, northern whites reacted in fear. Many of them perceived the influx of these visibly distinct Americans to be a threat to their social status. The employment of blacks threatened white workers with a status deprivation. In response, many whites struck out at the newcomers, rekindling racist fears of the past. For the emigrating blacks, the move north signaled a refusal to accept a caste system in the South which had excluded so many of them from the general prosperity of the nation. Tension mounted as black aspirations clashed with racial norms. The racial conflict which followed immediately became linked to the antiradical mood of the time. White mainstream America feared social upset from any source, whether it was black Americans or radical immigrants.

The mood of society in 1919 was as conducive to racial tension as it was to the Red Scare. Fueled by a witch hunt to weed out Bolsheviks and other radicals from America's inner fabric, racial prejudice became a natural extension of a patriotic call for complete Americanism. From Chicago to Tulsa, racial relations often became racial violence. It was in just such an atmosphere that the Ku Klux Klan experienced a rebirth.

Fighting for its own version of "one hundred percent Americanism," the Klan played upon the fears and hostility that existed between urban and rural America. Klan propaganda, advocating a concern that public morals were being weakened by the mixing of the races and by "red-inspired" trade unionism, sought to rally traditional Americans to its banner. The Klan's chief organizer, Edward Y. Clarke, roused his constituents against a "Jewish-Banker-Bolshevik conspiracy" that the Klan saw leading an international movement to take control of America. This fit right in with Palmer's warning that a Bolshevik uprising would occur on May Day, 1920. Racism was fused to anti-Bolshevism and all that it implied. Because Jews were perceived by many in rural Protestant America to be of foreign birth, the Klan's propaganda was received with patriotic fervor. Most rural Americans identified radicalism with foreigners. Jews, Catholics, and immigrants fit into this xenophobic milieu. By 1921, Klan membership reached the one million mark.

The Americanism crusade fit in nicely with concerns of American business over the growth of trade unionism. Strikes, after all, were a threat to profits, and American businesspeople were in no mood to have profits reduced. Labor organizers, in turn, called for a reorganization of the industrial system to promote workers to a position on par with the power and prestige of industrial capitalists. In a countervailing move against trade unionism, the business community called upon patriotism to defeat any "Bolshevik-inspired" labor organizing activity. Trade unionism was labeled as anti-American, radical, and foreign by design. American business viewed the struggle of the worker for better wages as the beginning of armed revolution in America. Anything or anyone associated with workers' rights was therefore anti-American and should be treated as such. If this meant intolerance of Constitutional guarantees, so be it.

Impact of Event

A search for a human rights perspective on the Palmer Raids revolves around three interrelated questions. First, what gave rise to the Red Scare which precipitated the raids? Second, why were the raids aimed for the most part at an alien component of the labor movement? Third, was the entire phenomenon an aberrant episode or an action which set the tone for the rest of the decade?

The Palmer raids became part of the "normalcy" of the Harding Administration. Antiradicalism continued to play a role throughout the decade in the agitation for immigrant restriction and as a catalyst for the business community's countervailing response of trade unionism. Significant anti-immigration activity resulted in the passage of the Johnson-Reed Immigration Act of 1924, which ended three centuries of free European immigration. This law laid the groundwork for continued anti-alien activity as some native-born Americans lashed out against those who, by their mere presence, challenged traditional norms.

Union activity was confronted by the emergence of the antiunion "American Plan," pursued by business throughout the decade. This effort, launched by employers to resist labor unionization on every front, included the use of labor spies to infiltrate the labor movement, the manipulation of public opinion through antiradical and anti-alien propaganda, and the hiring of strikebreakers to counter organized labor's ultimate weapon. A major force behind the plan was the National Association of Manufacturers (NAM). Throughout the decade, NAM expended a very large amount of money and political influence to lobby against trade unionism. Palmer's replacement, James Daugherty, complemented this activity in the courts. During his tenure in office, he was influential in obtaining many federal injunctions against work stoppages, forcing striking workers back to work. The courts also made it possible for trade union activities to be classified as a restraint of trade and therefore to be made illegal. The prevailing mood of the nation greeted such determinations with enthusiasm. At the beginning of the decade, 20 percent of all nonagricultural workers belonged to labor unions. By the end of the 1920's, because of a combination of antiradicalism, employer pressure, and unfriendly government activity, this percentage was cut in half.

Support for official antiradical activity also fanned the fires of nativism. The Palmer raids continued a wartime obsession for internal security. A postwar recession, high unemployment, and failures of international cooperation led to an overall atmosphere of an inability to confront emerging social pathologies. Antiradical and deportation remedies of the Departments of Justice and Immigration were part of the nativistic renewal of the period.

The Industrial Workers of the World (IWW, or Wobblies) played a key part in the postwar antiradical renewal. Communist influence within the group encouraged anti-Bolshevist passions to surface against it. Pursuit of the Wobblies had been going on since their organization in 1905. Their attempt to unite all workers into one big union, and their objection to and rejection of revered American values such as free enterprise and upward social mobility, painted an anti-American and therefore foreign picture of the organization. America saw the Wobblies as a threat to the internal security of the nation and as a conduit of alien ideas, and the IWW became a feared organization. Whether it deserved this reputation was not the point. Federal policies toward the group took on an antiradical and antialien tone. By the time of America's entry into World War I, the immigration, espionage, and sedition laws had been broadened to allow arrest and deportation of IWW officials. Many were jailed for conspiracy because of their opposition to the war. The organization's leader, William Dudley (Big Bill) Haywood, fled from the United States to the Soviet Union, where he died and was buried in the Kremlin wall.

IWW paranoia, and the fervent nativism which it helped to spawn, was reaffirmed after the war. Wobblies, particularly in the Pacific Northwest, were rounded up in antiradical and antialien crusades. The use of troops in the raids and the denial of legal rights to those arrested and held became at once an official answer to a nation's security problem and an appeasement to an insecure public's extreme xenophobia. This "normalcy" continued throughout the decade.

Bibliography

Allen, Frederick Lewis. *Only Yesterday: An Informal History of the 1920s.* New York: Harper and Brothers, 1931. Attempts to relate and interpret the story of the eleven years between the end of the war with Germany (November 11, 1918) and the stock market panic which culminated on November 13, 1929. Fully presents many events from this period which have never been completely chronicled. Indexed.

Higham, John. *Strangers in the Land.* New Brunswick, N.J.: Rutgers University Press, 1988. An "intellectual history" that encompasses and synthesizes political, economic, and social change by providing a summary of agitation for immigrant restriction and against immigration in the early twentieth century. Includes index and bibliographical notes.

Murray, Robert K. *Red Scare: A Study in National Hysteria, 1919-1920.* Minneapolis: University of Minnesota Press, 1955. Tells the story of the Red Scare following World War I. Suggests that this era was important because it provides an example of what happens to a democratic nation and its people when fear replaces ideals and reason. Includes index and bibliographical notes.

Preston, William, Jr. *Aliens and Dissenters.* Cambridge, Mass.: Harvard University Press, 1963. The significance of this study lies in its examination of the problems of aliens and dissenters. Deals with the period from 1890 to 1920, when the fear of foreigners and radicals increased in intensity. Concludes that such fears ultimately made aliens and radicals scapegoats for the country's ills. Includes index and bibliographical notes.

Tuttle, William M., Jr. *Race Riot: Chicago in the Red Summer of 1919.* New York: Atheneum, 1982. A history which attempts to explain the race riot and its causes in terms of individuals and groups. The analysis gets its foundation from a revealing overview of 1919's Red Summer and the Red Scare, detailing the racism and antiradicalism of that period. Includes index and bibliographical essay.

Wexler, Alice. *Emma Goldman in Exile: From the Russian Revolution to the Spanish Civil War.* Boston: Beacon Press, 1989. Details the last twenty years of the life of American anarchist Emma Goldman, who was deported from the United States to Russia in 1919, at the height of the anti-Communist movement. Presents the image of this radical feminist as "the most dangerous woman in America."

Thomas Jay Edward Walker

Cross-References

Congress Prohibits Immigration of Illiterates over Age Sixteen (1917), p. 231; The

SOLDIERS MASSACRE INDIAN CIVILIANS IN AMRITSAR

Category of event: Atrocities and war crimes
Time: April 13, 1919
Locale: Amritsar, Punjab, India

The Amritsar Massacre, or Jallianwalla Bagh massacre, was such an atrocious action that it can be singled out as spurring the Indian independence movement

> *Principal personages:*
> R. E. H. DYER (1864-1927), the officer who ordered a small force of Indian soldiers to open fire on a crowd of twenty thousand people
> SIR MICHAEL O'DWYER (1864-1940), the lieutenant governor of Punjab who approved of General Dyer's actions
> SAIF-UD-DIN KITCHLEW (1883-1963), a Kashmiri Muslim who was a coleader of agitation against the Rowlatt Acts in Amritsar
> DOCTOR SATYAPAL, a middle-class medical doctor who was a coleader for agitation against the Rowlatt Acts in Amritsar
> UDHAM SINGH (1899-1940), an Indian revolutionary who assassinated Sir Michael O'Dwyer

Summary of Event

Historian Alfred Draper titled one of his books *Amritsar: The Massacre That Ended the Raj.* The book's subtitle is correct, for it was that incident that galvanized sentiment to terminate British rule (the Raj) in India. Britain had ruled India for two hundred years, and India was considered the "jewel in the crown" of the British Empire. Under British rule, Indians had viewed the world through British spectacles. For the average Indian, there were two major powers in the world, Great Britain and Russia. Other European powers, except for Germany, a trading partner, were not considered relevant, nor was the United States.

In spite of this worldview, disenchantment had developed by the middle of the nineteenth century. The Mutiny of 1857 had exposed the exploitation of British rule, and although Queen Victoria had "added the Jewel to her Crown," Indian society was also combating philosophical and religious encroachment from the West. Revitalization movements developed to counter Christian and Western ideas. One reaction was the elimination of the *Brahmo Samaj* movement that had combined Christian doctrine and practices with Hindu philosophy. This was replaced by the *Arya Samaj,* or "Society of the Aryan People," which not only emphasized a return to Aryan foundations but also included personal relationships that were merged with Hindu traditions to develop a sense of superiority.

It was events after World War I, however, that altered the British-centric view held by Indians. The change was so rapid that within three months after the war, British prime minister Herbert Asquith stated that Indian questions would have to be approached from a new angle. Events in the world contributed to the loss of awe for British power. Stirrings of nationalism in Asia and the defeat of Russia by the Japanese showed that Europeans were not invincible. The Russian Revolution resulted in the collapse of a great reactionary power and of prewar ideas of world political relations. Also, the emergence of the United States and President Woodrow Wilson's Fourteen Points emphasized rights rather than the British ideas of concessions.

The change was not merely in attitudes or worldview. An educated leadership had emerged in India, many of whose members were educated in London and influenced by the political philosophies of John Locke and Karl Marx. It was these men, including Jawaharlal Nehru, who would later provide political leadership to the country. More immediate, however, was the treatment and attitude of the British after the war. At the outset of World War I, there was an outburst of loyalty for the British by the Indian people, but it diminished after the Allied victory.

A social gap had always existed between the British and the Indians; however, the gap increased with a change in the type of people in the Indian Civil Service (ICS). The old component had stayed on during the war, while younger people had served in the military, with the result that India, by the end of the war, was ruled by an old and tired bureaucracy. Furthermore, the Indian Civil Service lacked the ability it had had in early years; it lost its prestige, and the quality of its recruits decreased. Those in the ICS saw themselves as rulers of an inferior people and perceived themselves as fulfilling the "white man's burden" by administering to incompetent heathens.

The Indian contribution to World War I, especially from the Sikhs of Punjab, had been enormous. Sixty thousand men had been recruited from Patiala, and Sikh soldiers had fought on all fronts. Fourteen of the twenty-two military crosses awarded for gallantry went to Sikhs, whom police and local officials treated like rustics. When Sikhs faced discrimination in Canada and the United States, the British government did not come to their aid. Tales of discrimination and humiliation meted out to Sikh soldiers in Canada and California filtered back to villages in Punjab, and the Indians believed they had been betrayed by their British rulers. In spite of the sacrifices and support they had given to the Allied cause in the war, they did not receive promised reforms.

Dissatisfaction became rampant among the Indian overseas community in Canada and the United States. As a result, the Ghadr Party was formed in North America. The party sent money and fighters to spark an uprising, which did not materialize but was worrisome for the British administrators. In 1919, the harvest in Punjab was poor, land prices were high, productivity in the canal colonies decreased, and the cost of living rose. Not only were general economic conditions worse, but the oppressive Rowlatt Act was introduced in February of 1919 and passed in March. Actually, the Rowlatt Act was a collection of two acts that empowered police to arrest and search people without a warrant, detain suspects without a trial, and try people before special courts with neither juries nor rights of appeal. Interestingly, wild and fabricated stories spread about how a policeman who coveted a man's wife could get the husband out of the way because of the acts; a bride and bridegroom allegedly had to be inspected by a British doctor before a marriage could take place; and, it was rumored, a family would have to pay the government a sum of money equal to that spent on a wedding. The uneducated masses believed these rumors. Mohammed Ali Jinnah, an Indian politician who resigned from his post in protest, stated in his letter of resignation, "In my opinion a government that passes such a bill in times of peace forfeits the claim to be called a civilized government." This act energized the independence movement.

At that time, Sir Michael O'Dwyer was lieutenant governor of Punjab. O'Dwyer was a brilliant academic and a good sportsman who had entered the ICS full of confidence and imbued with the conviction that the British had the divine right to rule India. O'Dwyer was pugnacious and outspoken and had a disdain for the educated Indians. He detested and distrusted them and openly expressed his views. Thus, an equal disdain developed between him and the educated Indian class. Brigadier General Reginald Dyer came from a family with a long line of associations with India. His family had lived through the Mutiny of 1857, and the events were still in their memory, as was the fear of a fresh uprising. After graduating from Sandhurst, Dyer saw several campaigns; he was a swashbuckling character who had done well in fights and brawls.

In April of 1919, these two men were the principal British players in Punjab, as Mahatma Gandhi led the agitation against the Rowlatt bills in India. In fact, it was the oppressiveness of the Rowlatt Act and Gandhi's agitation against it that propelled Gandhi from his role as an obscure politician into national prominence. In the Punjab, protests were conducted in an orderly and peaceful manner until the police caused escalation in Amritsar. Peaceful demonstrations had been led by a Hindu and a Muslim, a fact that surprised the British but resulted in Hindu-Muslim unity. One leader was Saif-ud-Din Kitchlew, a Kashmiri Muslim who had been at the University of Cambridge with Jawaharlal Nehru. Kitchlew had a Ph.D. from Munster University and was considered pro-German. He was an eloquent speaker and supported home rule. The Hindu leader, Dr. Satyapal, was a medical doctor from a middle-class family. He was reserved, but he was a good orator and progressive nationalist who believed in peaceful and constitutional means to gain political freedom.

When the police arrested Kitchlew and Satyapal and whisked them away to Dharamsala, the news of their capture spread throughout the city, and crowds protested the action. The mob got out of hand, and in trying to disperse the crowd, the police killed six people and wounded more than thirty. As a result, the mob assaulted white people and set fire to English-owned banks, a church, and other establishments. Marcia Sherwood, a white Englishwoman, was caught in the mob and beaten. Sherwood was a well-liked doctor who had spent fifteen years helping the people of Amritsar. This event resulted later in the famous "crawl order" given by General Dyer. The order required every Indian passing the spot where Sherwood was assaulted to crawl along the street. Three British soldiers were stationed on the spot to enforce the order.

On April 12, 1919, when Brigadier General Dyer arrived from Jullundur with troops and armored cars, he was greeted in the bazaar by crowds shouting anti-British slogans. When he received information that telegraph cables had been cut and railroad tracks had been tampered with, he declared a state of emergency, which made all meetings illegal.

The local Congress Party had already called a meeting at Jallianwalla Bagh for the Baisakhi fair, and Sikhs were there to celebrate the birth anniversary of their *Khalsa*, the Sikh soldier-saint brotherhood. Many were unsuspecting villagers who came from outlying villages and were not aware of the events that had preceded their arrival at Amritsar. General Dyer took the attitude that it was best to use quick and strong force on such occasions, so when he heard of the April 13 meeting at the Jallianwalla Bagh, he marched troops over to the scene.

Jallianwalla Bagh was a seven-hundred-by-four-hundred-foot walled-in area with only one entrance, a seven-and-a-half-foot-wide passage. There was a large crowd of people in the courtyard; estimates of its size range from fifteen thousand to fifty thousand. A meeting was going on with pictures of Kitchlew prominently displayed. Speeches and poetry were read and a resolution passed calling for Kitchlew's release. At around 5:15 P.M., Dyer's troops surrounded the area. Seeing the soldiers, people rose to leave, but Hans Raj, a revolutionary leader, urged people to remain, arguing that the government would never fire on them.

Hans Raj was wrong. Dyer ordered his soldiers to fire. Fifty soldiers fired a volley of shots into the crowd, but Hans Raj continued to shout "they are only blanks" when he fell. As people fell dead and wounded, others made desperate attempts to escape, but they were trapped by the high wall surrounding the area. The only exit was blocked by soldiers firing at the crowd. Some climbed into a well but later drowned. Dyer ordered the soldiers to continue firing and to aim where the crowd was the most dense. There was no escape. Many innocent people, ignorant of the no-meeting order, were killed or wounded. The soldiers fired 1,650 rounds into the crowd, killing 379 and wounding more than 2,000. The cries of agony and thirst sounded long into the night as wounded lay dying among the corpses.

Impact of Event

It was not until the next day that people were allowed to pick up corpses and help the wounded. Repressive measures known as "Dyerarchy" were introduced. The term was coined in reference to the lawlessness of the British administrators. These measures were not excessive in physical pain or loss of money but in wounded pride. Indians meeting a white person were required to bow. Electricity was cut off in the Indian quarters, and a rigid curfew and other restrictive measures made normal existence impossible for the Indians. In the meantime, police had carte blanche powers to round up suspects and seemed motivated to obtain convictions at any cost. Indians were flogged without trial, and bicycles, carts, and vehicles not owned by Europeans were confiscated. Lawyers were commandeered as special constables and made to patrol the streets. Courts tried three hundred men and summarily sentenced fifty-one to death and others to imprisonment. Lahore, Kasur, Gujranwala, and most of Punjab suffered under martial law. In seven weeks, twelve hundred people were killed and thirty-six hundred wounded.

Public opinion was divided: The British community stood behind Dyer, and Indians were confused over what they saw as a change in British justice and administration. On April 19, when Dyer saw Sherwood in the hospital, in pain and her life in the balance, he was outraged and issued the famous crawl order. The summary courts that followed destroyed what faith the Indians had in British fairness. Punjabis were confused, for they had believed that, in spite of their faults, the British ruled with a semblance of fairness. They witnessed the opposite. The punishments were not countered by higher British officials, which surprised and bothered many Indians, especially the middle and upper classes who had grown up with a respect for English justice and fair dealings.

Publicity followed in the "Amritsar Leader Case," in which Satyapal and Kitchlew were tried for revolutionary plotting against the British. The trial did much to destroy British credibility and helped galvanize public opinion against Dyer's and O'Dwyer's actions. Nobel Prize winner Sir Rabindranath Tagore wrote to the viceroy and relinquished his knighthood, and Mahatma Gandhi returned medals he had received in honor of service to the British. The events aroused little interest in Britain, but in India they exposed to the Indian people a racist attitude. The Hunter Committee, composed of English and Indians, was formed to investigate the actions. During the testimony, Dyer displayed a callous attitude. After the hearings, on a train journey to Jullundur, Dyer talked freely about teaching the "bloody browns a lesson." He did not know that the man on the bunk above his was Jawaharlal Nehru, who was educated at Harrow and Cambridge and was the future prime minister of India. Nehru was appalled by Dyer's callousness, and his admiration for the British changed to animosity. Dyer was censured by the committee and subsequently relieved of his command.

The matter was debated in the British House of Lords and House of Commons. Dyer was vindicated by the House of Lords but censured by the House of Commons. Dyer's vindication had an adverse effect on British-Indian relations. In the meantime, O'Dwyer continued to proclaim his and Dyer's innocence. Eventually the matter went to court, and O'Dwyer came out victorious. Dyer had been in poor health during much of his time in India and died on July 23, 1927. A Sikh by the name of Udham Singh assassinated O'Dwyer on March 13, 1940. For this action Udham Singh became a hero among the Sikhs.

The results of the Amritsar Massacre were many. Gandhi, for example, was rocketed to national prominence. He inspired many to fight the British when he visited Punjab and encouraged patriots to be *nirbhai* (fearless). Gandhi was instrumental in the decline of the Chief Khalsa Diwan, a group that espoused Western ways, and in the creation of the Central Sikh League, a group more aligned with revolutionary ideology.

Racial tensions increased. The British feared the Indians and looked on their actions with suspicion, as they had after the Mutiny of 1857, when the British almost lost India in an uprising of Indian soldiers. On the other hand, the myth of British fairness and honor was destroyed. Even Indians who had been loyal to the Empire suffered and were victimized by O'Dwyer, who claimed that he had saved the Empire. In fact, he had alienated some of its most loyal supporters, especially the Sikhs, who had been crucial in maintaining British rule in India.

Bibliography

Colvin, Ian. *The Life of General Dyer.* Edinburgh: William Blackwood & Sons, 1931. A biography of General Dyer. It provides good insight into his life.

Draper, Alfred. *Amritsar: The Massacre That Ended the Raj.* London: Cassell, 1981. This is a well-researched and detailed account of the massacre.

Furneaux, Rupert. *Massacre at Amritsar.* London: Allen & Unwin, 1963. A well-researched and detailed account.

Singh, Khushwant. *A History of the Sikhs, 1839-1964.* Princeton, N.J.: Princeton University Press, 1966. The most authoritative account of Sikh history. The best summary source of the Amritsar Massacre and subsequent events.

Spear, Percival. "The First World War and the Great Leap Forward." In *A History of India.* Vol. 2. Baltimore, Md.: Penguin Books, 1965. An excellent history of India during the modern period, this chapter provides a good context for understanding the massacre.

Tinker, Hugh. "The Rise of Modern Social, Religious, and Political Movements." In *South Asia: A Short History.* Honolulu: University of Hawaii Press, 1990. This work is recognized as the most authoritative account of South Asian history. Tinker's chapter is the best explanation of the cultural conflict faced by Indians as they dealt with Western dominance.

Arthur W. Helweg

Cross-References

The Defense of India Act Impedes the Freedom Struggle (1915), p. 156; Gandhi Leads a Noncooperation Movement (1920), p. 315; Gandhi Leads the Salt March (1930), p. 447; India Signs the Delhi Pact (1931), p. 459; India Gains Independence (1947), p. 731.

THE LEAGUE OF NATIONS IS ESTABLISHED

Category of event: Peace movements and organizations
Time: April 28, 1919
Locale: Paris, France

The League of Nations was created in the attempt to preserve international peace by means of multilateral diplomacy and collective action against any state committing an act of aggression

Principal personages:
> WOODROW WILSON (1856-1924), the twenty-eighth president of the United States, who played the leading role in the creation of the League of Nations
>
> EDWARD M. HOUSE (1858-1938), a U.S. statesman who worked closely with President Wilson on the development of the new organization
>
> LORD ROBERT CECIL (1864-1958), a British statesman who served on the committee that drafted the organization's covenant
>
> JAN CHRISTIAN SMUTS (1870-1950), a South African statesman who served on the covenant committee
>
> LÉON BOURGEOIS (1851-1925), a former French prime minister and ardent proponent of the League of Nations, the chief French delegate on the covenant committee
>
> VITTORIO EMANUELE ORLANDO (1860-1952), the Italian prime minister and chief Italian delegate to the Peace Conference

Summary of Event

World War I was the single most important event leading to the creation of the League of Nations. Toward the end of the nineteenth century, many governments had anticipated the coming of a major war (although they did not imagine anything of the actual magnitude of World War I) and had taken a few steps to avoid it.

The First Hague Peace Conference was convened in 1899 and brought together twenty-six nations to explore what could be done to preserve peace and reduce armaments. Such a conference was unusual, perhaps even unprecedented, on such a scale, in that it was to devise procedures and possibly new international machinery not for the purpose of settling a specific problem but to maintain a stable and peaceful international order. Governments were acting preventively—a sign of progress. Unfortunately, the threat of war was not sufficiently imminent or international tension sufficiently great to impel the participants to be radically innovative. They did nothing to reduce the risk of war beyond making a rather bland attempt to improve international arbitration. Neither did they touch the issue of armaments. Ironically, they codified some of the laws and customs of war to reduce the inhumanity of armed conflict but did not interfere with the traditional right of states to resort to war.

They did agree, however, that meeting in such a fashion was desirable and should happen again. They could not be accused of being overly eager or driven by their sense of urgency; the Second Hague Peace Conference took place eight years later and, despite worsening international tensions, failed once again to devise new ways to protect world peace or to reduce armaments. Once again, the participants agreed to another meeting in about eight years, but World War I interrupted their leisurely process.

The terrible losses and the magnitude of the suffering caused by World War I drastically changed perceptions. By the end of the war, the idea of some sort of international organization or association of nations to prevent another world war was strong in many countries. U.S. President Woodrow Wilson made it one of his Fourteen Points and came to the Paris Peace Conference determined that this should be among the first questions raised. At the plenary meeting of January 25, 1919, it was agreed that a League of Nations should be created to provide safeguards against war and that it should be an integral part of the peace treaty. A commission was appointed, with Wilson as chair, to draft the covenant of the new organization. This was done in record time, in part because of the great amount of work done in previous years on the subject. The text of the covenant was adopted by a unanimous decision of the Peace Conference on April 28, 1919, but could only come into force as a part of the Treaty of Versailles, which went into effect on January 10, 1920. Implementation work, however, began immediately. Sir Eric Drummond was named as the organization's first secretary general, and a preparatory committee was appointed.

The peace conference specified that the league headquarters would be in Geneva, although the preliminary seat of the organization was in London. The main organs were the Assembly, the Council, and the Secretariat. The Assembly was composed of the entire membership (initially forty-one), but it never became global. The U.S. Congress refused to ratify the Treaty of Versailles and never joined the League of Nations; Japan, Germany, and Italy left the organization as a result of their expansionist policies. The Soviet Union became a member but was expelled when it invaded Finland in 1939.

Meeting once a year, the Assembly was empowered to discuss any issue brought to it by its members; however, it could only make nonbinding resolutions requiring unanimity among those who voted. Thus, in theory, any member could veto any recommendation. In practice, this rarely happened: Dissenting members would express their displeasure in committee meetings and simply abstain from voting in plenary sessions.

The Council was initially composed of four permanent members (France, Great Britain, Italy, and Japan) and four nonpermanent members, subsequently increased to six, nine, and finally eleven. Germany was made a permanent member in 1926. The Council developed the practice of having four regular meetings a year (and special meetings as needed). States regularly sent their foreign ministers or prime ministers, who developed the habit of working together as colleagues. The Covenant made no clear differentiation between duties of the Council and those of the Assembly. Both bodies had the right to deal with any matter of concern to the League of Nations but were only allowed to make nonbinding recommendations. The rule of unanimity applied in the Council, as in all League of Nations organs.

A small secretariat under the authority of the secretary general was given the duty of servicing the organization; it started with a staff of about one hundred in 1919, a number that rose to a maximum of about seven hundred in 1931. (The United Nations would have more than fifty thousand employees in various agencies around the world.) Under Drummond's leadership, the staff became a truly impartial and independent international civil service with high standards of efficiency. Members of the League of Nations, however, especially the most affluent, made determined efforts to cut expenditures to the bone.

The Paris Peace Conference had stipulated in its covenant that a Permanent Court of International Justice should be established, and it was left to the League of Nations to set it up. The structure of the court was approved by the Assembly in 1920, but it was kept independent of the League of Nations. It quickly became highly respected for the quality of its decisions; when the United Nations was created, the court was incorporated into its structure without any substantive changes.

The Treaty of Versailles also created another body, in many respects independent from the League of Nations but administratively tied to it, the International Labour Organisation (ILO), whose function was to promote the rights of working people around the world. Its structure was highly innovative: In contrast to other international organizations whose member states were represented by governmental personnel, national delegations to the ILO included representatives of employees and of employers, each group having the right to vote separately. The ILO became an agency of the United Nations.

The League of Nations rapidly became a complex structure, and subsidiary organs were created to address the many issues brought to it. These included the Permanent Mandate Commission to supervise the administration of the former colonies taken from the defeated powers, the minorities committees of the Council, and the committees concerned with military affairs and with the problems of disarmament. Even more numerous were the bodies dealing with economic and social matters, among them the Economic and Financial Organization, the Organization for Communications and Transit, the Health Organization, and the Intellectual Cooperation Organization as well as offices dealing with drug traffic, the protection of women, child welfare, the abolition of slavery, and refugee problems. Some of these had subsidiary organs of their own. They did an enormous amount of work that seldom made headlines but that affected the well-being of people around the world. Peace was beginning to be understood not simply in terms of power relationships, armaments, or political disputes but also in terms of the economic and social conditions of people in various parts of the world. Agencies integrated into an administrative system were for the first time available to deal with the needs of a growing global society. The world had come a long way from conferences at The Hague. Sovereign states remained the primary actors, but most of them now accepted the need to work together as members of permanent international structures.

Impact of Event

The League of Nations is seldom given credit for having done much for global society. It was created in an attempt to prevent the folly of another world war. World War II occurred nevertheless, and it is often said that the League of Nations failed. But did it really?

The League of Nations, imperfect as it was, provided all the machinery that was needed to curb the unbounded ambitions of Japan, Italy, and Germany. What was missing was the will to use it. The members of the League of Nations had pledged to act collectively under its covenant to stop aggression. When aggression was committed, however, they were not prepared to carry out under the banner of the League of Nations the kind of military action that was needed.

Without the will to act on the part of its members, no organization or governmental structure could work, and neither could the League of Nations. It is convenient to blame the machinery, but in this case it is an exercise in self-delusion: The governments that had pledged to protect peace and justice betrayed the trust that had been placed in them. Japan could have been stopped in its first act of aggression (perhaps teaching salutary lessons to future aggressors); Italy could have been stopped in its conquest of Ethiopia; Adolf Hitler himself was incredibly vulnerable when he gambled and remilitarized the Rhineland. None of the League of Nations members was willing to act in fulfillment of the covenant.

With regard to the process of world politics, the creation of the League of Nations represented a considerable improvement over the Hague Peace Conferences convened at eight-year intervals. It provided a permanent world forum in which every nation, the weak as well as the strong, could be heard. This was progress in a world in which smaller states tended to be ignored. Moreover, the League of Nations brought about a major change in the traditional right of states to go to war. For the first time in the history of the modern state system, organized society had taken the right to assess the legitimacy of recourse to force. No organization had ever had this option.

The League of Nations was a stepping-stone toward the more elaborate form of international organization created after World War II. As the world became more interdependent, states discovered that international institutions could help them meet the needs of their people. Economic and social issues were added to the agenda of diplomacy, with enormous benefits for ordinary people around the world. Dependent people were able to appeal in defense of their rights, refugees found more coordinated assistance, and workers gained better protection against a variety of abuses. It was the first time in the history of international affairs that such an array of public agencies had been made available to serve international society. The people of the world gained much from this experiment, despite the slowness or reluctance of some national governments to adjust to the new environment.

Bibliography

Cheever, Daniel S., and H. Field Haviland, Jr. *Organizing for Peace*. Boston: Houghton Mifflin, 1954. This thorough study gives an overview of the early development and creation of the League of Nations, examines its structure, and reviews the League of Nations' accomplishments in the areas of international security, economic cooperation, social and cultural activities, and dependent territories issues. Comparisons are made throughout between the League of Nations and the United Nations. Extensive bibliographies are provided.

Eagleton, Clyde. *International Government*. Rev. ed. New York: Ronald Press, 1948. Gives an excellent presentation of the historical background of the League of Nations and the international political context within which it operated. Discusses its work and compares it to the United Nations. A very good introduction to international organization. Provides text of the League of Nations' covenant.

Gathorne-Hardy, G. M. *A Short History of International Affairs, 1920-1939*. 3d ed. New York: Oxford University Press, 1942. An excellent review of the evolution of international politics during the era of the League of Nations. Provides the setting for the study of the League of Nations and its accomplishments. Very helpful to understand the issues facing the organization and how it performed.

Goodrich, Leland M. "From League of Nations to United Nations." In *International Organization: Politics and Process*, edited by Leland M. Goodrich and David A. Kay. Madison: University of Wisconsin Press, 1973. Contrasts the two world organizations in their character, structure, and functions in the realm of international security and in economic and social cooperation. This is a concise comparison by a long-established scholar in the field. Other studies in this volume are focused on the United Nations and provide an interesting contrast with presentations on the League of Nations by F. P. Walters and Alfred Zimmern.

The League of Nations in Retrospect: Proceedings of the Symposium Organized by the United Nations Library and the Graduate Institute of International Studies. New York: W. De Gruyter, 1983. Examines the institutional aspects of the League of Nations, its handling of security issues, and questions of financial, economic, social, and humanitarian cooperation. Although not comprehensive in their approach, the papers provide a useful perspective on the activities of the organization.

Rovine, Arthur W. *The First Fifty Years: The Secretary-General in World Politics, 1920-1970*. Leyden, The Netherlands: Sijthoff, 1970. Studies the activities of the three secretaries general of the League of Nations and their first three counterparts in the United Nations. Concludes with a lengthy overview of their role in world politics. Includes a bibliography.

Walters, F. P. *A History of the League of Nations*. New York: Oxford University Press, 1965. A classic study of the League of Nations. Comprehensive, detailed, and accurate. A superb historical presentation. Covers developments prior to World War I leading to the creation of the League of Nations and provides one chapter on the drafting of its covenant. Extremely useful.

Zimmern, Alfred. *The League of Nations and the Rule of Law, 1918-1935.* New York: Russell and Russell, 1969. An excellent study of the pre-World War I international setting leading to the creation of international organizations. Presents the various plans proposed for the League of Nations. The author examines the creation of the League of Nations and its major organs and explains how the world organization handled the problems brought to it. A superior historical work.

Jean-Robert Leguey-Feilleux

Cross-References

The Paris Peace Conference Includes Protection for Minorities (1919), p. 252; The International Labour Organisation Is Established (1919), p. 281; Germany Attempts to Restructure the Versailles Treaty (1925), p. 423; Japan Withdraws from the League of Nations (1933), p. 474; The United Nations Adopts Its Charter (1945), p. 657; Nazi War Criminals Are Tried in Nuremberg (1945), p. 667; The International Labour Organisation Wins the Nobel Peace Prize (1969), p. 1509.

STUDENTS DEMONSTRATE FOR REFORM IN CHINA'S MAY FOURTH MOVEMENT

Categories of event: Indigenous peoples' rights; revolutions and rebellions
Time: May 4, 1919
Locale: People's Republic of China, especially Beijing

The decision made at the Paris Peace Conference to give China's Shantung province to Japan enraged Beijing's college students and led to demands for international justice and domestic reforms

Principal personages:

CH'EN TU-HSIU (1879-1942), the dean of the School of Letters at National Beijing University and founder of *New Youth*, a magazine advocating reform

FU SSU-NIEN (1896-1950), a National Beijing University student, editor-in-chief of *New Tide* magazine

HU SHIH (1891-1962), a professor at National Beijing University, a supporter of academic freedom and advocate of language reform and the vernacular

LI TA-CHAO (1889-1927), the head of the library at National Beijing University, the first important Chinese to convert to Marxism

LO CHIA-LUN (1897-1969), a National Beijing University student, editor of *New Tide* magazine, and author of the May Fourth Manifesto

TS'AI YUAN-P'EI (1867-1940), the chancellor of National Beijing University who encouraged research and academic freedom

Summary of Event

The revolution of 1911 overthrew the Ch'ing dynasty and established the Republic of China. Without significant military power, Sun Yat-sen, father of the republic and founder of the Kuomintang (Nationalist Party), soon resigned as president of the Republic of China. The weak governments that followed were dominated by warlords. There were no democratic reforms, civil wars prevailed, and China's international position deteriorated.

In 1914, at the beginning of World War I, Japan captured from German forces the Shantung province of China, where Germany had established a sphere of influence and enjoyed political and economic rights extracted from a weak China in 1898. In 1915, Japan imposed the Twenty-one Demands on China that gave it extensive concessions in China and the right to assume permanently Germany's privileges in Shantung. Chinese warlord governments agreed to this and other Japanese demands in return for loans and Japanese support. Japan also secured secret agreements with Great Britain, France, and Italy and tacit approval from the United States that it should continue to control Shantung after Germany's defeat. In 1917, China declared war against Germany.

Chinese light industries boomed during World War I as a result of the decline of Western imports. This led to the development of a new entrepreneurial and managerial class in the industrial cities and the rise of a factory working class. New schools proliferated. In 1915, the Ministry of Education listed 120,000 government schools of all sorts. In addition, there were private schools, many run by Western missionaries. There thus emerged new social classes imbued with modern ideas. Most Chinese were excited about United States president Woodrow Wilson's Fourteen Points and his advocacy of national self-determination for oppressed peoples, which they thought should benefit them. Thousands of Chinese in many cities demonstrated joyfully at the end of World War I, anticipating a new dawning of justice for China.

At the Paris Peace Conference in 1919, China attempted to win back Shantung and sought an end to the unequal treaties that made it a quasi colony of powerful Western nations and Japan. United States president Woodrow Wilson agreed with British and French leaders to transfer Germany's rights in Shantung to powerful Japan rather than return the province to weak China, in violation of national self-determination and the human rights of the Chinese.

Chinese intellectuals who were dissatisfied with their inept government and China's low international status sought ways to reform and renew their national life. Many young men who had studied in Europe and the United States admired the democratic institutions and prosperous societies of the West. Ch'en Tu-hsiu, upon returning from studying in France, had founded a magazine called *New Youth* that championed political and social reforms. Hu Shih, a professor who had begun his advocacy of language reforms and the use of the vernacular instead of the classical written form while a graduate student in the United States, contributed articles to *New Youth*.

In 1916, Ts'ai Yuen-p'ei, who had participated in the 1911 revolution as a member of Sun Yat-sen's Kuomintang, became chancellor of National Beijing University. He implemented academic freedom and other reforms at the university so that the best faculty and brightest students flocked there.

In 1918, encouraged by Ts'ai, students at National Beijing University, among them Fu Ssu-nien and Lo Chia-lun, formed their own magazine called *New Tide*, committed to a critical spirit, scientific thinking, and a reformed style of writing. This magazine gave focus to student aspirations and won instant national recognition. *New Youth* and *New Tide* magazines became the standard bearers of the New Culture Movement, or Intellectual Revolution, in China.

When news of the Allied decision to award Shantung to Japan reached China, students at the National Beijing University organized a citywide student demonstration in protest. Five thousand student demonstrators from thirteen universities and colleges in Beijing assembled at the Gate of Heavenly Peace (Tiananmen) on May 4. They demanded that China not sign the Treaty of Versailles and that pro-Japanese officials who had signed secret treaties with Japan be punished. The rousing May

Fourth Manifesto called on Chinese to be ready to die for their nation but never to agree to give up their territory. A student delegation presented petitions of protest to the United States and British diplomatic missions. When the demonstrators passed the house of a pro-Japanese official, they broke into the home and set it afire. Police arrived and arrested ten students.

News of the arrests led to a strike of all students in Beijing. The strike quickly spread throughout major cities in China, where students also demonstrated to show solidarity with their fellows in Beijing. Many industrial workers struck, and merchants in key cities closed shops and boycotted Japanese-made goods in sympathy. Almost all newspapers supported the students and the patriotic movement they had unleashed. Sun Yat-sen also called for strong support for the students. All demanded that China refuse to sign the Treaty of Versailles. The government vacillated and authorized the Chinese delegation in Paris to use its discretion over signing the treaty. Chinese students in Western Europe then surrounded the hotel where the Chinese delegates stayed and physically prevented them from proceeding to Versailles when the signing ceremony took place.

In late May and June, student leaders assembled in Shanghai, formed an All China Student Union, and met in conference. Sun Yat-sen and other Kuomintang leaders met many students to persuade them that Sun's ideology of nationalism, democracy, and livelihood was crucial to China's national salvation. The warlord government in Beijing attempted to suppress the movement by imprisoning 1,150 students in Beijing. Since there was no jail space, it turned part of the National Beijing University's campus into a prison. A renewed wave of strikes and boycotts forced the government to capitulate. As the students marched triumphantly out of jail, the government apologized, the pro-Japanese officials were dismissed, and the cabinet resigned. The events are called the May Fourth Movement.

Impact of Event

The May Fourth Movement had far-reaching implications and results. It is recognized as China's first mass, student-led patriotic movement. Students became a new force in politics as nationalism became China's primary political issue. Anti-imperialism also acquired new emotional meaning. It inspired later generations of students to lead in demanding social reforms, democratization, and economic betterment as well as policies that would win equality and respect for China in world affairs.

In the United States, the blatant unfairness of awarding Shantung to Japan contributed to the Senate's rejection of the Treaty of Versailles. When Republican president Warren Harding called the Washington Conference in 1921-1922, he and the British delegation successfully pressured Japan to return Shantung to Chinese jurisdiction.

The May Fourth Movement had an important impact on China's political development. Sun Yat-sen immediately realized the potential of students in revitalizing his hitherto politically ineffective Kuomintang. He recruited many promising students to his cause and later, with Soviet help, restructured the Kuomintang to become a disciplined political party. Some intellectuals were profoundly disillusioned with the West as a result of China's treatment in Paris. They were particularly disappointed with Woodrow Wilson, whom they had hailed as the herald of a new, just world. As a result, some turned to Russia and to Marxism-Leninism, with its universalist explanation of history, its tight party organization, and its techniques of seizing power. Ch'en Tu-hsiu and Li Ta-chao formed a Marxist study club in Beijing in 1919; others were formed in several other cities. In 1921, Ch'en, Li, Mao Tse-tung (who had been hired by Li as library assistant), and others formed the Chinese Communist Party.

Socially, the May Fourth Movement led to intensified attacks on Confucianism and on traditional social and familial values and attitudes, such as the subordination of the young to old people and of women to men. Young people demanded and increasingly received the right to choose their careers and spouses; young women demanded emancipation and equality of rights and opportunities with men. Chancellor Ts'ai readily agreed to accept women students, admitting the first coeducational class after competitive examinations in 1920. Other universities and colleges quickly followed. After it gained power in 1928, the Kuomintang government adopted legislation and enacted laws that gave women equality for the first time in Chinese history.

The attack on Confucianism also stimulated a critical evaluation of China's past and inspired new scholarship in history, philosophy, archaeology, and other fields. It also opened minds to inquire about world cultural and philosophical trends. Enthusiastic audiences listened to lectures by noted scholars such as John Dewey, Bertrand Russell, and Rabindranath Tagore when they visited China in the early 1920's. The May Fourth Movement also gave impetus to the adoption of the vernacular by the popular press; it became the medium of instruction in schools in 1920. The importance of adopting the vernacular cannot be overemphasized, because it greatly facilitated the spread of popular education and modern ideas and ideals.

Thus, the May Fourth Movement had an important impact on many areas that range from political, social, and language reform to the emancipation of women. It also heightened the Chinese people's quest for international equality. For these reasons, it is an important turning point in modern China.

Bibliography

Chiang, Monlin. *Tides from the West: A Chinese Autobiography.* New Haven, Conn.: Yale University Press, 1947. Chiang was a scholar trained in the United States and a professor at Beijing University during the May Fourth Movement. Here he tells of his early experiences.

Chou, Min-chih. *Hu Shih and Intellectual Choice in Modern China.* Ann Arbor: University of Michigan Press, 1984. This well-researched book tells about the forces that molded Hu Shih's early life. It also explores his views on politics and literature.

Chou, Ts'e-tsung. *The May Fourth Movement: Intellectual Revolution in Modern China.* Cambridge, Mass.: Harvard University Press, 1964. This comprehensive book traces the background, development, and outcomes of the May Fourth Movement. It includes a detailed chronology of events, notes, and appendices.

Duiker, William J. *Ts'ai Yuan-p'ei: Educator of Modern China.* University Park: Pennsylvania State University Press, 1977. Details the important role Ts'ai played in fostering modern higher education and research in China, and in promoting academic freedom.

Grieder, Jerome B. *Hu Shih and the Chinese Renaissance: Liberalism in the Chinese Revolution, 1917-1937.* Cambridge, Mass.: Harvard University Press, 1970. An account of the traditional and new influences, and the political and social forces, that shaped the ideas of Hu and his friends.

King, Wunsz. *China at the Paris Peace Conference in 1919.* Jamaica, N.Y.: St. John's University Press, 1961. China's failure to achieve goals at the Paris Peace Conference that were thought legitimate by the Chinese precipitated the May Fourth Movement. This book details China's position in World War I, its postwar goals, and its treatment by the Allied Powers at Paris.

Schwarcz, Vera. *The Chinese Enlightenment: Intellectuals and the Legacy of the May Fourth Movement of 1919.* Berkeley: University of California Press, 1986. An interesting reevaluation of the May Fourth Movement and its impact, with emphasis on the students. A valuable work despite some factual errors.

Schwartz, Benjamin, ed. *Reflections on the May Fourth Movement: A Symposium.* Cambridge, Mass.: Harvard University Press, 1972. Many experts contributed their views and interpretations of an event that many consider to be the watershed of modern Chinese history.

Jiu-Hwa Lo Upshur

Cross-References

The Boxer Rebellion Fails to Remove Foreign Control in China (1900), p. 1; Sun Yat-sen Overthrows the Ch'ing Dynasty (1911), p. 116; The Paris Peace Conference Includes Protection for Minorities (1919), p. 252; Mao Delivers His "Speech of One Hundred Flowers" (1956), p. 958; Mao's Great Leap Forward Causes Famine and Social Dislocation (1958), p. 1015; The Chinese Cultural Revolution Starts a Wave of Repression (1966), p. 1332; Demonstrators Gather in Tiananmen Square (1989), p. 2483.

THE INTERNATIONAL LABOUR ORGANISATION IS ESTABLISHED

Category of event: Workers' rights
Time: June 28, 1919
Locale: Versailles, France

The ILO was established for the purpose of protecting the rights of workers, improving working conditions, and promoting social justice throughout the world

Principal personages:
> HAROLD B. BUTLER (1883-1951), the assistant secretary of the British Ministry of Labour
> EDWARD J. PHELAN (1888-1967), a civil servant in the British Ministry of Labour
> SAMUEL GOMPERS (1850-1924), the president of the American Federation of Labor
> ALBERT THOMAS (1878-1932), a leader of the moderate wing of the French Socialist Party, became the first director-general of the ILO in 1919

Summary of Event

The Industrial Revolution, combined with the drive for profits, caused profound social change. Throughout the nineteenth century, industrialization was accompanied by dangerous working conditions, minimal wages, exhausting hours, and child labor. It spawned destitution, squalid urban settlements, and the kind of human suffering so vividly portrayed by author Charles Dickens. Workers were sometimes viewed as expendable. The social consequences of the system were disastrous for the working class.

Social reformers, clerics, academics, and philosophers (among them Karl Marx) pressed for change. Trade unions were organized. Between 1871 and 1900, socialist parties were formed in more than twenty countries, and some labor legislation was enacted to begin protecting the human rights of the working class. Change was slow and piecemeal, and it increasingly was recognized that international action was needed. The First International (1864) and the Second International (1889) were efforts by labor unionists and socialists to organize at that level.

Switzerland was anxious to bring governments together to generate some form of international regulation to protect workers and, in 1889, suggested setting up an international organization for labor legislation. An international meeting resulted, but the participating governments were against adopting any labor convention, opposed the creation of any international machinery, and even turned down recommendations to hold periodic international meetings on labor issues. Trade unions tried to establish international links. The first international conference of trade union organizations was held in 1901; subsequent meetings defined tasks to be performed, such as exchanging information and providing assistance in industrial disputes. In 1913, the organization became known as the International Federation of Trade Unions.

World War I created profound changes in industry, including vastly increased production, expanded mechanization, and enlarged numbers of women in the work force. The working class contributed greatly to the war effort, and it wanted to be remembered in the creation of the new order that would result from the peace settlement. In 1916, an international trade union congress meeting in Great Britain drew up a detailed program of labor rights to be recognized by the peace treaty. It called for the creation of an international commission to ensure that these provisions would be implemented and advocated the establishment of an international labor office to study the development of labor legislation. Labor representatives of the Central Powers held a conference of their own in 1917 to elaborate a set of counterproposals for inclusion into the peace treaty.

The 1917 Bolshevik Revolution was another important factor leading the Paris Peace Conference to address labor concerns. The Russian upheaval helped to dispel complacency elsewhere. As World War I drew to an end, the British Ministry of Labour began to work on a detailed plan for an international labor organization. The Allies were committed to creating a world organization to achieve collective security, and it was considered inevitable that one of its organs would be concerned with labor issues. The Labour Ministry therefore began exploring, with the support of the British cabinet, what this structure should be. The peace conference would make that decision, but the Ministry of Labour wanted to propose a practical blueprint. Harold Butler, the assistant secretary, and Edward Phelan, an expert on foreign questions in the Intelligence Department, were the main architects of this document.

The 1919 Paris Peace Conference established a fifteen-member commission to draft the provisions concerning labor to be incorporated into the peace treaty. This body was headed by Samuel Gompers, president of the American Federation of Labor. As it turned out, none of the other national delegations had prepared any proposal as detailed and comprehensive as the British. The commission therefore decided to use that draft proposal for an international labor organization as the basis for discussion. The structure and organization developed by the commission and accepted by the peace conference became Part XIII of the Treaty of Versailles. This international organization was unprecedented but was seen as indispensable if grave labor disorders were to be avoided after the war. It did not meet all the objectives sought by workers' organizations, but it was capable of achieving progressive improvement in the condition of workers, human rights protection, and greater social justice.

The framework of the International Labour Organisation (ILO) was innovative in many respects. International organizations are usually composed of delegates of governments; the ILO had an unprecedented tripartite structure in order to foster communication among labor, management, and government. Each member-state was to send four delegates, two representing government and one each representing labor and management. About 150 nations had joined the ILO by 1990. The ILO remained independent from the United Nations (as it was from the League of Nations) but linked to it by an international agreement.

The ILO has three main organs. The International Labour Conference meets annually at the ILO headquarters in Geneva. All member-states are represented. It addresses problems faced by workers, develops labor standards to be applied worldwide, approves the budget, and decides on matters pertaining to the functioning of the organization. As a major departure from nineteenth century practice, decisions are made by majority votes (instead of unanimity); some require two-thirds majorities. Government, labor, and employer representatives vote in separate groups, another innovation of the tripartite system. Appropriate committees are used to share the organization's workload.

The second organ is the executive Governing Body, which meets three times a year to decide questions of policy and working methods. It is composed of fifty-six members, twenty-eight chosen from the government representatives and fourteen each from the employer and labor groups. The ten states of chief industrial importance (Brazil, China, France, Germany, India, Italy, Japan, the Soviet Union, the United Kingdom, and the United States) are given the privilege always to be represented on the Governing Body by one government delegate each. The other government seats, as well as the management and labor positions, are filled every three years by elections of peer groups (government, employer, and labor representatives, respectively) attending the International Labour Conference.

The third organ is the International Labour Office. It is the administrative infrastructure permitting the smooth functioning of the other organs and committees. It publishes a vast array of materials and employs a staff of about three thousand. Members of more than one hundred nationalities serve at headquarters in Geneva, in the forty field offices around the world, and in the countries in which the ILO is implementing projects. The staff is headed by the director-general, who is appointed by the Governing Body for a term of five years and who plays a crucial role in the fulfillment of the organization's mission. Albert Thomas, a prominent French labor activist passionately involved in the international worker movement, became the first director-general and established firm precedents of dynamic leadership.

The ILO's most important task is to develop international labor standards covering all work-related issues, such as hours of work, vacations, and social security. These standards are created by means of conventions and recommendations adopted by the International Labour Conference. Conventions require individual member-state ratification. A ratifying state undertakes the obligation of enacting whatever legislation may be needed to make the labor standards applicable as domestic law. Recommendations do not require ratification; they serve as guidelines for national labor policy. The ILO has developed procedures to monitor the implementation of its Labour Code and ensure that states fulfill their obligations.

Another important part of the ILO's program is provision of technical assistance to underdeveloped countries in labor-related matters. The ILO trains workers to increase their productivity and chances of employment. It assists countries in establishing their own training centers, particularly by providing much-needed equipment, such as computers, software, audiovisual materials, and tools. It acts as a clearinghouse for a large amount of information about occupational safety and health, promotes full employment, provides advice to governments, and fosters planning in all these matters. Hundreds of ILO experts are sent annually on temporary assignments around the world. Furthermore, the ILO does research, collects data on a vast variety of work-related issues, and publishes many studies, reports, guides, and manuals.

Impact of Event

The ILO has been remarkably successful in improving the condition of workers, protecting human rights, and fostering social justice in a global environment frequently hostile to social reform. The development of international labor standards implemented by the member-states' own legislation is a major achievement. The ILO had adopted 172 conventions and 179 recommendations by the early 1990's, covering major labor issues such as length of the workweek, the right to organize and engage in collective bargaining, equality of opportunity, just remuneration, employment security, weekly rest, occupational hazards, and social security.

The ILO programs of technical assistance to underdeveloped nations became increasingly more significant as former colonial possessions achieved full sovereignty. By the 1990's, about eight hundred ILO experts were working in about 140 countries on projects geared to local needs. Many of the projects are funded in large measure by the United Nations Development Program, with assistance from other U.N. agencies and independent contributors. The projects received $152 million from all sources in 1990. ILO assistance is especially effective in human resources development, particularly vocational training. This is accomplished by means of fellowships given to trainees from underdeveloped countries as well as through training local instructors and establishing training centers in the new nations. The ILO also provides instruction at its International Center for Advanced Technical and Vocational Training in Turin, Italy.

Assistance is also provided for the purpose of improving management performance in many fields, such as water supply, manufacturing, and transportation. This assistance has also been aimed at broadening the social role of managers, for example, by leading them to be more concerned about environmental protection. The ILO has launched a World Employment Program intended to increase employment opportunity in its member-states and consequently to reduce poverty.

The rapidly expanding use of highly complex technology and of dangerous materials in industrial production has led to large numbers of industrial accidents, including those causing permanent disability of workers. To remedy this problem, an international information center has been established along with an occupational hazard alert system. This system is responsible for examining and analyzing all the information on occupational safety appearing around the world for the purpose of making it available to all ILO members.

Among the ILO's many accomplishments, its extensive research and data gathering efforts stand out, together with its publication and information programs. Detailed analyses of labor problems and review of specific remedies actually developed in various parts of the world have been of enormous assistance to government and other agencies. Thousands of ILO publications are in print and distributed worldwide.

In 1969, the ILO was awarded the Nobel Peace Prize. This was a fitting recognition on its fiftieth anniversary of its remarkable accomplishments and a just reward for its ceaseless effort to improve the condition of workers everywhere, protect human rights, and promote social justice.

Bibliography

Alcock, Anthony. *History of the International Labor Organization.* New York: Octagon Books, 1971. The ILO commissioned the preparation of this official history as a fiftieth anniversary project. This thorough, well-documented study clearly shows the diplomacy of ILO activities and the difficulty of working with governments whose policies frequently clash. Gives insights into the accomplishments of the organization. Includes a comprehensive bibliography.

Galenson, Walter. *The International Labor Organization: An American View.* Madison: University of Wisconsin Press, 1981. A well-documented analysis of the work of the International Labour Organisation, what it does, the problems confronting it, and the issues leading to clashes between states, viewed from an American perspective. Discusses the problems that the United States has experienced within the organization, dissent over structure and operations, and the U.S. decision to withdraw from and subsequently to return to the ILO.

International Labour Office. *Report of the Director-General.* Geneva: Author, 1991. Part 2, *Activities of the ILO, 1990,* provides a most convenient official survey (in forty-nine pages, plus tables) of the current activities and accomplishments of the organization. It is sufficiently detailed to give a good idea of the scope and depth of the ILO's work. Gives statistical information. Annex 3 presents a list of ILO publications issued in 1990.

Johnston, George Alexander. *The International Labor Organization: Its Work for Social and Economic Progress.* London: Europa, 1970. Part 1 provides an overview of the origins of the ILO and its structure; Part 2 reviews the major problems facing the organization and the programs developed to address them. A substantial reference section supplies much useful information, including the full text of the ILO constitution, a chronology of major ILO events, and a short bibliography.

Landy, E. A. *The Effectiveness of International Supervision: Thirty Years of ILO Experience.* Dobbs Ferry, N.Y.: Oceana, 1966. This specialized volume examines the procedures used by the ILO to ensure compliance with the International Labour Code and analyzes the results. It reviews the strengths and the weaknesses of the system, the reasons for noncompliance, and the problems involved in effective supervision. Useful even though it covers only thirty years of ILO experience. Includes a bibliography.

Morse, David A. *The Origin and Evolution of the ILO and Its Role in the World Community.* Ithaca, N.Y.: Cornell University Press, 1969. A concise historical overview of the organization by one of its former directors. Clearly introduces the ILO and discusses its origins, structure, and evolution. Reviewing the changing needs of international society, it examines the organization's program and summarizes the ILO's contribution to social justice. Provides a short bibliography.

Shotwell, James T., ed. *The Origins of the International Labor Organization.* 2 vols. New York: Columbia University Press, 1934. The first volume gives a complete history of the pre-World War I background and a detailed account of the work done during the Paris Peace Conference. The second volume provides documents, fifty-four of which concern pre-World War I activities and negotiations at the peace conference.

Jean-Robert Leguey-Feilleux

Cross-References

Supreme Court Disallows a Maximum Hours Law for Bakers (1905), p. 36; The Bern Conference Prohibits Night Work for Women (1906), p. 75; Massachusetts Adopts the First Minimum-Wage Law in the United States (1912), p. 126; Great Britain Passes Acts to Provide Unemployment Benefits (1920), p. 321; Franklin D. Roosevelt Appoints Perkins as Secretary of Labor (1933), p. 486; The Wagner Act Requires Employers to Accept Collective Bargaining (1935), p. 508; Social Security Act Establishes Benefits for Nonworking People (1935), p. 514; Jouhaux Is Awarded the Nobel Peace Prize (1951), p. 873; The United Nations Adopts the Abolition of Forced Labor Convention (1957), p. 985; The Berlin Wall Is Built (1961), p. 1125; The International Labour Organisation Wins the Nobel Peace Prize (1969), p. 1509; Congress Passes the Equal Employment Opportunity Act (1972), p. 1650; Nigeria Expels West African Migrant Workers (1983), p. 2180.

THE SAINT-GERMAIN-EN-LAYE CONVENTION ATTEMPTS TO CURTAIL SLAVERY

Categories of event: Racial and ethnic rights; workers' rights
Time: September 10, 1919
Locale: Saint-Germain-en-Laye, France

The Saint-Germain-en-Laye Convention called for the suppression of slavery and the slave trade but made no provisions for implementation of its fiat

Principal personages:

ARTHUR BALFOUR (1848-1930), the British minister for foreign affairs, who headed his country's delegation

GEORGES CLEMENCEAU (1841-1929), the French premier, who headed his country's delegation

FRANK LYON POLK (1871-1943), the United States undersecretary of state, who headed his country's delegation

PAUL HYMANS (1865-1941), the Belgian minister for foreign affairs, who headed his country's delegation

ALFRED MILNER (1854-1925), the British minister for colonies, who represented both Great Britain and the Union of South Africa

TOMMASO TITTONI (1855-1931), the Italian minister for foreign affairs, who headed his country's delegation

AFFONSO DA COSTA (1871-1937), the head of Portugal's delegation

SUTEMI CHINDA (1857-1929), the head of Japan's delegation

JULES CAMBON (1845-1935), a French delegate to the conference

GUGLIELMO MARCONI (1874-1937), an Italian inventor who sat in his country's delegation

Summary of Event

The Convention of Saint-Germain-en-Laye was a link in the chain of the international diplomatic assault on slavery. The Congress of Vienna in 1815 began the international reprobation of the slave trade. Viscount Robert Castlereagh of Great Britain had eloquently pleaded for the end of that age-old abomination. His efforts, however, resulted only in denouncement of the slave trade "as inconsistent with the principles of humanity and universal morality." The Congress of Aix-la-Chapelle in 1818 also failed to suppress the slave trade. Likewise, the Congress of Verona in 1822 did nothing about the slave trade, despite Britain's plea.

In 1884, the Berlin Conference convened. Fourteen countries had representation: Austria-Hungary, Belgium, Denmark, France, Germany, Great Britain, Italy, The Netherlands, the Ottoman Empire, Portugal, Russia, Spain, Sweden and Norway, and the United States. In the Berlin Act of 1885, passed under British leadership, they condemned the internal as well as maritime slave trade. They also pledged to care for the moral and material improvement of "native tribes" and to help in suppressing slavery itself in the Congo basin. The United States did not ratify the Berlin Act. Moreover, most unfortunately, the Berlin Conference recognized the International Association of the Congo as a sovereign state. That state, popularly known as the Congo Free State, was the creature of King Leopold II of Belgium. He and his minions became known for the atrocities, including forced labor, that occurred there.

The European countries' imperialistic rivalry and opportunism in the partitioning of Africa led to the holding of the Brussels Conference in the winter of 1889-1890. Seventeen countries were present: Austria-Hungary, Belgium, the Congo, Denmark, France, Germany, Great Britain, Italy, The Netherlands, the Ottoman Empire, Persia, Portugal, Russia, Spain, Sweden and Norway, the United States, and Zanzibar. They proceeded to devise a detailed international code against the slave trade.

The Brussels Conference addressed the tremendous problems of the external and internal slave trade in Africa. Concerning the former, the conference's general act prescribed reciprocal rights of search and capture of vessels under five hundred tons within the "Maritime Zone." That area comprised the coasts of the Indian Ocean from Baluchistan to Quilimane (at eighteen degrees south latitude), including the Persian Gulf, the Red Sea, and Madagascar. The general act also placed strict regulations on the use of the flag of a signatory power and the carrying of African passengers in native vessels.

The Brussels Conference made detailed provisions to suppress the internal slave trade in Africa. These included the establishment of "strongly occupied stations" as refuges for the native population. Also approved was the use of cruisers, fortified posts, and expeditions to destroy the slave trade. Because the signatories considered the traffic in arms and liquor as adjuncts to the slave trade, they inserted in the conference's general act restrictions on the zones in which modern arms and distilled liquors could be sold.

All of the seventeen countries represented at the Brussels Conference signed its general act. Between late 1890 and 1896, three more countries became signatories: Ethiopia, Liberia, and the Orange Free State. By 1900, the work of the Brussels Conference had considerably eliminated large-scale slave raiding in areas under European control.

Nevertheless, the slave trade continued into the twentieth century. Slaves were exported to the Middle East. The import and export of slaves and slave raiding in Ethiopia lasted for many years. European contract labor traffic in Africa, a matter ignored by the Brussels Conference, continued to cover slaving operations. Furthermore, the illicit traffic in arms, which often intertwined with the slave trade, survived the strictures of the Brussels general act. Although less important as an international issue, the liquor trade also persisted as a problem in European colonies in Africa.

World War I definitely influenced the troika of slavery, the arms traffic, and the liquor trade. The Allies' victory meant the end of Germany's colonies. Victorious

Belgium, Great Britain, and France considered the acts of the Berlin and Brussels conferences to be outmoded. They viewed those acts as giving their World War I enemies—Germany, Austria, Hungary, and Turkey—and the neutrals in that conflagration—Denmark, The Netherlands, Norway, Persia, Spain, and Sweden—a right of intervention in their colonial dealings. Belgium, Great Britain, and France believed that the commercial clauses of the Berlin and Brussels conferences constituted infringement on their sovereign powers by limiting their right to control their own tariffs. Moreover, Belgium, Great Britain, and France claimed that the Brussels general act had solved neither the arms nor the liquor traffic. Furthermore, those three powers judged the slave trade to be so insignificant that the treaty had become a dead issue.

The three countries also recognized, however, the need for caution in jettisoning the Berlin and Brussels acts. The humanitarian principles of those acts, along with the free trade and navigation clauses, had cast a spell over the public, particularly in Great Britain and the United States. Additionally, the acts harmonized with the spirit embodied in the newly created and popular League of Nations. Thus, the Belgian, British, and French governments believed that they should not flout the United States, their own electorates, and interested neutral countries. Furthermore, the imperialistic Belgians, British, and French needed to exercise care in treating the Berlin and Brussels acts because they needed international public support in becoming the mandatory powers of the former German colonies.

The conclusion of World War I enabled the colonial powers to effect reconsideration of the Berlin and Brussels acts. Plans were made to replace the acts with treaties that would better suit the colonial powers themselves but still retain the model and many principles of the general act of Brussels. These conventions were signed on September 10, 1919, at Saint-Germain-en-Laye, France.

The first convention dealt with the arms traffic. It was signed by the United States, Belgium, Bolivia, the British Empire, China, Cuba, Ecuador, France, Greece, Guatemala, Haiti, Hedjaz, Italy, Japan, Nicaragua, Panama, Peru, Poland, Portugal, Romania, the Serb-Croat-Slovene State, Siam, and Czecho-Slovakia. The convention forbade the export of all modern arms except to signatories for their own use. No arms whatever were to be sent, except with permission, to Africa (excluding Algeria, Libya, and South Africa), the offshore islands of Africa, the Arabian peninsula, Persia, Transcaucasia, Gwadar, or former Ottoman Asiatic territories.

The second convention at Saint-Germain-en-Laye treated the liquor traffic in Africa, with some regions of the continent excluded. The signatories were the United States, Belgium, the British Empire, France, Italy, Japan, and Portugal. This agreement entirely prohibited "trade spirits," but left each territory free to define these liquors for itself. Other spirits would be levied customs duties.

The third convention at Saint-Germain-en-Laye revised the commercial clauses of the Berlin and Brussels acts. It was signed by the United States, Belgium, the British Empire (the United Kingdom, Canada, Australia, South Africa, New Zealand, and India), France, Italy, Japan, and Portugal. The leading participants were Arthur James

Balfour (Great Britain), Georges Clemenceau and Jules Cambon (France), Frank Lyon Polk (United States), Paul Hymans (Belgium), Alfred Milner (South Africa), Tommaso Tittoni and Guglielmo Marconi (Italy), Affonso da Costa (Portugal), and Sutemi Chinda (Japan). The agreement allowed Belgium, Great Britain, and France to fix their tariffs and fees for navigation in the basin of the Congo river. The signatory powers disposed of slavery and the slave trade in one sentence: "They will, in particular, endeavor to secure the complete suppression of slavery in all its forms and of the slave trade by land and sea." Thus, the Convention of Saint-Germain-en-Laye, like the Congress of Vienna more than a century earlier, treated slavery and the slave trade in a rhetorical manner only.

Impact of Event

Between 1815 and 1919, well-meaning diplomats in several international congresses took up the heinous, seemingly eternal problem of slavery. In 1815, at the conclusion of the Napoleonic Wars, the Committee of Eight of the Congress of Vienna issued a high-sounding declaration condemning slavery but supplied no mechanism for its enforcement. A century later, in 1919, the emissaries of twelve countries signed the third convention from Saint-Germain-en-Laye that likewise called for the suppression of slavery but again provided no machinery for implementation.

High hopes were placed in the Convention of Saint-Germain-en-Laye. Indeed, there rose the joyous claim that for the first time in history there was a definite commitment to the complete suppression of slavery and of the slave trade. The words "in all its forms" in the convention conceivably included forced labor, pseudoadoption, forced concubinage, and debt slavery. Moreover, the German and Ottoman empires, viewed in a number of circles as laggards in attempts to eliminate slavery, had ceased to be.

The particular convention of Saint-Germain-en-Laye dealing with slavery and the slave trade encountered serious problems. Two signatories did not ratify the agreement. One, the United States of America, refused because of its drift into isolationism. Another, Italy, manifesting jingoism, regarded the convention as an infringement on its sovereignty. Moreover, certain signatories that did ratify proved lukewarm in application of the convention. Belgium, France, and Portugal showed no eagerness in their colonial empires to eliminate forced labor, a situation that should have been understood as a form of slavery. South Africa, both in its provinces and in its mandate, former German Southwest Africa, displayed no enthusiasm.

Furthermore, in several ways the third convention of Saint-Germain-en-Laye, dealing with slavery and the slave trade, formed a retrogression from the general acts of the conferences of Berlin (1885) and Brussels (1890). Many states which signed or adhered to those acts did not sign or later adhere to this particular convention of Saint-Germain-en-Laye. They were Austria, Denmark, Ethiopia, Germany, Hungary, Liberia, The Netherlands, Norway, Persia, the Soviet Union (formerly Russia), Spain, Sweden, Turkey (formerly the Ottoman Empire), and Zanzibar. Noteworthy, also, was the failure of other successor states to the Austro-Hungarian, Ottoman, and

Russian empires to sign. They included Czechoslovakia, Poland, Yugoslavia, Egypt, Hedjaz, and Iraq.

Additionally, the 1919 Convention of Saint-Germain-en-Laye contained fundamental errors of omission. Article 22 of the General Act of the Conference of Brussels bound the signatory powers to the reciprocal right of visit, search, and seizure of vessels at sea engaged in the slave trade in the Indian Ocean, the Persian Gulf, and the Red Sea. That provision was not repeated in the Convention of Saint-Germain-en-Laye. Furthermore, Article 27 of the General Act of the Conference of Brussels provided for an international bureau at Zanzibar for the holding of documents and information on the suppression of the slave trade, which the signatory powers were pledged to forward. No such provision occurred in the Convention of Saint-Germain-en-Laye.

Indeed, the very legality of the Convention of Saint-Germain-en-Laye has been questioned. Officially that document styled itself as the "Convention Revising the General Act of Berlin, February 26, 1885, and the General Act and Declaration of Brussels, July 2, 1890." The General Act of Brussels had no provision authorizing any contracting state to denounce it. Thus, it could be abrogated only by securing the consent of all the states that had signed and ratified it. Only some of those states, however, signed the Convention of Saint-Germain-en-Laye. Consequently, one may argue that the Brussels Act remains in force.

Regardless of legalism, the Convention of Saint-Germain-en-Laye represents a minor event in the attack on slavery and the slave trade. Victims of those monstrous activities benefited very little from that document.

Bibliography

Coupland, Sir Reginald. *The British Anti-Slavery Movement.* London: Frank Cass, 1964. A brief, popular treatment of the campaign of a group of Britons for the abolition of slavery and the slave trade. Their approach represented humanitarian imperialism. Neglects economic factors. One-page bibliography.

Davis, David Brion. *Slavery and Human Progress.* New York: Oxford University Press, 1984. A detailed, scholarly telling of the "momentous shift from 'progressive' enslavement to 'progressive' emancipation." Excellent annotation and a helpful index.

Fischer, Hugo. "The Suppression of Slavery in International Law." Parts 1-2. *The International Law Quarterly* 3 (January-October, 1950): 28-51, 503-522. Discusses the problem of slavery in international law. Surveys slavery in customary international law, suppression of the West African slave trade, the fight against the East African and Central African slave trade, and the period between the world wars.

Greenidge, C. W. W. *Slavery.* London: George Allen & Unwin, 1958. A short, popular description of slavery and the antislavery movement by a longtime secretary of the Anti-Slavery Society. Advocates invocation of the machinery of the General Act of Brussels. Appendices include the Brussels Act of 1890, the Slavery Convention of 1926, and the Supplementary Convention of 1956.

Harris, John A. *A Century of Emancipation.* London: J. M. Dent, 1933. Popular, sympathetic narration of the antislavery movement. Stresses the aftermath of the Convention of Saint-Germain-en-Laye. Admirable index.

MacMunn, Sir George. *Slavery Through the Ages.* Westport, Conn.: Negro Universities Press, 1970. A well-written, detailed survey of slavery to 1938. Praises the Convention of Saint-Germain-en-Laye. Has illustrations and an index but no bibliography or annotations.

Miers, Suzanne. *Britain and the Ending of the Slave Trade.* New York: Africana, 1975. First-rate account. Questions the significance of the Convention of Saint-Germain-en-Laye in regard to attacking the slave trade. Scholarly and objective. Voluminous notes, superb bibliography, fine maps, and a model index. Includes the text of the Brussels Conference.

"Official Documents." *Supplement to the American Journal of International Law* (1921): 297-328. Complete text of the three conventions signed at Saint-Germain-en-Laye on September 10, 1919. Inadequate index.

Simon, Kathleen. *Slavery.* London: Hodder & Stoughton, 1930. Spirited story of slavery in the early twentieth century, by an Englishwoman. Simon shows high regard for the Convention of Saint-Germain-en-Laye. Well annotated, good print, serviceable index. Contains the text of the International Slavery Convention of 1926.

Erving E. Beauregard

Cross-References

Reformers Expose Atrocities Against Congolese Laborers (1903), p. 13; International Agreement Attacks the White Slave Trade (1904), p. 30; The Belgian Government Annexes the Congo (1908), p. 103; The League of Nations Adopts the International Slavery Convention (1926), p. 436; The International League for Human Rights Is Founded (1942), p. 590; Ethiopia Abolishes Slavery (1942), p. 607; The United Nations Adopts the Universal Declaration of Human Rights (1948), p. 789; The European Convention on Human Rights Is Signed (1950), p. 843; The United Nations Amends Its International Slavery Convention (1953), p. 902; The United Nations Adopts the Abolition of Forced Labor Convention (1957), p. 985; The U.N. Covenant on Civil and Political Liberties Is Adopted (1966), p. 1353; The Proclamation of Teheran Sets Human Rights Goals (1968), p. 1430; The OAU Adopts the African Charter on Human and Peoples' Rights (1981), p. 2136.

STEEL WORKERS GO ON STRIKE TO DEMAND IMPROVED WORKING CONDITIONS

Category of event: Workers' rights
Time: September 22, 1919-January 8, 1920
Locale: Pittsburgh, Pennsylvania, and other cities in the United States

Steel workers went on strike in 1919 to gain the right to some collective say on the terms of employment, only to see their strike defeated and their civil liberties suppressed

Principal personages:

WILLIAM Z. FOSTER (1881-1961), the secretary-treasurer of the National Committee for Organizing Iron and Steel Workers

ELBERT H. GARY (1846-1927), the chairman of the board of directors of the U.S. Steel Corporation, an advocate of the open shop

JOHN FITZPATRICK (1870-1946), the president of the Chicago Federation of Labor and Chairman of the National Committee for Organizing Iron and Steel Workers

SAMUEL GOMPERS (1850-1924), the president of the American Federation of Labor

MARY HARRIS "MOTHER" JONES (1830-1930), an indomitable labor organizer

Summary of Event

The steel industry in the early twentieth century United States was dominated by the United States Steel Corporation, the country's first billion-dollar conglomerate. Together with four or five smaller independent companies, it controlled U.S. production of steel. Profits were enormous and increased substantially during World War I. Elbert H. Gary, chair of the board at U.S. Steel, advocated the open shop, believing that labor organization was incompatible with low production costs and should be steadfastly resisted. Gary also adhered to the philosophy of corporate paternalism and was convinced that company-sponsored programs that provided recreational facilities, stock options, safety measures, limited company housing, and periodic wage increases would retain a loyal nonunion work force.

Workers were not satisfied. During wartime they increasingly saw themselves as patriotic producers and expected to be rewarded for their efforts. Instead, they found themselves forced to work twelve-hour days and six-day workweeks. Every second week, as they changed from day to night shifts, they worked between eighteen and twenty-four hours without any rest. Increases in the cost of living during World War I intensified dissatisfaction as it minimized the effect of prior pay increases and pressed many workers below the minimum level of subsistence. Without the legal right to engage in collective bargaining, workers felt betrayed and helpless. When the government, in March of 1918, recommended a wartime labor-management program that included the right of workers to organize into trade unions and to bargain with management (through shop committees, not union representatives), labor felt it was about to achieve long-denied rights and benefits.

Into this atmosphere came former labor radical William Z. Foster. Fresh from a successful organizing campaign among Chicago packinghouse workers (the first union victory in a mass-production industry during the war), this American Federation of Labor (AFL) organizer hoped to seize the opportunity presented by the wartime demand for workers and the sympathetic ear of government to press immediately for the organization of one-half million steel workers. With the support of the reform-minded and respected John Fitzpatrick, president of the powerful Chicago Federation of Labor, Foster managed to get the approval of AFL president Samuel Gompers and the national AFL convention to initiate an organizing drive among steel workers. A National Committee for Organizing Iron and Steel Workers was created on August 1, 1918, with Fitzpatrick as chair and Foster as secretary-treasurer and unofficial chief organizer. Foster began the organization drive in the region near Chicago and Gary, Indiana, under the banner of "eight hours and a union." Early success there encouraged him to move his headquarters to Pittsburgh, Pennsylvania, the center of the steel industry. Organizers fanned out through the steel towns of western Pennsylvania, eastern Ohio, and West Virginia. Foster was optimistic about organizing efforts, but an influenza epidemic struck the country during October and November of 1918 and forced the cancellation of meetings for weeks, allowing the steel companies time to consider their response. This was followed by the formal end of war in November, which brought into question the future of the entire labor relations program of the federal government.

Foster's biggest problem was the denial of the rights of free speech and assembly that his organizers were forced to confront in the steel regions, especially in the Pittsburgh area. Elected officials repeatedly passed ordinances requiring permits for labor meetings or refused to allow meetings to take place. Individuals who rented halls to labor organizers were pressured by politicians to cancel the leases. Pro-labor speakers were arrested as outside agitators and held in jail. Such actions were unconstitutional violations of First Amendment rights, but legal redress meant costly delays for the organizing effort.

Foster responded to the restrictions on free speech by organizing "flying squadrons" of organizers to target specific towns. They were arrested repeatedly and their meetings were disrupted by the police. The steel companies kept blacklists of union agitators, discharged workers for affiliating with the union, hired detectives to infiltrate the organizing campaign, and exerted considerable influence over the press, the police, local officials, and even church leaders. Pleas to the secretary of labor and to the governor of Pennsylvania brought promises of investigation but no meaningful response.

Despite the setbacks, organizers made progress. Organizing meetings were held in vacant lots outside towns, workers boycotted local businesses, and agitators, like the eighty-nine-year-old "Mother Jones" (Mary Harris Jones), refused to be intimidated. Workers began to join the new union in ever-increasing numbers. During the late summer of 1919 the organizing committee presented Elbert Gary with a list of twelve demands, including the right to collective bargaining, the eight-hour day, seniority rights, the reinstatement of workers discharged for their unionizing activities, the abolition of company unions, and wage increases, as the basis for negotiation. Gary rejected the demands. When pleas to President Woodrow Wilson for intervention on their behalf failed, the steel workers voted to go on strike beginning September 22, 1919.

Winning the support of workers and beating back assaults on the rights of free speech and assembly were only part of Foster's problems. The negative public reaction to the "Red Scare" and the high level of strike activity nationally allowed steel plant owners to link the organizing drive to "Bolshevism" and to paint Foster as a "red." Exaggerated newspaper accounts portrayed the steel districts as seedbeds of revolution. The owners added to the paranoia by generating their own propaganda, which alleged that steel workers were predominantly immigrant radicals. The Department of Justice, already combing the country for radicals, shifted its attention to the strike centers. Excerpts from Foster's own earlier writings (when he was a member of the Industrial Workers of the World) were reprinted and the charge made that he was really a syndicalist advocating the destruction of the capitalist system. Foster's refusal to repudiate all of his prior statements before a special Senate Committee investigating the strike in October, 1919, cost him not only the support of AFL president Samuel Gompers but also public support that was crucial to the success of the strike.

With the strike call the antiunion campaign became increasingly repressive. Mounted police rode into crowds of workers at outdoor rallies and clubbed participants, arrested organizers and charged them with disorderly conduct, and denied strikers the right to picket. Police forced people off the streets and clubbed those who resisted, broke up meetings, invaded homes, and even robbed strikers. Individuals were held in jail without definite charges being lodged against them. Foster produced hundreds of sworn statements charging criminal behavior on the part of police, but no one was prosecuted. The sheriff of Allegheny County in Pennsylvania brazenly deputized loyal employees of the steel companies for strike duty, prohibited any gathering of three or more people, and required that indoor meetings be conducted only in English. When strike leaders complained of terrorism and suppression of civil liberties to the Department of Justice, Attorney General A. Mitchell Palmer refused to get involved in what he considered to be a local matter. Recourse to the judicial system also failed to halt the repression, while appeals for a public outcry elicited no response outside the steel districts. Finally, after months of organized intimidation and the violation of basic human rights, an effective antiunion propaganda campaign, and refusal by the steel plant owners to accept any sort of compromise, the strike was called off on January 8, 1920.

Impact of Event

The steel strike of 1919 was important on several levels. Immediately following the strike, William Z. Foster published *The Great Steel Strike and Its Lessons* (1920), his personal account of the events in which he emphasized the utter disregard for basic human rights. To Foster, workers were helpless in defense of their individual freedoms when confronted with an organized opposition of state police, deputy sheriffs, city officials, company police and detectives, and armed strikebreakers. The public, primed to discount the opinions of a labor radical such as Foster, was provided startling confirmation of his charges by the respected Interchurch World Movement. Formed as an organization to represent American Protestantism in secular matters, it studied the strike through its own independent commission of inquiry.

When the Interchurch World Movement published its findings in the summer of 1920 it not only confirmed Foster's account but added new personal testimony of the substandard living and working conditions that had made the steel strike inevitable. The commission found that the arbitrary control exerted by the steel companies inside their plants was extended outside the factories to affect workers as citizens in their communities. The civil rights of free speech and assembly were nullified without just cause by local officials, while the personal rights of striking workers were violated by state police and sheriff's deputies. The report created a mild sensation, but its immediate impact was only to renew the debate over the existing twelve-hour workday. Under continued pressure, the steel industry finally agreed to establish the eight-hour day in 1923 but continued to bar unions from the industry.

The steel strike of 1919 also had impacts on labor relations during the 1930's. First, defeat in 1919 proved that some sort of governmental intervention would be necessary to guarantee fairness in the workplace. The expanded role assumed by the federal government during the New Deal made this intervention possible and eventually led to the passage of the Wagner Act in 1935. Second, the violation of civil liberties in 1919 served as the background for the investigation by the La Follette Civil Liberties Committee. This special Senate Committee, created in June, 1936, documented corporate violations of civil rights that interfered with the right of labor to organize and bargain collectively. The investigation attracted public attention, suggested that the government was lending further support to labor's organizing efforts, and contributed to the success of the second organizing campaign in the steel industry which began that same year.

Bibliography

Brody, David. *Labor in Crisis: The Steel Strike of 1919.* Philadelphia, Pa.: J. B. Lippincott, 1965. Revised and greatly expanded discussion of the 1919 steel strike from that presented previously in Brody's *Steelworkers in America* (1960). Focus shifts to the tortured process of unionization in the steel industry. New sources are examined.

_____. *Steelworkers in America: The Nonunion Era.* Cambridge, Mass.: Harvard University Press, 1960. A valuable account of how the working lives of steel workers were shaped during the first decades of the twentieth century. Examines the technological and managerial innovations in steel production, life in the mill towns, and the factors preventing unionization. Experience of steel workers during World War I is seen as primary cause of the 1919 steel strike.

Foster, William Z. *The Great Steel Strike and Its Lessons.* Reprint. New York: Da Capo Press, 1971. Impassioned account of the 1919 steel strike written immediately after the event. Examines conditions in the steel industry prior to the strike, the timing of the strike, tactics behind union organizing efforts and the strike itself, and internal and external reasons for defeat. Includes correspondence from leaders on both sides, details violations of civil rights and personal rights, and offers a valuable overview from someone at the center of the organizing and strike activities.

Lens, Sidney. *The Labor Wars: From the Molly Maguires to the Sitdowns.* Garden City, N.Y.: Doubleday, 1973. Includes an excellent account of the organizing drive in steel in 1919, the packinghouse strike that preceded it, and the role of William Z. Foster in both contests. Places events in context of ongoing battles that marked the rise of the American labor movement.

Olds, Marshall. *Analysis of the Interchurch World Movement Report on the Steel Strike.* New York: Da Capo Press, 1971. Detailed investigation of the 1919 steel strike from a neutral organization representing American Protestantism. Highly critical of the steel industry. Valuable statistical information regarding working and living standards among workers in the steel industry. Data include participation figures by geographic area and trade, organizational expenses, and testimony gathered from strike participants. Details violations of civil liberties.

Warne, Colston E., ed. *The Steel Strike of 1919.* Boston, Mass.: D. C. Heath, 1963. Includes an account of the basic structure of the steel industry, conflicting interpretations of events, the basic philosophies of the parties involved (Elbert Gary, John Fitzpatrick, and Samuel Gompers), samples of the industry's advertising campaign, testimony from residents of the mill towns, and conclusions from two strike investigation committees.

Steven L. Piott

Cross-References

Supreme Court Disallows a Maximum Hours Law for Bakers (1905), p. 36; Massachusetts Adopts the First Minimum-Wage Law in the United States (1912), p. 126; "Palmer Raids" Lead to Arrests and Deportations of Immigrants (1919), p. 258; The International Labour Organisation Is Established (1919), p. 281; The American Civil Liberties Union Is Founded (1920), p. 327; The Wagner Act Requires Employers to Accept Collective Bargaining (1935), p. 508; Social Security Act Establishes Benefits for Nonworking People (1935), p. 514; The Congress of Industrial Organizations Is Formed (1938), p. 545.

THE KU KLUX KLAN SPREADS TERROR IN THE SOUTH

Category of event: Racial and ethnic rights
Time: The early 1920's
Locale: The southern United States and many northern communities

Klan violence against both blacks and whites in the name of racial and moral purity reached a high between 1921 and 1924

Principal personages:

WILLIAM J. SIMMONS (C. 1880-1945), the founder of the post-World War I Ku Klux Klan and its driving force until 1922

EDWARD YOUNG CLARKE (1839-?), the publicity agent who raised Klan membership to the millions

HIRAM WESLEY EVANS (1881-C. 1940), the Imperial Wizard who wrested the Klan from Simmons and Clarke and ruled it until 1939

ROWLAND THOMAS, the reporter who exposed and publicized the Klan in 1921

DAVID C. STEPHENSON (C. 1885-C. 1962), a former Grand Dragon of Indiana who was sentenced to life in prison for the murder of his rape victim

Summary of Event

On Thanksgiving night in 1915, William Joseph Simmons led a group of twelve friends up to Stone Mountain, near Atlanta, Georgia, and before a burning cross swore them in as charter members of a secret fraternal organization dedicated to the ideals of racial purity and traditional morality. "The Invisible Empire, Knights of the Ku Klux Klan, Inc." was chartered as a new fraternal order by the state of Georgia on December 4. Simmons, its "Imperial Wizard," had served in the Spanish-American War as a private in an Alabama regiment; he was not trained for any career and was a member of numerous fraternal clubs.

Membership in the Klan cost a ten-dollar fee and the price of a white robe. Recruitment coincided with the Atlanta showing of a new film by D. W. Griffith, *The Birth of a Nation* (1915), which glorified the first Ku Klux Klan in the turbulent Reconstruction era after the Civil War. That original Klan had risen in the beaten South, and its goal had been to continue to "keep the Negro in his place"—in the fields and subordinate to whites. It was founded in 1866 by Confederate General Nathan Bedford Forrest, who disbanded it in 1871.

Conditions in the United States after World War I were conducive to the sort of thinking to which the Klan appealed. Returning doughboys were full of the extreme patriotism born of victory. They were greeted by the "Roaring Twenties," America's exuberant celebration of the truth of her "manifest destiny."

To the Klan, this exuberance seemed to undercut the old American morality. Moreover, blacks also returned from the war proud of their own distinguished service and filled with high expectations in peacetime. The hopes of America's blacks at the time were not very different from the dreams of the newly freed slaves that had called forth the original Klan.

In addition, the white, Anglo-Saxon, Protestant profile of America's population was changing. Whereas earlier immigrants had come primarily from Protestant Northern Europe, early twentieth century immigrants were mostly Italian, Irish, and Polish Catholics, Russian and Slavic Jews, and Asians. The Klan saw its role as that of the guardian of the old moral values in a radically changing American environment.

The new Klan objected to Catholics, perceiving their loyalty to a foreign pope as conflicting with their loyalty to the United States. Jews were similarly accused of an un-American devotion to their ancient beliefs. Asians, like blacks, suffered from the fault of looking "different." These groups became the targets of the Klan's literature of denunciation.

Beneath the rule of the Imperial Wizard, the Klan was arranged nationwide in eight "Domains," each under a "Grand Goblin." Each state was a "Realm" under a "Grand Dragon." Realms were divided into "Provinces" under "Great Titans," and Provinces into local Klans, each under an "Exalted Cyclops." The Imperial Wizard appointed a cabinet of twelve "Genii" and an assistant called the "Emperor." For his new Klan, Simmons had borrowed not merely the name but also the titles and secret language of the original Klan. These Klan features, as well as the costume, manual (the "Kloran"), ritual, and philosophy, were designed by Simmons as early as 1911.

The Klan's progress was slow, and Simmons did everything, even mortgaging his house, to keep his effort alive. In 1920, he contracted with Edward Young Clarke's Southern Publicity Association to build membership. Clarke was given the title of "Imperial Kleagle." Admittedly motivated only by hope of profit, Clarke and his partner, Elizabeth Tyler, soon discovered that they were most successful in recruiting when they emphasized the racial and religious "threats" to traditional American values posed by Catholics, Jews, blacks, and aliens. A membership sales force employed the concept of "pyramiding," with each officer receiving a portion of every ten-dollar membership sold by his team. The pair's plan of making the Klan prominent in the national press resulted in a great increase in Klan membership around the country; membership was estimated variously from two to five million by 1924.

The Klan was strongest in the South, in Alabama, Louisiana, Florida, North Carolina, Texas, Oklahoma, and Georgia; Atlanta was its "Holy City." It also had remarkable numbers in Oregon, Colorado, Kansas, Illinois, Ohio, and Pennsylvania, and was especially strong in Indiana. All strata of white male society could be found among its members, from Ph.D.s and state governors to rural and urban rowdies. There was much in the Klan's program that represented the feelings of Americans in the 1920's, a fact illustrated by the vicious, non-Klan-related race riots in Chicago and in Tulsa, Oklahoma, in 1919, and by the sharp increase in lynchings of blacks in the same year.

In the beginning, the Klan's activities consisted of nighttime violence against individuals or the threat of violence by means of parades as demonstrations of potential force. Actual violence was perpetrated by only a small minority of the millions of members. It is interesting to note that most Klan violence was directed not at blacks but at whites whose morals displeased the local Klan: men who the Klan alleged were unfaithful to their spouses, women who allegedly wore short skirts or "petted" in cars, and any white person who "fraternized" with blacks or patronized Jewish businesses.

Klan leaders Simmons, Clarke, and Tyler claimed that the twenty-one-day exposure of Klan violence by *The New York World* and its affiliate newspapers around the nation in September, 1921, actually was the catalyst that caused membership to burgeon. Indeed, the immediate reaction to the publicity was that more than two hundred applications for local chapters poured in, some on facsimile forms reprinted in the newspapers. In its series, *The New York World* enumerated 152 separate Klan outrages. Klan defectors provided information about forty-one floggings, twenty-seven tar-and-featherings, five kidnappings, forty-three persons forced to leave their towns, one case of branding with acid, and four lynchings. Most of the reported vigilante violence occurred in Texas between February and July, 1921. In addition, *The New York World* published an article divulging that Clarke and Tyler, known to have reaped great profits from their Klan activities, had in 1919 been implicated in a morals scandal, the police records of which had somehow disappeared.

Equally productive of new memberships was the publicity gained from the congressional investigation of the Klan in October, 1921. The Klan was thus in the headlines consistently for two months. Rowland Thomas, the writer of *The New York World*'s exposé, reviewed his case against the Klan and gave evidence about the Klan's religious and racist publications. He further presented proof that Simmons had boasted of having governors, members of Congress, and other officials in the "Invisible Empire" and under his orders. The last witness was Simmons himself, who for three days boldly denied that any of the violent acts were committed by Klansmen. Still, *The New York World* noticed that in three cases (in Mobile, Alabama, Pensacola, Florida, and Beaumont, Texas) Simmons had suspended or disbanded local chapters that had been accused of flagrant wrongdoing. He charged *The New York World* with being a stronghold of Jewish opinion. After the investigation, Simmons was able to assert, "Congress made us."

Impact of Event

Under Hiram Wesley Evans, who seized the leadership of the Klan in 1922 and forced the departure of Simmons and Clarke in 1924, the Klan renounced violence and worked at gaining power in the open political arena by campaigning and influencing legislation. The relocation of its offices to Washington, D.C., in 1925 was celebrated by a parade of forty thousand white-robed men and women down Pennsylvania Avenue. Thenceforth, the Klan emphasized the less controversial elements of its program and campaigned for education, donations to Protestant congregations, and morality.

Evans' plan was to distance the Klan from its many atrocities, such as that in August, 1922, when two farmers who had spoken out against the Klan were mutilated and murdered at Mer Rouge, Louisiana. Klan violence against Jews, blacks, and those allegedly involved in "vice" reached a high pitch that nearly plunged Oklahoma into civil war from 1921 to 1923. Finally, Governor John Walton installed martial law in the state, but he was soon removed from office. The Klan rejoiced.

Other events continued to show the Klan in a bad light. In March, 1925, David C. Stephenson, a Grand Dragon of the Indiana Klan who had become notoriously rich and powerful through his Klan activities, was convicted of murder when a woman died after being tortured and raped by him. His life sentence ended with his release after thirty-one years. In 1927, Evans entered a lawsuit against a group of seceding Pennsylvania Klansmen. In the ensuing courtroom battle, the Klan's "dirty linen" was divulged by secessionist witnesses and even by Simmons. One witness revealed the burning to death of an oil-doused Texan while hundreds of hooded Klansmen watched.

These and numerous other Klan outrages dominated headlines for months on end. By the end of the 1920's, the accumulation of Klan outrages took an inevitable toll on the Klan's popularity, effectiveness, and viability. When Evans announced in 1928 that the Klan would no longer use masks, it was too late to save the "hooded empire."

The Klan's entry into party politics proved damaging to the organization. Much infighting among Klansmen for nominations resulted. In some cases, however, the Klan could boast of having helped the election of an entire pro-Klan Republican slate. In 1924, the state of Oregon passed a compulsory public education bill that had been sponsored by the legislature with Klan backing. The measure effectively outlawed the existence of parochial schools and was one of the Klan's most notable successes. In the same year, the Klan helped elect eleven governors and sixteen members of Congress. After exercising great influence in the presidential election of 1924 and helping to defeat Alfred E. Smith in 1928, the Klan's importance and membership precipitously declined; by 1930, membership was down to between thirty and fifty thousand. Most observers thought that the decline was caused by the uninspiring ineptitude of the Klan's leaders in the open arena of political life.

Although Klan literature continued to attack Catholics, Jews, blacks, and foreigners, the Klan in the 1930's shifted its focus to assaulting communism and keeping blacks from voting. The Klan was never again the force in American life that it had been in the 1920's. In 1939, Evans sold the Klan to James A. Colescott, a veterinarian from Indiana. In 1944, the Klan was dissolved in lieu of payment of $685,000 in back taxes.

The Klan experienced sporadic revivals in later years, but it was always in splintered ineptitude and disrepute. Ultimately, Americans became disgusted with the Klan as an extremist group that trampled upon the freedom and rights of all Americans. Similarly, the Klan's false position as defender of the nation's morals was exposed by the greed and immorality of certain of its leaders.

Bibliography

Alexander, Charles C. *The Ku Klux Klan in the Southwest.* Lexington: University Press of Kentucky, 1965. Alexander's theme is "that the distinctive quality of the Klan in Texas, Louisiana, Oklahoma, and Arkansas was its motivation, which lay not so much in racism and nativism as in [Victorian] moral authoritarianism." Thus, most vigilantism was directed against whites. Alexander includes a glossary of Klan terminology and a useful annotated bibliography.

Allen, Frederick Lewis. *Only Yesterday: An Informal History of the Nineteen-Twenties.* New York: Bantam Books, 1931. Valuable as a virtually contemporary social history of the 1920's in the United States.

Cash, W. J. *The Mind of the South.* New York: Alfred A. Knopf, 1941. General introduction to the intellectual ethos of the American South. Allows the reader to understand better how the programs of the Klan might be representative of the general thinking of the populace of the South.

Chalmers, David M. *Hooded Americanism: The History of the Ku Klux Klan.* 1965. Rev. ed. Chicago: Quadrangle Books, 1968. One of the best general works on the Klan. Gracefully written, it gives a clear insight into the Klan mentality, the motivations that induced men and women of diverse backgrounds, urban and rural, northern and southern, to join the Klan. Contains a chapter on the original Klan of the Reconstruction era, focuses (Chapters 2-41) upon the Klan of the 1920's, and concludes with seven chapters on the Klan from 1929 to the 1960's.

Fry, Henry P. *The Modern Ku Klux Klan.* 1922. Rev. ed. New York: Negro Universities Press, 1969. The author was a Klan defector and a major source for *The New York World* of insider Klan information for its 1921 exposé. Devotes much space to *The New York World*'s coverage and to quotations from the depositions of witnesses at the congressional investigation that year.

Jackson, Kenneth T. *The Ku Klux Klan in the City, 1915-1930.* New York: Oxford University Press, 1967. Noting that the census of 1920 located more Americans in city environments than on farms, Jackson studied the Klan as an urban phenomenon and, for a time, as a political force. Many joined out of innocent patriotism and simply dropped out when Klan realities were revealed. Jackson believes that Klan violence has been overemphasized, and that in the cities the Klan was more often the victim. Excellent annotated bibliography.

Lutholtz, William. *Grand Dragon: D. C. Stephenson and the Ku Klux Klan in Indiana.* West Lafayette, Ind.: Purdue University Press, 1991. Examines the extraordinary political power wielded by Stephenson and the Klan in Indiana in the 1920's. The mayors of Indianapolis and Evansville and the governor of the state allegedly became clients of the Klan under Stephenson, but his moral reputation and an *Indianapolis Times* exposé spelled the Klan's demise in Indiana by 1928.

Rice, Arnold S. *The Ku Klux Klan in American Politics.* 1962. Rev. ed. New York: Haskell House, 1972. Provides a good, concise historical background of the Klan of the 1920's. Focuses, with numerous interesting details, on the Klan's political activities in local, state, and national elections and issues. Short and readable, it is vigorously anti-Klan.

Schlesinger, Arthur M., Jr. *The Crisis of the Old Order, 1919-1933.* Vol. 1 in *The Age of Roosevelt.* Boston: Houghton Mifflin, 1957. This volume purports to cover the age of Franklin D. Roosevelt; in effect, it is an excellent general treatment of American life and thought in the 1920's.

Daniel C. Scavone

Cross-References

The Immigration Act of 1921 Imposes a National Quota System (1921), p. 350; Martial Law Is Declared in Oklahoma in Response to KKK Violence (1923), p. 367; A U.S. Immigration Act Imposes Quotas Based on National Origins (1924), p. 383; The Congress of Racial Equality Forms (1942), p. 601; CORE Stages a Sit-in in Chicago to Protest Segregation (1943), p. 618; Race Riots Erupt in Detroit and Harlem (1943), p. 635; Truman Orders Desegregation of U.S. Armed Forces (1948), p. 777; The Civil Rights Act of 1957 Creates the Commission on Civil Rights (1957), p. 997; Eisenhower Sends Troops to Little Rock, Arkansas (1957), p. 1003; Meredith's Enrollment Integrates the University of Mississippi (1962), p. 1167; Congress Passes the Civil Rights Act (1964), p. 1251; Race Rioting Erupts in Detroit (1967), p. 1376; Jackson Becomes the First Major Black Candidate for U.S. President (1983), p. 2209; Wilder Becomes the First Elected Black Governor (1989), p. 2517.

ADVISORY COUNCILS GIVE BOTSWANA NATIVES LIMITED REPRESENTATION

Categories of event: Indigenous peoples' rights and political freedom
Time: 1920
Locale: Botswana (Bechuanaland Protectorate)

The Batswana attempted to use their advisory councils to shape colonial rule on key issues such as keeping South Africa from annexing them, but they faced British efforts to use the councils to legitimize tax increases and erode African rights

Principal personages:
KHAMA III (C. 1837-1923), the chief of the largest Batswana society, the BaNgwato
TSHEKEDI KHAMA (1905-1959), the regent of the BaNgwato (1925-1950) who offered the most sustained challenge to the councils' ability to influence important decisions
CHARLES F. REY (1877-1968), the British resident commissioner; sought to use the councils as a mechanism to legitimize his development policies
JULES ELLENBERGER (1871-1969), a colonial official who served as government secretary and then as resident commissioner

Summary of Event

British imperialism in southern Africa remained intertwined with the interests of the settler regimes in South Africa and Southern Rhodesia. Colonies like the Bechuanaland Protectorate (now known as Botswana) received little attention and often faced administrative decisions that inhibited development. The British were reluctant to expend resources in the protectorate because they anticipated no real gain from economic investments. They assumed that the territory would someday be transferred to South Africa.

The British sought to normalize their administrative and political position by instituting a government that was efficient yet inexpensive. They intended to provide better communication between the "colonized" and the "colonizer." After World War I, the British created the Native Advisory Council (after 1940, called the African Advisory Council) and the European Advisory Council as mechanisms to meet these objectives. These councils did not substantially enhance the rights of the indigenous people.

Perhaps the key issue that led British resident commissioner J. C. Macgregor to suggest the idea of councils related to tax increases. He had established the Bechuanaland Protectorate Native Fund, which taxed residents an additional three shillings. The African Advisory Council was to aid in collecting, administering, and disbursing this revenue. There was no high commissioner proclamation to give statutory authority to the councils, so the councils' advice would have no formal standing.

The councils did provide a forum for dissent and a basis for cooperation with the colonial administration. It was not until the 1950's and the formation of the Joint Advisory Council, however, that genuine collective actions occurred.

For the Batswana (the people of Botswana), the first session of the Native Advisory Council in 1920 at Gaborones raised fundamental questions about how effective this new colonial institution would work. In particular, there were serious concerns about its impact on local politics. Khama III, the most influential chief, refused to participate and sent no BaNgwato representatives because he believed that the council would undermine his authority and the limited autonomy of his people. Other chiefs wondered how the council could function if the largest Tswana group stayed away. Eventually, each of the major Tswana ethnic groups would participate in the council. Initially, the BaKwena, BaNgwaketse, BaKgatla, and BaMalete were joined by the BaTlokwa. By the third session, the BaRolong belonged. The BaTawana joined in 1931, while the BaNgwato waited until 1940 to become official members, although they regularly attended sessions before this.

The council considered some important issues and challenged the colonial administration to respond to Batswana needs. The key concerns surfaced quickly in the council deliberations. It became clear that the colonial administration primarily would address its own interests at Botswana's expense.

When the Batswana made demands that conflicted with neighboring South Africa, they encountered British priorities which were most often to South Africa's advantage. Discussions about transferring the colony to South African control, as a schedule to the 1909 South Africa Act delineated, indicated that the Batswana were united in their opposition to British-South African negotiations without their consent. The council provided an important forum on this issue. It showed that the Batswana had articulate spokespersons who understood South African policies. The debates on this topic seemed to indicate the potential for the council as a mechanism to shape colonial rule.

On other issues, Africans on the council were less effective in gaining British cooperation. Funding for the education of African children was limited. The government did not create an education department until 1935. Tribal treasuries were responsible for funding education out of their own scarce resources. African representatives to the council spoke about educational needs at each session, but the government proved unresponsive. Those few Africans who could afford to educate their children sent them to South Africa or Southern Rhodesia. There was no secondary school in Botswana in the 1920's and 1930's. Tiger Kloof, a mission school inside South Africa, served as the colony's best access to education. The council regularly recommended expenditures of their tax revenues to support the school, even though it was in South Africa.

The council supported the Batswana's most important economic concern, their cattle industry. They sought improved markets, expanded veterinary services, access to water, better breeding opportunities, and upgraded transportation links. The colonial administration acknowledged these needs but provided minimal assistance. When South Africa limited the colony's cattle market and embargoed Botswana's cattle, the Batswana received little support from the administration. In fact, the British sided with the South Africans on the embargo.

More general concerns about the protectorate's development found only marginal British support. Questions concerning exploitation of mineral deposits and other development schemes elicited responses indicating the limited capital funds available. In other words, the administration was unwilling to fund development.

The African Advisory Council made few inroads against the colonial administration. It provided an important forum for presenting issues of concern, although it did not empower the Batswana to alter British policy. It proved most useful in expressing distrust of South Africa.

The European Advisory Council was approved in 1920 and had its first meeting in 1921. The council was initially made up of three representatives of the European settlers, although the government had agreed to four members, a farmer and trader each from the North and the South. By the second session, the council had one representative each from the white land blocks of Gaborones, Tati, Tuli, Lobatse, and Ghanzi. By 1948, the council had expanded to eight members. Unlike the African Advisory Council, which initially met inside the protectorate, the European Advisory Council met in Mafekeng, the protectorate's administrative capital, located within South Africa's borders. Collaboration with the colonial administration, however, did not prove easy. Probably the most important objective for the European residents was the transfer of the colony to South African control. The European settlers pressured the government well into the 1950's to make this change. Most of their arguments were based on economic opportunities. Their underlying racial attitudes were always clear and often stated. In the 1920's and 1930's, they identified themselves closely with the South African white community.

The colonial administration responded to many of the settler demands. Education for white children received government financial support, although the children went to school outside the colony. The European cattle industry suffered from South African restrictions on the colony's beef, so efforts to use the council to lobby for change did not work well on this issue. In the early 1920's, the council successfully negotiated some loans for white farmers. The council asked the administration to reduce its allocation to fight lung sickness among diseased African-owned cattle. In this period, the European Council remained hostile to African priorities and showed no interest in working with the African Council.

The two councils shaped the debate over issues, but usually not the outcome. The European Council demonstrated little interest in cooperating with the Batswana until the 1950's. By then, the Joint Advisory Council had assumed the lead. In 1960, each of the councils was disbanded and a Legislative Council was created.

Impact of Event

The advisory councils were probably not pivotal in changing the course of events for human rights in Botswana. The councils did, however, provide an important dimension in the political struggles of the colony and created part of a legacy which influences Botswana even in the 1990's.

Tshekedi Khama, who became regent of the BaNgwato in 1925, worked outside the African Council to resist British attempts to move toward the transfer of the colony to South Africa. There can be no doubt that his efforts were most effective when the African Advisory Council followed his lead. In this way, that council served as an indispensable mechanism in pressuring the British. That the transfer never took place was largely the result of Tshekedi Khama's resistance, backed up by the African Council.

The strength of South Africa's influence over Botswana is indicative of the limitations of the colonial institutions. The European Advisory Council contributed to a closer economic relationship with South Africa. Its initiatives legitimized the colonial administration's attempts to make Botswana economically dependent on South Africa.

The British set up the councils in order to control events in the protectorate. They offered the Batswana and the European settlers a voice in administration, but it was clear that the British wanted to shape cooperation. Jules Ellenberger, a key colonial officer in the 1920's, had grown up in the midst of Tswana society and used his knowledge of it to weaken traditional institutions rather than to protect indigenous rights. Sir Charles Rey, the resident commissioner in the 1930's, followed a similar course. His aggressiveness in attacking the chiefs and their indigenous institutions in the name of economic development and modernization brought sustained resistance both inside and outside the African Council. It seemed as though Rey wished to restructure Batswana society by centralizing colonial institutions. Although he was unsuccessful in his political objectives, he did weaken local political institutions. His economic development plans suffered from a lack of resources and thus brought South Africa into a more dominant position.

In the 1950's, the councils offered a conservative model for political and economic development. Traditional chiefs had used the African Council to retain their influence. Settler leaders had shaped policies that maintained private holdings, close relations with South Africa, and race relations that preserved their privilege. The councils' legacy was preservation of this order for more than a decade past Botswana's 1966 independence.

Bibliography

Crowder, Michael. *The Flogging of Phinehas McIntosh: A Tale of Colonial Folly and Injustice, Bechuanaland, 1933.* New Haven, Conn.: Yale University Press, 1988. This terrific book demonstrates the tensions between Tshekedi Khama and those in the British colonial administration, especially Sir Charles Rey. It details the absurd lengths to which the British were willing to go in order to assert their political control over the Bechuanaland Protectorate in the 1930's. The volume is successful in showing the effectiveness of Tshekedi's leadership.

Morton, R. F., and J. Ramsay, eds. *Birth of Botswana: A History of the Bechuana-land Protectorate from 1910 to 1966.* Gaborone, Botswana: Longman, 1987. This text, by two academics who know Botswana well, is an excellent introduction to the country's history. It keeps the Batswana central to the country's history. It is used widely in higher education in Botswana.

Parsons, Neil. *A New History of Southern Africa.* London: Macmillan, 1982. This text is one of the best surveys of southern Africa. It is widely used in the region and emphasizes indigenous perspectives. It places Botswana in the larger context of the region.

Parsons, Neil, and Michael Crowder, eds. *Monarch of All I Survey: The Diaries of Sir Charles Rey.* London: James Curry, 1988. This volume is a splendid effort to edit the diaries of Sir Charles Rey. Their account provides Rey's views of events in the 1930's and his attitudes toward the Batswana. There are several accounts of and reflections on the councils.

Sillery, Anthony. *Botswana: A Short Political History.* London: Methuen, 1974. This short book is by a former British colonial administrator who served as resident commissioner in Botswana from 1946 to 1950. This imperial history expresses hints of paternalism while showing a genuine fondness for the Batswana.

Jack Bermingham

Cross-References

Reformers Expose Atrocities Against Congolese Laborers (1903), p. 13; The Belgian Government Annexes the Congo (1908), p. 103; The Atlantic Charter Declares a Postwar Right of Self-Determination (1941), p. 584; South Africa Begins a System of Separate Development (1951), p. 861; The Nonaligned Movement Meets (1961), p. 1131; Lutuli Is Awarded the Nobel Peace Prize (1961), p. 1143; The Organization of African Unity Is Founded (1963), p. 1194; Zimbabwe's Freedom Fighters Topple White Supremacist Government (1964), p. 1224; Students in Soweto Rebel Against the White Government (1976), p. 1882; The United Nations Imposes an Arms Embargo on South Africa (1977), p. 1937.

IRELAND IS GRANTED HOME RULE
AND NORTHERN IRELAND IS CREATED

Category of event: Political freedom
Time: 1920-1921
Locale: Ireland and Northern Ireland

After decades of discussion, the British parliament passed legislation granting home rule to Ireland in the form of two separate parliaments, which would govern domestic concerns

Principal personages:

DAVID LLOYD GEORGE (1863-1945), the British prime minister

SIR JAMES CRAIG (1861-1940), the first prime minister of Northern Ireland and a leading opponent of home rule

SIR EDWARD CARSON (1854-1935), a British political leader and head of Ulster opposition to home rule

EAMON DE VALERA (1882-1975), the head of the Sinn Féin republican movement

BONAR LAW (1858-1923), the leader of the Conservative-Unionists, a group opposed to home rule

MICHAEL COLLINS (1890-1922), a major figure of resistance to British rule but an opponent of De Valera concerning the 1921 treaty

Summary of Event

British influence in Ireland was of centuries' duration. Anglo-Norman aristocrats settled in Ireland among the native Celts in the twelfth century, and Protestants from England and Scotland were given lands there by British monarchs in the sixteenth and seventeenth centuries. It was not until 1800, however, that Ireland was fully integrated into the political system of the United Kingdom. Prior to that date, Ireland had its own parliament, although that body was often subject to the influence and control of the British authorities. The Act of Union in 1800 abolished the Irish parliament, leaving a single parliament for the entire United Kingdom.

Many in Ireland were dissatisfied with the union. Some wanted full independence, and this led to rebellions such as the nationalist Fenian movement of the 1860's. Other Irish people were willing to remain within the United Kingdom but wanted some sort of home rule, with a restored parliament in Dublin, for domestic matters. The most famous home rule advocate was Charles Stewart Parnell, an aristocratic Protestant landlord, whose supporters were, paradoxically, mostly Catholic farmers and shopkeepers.

The religious dimension is significant in any discussion of Ireland. Approximately three-quarters of the population at that time was Catholic, but the Protestant minority was concentrated in the north, in the province of Ulster, where they formed the majority. Home rule tended to be more popular among Irish Catholics than among Irish Protestants: Many of the latter feared that home rule would become Rome rule. There were other issues—Ulster was more industrialized than the agricultural South, and the majority in Ulster were descendants from Scottish and English immigrants— but religion was at the core.

Britain's Liberal Party twice introduced home rule legislation in the late nine- teenth century. It failed to pass both houses of Parliament so did not become law. After the second defeat, the movement for home rule waned. As a result of a parlia- mentary deadlock in 1910 between the two major political parties, Liberal and Con- servative, the issue of home rule returned. The Irish party supported the Liberals in exchange for Liberal backing for a new home rule bill. The third home rule bill was introduced in 1912, and as a result of legislation limiting the power of the House of Lords, the bill appeared destined to become law in 1914. Parnell's dream was about to be realized.

Many in Protestant Ulster, however, demanded that the union be maintained. Af- ter the bill was introduced, almost one-half million people in Ulster signed a Solemn League and Covenant against any home rule. A militia, the Ulster Volunteers, was created to fight the British government if necessary in order to stay within the United Kingdom. Weapons were smuggled into Ulster. Some British military officers sym- pathized with the Ulster position, as did many Conservative politicians, including Conservative leader Andrew Bonar Law and fellow Conservative Edward Carson, who accepted the leadership of the Ulster resistance. In the South, reacting to the events in Ulster, supporters of home rule formed their own volunteers to fight for the British government and for home rule. By the summer of 1914, it seemed that civil war might erupt. The outbreak of World War I in August, however, pushed the ques- tion of home rule into the background. Home rule legislation was passed but would not take effect until the war was over. The contentious issue of Ulster's relationship to home rule was left unresolved.

Most Irish, Catholics and Protestants alike, loyally supported Britain in the war against Germany. As the war dragged on and actual home rule remained in the future, the Irish home rule party began to lose influence. A violent uprising against British rule occurred on Easter Monday, April 24, 1916. A group of several hundred, inspired by earlier rebellions and committed to an independent republic, not home rule, occupied key locations in Dublin and proclaimed an Irish Republic. The re- bellion lasted less than a week, but hundreds died and much of central Dublin was destroyed. The rebels had little support, either during or after the rising, until the leaders were executed by the military authorities sent to restore order. As the list of martyrs lengthened, public opinion turned in favor of the rebels.

In a series of elections in 1917 and 1918, the Irish home rule party was regularly defeated by a new bloc, known as Sinn Féin, meaning "we ourselves" or "ourselves alone." Sinn Féin demanded not home rule but independence and identified itself with the Easter uprising. The most prominent of its members was Eamon De Valera, one of the leaders in 1916. The movement was not just political. The secretive Irish

Republican Brotherhood, who led the 1916 rebels, believed that force would be necessary to get rid of the British.

In December, 1918, at the end of World War I, a general election was held throughout the United Kingdom, including Ireland. In Ireland outside Ulster, Sinn Féin candidates swept away the old Irish home rule party, winning almost all the parliamentary elections. The victorious candidates, however, refused to take their seats in Parliament. Instead, they formed their own parliament, the Dail Eireann, in Dublin. It was outlawed by the British and could do little but issue proclamations and send delegations to the peace conference at Versailles and to sympathetic countries, particularly the United States with its large Irish community. Behind the Dail and its politicians was the military wing of Sinn Féin, which became known as the Irish Republican Army.

The wartime coalition government was headed by David Lloyd George, a Liberal, but was dominated by Conservatives strongly opposed to home rule, much less an independent republic of Ireland. Before becoming prime minister, Lloyd George had unsuccessfully attempted to negotiate an Irish settlement after the 1916 rebellion. As prime minister, in 1917 he urged the Irish to settle their own disputes. Sinn Féin refused to participate, and the unionists were obstructive. Lloyd George was sympathetic to home rule but more interested in preserving the unity of the United Kingdom. He moved cautiously to solve the Irish problem.

In 1919, the Conservatives still supported the Ulster unionist position but with less vehemence than before: As the dominant party in the coalition government, they needed Ulster less. James Craig, a decisive but less abrasive politician than Edward Carson, had taken over Ulster's defense. Craig's position was improved because the old home rule party had been replaced by the Sinn Féin republicans, who were unwilling or unable to negotiate with the British enemy. Some were in prison or in hiding, such as De Valera, who had been incarcerated in an English jail until his escape in February, 1919. In June, De Valera left for the United States to garner support. He did not return until December, 1920, a crucial period for Anglo-Irish relations.

In October, 1919, a British cabinet committee began to draft a bill to be submitted to Parliament. The assumption was that Ulster had to be treated separately from the rest of Ireland. Some suggested that each of Ireland's thirty-two counties decide by popular vote whether to accept home rule, but that proposal had no support within the cabinet. A decision was made to establish two home rule parliaments, one for Ulster and one for the rest of Ireland. This surprised the Ulster unionists: They had opposed any home rule parliament, and now they were being asked to have their own. They accepted what they initially did not want, concluding that having their own home rule parliament would in the long run protect them from the vagaries of future British governments that might give their rights away to the southern majority. Most members of the cabinet wished to include all nine Ulster counties in northern Ireland. Craig was opposed to this. He demanded only six. If the other three with their large Catholic majorities were included, he argued, in time a Catholic nationalist majority might emerge, willing to unite North and South. Even though only four of the six had Protestant majorities, Craig argued that those four counties would form too small a political unit and would not be viable. Ultimately, the cabinet bowed to Craig's demand for the six counties. The Government of Ireland Act of 1920 easily passed through Parliament and went into effect on May 3, 1921. Ireland had been partitioned, and Northern Ireland had come into existence with its own home rule parliament.

Impact of Event

The Government of Ireland Act of 1920 did not settle the Irish difficulties. The creation of Northern Ireland, which was two-thirds Protestant and in favor of the union with Britain, seemed to satisfy the majority in that province. In the rest of Ireland, however, troubles continued. Sinn Féin and the IRA refused to accept the act, which created a second home rule parliament, in Dublin. Their goal was complete independence. The violence which had broken out in 1919 was bloody and brutal. The IRA resorted to guerrilla tactics. To fight against the IRA, the British government enlisted former soldiers. Given makeshift uniforms, they became known as the "Black and Tans." Violence from one side led to reprisals by the other, resulting in incidents that went beyond the rules of war. On November 21, 1920, twelve British officers, members of a counterterrorist squad, were shot dead in Dublin. Later that same day, in retaliation, twelve civilians were killed at a football match. Civilian casualties in the first six months of 1921 numbered more than seven hundred dead and almost eight hundred injured, some by the British, some by the IRA.

By early 1921, the British government began to get the upper hand, but at considerable cost and with much criticism. On June 22, 1921, King George V, at the formal opening of the parliament of Northern Ireland, and with the support of Lloyd George, appealed for peace. Lloyd George followed up with a letter to De Valera, who responded in turn. On July 11, 1921, a truce was declared. Formal negotiations began in London in October.

The crucial issues were the relation of Ireland to the United Kingdom and of Ulster to Ireland. After hard negotiations, a treaty was agreed to on December 6, 1921. Dominion status was accepted by twenty-six southern counties, which would be known as the Irish Free State. The other six counties formed Northern Ireland. Lloyd George misleadingly intimated that a boundary commission would probably award enough of the territory of Northern Ireland to the Irish Free State to make the north untenable, thus leading to a unified Ireland. De Valera, however, opposed the treaty from Dublin, arguing for an external association with Great Britain instead of dominion status. Amid great controversy, the Dail approved the treaty in January by the narrow margin of sixty-four votes to fifty-seven. De Valera resigned and Griffith took his place.

The result was civil war. The IRA split between the pro- and antitreaty factions. In six months, the Irish Free State government executed seventy-seven antitreaty republicans, more than three times the number executed by the British government in two and one-half years. Griffith died of a heart attack, and in August, 1922, Collins was killed in an antitreaty ambush. De Valera was arrested by the Free State authorities and remained in jail for a year. In Northern Ireland, the police were given extensive powers to deal with the continuing violence. A special powers bill was passed giving the authorities almost unlimited authority. The worst casualty of the civil war was the cause of a united Ireland: The violence between the pro- and antitreaty groups in the Free State confirmed to the majority in Northern Ireland that the South could not be trusted. A partial peace came to the Free State with the defeat of most of the antitreaty forces during 1923. By then, the Protestant Unionist majority in Northern Ireland was in control of the province at the expense of the Catholics and Irish nationalists. In the South, Protestants faced less overt discrimination, but the bitterness over the treaty continued to divide Irish nationalists for decades to come.

Bibliography

Buckland, Patrick. *A History of Northern Ireland.* Dublin: Gill and Macmillan, 1981. This excellent short volume is more than a history of Northern Ireland. It includes material concerning the rest of Ireland and background to the continuing Irish conflicts. Contains a select bibliography and an index.

Coogan, Tim Pat. *Michael Collins: A Biography.* London: Hutchinson University Library, 1990. Biography of an ally of De Valera who differed with him over the 1921 treaty. The author argues that Collins was more pragmatic than De Valera, and that his death was a tragedy for Ireland. Includes biography and index.

Kee, Robert. *Ourselves Alone.* London: Penguin Books, 1989. First published in 1972 as the last book in a three-volume series entitled "The Green Flag." The author begins coverage in 1916 and continues through the civil war of 1922-1923. Well written, the work keeps an impartial tone in portraying the controversial events of those difficult years. Includes a bibliography and index.

Laffan, Michael. *The Partition of Ireland, 1911-1925.* Dundalk, Ireland: Dundalgan Press, 1983. Sponsored by the Dublin Historical Association, this brief volume is written for students and teachers of history. It is an excellent introduction to the formation of Northern Ireland. Contains a short bibliography and extensive footnotes with references.

Longford, Frank Pakenham, and Thomas P. O'Neill. *Eamon De Valera.* London: Hutchinson, 1970. The most readable biography of the key southern Irish figure, the work was published before De Valera's death and is not overly critical. Includes a bibliography, index, and numerous photographs.

Rowland, Peter. *David Lloyd George: A Biography.* New York: Macmillan, 1976. This work is the best single-volume biography of the most important British statesman during the crucial years after World War I. Much on the Irish imbroglio. Contains bibliography and index.

Stewart, A. T. Q. *Edward Carson.* Dublin: Gill and Macmillan, 1981. This short biography of a major anti-home rule politician is a sympathetic portrayal which

shows Carson as pro-United Kingdom but not anti-Irish. It is an excellent introduction to an important personage.

Eugene S. Larson

Cross-References

The Defense of India Act Impedes the Freedom Struggle (1915), p. 156; The Eas-
ter Rebellion Fails to Win Irish Independence (1916), p. 178; The Balfour Declaration Supports a Jewish Homeland in Palestine (1917), p. 235; Parliament Grants
Suffrage to British Women (1918), p. 247; The Paris Peace Conference Includes
Protection for Minorities (1919), p. 252; The League of Nations Is Established (1919),
p. 270; The Minimum Age for Female British Voters Is Lowered (1928), p. 442; The
Statute of Westminster Creates the Commonwealth (1931), p. 453; British Troops
Restore Order in Northern Ireland (1969), p. 1485; The Emergency Provisions (North-
ern Ireland) Act Is Passed (1973), p. 1720; Two Founders of Peace People Win the
Nobel Peace Prize (1977), p. 1932.

GANDHI LEADS A NONCOOPERATION MOVEMENT

Categories of event: Indigenous peoples' rights and political freedom
Time: 1920-1922
Locale: India

Gandhi organized the noncooperation movement in India in 1920 to transform the freedom movement from an elitist to a mass-based one and to actively and vigorously oppose British rule

Principal personages:
  MAHATMA GANDHI (1869-1948), the Hindu leader of the Indian nationalist movement, organized a noncooperation movement in opposition to British rule
  CHITTARANJAN DAS (1870-1925), an important leader of the Indian National Congress who agreed to support the noncooperation movement
  MOTILAL NEHRU (1861-1931), a moderate leader of the Indian National Congress in 1920

Summary of Event

Many Indians supported the British during World War I. These included Mohandas Kamarchand (Mahatma) Gandhi, who organized an ambulance brigade and recruited soldiers for the Indian Army. There were also many Indians, again including Gandhi, who believed that they could work with the British toward the granting of independence for India, which the British had promised in 1917 as a reward for Indian support during World War I. This feeling of goodwill on the part of Indians turned to distrust and outright hostility and opposition during the years 1918 to 1920. One reason was a 1919 massacre of Indian protesters in Amritsar. The British had passed new regulations which restricted Indian freedom, replacing strict laws passed during World War I that had expired. The Indians were protesting these new laws. Another source of hostility was the dismembering of the Ottoman Empire by the British and their allies, which upset India's Muslims (the *Khilafat* movement). A third was a series of new laws enacted just after the end of the war which reduced some of the civil liberties which the Indians had come to expect. Thus, on one hand, the British were making liberal constitutional changes, as in the Government of India Act of 1919 which gave more Indians the vote and allowed more of them to sit in regional and national legislatures. On the other hand, the British were also strengthening their own position through restrictive laws, such as those passed to control demonstrations in the Punjab against British rule, and through violence, such as the Amritsar Massacre. The result was that by July, 1920, Gandhi and many other Indian supporters of British rule had changed their minds about the British and come to believe that the British would not give equality, dignity, and freedom to Indians. Gandhi began to talk and write about his disaffection, saying that it was now his moral duty to work for the end of British rule since it had revealed itself to be evil.

More and more Indians joined the movement for independence in the first two decades of the twentieth century and expressed their opposition to British rule, but this was not a mass movement. The Indian National Congress party was run by an elite group of politicians who were mostly Western-trained lawyers. The main activity of the Indian National Congress was an annual conference which met in one of the major cities. It was not a well-funded organization, it did not have a mass following, and it did not have a local-level base. The British, on the whole, approved of the Congress, its members, and how they went about conducting political life. Gandhi was consciously and deliberately to change all this through the noncooperation movement of 1920.

Gandhi's aim during the movement was not only to change how the Indian National Congress operated and how the struggle for independence was being waged but also to transform the very style of Indian politics. He believed that Indians had become too Westernized and that they were cooperating too much with the British. He wanted to end British rule but wanted to achieve this peacefully, possibly with the collaboration of the British themselves. At the same time, Gandhi wanted to turn India away from the material values of the West and back to the simpler values of traditional India. He believed that, by returning to indigenous daily practices, Indians could undermine the British economy and transform their society. He revived the use of the spinning wheel, and the wearing of clothes made of hand-spun and hand-woven cloth (*khadi*) became a symbol of Congressmen. Hand-spinning and hand-weaving, he believed, would bring some relief from poverty and help to alleviate unemployment in the villages. Gandhi was, therefore, not only changing the way Indians saw themselves and how they acted; he was Indianizing the nationalist movement. This was further evidenced by the increasing use of Hindustani and other Indian languages rather than English. The end result was that Indians began to have more pride in their Indian heritage and their traditional way of life, and they began to believe that by following Gandhi they could fight for independence on their own terms and in their own style.

Gandhi, without prior consultation with the leaders of the Congress, announced on August 1, 1920, that the noncooperation movement would begin the following day. He knew that the British ruled India's millions on a day-to-day basis with only a small number of British officials and soldiers and that they did so with the cooperation of the Indians. If Indians withdrew their cooperation, then the British *raj* (rule) would fall. Gandhi called this technique of nonviolent resistance *satyagraha* (soul force).

Gandhi began the movement by returning the medals which he had received from the British government in thanks for his ambulance work in previous wars. He called for the boycott of schools and of law courts and he demanded the boycott of the forthcoming elections to the legislative councils. He asked Indians not to buy British-made goods and he asked them to surrender the titles and honorary offices which the British had given them. He called for the burning of British-made cloth and the wearing of hand-spun cloth, a call to which Indians responded in large numbers, so that the wearing of Indian-made clothes became a symbol of Gandhi and his followers.

At first, reaction to Gandhi's call for noncooperation was mixed. He had called for noncooperation, mostly through the press, before the Congress had a chance to meet and discuss the issue. Many Indians were unsure how to respond. Many of them had made careers and livelihoods for themselves and their families in the service of the British. In particular, lawyers such as Congress leader Motilal Nehru, one of the highest-paid advocates in India, had a very strong interest in the legal system. They did not want to lose their privileged position in society and the special relationship they had built up with the British. Indian politicians too had benefited from British rule, especially as the legislatures had just been reformed and they were to receive privileges which would enhance their status and their salaries. They had fought long and hard to get reforms from the British, and while they certainly wanted independence, many of them believed it would come slowly and only by cooperating with the British. They were also afraid that Gandhi's program would lead to social chaos and violence. The politicians came under pressure to support noncooperation, and they did not want to appear timid in the fight for freedom. The result was that over the next several months Gandhi won many to his cause, even if he did compromise by agreeing to the gradual rather than the immediate boycott of schools and courts.

Gandhi's call for noncooperation was heard all over India. People who had not been involved in politics before mobilized, invoked Gandhi's name, called for noncooperation, and even organized his campaign in the rural areas. The surprise was that the movement was most successful in those parts of India—Sind, Gujarat, Bihar, the United Provinces, and the Punjab—which for the most part had not been politically active in the past. In August, 1920, Congress approved the principle of noncooperation. Gandhi had persuaded the regular politicians, including the Congress leaders Motilal Nehru and Chittaranjan Das, however reluctantly, to support his movement. Gandhi, in fact, took over the Congress when his supporters were elected to all the important positions in the party. The noncooperation movement continued throughout 1921 and until 1922, when protests got out of hand and twenty-two policemen were trapped inside a police station and burned to death as a mob set fire to the building. Nonviolence was one of Gandhi's cardinal principles, and when he heard about the murder of these policemen he called off the nationwide movement, to the surprise and dismay of many of his supporters. Nevertheless, through the noncooperation movement the Indian National Congress and the nationalist movement had become Gandhian.

Impact of Event

Indians responded to noncooperation in many different ways, from wearing Gandhi caps and abstaining from alcohol to committing acts of violence such as murder and arson. In the end, not very many people resigned from their positions with the government, boycotted British schools, or gave up their legal careers, and the non-cooperation movement petered out after about a year. The psychological impact on India, however, was enormous. Indians, by refusing to pay rent, by refusing to obey police orders, by demonstrating in the streets, or by refusing to buy Western goods, realized they could oppose British rule on an everyday basis. Even more important, Indians began to think and talk about the end of British rule in India. Henceforth, the British would be on the defensive. When Gandhi started his movement again in 1930, the masses followed him in even larger numbers.

Through the movement Gandhi had become a national figure; by 1922 his reputation had spread throughout the subcontinent. Many Indians did not understand Gandhi's teachings, but they followed him. He came increasingly to be known as the *Mahatma* ("Great Soul") and revered as a saint. Gandhi, therefore, had become both political leader to Congress followers and holy man to the illiterate peasants. Both Gandhi and the British were amazed at how popular and renowned he had become not only in the big cities but also in the deepest countryside, where national politics had not penetrated before.

Charged with inciting disaffection toward the government, Gandhi was arrested on March 10, 1922. He pleaded guilty and was sentenced to six years' imprisonment, although he was released in 1924 because of ill health. After he left jail, he returned to his *ashram* (a spiritual retreat or commune) and did not take an active part in Indian politics until 1930. As he went to jail in 1922, not for the first time nor for the last, he left real changes behind him. India now had a national leader. Gandhi had increased the Indian sense of nationhood, and the Indian National Congress was increasingly a national political organization. Because of Gandhi it was difficult for any politician to operate in politics outside the Indian National Congress. The party was seen by many as the only representative of the people of India; it came to be identified with India itself. In addition, Gandhi was a very successful fund-raiser. Money flowed in to the party, and the Congress was able to fund a broad range of activities and to hire full-time workers. The party organization spread to the provincial level and was found in all the areas of British India.

The most important effect of all was that the depth of political awareness had increased dramatically. People of all classes were more politically aware, mobilized, and willing to engage in political activities. Their depth of consciousness in 1922 was greater than it had been in 1920, and while their political activity was to rise and fall depending on national politics and on how strongly they felt about local conditions and local issues, India would never be the same again. The movement not only raised people's consciousness about nationalism and the nationalist movement but also made them more aware of caste and community differences, especially the difference between Hindus and Muslims. As a result of the raising of political consciousness and the increase in passions people became more willing to fight to redress wrongs. This was eventually to lead the Muslims to demand a separate country for themselves, Pakistan.

Bibliography

Brown, Judith M. *Gandhi: Prisoner of Hope.* New Haven, Conn.: Yale University Press, 1989. Judith Brown has dedicated her career to the study of the life and career of Gandhi. The early chapters of this work aid the reader in understanding how Gandhi transformed the Indian political scene through his new idea of a noncooperation movement against British rule.

_____. *Gandhi's Rise to Power: Indian Politics, 1915-1922.* Cambridge, England: Cambridge University Press, 1972. This is the most detailed study of Gandhi's rise to prominence and political power in India, and it is also the most detailed study of the noncooperation movement of 1920 now available. It provides a very detailed background to the events of the noncooperation movement and gives almost a day-to-day account of the 1920 noncooperation movement.

Copley, Antony. *Gandhi: Against the Tide.* London: Basil Blackwell, 1987. This is the best short introduction to the life and career of Gandhi. For a very short study of Gandhi's noncooperation movement and his technique of nonviolent opposition, this is the book to read.

Erikson, Erik. *Gandhi's Truth: On the Origins of Militant Nonviolence.* New York: W. W. Norton, 1969. Gandhi was not a simple man with simple ideas. Gandhi was very concerned with the psychological effect his opposition would have on the British as well as on Indians. This work by a psychoanalyst gives a clear picture of Gandhi's psychology and describes in detail the inner workings of Gandhi's mind and how he wanted to change the way Indians saw themselves and the British. Part 3 of this book deals with the noncooperation movement and Gandhi's technique.

Fox, Richard G. *Gandhian Utopia: Experiments with Culture.* Boston: Beacon Press, 1989. Gandhi used traditional Indian concepts in his noncooperation movement. Through his clothing, prayers, actions, and language, not through Western concepts, Gandhi wanted to mobilize Indians. This work by an anthropologist shows how Gandhi used symbols based in traditional Indian culture, such as *ahimsa* (nonviolence), in his noncooperation movement of 1920.

Gandhi, M. K. *An Autobiography: The Story of My Experiments with Truth.* Boston: Beacon Press, 1957. Gandhi's autobiography, which he started writing in 1925 and originally published in 1929, is essential to an understanding of how Gandhi himself saw the issues of the times. Written in a simple style, it covers his life up to 1920. It does not deal with the noncooperation movement of 1920 but does describe other campaigns he conducted in South Africa. It expounds on the principles of nonviolence which were the backbone of the noncooperation movement of 1920.

Roger D. Long

Cross-References

The Muslim League Attempts to Protect Minority Interests in India (1906), p. 87;

GREAT BRITAIN PASSES ACTS
TO PROVIDE UNEMPLOYMENT BENEFITS

Category of event: Workers' rights
Time: 1920-1925
Locale: London, England

Between 1920 and 1925, Britain enacted several laws establishing a national system of unemployment insurance, laying the groundwork for a program of unemployment relief

Principal personages:

STANLEY BALDWIN (1867-1947), the prime minister and head of the Conservative Party (1923-1924 and 1924-1925), a strong advocate of labor's rights

NEVILLE CHAMBERLAIN (1869-1940), the minister of health from 1924 to 1929; enlarged the system of social security by passage of an old-age pension plan

WINSTON CHURCHILL (1874-1965), the president of the Board of Trade, a pioneer in unemployment insurance

DAVID LLOYD GEORGE (1863-1937), a Liberal Party prime minister (1916-1922), and an advocate of social reform, including unemployment insurance

RAMSAY MACDONALD (1866-1937), the prime minister of Great Britain during the first Labour Party government in 1924; extended insurance benefits to workers outside the trades

Summary of Event

In the post-World War I period, Great Britain's economic system faltered. Depression engulfed much of the nation in 1921, and unemployment reached unparalleled proportions. In response, the government expanded prewar social insurance legislation to provide relief for the unemployed. Between 1920 and 1925, fifteen acts of Parliament dealt with assistance to the unemployed. The changeover from the Labour Party to the Conservative Party government did not end the program of social reform. In 1925, when the British Labour party under Ramsay MacDonald lost power, the new Conservative government attempted to make the unemployment insurance programs affordable and, if feasible, self-supporting.

In the 1880's, Germany had legislated a much-admired social welfare system. The so-called Bismarckian program, however, had not dealt with unemployment. It was left for Great Britain to take the lead role in that category. The Unemployment Insurance Act of 1925 reflected Great Britain's prewar attempts to obtain relief for unemployed workers. Great Britain's modern welfare system began in the early twentieth century. In 1909, the Liberal Party had embarked on a far-reaching program of social reforms. A network of labor exchanges was set up to provide opportunities for employment. Two years later, the National Insurance Act Part II initiated unemployment insurance for workers in certain trades. The person most responsible for Part II was Sir Winston Churchill, president of the Board of Trade. Unemployment, he said, was the Achilles' heel of British labor, and he proposed a national minimum income to combat the problems presented by unemployment. The capstone to the welfare state the Liberals were building was the National Insurance Act Part II. An experimental program, it applied only to select trades where employment fluctuated the most, including building, auto manufacture, and shipbuilding.

The plan was contributory—employers, workers, and the state contributed a modest amount for every week of insured employment. Approximately 2.5 million workers, including 10,000 women, were covered. Churchill's plan, however, was delayed three years because of the outbreak of World War I. In 1916, coverage was extended to munitions workers, anticipating the return of peace and consequent unemployment of them. Unemployment within the covered trades was virtually nonexistent during the war, and the Unemployment Fund amassed a surplus of £15 million. After the armistice in 1918 until March, 1921, the state provided for unemployed civilians and exservicemen through "Out of Work Donations," special grants that were not part of the unemployment insurance. Most of the unemployed were entitled to the more generous "donations," and they preferred them to the insurance. Ironically, while Great Britain spent £62 million through the "donation" system, the Unemployment Fund saved money. The public attitude toward the state's responsibilities in dealing with unemployment in the postwar period was shaped by prewar experiments. The Liberals had established labor exchanges, introduced unemployment insurance, and started public works. The earlier programs were based on contributory insurance principles.

Because the wartime prosperity resulted in an Unemployment Fund surplus, Great Britain increased unemployment benefits without increasing the contributions. The program was further improved when the government passed the Unemployment Act of 1920, linking unemployment insurance with health insurance and extending the coverage nationwide. The Unemployment Act of 1920 became the "parent act" of the national system of unemployment insurance. Nearly all manual workers and all nonmanual workers earning less than £250 per year were included, extending the program to almost twelve million workers. The act provided for "covenanted" benefits earned through contributions, for a maximum of fifteen weeks. The 1920 unemployment act met little opposition because its basic principle had been set in 1911.

This extended coverage came just as the postwar depression hit Great Britain. When the act passed, fewer than one-half million workers were unemployed; in two months, the figure doubled. By the end of June, 1921, there were two million unemployed, apart from the part-time workers also making claims. Parliament responded with a new system of benefits in advance of contributions, called "uncovenanted" benefits, and converted the insurance year to two "special periods" of thirty-five weeks each. The maximum of fifteen weeks of benefits was extended to sixteen weeks in each of the "special periods." As the depression worsened, benefits were extended to twenty-two weeks during the "special periods," but benefit levels were reduced to those of 1920. Continued economic crises forced Parliament to enact the Unemployed Workers' Dependents Act. Intended to last only six months, the dependents' grant program became a permanent attachment to the 1920 parent act. The dual system of benefits enacted in 1922 included a "gap principle," which provided for fifteen weeks of "uncovenanted" benefits, broken by gaps of five weeks to help extend the relief over a thirty-week period. "Covenanted" benefits had no gaps. The 1923 Conservative government was forced to extend the uncovenanted benefits to eighteen weeks, subject to a two-week gap; covenanted benefits ran twenty-six weeks. Additional legislation provided for "benefit years" during which twenty-six weeks of uncovenanted benefits could be drawn.

The election of 1924 brought in the Labour Party, under Ramsay MacDonald. This first socialist government attempted to rebuild the entire benefits structure. It removed the gap of three weeks, granted uncovenanted (now "standard") benefits to all classes, extended benefits from twenty-six to forty-one weeks, and made "uncovenanted" (now "extended") benefits a statutory right, just as the standard benefits were. MacDonald, however, claimed that unemployment assistance was "never meant to be a living wage."

MacDonald's sudden dissolution of Parliament in October, 1924, returned Stanley Baldwin's Conservatives to power. The transfer of power, however, did not stop the process of change. The extended benefit ceased to be a statutory right, but to prevent thousands from starving and becoming paupers, the government was forced to waive rules that protected the Insurance Fund. The administrative waiver kept some two to three hundred thousand workers on the extended benefit rolls. The urgent need for relief forced the Conservative government to pass the Widows' and Orphans' and Old Age Contributory Act in 1925. Neville Chamberlain requested that Baldwin consider the four basic fears of the breadwinner: unemployment, sickness, old age, and death. Baldwin approved, and consequently, the 1925 legislation became the most comprehensive unemployment relief program yet enacted.

Based on the 1920 "parent act," the 1925 legislation continued unemployment benefits and the dependents' grant benefit as well as adding relief for widows, orphans, and aged citizens. For seven years, the Unemployment Insurance Act, not public works, provided relief for the jobless. Subsequent legislation enacted in 1927 and future unemployment relief measures of the 1930's were based on the "parent act" of 1920 and the other acts passed between that year and 1925.

Impact of Event

The international impact of Great Britain's experiment was significant. The scientific theory of unemployment insurance was the first of its kind in the world community. The Bismarckian social reforms of Germany had intentionally avoided unemployment remedies. Parliament saw that the nation could no longer ignore the plight of its jobless workers. Parliament's acceptance of a nation's responsibility for its workers served as a model for other nations, and many followed suit with their own programs. Great Britain became the bellwether in legislating relief benefits for the jobless.

By 1920, the principle of unemployment insurance had become nationally recognized as not only beneficial but necessary. In that year, nearly all workers were brought under the protection of the program, making the total number eligible for relief about eleven million. Changes made between 1920 and 1925 were mainly technical rather than substantive. In 1921, for example, the power to "contract out," whereby an industry could exempt itself from contributing to the insurance fund, was suspended; it was abolished in 1927. Aid to dependents of unemployed workers was added to relieve the suffering of families. Waiting periods for assistance were reduced, periods of eligibility were extended, and types of coverage significantly enlarged the relief measures.

The contributory insurance principle had been designed to cope with seasonal or cyclical unemployment. The chronic unemployment of the 1920's prevented the scheme from functioning as planned. The collapse of the postwar boom caused Great Britain's unemployment rate to rise to 11 percent nationwide, as compared to the 6 percent rate in the thirty years before World War I. Regional and industrywide jobless rates varied. The coal mining industry, after the strike of 1921, suffered from 23 percent unemployment, while 36 percent of the workers in shipbuilding and steel, industries relying heavily on coal, were jobless. Great Britain responded by increasing unemployment benefits and making them available to more unemployed workers.

Great Britain had abandoned the earlier "tiding over" concept of unemployment assistance to establish a minimum income for each worker. Under the act passed in 1920, weekly benefits were fixed at fifteen shillings for a man and twelve shillings for a woman, with half rates for young people. The Unemployed Dependents Act gave a married man eligible for benefit five shillings for his wife and one shilling for each dependent child under age fourteen, while an unmarried man was given the five shillings grant to pay for a housekeeper. At least one analyst has suggested that an unemployed man and his family possibly were better off than an unskilled laborer with a job. The Unemployment Act and the dependents' grant program were accompanied by housing, education, and health programs. The total effect was to provide considerable improvement in the standard of living for the jobless. The national insurance scheme provided medical care to nineteen million workers and dependents. Because of the relief measures, recipients were better fed and clothed, and saw improvements in their standards of health as the incidence of infectious diseases dropped. Although these relief measures were often ad hoc and full of inadequacies, they lessened the distress that came from illness, old age, and loss of a job.

Bibliography

Aldcroft, Derek H. *The Inter-war Economy: Britain, 1919-1939.* London: B. T. Batsford, 1970. A useful critical survey of the growth of Great Britain's economy, fluctuations in economic activity, and regional patterns of development. The emphasis, however, is on the Great Depression, at the expense of the 1920's. Includes an index and an extensive bibliography.

Beveridge, William Henry. *Unemployment: A Problem of Industry.* 3d ed. London: Longmans, Green, 1912. This dated work is still useful, for it presents a contemporary's view of the economic problems and the resulting legislation enacted to remedy those problems. Bibliography.

Cohen, Percy. *The British System of Social Insurance: History and Description.* New York: Columbia University Press, 1932. Written at the start of the Great Depression. The author looks at each specific event leading to the passage of unemployment insurance. Although dated, the book is useful in understanding the evolution of social reform legislation. Indexed, with a bibliography.

Garraty, John A. *Unemployment in History: Economic Thought and Public Policy.* New York: Harper & Row, 1978. This work includes a study of several industrial nations and their development of public policy to cope with unemployment. Includes the opposition that arose during the development and passage of social legislation. Index and references.

Gilbert, Bentley B. *British Social Policy, 1914-1939.* Ithaca, N.Y.: Cornell University Press, 1970. Comprehensive coverage of the Unemployment Insurance Committee and its report. Analytical and occasionally critical, it presents a serious in-depth study of British policy between the world wars. Includes an index and a bibliography.

Ogus, A. I. "Great Britain." In *The Evolution of Social Insurance, 1881-1981: Studies of Germany, France, Great Britain, Austria, and Switzerland,* edited by Peter A. Kohler and Hans F. Zacher. London: Frances Pinter, 1982. Provides an excellent comparison of the social insurance programs of European nations. The chapter on Great Britain surveys the evolution of unemployment insurance from England's 1834 Poor Law up to the late 1970's. It reflects a critical German point of view but succinctly covers the major legislation during the twentieth century. An unusual indexing allows the reader to compare easily all social insurance topics of each nation. Bibliography.

Walley, Sir John. *Social Security: Another British Failure?* London: Charles Knight, 1972. This book is most useful in studying the special contributions of Winston Churchill to social legislation. Examines the economic problems of the 1920's and 1930's from a British point of view. Includes a bibliography.

Winch, Donald. *Economics and Policy: A Historical Study.* New York: Walker, 1969. A good source for studying the ever-widening scope of the state's responsibility for economic affairs. Especially useful in comparing Great Britain's legislative process with that of the United States, including its effect on and implementation of policy formation. Index, no bibliography.

H. Christian Thorup

Cross-References

The British Labour Party Is Formed (1906), p. 58; Massachusetts Adopts the First Minimum-Wage Law in the United States (1912), p. 126; Steel Workers Go on Strike to Demand Improved Working Conditions (1919), p. 293; British Workers Go on General Strike (1926), p. 429; Social Security Act Establishes Benefits for Nonworking People (1935), p. 514; The First Food Stamp Program Begins in Rochester, New York (1939), p. 555.

THE AMERICAN CIVIL LIBERTIES UNION IS FOUNDED

Category of event: Civil rights
Time: January 19, 1920
Locale: New York, New York

The American Civil Liberties Union was founded to defend equal rights for all,
including rights to free speech, due process, and freedom of the press

> *Principal personages:*
> ROGER N. BALDWIN (1884-1981), the founder and until 1950 executive
> director of the American Civil Liberties Union
> ALBERT DE SILVER (1888-1924), a conservative and wealthy New York
> lawyer who substantially funded the ACLU and served as co-director
> ARTHUR GARFIELD HAYS (1881-1954), the general counsel to the ACLU
> for more than thirty years
> NORMAN THOMAS (1884-1968), a pacifist, socialist, and close friend of
> Baldwin
> CRYSTAL EASTMAN (1881-1928), a pacifist and social worker who, with
> Baldwin, established the Bureau of Conscientious Objectors
> JOHN HAYNES HOLMES (1879-1964), a pacifist Unitarian minister active in
> excluding the Communists from ACLU offices
> OSWALD GARRISON VILLARD (1872-1949), the editor of the *New York Post*
> and *The Nation*

Summary of Event

The violation of civil rights in World War I was common, and that era had the
worst record of abuse in the history of the United States according to many historians. Those who dissented or protested against the war, including pacifists, labor
groups of leftist ideological persuasion, socialists, communists, and those who actively opposed some aspect of the official policy of the war program, were all victims. This repression reached its climax, ironically, in the "Red Scare" after the war.
It was in 1920, at the height of the "Red Scare," that the American Civil Liberties
Union (ACLU) was founded.

The largest group opposed to the war was the American Union Against Militarism (AUAM), founded in 1914 by Lillian Wald and Paul U. Kellogg. Because of his
conscientious objection to the war, Roger N. Baldwin left St. Louis, where he served
as a social worker, to join the AUAM in New York in 1917. Baldwin explained his opposition in terms of Christian principles and the liberty of conscience as enshrined
in the U.S. Bill of Rights. With Crystal Eastman, he created the Bureau of Conscientious Objectors (BCO). After failing to prevent the passage of the conscription
bill (draft for military duty), Baldwin appealed to the Wilson Administration, par-

ticularly Secretary of War Newton D. Baker, for tolerant enforcement of the law. He urged upon the secretary a policy that would permit noncombatant duty or alternate service without punishment or dishonor for conscientious objectors, whether religious or political (socialists, pacifists, anarchists, and others). The administration adopted a rigid policy against exemptions, and in actual practice, at local army camps around the country, often engaged in harassment and punitive actions.

With the passage of the Espionage Act in June, 1917, members of the AUAM, especially Wald and Kellogg, became anxious about the organization's support of civil liberties and conscientious objectors. Was the AUAM in violation of the Act? To accommodate the internal dissention, a Civil Liberties Committee was created in July, 1917, to create distance between the AUAM and the work in defense of dissent. The separation was completed in October, 1917, when Eastman and Baldwin created the National Civil Liberties Bureau (NCLB). Wald was not prepared to oppose the government, whereas Baldwin was.

Publications expressing opposition to the war were barred from the mail, including Norman Thomas' "War's Heretics" and Baldwin's "The Truth About the International Workers of the World." So too was Thomas' *The World Tomorrow*. An issue of the *Nation* was barred because it was critical of Samuel Gompers, the American Federation of Labor leader who strongly cooperated with the war program. Postmaster General Albert S. Burleson was especially autocratic and high-handed in his censorship of the mail.

Agents of the Wilson Administration conducted raids against various groups considered suspect or groups which opposed the war, including, for example, the International Bible Students' Association. No group was more the object of assault than the International Workers of the World (IWW). Without attention to due process, the IWW was raided in September, 1917, resulting in 169 arrests, including that of William D. "Big Bill" Haywood. Raids and arrests of IWW members would continue throughout the "Red Scare." Baldwin contended that the IWW's protests and strikes were economically motivated; the Wilson Administration contended they were obstructionist actions against the war. In defending the IWW, the NCLB brought suspicion upon itself. The Military Intelligence Division prepared an attack upon the NCLB, and in late 1917 the Bureau of Investigation began spying on the NCLB. The New York office was raided by officers under the direction of Archibald Stevenson and its files were taken. Those files were later used by the New York Lusk Committee to define all pacifists and war critics as subversives. On October 7 the Justice Department decided against prosecution.

Baldwin enlisted the support of Fanny Witherspoon's Bureau of Legal First Aid, Harry Weinberger's Legal Defense League, and the Liberty Defense Union in defense of free speech. To win public support, he defined free speech in the context of the best of the American tradition, demanded respect be shown conscientious objectors, and insisted that due process of law be observed. His appeals were without much success, however, either with the public or with the government. Asserting the "clear and present danger" doctrine in the *Schenck* case, the Supreme Court affirmed the limits of free speech. Those serving jail sentences for speaking out against the war were left without recourse. In the *Abrams* case, Associate Justice Oliver W. Holmes, Jr., dissented, offering an impassioned defense of free speech. Defining free speech as "free trade in ideas," he wrote, "we should be eternally vigilant against attempts to check the expression of opinions that we loathe." Probably Holmes's dissent owed more to legal scholars than to the NCLB, but it did affirm the NCLB's struggle in behalf of free speech.

The NCLB's members were social workers, Protestant clergymen influenced by the social gospel, and conservative lawyers. Samuel Walker's *In Defense of American Liberties, A History of the ACLU* (1990) states that "over the next seventy years, this mixture of liberal social reformism and conservative faith in the promises of the Constitution remained the basic ingredient in the ACLU." NCLB lawyers Walter Nelles, Albert De Silver, and Harry Weinberger dealt with the legal issues of up to 125 cases a week involving conscientious objectors. When Congress extended the draft age to thirty-five, Baldwin himself was forced to register. At Local Board 129 he indicated his opposition to the war. He refused induction, presented himself for prosecution, and resigned from the NCLB. He was sentenced to one year in jail, from which he was released on July 19, 1919. Another opponent of the war, socialist labor organizer Eugene V. Debs, in court for his sentencing in Cleveland, best defined Baldwin's position: "While there is a lower class, I am in it; while there is a criminal element, I am of it; while there is a soul in prison, I am not free."

After his release from prison, Baldwin toured the West to study the conditions of American labor, joined the steel workers' strike in Pittsburgh, and worked as a manual laborer in St. Louis before returning to New York. The year that had passed while he was in jail was marked by an unprecedented wave of strikes, violence, and race riots. Labor radicals, aliens and immigrants—particularly those of Russian origin—socialists, and others considered "un-American" were often arrested without warrants and detained without cause. Unreasonable searches and seizures were made. The "Red Scare" of Attorney General A. Mitchell Palmer reached a climax in January, 1920. Under the Alien Act, 249 "undesirable aliens" were deported on the "Red Ark." In a separate incident, properly elected Socialist representatives were denied their seats by the New York legislature.

Baldwin returned to the NCLB intent upon taking up the cause of labor. Many members believed the NCLB was too closely identified with the cause of the conscientious objectors, so its future was uncertain. On January 12, 1920, the executive committee accepted Baldwin's plan for reorganization, and on January 19 the American Civil Liberties Union was founded. Baldwin and De Silver were named directors, immediately responsible to a local committee that met every Monday to report civil rights violations, and ultimately accountable to a larger national board. The $2 annual dues and one thousand members at the end of the first year failed to support a working budget of $20,000. Charles Garland, a young Bostonian who inherited wealth, extended a generous grant to the ACLU, establishing the American Fund for Public Service to support social reform and finance legal defense cases.

Impact of Event

The ACLU's immediate work was related to issues that had brought about its existence. It issued a "Report on the Illegal Practices of the United States Department of Justice," written by twelve prominent lawyers, which denounced the Department's anti-Red activities. "Illegal Practices" provoked a Senate investigation of the "Palmer raids," which documented civil liberties violations but prescribed no punishment. The ACLU struggled to secure amnesty, or at least commutation of sentences for time served, for those who had been imprisoned because of pacifism, political beliefs, opposition to the war, or labor activities. While presidents Warren G. Harding and Calvin Coolidge released numbers of them, including Debs, their citizenship was not restored until Franklin D. Roosevelt entered the presidency in 1933. The continuation of the campaign for free speech was seldom successful. Three examples will suffice: the arrest of author Upton Sinclair for attempting to read the First Amendment at an IWW rally; the prohibition on John Haynes Holmes speaking in a public school in New York City (later all ACLU members were excluded); and the ban on Margaret Sanger's attempt to speak on birth control in New York City in 1923.

In 1922, the ACLU created the Labor Defense Council. Its work included the cause of textile workers in Passaic, New Jersey, steel workers in Pittsburgh, marine workers at the Port of San Pedro in Los Angeles, and coal miners in the fields of West Virginia, among others.

The first decade marked few successes and frequent failures for the ACLU. Its leaders maintained faith in democracy and remained steadfast in their commitment that the Bill of Rights was the foundation of American liberties, despite the fact that the organization was under siege by the American Legion, by J. Edgar Hoover, who said it got money from Moscow, and by John L. Lewis of the United Mine Workers, who said it was communistic. In the years ahead, the ACLU would succeed in surrounding free speech with a body of legal precedents to safeguard freedom of expression, broadly defined to include the right to picket and demonstrate, for example.

The ACLU remained vigilant in defense of all civil liberties. Given that fact it is associated with some of the most important events and issues in American history. The ACLU initiated the 1925 Scopes "Monkey" trial concerning the right to teach evolution in schools. Providing legal counsel for the poor was a commitment of Baldwin from the beginning. Because the National Association for the Advancement of Colored People deferred, the ACLU initiated the challenge to segregation in the draft in World War II. It opposed separate-but-equal practices in the South, which made it a viable partner in the civil rights movement in the 1960's. It has affirmed the separation of church and state, opposing school prayer and defending Jehovah's Witnesses against any compulsory pledge of allegiance to the U.S. flag. It has defended the right of free expression of both the political left and right, including the Ku Klux Klan. It has defended the rights of the accused and has opposed the death penalty, in part because it falls much more heavily on the black, the poor, and the uneducated. The history of the ACLU is an affirmation of Baldwin's contention that civil liberties must be guaranteed to even the humblest member of American society.

Bibliography

Johnson, Donald. *The Challenge to American Freedoms: World War I and the Rise of the American Civil Liberties Union*. Lexington: University Press of Kentucky, 1963. An excellent work on the background of the ACLU, which links the issues of civil liberties to war mobilization. Baldwin is placed at the center of many of the events of critical importance.

Lamson, Peggy. *Roger Baldwin, Founder of the American Civil Liberties Union*. Boston: Houghton Mifflin, 1976. This work is less a biography than an oral history, an interview with Baldwin at the age of ninety. Its value lies in identifying many of the people associated with the ACLU and its exposition of Baldwin's point of view on many issues.

Murphy, Paul L. *World War I and the Origins of Civil Liberties in the United States*. New York: W. W. Norton, 1979. The author maintains that never before had the government intervened so extensively in civil liberties as during the war; never before had there been such a perversion of the rule of law. Discusses the range of repressive measures critical to an understanding of the origins of the ACLU.

Reitman, Alan, ed. *The Pulse of Freedom: American Liberties, 1920-1970's*. New York: W. W. Norton, 1975. A collection of essays by professional historians provides an excellent overview of the first fifty years of the ACLU. Its descriptive accounts include workers in the Great Depression, civil liberties in World War II, McCarthyism, and desegregation in the 1950's and 1960's. Foreword by Ramsey Clark.

Walker, Samuel. *In Defense of American Liberties: A History of the ACLU*. New York: Oxford University Press, 1990. Only a few pages are devoted to the origins of the ACLU, but no general survey of the ACLU provides a greater account of the issues and cases of the ACLU than this work. Excellent research and bibliography.

Whipple, Leon. *The Story of Civil Liberty in the United States*. New York: Vanguard Press, 1927. Sponsored by the ACLU. Vanguard, the publisher, was funded by the American Fund for Public Service (the Garland grant to the ACLU).

Jimmie F. Gross

Cross-References

"Palmer Raids" Lead to Arrests and Deportations of Immigrants (1919), p. 258; Steel Workers Go on Strike to Demand Improved Working Conditions (1919), p. 293; Sanger Organizes Conferences on Birth Control (1921), p. 356; HUAC Begins Investigating Suspected Communists (1938), p. 550; *Brown v. Board of Education* Ends Public School Segregation (1954), p. 913; *Gideon v. Wainwright* Establishes Defendants' Right to an Attorney (1963), p. 1182; *Miranda v. Arizona* Requires Police to

THE LEAGUE OF WOMEN VOTERS IS FOUNDED

Categories of event: Voting rights and women's rights
Time: February, 1920
Locale: La Salle Hotel, Chicago, Illinois

The League of Women Voters formed to carry on the struggle of the suffragists by educating and organizing voting women into an effective, nonpartisan political force

Principal personages:

CARRIE CHAPMAN CATT (1859-1947), the president of the National American Woman Suffrage Association and creator and founder of the League of Women Voters

WOODROW WILSON (1856-1924), the president of the United States at the time of the ratification of the Nineteenth Amendment

SUSAN B. ANTHONY (1820-1906), the most influential leader of the early suffragist movement

MAUD WOOD PARK (1871-1955), the first president of the League of Women Voters

Summary of Event

The last meeting of the National American Woman Suffrage Association (NAWSA) was held at Chicago's La Salle Hotel in February, 1920. Called the Victory Convention, in anticipation of the final ratification of the Nineteenth Amendment giving the women of the United States the vote, the meeting marked the birth of the League of Women Voters, an organization charged to "finish the fight" of the suffragist movement by educating and organizing the twenty million new voters into a formidable political force.

The fight the league hoped to finish had formally begun more than seventy years before, in 1848, when a group of determined women and men met in Seneca Falls, New York. The group drafted a Declaration of Sentiments listing women's grievances against men and laying out a series of eleven resolutions, all of which passed unanimously except one. The ninth, demanding the vote for women, seemed to many of the delegates to ask too much and passed by only a narrow margin.

One of the most influential leaders of the early women's suffrage movement, Susan B. Anthony, was herself skeptical at first of the need for women to vote, concentrating instead on crusades against alcohol and for property rights for women. She soon learned, as did a growing number of women, that social reforms were intimately tied to political power. Only with the vote would women be taken seriously.

One of the strongest roots of the suffragist movement was the antislavery cause, which many women's groups rallied around, especially during the Civil War years. When the Fifteenth Amendment was adopted in 1870, granting the vote to blacks but still excluding women, many of those groups realized that a persistent effort on their own behalf was necessary to win fundamental political rights for women.

The movement was anything but united, with as many different organizations of women as there were theories of how best to achieve political status for women. Some groups pushed for state-by-state reform, with women gaining the vote in a number of western states such as Wyoming and Utah. For others, that process proved tedious and discouraging. A national approach was called for. In 1878, Senator Aaron Sargent of California introduced a constitutional amendment granting voting rights to women. It became known as the Anthony Amendment, for Susan B. Anthony, its primary drafter and promoter. In 1890, Anthony oversaw the merging of the two most powerful (and often antagonistic) suffragist organizations into a united National American Woman Suffrage Association.

One of the delegates to the 1890 NAWSA convention was a young woman from Iowa, Carrie Chapman Catt. Catt represented the kind of woman America was seeing more and more of—well educated, socially progressive, able to earn a living, and frustrated by the limitations placed on women. She quickly proved her organizational and motivational powers, landing a series of responsible roles in the NAWSA, culminating with her appointment in 1900 as successor to Anthony in the role of NAWSA president.

The next twenty years brought the final uphill push for ratification of the Anthony Amendment. Catt knew that a cohesive approach was necessary to overcome the increasingly vocal, if less numerous, opponents to woman suffrage. President Woodrow Wilson came into office in 1913 as sympathetic to women's issues, yet falling short of supporting the vote for women. World War I seemed likely to postpone the suffrage effort; however, an undercurrent of support was swelling. Numerous demonstrations around Washington, D.C., took place during the war years. Many women were physically attacked by antisuffragists and forcibly arrested by authorities. Some went on hunger strikes in prison. The attendant publicity created visibility for the women's suffrage issue, which many politicians had hoped would quietly subside in the war effort. By war's end, more than half of the states had granted women the right to vote in some or all elections, a woman was serving in Congress (Jeannette Rankin of Montana), and Wilson had become a convert to the national woman suffrage cause.

In 1919, a constitutional guarantee of women's right of enfranchisement was all but inevitable. For Carrie Chapman Catt, the celebration was for something begun, not something completed. Already she was looking forward to work yet to be done. At the March NAWSA Jubilee Convention, held in St. Louis, Catt forwarded the proposal of a League of Women Voters responsible for educating the new electorate on its responsibilities and for promoting social and political issues pertinent to women and children. The approach would have to be nonpartisan in her vision, while still encouraging individual women to pursue active roles in party politics. It would be a difficult balance to maintain, but one necessary to keep the organization unified and critics at bay. The convention voted to dissolve the NAWSA when its function had been served and replace it with a league such as Catt had outlined. The next year was spent studying the goals and organization of such a group.

Partisan female leaders in both the major parties objected to the formation of the League of Women Voters. They argued that it represented a duplication of effort. Once the vote was won, it was up to women to become dedicated to participation in party politics to effect change, many among them believed. Further, critics of the proposed league stated that the nonpartisan restriction effectively denied league women any real power on controversial issues. Still others worried that agendas for state leagues would be at wide variance with national league objectives.

Throughout the storm of debate, Carrie Catt remained firm in her guidance of the new organization. She knew that the entire process of women voting would be a monumental experiment. Thus, Catt proposed that the league itself be established as temporary, pending a review after the first five years of existence. Whatever doubts there were about the viability of such a nonpartisan, yet politically active, organization, Catt wanted it to be tested before it was condemned. Above all else, Catt believed, the role of political educator could not be left to the parties. Women should enter party participation as independent thinkers, educated about and wary of long-established political structures.

The NAWSA convention in February, 1920, was persuaded by Catt's arguments and affirmed the formation of the National League of Women Voters. A constitution and bylaws were adopted, providing for a Washington, D.C., headquarters and a four-member executive board. Catt had never intended to head her own creation. From the four board members chosen, Maud Wood Park was prevailed upon to be the league's first leader. Park had graduated from Radcliffe College in 1898 and had soon after become a national organizer and leader of college equal suffrage leagues.

As new president of the League of Women Voters, Park would be challenged to carry forward the battle flag the older suffragists had passed on. The vote itself was merely a tool, albeit a crucial and hard-earned one, for effecting change concerning women's issues and general social problems of the country. The league became a focal point for critics and supporters alike in evaluating just what the vote would mean to women.

Impact of Event

In the November elections of 1920, fewer than half of the newly registered women voters went to the polls. Across the nation, critics of woman suffrage pounced on the turnout as proof of the meaninglessness of winning the vote. The League of Women Voters was left in a state of shock following the results. It had been the first test of women's enfranchisement, in a presidential election no less, and those who had worked so hard to win the vote felt betrayed by their own sisters. In truth, voter turnout was low in general for a variety of reasons, but that fact was little consolation to the league.

Eventually, the league saw the low turnout as proof of its very need. The vast majority of female voters had not shared in the knowledge and enthusiasm of the suffragists. The league's mandate was clear. It would need to focus on educating voters and improving political institutions, in that order.

The impact of the League of Women Voters was not immediately felt. Internally, the league suffered from disorganization which left many of the state-level affiliates, where the real grass-roots work needed to be done, ineffective. In the league's first year, forty-six states claimed to have organizations, but more than one-third of those survived in name only, if at all. The more powerful state leagues, such as that of Pennsylvania, often proved troublesome to national-level goals.

The league endured its awkward beginnings and began to develop a strong and educated base of members. Membership reached a peak of about 150,000 women (and men, starting in 1974) in the mid-1970's. One of its most visible educational vehicles commenced in 1976, with the sponsorship of televised presidential debates. Throughout its history, it held to the idea of educating the public on a nonpartisan basis.

The political activities of the league also garnered early results. In 1921, the league played a major role in passage of the federal Sheppard-Towner Maternity- and Infancy-Protection Act, which matched state funds for promoting maternal and infant hygiene. The League of Nations was also an early cause, although a much more frustrating one. Such legislative efforts continued, especially those emphasizing women's rights, child welfare, and world peace. Although the most visible efforts were at the national level, countless gains were also recorded at state and local levels in bettering the political and social environments for all voters, not merely women.

Perhaps the greatest threat to the league has been the very changes it sought to effect. As women became more empowered, both politically and economically, the volunteers on which the league traditionally depended became less available. Working women could no longer devote full-time energies to league work. The league suffered declines in membership and funding shortfalls in the 1980's. As the League of Women Voters entered the 1990's, it faced a new challenge of how to continue its work on social and political reforms with a dramatically different membership base.

Bibliography

Adams, Mildred. *The Right to Be People.* Philadelphia, Pa.: J. B. Lippincott, 1967. A review of the people and events leading to the passage of the Nineteenth Amendment, as well as a critical look at the impact of the vote for women from a 1966 perspective. The League of Women Voters is credited with major pushes toward equality for women beyond the vote, although the author emphasizes how much is yet to be done. Sources and index are provided.

Barry, Kathleen. *Susan B. Anthony: A Biography of a Singular Feminist.* New York: New York University Press, 1988. A well-researched account of Anthony's life as seen through the lens of modern radical feminism. Readers will find much critical discussion to fill in the blanks between narrative events; however, the work may seem overly academic at times. Extensive notes, bibliography, and index.

Buhle, Mari Jo, and Paul Buhle, eds. *The Concise History of Woman Suffrage.* Urbana: University of Illinois Press, 1978. An extremely useful collection of documents from the classic, original six-volume *History of Woman Suffrage*. Primarily covers the period leading up to the league's formation. Informative introductory material and index.

Catt, Carrie Chapman, and Nettie Rogers Shuler. *Woman Suffrage and Politics: The Inner Story of the Suffrage Movement.* New York: Charles Scribner's Sons, 1923. A firsthand account of the movement, dramatically told yet with intelligent assessments of the pertinent issues. Includes details of the legal machinations from both sides of the suffrage issue. Curiously omits any extensive discussions of the League of Women Voters' postratification role, perhaps because of Catt's own humility. Indexed.

Fowler, Robert Booth. *Carrie Catt: Feminist Politician.* Boston: Northeastern University Press, 1986. A thoughtful study of Catt's life, more critical than narrative. Focuses on Catt's leadership skills, organizational theories, and political savvy and how those elements intertwined with her personality. The work explains the organizational model behind the League of Women Voters. Thorough notes, bibliography, and index.

Harper, Ida Husted. *Life and Work of Susan B. Anthony.* 3 vols. Salem, N.H.: Ayer, 1983. A reprint edition of the original biography written both during (vols. 1 and 2, 1898) and after (vol. 3, 1908) Anthony's life. Gives a passionate (at times fawning) and in-depth account of this pivotal woman's life. Indexed, with many references to Carrie Chapman Catt.

Morgan, David. *Suffragists and Democrats: The Politics of Woman Suffrage in America.* East Lansing: Michigan State University Press, 1972. This study focuses on the political influence of the suffrage movement during presidential, congressional, and state campaigns in the crucial years leading to the ratification of the Nineteenth Amendment in 1920. Particularly strong in discussing President Wilson's conversion and subsequent maneuvering on behalf of woman suffrage. Bibliography and index.

Peck, Mary Gray. *Carrie Chapman Catt: A Biography.* New York: H. W. Wilson, 1944. Written by a close personal friend of Catt, this biography displays personal insights few other works on Catt could. Suffers sometimes precisely because of the proximity of the author to the subject as well as Catt's blatant reluctance to have herself memorialized, as this biography was written during her lifetime. Index.

Van Voris, Jacqueline. *Carrie Chapman Catt: A Public Life.* New York: The Feminist Press at the City University of New York, 1987. The "public life" of the subtitle comes from the biographer's admission that little substantive material on the private side of Catt is available. Thus, this work is a solid narrative account of Catt's prominent actions. Contains a brief discussion of the league's early, and quickly corrected, excursion into partisan politics. Notes, bibliography, and index.

Young, Louise M. *In the Public Interest: The League of Women Voters, 1920-1970.* New York: Greenwood Press, 1989. A primary source for any research about the league. Well researched and clearly presented with extensive endnotes, worth reading in their own right. Bibliography and index.

Christopher J. Canfield

Cross-References

The Pankhursts Found the Women's Social and Political Union (1903), p. 19; Finland Grants Woman Suffrage (1906), p. 70; Rankin Becomes the First Woman Elected to Congress (1916), p. 190; Parliament Grants Suffrage to British Women (1918), p. 247; The League of Nations Is Established (1919), p. 270; The Nineteenth Amendment Gives American Women the Right to Vote (1920), p. 339; Women's Rights in India Undergo a Decade of Change (1925), p. 401; Nellie Tayloe Ross of Wyoming Becomes the First Female Governor (1925), p. 412; The Minimum Age for Female British Voters Is Lowered (1928), p. 442; French Women Get the Vote (1944), p. 646; The National Organization for Women Forms to Protect Women's Rights (1966), p. 1327; Women in Switzerland Are Granted the Right to Vote (1971), p. 1605; The Equal Rights Amendment Passes Congress but Fails to Be Ratified (1972), p. 1656; A U.N. Convention Condemns Discrimination Against Women (1979), p. 2057.

THE NINETEENTH AMENDMENT GIVES
AMERICAN WOMEN THE RIGHT TO VOTE

Categories of event: Voting rights and women's rights
Time: August 26, 1920
Locale: Washington, D.C.

The Nineteenth Amendment to the U.S. Constitution, giving women the right to vote, was the culmination of several decades of struggle

Principal personages:
CARRIE CHAPMAN CATT (1859-1947), the president of the National American Woman Suffrage Association and founder of the League of Women Voters
ANNA H. SHAW (1847-1919), the president of the National American Woman Suffrage Association for eleven years
ALICE PAUL (1885-1977), an advocate of social reform, the founder of the National Woman's Party in 1906
ELIZABETH CADY STANTON (1815-1902), a leading spokeswoman for nineteenth century feminism; served as president of both major women's suffrage groups
SUSAN B. ANTHONY (1820-1906), a leading organizer of the suffrage movement, the cofounder and president of the National Woman Suffrage Association

Summary of Event

In 1890, the two wings of the women's suffrage movement (radical and moderate) merged to form the National American Woman Suffrage Association. Its first president was Elizabeth C. Stanton, long-time women's rights champion and social activist. Her leadership in the cause of woman suffrage was nearing an end, however, and younger women began replacing the aging stalwarts.

While not yet generally accepted, woman suffrage was no longer considered a fringe movement. It had influential friends in Congress as well as in state legislatures. This progress is attributable to the efforts of such veterans as Stanton (president of the National Woman Suffrage Association from 1869 to 1889), her close friend, cofounder and also president of the NWSA, Susan B. Anthony, and older allies such as Lucretia Mott and Lucy Stone. A younger generation was ready to advance the movement, confident that a growing social consciousness would aid their cause.

The ever-growing number of women moving into higher education and into the job market found enlarged horizons and new experiences and contacts. They developed programs for social reform as well as for personal development. The General Federation of Women's Clubs, formed in 1890, created a network of intelligent, capable women, able and willing to tackle serious social problems such as low wages, overcrowded tenements, and poor health conditions.

Carrie C. Catt served as president of the National American Woman's Suffrage Association from 1900 to 1904 and again from 1915 to 1920. She and Anna H. Shaw, president of the NAWSA from 1904 to 1915, epitomized the new leadership for women's rights. They stressed tighter organization, cohesion, and more propaganda as tools with which to broaden the movement's support. Catt, in particular, had a keen eye for detail and was responsible for recruiting and training suffragists. She proposed that suffragists do a systematic study of government, studying laws to note the unjust ones and ways to get them changed. Catt also proposed more visibility for the movement, through courting the press and establishing a finance committee to ensure a steady flow of funds.

Larger and better unified, the NAWSA of the early 1900's shifted its arguments, putting less stress on equal rights and more on the good that women could do for society as a whole. Female benevolence would have a wider outreach, the suffragists argued. They were helped considerably by meshing well with the Progressives' pre-World War I program of reform. The groups shared the same goals for society, such as an end to poverty, injustice, and corruption, so they cooperated in pressuring legislators for reforms such as cleaning up slums and sweatshops, expanding educational opportunities, and ousting corrupt political bosses.

Antisuffrage arguments took on new zeal between 1890 and 1919, as foes of woman suffrage defended the status quo. They pictured woman suffrage as an attack on traditional values and beliefs—the most basic ones asserting that the sexes had separate spheres and that the two must complement each other to keep society orderly. Foes of suffrage insisted that it would harm family and society, pitting wife against husband, disturbing the natural order. Also, women's traditional purity and moral superiority, they said, would suffer from the battles and tensions of politics.

Suffragists responded to their critics by shifting their emphasis to the altruism expected of women. The women's vote, they said, would purify politics and effect reforms nationwide. As one historian notes, the vote would not violate woman's sphere but rather "would consummate motherhood." Capitalizing on moral superiority and domestic ideals, the suffragists succeeded in broadening their support base.

In 1912, the Progressive Party endorsed woman suffrage, although candidate Theodore Roosevelt was a lukewarm advocate of the plank. Another victory came in 1914, when the General Federation of Women's Clubs passed a resolution supporting woman suffrage, giving the movement mainstream acceptability and respectability.

State campaigns were chalking up victories as well, particularly in the West. Anna H. Shaw, president of the NAWSA focused energies and funds into state campaigns with gratifying results. Between 1910 and 1914, seven Western states gave women the vote, and a new stage of the struggle began. Shaw's successor as president, Catt, concentrated on the federal level, working to win presidential and congressional support. Differing ideas of how to get that support sidetracked some of that effort.

Alice Paul, a political activist with a master's degree in sociology and a minor field in political science and economics, took leadership of the NAWSA's Congressional Committee in 1912. Its purpose was to lobby for suffrage on the federal level. More so than Catt or Shaw, Paul was adept at garnering publicity. The charismatic leader soon gathered a large number of young suffragists around her and formed the militant Congressional Union.

Older members of the NAWSA were annoyed by these tactics and, in 1916, Paul and her group left the NAWSA to found the National Woman's Party. One of their first public acts was to attack Woodrow Wilson and the Democrats, as the party in power, for denying women the vote. Paul and her followers picketed the White House and went on hunger strikes, both moves calculated to win attention and sympathy. Catt and the NAWSA avoided these tactics, not wanting to alienate friends in both parties.

Both the militants and the moderates used World War I to add "a few strings to the suffrage bow," as historian William L. O'Neill put it. When the United States entered the war in 1917, the NAWSA offered endorsement. Members sold bonds and organized benefits for the troops, as did millions of women nationwide. Catt argued that the fight for democracy at home was a matter of justice. Women were contributing immensely to the war effort and deserved a "reward."

Catt hoped to get a suffrage amendment through Congress, and her hopes rose after Wilson appeared at the 1916 NAWSA convention in June. While not committing himself, Wilson indicated that he saw success coming if the women persevered. Some of that success came from several states, which granted woman suffrage in presidential and municipal elections.

More pressure was brought on Wilson and Congress by the NAWSA and the Congressional Union's repeated charge that the United States was not truly a democracy as long as it denied a large percentage of citizens the vote. Embarrassed, Wilson urged the Senate to pass a woman suffrage amendment, calling it "vital" to winning the war. Catt was ecstatic when, on November 6, 1917, New York State passed a suffrage bill. She thought this would force Congress's hand, but it took several more months before Congress acted.

On January 10, 1918, the House of Representatives voted on the suffrage amendment. It was a close call: The amendment passed 274-134, barely gaining the required two-thirds majority. The Senate would prove to be an even tougher battleground.

Despite Wilson's personal appearance and plea before the Senate on September 30, 1918, the Senate voted down the amendment. On February 10, 1919, another vote was taken and again suffrage failed—by one vote. Catt was so sure that the next vote would bring victory that she began organizing the NAWSA's successor, the National League of Women Voters. She was determined that women be educated in how to use the vote and to be capable of full political participation.

The House of Representatives voted on woman suffrage May 21, 1919, with 304 for and 89 against. The Senate debate began on June 3, and late on June 4 the vote was taken: 56 for and 25 against. Victory had finally come.

Within the next four months, seventeen states ratified the Nineteenth Amendment, almost half the needed number. Catt and the NAWSA Executive Board were so certain of success that the NAWSA was dissolved in February, 1920. At the final meeting, Catt gave moving tribute to the pioneers who laid the groundwork for the final victory, naming in particular Susan B. Anthony and Anna H. Shaw.

On August 26, 1920, the Nineteenth Amendment became part of the United States Constitution. Catt, in Washington that day, was received at the White House by President and Mrs. Wilson. In New York the next day, she told a crowd of cheering women that they were no longer "wards of the nation." Rather, they were now "free and equal citizens." The long struggle was over.

Impact of Event

With the passage of the Nineteenth Amendment, the women's movement splintered into a variety of groups, each working for different concerns. The unifying cause of suffrage was won, and no new cause was able to galvanize women nationwide. Some positive immediate effects of the amendment did occur. Twenty states passed laws enabling women to serve on juries, for example. Congress, too, seemed eager to please women voters—at least temporarily.

In 1921, Congress passed the Sheppard-Towner Act to finance maternal education and child health-care programs. In 1924, Congress passed a child labor amendment, though it was never ratified. A Women's Joint Congressional Committee, representative of several major women's organizations including the Women's Christian Temperance Union, the General Federation of Women's Clubs, and the American Association of University Women, lobbied for desired bills. It became evident that expectations were too high: Woman suffrage would not solve all social problems.

One assumption common to both suffragists and antisuffragists was that women would vote in a bloc. Suffragists claimed they would thus purify politics and end war, crime, and injustice of all kind. Opponents foresaw domestic discord, excessive individualism, and even social anarchy. Statistics show that both sides were wrong. Women voted in smaller numbers than men and tended to vote the same way as male relatives. Part of the problem was a lack of women candidates and office holders. Women simply did not rally to "women's issues."

Catt saw this as stemming from the loss of a unifying cause. For decades, the struggle for suffrage had served to unify and energize women. With the coalition divided, factions split over such issues as protective laws and a newly-proposed equal rights amendment (pushed most strongly by Alice Paul). There was no common rallying point or broad consensus for women after 1920. Clearly, the Nineteenth Amendment did not give women much political power. What it did accomplish was a gradual attitudinal change: Women were now deemed able to be involved in public affairs, to act as agents of change. In reality, the suffrage struggle itself, as one historian notes, was "the basis for new social relations between men and women."

Among the varied women's organizations after 1920, the League of Women Voters did have some solid effects. In particular, state chapters for the League succeeded in decreasing the number of still-existent discriminatory marriage and property laws and, perhaps just as important, served to train women interested in politics. The League increasingly emphasized education rather than proselytizing for social reform, however, frustrating many former NAWSA members as well as Alice Paul and her activists. Factionalism grew, much of it focusing around the issue of social feminism.

There was widespread disagreement over what the term "feminism" should encompass. To Catt and pre-1920's suffragists, the new female image was one of women combining marriage and a career, of cooperating and competing with men in the professions. Many women gave more stress to marriage and motherhood and, thanks in large part to the growing advertising industry, were largely concerned with fashion, beauty, and sex appeal. It is not inconsequential that, in 1920, Atlantic City hotel owners promoted a beauty contest to select a Miss America. The new heroines were now likely to be movie stars and beauty queens rather than social activists such as Jane Addams or Alice Paul.

Bibliography

Barker-Benfield, G. J., and Catherine Clinton, eds. *From the Civil War to the Present.* Vol. 2 in *Portraits of American Women.* New York: St. Martin's Press, 1991. Very attractive format and geared to the general reader. Parts 5 and 6 give brief biographical sketches of leaders in the women's rights movement overall, highlighting such luminaries as Ida Wells-Barnett, Rose Schneiderman, and Alice Paul. Essays average eight to ten pages, with an introduction and chapter notes. No index or general bibliography.

Clinton, Catherine. *The Other Civil War: American Women in the Nineteenth Century.* New York: Hill & Wang, 1984. A comprehensive, chronological look at nineteenth century women, this brief text (202 pages) covers women's experiences with and contributions to the major campaigns and reforms of the 1800's. Alongside the usual women "stars," Clinton integrates "forgotten" women into her history: black women, poor women, Native American women, and lesbians. The book lays a good foundation for more detailed study. Includes a lengthy bibliographic essay (twenty-nine pages) and an index.

Flexner, Eleanor. *Century of Struggle: The Woman's Rights Movement in the United States.* Cambridge, Mass.: Belknap Press, 1977. A well-documented narrative of the women's rights movement in the United States. This study divides the material into three periods: 1800-1860, 1860-1890, and 1890-1920. Abundant quotes and anecdotes highlight each era as Flexner weaves together social, political, and economic developments affecting women's rights. Contains several pages of photos, chapter notes, and an index.

Harper, Ida Husted, ed. *The History of Woman Suffrage.* Vol. 5. New York: Arno Press, 1969. Very detailed, this 740-page book focuses on the years 1900-1920, giving reports of the annual national conventions of the National American Woman Suffrage Association. Many extracts from leading writers and speakers at both state and federal levels. Especially valuable chapters on the League of Women Voters and the War Service of Organized Suffragists. Uses material collected by Susan B. Anthony and Elizabeth Cady Stanton. Includes brief supplements for several chapters and a detailed index.

Van Voris, Jacqueline. *Carrie Chapman Catt.* New York: Feminist Press at the City University of New York, 1987. This biography focuses on Catt's work in the suffrage movement from 1900 to 1920. The last four chapters trace her efforts on behalf of international suffrage and world peace. Many excerpts from Catt's speeches and writings. Contains chapter notes, a lengthy bibliography, and an index.

Woloch, Nancy. *Women and the American Experience.* New York: Alfred A. Knopf, 1984. A lengthy (540-page) but selective survey of the history of American women, this text focuses on women's experiences in domestic and public life, with some attention to the impact of class and race. It alternates particular episodes with general surveys of an era. Four periods are covered: pre-1800, 1800-1860, 1860-1920, and post-1920. Several illustrations, suggested reading, and sources for each chapter. Includes an appendix giving charts, maps, and statistics, a bibliography, and an index.

S. Carol Berg

Cross-References

Rankin Becomes the First Woman Elected to Congress (1916), p. 190; The League of Women Voters Is Founded (1920), p. 333; Nellie Tayloe Ross of Wyoming Becomes the First Female Governor (1925), p. 412; Franklin D. Roosevelt Appoints Perkins as Secretary of Labor (1933), p. 486; The U.N. Convention on the Political Rights of Women Is Approved (1952), p. 885; The Equal Pay Act Becomes Law (1963), p. 1172; Congress Passes the Civil Rights Act (1964), p. 1251; Congress Passes the Equal Employment Opportunity Act (1972), p. 1650; The Equal Rights Amendment Passes Congress but Fails to Be Ratified (1972), p. 1656; O'Connor Becomes the First Female Supreme Court Justice (1981), p. 2141.

CAPITAL PUNISHMENT IS ABOLISHED IN SWEDEN

Category of event: Prisoners' rights
Time: 1921
Locale: Stockholm, Sweden

During a period of democratic reform and minority governments, Sweden's parliament enacted several human rights reforms, including abolition of the death penalty for peacetime offenses

Principal personages:

OSCAR VON SYDOW (1873-1936), a member of Parliament chosen by King Gustav V in 1921 to replace De Geer as prime minister

J. A. BOUVIN, introduced the abolition of the death penalty for peacetime offenses in Sweden's parliament in 1867

CARL ALBERT LINDHAGEN (1860-1946), a member of the Second Chamber of Parliament from 1897 to 1917 and of the First Chamber from 1919 to 1940

GERARD LOUIS DE GEER (1854-1935), a Liberal who headed a "caretaker" government in 1920 and 1921

KARL HJALMAR BRANTING (1860-1925), the prime minister of the first Social Democratic government in Sweden

Summary of Event

As early as 1855, Sweden had begun to adopt more humane treatment of its citizens. Punishments such as caning, whipping, and "church duty" (sitting in special pews at church, to be publicly ridiculed) were abolished. Limited religious freedom was granted in 1860. It was within this context of reform that the first attempt was made, in 1867, to abolish the death penalty for peacetime civil offenses and wartime offenses under the military penal code. J. A. Bouvin introduced a motion to abolish the death penalty into Parliament in that year, but it was defeated.

A restructuring of Sweden's political system was also under way. In 1866, Parliament began to revise its own structure and processes. The earlier four estates (nobles, the clergy, burghers, and landowners and the rural middle class) were replaced by the popularly elected Second Chamber (lower house) and a senatorial upper house. In 1907, manhood suffrage was broadened, and property qualifications generally were abolished.

During World War I, the Young Socialists, also known as Left-Socialists, continued to demand liberalization of the government and espoused Marxism. The Young Socialists were able to strengthen their political organization throughout the duration of World War I. When a potato famine in 1917 left Swedish farmers destitute, considerable public unrest threatened the government. Many non-Socialist party leaders, both Conservatives and Liberals, became concerned that the Socialists might lead the nation in a revolution similar to the Russian Revolution. Even if the Young

Socialists had developed a stronger leadership, however, their power base was too small to cause major disruption.

The end of World War I caught the Conservatives unprepared. The Liberal and Socialist parties, which had both gained strength in Parliament, took advantage of the moment to join forces. The two parties cooperated in order to continue their political reforms. This collaboration helped bring both political and social emancipation of women. When the 1921 Electorate Law went into effect, the number of eligible voters more than doubled, with women the clear majority. Numerous other political and humanitarian reforms were enacted, in part because they were a natural evolution of the great period of reform and in part as a means of undermining the growing strength of the Young Socialists by adopting some of their programs.

In 1920, Karl Hjalmar Branting became prime minister of Sweden's first Social Democratic government. As a single-party, minority government, it had little chance for a long tenure. When the election for the Second Chamber took place, six months after Branting's election, the Conservatives made a relatively strong recovery. Branting was forced to resign. The result of the shift in power, however, was that no party had a clear majority in the chambers, and none of the parties would form a government on a minority basis. The Liberals, the "middle" party, would cooperate with neither the right nor the left. King Gustav V therefore proposed a bureaucratic "caretaker" ministry under Gerhard Louis De Geer that would not be aligned with any of the parties. Only one member of Parliament served in De Geer's "professional" ministry.

Many reforms were introduced in Parliament during this critical period. Included in those reform measures was Proposition #144, which provided for the abolition of the death penalty for peacetime offenses. The measure was introduced in the First Chamber in 1921. De Geer, with the support of the Conservatives, attempted to block passage of the proposition. At the same time, parliamentary member Carl Albert Lindhagen put forth a motion to amend Proposition #144 to include the abolition of wartime offenses as well. Lindhagen's motion for amendment was defeated by a 46 to 32 vote. The unamended Proposition #144, which exempted peacetime offenses, passed through the First Chamber by a vote of 62 to 23.

When First Chamber elections were held in 1921, the Social Democrats gained more seats, although no political party had a clear majority. Once again, the king suggested a coalition government, but the parties would not comply. Largely because of his failure to show strong leadership, De Geer was replaced by Oscar von Sydow, another nonparty legislator. It was during the tenure of Prime Minister von Sydow that both the original Proposition #144 and Lindhagen's amendment were considered and acted upon in the lower house, or Second Chamber. The motion for complete abolition was defeated, but the original peacetime-only abolition was passed by a 116 to 48 vote. The failure of Parliament to approve Lindhagen's amendment can be attributed to the lack of a strong majority party and the concerns of the Swedish people about wartime offenses in the aftermath of a world war and a revolution in Russia.

The abolition of the death penalty for wartime offenses as well as for peacetime offenses was finally enacted in 1972 by a 266 to 37 vote. Sweden completed abolition of the death penalty for all offenses with the 1972 legislation.

Impact of Event

Until the beginning of the twentieth century, most governments accepted the death penalty as an effective and appropriate way to prevent and to punish crime. Executions were made to appear lawful and were justified by arguing that the supreme penalty was necessary, especially for the more serious offenses, for the good of society. Since 1867, when Bouvin introduced abolition legislation, there have been intermittent movements throughout Scandinavia and the Western world to abolish the death penalty, even as punishment for murder.

Sweden's 1921 Proposition #144 affirmed the value of human life and established a limit on what the state might do to its citizens. Some members of Parliament based their votes on the measure on political exigencies, attempting to avert further political crises. Many, however, cast their votes in a principled stand for human rights.

As one of the first nations to abolish the death penalty, Sweden exerted pressure on other Scandinavian and Western nations to reevaluate their own statutory punishments. The result has been the limiting of the numbers of offenses for which the death penalty may be demanded or the removal of that penalty entirely. Great Britain used Sweden's abolition of the death penalty and later reforms of alternative punishments as a yardstick to evaluate its own position on incarceration and executions. Great Britain's 1949-1953 Report of the Royal Commission on Capital Punishment examined the alternative punishments imposed by Sweden and expressed interest in the efficiency and humanity of Stockholm's Utrecht and Langholmen prisons, where psychiatric clinics worked with both convicted prisoners and suspects awaiting trial. The report concluded that available evidence showed that few released murderers committed further crimes of violence.

The prohibition of the death penalty became an integral part of the Instrument of Government of the Swedish Constitution. Chapter 8 states in Article 1 that no law or regulation may imply that a sentence for capital punishment can be pronounced. In 1976, this statement was moved to Chapter 2, which concerns fundamental liberties and rights. Its Article 4 states, "Capital punishment may not occur." Inclusion of the statement in Chapter 2 means that the abolition of the death penalty applies not only to Swedish citizens but also to alien residents, who are thus protected against extradition to nations where the death penalty is still practiced.

Although Norway preceded Sweden by removing the death penalty for peacetime offenses in 1905, that nation did not abolish all death penalties until after Sweden had done so. Denmark, in 1933, and Finland, in 1949, also abolished the execution of convicted offenders. By the end of the 1970's, many countries had abolished the death penalty as international public opinion generated pressure to stop executions. International human rights treaties have established restrictions and safeguards on the use of the death penalty in countries which have not yet abolished it.

Bibliography

Amnesty International. *When the State Kills . . . The Death Penalty: A Human Rights Issue.* New York: Author, 1989. A concise source for the status of capital punishment worldwide. Each nation is listed separately. The work presents a bias toward abolitionism but discusses arguments for and against capital punishment. The appendix includes extracts from various human rights conventions. No bibliography.

Aspelin, Erland, and Sten Hecksher, rapporteurs. *A New Penal System: Ideas and Proposals. Report No. 5.* Stockholm: Kristianstads Boktryckeri, 1978. This report for the National Council for Crime Prevention addresses the underlying principle that treatment should replace punishment. It is an excellent source for details on imprisonment, conditional sentences, probation, "open prisons," and other aspects of Sweden's penal system. No bibliography. Indexed.

Great Britain. Royal Commission on Capital Punishment (1949-1953). *Report.* London: Her Majesty's Stationery Office, 1953. This report is a detailed examination of the effectiveness of Sweden's penal system. It provides the most thorough analysis of the techniques employed. Extensive graphs and charts are useful in making comparisons with other nations' systems. Indexing is based on paragraphs, not page numbers.

Hadenius, Stig. *Swedish Politics During the Twentieth Century.* Translated by Victor Kayfetz. 3d rev. ed. Stockholm: Swedish Institute, 1990. A brief but scholarly analysis of the "Swedish model" of parliamentary government. It is especially useful because it includes a bibliography of recent English-language publications. No index.

Metcalf, Michael F., ed. *The Riksdag: A History of the Swedish Parliament.* New York: St. Martin's Press, 1987. This work presents an unbiased look at the evolution of Sweden's parliament, beginning in the thirteenth century. Includes maps, charts, and tables. The extensive topical bibliography is annotated, but many sources will be found only in the Swedish language. Indexed.

Scott, Franklin D. *Sweden: The Nation's History.* Minneapolis: University of Minnesota Press, 1977. Scott's work is probably the most comprehensive of the sources listed here. The evolution of Sweden's political parties is discussed in depth, with an extensive listing of references included. Although the death penalty is not specifically addressed, the work outlines the political setting for its abolition. The extensive bibliography contains many sources in the original Swedish. Indexed.

Verney, Douglas V. *Parliamentary Reform in Sweden, 1866-1921.* Oxford, England: Clarendon Press, 1957. Useful primarily for passages on the parliamentary reforms. This volume includes excellent biographical notes on many of the chief participants. Extensive bibliography.

H. Christian Thorup

Cross-References

China Initiates a Genocide Policy Toward Tibetans (1950), p. 826; The United Nations Sets Rules for the Treatment of Prisoners (1955), p. 935; The Iraqi Government Promotes Genocide of Kurds (1960's), p. 1050; The British Parliament Votes to Abolish the Death Penalty (1965), p. 1316; The Supreme Court Abolishes the Death Penalty (1972), p. 1674; The United Nations Issues a Declaration Against Torture (1975), p. 1847; Khomeini Uses Executions to Establish a New Order in Iran (1979), p. 2013; Amnesty International Adopts a Program for the Prevention of Torture (1983), p. 2204.

THE IMMIGRATION ACT OF 1921 IMPOSES A NATIONAL QUOTA SYSTEM

Category of event: Immigrants' rights
Time: 1921-1924
Locale: Washington, D.C.

Immigration legislation in 1921 created a quota system that favored the nations of northern and western Europe and put an end to the ideal of the United States as a melting pot

Principal personages:

WARREN G. HARDING (1865-1923), the twenty-ninth president of the United States (1921-1923); signed the restriction act of 1921 into law

WOODROW WILSON (1856-1924), the twenty-eighth president of the United States (1913-1921), an opponent of restriction who vetoed literacy test bills twice

ALBERT JOHNSON (1869-1957), a Republican representative from Washington State, chair of the House Committee on Immigration and Naturalization, a leading advocate of total restriction

ADOLPH SABATH (1866-1952), a Democratic representative from Illinois, born in Europe, a leading opponent of restriction in the House

LEBARON COLT (1846-1924), a Republican senator from Rhode Island, chair of the U.S. Senate Committee on Immigration, a supporter of restriction

WLLIAM P. DILLINGHAM (1843-1923), a Republican senator from Vermont, a leading advocate of restriction

MADISON GRANT (1865-1937), an author and lawyer, who wrote *The Passing of the Great Race in America* (1916), strongly advocating restriction

HENRY CABOT LODGE (1850-1924), a Republican senator from Massachusetts, chief advocate of a literacy test and supporter of restriction

KENNETH ROBERTS (1885-1957), a novelist and journalist who supported total restriction

Summary of Event

Throughout most of the nineteenth century, immigration to the United States was open to anyone who wanted to enter. By the 1880's, however, this unlimited freedom was beginning to disappear. The first law restricting immigration came in 1882, when Chinese were excluded from entering American territory. Hostility to Chinese workers in California sparked Congress to pass a bill amid warnings that Chinese worked for lower wages than whites and came from such a culturally inferior civilization that they would never make good Americans. The law became permanent in

1902. Five years later, under a gentlemen's agreement with the Japanese government, citizens of that country were added to the excluded list. The only other people barred from entering the United States were prostitutes, insane persons, paupers, polygamists, and anyone suffering from a "loathsome or contagious disease." Under these categories, compared to more than a million immigrants per year from 1890 to 1914, less than thirteen thousand were kept out annually.

The small number of those excluded troubled anti-immigrant groups, such as the American Protective Association, founded in 1887, and the Immigration Restriction League, created in Boston in 1894. Both organizations warned of the "immigrant invasion" which threatened the American way of life. These opponents of open immigration argued that since 1880, most new arrivals had come from different areas of Europe from that of the pre-1880 immigrants, who came largely from Germany, England, Ireland, and Scandinavia. The "new" immigrants—mainly Slavs, Poles, Italians, and Jews—came from poorer and more culturally "backward" areas of Europe. Many of these immigrants advocated radicalism, anarchism, socialism, or communism, and were unfamiliar with ideas of democracy and progress. Furthermore, they preferred to live in ghettoes in cities, where they strengthened the power of political machines and corrupt bosses. Those who considered themselves guardians of traditional American values found support for their position among trade unionists in the American Federation of Labor (AFL), whose president, Samuel Gompers, argued that the new immigrants provided employers with an endless supply of cheap labor, leading to lower wages for everyone.

Advocates of restriction found their chief congressional spokesperson in Senator Henry Cabot Lodge, a member of the Immigration Restriction League, who sponsored a bill calling for a literacy test. Such a law, which called upon immigrants to be able to read and write in their native language, was seen as an effective barrier to most "new" immigrants. Congress passed the bill in 1897, but President Grover Cleveland vetoed it, arguing that it was unnecessary and discriminatory. Cleveland believed that American borders should remain open to anyone who wanted to enter and that there were enough jobs and opportunities to allow anyone to fulfill a dream of economic success. Advocates of this vision of the American dream, however, were lessening in number over time.

The assassination of President William McKinley in 1901 led to the exclusion of anarchists and those who advocated the violent overthrow of the government of the United States. A more important step to a quota system, however, came in 1907, when the House and Senate established the United States Immigration Commission, under the leadership of Senator William P. Dillingham. The commission issued a forty-two-volume report in 1910, advocating a reduction in immigration because of the "racial inferiority" of new immigrant groups. Studies of immigrant populations, the commission concluded, showed that people from southern and eastern Europe had a higher potential for criminal activity, were more likely to end up poor and sick, and were less intelligent than other Americans. It called for passage of a literacy test to preserve American values. Congress passed legislation in 1912 calling for such a test, but President William Howard Taft vetoed it, saying that illiteracy resulted from lack of educational opportunity and had little to do with native intelligence. Open entrance to the United States was part of American history, and many of America's wealthiest and hardest working citizens had come without knowing how to read and write. If the United States barred such people, Taft argued, America would become weaker and less wealthy.

In 1915, Woodrow Wilson became the third president to veto a literacy bill, denouncing its violation of the American ideal of an open door. Two years later, in the wake of American entrance into World War I and growing hostility against foreigners, Congress overrode Wilson's second veto and the literacy test became law. Along with establishing a reading test for anyone over age sixteen, the law also created a "barred zone" which excluded immigrants from most of Asia, including China, India, and Japan, regardless of whether they could read. As it turned out, the test that asked adults to read a few words in any recognized language did little to reduce immigration. Between 1918 and 1920, less than 1 percent of those who took it failed. Representative Albert Johnson, chair of the House Committee on Immigration, had been a longtime advocate of closing the borders of the United States. In 1919, he called for the suspension of all immigration. Johnson's proposal was defeated in the House of Representatives.

In 1920, however, immigration increased dramatically, as did fears that millions of refugees from war-torn Europe were waiting to flood into the United States. Much of the argument for restriction was based on ideas associated with scientific racism. The Republican candidate for the presidency, Warren G. Harding, advocated restriction in several speeches, warning of the dangers inherent in allowing open admission. He called for legislation that would permit entrance to the United States only to people whose background and racial characteristics showed that they could adopt American values and principles. The next year, Vice President Calvin Coolidge authored a magazine article claiming that laws of biology proved that "Nordics," the preferred type, deteriorated intellectually and physically when allowed to intermarry with other races. These views reflected the growing influence of eugenics, the science of improving the human race by discouraging the birth of the "unfit." Madison Grant, a lawyer and secretary of the New York Zoological Society, and later an adviser to Albert Johnson's Immigration Committee, wrote the most influential book advocating this racist way of thinking, *The Passing of the Great Race in America* (1916). In it, he described human society as a huge snake. Nordic races made up the head, while the inferior races formed the tail. It would be this type of scientific argument, more than any other, that would provide the major rationale for creation of the 1921 quota system. The tail could not be allowed to rule the head.

Early in 1921, the House debated and passed Johnson's bill calling for a two-year suspension of all immigration. The Senate Committee on Immigration, chaired by Senator LeBaron Colt, held hearings on a similar proposal but refused to support a total ban after hearing arguments from business groups fearful that complete exclusion would stop all access to European laborers. Representatives from the National

Association of Manufacturers testified on the need to have access to inexpensive labor, even though some business leaders were beginning to fear that too many in the immigration pool were influenced by communism and socialism, especially after the communist victory in Russia in 1918. The possibility of thousands of radical workers with a greater tendency to strike coming into the country seemed too high a price to pay in return for lower wages. Unions, especially the AFL, continued to lobby for strict regulation of immigration. To keep wages high, Samuel Gompers told Congress, foreign workers had to be kept out. By 1921, the only widespread support for free and open immigration came from immigrant groups themselves. Although a few members of Congress supported their position, it was a distinctly minority view.

Senator William Dillingham, whose report in 1910 had renewed efforts to restrict immigration, offered a quota plan which he hoped would satisfy business and labor. He called for a policy in which each nation would receive a quota of immigrants equal to 5 percent of that country's total population in the United States according to the 1910 census. Dillingham's suggestion passed the Senate with little opposition and gained favor in the House. Before its final approval, however, Johnson and his supporters of total suspension reduced the quota to 3 percent and set 350,000 as the maximum number of legal immigrants in any one year. Woodrow Wilson vetoed the bill shortly before leaving office, but it was passed with only one dissenting vote in the Senate during a special session called by President Harding on May 19, 1921. The House approved the Emergency Quota Act the same day without a recorded vote. The only opposition came from representatives with large numbers of immigrants in their districts. Adolph Sabath, a Democratic congressperson from Chicago, led the dissenters, arguing that the act was based on a "pseudoscientific proposition" that falsely glorified the Nordic nations. His comments had little effect on the result. One of the most important changes in American immigration history went into effect in June of 1921.

Impact of Event

The Emergency Quota Act of 1921 severely reduced immigration into the United States. In 1922, its first full year of operation, only 309,556 people legally entered the country, compared with 805,228 the previous year. Quotas for Europe, the Middle East, Africa, Australia, and New Zealand were generally filled quickly, although economic depressions in England, Ireland, and Germany kept many potential immigrants at home. Less than half the legal number of immigrants came to America the first year; the southern and eastern Europeans filled almost 99 percent of their limit. No limits existed for Canada, Mexico, and other nations of the Western Hemisphere. To keep an adequate supply of cheap agricultural labor available to farmers in Texas and California, Congress refused to place a quota on immigration from these areas of the world. Japan and China were the only countries with a quota of zero, as Congress continued its policy of exclusion for most areas of Asia.

The 1921 act provided for "special preferences" for relatives of America citizens, including wives, children under eighteen, parents, brothers, and sisters. The commissioner of immigration was to make it a priority to maintain family unity; however, this was to be the only exception to the strict quota policy.

Congress extended the "emergency" law in May, 1922, for two more years. This move, however, did not satisfy Representative Johnson and others supporting complete restriction. Johnson's Immigration Committee continued to hold hearings and gather evidence supporting an end to all immigration. Johnson became increasingly interested in eugenics and remained in close contact with Madison Grant. In 1923, Johnson was elected president of the Eugenics Research Association of America, a group devoted to gathering statistics on the hereditary traits of Americans. He seemed especially interested in studies showing a large concentration of "new" immigrants in mental hospitals, prisons, and poorhouses. Such information led him to call for a change in the law. A reduction in the quota for "new" immigrants was necessary, he claimed, to save the United States from even larger numbers of paupers, mental patients, and criminals. The Immigration Committee voted to change the census base from 1910 to 1890, when there were far fewer southern and eastern Europeans in the country, and to reduce the quota from 3 percent to 2 percent. Congress would adopt those ideas in 1924.

Under the 1921 law, boats filled with prospective immigrants were returned to their homelands. These actions, however, were only the beginning, and the guardians of racial purity in Congress were already moving toward even tighter controls. Restrictionists had gotten most of what they wanted.

Bibliography

Bennett, Marion T. *American Immigration Policies*. Washington, D.C.: Public Affairs Press, 1963. Although written from a prorestriction point of view, this book contains useful information on all immigration laws up to 1962 and their effects on the numbers of people entering the United States. There is a brief but useful summary of arguments for and against the 1921 act. Includes an index and bibliography.

Divine, Robert. *American Immigration Policy, 1924-1952*. New Haven, Conn.: Yale University Press, 1957. An interesting, detailed account of the congressional movement toward restriction. Although mainly concerned with the 1924 law and its aftermath, there is a summary of attitudes in Congress and the rest of the United States that led to the 1921 act. Written from an antirestriction point of view. Contains an extensive and useful bibliography.

Garis, Roy. *Immigration Restriction*. New York: Macmillan, 1928. Written by an economist at Vanderbilt University in support of restriction. An old work but still useful in reflecting the attitudes of members of the Immigration Restriction League. Many charts and graphs. Contains an extensive bibliography prepared by the Library of Congress for the House Immigration Committee.

Higham, John. *Strangers in the Land: Patterns of American Nativism, 1860-1925*. New York: Atheneum, 1975. The classic account of anti-immigrant hostility in the United States from the Civil War to the final victory for restriction in the 1920's.

Presents a full account of the arguments for and against quotas, and contains an extensive discussion of the 1921 bill and the congressional debate on the subject. Includes a bibliography and an index.

Lipset, Seymour M., and Earl Raab. *The Politics of Unreason: Right-Wing Extremism in America, 1790-1970.* New York: Harper & Row, 1970. Although mainly focused on bigotry, the book contains a short discussion of restrictionist attitudes in many areas of the nation. The bibliography is helpful in finding sources for anti-immigrant ideas and values.

Solomon, Barbara. *Ancestors and Immigrants.* Cambridge, Mass.: Harvard University Press, 1956. A study of the Immigration Restriction League of Boston. Asserts that restrictionists perceived their world as crumbling under the influx of vast numbers of immigrants who knew nothing of democracy and liberty and were inferior intellectually and physically. Most of the study looks at attitudes before 1921—attitudes leading directly to the passage of the law.

Leslie V. Tischauser

Cross-References

Japan Protests Segregation of Japanese in California Schools (1906), p. 81; Congress Prohibits Immigration of Illiterates over Age Sixteen (1917), p. 231; "Palmer Raids" Lead to Arrests and Deportations of Immigrants (1919), p. 258; Congress Establishes a Border Patrol (1924), p. 377; A U.S. Immigration Act Imposes Quotas Based on National Origins (1924), p. 383.

SANGER ORGANIZES
CONFERENCES ON BIRTH CONTROL

Categories of event: Reproductive freedom and women's rights
Time: November 11-13, 1921, and March 25-31, 1925
Locale: New York, New York

Margaret Sanger brought European ideas on and methods of birth control to the United States, making it a respectable topic of the public health debate

Principal personages:
> MARGARET SANGER (1879-1966), a woman committed to spreading accurate information and methods of birth control
> PATRICK J. HAYES (1867-1938), the Roman Catholic archbishop of New York who attempted to restrict the free speech rights of birth control advocates
> HAROLD COX (1859-1936), a former British parliamentarian and editor of the *Edinburgh Review* whose 1921 speech on the morality of birth control was censored

Summary of Event

In the early twentieth century, great concern was voiced over the condition of working-class women and children. Social reforms such as protective labor legislation for women and children sought to alleviate conditions, but Margaret Sanger attempted a more radical reform through a single issue: birth control.

At that time, birth control and abortion were illegal in America, and most women had no access to reliable contraception. The 1873 Comstock laws forbade as obscene the dissemination of birth control information through the mail. Birth control was associated with licentiousness and immorality. It was argued by some that the use of contraceptives would eliminate the threat of pregnancy and would increase premarital sex. Others viewed the use of birth control devices as an unnatural act, an unholy effort to meddle with the will of God. Even feminists did not all support birth control, fearing that unrestricted sexuality would further oppress, rather than liberate, women.

The largely male middle-class medical community attacked birth control and abortion in the 1880's because the practices challenged the perception of motherhood as the proper role of women. Doctors saw women, especially middle-class women, who sought contraception as selfish, immoral, and threatening. As a profession, they opposed the study of contraceptive methods, although they did assist infertile women. Without access to preventive measures, many women, burdened by too many children and weakened by frequent pregnancy, turned to illegal abortionists in unhygienic conditions. The resulting deaths provided grist for attacks on birth control and abortion as unsafe.

Margaret Sanger was introduced to the harsh impact of these views on poor women while working as a visiting nurse in the Lower East Side of New York. There, women with large families and repeated pregnancies begged for some means to prevent additional children. When doctors refused them, Sanger took the matter into her own hands, embarking on a series of confrontational attempts to bring the pressing need for birth control to the attention of society.

Sanger traveled to Europe, where she learned the most accurate methods of birth control available at the time. She returned and, in 1914, published and distributed a pamphlet called *Family Limitation*, which provided practical instructions on how to prevent pregnancy. In 1916, she opened the first birth control clinic in the United States, in direct violation of New York State obscenity statutes. The clinic was quickly closed, and Sanger was tried, convicted, and sentenced to thirty days in prison. Although the final ruling allowed an exception to the obscenity rule for physicians, Sanger's conviction stood.

Sanger's strategy was to raise the level of debate over birth control to a scientific plane, where the value of contraception to public health could be demonstrated. She based her ideas on the European model, where the status of birth control was advanced compared to that of the United States. Although it had not yet been accepted fully by all governments or by all physicians, contraception enjoyed a more tolerated position in Europe. The first organization to promote birth control, the Malthusian League, was formed in England in 1877. Its platform, based on the economic theories of Malthus, held that controlling the population of the poor would lead to economic stability. The world's first birth control clinic was opened in Amsterdam in 1882 by Aletta Jacobs, Holland's first licensed woman doctor. Birth control devices, such as the pessary, invented by Karl Mensinga of Germany in the 1870's, were popular as contraceptives in Europe, though it was illegal to import them into the United States.

Sanger wanted to present the European ideas and methods to America in 1921, despite the fact that it was illegal to discuss birth control publicly. In seeking to have birth control treated with the same degree of respect and importance that it had in much of Europe, Sanger needed the support of physicians, scientists, and other respected members of the community. Her strategy was to create a public forum to demonstrate effective techniques of contraception to physicians, and in this way to disassociate birth control from the stain of immorality. Her vehicle was a conference.

The First American Birth Control Conference was held at New York City's Plaza Hotel, November 11-13, 1921, and was attended by doctors, academics, and scientists. Professional papers were presented on various aspects of the birth control debate including health issues, social problems, the relationship of overpopulation to war, and the legality of birth control. The sessions that Sanger viewed as most successful were those in which the latest European ideas and contraceptive techniques were demonstrated to American physicians. Sanger believed that once doctors were convinced of the reliability and safety of birth control, they would disseminate that knowledge to their patients.

Although the public discussion on birth control was couched in scientific terms, it did not slip past the notice of Sanger's powerful opponents. On November 13, 1921, the last day of the conference, Sanger was to introduce Harold Cox, a former member of the British Parliament, who would lead a mass meeting at Town Hall entitled, "Birth Control: Is It Moral?" The lecture had been widely publicized and a good crowd was expected, but when Sanger and Cox arrived at the meeting, they found their way barred by the police. On the orders of New York Archbishop Patrick J. Hayes, Captain Thomas Donohue marshaled police to break up the meeting before any law had been broken. Sanger telephoned police headquarters and discovered that no warrant or order had been issued for the action, so she defied the police, made her way inside the hall, and insisted on speaking until she and suffragist Mary Winsor were arrested. Released the next day and eventually acquitted of all charges, Sanger publicly condemned the attack on her right to free speech as well as church interference in public affairs.

The incident provided a groundswell of public support for Sanger and her cause. Many wealthy women publicly declared support for Sanger, as did members of the press and the legal profession, who defended her right to free speech. Sanger had effectively turned the attempt of Archbishop Hayes to suppress her speech into a powerful publicity vehicle. The mass meeting, rescheduled for November 18 at the Park Theatre, was held with a far larger crowd in attendance.

Only a few years after this event, Sanger organized another conference in New York City: the Sixth International Neo-Malthusian and Birth Control Conference (INMBC), held at the Hotel McAlpin on March 25-31, 1925. This conference, one of several Neo-Malthusian conferences convened sporadically since 1900, was the first of this type to be held in the United States. It effectively demonstrated Sanger's success at mobilizing American support for birth control. The Sixth INMBC was the largest and most internationally diverse of these conferences, with more than a thousand attendees from sixteen countries, including influential birth control advocates, Neo-Malthusians, physicians, and eugenicists. Among those who participated were Dr. Charles Vickery Drysdale, president of the British Neo-Malthusian League; Dr. Aletta Jacobs of Holland; and Gabriel Giroud, president of the French Malthusian League. In addition to medical papers on contraceptive techniques, papers were given by health workers, eugenicists, physicians, and social workers on the state of birth control in various nations.

Unlike the 1921 American conference, the 1925 international conference was not marred by censorship efforts. It became the impetus for greater American involvement in the international birth control movement.

Impact of Event

At the 1921 and 1925 birth control conferences, American physicians were exposed to the most advanced European theories and methods of birth control. These conferences established birth control as a scientific concern and an issue of public health, overriding the perceptions of it as an obscene and illegal practice. As wealthy and influential Americans began to support Sanger, the United States emerged as a leader in the international birth control movement.

The day before the first American conference, Sanger officially formed the American Birth Control League (ABCL), the first truly nationwide birth control organization in America. The ABCL provided a broad program of education, publicity, organization, and service, promoting scientific inquiry into and legalization of birth control and establishing a nationwide network of birth control clinics.

The controversy over the attempt of the Roman Catholic church to suppress the 1921 Town Hall meeting demonstrated American respect for the right to free speech, even in the case of an "immoral" subject. The Town Hall incident drew protests even from those who did not support birth control but believed that Cox and Sanger had the right to speak. In the end, the incident generated tremendous publicity for Sanger and the fledgling ABCL, most of it favorable. Many physicians who participated in the conference retained ties with the ABCL, serving on medical advisory boards and conducting scientific research. Upper-class women became actively involved in the organization of clinics all over the country.

Sanger utilized the conferences themselves to counter doctors' opposition to birth control and bring them into the movement. To further ensure their support, she vigorously pursued federal legislation for a "doctors-only bill," limiting the dispensation of birth control devices to physicians. Nevertheless, widespread acceptance of birth control as a health issue followed slowly, as did the removal of many legal obstacles.

Sanger was able to open the first legal, doctor-staffed birth control clinic in the United States in 1923. It was the first of many such clinics. It was Sanger's efforts, through vehicles such as the 1921 and 1925 conferences, that provided medical staff with the skills necessary to operate the clinics and conduct the contraceptive research that would affect the lives of women and their families the world over. Ordinary women, because of Sanger's work, eventually were able to limit the size of their families without stigma, without risking their health, and without violating the law.

The 1925 Sixth INMBC conference also dramatically underscored the changes that had taken place in American thought and attitudes since 1921. No police or church activity barred the smooth progression of the second, more widely attended conference, which paved the way for the growth of a strong international movement. Birth control advocates continued to meet and to share ideas and techniques. The immediate results of the 1925 conference were the formation of the International Federation of Birth Control Leagues and the convening of the 1927 World Population Conference in Geneva, which Sanger also organized. As post-World War II interest in population control swelled, these early advocates, joined by younger allies, formed the International Planned Parenthood Federation in 1952.

Bibliography

Gordon, Linda. *Woman's Body, Woman's Right: A Social History of Birth Control in*

America. New York: Grossman, 1976. A feminist reading of the American birth control movement. Gordon does not cover the conferences but provides a critical look at Margaret Sanger and the professionalization of the birth control movement by doctors and eugenicists. Index, footnotes, and references are provided.

Ledbetter, Rosanna. *A History of the Malthusian League: 1877-1927.* Columbus: Ohio State University Press, 1976. Provides a European background to the birth control movement, explaining the early work of Neo-Malthusians and their impact. Index, footnotes, and references are provided.

Reed, James. *The Birth Control Movement and American Society: From Private Vice to Public Virtue.* Princeton, N.J.: Princeton University Press, 1978. Provides background on the American birth control movement, though little on the conferences. Reed is especially useful for the relationship between the medical profession and the birth control movement. Index, footnotes, and references are provided.

Sanger, Margaret, ed. *International Birth Control Conference.* 4 vols. New York: American Birth Control League, 1925-1926. Provides abstracts of the papers given at the 1925 Sixth INMBC conference, as well as identification of participants. No references are provided.

_____. *Margaret Sanger: An Autobiography.* New York: W. W. Norton, 1938.

_____. *My Fight for Birth Control.* New York: Farrar & Rinehart, 1931. Autobiographical histories of Sanger and the birth control movement, including both conferences. The latter book contains greater detail on the conferences, but the former carries Sanger's story further. Neither book provide footnotes, but the former is indexed.

Cathy Moran Hajo

Cross-References

Sanger Opens the First Birth-Control Clinic in the United States (1916), p. 184; *Roe v. Wade* Expands Reproductive Choice for American Women (1973), p. 1703; Italy Legalizes Abortion (1978), p. 1988; Prolife Groups Challenge Abortion Laws (1989), p. 2443; The National Organization for Women Sponsors an Abortion Rights Rally (1989), p. 2489.

NANSEN WINS THE NOBEL PEACE PRIZE

Category of event: Refugee relief
Time: December 10, 1922
Locale: Oslo, Norway

Fridtjof Nansen won the Nobel Peace Prize for his humanitarian work, including arranging prisoner-of-war repatriation after World War I and assisting famine victims and refugees in the early 1920's

Principal personages:

FRIDTJOF NANSEN (1861-1930), a Norwegian polar explorer and scientist

PHILIP J. NOEL-BAKER (1889-1982), a British official at the Secretariat of the League of Nations and Nansen's assistant; winner of the Nobel Peace Prize in 1959

THOMAS FRANK JOHNSON (1887-1972), an official in the refugee agencies of the League of Nations from 1921 to 1936

LORD ROBERT CECIL (1864-1958), a British representative to the League of Nations and an advocate of its humanitarian work; winner of the Nobel Peace Prize in 1937

SIR ERIC DRUMMOND (1876-1951), the secretary-general of the League of Nations from 1919 to 1933

Summary of Event

On December 10, 1922, Fridtjof Nansen was awarded the Nobel Peace Prize for his completed humanitarian work, including organizing prisoner-of-war repatriation and aiding victims of the Russian famine. At the time of the award, Nansen held the post of League of Nations High Commissioner for Refugees. In this role, Nansen is credited both with helping thousands of uprooted people rebuild their lives and also with laying the legal and institutional foundations for future international refugee assistance efforts.

Nansen can be described as both a doer and a thinker. After earning a doctorate in zoology, Nansen initially achieved fame as a polar explorer. In 1888, he led the first expedition to cross Greenland successfully. Five years later, Nansen organized an even more adventurous project. In a specially built ship, the *Fram* (meaning "Forward"), Nansen and his companions set out across the frozen north. Soon the *Fram* became locked in the polar icecap. The ship and its crew returned home three years later. Nansen's ideas about Arctic drift were confirmed by his observations. During this journey, Nansen left the ship and attempted to reach the North Pole. Even though this effort failed, Nansen traveled farther north than had any other explorer until that date. He received a hero's welcome upon his return to Norway.

Although Nansen had always thought of himself as a scientist, his sense of duty and patriotism led him toward new challenges. In 1906 and 1907, he served as the first Norwegian ambassador to Great Britain. In 1917, Nansen interrupted his experiments once again to head a Norwegian commission charged with negotiating a food import agreement with the United States. Nansen's commitment to public service increased during World War I, as the death and destruction accompanying the conflict profoundly affected him. He believed that fundamental corruption in European civilization had caused the war, and that traditional methods of solving international problems needed to be changed. Nansen became a strong advocate for the League of Nations and served as the Norwegian delegate to it throughout the 1920's.

In 1920, the Council of the League of Nations called on Nansen to investigate the possibilities for prisoner-of-war repatriation in Europe. At that time, thousands of prisoners were stranded in the former Russian Empire and in Central Europe. Nansen persuaded governments to contribute funds and supplies, arranged for shipping, and coordinated the efforts of private agencies. He even negotiated with the Soviet Union at a time when mutual hostility existed between it and the members of the league. By the time Nansen finished his task, he had supervised the repatriation of about 425,000 prisoners at a cost of less than five dollars per person.

Although Nansen wanted to retire, he changed his mind in response to a series of tragic events. In the summer of 1921, it became obvious that a catastrophic famine was sweeping parts of Russia and Ukraine. In August, 1921, the International Committee of the Red Cross and other voluntary agencies asked Nansen to take charge of relief operations. Nansen accepted this challenge and immediately set up offices of the Nansen Mission in Berlin and in Moscow. At the Assembly of the League of Nations in September, 1921, Nansen, speaking as the delegate from Norway, made an impassioned plea on behalf of the famine victims. The government representatives, however, refused to grant official sanction to relief operations because the operations might inadvertently help the Soviet government. Undaunted, Nansen began raising funds from private sources. Although the assistance operations he directed are less well known than those conducted under the supervision of Herbert Hoover, they helped to save thousands of lives.

In the autumn of 1921, the Council of the League of Nations asked Nansen to take on one more humanitarian project. At the time, approximately one million White Russian refugees were scattered around the periphery of the former Czarist empire. These refugees lacked food, clothing, and shelter; many lived in desperate poverty. Moreover, these refugees could not easily return to their home country because of the Russian Revolution, civil war, and famine, and legally they could not travel to another country. After the urging of officials in the League of Nations Secretariat, Nansen gave up his retirement to become the League of Nations High Commissioner for Russian Refugees. In doing so, he became the first international civil servant to be charged with refugee assistance.

As high commissioner, Nansen's official job description included providing legal protection for and arranging either the repatriation or the employment of the refugees. His first task was to establish an organization capable of assisting one million refugees without exceeding tight budgetary constraints. The League of Nations allocated only $20,000 for refugee assistance. Nansen began by recruiting a small staff, including Philip J. Noel-Baker and Thomas Frank Johnson, to run the Geneva office and to keep in contact with donor governments. He also appointed delegates in host countries and created an advisory committee of voluntary agencies. Through these varied sources, the Nansen organization benefited from the input of government officials in host and donor countries, refugees in host countries, and volunteers engaged in refugee aid.

Shortly after assuming his post as high commissioner, Nansen faced a major refugee crisis in Constantinople. This city, then under Allied control, had become a dumping ground for the defeated White Russian forces and the civilians under their protection. In September, 1921, almost thirty-five thousand refugees, many on the brink of starvation, had been left there. Although the League of Nations had not authorized Nansen to provide material assistance to refugees, he decided that it would be useless to find jobs for the refugees while they still needed food and shelter. Using his skills as a fund-raiser, Nansen secured enough money from governments and private organizations to evacuate more than twenty thousand refugees to forty-four different countries. Almost a year later, in October, 1922, Nansen responded to the refugee crisis produced by the Greco-Turkish war. In this case, Nansen helped to coordinate relief efforts for more than one million refugees in Greece and Turkey.

Nansen was concerned not only with the emergency needs of refugees but also with their long-term problems. Paramount among these was their lack of passports and other documents which would provide them with a secure legal position in host countries. In July, 1922, Nansen called an intergovernmental conference to examine the legal status of Russian refugees. As a result of this conference, a special certificate of identity for refugees, commonly called a "Nansen passport," came into being. Although this document was not an official passport, it gave refugees a legal identity and made it easier for them to travel internationally in order to join friends or accept jobs. Eventually, more than fifty countries accepted this system. Its provisions expanded to cover other refugee groups, including Armenians (1924), Assyrians, Assyro-Chaldeans, and Turkish refugees (1928), and Saarlanders (1935).

After receiving the Nobel Peace Prize in December, 1922, Nansen focused his efforts on helping Russian and other refugees to find permanent homes. Until 1924, he retained hope that many Russian refugees would return to their home country, even though many émigré organizations opposed repatriation. Despite his efforts to arrange repatriation, only about six thousand refugees returned to the Soviet Union before a deterioration in relations with the government ended negotiations. After the Greco-Turkish war, Nansen proposed that an international loan be used to help Greece deal with the more than one million refugees who had recently arrived on its shores. This suggestion became the embryo which eventually grew into the Greek Refugee Settlement Commission, a joint venture between the Greek government and the League of Nations. By the time it had concluded its work in 1930, about six hundred thousand rural and urban refugees had been given new homes. During the last years of his life, Nansen attempted to arrange a major settlement project for

Armenian refugees in Erivan (Soviet Armenia). In this case, Western opposition to any projects inside the Soviet Union rendered Nansen's pleas on behalf of the Armenian cause useless.

In May, 1930, Nansen died while reading a newspaper at his home in Norway. The League of Nations created the Nansen International Office and charged it with carrying on his work. Although this organization won the Nobel Prize in 1938 for its refugee assistance programs, it did not provide the world with Nansen's moral leadership or his creative approach to problem solving. In the words of Lord Robert Cecil, Nansen's friend and a British delegate to the League of Nations, "It was a bad day for Peace, Humanity and the League when he died at a comparatively early age. He has left no successor."

Impact of Event

Nansen's humanitarian career had both an immediate and also a lasting impact on human rights. First and foremost, his work was of a practical nature, aimed at improving the lives of people who were in prison, homeless, starving, insecure, or poor. As a leader who organized several international assistance efforts, he saved and improved the lives of thousands of people. Nansen's contributions to human rights, however, go beyond the immediate impact he had in the 1920's.

Nansen's work for the League of Nations showed that an international organization could be effective in carrying out humanitarian work. Although this may be taken for granted, at that time many believed that the league should confine itself to military and political issues and leave "charity" to private groups. The success of prisoner-of-war repatriation and refugee assistance programs helped to change attitudes about what constituted the proper scope of international cooperation.

As high commissioner for refugees, Nansen established an institutional structure that would later be adopted by the United Nations High Commission for Refugees (UNHCR). The UNHCR also has a high commissioner in Geneva, delegates in host countries, and close relations with international nongovernmental organizations. From a human rights perspective, the delegates in host countries are especially important: They help to ensure that the human rights of refugees actually are protected at the local level. Many of Nansen's delegates were familiar with the languages and cultures of the people they helped because they were refugees themselves. Unfortunately, this opportunity for refugee participation in decision making was lost after Nansen's death. In 1938, the League of Nations fired all refugee employees in response to pressure from the Soviet Union.

In addition to establishing institutions, Nansen is also known as the founder of international refugee law. Although the tradition of asylum has a long history in international law, it was not until the 1920's that governments reached formal agreements about the legal status of refugees. Although the Nansen passport system initially was not binding, it became codified in the 1933 Refugee Convention, the first comprehensive treaty dealing with refugees. This document, in turn, served as the basis for the 1951 United Nations Convention Relating to the Status of Refugees.

Finally, Nansen left a legacy in the personal example he set for all leaders in the humanitarian field. Nansen never accepted any salary as high commissioner, rode third class on trains, and shunned the frills associated with public life. Characteristically, he donated the monetary award from the Nobel Prize to Greek refugees and to an agricultural research station in the Soviet Union. His approach to refugees resembled his approach to life. Instead of seeing problems, he saw opportunities for the improvement of the world. Sometimes, Nansen's idealism led him to underestimate the political obstacles to a particular project. The Armenian settlement scheme is a case in point. More often than not, however, his creative approach to providing durable solutions for refugees met with positive results. Consequently, Nansen made a lasting contribution to the cause of human rights.

Bibliography

Cecil, Robert Gascoyne-Cecil. *A Great Experiment: An Autobiography.* London: Jonathan Cape, 1941. This autobiography gives an account of Cecil's experience with the League of Nations, including his personal and working relationship with Nansen.

Holborn, Louise W. *Refugees, a Problem of Our Time: The Work of the United Nations High Commissioner for Refugees, 1951-1972.* Metuchen, N.J.: Scarecrow Press, 1975. Although this book is primarily a history of the UNHCR, it covers Nansen's role as high commissioner and the early days of refugee assistance at the League of Nations. The book assesses both the strengths and also the weaknesses of the league's refugee programs, and evaluates the contribution of Nansen and the League of Nations to the refugee work of the United Nations.

Hoyer, Liv Nansen. *Nansen: A Family Portrait.* Translated by Maurice Michael. London: Longmans, Green, 1957. A very personal account of Nansen's life, written by his daughter.

Johnson, Thomas F. *International Tramps: From Chaos to Permanent World Peace.* London: Hutchinson, 1938. This is Johnson's own account of his fifteen-year career with the refugee agencies of the League of Nations. It provides its reader with personal insights about Nansen and the League of Nations not available elsewhere. The book, however, is limited in that it presents only Johnson's viewpoint on particular issues.

Marrus, Michael R. *The Unwanted: European Refugees in the Twentieth Century.* New York: Oxford University Press, 1985. Gives a comprehensive summary of the plight of European refugees from the early twentieth century through the Cold War era. It discusses Nansen and others who contributed to the League of Nations' refugee work. The book is an excellent source of historical information, although Marrus' account is based largely on secondary, not primary, resources.

Nansen, Fridtjof. *Adventure, and Other Papers.* London: Hogarth Press, 1927. This small volume gives the text of several of Nansen's most famous speeches, including the one he gave upon acceptance of the Nobel Peace Prize. The speeches are invaluable in providing important insights into Nansen's views on human nature and on the issue of war and peace.

_____. *Russia and Peace.* London: Allen & Unwin, 1923. Nansen presents his controversial ideas about the role of the Soviet Union in the post-World War I era. He argues that the newly formed country should be encouraged to become an integral part of Europe.

Simpson, John Hope. *The Refugee Problem: Report of a Survey.* London: Oxford University Press, 1939. Contains the results of an extensive survey undertaken by the Royal Institute of International Affairs, London, on the refugee problem in Europe. It includes extremely valuable information about Nansen as high commissioner and the institutions that carried on his work after his death. The survey also includes the most comprehensive statistical data published on the major refugee groups of the period.

Skran, Claudena M. "Profiles of the First Two High Commissioners." *Journal of Refugee Studies* 1, no. 3/4 (1988): 277-296. Based on archival and other primary sources of information, this article focuses on Nansen's role as high commissioner and evaluates his contributions to the development of international refugee assistance programs.

Sörenson, Jon. *The Saga of Fridtjof Nansen.* Translated by J. B. C. Watkins. London: Allen & Unwin, 1932. One of the best biographies of Nansen ever written. It includes information on his career as an explorer and on his humanitarian work.

Claudena M. Skran

Cross-References

Lenin and the Communists Impose the "Red Terror" (1917), p. 218; Lenin Leads the Russian Revolution (1917), p. 225; The Immigration Act of 1921 Imposes a National Quota System (1921), p. 350; A U.S. Immigration Act Imposes Quotas Based on National Origins (1924), p. 383; The United Nations Creates an Agency to Aid Palestinian Refugees (1949), p. 814; The United Nations High Commissioner for Refugees Statute Is Approved (1950), p. 855; The U.N. Convention Relating to the Status of Refugees Is Adopted (1951), p. 867.

MARTIAL LAW IS DECLARED IN OKLAHOMA
IN RESPONSE TO KKK VIOLENCE

Categories of event: Racial and ethnic rights; civil rights
Time: 1923
Locale: Oklahoma

Oklahoma governor John Walton's declaration of martial law, in response to Ku Klux Klan terrorism, led to a controversy that resulted in his impeachment and removal from office

Principal personages:
>   JOHN "JACK" WALTON (1881-1949), the governor of Oklahoma who placed the state under martial law
>   EDWIN DE BARR (1859-1950), the vice president of Oklahoma University who served as the first Grand Dragon, or head, of the Oklahoma Ku Klux Klan
>   N. CLAY JEWETT, an Oklahoma City businessman who succeeded De Barr as Oklahoma Grand Dragon in 1923
>   MARTIN E. TRAPP (1877-1951), the lieutenant governor of Oklahoma; succeeded Walton as governor

Summary of Event

The original Ku Klux Klan began in Tennessee in late 1865, shortly after the Civil War. A secret organization whose members wore masks, hoods, and robes, it spread throughout the South, using threats, beatings, and murder to prevent recently freed slaves from exercising their newly won political and civil rights. The federal government, in the early 1870's, forcibly suppressed the first Klan movement, yet racial violence continued. By the turn of the century, Southern blacks had lost virtually all of the rights supposedly guaranteed under the 1868 Fourteenth Amendment (equal citizenship) and the 1870 Fifteenth Amendment (suffrage).

In 1915, William J. Simmons organized a second Ku Klux Klan organization in Atlanta, Georgia. By 1920, it had spread beyond the old Confederacy and found varying degrees of support throughout the nation. Targets included not only African Americans but also Catholics, Jews, and aliens as well as native-born Americans who violated the moral code of rural, Protestant America. By the mid-1920's, the Klan had attained a membership of several million and exercised political influence in a number of states and communities.

The Klan became a visible presence in Oklahoma in 1921. This former Indian territory, admitted to statehood in 1907, had a tradition of frontier vigilantism, lynchings, labor tensions, and mistreatment of its large Native American population, which was systematically cheated of its land. Blacks in 1920 formed about 7 percent of Oklahoma's two million residents and had been subjected to disfranchisement and racial segregation well before the Klan's arrival. In the spring of 1921, lynching rumors triggered a Tulsa race riot in which nearly eighty people, mostly blacks, perished. Catholics, Jews, and aliens were few in number and were regarded with some suspicion by the white Protestant majority.

Under the leadership of its first Grand Dragon, Edwin De Barr, a chemistry professor and vice president of the University of Oklahoma, the Oklahoma Klan by the spring of 1922 reached a membership of seventy thousand. Unlike many of its sister organizations in other states, it focused little attention on Catholics, Jews, and aliens and generally refrained from initiating economic boycotts against these groups. Although the Klan played no clear role in the Tulsa riot, it occasionally targeted blacks. In El Reno, a black hotel porter was whipped for being insufficiently deferential toward white guests, and in Enid the Klan drove out more than twenty blacks whom its members viewed as posing a criminal threat. In 1922, a prominent Tulsa black was whipped and mutilated for attempting to register blacks to vote.

The primary targets of Klan violence, however, were native-born whites. The oil boom of the early twentieth century had generated rowdy boomtowns, with an upsurge of crime, vice, and labor strife. State "dry laws" and national prohibition were flagrantly violated. Oklahoma was thus fertile ground for Klan recruiters who pledged to restore order and reaffirm traditional values. Local whipping squads formed, and alleged adulterers, loose women, wife beaters, bootleggers, and criminals were abducted and beaten. The first evidence of the Klan in Oklahoma was the July, 1921, abduction and whipping of a Muskogee dishwasher accused of criminal behavior. Later that year, a shoot-out in Wilson between Klan members and suspected bootleggers left three of the latter dead. Although hundreds of floggings occurred, victims feared reporting the incidents, since many officials and police had Klan affiliations.

Indeed, by 1922 the Klan in Oklahoma had become a significant political force, locally and on the state level. Klansmen dominated the state legislature. At first, there was little open opposition to the Klan, but this would change under the administration of Governor John "Jack" Walton.

As mayor of Oklahoma City, Walton had earlier expressed opposition to the Klan. He had warned police that he would not tolerate their membership in the order, and he had launched an investigation of Klan use of the local fairgrounds. Following his successful 1922 gubernatorial election campaign, backed by the Democratic party and the new Farmer-Labor Reconstruction League, Walton made an effort to conciliate the diverse elements of his constituency, which included not only the reformist Leaguers who were anti-Klan but also a significant proportion of Klansmen. Walton opportunistically appointed Klansmen to state positions and even secretly joined the order. He used patronage ineptly and caused an outrage when he appointed a poorly qualified Reconstruction League leader as president of the Agricultural and Mining College. Walton's efforts to please all sides backfired. Rumors circulated that Walton had taken money from the oil interests and had misappropriated state funds. By the spring of 1923, there was considerable talk of impeachment.

At the same time, there was a new outbreak of masked attacks. Walton announced that if local law officers failed to correct this problem, he would employ the National Guard. On June 26, he briefly imposed martial law in Okmulgee County. In August, six unmasked men kidnapped and severely whipped Nate Hantaman, a Jewish boardinghouse operator in Tulsa suspected of dealing in narcotics and liquor. There was evidence of possible police collusion with the kidnapping. After officials failed to apprehend Hantaman's assailants, Walton on August 13 placed Tulsa under martial law, sending in National Guards and then establishing a court of inquiry that indicted several floggers. Such actions won praise from both the Oklahoma and national press, but then Walton seemed to abandon all restraint. On August 30, in violation of the state constitution, he announced a suspension of habeas corpus for the entire county and sent two hundred more guards. When the *Tulsa Tribune* protested, Walton briefly placed the paper's editorial page under military censorship. He advised citizens to shoot any masked men who attempted to assault them, promising them a pardon.

Open warfare ensued between Walton and the Klan. N. Clay Jewett, an Oklahoma City businessman who had recently replaced De Barr as Grand Dragon, declared that Walton would never break the Klan's power in Oklahoma. Walton then ordered a statewide ban on Klan parades and demonstrations, threatening to place the entire state under martial law if his order were disobeyed. Jewett shrewdly complied and exhorted his followers to refrain from vigilante action. On September 15, just as a grand jury was to convene to investigate the governor's misuse of power, Walton placed all of Oklahoma under martial law. Labeling Klansmen enemies of the state, he called up six thousand additional Guards and forcibly prevented the grand jury from proceeding with its investigation. Testimony given before an Oklahoma City military court revealed that high local officials had joined the Klan. The general sentiment, however, was that the governor had gone too far.

By now, there was a determined effort to impeach Walton. The governor used threats, military force, and legal action in a desperate attempt to prevent such action, but on October 2 Oklahoma voters overwhelmingly approved an initiative proposal permitting a special legislative session in which the issue of impeachment and removal could be considered. On October 8, the governor terminated military rule in Oklahoma. Three days later, he convened the legislature to consider anti-Klan proposals, but when the lower house met, it made impeachment proceedings its first priority and adopted twenty-two charges against Walton. In November, the senate upheld eleven of these charges by the two-thirds majority needed for conviction and removal from office. These included the suspension of habeas corpus, use of the National Guard to prevent a grand jury from convening, misuse of state funds, excessive use of pardons, and incompetence.

Impact of Event

Governor Walton's decision to invoke martial law provoked considerable controversy. Oklahomans had been sharply divided on the Klan issue, with the organization receiving its greatest support in the central, northern, and eastern sections of the state. Among followers of the Reconstruction League, with its strongest base in southern Oklahoma, there was deep opposition to the hooded order. The League condemned the Klan as antilabor and denounced its violence and bigotry, and at least initially supported Walton's war on the Klan. Most Oklahomans, however, recoiled at the governor's decision to invoke martial law. Tulsans, for example, found it insulting to have Guards patrolling their streets and to be subjected to sundown curfews. On the eve of the October 2 initiative election that ultimately paved the way for Walton's ouster, the governor proclaimed a postponement of the balloting and threatened that Guards and police were prepared to shoot those who went to the polls. Nevertheless, more than half of the eligible voters defied the threat and voted 209,452 to 70,638 in favor of the proposal.

Many Oklahomans, including members of the Reconstruction League, concluded that Walton posed a greater menace than did the Klan, and they rallied around the cry that they wanted "neither Klan nor king." Historians generally agree that Walton used his war on the Klan to divert attention from his own corruption and incompetence. Tactics nominally directed against the Klan in actuality posed threats to the constitutional rights of all Oklahoma citizens. Moreover, at the time of his ouster, politically and numerically the Oklahoma Klan was stronger than ever: In 1924 its membership hit a peak of more than 100,000, placing the state near the nation's top in terms of its percentage of Klansmen. The unpopularity of Walton's actions may well have bolstered the Oklahoma Klan, which had seemed to be waning prior to his declarations of martial law.

At the same time, however, Klan abuses clearly warranted corrective action. Oklahoma's Klan reputedly was the most violent in the nation, and local authorities were either ineffective in controlling it or sometimes collaborated with the hooded order. Oklahoma military court hearings admittedly yielded few convictions, but the several floggers who were indicted and convicted were probably the first Klansmen whose guilt was clearly demonstrated by a court of law.

Under Walton's successor, Martin Trapp, the legislature in late 1923 adopted a moderate bill that regulated the wearing of masks and slightly increased the penalties for masked offenses. Furthermore, as most Oklahomans came to reject the excesses of vigilantism, Klan leaders like Jewett attempted to discourage such activities, and the Klan wave of terror ceased. The Klan's political success also proved fleeting. The majority of Oklahoma Klansmen were Democrats who took offense when Jewett, a Republican, engaged in machinations designed to benefit his own party. Klansmen also tired of the order's internal bickering, its authoritarian structure, and the continual financial burdens of dues and "taxes." As in other states, the Klan failed to deliver politically despite its nominal control over the legislature. As the decade ended, the Oklahoma Klan was a virtually powerless force claiming only two thousand members.

Oklahoma's black population continued to hold a subordinate social and political position until the civil rights revolution of the 1950's and 1960's. A third Klan movement, with a penchant toward violence, developed in reaction to these human rights advances, but both in scale and in political influence it never came close to approaching the Klan of the 1920's.

Bibliography

Alexander, Charles C. *The Ku Klux Klan in the Southwest.* Lexington: University of Kentucky Press, 1965. Alexander contends that the Klan's appeal in southwestern states like Oklahoma rested primarily on its attempt to enforce crumbling Victorian values. His detailed account of Walton's war on the Klan rests on the premise that the governor's actions were an insincere attempt to cloak the ineptness and corruption of his own administration. References and index.

Chalmers, David M. "Mayhem and Martial Law in Oklahoma." In *Hooded Americanism: The History of the Ku Klux Klan.* 2d ed. New York: F. Watts, 1981. This chapter in the standard survey of the second Klan movement, which flourished in the 1920's, offers a useful, brief introduction to the topic but not much in the way of analysis. Has bibliography and index.

Morgan, H. Wayne, and Anne Hodges Morgan. *Oklahoma: A History.* New York: W. W. Norton, 1984. This work includes a clear, concise consideration of the Klan's rise in Oklahoma and Walton's crusade against the organization. The Morgans argue that Walton lacked the experience and intelligence to govern the state, and that the alliance formed to remove him from office served to fortify the Klan politically, at least temporarily. References and index.

Neuringer, Sheldon. "Governor Walton's War on the Ku Klux Klan: An Episode in Oklahoma History 1923 to 1924." *Chronicles of Oklahoma* 45 (Summer, 1967): 153-179. This article has little information about the Oklahoma Klan but provides a detailed and balanced assessment of Walton's political struggle against the Invisible Empire. The author suggests that initially there was some justification for establishing military courts; however, Walton resorted to measures that were clearly unconstitutional, unwarranted, and counterproductive. Contains references.

Oates, Stephen B. "Boom Oil! Oklahoma Strikes It Rich." *The American West* 5 (January, 1968): 11-15, 64-66. A lively account that explains how the rowdiness and lawlessness of the boomtowns persuaded thousands of Oklahomans to embrace the Klan in an effort to restore order and traditional values. Illustrations.

Scales, James R., and Danney Goble. *Oklahoma Politics: A History.* Norman: University of Oklahoma Press, 1982. This study includes a useful analysis of Oklahoma politics of the 1920's and portrays Walton's war on the Klan as a largely ineffective political maneuver. The authors argue that "the Klan richly deserved punishment, but not subversion of civil liberties with unparalleled ruthlessness." Has references, illustrations, and index.

Tucker, Howard A. *History of Governor Walton's War on Ku Klux Klan, the Invisible Empire.* Oklahoma City: Southwest, 1923. Written by an Oklahoma journalist shortly before Walton's impeachment, this brief work provides a vivid if disjointed depiction of Klan violence, often through the testimony of its victims. Marred by some inaccuracies and dubious claims, it presents Walton's behavior in a more sympathetic light than most later sources. Lacks references and index.

Allen Safianow

Cross-References

Black Leaders Call for Equal Rights at the Niagara Falls Conference (1905), p. 41; "Palmer Raids" Lead to Arrests and Deportations of Immigrants (1919), p. 258; The Ku Klux Klan Spreads Terror in the South (1920's), p. 298; Race Riots Erupt in Detroit and Harlem (1943), p. 635; The Civil Rights Act of 1957 Creates the Commission on Civil Rights (1957), p. 997; Eisenhower Sends Troops to Little Rock, Arkansas (1957), p. 1003; Meredith's Enrollment Integrates the University of Mississippi (1962), p. 1167; Congress Passes the Civil Rights Act (1964), p. 1251; African Americans Riot in Watts (1965), p. 1301; The Kerner Commission Explores the Causes of Civil Disorders (1967), p. 1370; Race Rioting Erupts in Detroit (1967), p. 1376; Race Riot Breaks Out in Miami, Protesting Police Brutality (1980), p. 2101.

NEVADA AND MONTANA INTRODUCE THE OLD-AGE PENSION

Categories of event: Older persons' rights and workers' rights
Time: March 5, 1923
Locale: Nevada and Montana

The United States trailed far behind the rest of the industrial world in providing relief for older citizens until Nevada and Montana approved old-age pensions in 1923

Principal personages:

JOSEPH M. DIXON (1867-1934), the progressive Republican governor of Montana in 1923

ABRAHAM EPSTEIN (1892-1942), a founder of the American Association for Old Age Security and the principal crusader for old-age pensions

JAMES C. SCRUGHAM (1880-1945), the Democratic governor of Nevada in 1923

Summary of Event

At the same hour and on the same day, March 5, 1923, Montana governor Joseph M. Dixon and Nevada governor James C. Scrugham signed the first old-age pension legislation in the United States. The issue of providing a pension for America's older population had become prominent in the years after World War I. Proponents of old-age pensions, propelled to a great extent by the politics of Progressivism, pointed to the fact that the United States stood alone among the industrial nations in refusing assistance to those considered too old to hold regular jobs. The United States continued to apply the nineteenth century doctrine of laissez-faire at a time when circumstances cried out for assistance to retired wage earners. It was no longer realistic to expect that lifelong wage earners could set aside enough money to live comfortably in their retirement years.

Supporters of old-age pensions had statistics on their side, and they used them effectively. In 1880, 3 percent of America's population was sixty-five or older, but by 1920 the percentage of older persons had risen to five. In addition, more people than ever before worked for a wage, the average lifespan was increasing rapidly, businesses tended to retire workers forcibly, and industrial society had brought about a greater dispersal of family members. With these facts in mind, there could be little doubt that the need for old-age pensions was going to increase in the future. As Abraham Epstein, the leading advocate of old-age relief, expressed in the 1920's, "If the sunset of life is to continue unproductive, wretched and humiliating, is it worth prolonging?"

Much of the information used to expose the problems of America's retired workers came from a legislative commission created in Pennsylvania in 1917. It was not in Pennsylvania, however, or in any other highly industrialized northeastern state that an old-age pension bill was first enacted. Instead, it was the underpopulated and far less industrialized states of Montana and Nevada that led the way. The circumstances under which these two states first provided old-age assistance included staggering local economies, progressive politics, and inadequate care facilities for the destitute elderly. Like many other states, Montana and Nevada had a certain number of county homes to house the old and poor. These were roughly modeled along the lines of the poorhouses prescribed by the 1834 New Poor Law in England. Although some of the more onerous aspects of the poorhouses had been eliminated, the county homes were scarcely desirable residences. Moreover, with physician fees and food costs, they were expensive to maintain, and the number of persons seeking refuge had continued to increase. It was evident that the county homes would soon be incapable of handling the demands placed upon them. Those who supported the creation of old-age allowances made compelling economic and humanitarian arguments against the county homes. They pointed out that the homes were becoming too expensive to maintain and that, because of the notorious condition of many of the homes, people feared going into one of them more than they did starving.

Early in 1923, the Montana and Nevada legislatures began to consider another kind of relief for the retired and poor. In each state, the presence of a governor who favored social reform contributed to the momentum for new measures. In Montana, Governor Joseph M. Dixon, a longtime Republican progressive who had served in the United States House of Representatives (1902-1904) and the United States Senate (1905-1917) and managed Theodore Roosevelt's 1912 presidential campaign, gave his support to a pension plan that allowed individual counties to provide relief for persons seventy years of age and older with incomes of less than three hundred dollars per year. Each person given a pension had to have been a citizen of the United States and a resident of Montana for at least fifteen years. The maximum that any person could receive was twenty-five dollars each month. The Montana law placed the burden for administering and financing the pension in the hands of county officials. County commissioners were to decide who qualified for the old-age pension and how much each pensioner would receive. There was no state authority to oversee the pension plan, nor did the state reimburse counties for the pensions they paid.

In Nevada, the old-age pension bill gained the support of Democrats and progressive Republicans. The Democratic governor, James C. Scrugham, gave his approval to the measure as it proceeded through the state legislature. The Nevada law provided for a much different form of administration from that approved in Montana. In Nevada, the governor, lieutenant governor, and attorney general were established as the State Old Age Pension Commission. The governor then appointed three residents from each county to serve on county pension boards. These boards received applications for relief from eligible persons and then made recommendations to the state commission. Pensions could be granted to individuals sixty years of age or older who had been United States Citizens for at least fifteen years and residents of Nevada for at least ten years. No one could be given an old-age allowance in excess of one dollar per day. If an applicant owned property valued at three thousand dollars or more, that applicant was automatically disqualified. The money to support the Nevada system came from a special tax of 2.5 mills on each hundred dollars of taxable property within each county. It remained to be seen whether the centralized Nevada system or the decentralized Montana system would work more efficiently.

Impact of Event

Supporters of old-age pensions from around the nation were buoyed by the legislation enacted in Montana and Nevada. Beginning with Pennsylvania in May, 1923, many other states passed similar legislation. In the specific cases of Montana and Nevada, however, the impact of the 1923 old-age pension measures appears to have been slight. A survey of Montana counties undertaken by Abraham Epstein in 1926 is quite revealing in this regard. Epstein received information from fifty-one of the state's fifty-six counties. Fourteen counties did not participate in the system because they had either no applications or no money to provide pensions. The largest county, which included the city of Butte, fell into the latter category. The information further revealed that, in the counties responding, only 2.6 out of every 1,000 eligible inhabitants applied for old-age pensions. At the end of 1926, there were only 448 pensioners in the thirty-two counties reporting that they had granted any pensions. Statistics gathered from the Associated Industries of Montana and the United States Department of Labor showed that each citizen of the participating counties paid about twenty-eight cents per year to support the pension plan and that money spent on old-age relief was less than a quarter of that spent to maintain the county homes.

The Nevada old-age pension law was so ineffective that it was repealed by the state legislature early in 1925. In March of that year, a new bill was passed that adopted the Montana system of putting all decisions in the hands of county officials. The state no longer supervised the granting of old-age allowances. The 1925 Nevada legislation raised the eligible age for assistance to sixty-five. A survey undertaken in 1926 could find only one person in the entire state who had been granted an old-age pension. In both Montana and Nevada, as well as in other states, private insurance interests tried to discourage implementation of the pension laws.

The Montana and Nevada laws did not have much impact within the respective populations of those states, but on a national level the legislation gave momentum to the old-age pension cause. Legislators in highly populated industrial states were embarrassed that sparsely populated Montana and Nevada had taken the first steps to provide relief for the aged poor. Ultimately, it took the Great Depression, when many well-to-do elderly lost their savings, to force the national government to abandon the notion that individuals should save their earnings for old age. The result was the national Social Security Act passed during the Franklin D. Roosevelt Administration.

Bibliography

Douglas, Paul H. *Social Security in the United States.* 1936. Reprint. New York: Da Capo Press, 1971. A comprehensive, if somewhat thin, look at efforts to provide relief for the nonworking aged. Douglas explains why employers in every state opposed, on the basis of cost, pension legislation. Includes an appendix and an index.

Elliott, Russell R. *History of Nevada.* Lincoln: University of Nebraska Press, 1973. A splendid general history of Nevada. The author is at times overly allusive, and discussions of political events are not always well focused. There is no discussion of the pension laws, but the work contains an amazing, and extremely important, annotated bibliography. There is an index.

Epstein, Abraham. *The Challenge of the Aged.* 1928. Reprint. New York: Arno Press, 1976. By a wide margin, this is the most useful and significant work on the plight of the aged through 1927. Epstein was a leader in the campaign for old-age relief, and his work is full of information and statistics that illuminate the subject. It is clearly written and well organized. Very highly recommended. The work contains notes, an appendix, and an index.

Karlin, Jules A. *Joseph M. Dixon of Montana.* 2 vols. Missoula: University of Montana Press, 1974. This is a well-researched and inclusive biography of one of Montana's most important politicians. Although Karlin does not discuss the old-age pension laws, he describes convincingly the circumstances in Montana from which a pension law emerged. The organization of the biography is sometimes confusing, and it is not attractively printed. There is an excellent bibliography and index.

Spense, Clark C. *Montana: A History.* New York: W. W. Norton, 1978. This is one of the state histories published by Norton for the bicentennial celebration. The publisher placed strict limits on the number of pages for each book; therefore, this study is not as useful as it might have been. Nevertheless, Spense does provide a very good introduction to Montana's politics and society. There is an excellent section devoted to suggestions for further reading and also an index.

Ronald K. Huch

Cross-References

Massachusetts Adopts the First Minimum-Wage Law in the United States (1912), p. 126; Social Security Act Establishes Benefits for Nonworking People (1935), p. 514; The Congress of Industrial Organizations Is Formed (1938), p. 545; The First Food Stamp Program Begins in Rochester, New York (1939), p. 555; Congress Enacts the Age Discrimination in Employment Act (1967), p. 1397; Oregon Legislates Guaranteed Basic Health Care for the Uninsured (1989), p. 2437.

CONGRESS ESTABLISHES A BORDER PATROL

Category of event: Immigrants' rights
Time: May, 1924
Locale: Washington, D.C.

Congress established the United States Border Patrol to prevent undocumented immigrants from Latin America and Canada from entering the United States

Principal personages:
> JOHN BOX (1871-1941), a United States congressman from Texas, supporter of legislation to restrict Mexican immigration
> JAMES J. DAVIS (1873-1947), the U.S. secretary of labor (1921-1929), an advocate of strict control of immigration
> WILLIAM GREEN (1872-1952), the president of the American Federation of Labor
> CLAUDE HUDSPETH (1877-1941), a United States congressman from Texas who introduced a bill creating the United States Border Patrol
> CHARLES EVANS HUGHES (1862-1948), the U.S. secretary of state (1921-1925); argued against immigration restriction for the Western Hemisphere

Summary of Event

The United States Border Patrol was created in 1924 to curtail illegal immigration from Latin America and Canada. Previously, a force of fewer than forty mounted inspectors rode the borders looking for Chinese migrants attempting to enter the country in violation of the 1882 Chinese Exclusion Act. Mexican workers proved so valuable to the economy of the American Southwest that little effort was made to prevent them from crossing the Rio Grande to work for cotton and sugar beet growers and as agricultural laborers. A literacy test passed in 1917 during World War I made it more difficult for farm hands to enter, but the test could be avoided easily by sneaking into the country at night. Enforcement was lax because of protests from growers and farmers who depended on a cheap labor supply for their economic livelihood.

In the early 1920's, illegal immigration from Mexico far exceeded the average of fifty thousand legitimate immigrants per year. In 1921, Congress adopted a restrictive immigration policy based on a national quota system. Supporters argued for including the peoples of the Western Hemisphere in the limitations but did not succeed because of opposition from the State Department and agricultural interests in Texas, Arizona, and California. Secretary of State Charles Evans Hughes told Congress that limiting Latin American immigration would harm attempts to improve diplomatic relations with that part of the world, while farmers and growers claimed that a steady supply of migrants from south of the border was necessary to keep them in business. For these reasons, both the Senate and the House agreed to put no restrictions on New World peoples.

When Congress passed a law in 1924 establishing a national origins system for immigrants, it again excluded people from the Western Hemisphere. A proposal to include Latin Americans and Canadians under this more restrictive policy failed by large margins in the House and Senate. Hughes once again testified in opposition to the amendment and repeated his statement that the foreign policy of the United States demanded favorable treatment for migrants from Western nations. A new element entered this debate in Congress, however, as several congresspeople, led by Representative John Box of Texas, emphasized what they perceived as the racial and cultural inferiority of the Mexican population. The discussion in Congress focused on Mexicans because they made up the largest portion of immigrants from the New World. Almost 100,000 had crossed the border legally in 1924. Thousands more had entered illegally to escape paying the eighteen-dollar visa fee required of all immigrants under the new law. The flow of Central and South Americans coming into the country numbered fewer than five thousand that year and was not perceived as a threat.

Advocates of ending the flows of both legal and illegal immigration argued that Mexicans were taking away American jobs and working for starvation wages. The American Federation of Labor, under its new president, William Green, and the American Legion were major proponents of this viewpoint. "Scientific racists," who believed that white America was disappearing, argued about the dangers of "colored blood" polluting America and contaminating its way of life. Most Mexicans had Indian blood in them. According to racial theorists of the time, Indians were inferior to Nordic types in intelligence and physical ability. The 1924 law was aimed at keeping the inferior races of southern and eastern Europe out of the country. It made no sense, therefore, to allow free access to inferiors from other parts of the world. These arguments had been successful in winning approval of the 1921 quota system, whereby each nationality group in the United States was limited in immigration each year to 3 percent of its total number in the United States according to the 1910 census. The 1924 law reduced the total to 2 percent of the population according to the census base of 1890. Congress decided to remove Latin America and Canada from these restrictions principally because of the belief that cheap Mexican labor was necessary to keep American farmers prosperous.

Labor unions had frequently challenged that view. During the 1921-1922 depression in the United States, they began a campaign to include Latin Americans under the quota system. They had a strong ally in Secretary of Labor James J. Davis, a former union president. He ordered all unemployed Mexicans to leave the United States in 1922. Resentment and violence mounted because of the economic hard times, and in some Texas towns starving Mexicans were physically expelled. When the short depression ended and job opportunities opened, agricultural interests petitioned Congress to reopen the borders. Mexican labor was too valuable to the economy to exclude completely, because Mexicans did the jobs Americans simply would not do, and for wages Americans would not accept. The Spanish-speaking aliens would not become permanent residents, Congress was reassured, and they offered no political threat since the poll tax still in effect in Texas and other southern states prevented them from voting. The sugar beet growers and cotton farmers tried to appease the labor unions by arguing that the aliens were unskilled laborers and therefore were not a threat to American workers.

The same reasoning kept Canadians from inclusion in the new immigration system. These immigrants were mostly from French-speaking Quebec and worked in New England textile mills for very low wages. Most of the congressional debate centered on Mexicans, and there was little discussion of immigration from the north. Congress' major fear seemed to be that large numbers of "peons" from south of the border were entering the United States illegally and that they posed a threat to American values and customs because they were Catholics and spoke a foreign language. Something had to be done to stop that flood, but the economic interests of southwestern farmers would also have to be protected. If, for foreign policy and economic reasons, Latin Americans could not be in the quota system, the reasoning went, perhaps the borders of the United States could be secured from illegal immigration by tighter controls. Smuggling of impoverished workers from south of the border was a major problem, and no agency of the American government existed to control it.

Concern over the flow of laborers from the south led to the establishment of the United States Border Patrol on May 8, 1924. Congressman Claude Hudspeth of Texas, who owned a large farm in East Texas but who was not dependent on Mexican labor, proposed its creation and got Congress to provide $1 million for this new branch of the Bureau of Immigration and Naturalization in the Department of Labor. The Patrol had 450 officers, whose main job was to ride the Mexican border on horseback seeking out smugglers and the hiding places of illegal aliens. Opposition to the Patrol proved to be considerable. Ranchers and farmers protested and interfered with the arrests of their laborers. Patrol officers were told to expel any alien who could not prove that he or she had paid the visa fee.

The growers bitterly assailed the increasingly difficult requirements for legal immigration. The 1924 law mandated not only a ten-dollar visa fee, which had to be paid to an American consul in the nation of origin, but also a six-dollar head tax for each applicant. Few Mexicans could afford these fees because their average wage was twelve cents for a ten-hour day in their homeland. These fees thus encouraged illegal entry and the smuggling of laborers. For a small sum paid to smugglers, Mexican peasants could avoid the fees and the literacy test and easily find jobs paying $1.25 a day in Texas, Arizona, and California. In its first year of operation, the small Border Patrol staff reported turning back 15,000 aliens seeking illegal entry, although an estimated 100,000 farm workers successfully evaded the border guards. For that reason, in 1926 Congress doubled the size of the Patrol and made it a permanent part of the Bureau of Immigration and Naturalization.

Impact of Event

During its first three years of operation, the Patrol turned back an annual average of fifteen thousand Mexicans seeking illegal entry. It did not have enough personnel to end all illegal entry, and Mexican workers were too valuable to the economy of the Southwest to eliminate completely. Ranchers and farmers who benefited greatly by using Mexican labor continued to oppose the picking up and deporting of field hands who preferred to deal with smugglers rather than paying the visa fee and head tax.

In 1926, the Immigration Service backed away from strict enforcement of the law and entered into a "Gentlemen's Agreement" with agricultural interests in California and Texas. This called for registration of all Mexican workers in the states. They would each receive an identification card that allowed them to work, in exchange for an eighteen-dollar fee payable at three dollars per week. When Congressman John Box of Texas heard about "immigration on the installment plan," he was outraged and called for an end to this "outlaw's agreement." He denounced Mexicans as racially inferior to white Europeans, since they were mainly Indian, and warned that their illegal influx had been so large that they threatened to reverse the results of the Mexican War of 1846-1848. After that conflict, the United States had acquired California, Arizona, and much of the Southwest, but now, according to Box, "bloodthirsty, ignorant" bandits from Mexico were becoming the largest population in those areas and retaking them.

Because of such fears, Congress, in 1929, voted to double the size of the Border Patrol and demanded a crackdown on illegal entry. Congress was also responding to union demands for increased border security. Steel corporations had recently begun to recruit Mexicans from the Southwest to work in places such as Chicago and Gary, Indiana, where they would be paid less than Anglo-Americans. As European labor became more restricted because of the national origins requirement, Mexico and Latin America were seen by northern industrialists as new sources of cheap labor, much to the annoyance of labor unions. For many impoverished agricultural workers, the economic rewards seemed worth the risk. Many Mexicans moved north to Illinois, Michigan, and Ohio. In response, the Texas legislature passed a law charging a $1,000 fee for labor recruiters before they could begin operating in the state. The growers and farmers did not want all their cheap labor to move north.

A new law, suggested by the State Department, said that anyone caught entering the United States after having been deported previously would be charged with a felony and be liable for up to two years of imprisonment. This legislation greatly decreased illegal entry into North America. The Patrol was also authorized to cover the borders of Florida and Canada. The Gentlemen's Agreement was ended, and the full eighteen-dollar fee was again required. These measures, plus the economic insecurity brought about by the worldwide depression beginning in 1929, temporarily ended the conflict over illegal immigration from Mexico and other nations of the Western Hemisphere. The issue would not reemerge as an important problem until after World War II. The most important impact of the creation of the Border Patrol was to make illegal entry into the United States much more difficult than it ever had been before. A government agency now had the authority to arrest and deport illegal aliens.

Bibliography

Bennett, Marion T. *American Immigration Policies.* Washington, D.C..: Public Affairs Press, 1963. Has a brief discussion of the various and changing policies toward Latin Americans and Canadians. Generally, a useful summary of congressional action on immigration law. Nothing specific on the creation of the Border Patrol. This was, in 1991, the most recent history of United States immigration policy. Includes an index and extensive bibliography.

Divine, Robert. *American Immigration Policy, 1924-1952.* New Haven, Conn.: Yale University Press, 1957. Has some useful comments on congressional attitudes toward Mexicans. Little to say about the Border Patrol. Critical of racist attitudes and their influence on lawmakers. Gives a detailed history of immigration policy and law, the national origins debate, and the attempt to include the Western Hemisphere under immigration law provisions. Good background material on the most significant immigration laws and their enforcement. Contains an extensive bibliography and index.

Fogel, Walter. *Mexican Illegal Alien Workers in the United States.* Los Angeles: Institute of Industrial Relations, University of California, 1979. A short description of the activities and purpose of the Border Patrol. Gives a very brief survey of its history. Contains useful information on the attitudes of Mexican workers and their reasons for illegally entering the United States. Contains useful statistics concerning apprehensions and deportations. Focuses mainly on California. No bibliography or index.

Higham, John. *Strangers in the Land: Patterns of American Nativism, 1860-1925.* New York: Atheneum, 1975. The classic account of antiforeign and anti-immigrant hostility. Describes the attitudes of Texans and Californians to their neighbors south of the border but has little to add concerning the organization of the Border Patrol. Discussion is extensive concerning anti-Catholic motivations for restriction. Presents a firm denunciation of bigotry and prejudice. Nothing specific to say about the creation of the Border Patrol. Includes an index and a useful bibliography.

Perkins, Clifford A. *Border Patrol: With the U.S. Immigration Service on the Mexican Boundary, 1910-1954.* El Paso: Texas Western Press, 1978. The recollections and adventures of a former district officer. Discusses the founding, staffing, and organization of the Patrol and the contributions of some of its early members. Useful information on the education, attitudes, and responsibilities of officers. Told from the point of view of an officer who supported the mission of the Patrol. Many anecdotes concerning the methods used by enforcement officers. Has little to say in favor of open borders and free migration. No index or bibliography.

Reisler, Mark. *By the Sweat of Their Brow: Mexican Immigrant Labor in the United States, 1900-1940.* Westport, Conn.: Greenwood Press, 1976. A detailed, well-written history of Mexican immigration and the problem of illegal aliens. Discusses the organization and purpose of the Border Patrol and summarizes its accomplishments and problems. Provides a useful description of the attitudes of agricultural interests, labor unions, and immigrants. The only book covering this period of Border Patrol history. Presents the best discussion of the motivations of the growers and the restrictionists and has complete statistics on the impact of enforcement on the movement of people across the border. Has an extensive bibliography and an index.

Leslie V. Tischauser

Cross-References

Congress Prohibits Immigration of Illiterates over Age Sixteen (1917), p. 231; "Palmer Raids" Lead to Arrests and Deportations of Immigrants (1919), p. 258; The Immigration Act of 1921 Imposes a National Quota System (1921), p. 350; A U.S. Immigration Act Imposes Quotas Based on National Origins (1924), p. 383; HUAC Begins Investigating Suspected Communists (1938), p. 550.

A U.S. IMMIGRATION ACT IMPOSES QUOTAS BASED ON NATIONAL ORIGINS

Category of event: Immigrants' rights
Time: June, 1924
Locale: Washington, D.C.

The Immigration Act of 1924 created a quota system based on national origins that severely restricted the number of immigrants allowed to enter the United States

Principal personages:

ALBERT JOHNSON (1869-1957), a Republican representative from Washington State, chair of the House Committee on Immigration and Naturalization, a leading advocate of total restriction

HENRY CABOT LODGE (1850-1924), a Republican senator from Massachusetts, the key supporter of the national origins idea in the Senate

ADOLPH SABATH (1866-1952), a Democratic representative from Illinois, the leading spokesperson for the opponents of restriction and the national origins idea

CHARLES EVANS HUGHES (1862-1948), the U.S. secretary of state (1921-1925); argued against quotas and the ban on Japanese and Chinese immigration

CALVIN COOLIDGE (1872-1933), the thirtieth president of the United States, (1923-1929), an advocate of immigration restriction

Summary of Event

In 1921, Congress, for the first time in American history, passed a bill severely restricting immigration to the United States. The new system reversed a traditional policy of open admission. Based on national quotas, the law limited immigrants to 358,000 per year. Each nationality would be restricted to 3 percent of the total number the group had in the United States according to the 1910 census. Nations of the New World, including Mexico and Canada, were excluded from the quota system. Supporters hoped the measure would prevent southern and eastern Europeans from coming into the United States. Most of these people were "unfit" to be American, restrictionists argued, and would destroy American values and culture. The 1921 law led to a significant decline in immigrants, but the reduction was not enough to satisfy enemies of open borders. They sought and ultimately achieved even tighter restrictions three years later.

In his inaugural address, President Calvin Coolidge presented the case for tighter restrictions by arguing that new arrivals "should be limited to our capacity to absorb them into the ranks of good citizenship. America must be kept American." Coolidge voiced the views of many citizens by arguing that "biological laws" showed that people from northern Europe, mainly of English, Irish, and German descent (the

"Nordic" races), degenerated when mixed with southern and eastern Europeans. To promote growth and racial "purity," barriers to American society would have to be erected even higher.

In 1922, Congress had extended the 1921 law for two more years. Some of its supporters believed that the bill still allowed too many immigrants of "inferior" races. Representative Albert Johnson, chair of the House Committee on Immigration and Naturalization, wanted even tighter restrictions. In 1922, his committee began holding hearings and gathering proof to support tighter controls. Johnson appointed Harry H. Laughlin, an advocate of eugenics, as the committee's chief scientific adviser. Eugenicists believed that the human race could be improved through selective breeding, much as herds of cattle could be made stronger by eliminating the weak cows. Laughlin supervised the Eugenic Records Office in New York, which collected statistics on the hereditary traits of Americans. On frequent occasions, he testified before the Immigration Committee about the "bad breeding stock" that was being allowed to enter the United States. Studies by his organization showed, he claimed, that an overwhelming proportion of the inmates of prisons, mental hospitals, and poorhouses belonged to nationality groups coming from eastern and southern Europe, principally Italians, Poles, Jews, and Slavs. Crime and poverty were linked to inherited traits in populations and eventually could be bred out of existence by allowing only the "higher" races entrance to America. Use of the 1910 census had allowed too many "inferior people" into the United States, he concluded.

Based on this evidence, Johnson, in 1923, asked Congress to change the census base to 1890. Since most immigrants from southern and eastern Europe had come into the country after that date, this change would severely reduce their numbers. To further guarantee extremely limited immigration, Johnson also demanded that the quota be cut from 3 to 2 percent for each nationality. The proposal would cut Italian immigration from 41,000 to 4,000; Polish from 31,000 to 6,000; and Greek from 3,000 to 100. This proposal continued the total exclusion of Chinese and Japanese citizens, a policy which had been in effect since 1882 for China and 1907 for Japan.

Opposition to the reductions was minimal during committee debate. New evidence from intelligence tests given to recruits in World War I was used to help make the case for tighter restrictions. Johnson cited evidence from Army tests that claimed to show that the mean "mental age" for officers differed significantly by race. White officers averaged 17.26 years, Italians measured 11.8 years, southern African Americans 10.3 years, and German Americans 12.83 years. Other tests purported to show the lower level of intellectual accomplishment of "new" immigrant groups. The question of whether the tests were culturally biased was not raised. Most members of Congress accepted the results without challenge and concluded that to preserve the quality of American life, "lower races" had to be kept out. The argument made by Representative Adolph Sabath, one of Johnson's chief opponents, that restriction bred disunity in the United States by setting the peoples of northwestern Europe against southerners and easterners, had little effect on the result. Johnson's bill to change the census base to 1890 passed by a large majority. The Senate, however, balked at the House measure and established an entirely new method of controlling immigration.

Some opponents of immigration argued that, eventually, the quota system should be changed because it was based on the number of foreign-born in a given census year, so it did not reflect the current population. To replace this "biased" system, Senator David A. Reed proposed a "national origins" method of selection. By completing a study of the total American population, every citizen's or resident's ancestors would be counted and the new quotas would relate directly to an accurate picture of American society. With the support of Senator Henry Cabot Lodge, Reed got the Senate to adopt his idea with only six votes in opposition. According to the Senate proposal, a 2 percent quota based on the 1890 census would be in effect until 1927. Meanwhile, the Bureau of the Census and the commissioner-general of immigration would survey the population to determine national origins.

The new law reduced the yearly maximum immigration to 164,447 and limited immigration to 2 percent of the 1890 census for any nationality. After 1927, the annual quota for any nationality would be proportional to that nationality's representation in the U.S. population as of 1920. The total number of immigrants would be limited to 150,000. Nationality was to be determined by birthplace or by descent. A person of Polish or Hungarian heritage born within the borders of Germany, for example, would be counted as a German. The House agreed to this new system after a short debate, and President Coolidge signed it into law on May 26, 1924.

Impact of Event

The new law achieved its intended effect: severely and quickly reducing American immigration. The number of immigrants from Europe fell to fewer than 150,000 per year by 1929. Countries in the Western Hemisphere were not included in this new system as they had been under the 1921 law. Farmers in the southwestern United States depended on Mexican laborers to harvest their crops, and a proposal in the Senate to establish quotas for Central America failed by a wide margin. Canadians, who formed a large part of the work force in New England textile mills, also could enter the country free of any quota. Each nation of the world, with two exceptions, received a minimum allotment of one hundred immigrants to the United States regardless of whether it had a resident population in America. The Japanese and Chinese remained barred.

Secretary of State Charles Evans Hughes had asked Congress to repeal the ban on these two groups, but to no avail. As a result, bitterness toward America increased in both countries. The Japanese deeply resented being excluded deliberately and held a National Humiliation Day in Tokyo on July 1 as "hate America" rallies were mounted in dozens of Japanese cities. Relations between the two countries had improved slightly the previous year because of American assistance sent after the great Tokyo earthquake, but the continued ban on Japanese workers ended that brief period of good relations. The ban on Chinese and Japanese citizens would not be terminated by Congress until 1952.

Determining national origins was assigned to a committee of experts and proved a difficult responsibility; hence, implementation of the national origins criteria was delayed until 1929. No records of nationality had been kept before 1820, and the country of origin for individuals was not listed until 1850. The country of origin of foreign-born parents was listed only after 1890. The Committee on Linguistic and National Stocks in the Population of the United States, made up of social scientists and population experts, resorted to a crude statistical analysis of census figures from 1790. They determined origins by counting surnames listed on census manuscripts. "Smith," for example, was counted as English, although it once might have been the German "Schmidt" or even an African-American name. Using this method, the British ended up with 57 percent of the quota, whereas the 1890 census allowed them only 21 percent. German Americans and Scandinavians protested this method, since their numbers were slightly reduced. Among the major losers under the new method of counting immigrants were southern and eastern Europeans, who received only 12 percent of the allotments. Exemptions were difficult to get and were generally given only to wives and children of those who were already citizens of the United States. Economic catastrophe also worked to reduce the supply of potential migrants. The Great Depression had a devastating effect on movement of people throughout the world, as only the well-to-do could afford to leave their homelands. Very few countries filled their quotas in the 1930's. American consular officials in charge of issuing visas were advised by the State Department to be vigilant in keeping out potential paupers. Unemployment rates approaching 30 percent in the United States encouraged militancy of congresspersons and immigration officials in excluding foreigners, lest they add even more bodies to the relief lines.

Strict application of this system had deadly consequences for many German Jews. Because the new law did not distinguish between immigrants and refugees, thousands of Jews who applied for American visas were denied them by consular officials, who determined that the applicants were ineligible since they had little money and no jobs lined up, and thus appeared headed for the relief rolls. Ironically, the quota for Germany, around six thousand per year, was never filled. The Immigration and Naturalization Service refused to make any exceptions, and Congress supported the agency in its decisions. The idea that the United States stood as a refuge for the oppressed and dispossessed of the world had lost its meaning. Passage of the bill and implementation of the national origins idea represented the final and most significant victory for enemies of free and open American borders. In the 1930's, for the first time in American history, more people left the country than entered.

Bibliography

American Council of Learned Societies. "Report of the Committee on Linguistic and National Stocks in the Population of the United States." In *Annual Report of the American Historical Association by the American Historical Society.* Washington, D.C.: Government Printing Office, 1932. Contains the findings of the committee assigned to determine the national origins of the population of the United

States. Useful for discovering the methods used by social scientists to circumvent problems resulting from lack of information in early census data.

Bennett, Marion T. *American Immigration Policies.* Washington, D.C.: Public Affairs Press, 1963. Although written from a prorestriction point of view, this book contains useful information concerning immigration laws. There is a useful summary of the national origins debate in Congress and other provisions of the 1924 immigration law. Includes an index and an extensive bibliography.

Divine, Robert. *American Immigration Policy, 1924-1952.* New Haven, Conn.: Yale University Press, 1957. An interesting, detailed account of the legislative history of the 1924 immigration law. There is a detailed summary of the attitudes of both restrictionists and their opponents. The reasons behind the move to a national origins system are described and criticized. Written from an antirestriction point of view. Contains an index and complete bibliography.

Garis, Roy. *Immigration Restriction.* New York: Macmillan, 1927. Written by a Vanderbilt University economist who supported restriction and the national origins system. An old work, but useful for portraying a prorestrictionist perspective. Some of the charts and graphs in the book were used by the Senate and House committees to support a change from the 1921 method of using the census. Contains an index and a bibliography prepared by the Library of Congress for Congress.

Higham, John. *Strangers in the Land: Patterns of American Nativism, 1860-1925.* New York: Atheneum, 1975. The classic account of antiforeign and anti-immigrant hostility in the United States from the Civil War to the imposition of the national origins system. Gives a complete account of the congressional struggle for immigration restriction and presents a detailed analysis of the 1924 legislative victory. Includes an index and a very helpful bibliography on its subject.

Howland, Charles P. *Survey of American Foreign Relations, 1929.* New Haven, Conn.: Yale University Press, 1929. A good, concise history of restriction legislation. Especially useful since it contains a record of the reaction to American immigration policy in the Far East and Europe.

Lipset, Seymour M., and Earl Raab. *The Politics of Unreason: Right-Wing Extremism in America, 1790-1970.* New York: Harper & Row, 1970. Deals with bigotry and the attitudes of those calling for restriction. Has a lengthy bibliography and an index. Chiefly useful for understanding the psychology of bigotry and the political values of those associated with anti-immigrant hatred.

Solomon, Barbara. *Ancestors and Immigrants.* Cambridge, Mass.: Harvard University Press, 1956. A history of the Immigration Restriction League of Boston. Ends before passage of the national origins act, but its description of Henry Cabot Lodge's attitudes toward immigration is very useful in helping to understand the restrictionist point of view. Contains an index and a short bibliography.

Leslie V. Tischauser

Cross-References

Japan Protests Segregation of Japanese in California Schools (1906), p. 81; Congress Prohibits Immigration of Illiterates over Age Sixteen (1917), p. 231; "Palmer Raids" Lead to Arrests and Deportations of Immigrants (1919), p. 258; The Immigration Act of 1921 Imposes a National Quota System (1921), p. 350; Congress Establishes a Border Patrol (1924), p. 377.

HITLER WRITES *MEIN KAMPF*

Categories of event: Atrocities and war crimes; racial and ethnic rights
Time: June-October, 1924 (volume 1), and July-August, 1925 (volume 2)
Locale: Landsberg Fortress and Berchtesgaden, Germany

In Mein Kampf, *Hitler outlined the plan he later followed to eliminate many of the basic rights of large segments of the populations of Europe*

Principal personages:
ADOLF HITLER (1889-1945), the Führer (leader) of the Nazi Party at the time *Mein Kampf* was published; dictator of Germany (1933-1945)
RUDOLF HESS (1894-1987), the deputy Führer of the Nazi Party who helped Hitler articulate many of his ideas
HOUSTON STEWART CHAMBERLAIN (1855-1927), a philosopher and historian whose work influenced Hitler's own worldview
ALFRED ROSENBERG (1893-1946), the official "philosopher" of Nazism, later commissioner of the conquered territories in the Soviet Union

Summary of Event

On November 8-9, 1923, Adolf Hitler and a number of his followers tried unsuccessfully to seize control of the Bavarian government as a prelude to overthrowing the German republic. Hitler and many other Nazis were captured and tried for high treason in Munich during the early months of 1924. After his conviction, a judge sentenced Hitler to five years' imprisonment in Landsberg Fortress, just south of Munich. Hitler actually spent less than a year in prison, gaining parole just before Christmas in 1924. Hitler used the leisure time provided by his incarceration to dictate a semiautobiographical political testament to his private secretary, Rudolf Hess, and his chauffeur and former company sergeant, Emil Maurice.

Hitler originally intended to entitle the book "Four and a half years of struggle against lies, stupidity, and cowardice," but another associate, Max Amann, convinced him to shorten the title to *Mein Kampf (My Struggle*; English translation 1933), subtitled *A Reckoning.* The book outlined Hitler's plan to overthrow the existing government of Germany and create a new reich based on a racial, eugenicist, and social Darwinist interpretation of history which the author had developed from wide but indiscriminate reading. Hitler unapologetically called for aggressive war to conquer living space for his new reich's excess population, for denying citizenship and civil rights in his new Germany to all "non-Aryans," for eliminating all political parties that opposed his will and thus destroying political freedom for all Germans, for implementing eugenics policies that would result in the mandatory sterilization of all persons judged physically, mentally, or morally inferior, and for enforcing a rigid morality on the entire population. *Mein Kampf* reserved special treatment for the Jews of Germany and Europe. Hitler considered the Jews to be the cause of most of the world's problems. Accordingly, he expressed the intent to exclude them from the cultural and political life of his rejuvenated Germany and to deny them economic freedom as well. Taken in total, *Mein Kampf* is the most complete rejection of the concept of basic human rights ever written.

The autobiographical sections of Hitler's book provide clues as to how he arrived at his radical positions and to his own justifications. Klara Hitler gave birth to her fourth child, Adolf, on April 20, 1889, in the small town of Braunau in Austria. Hitler's father, Alois, was a middle-level bureaucratic official in the Austro-Hungarian customs service. The elder Hitler intended for Adolf eventually to pursue a career in the bureaucracy and sent him to a suitable preparatory school. The younger Hitler did not excel at his studies, however, except for gymnastics and history. His history teacher was an ardent pan-German nationalist who advocated that all Germans (including those within the Dual Kingdom of Austria-Hungary) be united in one great fatherland. These early history lessons were apparently the ultimate source of Hitler's extreme nationalism.

Four years after his father's death in 1903, Hitler convinced his mother to allow him to move to Vienna to study art without graduating from high school. After being rejected by his chosen art school, Hitler stayed on in Vienna. He began to read widely in the Vienna library and came into contact with the Viennese gutter press as well. He was greatly impressed with the history and philosophy of Houston Stewart Chamberlain, who presented a grandiose racial interpretation of history arguing that the Aryan race had been responsible for almost all the great technical and cultural achievements of history. Chamberlain's work also contained a mystical element suggesting that Aryans had a duty to lift humankind toward some unknown purpose decreed by God. These ideas had an enormous influence on Hitler and are clearly reflected in *Mein Kampf.*

During his years in Vienna, Hitler also encountered the judeophobic gutter press that denounced all Jews as destroyers of culture, parasites who were responsible for most of the evils of modern society. Hitler also learned the potential political power of anti-Semitism through observing the popularity of Vienna's judeophobic mayor, Karl Lueger. The most recurrent theme in the first volume of *Mein Kampf* is Hitler's conviction that Germany could be rebuilt only if the power and influence of the Jews were eliminated. Hitler also encountered and came to detest Marxism while living in Vienna. He came to regard Marxism as being nothing more than a Jewish ploy to seduce German workers away from their fellow Germans, and thus resolved in *Mein Kampf* that Marxism must be destroyed. In the second volume of his book (devoted primarily to the foreign policy of his new reich), he combined his anti-Marxism with the need to conquer new living space for the German nation, advocating an invasion of the Soviet Union that would allow the annexation of vast territories in the Ukraine and at the same time crush Marxism at its foundation in Moscow.

Hitler also encountered the writings of German eugenicists during the period 1907-1914, although exactly what he may have read is uncertain. The modern eugenics movement began in England during the latter half of the nineteenth century, fueled by the works of Francis Galton, a cousin of Charles Darwin. In several influential books published between 1869 and 1889, Galton advocated applying knowledge of heredity to the improvement of the human race. He suggested that selective breeding techniques long employed to produce superior livestock strains be adopted to elevate the mental and physical qualities of future generations of humankind, thus giving evolution a helping hand. Galton's ideas spread slowly throughout the Western world and eventually influenced legislation in many countries (including the United States) that established mandatory sterilization of mentally and physically defective individuals and restricted immigration.

All these ideas internalized by Hitler before 1914 were reinforced by his experiences during World War I and the German revolution that followed it. Hitler became more convinced than ever that a gang of Marxist and Jewish traitors had deliberately betrayed Germany for their own gain. The final element of Hitler's philosophy came to him through Alfred Rosenberg, a Baltic German who fled from the Bolshevik Revolution in Russia and came to Munich in 1918. Rosenberg brought with him a document entitled *The Protocols of the Elders of Zion*, which contained a purported Jewish plan for world domination. Hitler's view of the world and human history was now complete. The Jews, an evil, parasitic, and destructive race, had deliberately provoked World War I in order to destroy the superior Aryan race and advance their own plans of world conquest. International Marxism was simply a creation of the Jews meant to weaken the other races of the world. Jewish economic, political, and cultural power must be destroyed in Germany and Europe as a prelude to Aryan realization of the special mission decreed for them by the creator. If one accepts these premises, as Hitler did, then the massive demolition of human rights advocated in *Mein Kampf* is justified.

Impact of Event

Mein Kampf eventually sold more than ten million copies in sixteen languages. Many people in Germany and the rest of the Western world were convinced that Hitler's programs would produce a better society, even though they might not agree with every particular idea expressed in the book. After he came to power in Germany in 1933, Hitler proceeded to implement the policies advocated in his book with a consistency rarely seen among politicians and with disastrous effects for millions of people.

By 1935, Hitler had dissolved all political parties except his own. The Nazis arrested the leaders of many of the German political parties, especially the Marxist parties, and incarcerated them in concentration camps. Hitler also ordered the dissolution of German trade unions and outlawed collective bargaining. Concurrently, Nazi economic policies managed to extricate Germany from the Great Depression and to provide jobs and an improved standard of living for most Germans. The loss of political freedom seemed, to many of those living in the new reich, a small price to pay for economic prosperity and the new national pride engendered by the Nazis.

In 1935, the docile German parliament passed the first of what came to be called the Nuremberg Laws, which systematically deprived the Jews in Germany of their civil rights—first revoking their citizenship and expelling them from the civil service, then limiting their access to education and excluding them from ownership of newspapers and other media. Eventually, during World War II, the Nazis sent almost all the Jews of Germany and Nazi-occupied Europe to concentration camps, where they were used as slave labor under very harsh conditions. Hundreds of thousands of Europe's Jews died in those camps, including many who were executed simply because they were Jews, in a nightmarish realization of the eugenicist call to eliminate inferior human breeding stock. Radical eugenics was also applied to the Aryan population of Germany during the first years of World War II, when thousands of Germans deemed incurably insane or terminally ill were put to death in German hospitals by German doctors.

Many "Aryan" Germans fared little better than the Jews under the Nazi rule. Homosexuals also found themselves in forced labor camps, as did Gypsies, members of the clergy who refused to follow the Nazi party line, and "social malcontents" who refused to conform to Hitler's views of proper behavior. An entire generation of German children underwent indoctrination with Hitler's ideas during their forced membership in the Hitler Youth.

Hitler's foreign policy was a major factor in the outbreak of World War II. During that war, he ordered his armies to invade the Soviet Union, true to the course of action outlined in *Mein Kampf.* Intending to crush Marxism and conquer living space for the German people, Hitler's invasion resulted in the deaths of more than twenty million Russians and perhaps six million Germans. Ultimately, the war resulted in the near-destruction of the German nation and the German people—exactly the reverse of what Hitler promised to achieve. The basic antihumanitarian ideas in *Mein Kampf* ultimately resulted in one of the greatest disasters in history for human rights.

Bibliography

Baynes, Norman H., ed. *The Speeches of Adolf Hitler, April 1922-August 1939.* New York: H. Fertig, 1969. Includes translations of all Hitler's important speeches from 1922 to the outbreak of World War II. The various speeches, many of them very long, elaborate and expand upon the topics emphasized in *Mein Kampf* in language often much more graphic than the turgid prose of the book. Baynes's commentary is perceptive and illuminating.

Bracher, Karl Dietrich. *The Germany Dictatorship: The Origins, Structure, and Effects of National Socialism.* New York: Praeger, 1970. The definitive work on Nazi Germany. Contains chapters concerning the origins of Hitler's ideology, the writing of and meaning of the ideas expressed in *Mein Kampf,* and the effects of those ideas in practice. The bibliography on Hitler and Nazism is the most complete in English. Bracher offers insights into the nature of National Socialism and into Hitler's personality not available in any other work.

Hauner, Milan. *Hitler: A Chronology of His Life and Time.* New York: St. Martin's

Press, 1983. A very detailed chronology of the major events in Hitler's life and the rise and fall of National Socialism in Germany. Quotes extensively from *Mein Kampf* and from Hitler's speeches to illuminate the ideological underpinnings of many of the otherwise enigmatic policies adopted by Hitler and the Nazis. The index is not as comprehensive as might be desired, and most of the bibliographical entries are for German-language sources.

Hilberg, Raul. *The Destruction of the European Jews.* Chicago: Quadrangle, 1961. Despite many inaccuracies and flawed interpretations, still a comprehensive account of Nazi treatment of the Jews of Germany and Nazi-occupied Europe. Graphically illustrates how the ideas Hitler expressed in *Mein Kampf* led directly to unspeakable suffering for millions of people. Contains an excellent bibliography and an adequate index.

Hitler, Adolf. *Mein Kampf.* Translated by Ralph Manheim. Reprint. Boston: Houghton Mifflin, 1971. No commentary can illustrate Hitler's ideas as well as *Mein Kampf* itself. Hitler's clumsy and often pompous prose does not prevent the reader from understanding that Hitler's program called for the destruction of many basic human rights, including freedom of the press, freedom of speech, freedom of association, free enterprise, and sexual freedom. The reader may never understand, however, why these ideas had such great attraction for so many people. Manheim's translation is the best available, and his subject index is adequate.

Maser, Werner. *Hitler's Mein Kampf: An Analysis.* London: Heinemann, 1974. Shows that many of the autobiographical details in Hitler's account of his early life are inaccurate and misleading. Tries (often unconvincingly) to explain many of the obscure references in Hitler's book and to extrapolate the sources of some of the ideas expressed therein. Concludes that Hitler tried dogmatically to implement all the major programs he espoused in *Mein Kampf* and that his ideas did not change substantially from the time the book was written until his death. The bibliography contains mostly German-language references, but the index is helpful.

Pulzer, Peter G. *The Rise of Political Anti-Semitism in Germany and Austria: 1867-1918.* New York: John Wiley, 1964. Examines the origins and evolution of anti-Jewish feeling immediately before and during Hitler's formative years. Shows that the ideas concerning Jews in *Mein Kampf* were by no means unique to Hitler, and in fact were widely shared. Also analyzes the reasons why judeophobia became so widespread in Germany and Austria. Good bibliography and index.

Toland, John. *Adolf Hitler.* New York: Praeger, 1976. The most accurate, the most comprehensive, and the most objective of the many biographies of Hitler. Devotes many pages to analyzing the ideas Hitler expressed in *Mein Kampf* and echoed in his speeches. Exhaustive bibliography and excellent index.

Paul Madden

Cross-References

Germans Revolt and Form Socialist Government (1918), p. 241; Mussolini Seizes

MUSSOLINI SEIZES DICTATORIAL POWERS IN ITALY

Category of event: Political freedom
Time: 1925-1926
Locale: Italy

Benito Mussolini's seizure of power in the 1920's led to a dictatorship that destroyed political freedom in Italy and threatened international peace and stability during the 1930's

> *Principal personages:*
> BENITO MUSSOLINI (1883-1945), the founder and leader of the National Fascist Party; called on by King Victor Emmanuel III in October, 1922, to become prime minister of Italy
> VICTOR EMMANUEL III (1869-1947), the king of Italy from 1900 to 1946
> GIACOMO MATTEOTTI (1885-1924), an attorney and socialist representative in the Italian parliament

Summary of Event

Italy made slow but notable progress in human rights during the first decades of the twentieth century. Under a constitutional monarchy, Italians shaped a limited parliamentary democracy similar to those of other Western European nations. By the early 1900's, the working class had won the right to organize and strike. Socialist labor unions vigorously advanced both economic and political goals. A lively, diverse press gave voice to a wide range of political opinion, although the more radical publications were often restrained by government censorship and the moral condemnation of the Catholic church. Universal male suffrage, enacted in 1913, underscored the nation's political progress. Women, although denied the vote, acquired important legal and property rights in 1919. The emergence of mass political parties after World War I heralded the prospects for democratic reform.

The post-World War I years offered new opportunities to create a more equitable, democratic society. The war also jeopardized Italy's progress by creating grave economic and political instability. Conservative government leaders, business people, and landowners feared a communist revolution similar to that of Russia in 1917. Benito Mussolini's National Fascist Party compounded the political crisis with its revolutionary program and its violence against political opponents. Mussolini, a former socialist party leader and newspaper editor, had founded the Fascist movement immediately after the war. His virulent nationalism, anticommunism, antidemocratic politics, and appeal to violence attracted a large following of war veterans and political malcontents. Fascist paramilitary units, known as *squadristi*, carried out "punitive expeditions" against their rivals, primarily the socialist party and labor unions. Their brutal assaults and destruction of property, often unopposed by local government authorities, brought the country to the brink of civil war in the early 1920's.

The political crisis in Italy culminated in October, 1922, with the "March on Rome." Benito Mussolini orchestrated this threat to occupy the nation's capital with his party's paramilitary forces. While threatening armed conflict, he negotiated with influential business and political leaders and pressured King Victor Emmanuel III to invite him to form a new government. Mussolini assumed the position of prime minister and organized a coalition cabinet, filling the ministerial posts with members of his own and other conservative parties. Although the Fascists were a minority party, they achieved political dominance in the parliament following the elections of April, 1924. Under a new election law, the party receiving the most votes was given two-thirds of the seats in the Chamber of Deputies.

Mussolini's new government contended with a large, but divided, parliamentary opposition on the political left—democrats, socialists, and communists. One of his most persistent and outspoken adversaries was Giacomo Matteotti, leader of the reformist socialist party and a member of Parliament. Matteotti gained a reputation as Mussolini's most dangerous critic by carefully documenting specific cases of abuse and corruption in the government. His report on the 1924 elections revealed widespread election fraud and violence by the Fascist party. Despite personal threats from Fascist leaders, including Mussolini, Matteotti continued to denounce the government from his seat in Parliament and to collect information about financial improprieties of government officials.

Matteotti's disappearance on June 10 immediately raised allegations of government involvement, and several witnesses later verified his kidnapping by Fascist *squadristi*. Although Matteotti's body was not discovered until mid-August, most of the public assumed that his abduction and murder had been sanctioned at the highest level of Fascist party leadership, perhaps by Mussolini himself. The Matteotti affair provoked a spontaneous outpouring of popular protest against the government. Labor unions organized political strikes and public demonstrations. More than one hundred deputies from opposition parties refused to participate in parliamentary proceedings, declaring that Mussolini had lost all moral and political right to govern. The "Aventine Secession"—alluding to similar protests during the ancient Roman Republic—gave the outward appearance of solidarity on the political left. Even leading conservatives, who had previously supported Mussolini's government, now called for his resignation.

The overwhelming protest initially paralyzed Mussolini, belying his reputation as a man of action. He attempted to mollify the political right—the king, influential businesspeople, and senators—by reshuffling his cabinet and replacing Fascist ministers with well-respected conservatives. This compromising outraged Fascist militants, especially the local party leaders who demanded a "second wave" of violence to destroy the remnants of political opposition and the pretense of parliamentary government. They confronted Mussolini and threatened him personally in several heated party meetings. Defiance to his authority within the Fascist Party as well as in the government compelled him to take action.

On January 3, 1925, Mussolini made a dramatic speech in the Chamber of Deputies in which he assumed complete responsibility for the violence committed by the Fascists, including the murder of Matteotti. He challenged the members of the parliament to impeach him, and with a threatening overtone announced that the situation would be "cleared up all along the line" in the following forty-eight hours. This speech marked the beginning of Mussolini's dictatorship. Within hours, local authorities began closing down the meeting halls of opposition groups and suppressing antigovernment publications. More than one hundred political dissidents were arrested. The *squadristi* unleashed a "second wave" of violence, destroying opposition presses and using intimidation and physical assaults to silence protest. The anti-Fascist opposition, contentious, divided, and unable to agree on a course of action, offered little effective resistance to Mussolini's seizure of power.

Mussolini's personal dictatorship gradually took shape over the next two years. He established his authoritarian rule through rigorous enforcement of existing laws, new restrictive legislation, and special executive decrees. After several unsuccessful assassination attempts against Mussolini in 1925 and 1926, the government passed a series of "exceptional decrees" that formally outlawed all political parties, banned anti-Fascist organizations and publications, and cancelled all passports. The participants in the Aventine Secession were stripped of their parliamentary immunity and barred from taking their seats in the Chamber of Deputies. Local elected governments were eliminated and replaced by state-appointed administrators.

The exceptional decrees created the Special Tribunal for the Defense of the State, a military court that functioned outside the normal judicial process and allowed the arbitrary arrest and imprisonment of more than five thousand government opponents. The death penalty, which had been abolished in 1890, was reintroduced. Giovanni Amendola, Piero Gobetti, Antonio Gramsci, and several other prominent anti-Fascists died as a result of street beatings or lengthy prison terms. Hundreds of others fled the country in order to escape the *squadristi* violence or imprisonment.

The government decrees sanctioned the operations of a secret state police, identified by the sinister, but apparently meaningless, acronym OVRA. Under the efficient direction of Arturo Bocchini, the police monitored antigovernment activity and used their authority to place individuals under house arrest or send them into "internal exile" in remote villages or on coastal islands. Mandatory identity cards allowed the police to control personal movement, employment, and access to public services. By 1927, Mussolini's regime had eliminated most vestiges of political freedom in Italy. Discarding the parliamentary designation of prime minister, he referred to his position as "head of state" and adopted the title *Il Duce*—the Leader. Through his dictatorship, he sought to fulfill his own maxim: "Everything in the State, nothing outside the State, nothing against the State."

Impact of Event

Mussolini's seizure of power marked a disturbing political development in the modern world. It repudiated more than a century of European progress toward greater political democracy and individual liberty and introduced the term "totalitarian" into modern political vocabulary. Although Mussolini's regime never achieved the totalitarianism of Adolf Hitler's Germany or Joseph Stalin's Soviet Union, the results of his dictatorial rule proved devastating to a free society. The ban on political parties and elections destroyed democratic politics; the abolition of labor organizations stripped workers of their right to seek economic redress; and the purging of the state bureaucracy and the courts ensured total government acquiescence to Mussolini's authority.

The establishment of the Special Tribunal allowed the regime to bypass regular judicial procedures and arrest, imprison, or exile thousands. Many Italians defied the government by leaving the country on their own accord. During the 1920's and 1930's, Italy lost some of its most talented citizens to immigration, including the nuclear physicist Enrico Fermi and the renowned orchestral conductor Arturo Toscanini. The elimination of a free press, strict control of the media and education, and the use of secret police to stifle political dissent further eroded individual freedoms.

The goal of creating a totalitarian state represented an unprecedented degree of government intrusion into the daily lives of citizens. Even organized sports, recreational programs, youth groups, artistic activities, and professional associations fell under government supervision. Only the conservative institutions that lent timely support to Mussolini in his first years—the military, the monarchy, and the Catholic church—retained a large degree of autonomy under the Fascist regime.

Mussolini's success in Italy inspired similar "fascist" movements in several European countries. Each had its own identity, but they all shared an affinity for political violence and an abiding contempt for democracy and individual civil rights. In Germany, the Nazis imitated and refined the methods of the Italian Fascists. Their success brought Adolf Hitler to power in 1933 and marked the beginning of an unparalleled disaster for human rights and international peace.

Mussolini's belligerent foreign policy effectively destabilized international relations at a time when most nations were seeking ways to ensure peace. In the years following World War I, European diplomats had worked diligently to limit armed conflict through the newly founded League of Nations, naval disarmament treaties, and collective security agreements. With his invasion of Ethiopia in 1935, Mussolini challenged the League of Nations and revealed its impotence against military aggression. He defied the Geneva Convention's ban on poison gas and used it with devastating results against Ethiopian troops. His military assistance to Francisco Franco in the Spanish Civil War helped destroy democratic government in Spain and install a dictatorial regime that remained in power for more than thirty-five years. Mussolini's military success in Africa encouraged Hitler's ambitious plans for German territorial expansion. With the Pact of Steel in 1939, the two men cemented a military alliance that brought on the greatest human catastrophe in modern history, World War II.

Bibliography

Cannistraro, Philip V., ed. *Historical Dictionary of Fascist Italy.* Westport, Conn.: Greenwood Press, 1982. The standard reference for individuals, institutions, and events in Italy under Fascist rule. Includes informative entries on the anti-Fascist movement. The appendix contains a complete listing of government ministers who served in the Fascist government.

Collier, Richard. *Duce! A Biography of Benito Mussolini.* New York: Viking Press, 1971. A lively biography, somewhat sympathetic to its subject. Collier casts Mussolini in the tragic-heroic mold and draws from several hundred interviews to give his biography an informal, narrative style.

De Grand, Alexander. *Italian Fascism: Its Origins and Development.* 1982. 2d ed. Lincoln: University of Nebraska Press, 1989. A concise, thoughtful, and well-organized introduction to Italian Fascism. The bibliographical essay has been updated for the second edition and is particularly helpful for those not familiar with the historiography of Italian Fascism.

Lyttelton, Adrian. *The Seizure of Power in Italy, 1919-1929.* 1973. 2d ed. London: Weidenfeld & Nicolson, 1987. A brilliant study, the best work available in any language on Mussolini's "seizure of power." Lyttelton focuses on the intricate personal and institutional relationships that brought Mussolini to power and maintained his dictatorship for almost twenty years.

Mack Smith, Denis. *Mussolini.* New York: Alfred A. Knopf, 1982. The best of several modern biographies available in English. Thoroughly researched from a wide range of archival and secondary sources. The author's highly critical, even derisive, assessment of Mussolini strips away the mythology of *Il Duce* and Fascist revolution to reveal a corrupt, unscrupulous, and often inept political leader.

Matteotti, Giacomo. *The Fascisti Exposed: A Year of Fascist Domination.* New York: Howard Fertig, 1969. First published clandestinely in 1923, Matteotti's report documents in detail the terrorism of the *squadristi*, the complicity of government authorities in the Fascist violence, and the political corruption during Mussolini's first year in power. This impressive exposé established Matteotti's reputation as Mussolini's most dangerous critic and eventually led to his murder by Fascist agents.

Salvemini, Gaetano. *The Fascist Dictatorship in Italy.* New York: Howard Fertig, 1967. First published in 1927 by one of the most important anti-Fascist historians, Salvemini's work weaves pointed commentary with extracts from contemporary documents (some taken from Matteotti's exposé) to underscore the criminality of the Fascist movement and its leadership.

——————————. *The Origins of Fascism in Italy.* New York: Harper & Row, 1973. Written in 1942 and based on Salvemini's lectures at Harvard University, this book remained unpublished until after the author's death. Salvemini goes beyond his earlier polemic against the Fascist regime and explores the conditions in Italy that made Fascism possible. Chapter 26 provides a good summary of the political infringements resulting from the creation of Mussolini's totalitarian state.

Seton-Watson, Christopher. *Italy from Liberalism to Fascism, 1870-1925.* London: Methuen, 1967. Although somewhat dated, this remains the best survey of modern Italy up to the Fascist period. Seton-Watson traces the triumph of Fascism to the failure of liberalism during the post-World War I political crisis. Includes an annotated bibliography and a helpful reference listing of the many Italian governments and their cabinet ministers during the years 1871-1925.

Michael F. Hembree

Cross-References

Hitler Writes *Mein Kampf* (1924), p. 389; Germany Attempts to Restructure the Versailles Treaty (1925), p. 423; Hitler Uses Reichstag Fire to Suspend Civil and Political Liberties (1933), p. 480; Nazi Concentration Camps Go into Operation (1933), p. 491; Corporatism Comes to Paraguay and the Americas (1936), p. 533; Nazi War Criminals Are Tried in Nuremberg (1945), p. 667; Italy Legalizes Abortion (1978), p. 1988.

WOMEN'S RIGHTS IN INDIA
UNDERGO A DECADE OF CHANGE

Category of event: Women's rights
Time: 1925-1935
Locale: India

The status of women in traditional Indian society underwent substantial change as a result of specific legislative measures as well as the growth of social consciousness

Principal personages:

RAJA RAM MOHAN ROY (1774-1833), a prominent social reformer of the nineteenth century, and founder of the "Brahmo Samaj," a reformist organization

LORD WILLIAM BENTINCK (1774-1839), the governor-general of India, one of those responsible for abolishing *sati*

MAHATMA GANDHI (1869-1948), a prominent nationalist leader and social reformer

ANNIE BESANT (1847-1933), a British theosophist, active in the struggle for freedom and women's rights

Summary of Event

The status of women in India traditionally had been defined by the patrilineal structure of society. Religion and custom provided the guidelines for restricting women's rights and prescribing their conduct. Hindu and Muslim women were equally affected by these factors, although in somewhat different ways. Muslim women were subject to many strictures, the most visible being segregation of female children and adults and the practice of *purdah* ("curtain"), which required Muslim women to be veiled when in public. This custom eventually spread to upper-class Hindu women in northern India. Hindu women were governed by the tenets of their religion, which restricted their rights regarding inheritance, possession of property, and divorce, among others.

By the nineteenth century, the cruel suppression of fundamental rights was accepted as a norm of society rather than a cause for concern. The vast majority of women had no control over their destinies. Women had no choice in selecting their husbands; this was done by the family or community, often at birth. Child marriages were widely practiced, and polygamy was prevalent among several groups in society. Marriages were governed by caste and community restrictions, and intercaste marriages were not recognized. A particularly abused custom was that of dowry and its attendant assumption that the bride's family would pay for a lavish wedding. The birth of several daughters was a financial liability, and female infanticide was not unknown. Many tragic incidents resulted from the inability of some families to meet these often unreasonable expenses. The practices of dowry payment and extravagant weddings drew public attention and protest when the press reported an incident in 1914 in which a young Bengali girl committed suicide. Upon learning that her father had mortgaged his home in order to provide for her dowry, the young woman set fire to herself. The popular indignation aroused by this story led to a short-lived trend of refusing dowries; however, in the absence of specific legislation to outlaw the practice, the custom continued as before.

The practice of *sati* (widow burning) continued in many northern communities despite the 1829 legislation declaring it to be illegal. The condition of widows in society reflected the inhumanity of custom. Even if a widow were allowed to survive her husband's death, she was treated as a menial in the household and denied adequate food and simple pleasures such as new clothing, ornaments, and entertainment. The practice of shaving off a widow's hair was part of this denial of life. Thus, widows could either literally die with their spouses or endure a living death. This was the logical outcome of a system in which the wife's dependence on her husband was so complete that his death left her no alternative means of survival.

Efforts to change this state of affairs intensified during the nineteenth century, when the spirit of social reform gained momentum along with a rise in public consciousness. During this period, the energies of several individuals and organizations were directed toward an improvement of conditions of society in general and women in particular. Many significant changes occurred during this period, partly as a result of the promotion of social causes by various reform organizations and partly as a result of the passage of specific legislation to make some of the inhumane practices illegal and punishable. The change in public opinion toward women's rights far outpaced the actual legislation that was passed. The growing involvement of women of all social classes in the freedom struggle also gave impetus to the forces of reform in society.

Many of the legislative measures that were proposed failed to pass or were postponed for later consideration, but enough legislation did pass to set a trend in equalizing the status of women with that of men. Even the unsuccessful measures reflected a variety and scope that ranged from Viththalbhai Patel's bill to recognize intercaste marriage (1918) to the civil marriage legislation (1911, 1922) that was eventually passed in modified form in 1923. Monogamy and divorce bills introduced at this time also failed initially. Opposition to reform came from conservative elements of society.

The cause of women's education had been greatly enhanced by the government's resolution on educational policy in 1904. Commenting on the lack of encouragement and limited opportunities for educational and professional training of girls, the report cited the noticeably small proportion of females—less than 10 percent of enrollment—in public schools. The pace of change in this area was slow. The percentage of girls attending educational institutions had risen only slightly, from 1.58 percent in 1886 to 2.49 percent in 1901. The founding of Lady Hardinge Medical College in Delhi and the Women's University in Poona in 1916 initiated a new phase in the opportunities available to women.

A number of other progressive measures contributed to the currents of change. These included a law restricting dowries (1916), the establishment of several children's homes following the lead taken by the Indian Women's Association (1923), and the founding of the Birth Control League (1924) to address issues of population control. Equally important was a measure that curbed the prostitution (1925) that flourished under the shelter of *Devadasi*, the traditional institution of temple service. Muslim ladies took a decisive step when they decided to abolish *purdah* by a resolution adopted at the All India Women's Congress in 1928.

Two acts of legislative reform stand out in the decade of change from 1925 to 1935. The first was the Sarda Act of 1929, which tackled the issue of child marriage. It applied equally to all religious and caste groups and expressly forbade the marriage of girls under the age of fourteen and boys under the age of eighteen. Child marriage was made an offense punishable by imprisonment, a substantial fine, or sometimes both. Anyone identified as performing, directing, or in any way encouraging child marriage was subject to severe penalties. This included parents and any male over the age of twenty-one who was a party to the marriage. This represented a tremendous achievement in the struggle for women's emancipation.

The Government of India Act of 1935 was the second measure that resulted in significant gains for Indian women. Several provisions of the act served to extend the political rights of women. A number of seats were allocated specifically for women in the federal and provincial assemblies and the Federal Council of State. A total of forty-one seats were set aside in the assemblies of eleven provinces. In addition, nine seats were allocated for women in the Federal Assembly and six seats in the Federal Council of State. The numbers may not appear to be large, but their symbolic value was substantial, as an acknowledgment of women's right to represent and to be represented in government. Women could at last participate in the decisionmaking process themselves rather than rely on the efforts of male legislators. A further gain was achieved by the amendment of qualifications for exercising the franchise. This enabled more than six million women to exercise their political prerogatives.

Impact of Event

The immediate impact of these changes was to free women from the confines of the religious codes and traditional custom. Through a process of steady consolidation, some of the objectives of the social reformers of the nineteenth century were finally realized. The decade of change represented one significant phase in the ongoing process of social change. The most valuable gain was a recognition that a new social order could not be established while a large proportion of the population continued to occupy a subordinate status. The value of women as a human resource was being acknowledged by enlightened individuals, both British and Indian. Women themselves, through their organizations and through their active participation in the civil disobedience movement for independence, demonstrated their capability for helping their own cause. Women of all social classes and religious persuasions set aside their traditional roles to participate in the freedom struggle alongside men, endured imprisonment, and simultaneously continued to organize themselves to deal with women's issues. The role of women in the freedom struggle was both a consequence of and an impetus for social change.

In order to achieve equality, women had to challenge some of the fundamental assumptions underlying the social order as it had functioned for centuries. The patrilineal structure and caste system had drawn their legitimacy from ascribed status. This created closed groups that were ranked in a specific hierarchy and maintained through rules for permissible marriages. Most of these assumptions were challenged by the reforms relating to the position of women in society, since these reforms introduced the validity of achieved status in a traditional culture. This, in turn, presaged the weakening of the caste system over time. Even the "untouchables" could look to the position taken by women as precedent for change.

The groups that benefited the most were the educated, the urban dwellers, and the upper classes. The poor, the rural inhabitants, and the uneducated continued to lag behind. The success of the reforms cannot therefore be stated in easily measurable terms. Public attitudes and practices far outweighed the specific acts of legislation that were passed. This explains the persistence of some customs despite statutes declaring them to be illegal, and it also explains why women could play an active role in the freedom struggle despite the presence of traditional barriers. Attitudes varied according to social class and education. While the upper and middle classes pressed ahead with reforms, many of the less advantaged required the inspired leadership of individuals such as Mahatma Gandhi. The seeds had already been sown by earlier reformers such as Raja Ram Mohan Roy and Sir William Bentinck, whose anguish at the practice of customs like *sati* set them apart from their contemporaries. The decade of change saw the realization of their efforts. As a result, some Indian women could aspire to be educators, physicians, scientists, and even prime ministers. Women could reasonably aspire to equal rights in society, but an occasional instance of *sati* was still possible. Social reforms continued to be an important concern.

Bibliography

Brown, Judith M. *Modern India: The Origins of an Asian Democracy.* Delhi, India: Oxford University Press, 1985. The author's astute analysis of the foundations of Indian society is helpful in understanding the background of social reform. A valuable general source that does not directly concentrate on the issue of women's rights.

Majumdar, R. C., ed. *Struggle for Freedom.* Vol. 11 in *The History and Culture of the Indian People.* Bombay: Bharatiya Vidya Bhavan, 1978. The most detailed source for the history of the freedom struggle from the Indian perspective. It takes a comprehensive look at social reform in general and women's issues in particular. An invaluable resource for the specialist as well as the general reader.

Majumdar, R. C., H. C. Raychaudhuri, and Kalikinkar Datta. *An Advanced History of India*. London: Macmillan, 1951. One of the best general histories of India, with a level of detail not often found in works of this breadth. Written from the indigenous perspective.

Panikkar, K. M. *The Foundations of New India*. London: Allen & Unwin, 1963. An eminently readable account of the course of modernization in India. Written for the general reader.

Philips, C. H., ed. *The Evolution of India and Pakistan, 1858 to 1947*. Vol. 4 in *Select Documents on the History of India and Pakistan*. London: Oxford University Press, 1962. A well-chosen collection of source materials relating to the formative period in the history of the modern nations of India and Pakistan. These selections are a ready source of reference both for specialists and for interested general readers.

Spear, Percival. *The Oxford History of Modern India, 1740-1947*. Oxford, England: Oxford University Press, 1978. This book is a reprint of part 3 of the third edition of the *Oxford History of India* (1958). This fully revised and rewritten version concentrates on the process of social change in a modernizing nation. Brilliantly traces the interaction of Western influences and Indian forces as they transformed Indian society.

Sai Felicia Krishna-Hensel

Cross-References

The Pankhursts Found the Women's Social and Political Union (1903), p. 19; The Muslim League Attempts to Protect Minority Interests in India (1906), p. 87; Women's Institutes Are Founded in Great Britain (1915), p. 167; Parliament Grants Suffrage to British Women (1918), p. 247; Gandhi Leads a Noncooperation Movement (1920), p. 315; The Minimum Age for Female British Voters Is Lowered (1928), p. 442; Gandhi Leads the Salt March (1930), p. 447; India Signs the Delhi Pact (1931), p. 459; The Poona Pact Grants Representation to India's Untouchables (1932), p. 469; India Gains Independence (1947), p. 731; The Indian Government Bans Discrimination Against Untouchables (1948), p. 743; The U.N. Convention on the Political Rights of Women Is Approved (1952), p. 885; The Indian Parliament Approves Women's Rights Legislation (1955), p. 924; Indira Gandhi Is Assassinated (1984), p. 2232; Benazir Bhutto Becomes the First Woman Elected to Lead a Muslim Country (1988), p. 2403.

THE PAHLAVI SHAHS ATTEMPT TO MODERNIZE IRAN

Categories of event: Political freedom and religious freedom
Time: 1925-1977
Locale: Iran

The numerous social and economic reforms instituted by the modernizing Pahlavi shahs over a forty-year period were imposed at the expense of political freedom and social justice

Principal personages:
> REZA SHAH PAHLAVI (1878-1944), the first ruler of the new Pahlavi dynasty, crowned in 1926
> MOHAMMAD REZA (SHAH) PAHLAVI (1919-1980), the son of Reza Shah; ruled Iran from 1941 until 1979, when forced to flee Iran in the wake of the Islamic Revolution
> JOHN F. KENNEDY (1917-1963), the president of the United States, partially responsible for some of Mohammad Reza's reforms in the 1960's

Summary of Event

On February 21, 1921, General Reza Khan led a *coup d'etat* in Iran, effectively ending the rule of the Qājār dynasty. By the time of his coronation, in 1926, as the first ruler of the Pahlavi dynasty, his reform program was well under way. Both Reza Shah (he gave himself the title of shah) and his son, Mohammad Reza, who succeeded him in 1941, believed that Iran should become part of the modern world as quickly as possible. Although Reza Shah repeatedly emphasized the need to be rid of foreign influence, even rejecting foreign loans, the Pahlavi shahs were convinced that modernization meant Westernization.

The challenges of modernization were great. Iran had experienced little economic development before 1925, and the country was on the verge of bankruptcy when Reza Khan ascended to the throne. There was little centralization of services; a small, ineffective army tried to keep order; the Muslim clergy's influence was pervasive; and only slightly more than half of the population was educated. The Pahlavi shahs turned Iran around through their policies of nationalism, industrialization, centralization, secularization, and emancipation of women.

One of Reza Shah's first reforms was to establish a centralized bureaucracy. This centralization was further expanded under Mohammad Reza, so that by the mid-1970's, Iran had nineteen ministries with 560,000 civil servants whose authority reached out to all aspects of Iranian life.

Until 1920, there was no national army in Iran. To keep internal order and fend off foreign invasion, Reza Shah created a large army equipped with modern weapons. Mohammad Reza was even more obsessed than his father with having a large, well-equipped army. The Iranian army grew from 23,000 in 1920 to 410,000 in 1977. Mohammad Reza built his regime around the army and used the army to suppress opposition to his regime.

In order to accomplish his goal of creating a unified state, Reza Shah emphasized the importance of the Persian language. Non-Persian languages were forbidden, and schools and printing presses using other languages were closed. Ethnic differences were to be eradicated by creating a genuine Iranian identity (modeled on the West). Consequently, the Iranian parliament (Majles) passed the Uniform Dress Law, which made wearing of Western clothes compulsory. In 1928, Reza Shah ordered every adult male in Iran, with the exception of the clergy, to wear the rounded, peaked Pahlavi cap. Eight years later, he decreed that all men must replace the Pahlavi caps with European felt hats. This law created great opposition among devout Muslims, who found it impossible to pray with the new hat on their heads. When Muslims defied the order, troops were dispatched to make sure they obeyed.

Closely related to nationalism were Reza Shah's policies toward the tribes. He considered nomadic tribes, a key group in rural Iran, to be a serious impediment to creating a modern state. At the beginning of the twentieth century, Iran's nomadic tribes accounted for almost one-fourth of the total population. Tribal leaders were very powerful and posed a threat to the shah's one-man rule. Consequently, in 1933, Reza Shah embarked on a policy of settling the nomadic tribes in order to bring them under control of the central government. This policy was continued under Mohammad Reza, so that by 1979, the tribal population had dwindled to one percent of the total population. Under the policy of forced sedentarization, grazing lands were confiscated, depriving tribes of a means of support, and tribal leaders were often imprisoned and executed.

Reza Shah opened up society to Iranian women. Traditionally, women were confined to the home, married off at an early age, and rarely given an education. Both shahs are credited with increasing women's opportunities for education, although the benefits of higher education often accrued to middle- and upper-middle-class urban women.

In 1936, Reza Shah banned women's wearing of the *chador* (a head-to-foot black veil covering everything but the face). This law was often implemented mercilessly. Women wearing the *chador* were not permitted in movie theaters or in public baths, and taxi and bus drivers could be fined for accepting veiled women in their conveyances. After 1935, government officials could be dismissed unless they brought their wives, unveiled, to office parties. There were even recorded instances of police forcibly ripping off the *chadors* of women who defied the order.

In 1963, women were permitted to vote and to hold public office, and in 1967 important reforms were made in marriage and divorce under the Family Protection Law. These were violently opposed by the clergy.

The reigns of both shahs were weakened and strained by their relations with the Muslim clergy. Both shahs endeavored to break the power of the religious hierarchy, which often resisted their reforms. From the onset, Reza Shah's policies emphasized creating an Iranian nationalism distinct from Islam.

From 1925 to 1928, he replaced Sharīa (religious law of Islam) with civil codes modeled on the French. State courts were created, weakening the power of religious courts. The educational system and registration of documents, formerly the province of the clergy, were turned over to secular authorities, depriving many clerics of jobs.

General restrictions on religious observance were instituted. Public demonstrations on certain religious holidays were forbidden. Exit visas were denied for those wishing to make religious pilgrimages. The economic strength of the clergy was weakened when the government seized control over the administration of the *vaqfs* (large religious endowments).

When the secular reforms were greeted with violent opposition by the clergy, the shah's army units did not hesitate to use force. Reza Shah himself once entered the shrine at Qom without removing his boots and personally flogged the *mujtahid* (religious leader), who had dared to criticize the queen for removing her veil.

Mohammad Reza continued the antagonization of religious authorities begun by his father, seizing control of virtually all religious education, cutting subsidies to the clergy, and replacing the Islamic calendar with a royal calendar.

The bazaar is a cluster of small shops, sometimes numbering in the thousands, in a particular section of an urban area. The shops contain merchants, money lenders, commodity producers, salespeople, and shop assistants; street vendors and canvassers work outside. The bazaars played a crucial role in Iran's economy, but Mohammad Reza claimed they were relics of the past and obstacles to modernization. In actuality, he felt threatened by their independence from the state and their close alliance with the religious elements. With the creation of new companies, the proliferation of modern financial institutions, and the invasion of foreign consumer goods sold in modern supermarkets, the bazaar's monopoly over the economy was gradually weakened. Bazaar merchants began to speak out against rapid modernization.

This infuriated the shah. He embarked on an antiprofiteering campaign to scapegoat bazaars for inflation. The government planned to build a superhighway right through the Teheran bazaar. To further weaken bazaar wholesalers and retailers, the government created state purchasing corporations for such essentials as wheat, meat, and sugar. Neighborhood shops were often replaced with supermarkets that received cheap bank credit. When economic pressures on the bazaars failed to eliminate them, the government took more drastic steps. During the antiprofiteering campaign of 1975, forty thousand shops were closed and more than eighty thousand bazaar shopkeepers were imprisoned or exiled.

With the creation of new industries, growth exceeded expectations. From 1925 to 1976, gross national product multiplied seven hundred times, per-capita income two hundred times, and imports almost one thousand times. Although industrial development was important to Iran's modernization, it often led to exploitation of workers under both shahs. Under Mohammad Reza, the state supported workers' demands for higher wages but kept them from creating independent unions. Workers were allowed to enter only state-created labor unions. Savak, an intelligence agency, set up branches in factories to harass workers and suppress strikes, using violence if necessary.

Although Reza Shah pursued a vigorous industrialization policy, his agricultural policy continued traditional practice. Large landlords were allowed to remain in possession of their lands and wealth. By 1941, Reza Shah, who did not have any property before coming to power, possessed 2,670 villages. At the end of his reign, Iran remained basically a semifeudal agricultural system.

It fell to Mohammad Reza to break up the traditional landholding system. In 1963, acting upon pressure from U.S. President John F. Kennedy for reform, the Shah issued an ambitious program of reforms known as the White Revolution. Particularly noteworthy was the land reform program by which Mohammad Reza hoped to destroy the influence of the landlords, improve agricultural output, and create a base of support for his regime among the peasants and the working class.

Before land reform, less than one percent of the total population owned close to sixty percent of the land under cultivation, and the vast majority of tenants lived at subsistence level. Under the land reform policy, landlords' holdings were cut to one village. All other holdings were to be sold to farmers who were already tilling the soil. Approximately eight thousand villages, or one-seventh of the total number, were affected by the reforms. Under later phases, farmers were given leasing options. During the third phase, agricultural corporations were established to improve farming methods.

Impact of Event

The Pahlavi shahs' reforms radically transformed Iran within a relatively short time from a backward Middle Eastern outpost into a thriving modern country. Although the oil flowed, bringing great wealth, and state-of-the-art weapons poured in, the impact of too-rapid modernization eventually tore Iranian society apart and was partially responsible for the revolution in 1979 which overthrew the Pahlavi regime and established an Islamic republic.

The land reform program was a dismal failure. The best land in the country was chopped up into inefficient small pieces, and productivity declined. In the end, only a small group of peasants benefited from land distribution. Two-thirds of the peasants did not acquire land or received minuscule plots. The majority of the peasants who gained land later lost it because they could not obtain enough credit or because they could not keep up with the rising cost of agricultural production. Peasants were forced to join cooperatives, in which they were excluded from making decisions by government bureaucrats who had in fact assumed the role of the former landlords. Richer peasants were soon buying out poorer peasants and creating a new small landlord class. Millions of peasants left the farms and flocked into the cities to become discontented laborers for the new agribusinesses, often living in shanty towns of cheap houses lacking electricity, water, and gas.

Although economic growth was impressive, the political apparatus of the state continued to be underdeveloped and unable to serve the needs of a modern society.

The drive for modernization lacked a wide base of support and a prominent ideology. The newly emancipated modern middle class demanded political rights and institutions to channel its views. The shahs refused to grant these, and those who were foolish enough to speak out against the shahs' reforms were brutally suppressed. As alienation to the regime increased, Mohammad Reza began to rely more and more on repression and foreign support. Like his father, Mohammad Reza instituted reforms under a dictatorship backed up by the army and Savak.

The shah's internal policies widened the existing cleavages in society. Nikki Keddie has pointed out that the rapid modernization from above and secularization created two cultures. The upper class and new middle classes became increasingly Westernized and unwilling to understand the traditional and religious values of the peasants and traders in the bazaars. As the pace of social change accelerated and traditional values were frowned upon, the family and ethical values began to disintegrate.

The campaign against the religious authorities begun under the first shah intensified during the latter part of his son's reign. The increasing Westernization and secularization of society, along with suppression of the clerical class and expropriation of their lands, increased the hostility of this group toward the regime and resulted in its alliance with other alienated groups in society to undermine the Shah's rule. The Shah had failed to realize that the majority of Iranians were attached to the Islamic part of Iranian culture.

The shahs' emphasis on nationalism was contradicted by their dependence on Western values and advisers. As more and more of Western culture was imported, Iranians became increasingly alienated from their roots. Resentment built against the shahs' foreign consultants, who took away jobs, caused rents to soar, and often displayed an acute insensitivity to traditional Iranian cultural mores and religious beliefs. Demands on the government intensified. In the end, by resorting to political repression and overly rapid modernization, Mohammad Reza could not deliver the better life he had promised. He succumbed to a revolution headed by Islamic leader Ayatollah Ruhollah Khomeini and fled Iran in 1979.

Bibliography

Abrahamian, Ervand. *Iran Between Two Revolutions.* Princeton, N.J.: Princeton University Press, 1982. An analysis of the social bases of Iranian politics, focusing on how socioeconomic development gradually transformed the shape of Iranian politics from the late nineteenth century to 1979.

Arjomand, Said Amir. *The Turban for the Crown.* New York: Oxford University Press, 1988. Excellent chronology of significant events in Iranian history. Chapters deal with the rise of the modern state, constitutional revolution, formation of a modern bureaucratic state, and the Islamic Revolution. Excellent appendix including tables and charts showing Iranian institutions and economic sectors before and after reforms.

Banani, Amin. *The Modernization of Iran, 1921-1941.* Stanford, Calif.: Stanford University Press, 1961. Based primarily on Persian sources, this book examines the reforms instituted by Reza Shah and evaluates the consequences of Westernization in general.

Keddie, Nikki. *Roots of Revolution.* New Haven, Conn.: Yale University Press, 1981. An in-depth study of the tensions in Iran between the secularized middle and upper classes and the religiously oriented bazaar class.

Lenczowski, George, ed. *Iran Under the Pahlavis.* Stanford, Calif.: Hoover Institution Press, 1978. A compilation of articles, written by a team of international scholars, portraying and evaluating the changes that occurred in Iran after the Pahlavi dynasty came to power. The authors are generally favorable to the shahs and conclude that the Pahlavis brought a real revolution.

Pahlavi, Mohammad Reza Shah. *Mission for My Country.* New York: McGraw-Hill, 1961. In this autobiography, the Shah, in addition to his life story, discusses Iran's social and political problems and his views on various issues such as land reform, education, the role of women, and modernization.

Renée Taft

Cross-References

The Iranian Constitution Bars Non-Muslims from Cabinet Positions (1906), p. 52; The United Nations Issues a Declaration Against Torture (1975), p. 1847; Carter Makes Human Rights a Central Theme of Foreign Policy (1977), p. 1903; Khomeini Uses Executions to Establish a New Order in Iran (1979), p. 2013; Iranian Revolutionaries Hold Americans Hostage (1979), p. 2045; Sixty-three Persons Are Beheaded for Attacking Mecca's Grand Mosque (1980), p. 2095.

NELLIE TAYLOE ROSS OF WYOMING
BECOMES THE FIRST FEMALE GOVERNOR

Category of event: Women's rights
Time: January 5, 1925
Locale: Wyoming

Nellie Tayloe Ross became the first female governor in United States history when she was inaugurated as governor of Wyoming on January 5, 1925

Principal personages:
> NELLIE TAYLOE ROSS (1876-1977), the first woman to be inaugurated as a governor in the United States
> WILLIAM BRADFORD ROSS (1873-1924), the husband of Nellie Tayloe Ross; elected as governor of Wyoming in 1922
> EUGENE J. SULLIVAN, Nellie Ross's Republican opponent in 1924

Summary of Event

The unexpected death of Governor William Bradford Ross on October 2, 1924, provided the opportunity for his wife, Nellie Tayloe Ross, to establish her place in the history of Wyoming and the United States. William B. Ross, a Democrat, had been elected to a four-year term as governor in November, 1922. His victory resulted from a split in Wyoming's dominant Republican Party between liberals and conservatives. The liberal Republicans decided to support Ross, and thus a Democrat was elected governor of a state where nearly 70 percent of the voters considered themselves to be Republicans. Ross saw himself as a political progressive, but he focused heavily on such traditional Wyoming interests as farm policies and law and order.

Although he confronted a solidly Republican state legislature, Ross remained a popular governor when he was stricken with appendicitis in late September, 1924. Surgeons removed his appendix, but the surgery brought about a secondary infection that caused his death on October 2, 1924. Ross's death came as a shock to Wyoming citizens, who poured out their sympathy to Ross's widow. It was primarily this sympathy, and the Democratic Party's wish to take advantage of it, that brought Nellie Tayloe Ross to the nation's attention.

Within days of her husband's funeral, Nellie Ross was beseeched by state Democratic leaders to consider fulfilling the remainder of her husband's term. The state's attorney general had ruled that a new governor would need to be elected at the next scheduled general election, which was less than five weeks away. Although she expressed doubts about her ability to carry out the duties of a governor, Ross made no attempt to stop her nomination by the state Democratic convention on October 14.

Nellie Davis Tayloe was born in St. Joseph, Missouri, to parents of considerable wealth and station. She was educated as a kindergarten teacher and taught for a brief time in Omaha, Nebraska, before meeting William Bradford Ross while on a visit to her father's family in Tennessee. A romance quickly developed, and they were married in Omaha in 1902. The new Mrs. Ross then surrendered her teaching position and moved to Wyoming with her politically ambitious husband. As William Ross's career moved forward, Nellie Ross devoted herself to rearing three children (a fourth child died at the age of ten months). As she once said, until her husband died the thought of a vocation outside the home never entered her mind.

What Nellie Ross knew about politics came through years of observing her husband's political career. She admitted that she was bereft of political experience, but she believed that she had "unconsciously absorbed" knowledge of what it meant to be chief executive of a state government. Nevertheless, Ross was reluctant to test her understanding of politics in the crucible of an election campaign. She chose instead to remain at home during the days prior to the November 4 election. She was confident that the voters of Wyoming would pay tribute to her husband's memory by electing her. It was left to other Democratic Party leaders to explain that Ross intended to follow the policies initiated by her husband.

The Republican nominee, Eugene J. Sullivan, was a New Hampshire-born attorney. He found it very difficult to campaign against a candidate who was in mourning and who refused to leave her house. Sullivan had close ties with major oil companies, and Democrats repeatedly suggested that whereas Ross would continue her husband's practice of fighting for the "little fellow," Sullivan would support big business interests.

During the three-week campaign, Democrats worked to capitalize on the fact that Wyoming could make history by being the first state to have a female governor. This, they argued, would be in keeping with Wyoming's reputation for granting political rights to women. In 1869, the first legislature of the Wyoming Territory had given women the right to vote and to hold office. (Two male suffragists had convinced the tiny legislature that providing rights for women would attract more females to the West.) Ross's supporters also used the slogan Beat Texas to It, a reference to the campaign of Miriam F. "Ma" Ferguson, who was expected to win the election for governor in Texas. Ferguson was elected in Texas (she was also campaigning for an office left vacant by her husband's death), but the inauguration there was scheduled for three weeks later than Wyoming's.

In the last days of the campaign, it was apparent that Ross held the advantage. The Republicans were hurt by Sullivan's association with big business and by the continuing sympathy for Ross generated by her husband's death. Many Republicans joined with Democrats in placing newspaper advertisements supporting Ross. On the eve of the election, an editorial in the *Wyoming Labor Journal* noted that tea parties in the state capitol certainly would be preferable to "Teapot Dome" parties.

The results of the election showed Nellie Tayloe Ross winning handily. She reacted to her victory by pointing out that a peculiarly tragic turn of events had made her governor. Ross reiterated that she would never have sought the governor's office of her own volition. She had taken on the challenge because so many friends had told her that only she could guarantee the attainment of her husband's legislative programs.

Nellie Tayloe Ross served out the remaining two years of William Ross's term and then was defeated in an attempt to gain reelection. Her two years as governor were undistinguished. She found it nearly impossible to work with the Republican-dominated legislature. During the course of the 1926 campaign, in which Ross did take to the stump, she discovered that the sympathy votes she had had in 1924 were no longer there. Women's rights advocates complained that while she was governor Ross had shown no interest in advancing their cause, a charge that Ross did not deny. Republicans who had supported her during her first campaign now gave their votes to their own party's candidate.

Her defeat in 1926 did not end Ross's involvement in politics. The two years in the state capitol had convinced her to become an activist on behalf of the Democratic Party. In 1928, she was vice chair of the Democratic National Convention and seconded the nomination of Alfred Smith for president. In that same year, she moved to Washington, D.C., and directed the national efforts of Democratic women. She was especially prominent in the campaign of Franklin Delano Roosevelt in 1932. As a reward for her efforts, Roosevelt appointed her the first female director of the United States Mint. She held this post until 1953. When her duties permitted, Ross wrote political articles for a variety of women's magazines and supervised a large tobacco farm she had purchased in Maryland. Although she had much success as a businesswoman and as a government officeholder, Ross never spoke out forcefully for more opportunities for women.

Impact of Event

The election of Ross, along with that of Ferguson in Texas, created a stir in the nation's press. Most of the commentary was far from positive. It was widely reported that Ross had achieved election on the basis of sentiment and that she had no political expertise in her own right. There were doubts that Ross or Ferguson would ever carry out anything more constructive than baking a pie or making a bed. A writer for the Consolidated Press Association hoped that Ross would "keep house" for the state by following the "homely virtues of rigid economy, neatness, orderliness, and efficiency." On the other hand, there were those who observed that both women had been freely elected and that this had to mean an improved image for females in politics.

Wyoming citizens seemed proud of the fact that the first female governor had been inaugurated in their state; they especially enjoyed the attention Wyoming received in the Eastern press. It seemed to confirm that Wyoming really was the "Equality State," an appellation given to Wyoming as a result of the women's suffrage bill passed by the territory's first legislature in 1869. That bill, in fact, gained more favorable interest from feminists across the country than did Ross's election.

The long-range impact of Ross's election on the course of the women's rights movement appears to have been negligible. As T. A. Larson notes in his bicentennial history of Wyoming, the state has consistently lagged behind even neighboring states in granting opportunities to women. In the 1970's, the federal government pressured Wyoming to move more swiftly to diminish sexual discrimination. Ross's election to the governor's office did not change basic attitudes toward women in male-dominated Wyoming.

On a national level, there is no way to gauge the effect of Ross's election. Surely her victory showed that in very special circumstances women could be elected to high office. This may well have encouraged other women to pursue political ambitions. The fact remained, however, that by the last decade of the twentieth century it still was considered unusual for a woman to be voted into high political office.

Bibliography

Aslakson, Barbara Jean. *Nellie Tayloe Ross: First Woman Governor.* Laramie: University of Wyoming, 1960. This master's degree essay is the only attempt to provide an account of Ross's career as governor. The work is strongest when Aslakson writes about Ross's problems while in office.

Brown, Dorothy M. *Setting a Course: American Women in the 1920s.* Boston: Twayne, 1987. A comprehensive study of women in the 1920's by a professor of history at Georgetown University. Brown discusses the wide variety of female experience in the 1920's, experience that involved church, politics, education, and work. Although the book may be overly allusive in places, it is well worth reading. It will change some ideas about the flapper age. A note on sources, endnotes, and index.

Flexner, Eleanor. *Century of Struggle: The Women's Rights Movement in the United States.* Cambridge, Mass.: Harvard University Press, 1959. A breakthrough book in the study of women's history in America. The author recounts the efforts of women to extend their rights and opportunities and especially to gain the franchise. Flexner does not ignore the considerable achievement of black women under adverse circumstances. She gives some attention to Wyoming's role in opening the door to female voters but places this event in perspective. A respected account that is highly recommended. Bibliographical summary, notes, and index. The work was reprinted in paperback by Atheneum in 1970.

Gilmore, Inez Haynes. *Angels and Amazons: A Hundred Years of American Women.* Garden City, N.Y.: Doubleday, 1934. A pioneering study of the progress of women in America from 1833 to 1933. Irwin discusses the struggle for female opportunities in education, politics, and the workplace. The book is especially strong in discussing the many organizations formed to advance the cause of women. The author perhaps places more importance on Wyoming's extension of suffrage to females in 1869 than is justified. Written in a lively style, the work contains an appendix and index but no bibliography or notes.

Gould, Lewis J. *Wyoming: A Political History, 1868-1896.* New Haven, Conn.: Yale University Press, 1968. A well-researched and well-written account of early politics in Wyoming. Gould discusses the territorial legislature that startled the country by allowing women to vote and to hold office.

Larson, T. A. *Wyoming: A Bicentennial History.* New York: W. W. Norton, 1977. Larson's work is the best general history of Wyoming's politics and culture. The author puts in perspective Wyoming's claim to be the "Equality State." His discussion of Ross's election is slight but on the mark.

Ronald K. Huch

Cross-References

Rankin Becomes the First Woman Elected to Congress (1916), p. 190; The League of Women Voters Is Founded (1920), p. 333; The Nineteenth Amendment Gives American Women the Right to Vote (1920), p. 339; Franklin D. Roosevelt Appoints Perkins as Secretary of Labor (1933), p. 486; The U.N. Convention on the Political Rights of Women Is Approved (1952), p. 885; The Equal Pay Act Becomes Law (1963), p. 1172; The National Organization for Women Forms to Protect Women's Rights (1966), p. 1327; The Equal Rights Amendment Passes Congress but Fails to Be Ratified (1972), p. 1656; Congress Votes to Admit Women to the Armed Services Academies (1975), p. 1823; O'Connor Becomes the First Female Supreme Court Justice (1981), p. 2141.

JAPAN ENDS PROPERTY RESTRICTIONS ON VOTING RIGHTS

Category of event: Voting rights
Time: May 5, 1925
Locale: Tokyo, Japan

In the decade following World War I, Japan allowed increased political participation, epitomized by the passage of a universal manhood suffrage act that removed property qualifications

Principal personages:

KEI HARA (1856-1921), a politician who helped build up political party organizations and, as prime minister, helped parties gain access to executive power

TSUYOSHI INUKAI (1855-1932), an early and consistent backer of universal manhood suffrage

SAKUZO YOSHINO (1878-1933), a liberal scholar and major spokesperson for increasing democracy within the Japanese political system of the 1920's

SHIMPEI GOTO (1857-1929), a bureaucrat in both the Meiji and Taisho eras who promoted universal manhood suffrage

SEIGO NAKANO (1886-1943), a liberal journalist and politician who advocated extension of voting rights and espoused a philosophy of "spiritual individualism"

RYUTARO NAGAI (1881-1944), a politician, journalist, and educator who espoused extension of popular participation in politics

KOMEI KATO (1860-1926), the prime minister when the 1925 Universal Manhood Suffrage Law was passed

Summary of Event

Japan began the long process of building a modern nation-state in 1868 with a revolt against the feudal authorities that had ruled for more than 250 years. The Meiji Restoration established the emperor as head of state. There was little disagreement concerning the necessity of quickly building a rich country and strong military in the face of the imperialist threat from the West. The feudal class structure was dismantled, a national tax structure was instituted, a modern army and navy were planned and begun, a public school and university system was built, a modern bureaucracy was put into place, and efforts to industrialize were begun.

In the beginning, there was no real widespread philosophical debate over the form government would take. To offset feudal divisions, the emperor was elevated as the embodiment of the state, and the men who engineered the revolution emerged as the de facto executive decision makers acting in the name of the emperor. The mass of people, as the emperor's subjects, were expected to pay their taxes, serve in the military, and obey the law because they were a self-contained island people whose homeland faced a hostile world, because their crowded communities demanded a predictable order, and because their life opportunities depended on an expanding industrial economy. Citizen participation, the vote, and representation did not become issues until the 1880's.

The executive oligarchy ruling in the emperor's name, who came to be known as the "elder statesmen," came under attack in the 1880's from political associations led by men who had been part of the inner circle but had left in disagreement. The issues were foreign policy and financial scandals, but the basic disagreement concerned division of political power in a rapidly modernizing country. The political associations, gradually acquiring the character of political parties, agitated for representative institutions and a constitution similar to those of Western Europe. The Elder Statesmen, eager to maintain a strong state and harmony and to avoid a more radical redistribution of power, moved to formulate a constitution that protected the imperial executive primacy while allowing an elected lower house of representatives in a parliament called the "Diet." A broad range of citizens' civil rights were laid out, but the theoretical basis of government was still the primacy of the emperor's ultimate executive power. The Meiji Constitution was promulgated as a gift from the emperor in 1889. Voting was restricted to males above age twenty-five paying at least fifteen yen national or land tax. This was about 1.5 percent of the population or roughly four hundred thousand voters, mainly in rural areas.

By the end of World War I, another turning point was reached in the evolution toward increased democracy. The original mission of the Meiji oligarchy—"rich country, strong military"—seemed well on its way to fulfillment, since Japan was entering the ranks of the major powers. At the same time, a whole range of new groups and interests emerged, clamoring to be served, who could not be brought to support national goals by the old ruling style of the Elder Statesmen. The growth of industry produced a new kind of prosperity, but the gap between rich and poor grew. As peasants migrated into industrial centers, urban population grew but agriculture stagnated. Agrarian discontent grew alongside labor unrest. Wartime and empire expenses called for yearly increases in the budget. Appropriations were made by the House of Representatives of the Diet, which was elected. The legislature's leverage within the government grew in relation to the executive oligarchy and bureaucracy. Larger budgets meant higher taxes, and pressure grew to broaden the franchise to compensate for tax increases. The Elder Statesmen, growing older and dying off gradually, began to lose influence.

Until 1918, political parties' power to influence policy was confined to the Diet. Prime ministers were chosen by the Elder Statesmen. The prime minister, his cabinet, and the bureaucracy exercised executive functions largely insulated from legislative pressures. The prime minister could dissolve a hostile Diet or manipulate Diet elections. With the pressures mentioned above, however, including needs for larger budgets, cabinets found it more and more difficult to govern. In 1918, a series of major riots over the price of rice occurred, and the head of the Seiyukai Party, Kei

Hara, was made prime minister. From 1918 until his assassination in 1921, Hara created a party-dominated cabinet and made the bureaucracy more responsive to party policies. Although the parties were conservative and not particularly broad-based in membership, this change brought Japan closer to the responsible cabinet model, wherein cabinet policy-making responded to legislative majorities, as in Great Britain, for example.

In the evolution of Western democracies, the development of political party power brought pressures to extend the vote, but in Japan the regular parties and Hara himself seemed inclined not to want to share constituent input too widely. In 1900, there had been a reduction of property qualifications from fifteen to ten yen in taxes, which brought the franchise to 2 percent of the population. Universal manhood suffrage—the elimination of property qualifications—was rejected in the Diet, however, despite growing demands from the general public.

Foremost among the intellectuals arguing for universal manhood suffrage was Sakuzo Yoshino, a professor at Tokyo University, who wrote influential articles arguing for *minponshugi* ("the people's will as a basis of government"). While accepting the emperor's position, he held that extending suffrage would reinforce the Diet as the true center of politics and act as a better reinforcement for imperial power than the small ruling oligarchical clique. Seigo Nakano, a liberal journalist and politician, also argued for universal manhood suffrage, out of a commitment to individualism and as a way to transcend growing class differences. Ryutaro Nagai, another journalist-politician, pointed out that the spread of education (90 percent of male children were in school by the 1920's) made removal of property qualifications a common sense means to offset privileged classes. He claimed it would be impossible to re-form politics without a mass electorate. He even advocated the vote for women. Among progressive bureaucrats backing universal manhood suffrage was Shimpei Goto, who noted in his visits to the United States the potential for an "emergence of mass power" in a mass electorate. Noting a lack of trust in corrupt party governments, he believed that the citizenry could be better mobilized to support broad change if they voted.

In 1923, Komei Kato became prime minister. Along with Tsuyoshi Inukai, a long-time supporter of universal manhood suffrage, he had formulated a new party, the Kenseikai, to challenge the Seiyukai. The competition caused the Seiyukai to swing over to support new voting rights. An "enlightened conservative," Kato, with Inukai's support, pushed through a bill in the Diet in 1925 that removed property qualifications from the franchise. All males over age twenty-five who were not indigent could vote. The electorate increased from three million to about fourteen million (about 20 percent of the population). Accompanying the new franchise extension, however, was the Peace Preservation Law of 1925, which allowed the government to crack down on associations that sought any radical change. It broadened censorship powers and police discretion in limiting rights of assembly. As a political control measure, it constrained much of the purely democratic thrust of universal manhood suffrage.

Impact of Event

The suffrage law of 1925 was unquestionably a step toward political progressivism. It was enacted partly in response to persuasion by genuine idealists, partly out of the pressure of political competition, and partly to forestall rising discontent. It was ironic, however, that its immediate effects in realigning Japanese politics were minimal, and the longer-term course of Japanese politics in the 1930's would ultimately turn in an undemocratic direction.

Universal manhood suffrage did not push Japan decisively toward increased democracy as a result of a number of factors. First, many within the parliamentary "regular" parties remained suspicious of accommodating the needs of the new masses brought into the electorate. Both the main party alignments had become groupings of factions based on local loyalties and special-interest favor-mongering. They were narrow but manageable. The idea of input from the masses made the party leaders uncomfortable. Liberals such as Inukai were the exception.

New political parties built around the grievances of labor or small farmers or tenants had already emerged as a kind of mass-based alternative to regular parties. Largely left-wing, they seemed at first glance to be well-positioned to benefit from universal manhood suffrage in 1928, the first national election in which the new rules were implemented. They proved to be divided ideologically, however, and were outmaneuvered by the regular parties, capturing only 5 percent of the total vote. In the wake of the 1928 election, the interior minister rounded up 1,250 leftists under the Peace Preservation Law. It was clear that the regular parties, which could have built support based on the foundation of a broad suffrage, chose instead the narrower but more manageable conservative strategy.

Universal manhood suffrage did break the stranglehold that rural bosses—the core of the regular parties—had on small farmers and tenants. The farmers and tenants, however, although anticapitalist, did not support the democratic mass parties but instead turned increasingly to the radical ultranationalist right wing. The ideal of universal suffrage was that individuals acting in enlightened self-interest could produce the best government for the greatest number. Rural communalism, inherent in Japan, undercut this ideal.

The military coup in Manchuria in 1931 signaled a new era in Japanese politics wherein the military, speaking to national defense fears and expansionist fervor, came to exert more control over government decisions. The military gained more and more public support, including that of many regular party members. Inukai, as prime minister, was assassinated in 1932 by army officers. Nagai and Nakano, among many other liberals, came to support a more state-centered political view.

The regular parties survived and even abetted the establishment of a garrison state until 1940, when they were merged into a single government party, the Imperial Rule Assistance Association. Thus, universal manhood suffrage and the promise of mass politics in 1925 produced no profound transformation of electoral behavior or of political alignments in Japan. It is clear that Western-style individualistic democracy faced an uphill battle even in the 1920's and much more so under the wartime conditions that followed. The foundations of democracy were laid, however, and in the vastly changed milieu after 1945, a new politics was made possible by universal manhood suffrage.

Bibliography

Duus, Peter. "The Era of Party Rule: Japan, 1905-1932." In *Modern East Asia: Essays in Interpretation*, edited by James B. Crowley. New York: Harcourt, Brace & World, 1970. This chapter is one of the best summary surveys of most of the political themes dealt with in this article. Focuses mostly on party evolution. Includes selected readings.

_____. *Party Rivalry and Political Change in Taisho Japan.* Cambridge, Mass.: Harvard University Press, 1968. This is the fullest treatment of the whole context of 1920's politics. It sees universal manhood suffrage as the major landmark accomplishment of the regular parties (Duus disagrees with Toriumi, below). Contains an index, a glossary, and a bibliography.

Havens, Thomas R. "Japan's Enigmatic Election of 1928." *Modern Asian Studies* 11 (1977): 543-555. This is a crisply written piece that focuses on the outcome of universal manhood suffrage in the first national election in which it was implemented. It expresses an important point regarding Japanese democratic evolution—that the mass parties failed to benefit from suffrage extension even before the 1930's.

Najita, Tetsuo. *Hara Kei in the Politics of Compromise, 1905-1915.* Cambridge, Mass.: Harvard University Press, 1967. Growing out of a dissertation, this remains the only monograph in English on Hara. It illustrates the crucial developments in parties in the early 1920's in laying the groundwork for suffrage extension. Contains an exhaustive bibliography, glossary, and index.

Scalapino, Robert A. *Democracy and the Party Movement in Prewar Japan: The Failure of the First Attempt.* Berkeley: University of California Press, 1953. Scalapino is the senior scholar of Japanese prewar politics. He draws in background all the way to the feudal era to try to answer the question of why Japanese parties "failed" in the militarist era. Contains a glossary, a bibliography, and an index.

_____. "Elections and Political Modernization in Prewar Japan." In *Political Development in Modern Japan*, edited by Robert E. Ward. Princeton, N.J.: Princeton University Press, 1968. This chapter is a survey of elections and voter behavior that traces the transition from the Meiji era to World War II. Scalapino concludes that the Japanese had developed a system of "guided democracy."

Toriumi, Y. "The Manhood Suffrage Question in Japan After the First World War." *Papers on Far Eastern History* 11 (March, 1975): 149-168. This covers the cabinet just before Kato's, arguing that universal manhood suffrage had the support of progressive bureaucrats like Goto and that parties and intellectuals were not the only proponents.

Totten, George O. *The Social Democratic Movement in Prewar Japan.* New Haven, Conn.: Yale University Press, 1966. This is the best single source on the mass parties, looking at the prospective benefits these organizations hoped to achieve through universal manhood suffrage. Growing out of a dissertation, it contains an index and appendices.

David G. Egler

Cross-References

Parliament Grants Suffrage to British Women (1918), p. 247; The Nineteenth Amendment Gives American Women the Right to Vote (1920), p. 339; French Women Get the Vote (1944), p. 646; The Twenty-fourth Amendment Outlaws Poll Taxes (1964), p. 1231; Congress Passes the Voting Rights Act (1965), p. 1296; Women in Switzerland Are Granted the Right to Vote (1971), p. 1605; Congress Extends Voting Rights Reforms (1975), p. 1812; Congress Requires Bilingual Elections to Protect Minority Rights (1975), p. 1817.

GERMANY ATTEMPTS TO RESTRUCTURE THE VERSAILLES TREATY

Category of event: Civil rights
Time: October, 1925
Locale: Locarno, Switzerland

Germany initiated the Locarno Conference to reduce the German debt, offering reassurances of security for France in exchange

Principal personages:
>GUSTAV STRESEMANN (1878-1929), the foreign minister of Germany whose diplomacy resulted in the Locarno Pact
>ARISTIDE BRIAND (1862-1932), the foreign minister of France whose vision of world peace and a united Europe facilitated the Locarno Pact
>CHARLES G. DAWES (1865-1951), the American vice president who introduced the Dawes Plan in 1924
>AUSTEN CHAMBERLAIN (1863-1937), the British foreign secretary who represented Great Britain at the Locarno Conference

Summary of Event

The Treaty of Versailles, which concluded World War I, left Europe in an uneasy state. France and Great Britain had, with American backing, imposed upon Germany an immense war indemnity. The German people felt grievously and unjustly persecuted, and the French dreaded Germany's recovery and possible vengeance.

This was the situation addressed when delegates from Germany, France, Great Britain, Italy, Belgium, Poland, and Czechoslovakia met in Locarno, Switzerland on October 5, 1925. On October 16, seven treaties were signed. The principal document was a Treaty of Mutual Guarantee signed by France, Great Britain, Belgium, Italy, and Germany. Also called the Rhineland Security Pact, it guaranteed that the fifty-kilometer zone in Germany east of the Rhine would remain demilitarized and that Germany would honor its Belgian and French frontiers. By two separate treaties, Germany pledged not to make war on Belgium or France except in legitimate defense or in a League of Nations action and to settle disputes by arbitration. In the east, however, German foreign minister Gustav Stresemann refused to pledge the same boundary guarantees as in the west. Rather, Germany signed treaties of arbitration with Poland and with Czechoslovakia. France also signed treaties with Poland and Czechoslovakia against the possibility of German aggression. The treaties were formally signed in London on December 1, 1925, effective as soon as Germany entered the League of Nations (September 8, 1926). For the first time since World War I, Germany was treated as a friendly nation.

In order to appreciate better the meaning of the Locarno Treaty of 1925, it is necessary to review the events leading to World War I and the Versailles Treaty of

1919. One interpretation says that the major impetus to war was the aggressive posture of Germany, unified as a nation only in 1870 and impatient to gain respect and territory on a par with her well-established and prestigious neighbors, Great Britain and France. This interpretation, which became operative after the victory of Britain and France in World War I, was not by any means clear and unambiguous fact.

Animosities between England and Germany did play their part in establishing a general war mood. Eager to catch up, Germany embarked at the turn of the century upon a program of rapid naval construction, including thirty-eight battleships. This was perceived in world opinion as a challenge to traditional British supremacy on the high seas but in Germany as a security measure appropriate for a full-fledged nation.

Another area of Anglo-German rivalry was Germany's expansion as a colonial power in Africa, the South Pacific, and especially the Middle East. The contract of the Deutsche Bank with the Turkish government (November 27, 1898) to construct a railroad from Istanbul to Baghdad was initially favored by Great Britain, which hoped to use Germany as a foil to Russian expansionism in Turkey. British public opinion discouraged British banks from accepting a German request to finance the project jointly. As the railway subsequently resulted in a nearly monopolistic German influence in the economic and political life of Turkey, Great Britain came to view it as a threat to its lifelines in Egypt and India.

Franco-German relations had long been strained. Since the humiliation of France in the Franco-Prussian War of 1870, the French nationalist press had demanded a war of revenge. A spirit of resentment toward Germany persisted in France. At the same time, the French felt alarmed and threatened by Germany's already superior numbers and the rapid growth of its naval power.

The June 28, 1914, assassination in Sarajevo of the heir to the throne of Habsburg Austria, Archduke Francis Ferdinand, and his wife, by a Serbian citizen, Gavrilo Princip, was only the trigger which set in motion a series of responses culminating in the war. Princip's deed was the final event in a history of small Eastern European wars and of a dangerous animosity between Serbia and Austria.

The South Slavic peoples residing in the Austro-Hungarian Empire in the nineteenth century had long agitated for independence, with moral support from czarist Russia. In 1867, Hungary had satisfied its nationalist aims through the creation of a new national entity, Austria-Hungary. Both Serbia and Montenegro achieved a land-locked independence from Turkey at the 1878 Congress of Berlin, but concurrently the South Slavs of Bosnia and Herzegovina were annexed by Austria. Serbia claimed a right to rule these formerly Turkish provinces based upon their ethnic relationship and, in anticipation of Russian support, gradually prepared for a possible war with Austria. In deference to a German demand, however, Russia officially, at least, ceased support of Serbia and recognized Austria's possession of Bosnia and Herzegovina in 1909.

Two Balkan Wars in 1912 and 1913 added fuel to Serbia's animosity toward Austria-Hungary. Victorious in the second of these wars, Serbia gained parts of Macedonia, but Austria-Hungary fiercely opposed acquisition of lands bordering on the Adriatic which would allow Serbian access to the sea. That corridor was filled by Albania, newly created by the great powers by means of the 1913 Treaty of London.

Opinions differ about the rush of events after the assassination of the Habsburg heir. One question was whether Serbian leadership sponsored the assassination, or knew of it in advance. Austria demanded satisfaction, as if there had been official Serbian complicity. Although involvement of the Serbian leaders remains questionable, Serbia acceded to nearly all the Austrian demands. Austria rejected the Serbian response as unsatisfactory. Russia was committed to defense of Serbia. Germany, it was clear to all, would support fellow Germans in Austria.

Germany was thus, by some accounts, no more guilty as a cause of World War I than any other European state. Nevertheless, Article 231 of the Versailles Treaty proclaimed that defeated Germany accepted guilt for the war. Other articles outlined the exorbitantly high indemnity that the new Weimar government of Germany acknowledged it must pay. Aggravating this not-clearly-deserved war debt, Germany was deprived of a nation's normal means of generating revenue, natural energy resources and overseas possessions as markets and sources of raw materials. Germany had to cede the rich coal-producing Saar Basin to France and return other disputed lands won by Germany in the Franco-Prussian War of 1870. Article 119 of the Versailles Treaty took away all of Germany's overseas possessions.

After the war, Kaiser Wilhelm II of Germany had fled to Holland. The Weimar regime's acquiescence to the stipulations of the Versailles Treaty exposed it to criticism. No doubt the new republican government anticipated actual reparations to be lenient, since it had had no part in Germany's role in the war. That was not the case. Much discussion has been devoted to the question of whether the Allies' lack of consideration for the Weimar democracy promoted the German nationalism of the 1930's.

In the years that followed the Versailles Treaty, the Allies sensed the extent to which it had been excessively harsh and that the Germans must in time seek satisfaction. British foreign secretary Lord Arthur Balfour announced in 1922 that if the United States, which had claimed no part of Germany's reparations payments, would cancel European debts, then Great Britain would discontinue demanding German payments. The United States, however, viewed reparations and inter-Allied debts as entirely separate problems. Britain then offered a unilateral cessation of her claims. France, with a debt to Britain much less than its anticipated reparations from Germany, refused to grant a moratorium.

British goodwill toward Germany left the French government feeling increasingly isolated and insecure. The solution of French prime minister Raymond Poincaré was to maintain and even increase the obstacles to German growth. Thus, in 1923 France occupied Germany's mineral-rich Ruhr basin on the pretext that Germany had become delinquent in deliveries of timber. The response of the Weimar government, now even more profoundly prevented from generating the wealth with which to make payment, was "passive resistance." This took the form of issuing worthless paper marks for the purpose of making the requisite payments.

The French, British, and American governments, banks, and private speculators worsened the situation by purchasing German marks at current low exchange rates, planning to sell them back when the mark stabilized at its normal higher value. Instead, the resultant flood of marks into the money market led to the collapse of the German monetary system in 1923. By then, the mark was worth as little as 4.2 trillion to the dollar, less than the paper it was written on. A disastrous general European inflation had set in, and a worldwide financial collapse seemed imminent.

The 1923-1925 period saw massive efforts to rectify matters. Stresemann designed a plan to convert old German marks into strongly backed Rentenmarks at a rate of a trillion to one. This was the major step in alleviating the world's general inflation. In 1924, the Dawes Plan, proposed by U.S. vice president Charles Dawes, provided for a large Allied loan to help stabilize the mark and regulate the amounts of reparations required. Finally, a British-sponsored Geneva Protocol attempted to define aggression and provide for peaceful settlement of international disputes. Although never implemented, it established a spirit for Locarno.

France sought to contain Germany by preponderant force, while Britain worked at conciliation, removing the causes of German dissatisfaction. Britain constantly tried to keep France from provoking Germany. The French could charge that Germany's resentment was the result of Britain destroying Germany as a world power, taking its colonies, dismantling its navy, and seizing its capital holdings abroad. It was unfair, said the French, of Britain to ask France, Poland, and other continental powers to make concessions while Britain made none.

Impact of Event

In February, 1925, Stresemann had expressed to France his government's desire to guarantee the Franco-German Rhine frontiers as established by the Versailles Treaty. The Germans regarded as great sacrifices their acknowledgment of French possession of Alsace-Lorraine and their promise not to use force in Eastern Europe. Perhaps these sacrifices would alleviate France's fear of its more populous neighbor, assure France of Germany's peaceful stance, and thereby meet the French need for security. If successful, Germany could hope in return for a reduction of its war indemnity and possibly, in time, even a dismantling of other provisions of the Versailles Treaty.

Locarno was regarded as marking the start of an era of goodwill and as the reconciliation of former enemies of World War I. The high hopes of the moment were reflected in the Nobel Peace Prize awarded to Aristide Briand of France, Austen Chamberlain of Great Britain, and Gustav Stresemann of Germany. One assessment regards Locarno as the true end of World War I.

What precisely did Locarno do, and how did it affect the sense of security of the peoples of Europe and the world? After a war that had surpassed all fears, and after an inflation that had destroyed the savings and economic security of countless middle-class families, the world was sorely in need of good news. The Locarno Treaties offered hope of a peaceful future.

The Locarno Treaties have also received a negative interpretation, which to some extent may reflect the true state of affairs. Such an interpretation came only after the treaties were known to have failed to bring permanent peace and after Stresemann's private papers had been published. Was Locarno a screen behind which Stresemann actually supervised German rearmament? Did Stresemann's trade and nonaggression pacts with the Soviet Union after Locarno prove Germany's hypocrisy?

Disillusionment exists even regarding the motivations of the Allies. It is argued that Locarno reflected Great Britain's desire to keep continental commitments at a minimum. Great Britain's unwillingness to concern itself with Eastern Europe seemed to be a portent of its attitude in 1938, and was so assessed by Adolf Hitler. The West, through the Locarno Treaty, may simply have been protecting itself by turning German ambitions eastward against the Bolsheviks. The Soviet Union did in fact see the treaties as a hostile scheme against it, since Germany's eastern frontiers were not guaranteed. Finally, in both Germany and France nationalists attacked the treaties.

For ten years, Locarno represented a ray of hope. Hope proved illusory, however, when Hitler violated the pacts in March, 1936. A week later, the other powers voted to condemn Germany but took no punitive action.

Bibliography

Borsody, C. Stephen. *The Triumph of Tyranny.* New York: Macmillan, 1960. Argues that the Allied purpose at Locarno was to keep Germany and the Soviet Union apart and that, perceiving this, the Soviets viewed it as portentous of a new European war.

Eyck, Erich. *A History of the Weimar Republic.* 2 vols. New York: John Wiley & Sons, 1967. The best general history of the Weimar period. Volume 2 has extensive and incisive detailed material on Locarno.

Jacobson, Jon. *Locarno Diplomacy: Germany and the West, 1925-1929.* Princeton, N.J.: Princeton University Press, 1972. Explores the personalities and diplomacy of the Locarno era and offers an interpretation by means of newly released American, British, and German state documents and contemporary private documents, including Stresemann's private papers. Jacobson views Locarno as a sinister diplomatic duel between Briand and Stresemann. Extensive bibliography.

Marks, Sally. *The Illusion of Peace: International Relations in Europe, 1918-1933.* New York: St. Martin's Press, 1976. Views the period as extremely unstable and inevitably explosive because the Versailles Treaty was so unfair to Germany. Useful chronology of important events from 1915 to 1937.

Nicholls, A. J. *Weimar and the Rise of Hitler.* New York: Macmillan, 1968. An analysis of the failure of the Weimar government. Regarding Locarno, Nicholls presents Stresemann's argument that the eastern arrangements left Germany free to resort to war there. Stresemann believed Locarno would forestall a bilateral Anglo-French treaty and saw it as the beginning of the dismantling of the whole Versailles Treaty. Useful chronology of events from 1918 to 1933.

Taylor, A. J. P. *The Origins of the Second World War.* New York: Atheneum, 1983.

Praises Stresemann and Briton Ramsay MacDonald for their peacekeeping roles between the wars. Stresemann's posthumous papers prove that he wanted to destroy the Versailles Treaty. It had to be revised, by peace or war; Stresemann sought peace.

Wolfers, Arnold. *Britain and France Between Two Wars.* New York: Harcourt, Brace, 1940. Good general introduction to the diplomacy of the period after World War I. Points up the high level of friction that developed between the two allies with reference to Germany.

Daniel C. Scavone

Cross-References

Legal Norms of Behavior in Warfare Formulated by the Hague Conference (1907), p. 92; Germany First Uses Lethal Chemical Weapons on the Western Front (1915), p. 161; Lenin and the Communists Impose the "Red Terror" (1917), p. 218; Lenin Leads the Russian Revolution (1917), p. 225; Germans Revolt and Form Socialist Government (1918), p. 241; The Paris Peace Conference Includes Protection for Minorities (1919), p. 252; The League of Nations Is Established (1919), p. 270; Hitler Writes *Mein Kampf* (1924), p. 389; Mussolini Seizes Dictatorial Powers in Italy (1925), p. 395; Hitler Uses Reichstag Fire to Suspend Civil and Political Liberties (1933), p. 480.

BRITISH WORKERS GO ON GENERAL STRIKE

Category of event: Workers' rights
Time: May 4-12, 1926
Locale: London and other major cities, United Kingdom

Led by the coal miners, British unions unsuccessfully attempted to improve wages and working conditions during the economic hard times between World War I and World War II

Principal personages:

STANLEY BALDWIN (1867-1947), the Conservative prime minister (1923-1929 and 1935-1937), a leading figure in British politics between the wars

HERBERT SMITH (1862-1938), the president of the Miners' Federation of Great Britain (1921-1938)

ERNEST BEVIN (1881-1951), a labor leader and member of the Trades Union Congress' General Council (1921-1940), later foreign secretary in the Labour government (1945-1951)

WALTER CITRINE (1887-1983), an effective administrator of British trade unions, general secretary of the Trades Union Congress (1926-1946)

J. H. THOMAS (1874-1949), the leader of the National Union of Railwaymen and a key official in the Trades Union Congress

A. J. COOK (1884-1931), the secretary of the Miners' Federation of Great Britain (1924-1931)

WINSTON CHURCHILL (1874-1965), the controversial chancellor of the exchequer (1924-1929) who later became Great Britain's prime minister (1940-1945 and 1951-1955)

SIR HERBERT SAMUEL (1870-1963), the chair of the Royal Commission on the Coal Industry (1925-1926)

SIR ALFRED MOND (1868-1930), an industrialist and creator of Imperial Chemical Industries who sponsored talks between labor and management in 1928

Summary of Event

The General Strike of 1926 was a nine-day strike of about three million British miners, transport workers, dockers, printers, steel and chemical workers, power plant workers, and builders. It brought British economic, social, and political life to a halt during its course and was the most spectacular and extensive work stoppage in the history of British industrial relations. The strike had been called by the general council of the Trades Union Congress (TUC) in support of the Miners' Federation of Great Britain, which had been locked out by mine owners for refusing to accept longer hours of work for lower pay. Political and business leaders feared that the

General Strike was a prelude to violent revolution on the Russian Bolshevik model, and Prime Minister Stanley Baldwin determined to crush it. After nine days, the TUC called off the strike, but the miners remained out for nine more months.

The idea of the general strike was first expressed by William Benbow, a Quaker radical, in 1832. Benbow argued that the vast majority of workers produced goods for the benefit of a few employers. If they organized and proclaimed a "Grand National Holiday" in which everyone stopped working, then the economy would grind to a halt, public services and the government would cease functioning, and employers would be forced to grant equal political and economic rights to workers. Benbow's ideas were ignored in Britain but became popular in French labor and socialist circles, where they became the cornerstone of the syndicalist movement. The first fourteen years of the twentieth century saw almost continuous unrest among British dockers, transport workers, and coal miners. As industrial relations increasingly worsened, the labor movement shifted sharply to the political left and adopted the idea of the general strike.

Although World War I put a temporary end to industrial disputes, the miners did not give up their long-range goals: nationwide rather than regional pay agreements and nationalization of the mines. The British government refused to retain the wartime state operation of the mines, however, and the coming of peace led to a collapse of the coal market. The mine owners cut wages and increased hours of labor, which resulted in a nine-month strike in 1921 that the union lost. A momentary upturn in the export market for British coal was ended when Prime Minister Stanley Baldwin's Conservative government returned in 1925 to the gold standard, which overvalued the British pound and destroyed coal's competitive edge in international markets. The owners announced sweeping paycuts, but pressure from the TUC forced the government to subsidize wages at their existing levels for nine months and to establish a commission to study the mining industry.

The commission, chaired by Sir Herbert Samuel, a prominent Liberal statesman, reported in March, 1926. It recommended some of what the miners wanted, such as a national wages board, family allowances, improved working conditions, and the nationalization of coal royalties. It opposed continuation of the government subsidy, however, and recommended that either wages should be cut or the working day lengthened. The Miners' Federation, led by Herbert Smith and A. J. Cook, refused to negotiate, declaring "Not a penny off the pay, not a minute on the day." Neither the miners' union nor the mine owners were prepared to yield. When lockout notices went up at the mines, the TUC voted to strike in sympathy with the miners and gave full power to its general council to settle the dispute.

The TUC leaders, Ernest Bevin and Walter Citrine, wanted to avoid a strike and succeeded in hammering out an agreement with Baldwin early on Sunday morning, May 2. Unfortunately, a series of confusing circumstances prevented the agreement from being accepted. Miners' union officials, who needed to approve the agreement, had left London the night before; the officials were recalled but did not get back until Sunday evening. Then, just as the TUC representatives were about to sign the precise terms of the agreement, Baldwin complained that strikes had already taken place and declared that his government would not resume negotiating until the TUC repudiated the unofficial strike actions and withdrew the order for a general strike. Bevin and Citrine drafted a statement denying responsibility for the actions, but when they returned to the negotiating room they found the lights off. Thus the General Strike began at midnight, May 4, 1926.

The General Strike of 1926 was surely one of the oddest general strikes on record. In theory, general strikes were revolutionary actions to bring down government, yet the TUC denied any revolutionary intent. Rather, it claimed, in J. H. Thomas' words, that the strike was "merely a plain, economic, industrial dispute." Certainly the labor movement was unprepared for a general strike, thereby lending credence to Thomas' view. It had no plans whatsoever as to how to organize a general strike; many important decisions about which activities to strike and which to exempt from strike were made on the spot by local organizers.

Nor was the General Strike really general. It did affect about three million of the 4.3 million workers in unions affiliated with the TUC. Since the workers involved were crucial, especially the power-plant workers, the printers, and the transport workers, daily life was affected. Electricity became hard to obtain, no newspapers were printed, and commuters had a hard time getting to work. Many millions of workers, both working class and middle class, did continue to work during the strike. The banks never closed, nor were telephones and telegraphs shut down. The strike's effectiveness varied from place to place. Mining regions saw the most complete compliance with the strike. Urban transportation was shut down altogether in Manchester, Newcastle-on-Tyne, and Hull. Only five hundred of London's thirty-three hundred buses ever got on the streets. Compliance was more limited in other areas. Bus services were restored to normal in Cardiff, Chatham, Southampton, and Portsmouth, and were never interrupted in Oxford and Bristol.

The Baldwin Cabinet maintained from the beginning that the General Strike in fact was an unconstitutional attempt to coerce, and perhaps even to overthrow, parliamentary constitutional authority. Otherwise, argued the government, why have a General Strike at all? On this point, the government won the battle of public opinion. Chancellor of the Exchequer Winston Churchill proclaimed that a labor victory would result in the replacement of the existing constitution by "some Soviet of trade unions." More soberly, the Liberal lawyer Sir John Simon declared that the strike was illegal. Baldwin himself gave several influential fireside addresses over the British Broadcasting Corporation (BBC) radio which convinced many of the General Strike's unconstitutional and potentially revolutionary nature. A measure of his speeches' effects is the fact that the number of volunteer strikebreakers increased after he gave them. Moreover, in contrast to the labor movement, the government was prepared for a general strike, having laid plans to maintain essential services in the event of a general walkout after the 1921 miners' strikes.

In many ways, the General Strike seemed to be a conflict of personalities. On the union's side, Herbert Smith appeared the very image of the taciturn labor leader with his standard response to compromise, "Nowt doin." On the government side, Winston Churchill took a visible role in leading organized opposition to the General Strike. He published a government-printed newspaper, the *British Gazette*, which called for total defeat of the working-class enemy in the most extravagant language of class warfare. Caught in between were Bevin and Citrine of the TUC General Council, pragmatic men who were committed to negotiation and who did not want the strike, but who had to see it through.

The General Strike entered the British public imagination and became one of the great myths of the twentieth century. Stories abound of strikers playing soccer with police, of undergraduates and socialites running buses, trucks, and even railway trains. Certainly for many it was a lark. For many more, however, the days of the General Strike were fearsome ones in which getting to work and finding food were difficult tasks and when revolution seemed to be at hand. Lacking newspapers and doubting what they read in both the government *British Gazette* and the unionist *British Worker*, the general public at first was confused with rumor. Radio thus became increasingly important. The BBC was in its infancy in 1926. John Reith, its first director-general (1922-1938), personally sympathized with the miners' plight and in politics favored the Labour Party, but as a professional he was concerned about maintaining the BBC's reputation for impartiality and independence. He resisted Winston Churchill's attempts to commandeer the BBC and turn it into a government mouthpiece. The price of maintaining independence, though, was to hew closely to the government's line by reporting the news in a way that was fundamentally favorable to the government's position. Moreover, once the British High Court of Justice had declared the strike to be illegal, Reith believed that the BBC was enjoined from broadcasting anything that might justify or prolong the strike. On those grounds, Reith refused to broadcast a sermon by the Archbishop of Canterbury that proposed the resumption of negotiations because the Archbishop's suggestions did not fit into the government's plans. Thus it was that the government was in a much better position to mold public opinion.

One myth that attained special prominence in the British mind was that the General Strike passed without violence. The government certainly was prepared to use force to maintain essential services. Army regiments armed with machine guns guarded trucks as volunteers loaded them with food in the docks, and more soldiers escorted convoys of food-laden trucks through the streets of London. A battleship anchored off the port of Liverpool and trained its guns on the docks. The government enrolled 200,000 special constables to assist the police, formed a special steel-helmeted police reserve, and even considered mobilizing the Territorial Army (Britain's equivalent of the U.S. National Guard). Although the army never used its guns on the strikers, there was violence between strikers and police in several cities. About four thousand people were arrested, but there were no deaths on account of the strike.

The resolve of the miners to strike never wavered, and other workers in the so-called "second line" of the steel, shipbuilding, and textiles industries wanted to be called out in support of the miners. Citrine and Bevin of the TUC General Council had never given up hope of negotiating an end to the strike, however, and on May 11 proposed that the strike be called off on the basis of a memorandum drafted by Sir Herbert Samuel. Samuel's memorandum proposed that any reduction of wages in the coal mines should await adoption of the Samuel Commission's proposals to re-organize the industry. Baldwin never stated that he accepted the memorandum, and the Miners' Federation rejected it out of hand, but the TUC General Council ac-cepted it as the basis for calling off the strike. This it did at noon on May 12, and the General Strike was officially over. The miners carried on their strike for a further nine months, but growing hardship and demoralization drove the last of them back to the mines in November, accepting lower pay and longer hours. Their cause had suffered total defeat.

Impact of Event

Stanley Baldwin, who hailed the General Strike's end as a victory for constitu-tionalism, emerged with unparalleled prestige in the eyes of the British public. The TUC attempted to portray the strike's end as a victory for labor, but few workers accepted that interpretation. They returned to work slowly, bewildered at the defeat of what they thought was a just cause and troubled by what they thought had been betrayal by union leadership. Many workers were humiliated, and even punished, by their employers when they returned.

Baldwin and the Conservatives could have used their strong position to deal con-structively with the problems faced by the mining industry, but they chose to do nothing. Doing nothing would have been the correct policy if the General Strike had been motivated primarily by a revolutionary desire to overthrow the constitution. On the other hand, if the strike's causes rested primarily in the day-to-day difficulties of the British economy, as seems probable, then a more statesmanlike policy would have been to address those difficulties. In fact, Baldwin neither seriously attempted legislation along the lines suggested by the Samuel Commission nor encouraged constructive negotiations between miners and owners. Rather, he directed his ener-gies mainly toward punishing the labor unions. His government introduced the Trades Disputes Act of 1927, which declared general strikes illegal and forbade trade unions to collect political funds from their members unless they first obtained written per-mission to do so from each member individually.

Having tasted bitter defeat in the General Strike, the labor movement lost faith in united industrial action, and even the use of the ordinary strike declined during the later 1920's and the 1930's. Instead, labor leaders turned to improving working con-ditions through negotiations and conciliation. Citrine, the general secretary of the TUC, and Ben Turner, the TUC's chair, cosponsored a series of conferences with Sir Alfred Mond, the creator of the giant Imperial Chemical Industries and the leading industrialist of the day. These Mond-Turner conferences, attended by TUC officials and industrial executives, promoted cooperation and consultation between employers and labor and recommended the creation of a national industrial council to solve economic disputes through negotiation. Although nothing came of this specific proposal, the Mond-Turner talks did lead to regular negotiations between employers and employees in some industries.

Economic troubles continued throughout the rest of Baldwin's government, which fell in 1929 as a result of the Great Depression. Basic industries—coal, iron, steel, and textiles—continued to decline in world markets under the impact of foreign competition. Baldwin's government took the position that there was no remedy other than time. Given such a do-nothing policy, it is not surprising that the Conservatives lost the general election of 1929.

The Labour Party government formed in 1945 sought to make real the dreams of the general strikers of 1926. Many of the strike leaders found themselves in high office: Ernest Bevin became foreign secretary, and Aneurin Bevan, who had organized the strike in South Wales, was the minister responsible for creating the National Health Service. Two of the first acts of the Labour government were to repeal the Trades Disputes Act and to nationalize the coal mines. The government went on to create a welfare state that offered full employment, basic social security, educational opportunity for all, and the reduction of class distinctions. Looking back twenty years, the labor movement remembered the General Strike of 1926 as the first thoroughgoing attempt to create a more just society, one in which workers could deal with their employers with dignity and as equals.

Bibliography

Farman, Christopher. *The General Strike, May 1926.* London: Rupert Hart-Davis, 1972. A straightforward and readable account that attempts to tell the story without ideological bias. Focuses on personalities and includes illustrations of the principal personages and scenes.

Graves, Robert, and Alan Hodge. *The Long Week-End: A Social History of Great Britain, 1918-1939.* New York: W. W. Norton, 1963. This book is a delightful and fascinating account of daily social life between the wars, focusing on fads, fancies, controversies of the day, fashions, entertainment, sports, and all the activities that ordinary people think important but that historians sometimes miss in their focus on politics. Its chapter on the General Strike is written from the perspective of how the events affected people's daily lives.

Havighurst, Alfred F. *Twentieth-Century Britain.* 2d ed. New York: Harper & Row, 1962. This straightforward, clearly written general account of British political history from the death of Queen Victoria in 1901 to the end of the 1950's is especially good for the interwar years.

Morris, Margaret. *The British General Strike, 1926.* London: The Historical Association, 1973. A brief, objective survey, clearly written but with a now-outdated bibliography.

Renshaw, Patrick. *Nine Days That Shook Britain: The 1926 General Strike.* Garden City, N.Y.: Anchor Press, 1976. A readable survey of the General Strike's background, course, and consequences, placed in the context of the history of coal mining. Includes a chronology of events and a comprehensive and useful bibliography. The best source to start research.

Skelley, Jeffrey, ed. *The General Strike, 1926.* London: Lawrence and Wishart, 1976. This collection of essays seeks to bring regional and personal perspectives to the study of the General Strike. The book's core is made up of regional studies of the strike in Scotland; the North, Midlands, and South of England; and South Wales. Several essays take a national perspective. Many of the essays focus on the role that the Communist Party of Great Britain played in the strike.

Taylor, A. J. P. *English History, 1914-1945.* Vol. 15 in *The Oxford History of England*, edited by Sir George Clark. New York: Oxford University Press, 1965. Covering the period from the beginning of World War I to the end of World War II, this book reaches the highest standards of objectivity while offering the lively writing that one expects from the author. A. J. P. Taylor, sometimes controversial but always stimulating, deals with social and economic developments as well as with political history. This book is indispensable for background to the period. Includes a bibliography, a list of cabinets, and maps.

D. G. Paz

Cross-References

The British Labour Party Is Formed (1906), p. 58; The International Labour Organisation Is Established (1919), p. 281; Steel Workers Go on Strike to Demand Improved Working Conditions (1919), p. 293; Great Britain Passes Acts to Provide Unemployment Benefits (1920), p. 321; The Wagner Act Requires Employers to Accept Collective Bargaining (1935), p. 508; Social Security Act Establishes Benefits for Nonworking People (1935), p. 514; The Congress of Industrial Organizations Is Formed (1938), p. 545; Solidarity Leads Striking Polish Workers (1980), p. 2112; Solidarity Regains Legal Status in Poland (1989), p. 2477.

THE LEAGUE OF NATIONS ADOPTS THE INTERNATIONAL SLAVERY CONVENTION

Category of event: Civil rights
Time: September 25, 1926
Locale: Geneva, Switzerland

The 1926 International Slavery Convention was part of an effort begun by colonial nations a century earlier to suppress slavery in all of its forms

Principal personages:

PAUL HYMANS (1865-1941), a delegate to the League of Nations from Belgium

FREDERICK J. LUGARD (1858-1945), the United Kingdom's delegate on the Temporary Slavery Commission

HENRY MORTON STANLEY (1841-1904), a British subject, writer, and explorer; his expeditions helped reveal the extent of slavery in Africa

Summary of Event

The ancient Greeks believed in natural slavery, especially for people who did not speak Greek, who were referred to as "barbarians." With the advent of Christianity and the nation-state, a variety of justifications were used to harmonize slavery with the teachings of the Bible. Christians, for example, justified enslaving people who practiced cannibalism and human sacrifice.

The philosophers of the American and French revolutions did much to discredit slavery by condemning it for destroying the natural liberty of human beings. In the aftermath of the Napoleonic Wars, at the Congress of Vienna on February 8, 1815, the victorious nations declared their intention to suppress the slave trade. The powers with colonial possessions were advised of their obligation and duty to abolish the slave trade. The slave trade was by then in retreat in Europe and North America; however, the institution of slavery itself, in the form of plantation slavery in the British possessions and in the United States, was virtually untouched.

None of the nations at the Congress of Vienna in 1815 was willing to trespass on the sovereignty of other states to end any form of domestic slavery. Nevertheless, the Congress of Vienna was a major step toward engendering an agreement among European nations to work to abolish the international traffic in slaves, especially the trans-Atlantic trade.

Colonialism could be justified, according to Sir Frederick Lugard, who had served for many years in Africa as a colonial administrator, only if it provided mutual advantages for the colonized "natives" and for the world. Colonialism was a "school" to Christianize and civilize "savage" peoples. In return, the colony would provide European capitalists with raw materials for their industries and markets for their manufacturers.

In 1885, European nations held the African Conference at Berlin. That conference called for the suppression of slavery and specifically of "the Negro slave trade," but the act passed by the conference applied only to the Congo Basin. It was an important development in creating a body of international law which was militantly opposed to slavery.

Explorers, such as Henry Morton Stanley, had discovered and publicized the existence of a vast area in Africa that was controlled by Arab slave raiders. Arab traders, such as Tippu Tib, actually posed a military threat to the tribes of the region and even to the Belgian military. Strong military operations were necessary in the Congo and elsewhere in Africa to defeat combative slave traders. The parties to the African Conference, in an 1886 decree, provided for penal servitude for slave traders.

Slave caravans penetrated the interior of Africa from the shores of the Mediterranean, the Red Sea, the Persian Gulf, and the Indian Ocean. The traffic in slaves encompassed the modern countries of Nigeria, Sudan, Ethiopia, Ghana, Burundi, and Zaire, among others. Slaves brought to trading centers in northern and eastern Africa were sold for local use or, as was more often the case, were sent to Turkey, Arabia, Iran, and other eastern countries. Another decree in 1888 regarding labor contracts prohibited the enslavement of natives by nonnatives. The colonial powers were trying to abolish slavery indirectly by abolishing the slave trade.

There were difficulties connected with the outright abolition of domestic slavery (that is, slavery within a colony) and forced labor, and an international consensus did not yet exist for a frontal attack on slavery and its analogous forms. An impressive step was taken to suppress slavery at the Second Brussels Conference of 1890. The General Act of Brussels, signed on July 2, 1890, as a result of that conference, had more signatories than earlier international conventions on the suppression of slavery; it also had more enforcement requirements in its articles than did preceding conventions. The nations meeting at Brussels included all of the major European nations, as well as the United States, Turkey, Iran, and Zanzibar. The General Act of Brussels prescribed specific measures for the acceding nations to take against slave raiding and trading in the territory under European control.

The measures enacted by the antislavery alliance were designed to spur the parties to organize the administrative, judicial, and military services of government in their territories of Africa so that they could more effectively regulate the slave traffic. The General Act of Brussels required the establishment of military posts in the interior, where slave raiders collected slaves for overland transit to the coasts for shipment to eastern countries; an increase in the use of steamships manned by soldiers on navigable waterways and lakes, thus expanding the presence of the central government throughout the region; more operations by "flying columns" of soldiers to maintain contact between various military posts; and the installation of telegraphs as a means of linking isolated areas to the provincial capital to monitor movements of slave traders and to allow for a more rapid deployment of military forces.

The articles of the General Act of Brussels were meaningful in setting the foundation for more expansive efforts toward suppressing the slave trade, domestic slavery, and many of the forms of forced labor. Belgium employed military force against slave raiders to gain control of the interior and to suppress slavery. In time, with the use of native troops and modern weapons, the Belgians secured the interior from large-scale raids from outside the Congo Basin, at a cost of considerable losses of Belgian soldiers. The problem of domestic slavery was left to languish. It was difficult to differentiate between slavery, according to many European apologists, as an acceptable social institution and slavery as a barbaric and cruel method of employment of individuals against their will. Domestic slavery was seen as inevitable but susceptible to gradual elimination through "civilizing" of native people by European colonizers. Enslavement of natives by natives was considered by Europeans to be beyond the realm of their control, while slavery imposed by nonnatives on natives was strictly prohibited as odious to all civilized people and was punishable by law.

World War I interrupted the international efforts to stop slavery and the continuing endeavor at enforcement of the precepts of the General Act of Brussels. The victorious allies—Belgium, the United Kingdom, France, Italy, Japan, Portugal, and the United States—signed a new compact at Saint-Germain-en-Laye on September 10, 1919. The new convention was formulated to complete the work started by the General Act of Brussels.

The Saint-Germain-en-Laye Convention was short-lived. It was superseded by antislavery activities of the newly founded League of Nations. The League of Nations confirmed the previous antislavery declarations and proclaimed its own intent to achieve the complete suppression of slavery "in all of its forms and of the slave trade by land and sea."

In 1924, the League of Nations appointed a Temporary Slavery Commission of eight experts to compile information on slavery, so-called domestic slavery, slave raiding, serfdom, purchase of girls as brides, simulated adoption of children for purposes of sexual exploitation, varied forms of indenture, and compulsory labor by state and private employers. Sir Frederick Lugard, perhaps the most influential and respected member of the Temporary Slavery Commission, helped to craft the commission's report to the Council of the League of Nations. Sir Frederick's broad experience and practical approach to the suppression of slavery assured the report's adoption by most of the member states of the League of Nations. His suggestions moved the members to moderate positions while retaining the goal of the eventual end of de facto slavery through a process of transition and the development of new modes of employment.

Paul Hymans, the Belgian delegate to the League of Nations in 1926, personified the efforts by Belgium to establish an unambiguous posture toward the suppression of the slave trade and nonnative enslavement of natives. He was reluctant, as were most members, to grapple with the question of forced labor and domestic slavery. The Belgians were, to a good extent, successful in suppressing the slave trade in the Congo Basin.

The report of the Temporary Slavery Commission stated the objectives of the commission. It defined "enslavement," made proposals for regulating and punishing persons engaged in slave-raiding and the slave trade, and addressed "slave dealing" and the more controversial domestic slavery issue. In an auxiliary category, the report discussed the acquisition of girls by purchase, disguised as payment of dowry, and adoption of children "with a view to their virtual enslavement or the ultimate disposal of their persons."

The Temporary Slavery Commission was shrewdly cautious on the question of forced labor: Its abolition was desirable but not achievable given the provisions of the Covenant of the League of Nations, which prohibited intervention by member states into the domestic affairs of any state. In addition, the commission recognized a need for compulsory native labor in an environment that was inhospitable to white workers. According to the adopted Convention on Slavery, signatories recognized the need for governments to use compulsory or forced labor for public projects but urged that such use should be transitional and should be put to end as soon as possible. Signatories were allowed to accept all or only some of the provisions of the convention, significantly weakening its impact. It was more moral suasion than enforceable law, but it represented a goal to be striven for by many members of the League of Nations.

Impact of Event

The 1926 Slavery Convention defined slavery as "the status or condition of a person over whom any or all of the powers attaching to the right of ownership are exercised." The convention required the former colonies of Germany and the Ottoman Empire, now mandates of the League of Nations, to suppress slavery and to prepare the people of the mandates for active participation in their own political affairs.

Ethiopia was denied entry into the League of Nations until it formulated a definite plan to eliminate all forms of slavery, which it finally accomplished to a limited extent in the official abolition of slavery in 1942. Liberia, the other recalcitrant slave state, was pressured by the League of Nations to outlaw intertribal slavery and to abolish some other forms of servitude.

The most significant impacts of the 1926 Slavery Convention were on slave raiding and the de jure abolition of slavery in Ethiopia and Liberia. The mandate system also gave the League of Nations moral clout and some circumscribed political leverage in suppressing domestic slavery and specific forms of forced labor.

It was the transition from slavery to certain forms of servile labor, including debt bondage and contract labor, that undermined the effects of emancipation of slaves around the world. Two strategies emerged to replace de facto slavery. One was to entice new labor from other areas by means of indentures, or contracts to work for specific periods of time. This system often involved the accumulation of debts by the laborer. The other form, emerging in the aftermath of emancipation, was peasant bondage, which used former slaves on small land holds and on large projects, such as road building and railroad construction. Peasant bondage was a form of virtual slavery in which workers were "paid" in the form of training or provisions. Both systems, in many variations, are indirect forms of slavery, or servitude. In the United States, servile labor took the form of sharecropping and share tenancy, in which workers paid part of their harvest as rent. In the Caribbean, it was in the form of contracted labor from India and the Middle East.

The 1926 International Slavery Convention had an important impact, as laying the foundation for continuing struggle against de jure slavery and in establishing continual international opposition to all forms of slavery. It did not, however, immediately end all forms of unequal and exploitive labor arrangements.

Bibliography

Barnes, Anthony J. *Captain Charles Stuart: Anglo-American Abolitionist.* Baton Rouge: Louisiana State University Press, 1986. A solid biography of a relatively obscure militant abolitionist. His attack on gradualists in the movement convinced people like William Lloyd Garrison to take a more militant stance.

Drescher, Seymour. *Capitalism and Antislavery: British Mobilization in Comparative Perspective.* London: Macmillan, 1986. This revisionary account of black slavery in the Americas and in Africa is convincing. Drescher's assessment of the historiography on slavery is broad and powerfully written. Drescher explains English law and slavery.

Ennew, Judith. *Debt Bondage.* London: Anti-Slavery Society, 1981. A survey of contemporary debt bondage throughout the world. This report shows graphically the persistence of contract labor and the little progress being made to end it.

Koger, Larry. *Black Slaveowners: Free Black Slave Masters in South Carolina, 1790-1860.* London: McFarland, 1985. There have been several works on free blacks owning slaves in the antebellum South. This is the first study to show that free black masters behaved similarly to white slaveowners. Both exploited slaves for profits.

Lordell, Richard A. *Economic Structure and Demographic Performance in Jamaica, 1891-1935.* New York: Garland, 1987. The author is interested in two major socioeconomic characteristics of Jamaica—the demography of the island and the plantation system. His main contribution is his finding that death rates tended to be higher for workers who dealt with certain staple crops.

Watson, Alan. *Roman Slave Law.* Baltimore: The Johns Hopkins University Press, 1987. The author maintains that in a strict sense there was scarcely any such thing as "Roman slave law"; rather, every category of the law was affected by the fact of being a slave.

Claude Hargrove

Cross-References

Reformers Expose Atrocities Against Congolese Laborers (1903), p. 13; International Agreement Attacks the White Slave Trade (1904), p. 30; The Belgian Government Annexes the Congo (1908), p. 103; The Paris Peace Conference Includes Pro-

THE MINIMUM AGE FOR FEMALE
BRITISH VOTERS IS LOWERED

Categories of event: Voting rights and women's rights
Time: July 2, 1928
Locale: London, England

The 1928 Representation of the People Act lowered the age at which women could vote from thirty to twenty-one, thereby granting them suffrage at the same age as male voters

Principal personages:
LADY NANCY ASTOR (1879-1964), the first female member of the House of Commons
STANLEY BALDWIN (1867-1947), the British prime minister in 1928, chiefly responsible for the equal-suffrage legislation
WINSTON CHURCHILL (1874-1965), the chancellor of the exchequer in 1928 and leader of cabinet opposition to the equal-suffrage legislation
ELEANOR RATHBONE (1872-1946), the president of the National Union of Societies for Equal Citizenship
LADY MARGARET RHONDDA (1883-1958), the leader of the Equal Political Rights Campaign Committee

Summary of Event

In 1918, the British Parliament passed the Representation of the People Act, which gave men the right to vote at age twenty-one but restricted suffrage for women to those qualified to vote in local elections and aged thirty and over. This step was welcomed by women's suffrage organizations, since it conceded the principle of women's suffrage, but as women remained second-class citizens it did not fulfill their objective of equal suffrage rights. Therefore, almost immediately after celebrating their partial victory, women's suffrage organizations began preparing for a new campaign to obtain the vote on the same terms as men.

Women sought equal suffrage for a variety of reasons. It was viewed by many as an insult to women that they should not be trusted with the vote until they reached the age of thirty, whereas men could vote at the age of twenty-one. Unequal suffrage was seen as a symbol of the wider pattern of sex-differentiated policies that hampered women's opportunities in employment and in public life in general. Jobs were generally sex-segregated, with the higher-status and higher-paying positions reserved for men. Even in those few areas, such as teaching and the civil service, in which women did the same work as men, they received lower pay. In many areas, employers imposed a marriage bar that forced female employees to resign from their positions if they married. In addition, the government refused to allow doctors at public health clinics to provide married women with birth-control information. Women hoped that the additional political power they would gain from equal suffrage rights would enable them to change these discriminatory policies.

The postwar campaign for equal suffrage was conducted primarily by women's organizations that had fought for woman suffrage before the war. The largest and most important of these was the National Union of Societies for Equal Citizenship (NUSEC), which was known as the National Union of Women's Suffrage Societies until 1918. Led by Eleanor Rathbone, NUSEC worked for reform by quietly lobbying political leaders rather than by using the more militant, and more public, methods associated with the prewar suffragettes.

NUSEC's efforts to get a commitment from the Conservative Party to act on the issue benefited from the assistance of the first female member of the House of Commons, Lady Nancy Astor. An American who had married the wealthy British member of Parliament David Astor, Lady Astor was elected to the House of Commons as a Conservative in 1919. She viewed herself as a spokesperson for women and was taken seriously in this role by politicians seeking support from female voters. Those who find it curious that equal suffrage was eventually enacted by a Conservative government should bear in mind Lady Astor's persistent lobbying for that reform within her own party.

During the 1924 election campaign, under prodding from NUSEC and other women's groups, the Conservative Party leader, Stanley Baldwin, pledged that if his party were returned to office, it would sponsor a special parliamentary conference on the equal-suffrage issue. This was understood by women as a commitment to introduce equal-suffrage legislation, although some Conservatives who opposed that reform thought it a clever way of attracting female votes without promising to do anything more than hold a conference to discuss the issue. Thus, the Conservative government did not become unequivocally committed to proceed with equal suffrage until 1925, when a cabinet minister, William Joynson Hicks, pledged that the government would act on the matter before the end of the current Parliament.

When the government failed to take action during the next two years, women's groups began to fear that they had been deceived. NUSEC joined with more than forty other women's organizations on July 3, 1926, in sponsoring a march through London to Hyde Park to demonstrate the degree of support among women for equal suffrage. Although some speakers warned that there could be a revival of suffragette tactics if the government did not proceed with reform, Lady Astor privately discouraged militant action. She claimed that suffragette violence would make it impossible for the government to proceed with legislation, as it would appear that the politicians were giving in to force. Reluctantly, Lady Margaret Rhondda accepted this advice, but her dissatisfaction with NUSEC's backstage lobbying tactics led her to form a new group, the Equal Political Rights Campaign Committee, to increase pressure on the government.

The suffrage reformers were correct in believing that prominent members of the cabinet were seeking a way to avoid honoring the government's pledge on equal suffrage. The cabinet committee appointed by Baldwin to draft a bill devoted most of its time to trying to find some reason for not proceeding with it. One of the cabinet ministers most adamantly opposed to legislation, Winston Churchill, feared that granting the vote to women at age twenty-one would be a political disaster for the Conservative Party, as he anticipated that most of the newly enfranchised women would vote for the rival Labour Party. Other Conservatives opposed reform on the ground that it meant enfranchising "flappers," a pejorative term implying immature, empty-headed females who knew nothing about politics or life and who would likely cast their votes for the most attractive male candidate. Underlying the various arguments opposing equal suffrage was an awareness that it would make women the majority of the electorate; some Conservatives feared that women would be less willing than men to vote for policies running the risk of war to protect the British Empire.

Despite the strong resistance within his party, Baldwin insisted that the government proceed with legislation. He was aware that if the Conservatives did not act, the Labour Party would make an issue of it at the next general election and might gain enough female votes to defeat the Conservatives. Since a Labour government would then almost certainly introduce equal suffrage, Baldwin believed that reform was inevitable and that inaction by the Conservative government would only improve the Labour Party's election prospects. He was also convinced that a majority of the newly enfranchised women would become Conservative voters, given the party's special interest in promoting home and family life.

As a result of Baldwin's support, the government finally introduced its equal-franchise bill in 1928. It granted women the right to vote at age twenty-one on the same terms as men. Once it was introduced in Parliament, the outcome was never in doubt, in part because opponents feared that speaking against the bill could antagonize existing female voters. The bill was supported by the Labour and Liberal parties, and thus the only opposition came from a handful of diehard Conservatives. The antisuffragists' dire predictions of the consequences that would follow if the bill passed seemed so outdated that they provoked laughter rather than serious discussion from the members supporting the measure. Late in March, 1928, the House of Commons voted overwhelmingly for the bill: 387 endorsed it with only 10 opposing. When a majority of the House of Lords also voted for it, the Representation of the People (Equal Suffrage) Act became law on July 2, 1928.

Impact of Event

The equal-suffrage act removed one of the most important remaining symbols of women's inferior position under British law. Baldwin described the act as the final step in granting women equal rights. Many women accepted this claim and withdrew from women's reform organizations to devote themselves to their families and private lives. Women viewed the act as the culmination of a movement for political rights begun nearly sixty years earlier. Some, like Millicent Fawcett, had devoted most of their adult lives to the suffrage campaign. It should not be surprising, therefore, that for many women the sense of elation was mixed with a feeling of relief that the struggle was finally over.

Although antisuffragists had predicted that equal suffrage would bring radical change to British political life, this expectation proved mistaken. About five-and-one-half million women gained the right to vote as a result of the act. Although the act is usually described as having granted the vote to women between the ages of twenty-one and thirty, nearly one-third of those who gained the franchise were over thirty and had been prevented from voting by the property-owning requirements of the previous electoral law. As a result of the act, women became a majority of the electorate; at the next general election, held in 1929, 52.7 percent of the voters were female.

Nevertheless, only 14 women were elected to the House of Commons in 1929 as compared to 601 men. The new women members were absorbed into the existing political parties and voted as the male members of their parties did; they did not form a distinct women's group in Parliament. Women voters did not vote as a bloc but divided their votes among the three major parties much as men did. Although some claimed that the new female voters were responsible for Labour's victory in the 1929 election, this has not been proven. Most studies have shown, on the contrary, that women were slightly more likely than men to vote Conservative.

In the short term, women gained few direct benefits from equal suffrage. The newly elected Labour government was surprisingly indifferent, if not openly hostile, to women's issues. It took no steps to protect women's rights to work when rising male unemployment stimulated public criticism of women workers. Although Minister of Labour Margaret Bondfield was the first female cabinet minister, she was directly responsible for legislation that deprived many married women of their right to unemployment benefits. The Labour government did nothing to assist the campaign for family allowances that had been so important to Labour Party women in the 1920's. Finally, the Labour government resisted women's demand that public health clinics be allowed to provide birth-control information to married women and permitted this change to be introduced only when Labour-controlled city councils joined in the campaign.

One of the most important consequences of equal suffrage was the withdrawal of women from active campaigning for sex equality. After 1928, the membership of the largest feminist organization, the National Union of Societies for Equal Citizenship, declined rapidly. By the early 1930's, it had become a much smaller and much less influential organization.

Bibliography

Adam, Ruth. *A Woman's Place, 1910-75.* London: Chatto & Windus, 1975. A well-written, lively history of British women for the general reader. It includes a good summary of developments affecting women in the 1920's and relates the suffrage campaign to other women's issues. Contains an index and endnotes but no bibliography.

Alberti, Johanna. *Beyond Suffrage: Feminists in War and Peace, 1914-28.* New York:

St. Martin's Press, 1989. A well-informed study of British feminists in the 1920's. Makes extensive use of manuscript material to add to the understanding of the women involved in the campaign. No bibliography, but provides an appendix with useful biographical information on the major feminists.

Harrison, Brian. *Prudent Revolutionaries: Portraits of British Feminists Between the Wars.* Oxford, England: Clarendon Press, 1987. Contains excellent biographical studies of many of the women involved in the equal-suffrage campaign. Includes much new information, especially on their personal lives. Outstanding index and valuable bibliographical essay.

Middlemas, Keith, and John Barnes. *Baldwin: A Biography.* London: Weidenfeld & Nicolson, 1969. The fullest biography of the prime minister responsible for the 1928 suffrage act. It examines the conflict within the Conservative Party on the issue and Baldwin's reasons for proceeding with it against the strong opposition of prominent members of his own party. Contains an index and a brief list of references.

Smith, Harold L., ed. *British Feminism in the Twentieth Century.* Amherst: University of Massachusetts Press, 1990. A collection of original essays on various aspects of British feminism. Has chapters on feminism in the 1920's and on Eleanor Rathbone that provide the context for the 1920's suffrage campaign. Has an index and a brief bibliography.

Strachey, Ray. *The Cause: A Short History of the Women's Movement in Great Britain.* 1928. Reprint. London: Virago, 1978. An important study by a prominent figure in the largest women's suffrage organization. Rather bland and not as revealing as it could have been. Useful as a detailed narrative of what happened and women's perceptions of events. Includes an index, but the brief bibliography is badly dated.

Harold L. Smith

Cross-References

The Pankhursts Found the Women's Social and Political Union (1903), p. 19; Women's Institutes Are Founded in Great Britain (1915), p. 167; Parliament Grants Suffrage to British Women (1918), p. 247; The Nineteenth Amendment Gives American Women the Right to Vote (1920), p. 339; Women's Rights in India Undergo a Decade of Change (1925), p. 401; French Women Get the Vote (1944), p. 646; The U.N. Convention on the Political Rights of Women Is Approved (1952), p. 885; The United Nations Issues a Declaration on Equality for Women (1967), p. 1391; Women in Switzerland Are Granted the Right to Vote (1971), p. 1605; Thatcher Becomes Great Britain's First Female Prime Minister (1979), p. 2024; A U.N. Convention Condemns Discrimination Against Women (1979), p. 2057.

GANDHI LEADS THE SALT MARCH

Categories of event: Indigenous peoples' rights and political freedom
Time: 1930
Locale: India

Gandhi organized the Salt March in 1930 to protest British actions in India and to start a mass campaign of noncooperation

Principal personages:

MAHATMA GANDHI (1869-1948), the Hindu leader of the Indian national-ist movement who began the Salt March in 1930 to restart mass op-position to British rule

SUBHAS CHANDRA BOSE (1897-1945), a young radical Congressmember who saw that opposition to Gandhi was impossible

LORD IRWIN (1881-1959), the viceroy of India from 1926 to 1931

JAWAHARLAL NEHRU (1889-1964), a socialist and a believer in Western science and technology; one of Gandhi's principal followers during the Salt March

MOTILAL NEHRU (1861-1931), the founder of the "Nehru dynasty" who gave up his moderate politics to join Gandhi in the Salt March

Summary of Event

Mohandas Karamchand Gandhi was released from prison in 1924, having been incarcerated for nearly two years for his part in the illegal activities of the non-cooperation movement, which he started in 1920 in a successful attempt to arouse opposition to British rule. Gandhi (known as Mahatma, or "Great Soul") retired from politics upon his release and returned to his *ashram* (commune) to devote himself to spinning *khadi* (homespun cloth) and to fostering Hindu-Muslim unity, prohibition, and the moral and economic uplift of village life. As a result, politics entered a lull and the Indian nationalist movement, which had gathered strength during the last part of the nineteenth century and become strong during the twen-tieth century, was left without an active national leader. Nevertheless, all members of the Indian National Congress, the most important political party in India, knew that Gandhi was the most widely accepted leader in the country. Even during his period of retirement, political leaders constantly kept in touch with him, and a volu-minous correspondence was exchanged. Party officials urged him to return to active politics and again to lead the nationalist movement. The Congress organization was passing into the leadership of a new generation—Jawaharlal Nehru and Subhas Chandra Bose—who wanted to start a new noncooperation movement, but Gandhi was the only person who could lead such a movement.

The nationalist movement had not been very vigorous since Gandhi's retirement from politics, and many Indians had cooperated with the British and now served in government legislatures and agencies. As a result of this lack of active opposition by Indian politicians, the British continued to ignore Indian rights. Indians did not, for example, have control of the legislative councils which the British had introduced in 1923; the British and their appointees dominated the councils. The legal system was controlled by British judges, and all the senior policemen and officers in the army were British. On a daily basis, the British continued to show disrespect to Indians by barring them from almost all British social clubs and by shunning their company except on special occasions. In short, Indians were treated as foreigners in their own land and kept down by a British *raj* (rule) which was backed up by a strong police force and army that Indians themselves had to finance through their taxes.

It was only through opposition by the Indians that this would change. The occasion for the resurgence in the nationalist movement came with the appointment of the Simon Commission in 1928. This was a committee made up of British politicians and sent to India to assess how the constitution of 1919 was working. It was to decide how the next step of reforms should take place. The British had created anger by not appointing a single Indian to the commission. This was perceived as a racist slight, and to show disapproval of it, the Indian National Congress refused to attend the first session of the Round Table Conference, which was held in 1930 in London to allow Indians representing various religious and interest groups to discuss with the British how a new constitution should be written. In the meantime, Congress had, in fact, produced its own draft of a constitution (Motilal Nehru's *Nehru Report* of 1928) and threatened that if the British did not give India dominion status, which would have made India as free as Australia, Canada, or New Zealand, India would demand complete independence. This was the background to Gandhi's return to active politics at the end of 1928.

The Congress and Gandhi met in December, 1929, and decided to start a civil disobedience campaign similar to the noncooperation movement of 1920 in order to force the British to take notice of Indian demands for rights and freedom. It was left to Gandhi to decide how and when the campaign would start. He decided it would be over salt. Many were amazed that Gandhi had chosen this issue over which to oppose imperial rule, but salt was a heavily taxed government monopoly and therefore any protest over it would be understood easily by all Indians. Before Gandhi began the movement, he offered peace to the government through his "eleven points," a series of demands that included social reforms and economic reforms such as reduction of military expenditures. These demands were rejected by the British.

On March 5, Gandhi announced to his *ashram* that he and a group of his followers would march to the coast carrying copies of the *Gita* (a Hindu holy book), and once they had arrived at the sea they would break the law by making salt. This was a deliberate campaign to confront British rule in India. Gandhi informed the Viceroy, Lord Irwin, that he proposed to start a civil disobedience campaign on the salt tax issue, and on March 12 he and seventy-nine followers began their trek to the sea. They made the 240-mile trip in twenty-five days, arriving at Dandi, on the Indian

Ocean, on April 5. Early the following morning they went down to the beach, picked up some salt-encrusted mud, boiled it, made salt, and thus broke the salt laws. Salt had now become the symbol of India's fight for freedom.

The salt campaign that began with Gandhi's month-long march lasted another two months, until the beginning of the monsoon season. At first the British did not respond to Gandhi's breach of the law, but when he wrote to the Viceroy and informed him of plans to raid the Dharsana Salt Works nearby, he, along with all the Congress leaders, was arrested on May 5. Gandhi was incarcerated under an 1827 regulation which did not require a trial or a fixed sentence. He was held in prison for nearly a year, until January 26, 1931.

The Salt March and the noncooperation movement which followed coincided with the worldwide depression. Importers could not sell their stocks, tenant farmers could not earn enough from their crops to pay their rents, landlords and cultivating owners could not cover their land revenue, and even the government had to cut back staff and reduce salaries. The salt march started off a civil disobedience movement joined by large numbers of these disaffected people.

The salt *satyagraha* (nonviolent civil disobedience campaign) affected almost every province in the country. People even marched down to local rivers to boil the water in a symbolic gesture of solidarity with Gandhi. The government was put on the defensive. Rings of Congress volunteers surrounded the people making salt so that it became impossible to arrest the lawbreakers without resorting to great violence; any violence was publicized by the Congress in great detail. A tremendous amount of enthusiasm and a contempt for the government were generated through this campaign. Gandhi had once again seized the political initiative for the Congress party, and all of India was motivated to fight for freedom.

Salt was the symbol of the campaign but it was not the only part of the civil disobedience movement. The salt campaign was localized along the coast, but the boycott of foreign cloth became a very forceful India-wide offensive. Social pressure was applied to vendors and buyers by protesters who sealed foreign cloth stocks and physically, in a nonviolent manner, blocked merchants who attempted to move them. The major centers of India's foreign cloth trade came to a virtual halt for most of the year and imports dropped dramatically.

There were also campaigns which varied from province to province and were related to local grievances. In the west of India, in Gujarat, people refused to pay their land revenue tax and started a social boycott of government workers. Many of those workers resigned from their positions. In the Central Provinces, people burned trees and cut grass in defiance of forestry regulations, and in Bihar people broke liquor laws. In the city of Bombay, the Congress practically took over the city. As the government official responsible for domestic affairs noted, "The numbers, the discipline, the organization and the brushing aside of the ordinary functions of police control of traffic have combined to produce a vivid impression of the power and the success of the Congress movement." The British administration hovered on the brink of collapse for months.

Impact of Event

Gandhi had inspired and started a mass movement in a manner never before seen in India. Sixty thousand people were imprisoned by the British, but millions more heard of the campaign, avoided buying foreign cloth, made donations to the Congress, or attended one of innumerable meetings. Some soldiers in the army refused to obey orders to fire on unarmed demonstrators. The government was concerned that for the first time protest had become a rural movement as well as an urban one. Very significant also was the fact that upper-class and educated women participated in politics for the first time in history. Women continued the work of husbands or male members of the family who went to prison. Some of them even went to prison themselves. This reflected an incredible change in attitude. Before Gandhi led the nationalist movement, going to prison would have been a mark of terrible shame. Now people were willingly defying the police and committing crimes in the name of freedom. Further, the movement involved people of all ages, as even children became "freedom fighters."

With the involvement of so many people of all classes and ages, the Congress' prestige grew immensely as people proudly called themselves followers of Gandhi. People began to sense that independence was near and began to talk about what was going to happen after the British had left. Those politicians who had not supported the movement and who were cooperating with the British to reform the constitution were embarrassed to be seen as collaborators and were pushed unwillingly into opposition to the British. At this juncture, one of the most important of the Muslim leaders of the country and one who had always opposed Gandhi's tactics, Muhammad Ali Jinnah, left India and settled in England.

The Salt March and the movement it started were an enormous success. The British government increasingly had to use force to maintain law and order; this use of force put it more and more in the wrong with the Indian people. Slowly, it lost all moral authority in the land. Congress increasingly came to be identified with the nation itself.

The psychological impact of the movement was enormous. Indians of all classes and ages became willing to stand up for their rights. Large numbers of women were involved in a political movement for the first time in history. The whole nation had been mobilized, and the image of Gandhi marching to the sea in defiance of the British Empire became front page news in all the major newspapers of the world. Gandhi became a hero to nationalists everywhere, receiving the admiration of many people even in England.

By 1931, the movement had exhausted both the British and the Indians. After Gandhi and the leaders of the Congress had been released from prison, he wrote asking the Viceroy for a meeting and a truce. Lord Irwin willingly agreed. The result was the Gandhi-Irwin Pact (the Delhi Pact) of March 5, 1931.

The noncooperation movement started by the Salt March mobilized an entire continent, established Gandhi as an international figure, and made the world's largest empire come to terms. Indians had become too strong for the British to trample on their human rights as they had in the past: India had been awakened.

As a result of the Gandhi-Irwin Pact, Gandhi was invited to attend the Second Round Table Conference. He did so as the sole representative of the Congress. Although Gandhi did not get what he wanted and considered the conference a failure, the Government of India Act of 1935 which emerged from it gave virtual independence to the provinces and planned for independence at the center as well. The British still ruled India, but Gandhi had mobilized the Indians to such an extent that the days of foreign dominance over this vast land were clearly numbered.

Bibliography

Brown, Judith M. *Gandhi: Prisoner of Hope.* New Haven, Conn.: Yale University Press, 1989. This is not a detailed account of the Salt March, but it does discuss the period and will place it in broader context. Brown has dedicated her academic career to studying the life of Gandhi. This is a very authoritative book and can be considered a basic work on Gandhi.

_____. *Gandhi and Civil Disobedience: The Mahatma in Indian Politics, 1928-34.* Cambridge, England: Cambridge University Press, 1977. For the most detailed account of the Salt March available, this is the book to read. It is highly detailed and almost a week by week account of Gandhi's activities during the period 1928-1934.

Copley, Antony. *Gandhi: Against the Tide.* London: Basil Blackwell, 1987. To place the accounts of the Salt March in context and within an understanding of Gandhi's life work, this is the quickest book to consult. Very short, it is a handy quick reference.

Erikson, Erik. *Gandhi's Truth: On the Origins of Militant Nonviolence.* New York: W. W. Norton, 1969. Gandhi's aim during the Salt March was not only to mobilize Indians against the British but also to raise the consciousness level of Indians and to give them a psychological lift. This is a book by a psychoanalyst who describes Gandhi's attempts during the Salt March to change the psychology of Indians and to make them less passive.

Fox, Richard G. *Gandhian Utopia: Experiments with Culture.* Boston: Beacon Press, 1989. Gandhi was not only aiming at freedom for Indians but also wanted to influence India's cultural and social life. This is a work by an anthropologist who discusses the cultural dimensions of Gandhi's work during the Salt March.

Gandhi, M. K. *An Autobiography: The Story of My Experiments with Truth.* Boston: Beacon Press, 1957. Gandhi stops his autobiography when he reaches the year 1920, but this book is essential to understanding Gandhi's ideas as he developed them in his early life.

Nehru, Jawaharlal. *Toward Freedom: The Autobiography of Jawaharlal Nehru.* 1941. Reprint. Boston: Beacon Press, 1963. In some ways Nehru, an internationalist who was considered a radical, was the opposite of Gandhi, yet for a variety of reasons he became one of Gandhi's most devoted followers. This autobiography reveals the remarkable power Gandhi had over Indians and how modernists like

Nehru were flabbergasted when Gandhi came up with the idea of the Salt March but later conceded that Gandhi had chosen the exact symbol with which to arouse opposition to the British. This is a classic account, by a participant, of the events of the time.

Roger D. Long

Cross-References

The Muslim League Attempts to Protect Minority Interests in India (1906), p. 87; The Defense of India Act Impedes the Freedom Struggle (1915), p. 156; Soldiers Massacre Indian Civilians in Amritsar (1919), p. 264; Gandhi Leads a Noncooperation Movement (1920), p. 315; India Signs the Delhi Pact (1931), p. 459; The Poona Pact Grants Representation to India's Untouchables (1932), p. 469; India Gains Independence (1947), p. 731.

THE STATUTE OF WESTMINSTER
CREATES THE COMMONWEALTH

Category of event: Political freedom
Time: 1931
Locale: London, England

By recognizing the constitutional equality of the Dominions of the British Empire with Great Britain, the Statute of Westminster symbolized the evolution of the Empire into the Commonwealth of Nations

> *Principal personages:*
> ARTHUR BALFOUR (1848-1930), a former Conservative British prime minister; presided over the 1926 Imperial Conference and drafted much of the Statute of Westminster
> JOSEPH CHAMBERLAIN (1836-1914), a Conservative British colonial secretary (1895-1903)
> JOHN GEORGE LAMBTON, LORD DURHAM (1792-1840), a British statesman who, as governor-general of Canada, wrote the Durham Report
> SIR WILFRID LAURIER (1841-1919), the prime minister of Canada (1897-1911); advocated the growth of Dominion self-government within a loosely organized British Empire
> JAN CHRISTIAN SMUTS (1870-1950), a South African statesman who suggested changing the name of the British Empire to the British Commonwealth of Nations

Summary of Event

At the turn of the century, the British Empire covered more than one-fourth of the land area of the world. Since that time, most of Great Britain's colonies have become independent nations. The British Empire, the greatest the world had ever seen, is no longer called an "empire"; it has become, instead, the Commonwealth of Nations, and the United Kingdom is only one of its many members. Historians and politicians continue to disagree about the reasons for the evolution of the Empire into the Commonwealth and whether the consequences have been harmful or beneficial. Few, however, would dispute that one of the most significant events in this development was the enactment of the Statute of Westminster in 1931.

Ironically, the statute did little to alter relationships within the Empire; rather, it recognized and gave clear legal form to changes that had already occurred. Although its enactment encouraged further modifications in the fabric of the Empire, it was itself the result of a long process of struggle and compromise, disagreement and consensus. An understanding of how the statute became a symbol for the end of the Empire and the beginning of the Commonwealth requires background knowledge of the history of the British Empire.

England (or Great Britain, as the central Empire became known after the creation of the United Kingdom in 1701) first began expanding overseas in the 1500's. Nearby Ireland was the first acquisition in this expansion, but British ships were soon venturing to the Americas and around the world. Wherever they went, colonies were planted, all ultimately under the authority of the British Parliament in London. In some areas, such as Australia, New Zealand, Canada, what would become the United States, and the Cape Colony at the tip of southern Africa, the native inhabitants were few or unable to resist settlement by the English. In these colonies, large numbers of immigrants soon arrived, creating thriving new societies. In the period before the American Revolution, in accordance with the prevailing economic philosophy of mercantilism, Great Britain attempted to control the governments and economies of these colonies tightly.

When the United States successfully rebelled against this policy and left the Empire, however, the British began to reassess their domination of the other colonies, for they did not wish to lose any more of them. In addition, mercantilism was being abandoned in favor of the idea of free trade, which asserted that attempts to control colonial commerce were counterproductive.

After an abortive rebellion in Canada in the 1830's, a new governor-general, Lord Durham, was sent from London to survey the situation. The report that Durham issued in 1839 insisted that the only way in which the Empire could be preserved was to begin a process of gradually granting "responsible government" (self-government) to Canada and the other colonies populated largely by European settlers. The Durham Report led to the passage of the British North America Act of 1867, under which the British Parliament gave up many of its powers over Canada. This law became the model for the development of self-government in Australia, New Zealand, and the Cape Colony. These colonies were now called dominions. Because British armed forces, especially the Royal Navy, continued to protect them, however, the United Kingdom continued to control their foreign policy. In addition, various laws, especially the Colonial Laws Validity Act of 1865, decreed that any legislation passed in the dominion parliaments had to be submitted to the British Parliament for approval before it could become law.

Increasingly, the dominions chafed under these restrictions and demanded that London relinquish its supervision over their legislative powers. In effect, they began to present Great Britain with a difficult choice: Either to allow the dominions to become fully equal with the United Kingdom as self-governing nations or to face the strong possibility that, like the United States, they might become independent republics and leave the Empire.

From 1887 onward, the British government attempted to find a solution to this problem by holding a series of colonial and imperial conferences. Key British cabinet ministers and the prime ministers of the dominions gathered in London to discuss policy for the Empire as a whole. The British government was especially concerned to maintain the unity of the Empire and its resources because the economic and political position of the United Kingdom was being threatened by the growing strength of the United States and Germany. Without support from the dominions, both Great Britain and its Empire might collapse.

At a colonial conference held in 1897, the British colonial secretary, Joseph Chamberlain, advocated that such conferences become the basis for a more fully unified Empire, a kind of federated superstate. Trade and tariff preferences would be given to members, and all would contribute to imperial defense. Chamberlain's ideas caused a storm of controversy in Britain and in the dominions. Although he had many supporters, strong arguments were offered against his concept. In the first place, none of the dominions was willing to give up what they saw as their natural political evolution toward full independence. In addition, the economic interests of the dominions and the United Kingdom were highly dissimilar—Canada, for example, was not willing to give up her close trade ties to the United States. Finally, since the eighteenth century, Great Britain's economic strength had been based on free trade; to reverse course seemed almost sacrilegious.

Dominion prime ministers were almost uniformly hostile to Chamberlain's approach. Sir Wilfrid Laurier, the prime minister of Canada, suggested instead that the Empire should move away from central control from London and toward a loosely organized and largely undefined association—what would eventually become the Commonwealth.

Chamberlain's idea was buried in 1905 when an election brought a new government to power in Britain. The ruling Liberal party was strongly in favor both of maintaining free trade and reducing Great Britain's international commitments. Thus, by the beginning of World War I in 1914, it was generally acknowledged—though not clearly indicated in any kind of legislation—that the dominions were self-governing, even in the areas of foreign policy and trade.

Tensions between the dominions and the United Kingdom were largely shelved for the duration of World War I (1914-1918), and the dominions quickly placed their resources at the disposal of the mother country. Their contribution to the Allied victory was so obvious that, at the peace conference of 1919, no one questioned their right to representation as separate nations. Thus, delegates both from the British Empire as a whole and from each of the dominions signed the Treaty of Versailles. In addition, when the League of Nations was set up in 1919, each of the dominions sent its own delegation.

To the world outside the Empire, the dominions were already independent nations. This status had become manifest in Great Britain, too, in 1917, when an Imperial War Cabinet, which included the prime ministers of the United Kingdom and the dominions, was formed to determine war policy. That same year, during an Imperial War Conference held to discuss Empire relations, a resolution was passed declaring that, after the end of the war, the authority of the dominions to determine their own individual foreign policies should be recognized. In a speech to the British Parliament at the end of the conference, Jan Smuts, a South African delegate, asserted that Great Britain and the dominions were equal members of an association which he preferred to call the "British Commonwealth of Nations," rather than the

British Empire. In subsequent conferences, as well as official documents, Smuts's term came into increasing use.

In the post-World War I period, the dominions continued to demand a more precise constitutional acknowledgment of their free and equal status within the Empire. Finally, in 1926, Arthur Balfour, a former British prime minister who presided over the Imperial Conference of that year, wrote in the conference report that the self-governing dominions were recognized by the British government as, essentially, independent nations in no way subordinate to Great Britain or one another and associated only by their common allegiance to the Crown and their membership in the British Commonwealth of Nations. Another conference, in 1930, formalized Balfour's conclusions in the form of legislation, the Statute of Westminster. Great Britain and all the dominions formally enacted the statute in 1931.

Impact of Event

Although the Statute of Westminster did not create the Commonwealth, it is generally regarded as the single great legal landmark in the history of that organization. It not only defined the Commonwealth and explained the constitutional relationship among its members but also helped to determine how the Commonwealth would develop in the future. Specifically, it included two points: first, that the Commonwealth was a free association of self-governing nations united by their common allegiance to the British Crown; and second, that the Parliament of the United Kingdom could not legislate for the dominions without the request and consent of their own parliaments. In simple terms, what the Statute did was acknowledge the constitutional equality of the dominions with the United Kingdom; Great Britain no longer had any authority over these nations. Thus, it may be reasonably said that the statute legally recognized that the Commonwealth existed.

To many historians of the Commonwealth, the Statute of Westminster also symbolized the victory of liberal democracy over imperial tyranny. In its long history, Great Britain had been a pioneer in the development of the institutions of constitutional democracy. In the nineteenth century, British statesmen frequently claimed that one of the goals of the Empire was to bring the blessings of such institutions to the nations under its control. They believed, or at least said they believed, that the Empire was serving a moral purpose, spreading civilization and good government. This claim was belied by the fact that, throughout the world, the Empire was maintained by the force of British arms. How could an Empire that existed through coercion claim to be democratic? Faced with this dilemma, the rulers of the Empire stumbled gradually toward the idea of a commonwealth, a voluntary association of equals.

At first, most statesmen believed that the Commonwealth consisted only of the United Kingdom and the dominions—in other words, nations whose people were primarily whites and whose culture was European in origin. The example set by the dominions, however, was not lost on Britain's other colonies. In fact, the majority of the population of the Empire was not descended from Europe. The so-called "jewel" of the Empire, for example, was India, a country whose immense population was considered by the British of the time to be uncivilized. Although the British rulers of India had begun in the early 1800's to set up schools, send Indians to British universities, and even give them important administrative posts in the government, few British statesmen were ready to recognize India as a dominion. Indian nationalists, like their dominion counterparts, had long agitated for self-government or even complete independence. Once the Statute of Westminster recognized the principle that the Empire-Commonwealth was a flexible organism, many British leaders came to the conclusion that it was flexible enough to acknowledge India's claims. Eventually, in 1947, India gained its independence as a republic and refused to accept even the allegiance to the Crown that formed a part of the Statute of Westminster. The new Indian government sought to remain a part of the Commonwealth, and the British cabinet acceded to the request.

In the decades after India gained its independence, nearly all the other British colonies also became independent, but most of them remained as members of the Commonwealth, whatever their form of government. The principle that the Commonwealth, as a voluntary association with the British monarch as its purely symbolic head, can accommodate such variety has allowed it to grow and continue. Commonwealth conferences continued to meet annually. Whether the Commonwealth has any real purpose or function, however, remains a matter of debate among both its leaders and its historians.

Bibliography

Barnett, Correlli. *The Collapse of British Power.* New York: William Morrow, 1972. An analysis of how various aspects of British power operated and why they failed in the twentieth century. Barnett asserts that the decline and fall of the British Empire involved military, diplomatic, social, economic, and even religious factors, and that, taken together, they show a failure of British national character.

Bowle, John. *The Imperial Achievement: The Rise and Transformation of the British Empire.* Boston: Little, Brown, 1974. While Barnett concentrates on the reasons for British decline, Bowle emphasizes British successes in creating a flexible imperial system open to new relationships and able to withstand the development of democracy and self-government among Britain's former colonies. Provides a good survey of the history of the Empire-Commonwealth from its origins to the 1970's.

Hancock, W. K. *Problems of Nationality, 1918-1936.* Vol. 1 in *Survey of British Commonwealth Affairs.* London: Oxford University Press, 1937. Although somewhat dated, Hancock's summary of the constitutional evolution of the Commonwealth in the period covered is probably still the best available. Makes the complexities of imperial constitutional law clear even to the nonspecialist reader.

Holland, R. F. *Britain and the Commonwealth Alliance, 1918-1939.* London: Macmillan, 1981. A study of what the Commonwealth relationship meant to British policymakers, how their views of this relationship changed, and how the policies that resulted also evolved. Holland's main theme is that the creation of the Commonwealth was one way in which British states attempted to stem the decline of the Empire after World War I. Excellent bibliography.

Hussey, W. D. *The British Empire and Commonwealth, 1500-1961.* Cambridge, England: Cambridge University Press, 1963. An excellent introductory survey text for the general reader. Devotes substantial attention to the history of individual colonies and dominions. Includes a glossary and bibliography.

Judd, Denis, and Peter Slinn. *The Evolution of the Modern Commonwealth, 1902-80.* London: Macmillan, 1982. A brief summary of the evolution of the Empire into the Commonwealth and the changes in the Commonwealth since World War II. Includes incisive discussions of British "imperialism" and the events and personalities leading to the creation of the Statute of Westminster. Excellent bibliography.

Mansergh, Nicholas. *The Commonwealth Experience.* 2d ed. 2 vols. London: Macmillan, 1982. Mansergh is generally regarded as the best historian of the Commonwealth, and these two volumes are viewed as his finest work. Useful to both specialists and general readers.

_____. *Survey of British Commonwealth Affairs.* London: Oxford University Press, 1952. Very detailed examination of the development of dominion status, the foreign policy of the Commonwealth as a whole, and the external policies of individual dominions. May be somewhat difficult for those without sufficient background in British and Commonwealth history, but extremely valuable for its discussion of the Statute of Westminster.

Thomas C. Schunk

Cross-References

The Defense of India Act Impedes the Freedom Struggle (1915), p. 156; The Easter Rebellion Fails to Win Irish Independence (1916), p. 178; Soldiers Massacre Indian Civilians in Amritsar (1919), p. 264; Ireland Is Granted Home Rule and Northern Ireland Is Created (1920), p. 309; Gandhi Leads a Noncooperation Movement (1920), p. 315; Gandhi Leads the Salt March (1930), p. 447; India Signs the Delhi Pact (1931), p. 459; The Poona Pact Grants Representation to India's Untouchables (1932), p. 469; India Gains Independence (1947), p. 731; Hong Kong Residents Pressure Great Britain on Passport Issue (1980's), p. 2073.

INDIA SIGNS THE DELHI PACT

Categories of event: Indigenous peoples' rights and civil rights
Time: March 5, 1931
Locale: India

Mahatma Gandhi and the viceroy of India agreed to the Delhi Pact, which ended a civil disobedience campaign and provided for talks between the Congress Party and the British

Principal personages:

MAHATMA GANDHI (1869-1948), the Hindu leader of the Indian National Congress who met with Viceroy Lord Irwin to end the civil disobedience movement

LORD IRWIN (1881-1959), the viceroy of India from 1926 to 1931, with whom Gandhi signed the Delhi Pact

JAWAHARLAL NEHRU (1889-1964), the son of the founder of the "Nehru dynasty" who at first opposed Gandhi's signing of the Delhi Pact

Summary of Event

In 1928, Mohandas Kamarchand (Mahatma) Gandhi and the Indian National Congress Party decided to oppose vigorously the appointment of the Simon Commission, which was sent to India to decide how the next step of constitutional reforms should take place. Gandhi decided that the opposition would take the form of a noncooperation movement. This would be a movement of civil disobedience begun with deliberate breaking of the salt laws. Accordingly, on March 12, 1930, Gandhi and his followers started a twenty-five day march to the sea to collect salt and to break the law. The Salt March started off a nationwide protest over a wide variety of issues involving millions of Indians of all ages, classes, and religions. On May 5, Gandhi and the leaders of the Congress party were arrested and imprisoned. Eventually, more than sixty thousand people were incarcerated by the British as a means of stopping this protest movement which led people to block streets, disobey police orders, and march through city centers curtailing business and completely disrupting all normal activities.

The Congress leaders were held in prison for nearly a year, until January 26, 1931, when they were released by the viceroy, Lord Irwin. They were set free because the British wanted a truce with the Congress. The British were anxious to bring the Congress into the ongoing constitutional discussions—the Second Round Table Conference, to be held in London at the end of the year—so that the new constitution which the British wanted to introduce into India would be accepted by the country. Because of this, they needed an end to the civil disobedience movement and Gandhi's participation and cooperation.

The Congress saw the noncooperation movement as a success, achieving a response never before seen in India, but many people, including Gandhi, were exhausted and ready for peace with the government. The rank and file members of the Congress who had led the demonstrations against the government were tired, and Indian businesspeople, who had in some cases lost a substantial sum of money because they were stopped from selling British products, wanted an end to disruptive practices. At this time, one of the most radical members of the Congress, Jawaharlal Nehru, came firmly under Gandhi's influence after the death of his father, Motilal Nehru. In addition, many of the more moderate politicians in India wanted an end to illegal activities. The result was that Gandhi responded positively to Irwin's January 17 invitation to talks.

The formal meetings between Gandhi and Irwin began in New Delhi on February 17, 1931. There was a total of eight meetings over a period of three weeks. Gandhi and Irwin got along well together, as both men were very religious and appreciated that quality in each other. The talks represented the highest point of Gandhi's political career and led to the Delhi Pact (popularly known as the Gandhi-Irwin Pact) of March 5, 1931.

The meetings did not meet with everyone's approval. Many Indians, including one of the most radical and forceful advocates of violent opposition to the British, Subhas Chandra Bose, wanted total opposition to British rule instead of talks and cooperation. Even they saw that opposition to Gandhi, who was immensely popular among the elite politicians as well as among the masses, would weaken their own position. Many conservatives in England were also strongly opposed to the meetings. Winston Churchill, the leading opponent in the Conservative Party, made the most famous comment when, referring to Gandhi, he complained about "the nauseating and humiliating spectacle of this one-time Inner Temple lawyer, now seditious fakir, striding half-naked up the steps of the Viceroy's palace there to parley on equal terms with the representative of the King-Emperor."

This comment revealed the new reality of the political situation in India and the significance of the Delhi Pact: An Indian was talking as an equal with the British viceroy for the first time in history. Through their noncooperation movements and through their mass opposition, Indians, under the leadership of Gandhi, had forced the British to establish a new relationship between themselves and the colonized people. Gandhi had aroused too much opposition to the British *raj* (rule) and India was no longer the docile and profitable country it had once been. The British knew they could no longer ignore Indian public opinion or ride roughshod over Indians' civil rights. As a result, they seriously planned to hand over the government of India to the Indians. The end of nearly two hundred years of foreign rule was clearly near.

Gandhi and the viceroy discussed a large number of issues. In the end they came to an agreement on most and agreed to disagree on the others. The agreement began over the salt laws. The salt laws were not repealed, but local residents of areas where salt was made were allowed to produce some for domestic consumption and for sale within their village. They were not, however, allowed to sell or trade their salt outside their village. An amnesty was given to the many thousands of people arrested during the noncooperation movement who were not guilty of violent crimes, and all special ordinances passed to control the campaign were withdrawn. Those properties which were confiscated, forfeited, or attached because of a failure to pay fines and had not yet been sold by the government were restored to their owners. People were given back their government jobs if they had resigned from them as part of the noncooperation movement, provided that the jobs had not been offered to someone else in the meantime. Gandhi demanded an inquiry into police behavior during the campaign, but Irwin refused. Gandhi gave in on this point.

Gandhi agreed that civil disobedience would be stopped. In particular, organized defiance of any law, the movement for the nonpayment of land revenue and other legal fees, the publication of news sheets in support of civil disobedience, and the attempts to influence civil and military officials or to persuade them to resign, were to cease. Gandhi also agreed that Congress would attend the second meeting of the Round Table Conference, to be held in London in the fall, to discuss a new constitution. Gandhi's comment after the talks were over was that Indians now had proof that the British were serious about giving them freedom and self-government.

The Delhi Pact was an important breakthrough with regard to the rights of Indians. Gandhi and the Congress, which represented the majority of Hindus in India, had in the past been the major opponent of British rule. Previously, the British had ignored this opposition as much as they could. This was no longer possible. The Delhi Pact, which resulted from the Salt March and the noncooperation movement, created a new relationship between Indians and the British. The British had to respect Indians' civil rights in a way they never had in the past.

Impact of Event

The impact of the Delhi Pact on the Congress was to change its policy of noncooperation with the British to that of working with them to write a new constitution and of taking part in the government under that new constitution. The impact on the British was that it increased their determination to work out a constitution which would be acceptable to Indians and one which would prevent any reoccurrence of a noncooperation movement.

Gandhi attended the second session of the Round Table Conference, which opened in September, 1931, as the sole representative of the Congress. He did not get everything he wanted, but the Government of India Act of 1935 which followed from the conference provided for representative government in the provinces and planned for independence at the center as well. One British concession at the conference was that minorities such as the Muslims were given special representation in regional parliaments and the national assembly. This increased their civil rights considerably. The pact established a new relationship between Indians and the British—they were now partners and not master and servant in the government of India.

The Government of India Act of 1935 called for general elections to be held in all the provinces of British India. These were held at the end of 1936 and the beginning of 1937. The Congress scored a major triumph, securing power in most of the provinces, and essentially ran the country from 1937 to 1939. The Congress members resigned from their government positions then because the British had declared war on behalf of India without consulting them. This had the unforeseen result of alienating elite Muslims, who believed they were excluded from government positions and contracts by the Hindus, who now had most of the power and patronage. In March, 1940, the leading Muslim political party, the All-India Muslim League, called for the creation of a separate country for Muslims. When India received its independence in 1947, the country was split up into the Hindu area of India and the Muslim area of Pakistan.

The Delhi Pact was a turning point in Indian history because it established a new relationship between the British and the Indians. The agreement of a viceroy of the world's most powerful empire with Gandhi, a small man who dressed and acted as a saint, symbolized the triumph of Gandhi's ideas of nonviolence and civil disobedience.

Bibliography

Brown, Judith M. *Gandhi: Prisoner of Hope*. New Haven, Conn.: Yale University Press, 1989. This signing of the Delhi Pact by Gandhi, Brown maintains, was the highpoint of Gandhi's career. This book by the leading Western Gandhi scholar places the Delhi Pact within the context of Gandhi's long, complex political life.

_____. *Gandhi and Civil Disobedience: The Mahatma in Indian Politics, 1928-34*. Cambridge, England: Cambridge University Press, 1977. For a detailed account of the Delhi Pact and the events surrounding it, this is the book to read.

Copley, Antony. *Gandhi: Against the Tide*. London: Basil Blackwell, 1987. This is a good, short life history of Gandhi which shows the place of the Delhi Pact within the framework of the struggle for freedom. A useful quick reference.

Erikson, Erik. *Gandhi's Truth: On the Origins of Militant Nonviolence*. New York: W. W. Norton, 1969. Gandhi had many interests and was a very unusual man. This book is by a psychoanalyst who looks at the psychology of Gandhi's actions and the psychological dimensions of his relationship with the British. He analyzes the psychology behind Gandhi's decision to enter into negotiations with the British and the reasons for the Delhi Pact.

Fox, Richard G. *Gandhian Utopia: Experiments with Culture*. Boston: Beacon Press, 1989. This anthropologist shows how Gandhi was not only attempting to come to political decisions with the viceroy through the Delhi Pact but was also trying to define the Indian nationalist movement in cultural terms congruent with traditional Indian culture.

Gandhi, M. K. *An Autobiography: The Story of My Experiments with Truth*. Boston: Beacon Press, 1957. Gandhi's coming to terms and negotiating with his opponents had its origins in his movement in South Africa. While Gandhi's autobiography ends in 1920 and does not cover the Delhi Pact, it is essential reading for understanding Gandhi and how politics was a part of his life.

Nehru, Jawaharlal. *Toward Freedom: The Autobiography of Jawaharlal Nehru*. 1941. Boston: Beacon Press, 1963. This is an insider's account of the Delhi Pact of 1931. Nehru, even though he had different ideas on economics and was the opposite of Gandhi in many respects, was one of Gandhi's most loyal followers. This book is a classic in its own right and is essential for a firsthand account of the Indian nationalist movement of the 1920's and 1930's.

Parekh, Bhiku. *Colonialism, Tradition, and Reform: An Analysis of Gandhi's Political Discourse*. Newbury Park, Calif.: Sage Publications, 1989. Parekh analyzes Gandhi's political technique and explains how Gandhi was careful to use Indian symbols during his negotiations that led to the Delhi Pact. This is a rich analysis by a renowned Indian thinker.

Rudolph, Susanne Hoeber, and Lloyd I. Rudolph. *Gandhi: The Traditional Roots of Charisma*. Chicago: Chicago University Press, 1983. During the negotiations which led to the Delhi Pact, Gandhi used his charisma and his ideas of ethical universalism to appeal to Viceroy Lord Irwin, who was also a deeply religious man. For Gandhi, means were more important than ends. The authors describe Gandhi's appeal and show how he used all kinds of symbols, from the political to the religious to the traditional, as part of his message.

Roger D. Long

. **Cross-References**

The Muslim League Attempts to Protect Minority Interests in India (1906), p. 87; The Defense of India Act Impedes the Freedom Struggle (1915), p. 156; Soldiers Massacre Indian Civilians in Amritsar (1919), p. 264; Gandhi Leads a Noncooperation Movement (1920), p. 315; Gandhi Leads the Salt March (1930), p. 447; The Poona Pact Grants Representation to India's Untouchables (1932), p. 469; India Gains Independence (1947), p. 731.

EL SALVADOR'S MILITARY MASSACRES CIVILIANS IN *LA MATANZA*

Categories of event: Atrocities and war crimes; revolutions and rebellions
Time: January-February, 1932
Locale: El Salvador

The massacre of up to thirty thousand peasants by the army ended a radical reform movement in the Salvadoran countryside and ushered in fifty years of repression and military rule

Principal personages:
>AGUSTÍN FARABUNDO MARTÍ (1893-1932), a principal leader of the Salvadoran Communist Party
>MAXIMILIANO HERNÁNDEZ MARTÍNEZ (1883-1966), the military dictator of El Salvador who ordered the 1932 bloodbath
>ARTURO ARAÚJO (1877-1967), the reform-minded civilian president of El Salvador, unseated by a right-wing coup that transferred power to General Martínez

Summary of Event

Social relations in El Salvador in the first decades of the twentieth century were characterized by a wide division in power. The peasant masses, who had once enjoyed communal property rights as part of an ancient landholding system, had seen these rights taken away in the late 1800's by a powerful clique of coffee planters. Behind a shield of "liberal" legislation, these growers had succeeded in expanding their holdings to encompass nearly all of the country's arable land. They modernized the economy by tying their fortunes to the exclusive cultivation of coffee, for which a large international market existed.

Such modernization carried with it a high cost in human terms. The peasants, most of whom were Pipil Indians, had an almost mystical reverence for their cornfields. The disestablishment of their communal system had a psychological, as well as a material, effect on their lives. Without access to land, they had no options other than to work on the coffee plantations as *colonos*, receiving in exchange tiny plots for their own subsistence along with a miserable wage, often issued in kind. Once-independent peasants were thus reduced to debt peons.

For their part, the coffee growers, or oligarchs, took advantage of a seemingly limitless world demand for their product. The coffee boom, which lasted throughout the 1920's, stimulated urbanization, brought railways and telegraph lines to the interior, and widened the economic gap between the coffee growers and the peasantry. The wealthy lived in regal splendor while the poor seethed in their poverty.

The rural environment of El Salvador had little in it of philanthropy. The planters kept wages low and they paid almost no taxes that might support social services.

Discontent among the poor was widespread in consequence, and isolated uprisings occurred frequently. The rural constabulary and the National Guard smashed all of these movements. As time went by, the oligarchs came to rely more and more on coercion to maintain the status quo in the countryside.

The Great Depression of 1929 provided the catalyst for a social explosion. The demand for coffee on the world markets collapsed. With prices falling, the *colonos* lost the opportunity to find work. Wages fell 60 percent. In the cities, the Depression gave rise to a period of intense political discussion, with younger members of the oligarchy expressing some doubts as to whether the traditional order could contain the social crisis. A few individuals looked to reformist solutions.

Among their number was Arturo Araújo, an admirer of Britain's Fabian Socialists. Araújo was something of a wild card in Salvadoran politics, and the *Partido Laborista* he founded reflected an eclectic blend of mysticism, anti-imperialism, and what was termed *vitalismo mínimo*—the idea that every citizen deserved a "vital minimum" of goods and services necessary to a happy life. Such sentiments appealed to many, especially in the cities, where trade unionists and middle-class professionals lent avid support to Araújo.

The Communist Party of El Salvador also favored this wayward son of the oligarchy. In this instance, however, their support was conditional, since the communists, led by veteran activist Agustín Farabundo Martí, feared that Araújo's popularity might overshadow their own plans to carve a measure of power from the country's difficulties. As it turned out, they needed to fear something far more sinister.

Despite the misgivings of most oligarchs, the government held free elections in January, 1931. Five presidential candidates, most of whom represented conservative coffee interests, entered the field against Araújo. The latter went on to win anyway and took office at the beginning of March. Problems plagued Araújo from the beginning. The Depression hit the country people very hard. Although he had made vague promises as to land reform, the new president simply could not deliver on these while simultaneously safeguarding the privileges of the elite.

The lack of direction displayed by Araújo was evident from the beginning. The oligarchs, who had previously thought Araújo merely risky, now saw him as positively dangerous and looked to anyone who might deliver them from his influences. The peasants and the trade unionists also became disillusioned. Seeing that their support had brought them repression and not reform, they began to consider more radical solutions, particularly those espoused by Farabundo Martí and the communists. Several strikes by *colonos* in April and May were brutally crushed by forces under War Minister (and Vice President) Maximiliano Hernández Martínez. Widespread rebellion now seemed likely.

Of all the groups opposed to Araújo, clearly the most willing to act upon its grievances was the military. The president had tried to reduce the army's budget by 25 percent and tried to retire a number of senior officers. Most crucial, however, was his inability to pay his soldiers. In normal times, export duties paid the greater part of government expenses, but with coffee exports at rock bottom, Araújo's administration was delinquent in its payments to all officials.

The end came swiftly. On December 2, 1931, army units loyal to General Martínez seized control of San Salvador and other major cities. Only Araújo loyalists initially condemned the attack. Most political parties, including the communists, gave their tacit approval. They felt reassured when Martínez announced that municipal elections scheduled for January, 1932, would go forward. The Left then organized meetings and street demonstrations, distributed leaflets, and prepared for the elections. Few doubted that Martínez would keep his word.

The general, however, had his own ambitions. A man of a mystical frame of mind who would later conduct seances in the presidential palace, Martínez felt certain that he acted with divine aid. Having identified all opposition organizers, he cancelled the elections and began a massive repression. Realizing that they were moving in the eleventh hour, the communists launched an urban revolt on January 22, supposedly set to coincide with a rural insurrection in the western departments of Santa Ana, Ahuachapán, and Sonsonate. The Indian leaders of those areas had tenuous ties to Farabundo Martí, even though they had no use for communists generally. They nevertheless decided that a revolt offered them their last chance of deliverance.

They were wrong, tragically so. The army quelled the urban uprising in a matter of hours, police agents having already penetrated the revolutionary cells. They had previously detained Farabundo Martí. A policy of summary execution began that included even suspected members of opposition groups. Martí received unusual treatment: He was given a brief trial before he faced the firing squad.

The rural districts experienced the full fury of the repression. The peasant rebels, armed with machetes, managed to hold out for forty-eight hours. They killed some fifty policemen. The army and the irregular forces set up by the landowners exacted an awesome revenge in what Salvadorans still refer to simply as *la matanza*, the massacre: The army regarded anyone with Indian features as being automatically guilty and liable for the ultimate penalty. Whole villages were razed. Hospitals were checked and the wounded dragged out and killed. Women, children, and dogs were shot along with men. The corpses soon became so numerous that they could not be buried and were simply left in ditches along the roads. As one witness later observed, only the vultures ate well that year. Before the violence had run its course in February, as many as thirty thousand people had died. The massacre left a legacy of violence in Salvadoran politics that sixty years later had yet to be overcome.

Impact of Event

La matanza left a deep scar in Salvadoran society. Virtually every family in the western part of the country lost someone to the army terror. The effects of the repression went even further, however, than the loss of life.

There were cultural losses. Because Martínez and the army chose to identify the Pipil Indians as part of a wide communist conspiracy, most Indian survivors rushed to deny their Indian identity. They abandoned the use of native garb, which they saw as a provocative symbol of resistance likely to bring down the wrath of the police.

Indians encouraged their children to avoid speaking Pipil except at home, and then only in hushed tones.

There were social losses. With the members of many families serving in the army or among the rebels, the repression could not help but have a divisive impact. It became impossible to trust anyone. All of the traditional foci of rural authority and trust—the church, and more importantly, the socioreligious brotherhoods (*cofradías*)—lost the popular support they had once enjoyed. Fear dominated the peasant landscape. Only the oligarchs could claim that *la matanza* had increased the level of solidarity in their ranks. It also taught them the false lesson that class solidarity outweighed national reconciliation and that their survival depended on the subordination of the peasants.

Finally, the repression brought political losses. General Martínez followed *la matanza* with a twelve-year dictatorship that brooked little opposition, even from the oligarchs. Although civilian vigilantes conducted much of the 1932 slaughter, its political outcome confirmed the army's claim on power. Martínez was only one of many military presidents who were to rule El Salvador during the twentieth century. As an institution, the Salvadoran armed forces consistently resisted pressures to make room for civilian participation in politics. When open application of force has been inadvisable, the military has acted in collusion with the oligarchs to create death squads, which, by the 1990's, essentially had become institutionalized.

For their part, the peasant masses in the El Salvador of the 1990's became caught between two polar extremes. They could either join the ranks of the army and the elites, who perceived the struggle as an anticommunist crusade, or they could join with the Farabundo Martí National Liberation guerrillas, the ideological descendants of Martí, and fight to establish the kind of Leninist regime that had been repudiated throughout the Eastern Bloc. In either direction, death threatened the average citizen. The greatest and most frightening legacies of *la matanza* are the effects that it left in the popular mind and the knowledge that it can happen again.

Bibliography

Anderson, Thomas P. *Matanza: El Salvador's Communist Revolt of 1932.* Lincoln: University of Nebraska Press, 1971. Despite its inaccurate title, this work is still rightly considered the classic English-language account of the repression. It is also the most thoughtful and the least pedantic. Anderson conducted extensive interviews with participants and made use of little-known manuscript materials. Includes map, footnotes, extensive bibliography, and index.

Dalton, Roque. *Miguel Marmol.* Willimantic, Conn.: Curbstone Press, 1987. This is a unique and fascinating account of *la matanza*, based on extensive interviews with an active organizer of the Salvadoran Communist Party who was himself shot and left for dead in 1932 and who later spent many years in exile in the Soviet Union. Marmol's Stalinist attitude dates him, but his comments about sacrifice and struggle still ring true. Dalton, an important poet and member of the revolutionary underground, was murdered in 1975 by a rival leftist faction. Includes three letters from Marmol as well as an October, 1986, interview.

McClintock, Michael. *State Terror and Popular Resistance in El Salvador.* Vol. 1 in *The American Connection.* London: Zed Books, 1985. This thorough examination of U.S. military and economic aid to El Salvador contains some useful references to the 1932 massacre, including some of the comments of the American military attaché in San Salvador at the time. Includes endnotes, bibliography, and index.

Montgomery, Tommie Sue. *Revolution in El Salvador: Origins and Evolution.* Boulder, Colo.: Westview Press, 1982. This insightful history of the Salvadoran struggle for justice focuses more on the 1970's and 1980's than on *la matanza.* Nevertheless, its detailed account of the antecedents of the quagmire of the 1990's marks it as a key source of information for understanding modern El Salvador. Includes photos, maps, tables, index, and bibliography.

North, Liisa. *Bitter Grounds: Roots of Revolt in El Salvador.* 2d ed. Westport, Conn.: Lawrence Hill, 1985. Chapter 3 covers the 1932 peasant revolt and its bloody aftermath. The study as a whole is a brief but concise treatment of Salvadoran politics in the twentieth century. It is especially strong on economic questions. Includes maps, tables, notes, index, bibliography, and appendices.

Parkman, Patricia. *Nonviolent Insurrection in El Salvador: The Fall of Maximiliano Hernández Martínez.* Tucson: University of Arizona Press, 1988. This is a valuable and well-researched account of the Martínez regime, concentrating more on his ouster in the mid-1940's than on *la matanza.* It is based largely on materials drawn from the archives of the Department of State and on interviews. Includes maps, illustrations, endnotes, and bibliography.

Russell, Philip L. *El Salvador in Crisis.* Austin, Tex.: Colorado River Press, 1984. Like most "committed" historical works, this study favors a leftist solution for the Salvadoran problem. It is quite thorough and well-researched in its treatment of the 1932 bloodbath, although it cannot boast the depth of Anderson's account. Includes maps, tables, illustrations, graphs, endnotes, bibliography, and index.

Thomas L. Whigham

Cross-References

Armenians Suffer Genocide During World War I (1915), p. 150; The Sudanese Civil War Erupts (1955), p. 941; Papa Doc Duvalier Takes Control of Haiti (1957), p. 1009; Brazil Begins a Period of Intense Repression (1968), p. 1468; An Oppressive Military Rule Comes to Democratic Uruguay (1973), p. 1715; Allende Is Overthrown in a Chilean Military Coup (1973), p. 1725; East Timor Declares Independence but Is Annexed by Indonesia (1975), p. 1835; The United Nations Issues a Declaration Against Torture (1975), p. 1847; The Argentine Military Conducts a "Dirty War" Against Leftists (1976), p. 1864; Indigenous Indians Become the Target of Guatemalan Death Squads (1978), p. 1972; Argentine Leaders Are Convicted of Human Rights Violations (1985), p. 2280.

THE POONA PACT GRANTS REPRESENTATION TO INDIA'S UNTOUCHABLES

Categories of event: Racial and ethnic rights; civil rights
Time: September 25, 1932
Locale: Poona, India

The Poona Pact was a compromise measure rescinding an award of separate electorates to Depressed Classes but giving them reserved seats through an electoral college

Principal personages:

MAHATMA GANDHI (1869-1948), the leader of the Indian National Congress and signatory to the Poona Pact

RAMSAY MACDONALD (1866-1937), the prime minister of England at the time of the second Round Table Conference

BHIMRAO RAMJI AMBEDKAR (1892-1956), the leader of the Depressed Classes and founder of the All-India Depressed Classes Federation, a signatory to the Poona Pact

RAO BAHADUR M. C. RAJAH, the president of the All-India Depressed Classes Conference and a follower of Gandhi

Summary of Event

The second Round Table Conference, called to frame a new constitution for British India and establish gradual self-government leading to dominion status and then independence, was held in 1932, in London. Members of the British government, including Prime Minister James Ramsay MacDonald, and representatives of the Indian National Congress Party met to discuss the matter of constitutional safeguards to protect the status of minority communities in India on the provisional and central legislatures being established. Muslims, and the All-India Muslim League, had successfully convinced the British government that there should be such safeguards to protect the political, economic, and educational interests of India's minority communities, including Muslims. As a result of recognition of the validity of this claim, other communal groups, including Sikhs, Indian Christians, Mahrattas, Anglo-Indians and members of the European community, so-called "backward classes," and women, also petitioned the government for special representations to be set aside for them in the 1935 Indian Constitution. One such religious group was the Untouchables, the Hindu "outcastes" also known by their more political names of "Scheduled Castes" or "Depressed Classes," or as Gandhi referred to them, the *Harijans*, or "children of God." The untouchable classes were divided into three categories—Untouchables, Unapproachables, and Unseeables. In 1962, the number of untouchables was estimated at about sixty million out of three hundred million Hindus.

It was very difficult for the Congress to accept the idea that there were two communities in India whose interests were divergent, namely the Hindus and the largest minority, the Indian Muslims. Now it was being asked to recognize differences within Hinduism between Caste Hindus and the group historically known as the Untouchables. Mohandas K. Gandhi, in Yeravda Prison for civil disobedience activities at the time of the August 4, 1932, Communal Decision that made communal awards not only to Muslims but to Depressed Classes, among others, reacted very strongly to the granting of separate electorates to the Depressed Classes and government recognition of their seemingly separate destinies from Caste Hindus. He began a fast that he vowed to continue until his death if separate electorates were not lifted. He saw the separate electorates as part of a "divide and conquer" strategy to separate the Untouchables from the main body of Hindus. In essence, Gandhi wanted one electorate, composed of both "touchables" and "untouchables." He wanted Caste Hindus to recognize independently their moral and social responsibilities toward eradicating untouchability and bringing "outcaste" persons into the fold.

Prime Minister MacDonald, in explaining the Communal Decision to Gandhi, did not make things easier for the Congress to swallow when he said that the Depressed Classes would have in effect two votes. Gandhi declared this "the last straw." In a statement on September 16 announcing his fast, he said he would end it as soon as the threat of separate electorates was removed once and for all. As a prisoner, he considered himself unfit to set forth his proposals. He agreed to accept any agreement made on the basis of joint electorate that was arrived at between the responsible leaders of caste Hindus and the Depressed Classes and which was accepted by mass meetings of all Hindus. Apart from the political aspects of the Communal Decision, what was at stake was the removal of inequality and elements attached to untouchability that condemned this group of Hindus to a permanent underclass with few, if any, means for group or even individual advancement.

The Poona Pact, also known as the Yeravda Pact, was an agreement reached on September 24 and signed on September 25, 1932. Dr. Bhimrao Ramji Ambedkar, representing the Depressed Classes, agreed to the pact on September 26. Although he was a highly educated and renowned member of the Depressed Caste, he was stigmatized in spite of his personal accomplishments by what was clearly an outdated form of Indian social, economic, and discriminatory distinction. The pact was seen as a compromise: While still recognizing the special status of the Depressed Classes, it would not award them separate electorates but instead joint electorates with the general population along with an electoral college of Depressed Classes members who would elect four candidates from their group for primary elections for reserved seats for that community. Those winners of the primary elections would then constitute the candidates to be voted upon by the general electorate. This provision's term was ten years, but it could be abolished earlier. The pact also provided, in every province, money for the establishment of educational facilities for members of the Depressed Classes and the removal of political disabilities because of untouchability in appointments for public service jobs. The scheme for primaries, in which only the Depressed Classes would have a vote, was proposed by Sir Tej Bahadur Sapru and made the compromise more palatable to Ambedkar.

Although the Poona Pact, which later became part of the 1935 Indian Constitution, offered the Depressed Classes less than the Communal Decision, Ambedkar had proven himself to be an effective voice for the Untouchables by winning the right to separate electorates in the first place. It was a move that had religious as well as political implications, as did most things in India. Gandhi himself said that he saw it as a religious matter and moral issue, however, and as something only to be corrected by Hinduism itself rather than by what he called "political constitutions." The Communal Decision gave legitimacy to the idea that the caste system in India was unfair and certainly outdated.

Gandhi referred to the Untouchables as the "Suppressed" rather than the "Depressed" classes and in 1933 began calling them *Harijan*. After the Poona Pact was signed, Gandhi attempted to eradicate the social and religious debilitating effects of untouchability by opening Hindu temples to Untouchables. He remained opposed to interdining and intermarriage which, however, eventually also took place. It has been suggested that Gandhi, by not endorsing the interdining and intermarriages which were in fact taking place, sent ambiguous signals to people who wished to follow his example.

Impact of Event

The most immediate consequence of the acceptance of the Poona Pact was the ending of what has been called the "epic fast" and the saving of Gandhi's life. The Mahatma himself indicated, at the time of his fast, that it was not a response to those who disagreed with him but rather a way to force his supporters to confront an issue, untouchability, that had disturbed him since he was a young man. To put his life on the line over this matter was a way to show how deeply he was affected by its continuance. He was unwilling, however, for the caste system to be abolished entirely because it was so central to the historical and religious nature of Indian culture and society. Some saw the caste system's removal as the only way untouchability would disappear.

In terms of its political and social impact, the Poona Pact did get the Indian National Congress to put untouchability on its agenda. Untouchability thus became a concern of the reformist movement. There had been other movements in the past seeking to ameliorate the situation of the Depressed Classes by eliminating subcastes, relaxing caste restrictions, or even abolishing caste altogether. The Poona Pact opened some temple doors previously closed to Untouchables. There were also private efforts at interdining between the Depressed Classes and the "Sanatanists," or orthodox Hindus. In 1932, the All-India Anti-Untouchability League, an organization to assist Scheduled Castes, was founded. In 1933, Gandhi renamed the league the *Harijan Sevak Sangh*. That same year, a new weekly paper, *Harijan*, was also started. The paper published graphic drawings of the miserable habitations in which these "outcastes" lived. Their disabilities were listed at length: In some parts of the country they were denied access to village wells, schools, and post offices, and were prevented from using umbrellas and wearing sandals.

The Poona Pact could not end the curse of untouchability, which was more than three thousand years old. Access to a temple is not access to a good job. The *Harijans* remained at the bottom of Indian society. Segregation and discrimination did not end when Gandhi ended his fast. After the fast and the signing of the Poona Pact, untouchability lost its public approval. The concept was recognized as morally illegitimate.

The impact of this human rights event can be measured by remarks and speeches by Ambedkar in 1950, after India's independence, comparing Hinduism to Buddhism. He, and many in the Depressed Classes, saw Buddhism as the religion of equality while Caste Hinduism was seen as the religion of inequality. In several speeches that year, Ambedkar urged members of the Depressed Classes to convert to Buddhism and asked Buddhists to accept them. Ambedkar called for the resurgence of Buddhism in India, the land of the Buddha's birth, and inserted provisions into the constitution of independent India regarding the study of the language, Pali, which would complement the religious resurgence. On October 14, 1956, Ambedkar became a Buddhist, showing his followers the road he decided to take toward full equality, a path he thought all of India should take to achieve true democracy.

It would be fair to say that Ambedkar, who died shortly after his formal conversion, had decided after many years of study and contemplation that as long as there was a caste system, untouchability would exist. That status would be accompanied by social, educational, economic, and religious disabilities. It would appear that the only means of gaining equal status and the human dignity traditionally denied to persons considered to be "outcaste" was to leave Hinduism and to be in the vanguard of the revival of Buddhism in the land of its birth.

Bibliography

Coupland, Reginald. *The Indian Problem: Report on the Constitutional Problem in India.* New York: Oxford University Press, 1944. Discusses British India's constitutions of 1919 and 1935 and the Round Table Conferences which led to the latter statute. Good background for the constitutional problems with untouchability, including itemization of political liabilities of the Depressed Classes.

Desai, A. R. *Crusade Against Untouchability: Social Background of Indian Nationalism.* 3d ed. Bombay: G. R. Bhatkal, 1959. Provides glimpses of the history of untouchability and what it means as a cultural principle and also a brief history of reform movements that attempted to improve the situation of people who suffered under it. Desai also shows the economic basis of untouchability, which historically has favored Caste Hindus.

Fischer, Louis. "Climax." In *The Life of Mahatma Gandhi.* New York: Harper & Brothers, 1950. A chapter in an interesting biography of Gandhi which gives an almost insider's view of what the Mahatma was thinking during his fast for the removal of separate electorates for the *Harijans.*

Keer, Dhananjay. *Dr. Ambedkar: Life and Mission.* Bombay: Popular Prakashan,

1962. A biography of the leader of the Depressed Classes with a detailed account of the activities of Ambedkar and Gandhi during the second Round Table Conference which led to the Poona Pact and the politicization of the untouchability issue in India and within the Indian National Congress. Particularly interesting is the recounting of pressures on Ambedkar to accept the Poona Pact and thus end Gandhi's fast.

Majumdar, R. C., ed. *Struggle for Freedom.* Vol. 11 in *The History and Culture of the Indian People.* Bombay: Bharatiya Vidya Bhavan, 1969. Good encyclopedic review of British Indian nationalism with an interesting and slightly polemic view of Gandhi's motivations in fighting against untouchability. Discusses at length pre-Gandhi social reforms against this practice.

Nanda, Bal R. "Harijans." In *Mahatma Gandhi: A Biography.* Boston: Beacon Press, 1958. The biographer strongly makes his point that Gandhi, throughout his life, was very much against untouchability. Nanda suggests that fasting might have been a form of coercion, but if so it was directed at Gandhi's followers rather than those wanting separate electorates—that it was "to sting the conscience of the Hindu community into right religious action."

Nancy Elizabeth Fitch

Cross-References

The Muslim League Attempts to Protect Minority Interests in India (1906), p. 87; Gandhi Leads a Noncooperation Movement (1920), p. 315; Gandhi Leads the Salt March (1930), p. 447; India Signs the Delhi Pact (1931), p. 459; India Gains Independence (1947), p. 731; The Indian Government Bans Discrimination Against Untouchables (1948), p. 743; Sikhs in Punjab Revolt (1984), p. 2215.

JAPAN WITHDRAWS FROM THE LEAGUE OF NATIONS

Categories of event: Political freedom and indigenous peoples' rights
Time: February 24, 1933
Locale: Geneva, Switzerland

Japan withdrew from the League of Nations over the Lytton Commission Report, which criticized Japan's actions in Manchuria

Principal personages:
CHIANG KAI-SHEK (1887-1975), a military strongman and titular leader of China
YOSUKE MATSUOKA (1880-1946), the chief delegate to the League of Nations from Japan; led Japan's withdrawal from the League
TSUYOSHI INUKAI (1855-1932), the prime minister of Japan who was assassinated for his refusal to recognize Manchukuo
EARL OF LYTTON (1876-1947), the delegate from Great Britain and president of the Commission of Inquiry into the Manchurian Incident
"HENRY" PU-YI (1906-1967), the "Last Emperor" of the Ching (1644-1911) Dynasty in China and the puppet "Emperor" of Manchukuo

Summary of Event

On February 24, 1933, Yosuke Matsuoka, the chief Japanese delegate to the League of Nations, read a long and impassioned plea to the General Assembly in Geneva. He implored the League not to give sanction to its own Lytton Commission Report, which criticized Japan's actions in the so-called Mukden Incident of 1931 and its subsequent actions in relation to the establishment of the Japanese puppet regime in Manchukuo in 1932. When the League ignored his plea and voted to sustain the report, Matsuoka turned on his heel, summoned his Japanese colleagues to follow, and stalked dramatically out of the meeting hall. In so doing, he gave a visible image of Japan's eventual official withdrawal from the League and, some historians have argued, to the beginning of World War II.

Without doubt, it was a watershed event in Sino-Japanese relations and in the history of human rights in Manchuria as well. It was also an event that contributed to the destruction of civilian democratic government in Japan and drew a suffocating pall over the possibilities of democracy in China as well.

Japan's withdrawal from the League can be traced directly to the Mukden Incident on the evening of September 18, 1931. The Japanese Kwangtung Army stationed in Manchuria feigned a Chinese attack on the Japanese-owned South Manchuria Railroad as part of a strategy to overrun all of Manchuria and parts of northeast China. The antecedents of the 1933 withdrawal can also be traced to Japanese attempts to win supremacy in Manchuria as early as the First Sino-Japanese War of 1894-1895.

For the next thirty years, Japan attempted to wrest control of that mineral-rich area from China. By the time that the Japanese Kwangtung Army precipitated the Mukden Incident, Japan had come to believe that it possessed "special interests" and rights there. In fact, only three years before, the army had attempted to create cause for military intervention by assassinating their own military protégé, the Manchurian warlord Zhang Zuolin. When the army "responded" to the alleged Chinese attack on the railroad, it was the culmination of a long-desired wish to separate Manchuria from China.

Before the Japanese government could reestablish control over its own troops, the Kwangtung Army had driven before it most of the Chinese troops in the area as a "protective reaction." A week after the beginning of the incident, most of Manchuria and parts of North China were firmly in the possession and control of the Kwangtung Army. The army had in effect conducted its own foreign policy and now dared the Japanese civilian government to negate a victory for which the Japanese people showed great support and enthusiasm.

The government was confronted with a nearly impossible situation. On one hand, it faced a military which was split internally on many issues (Army versus Navy, "Old" Army versus "Young Officer Movement") but solidly united against the idea of returning Manchuria to a corrupt Chinese government. On the other hand, the government was assailed by opposition parties that wished to use the crisis for political reasons. To criticize the government for weak foreign policies had been the time-tested weapon for opposition parties in Japan for half a century. To its credit, the government tried to manage the crisis by attempting to reach a compromise with Chinese strongman Chiang Kai-shek. The Kwangtung Army, however, continued to make matters worse. The army leadership recognized that if something was not done quickly to destroy the chances for an agreement, all their hard-won territory might be returned to Chinese sovereignty. Despite explicit government orders not to precipitate more problems, the army began to manuever to create an "independent" regime which it could control.

China, like Japan, was a member of the League of Nations and therefore appealed to the League for redress. The League began to investigate the matter, and after nearly a year of preparation it appointed a commission led by the British delegate, the Earl of Lytton, to investigate and recommend a course of action.

Before that commission could accomplish its tasks, however, the Japanese government collapsed, in mid-December, 1931. It was replaced by one led by Tsuyoshi Inukai, who five months later was gunned down by militarists in May, 1932, ushering in what one historian has called government by assassination.

As busy as the military was in coercing political change by threat and intimidation in Japan, its branch in Manchuria was intent on extending its power and control. In a series of rapid strikes, it secured the strategic strongholds of the area. In March, 1932, it engineered a Kwangtung Army-inspired "spontaneous" native Manchu revolution and declared an independent state of Manchukuo. The army installed "Henry" Pu-yi, the "Last Emperor" of the Chinese Ching Dynasty, as the "Emperor of Manchukuo." Inukai was assassinated in part because he refused to recognize this travesty of a government. His successor extended full diplomatic recognition in September, 1932, almost exactly one year after the Mukden Incident.

As for the political and human rights of the Manchurians, the Japanese military already had an imperialist blueprint for treatment of subjugated people. Like the Taiwanese (since 1895) and the Koreans (since 1910), Manchurians became second-class citizens in their own homeland. The heretofore untapped major mineral and commercial sectors of their economy were controlled outright by the Japanese, and nearly all forms of political expression were brutally suppressed.

Manchuria had been controlled previously by a mixture of feudal warlords, former members of the Chinese Imperial government, and members of the landed elite. Most of this sociopolitical leadership had fled with the retreating Chinese army in September, 1931. Those who had not were closely watched, imprisoned, or both. The Manchurian government, which mirrored Japan's own, was in fact totally controlled by Japanese "advisers," and all decisions were made by the commander of the Kwangtung Army. A few Manchurian collaborators were used as puppets, but the Manchurians were in the main relegated to subservient positions.

A second year went by as the Lytton Commission went about its task. Japan attempted to coerce the Chinese government into recognizing Manchukuo, but China preferred to await the final League disposition of the case. Finally, in late September, 1932, the Lytton Commission reported that "without any declaration of war, a large part of Chinese territory has been forcibly seized and occupied by Japanese troops . . ." It recommended that the Kwangtung Army return to its position and function as of September 17, 1931, and that all actions taken subsequent to that date not be recognized or sanctioned by the League.

Japan's chief delegate to the League, Matsuoka, scrambled to try to have the report tabled pending a trilateral agreement between Japan, China, and Manchukuo (which he knew to be unlikely if not impossible). The League, after some deliberation, decided to vote on whether to accept the Lytton Report. At this point, Matsuoka made his quixotic and impassioned speech to the General Assembly in which he implored it not to accept the report "for the sake of peace in the Far East and for the sake of peace in the world." Unconvinced, the General Assembly voted to accept the report by an overwhelming majority (forty-six to one, with Siam abstaining). Matsuoka and the Japanese delegation then made their dramatic and symbolic exit. One month later, on March 27, 1933, the Japanese government officially notified the League of its intention to withdraw from that body.

Manchukuo remained a nation in name only, with only Japan, Italy, Germany, and a few other nations extending diplomatic recognition. It became part of Japan's wartime Greater East Asia Co-Prosperity Sphere and was returned to Chinese control with the defeat of the Japanese Empire in August, 1945.

Impact of Event

In Manchuria, Japan began a concerted effort to colonize the country with nearly one-half million Japanese immigrants who found ready employment as managers in companies "jointly owned" by Japanese financial interests and the government of Manchukuo. All political parties, with the exception of the *Hsieh Ho Hui* (Concordia Association), were outlawed. All other forms of political expression, including the few remaining Manchu language newspapers, were completely stifled or tightly controlled.

By 1937, the country had become part of Japan's fancifully named Greater East Asia Co-Prosperity Sphere. A corporation was established in October, 1937, to help supply Japan with war materials. The corporation, like the government of Manchukuo, was under the complete control of the Kwangtung Army. The bulk of Manchuria's natural resources were exported to Japan for the war effort.

The government of Manchukuo was modeled on that of Japan, but in reality the organs of government were firmly in the hands of the Japanese. In fact, virtually every aspect of Manchurian society was controlled by the Kwangtung Army. The "Emperor" Pu-yi was never allowed even the semblance of power. The thirty million Manchurian people were limited to working for Japanese-owned and -controlled companies, their every political, civil, and human right suppressed by the brutal military government. Hundreds of thousands of them were imprisoned or forced to work as slave laborers during the war. Estimates of Manchurian deaths by starvation, torture, malnutrition, and execution ranged between eighty thousand and one hundred thousand.

Between 1931 and 1945, Manchurians were denied the rights to own property, to assemble and speak freely, to vote, to a fair trial, to sue, to emigrate, and even to divorce their spouses. In short, Manchurians were denied virtually every conceivable human and civil right by their Japanese masters.

At home, the Japanese military continued to threaten and assassinate its civilian and even its own military leaders. In mid-1937, a military-controlled Japan began another war with China, a conflict that would last until Japan's defeat in August, 1945.

Japan's political party system, which had been the first in East Asia and had showed promise, was dismantled. All political parties were coerced into "cooperating" with the military during the war. They disbanded and joined the Imperial Rule Assistance Association (*Taisei yokusankai*), which acquiesced in Japan's eventual extension of the war with China to include the United States, Great Britain, and the other Allies. Thousands of Japanese dissidents were rounded up and imprisoned without trial and hundreds more simply disappeared, probably assassinated by the secret police forces of the army. Opposition newspapers were closed down and their editors imprisoned, political rallies of all sorts were outlawed, and legal and civil rights were suspended for the duration of the war.

It may be fairly said then that the Mukden Incident of September 18, 1931, led directly to the establishment of Manchukuo. Both, in turn, contributed to withdrawal of Japan from the League of Nations. The incidents foisted upon a hapless Japanese civilian government by the Kwangtung Army and its supporters in Japan helped to discredit, destabilize, and ultimately destroy the political party-style democratic government in Japan.

Bibliography

Borg, Dorothy. *The United States and the Far Eastern Crisis of 1933-1938.* Cambridge, Mass.: Harvard University Press, 1964. Concerned primarily with the effects of the crisis on American foreign policy. Excellent analysis and masterful integration of both Japanese as well as American sources. Valuable bibliography, especially for access to the Tokyo war crimes trial documents.

Byas, Hugh. *Government by Assassination.* New York: Alfred A. Knopf, 1942. Although suffering from a dearth of Japanese sources and a lack of objectivity (written by a journalist-turned-historian in the middle of the war), it is still valuable for the description of Japanese domestic politics.

Crowley, James B. *Japan's Quest for Autonomy: National Security and Foreign Policy 1930-1938.* Princeton, N.J.: Princeton University Press, 1966. A superb work that integrates the crises into the greater history of Japan's foreign policy. Chapter 3, "Withdrawal from the League," is truly masterful. Excellent bibliography.

Jones, Francis C. *Manchuria Since 1931.* London: Royal Institute of International Affairs, 1949. The best study of the effects of the crises on Manchuria. Excellent chapters on "Japanese Immigration and Settlement" and on "Treatment of Racial Minorities." Extensive charts, maps, and statistical tables.

League of Nations. *Official Journal: 1931-1933.* Geneva: Author, 1933. Contains official proceedings, deliberations, speeches, and the extensive Lytton Commission Report. Wordy and difficult to use, but invaluable for particulars as well as detailed maps. No index.

Ogata, Sadako N. *Defiance in Manchuria: The Making of Japanese Foreign Policy, 1931-1932.* Berkeley: University of California Press, 1964. Valuable for its time, but superseded two years later by Crowley's work. Good use of Japanese documents. Valuable bibliography, well-indexed.

Smith, Sara. *The Manchurian Crisis, 1931-1932: A Tragedy in International Relations.* New York: Columbia University Press, 1948. Dated, but still valuable as an example of the argument that the crisis exposed the League's weaknesses and led Mussolini and Hitler into their own foreign adventures. Uses no Japanese sources.

Thorne, Christopher. *The Limits of Foreign Policy: The West, the League, and the Far Eastern Crisis of 1931-1933.* London: Hamish Hamilton, 1972. Perhaps the definitive monograph of the subject from the Euro-American perspective. Relies heavily on the translated works of Japanese historians. Excellent bibliography.

Yoshihaski, Takehiko. *Conspiracy at Mukden: The Rise of the Japanese Military.* New Haven, Conn.: Yale University Press, 1963. Concerned with the crisis up to the fall of the Japanese government in December, 1931. Uses the crisis as a case study for the rise of militarism in Japan. Handy chronology, good bibliography and index.

Louis G. Perez

Cross-References

The Boxer Rebellion Fails to Remove Foreign Control in China (1900), p. 1; The League of Nations Is Established (1919), p. 270; Japanese Troops Brutalize Chinese After the Capture of Nanjing (1937), p. 539; Roosevelt Approves Internment of Japanese Americans (1942), p. 595; A Japanese Commander Is Ruled Responsible for His Troops' Actions (1945), p. 662.

HITLER USES REICHSTAG FIRE TO SUSPEND CIVIL AND POLITICAL LIBERTIES

Categories of event: Political freedom and civil rights
Time: February 27, 1933
Locale: Berlin, Germany

Adolf Hitler used the burning of the German parliament (Reichstag) building as an excuse to limit civil and political liberties granted under the Weimar constitution

Principal personages:

ADOLF HITLER (1889-1945), the chancellor of Germany and leader (Führer) of the Nazi Party

HERMANN GÖRING (1893-1946), the Prussian minister of the interior, president of the Reichstag, and prosecutor at the Reichstag fire trial

JOSEPH GOEBBELS (1897-1945), the Nazi propaganda leader and, after March 13, 1933, the German minister of propaganda

MARINUS VAN DER LUBBE (1909-1934), the Dutch arsonist who burned the Reichstag building

GEORGI DIMITROV (1882-1949), a Bulgarian defendant at the Reichstag fire trial, later secretary-general of the Communist International

ERNST TORGLER (1893-1963), a German Communist representative to the Reichstag and defendant at the trial

Summary of Event

The years following World War I were a period of chaos in Germany. Defeat in war and the humiliation of the peace at Versailles made the populace bitter, frustrated, and angry. They vented their frustration on the Allies, on Jews and other non-German peoples, and above all on the Weimar republic created to replace the monarchy. The first wave of turmoil arose from 1918 to 1923, but it subsided with improving economic conditions in the second half of the 1920's. The Weimar constitution appeared to be working very well. With the outbreak of the depression in 1929, however, a new swell of political agitation based on race and class hatred gained momentum.

The turbulent years immediately after the war saw the rise of extremist parties on the left and right. From 1919 to 1923, the German Communist party initiated three uprisings. Nationalist, anti-Communist, and anti-Semitic groups also on several occasions attempted to overthrow the republic and committed acts of terror against its officials. The most infamous uprising of the political right in those years occurred in Munich in October, 1923—the unsuccessful "Beer Hall Putsch" of Adolf Hitler, leader of the National Socialist German Workers' Party, the Nazis. In the lull of 1925-1929, the party did not fare well, but with the depression, all extremist parties and organizations gained support. Hitler found his star on the ascendant.

As conditions in Germany worsened and political haggling in the parliament (Reichstag) accomplished little, the aged and reactionary president of the republic, former Field Marshal Paul von Hindenburg, disregarded the principles of democratic government. He relied solely on his aristocratic cronies to rule, principally Baron Franz von Papen, who assumed the chancellorship in 1932. The latter, however, found himself stymied by the Communists and the Nazis, whose strength in the parliament had increased with the depression. Preferring the right, von Papen came to an agreement with Hitler, whom he hoped to control. Thus, after a number of back-room deals, on January 30, 1933, von Papen convinced von Hindenburg to appoint Hitler as the new chancellor of Germany.

Hitler's chancellorship came through neither a mass revolution nor the ballot box. Although the Nazi party had grown rapidly in strength since 1929, Hitler had lost the presidential election to von Hindenburg in 1932. Likewise, his Nazis, although gaining a plurality, were able to win only thirty-seven percent of the vote in the parliamentary elections of July, 1932. Without sufficient popular support, Hitler needed a different way to break out of the restrictions which von Papen had imposed on him.

In one of his first acts as chancellor, Hitler used emergency decrees provided by the constitution to replace the democratically elected Socialist government of the Prussian state with one led by Hermann Göring, a Nazi minister without portfolio in the national cabinet. Hitler also took measures against the Communists, who were calling for resistance although not actually carrying out any overt acts. Göring raided Communist headquarters in Berlin and closed their printing presses. Many did not see Hitler's chancellery as a threat until then because the Nazis remained a minority in the government. The left now became alarmed, and apprehension concerning the Nazis spread.

On February 25, the day after Göring's raid, three attempts to start fires in government buildings were aborted. The next day, Hitler's astrologer, Erik Hanussen, predicted a building would soon go up in flames. On Monday, February 27, a Dutch arsonist, Marinus van der Lubbe, perpetrator of the February 25 attempts, purchased some incendiary materials and went to the Reichstag. After surveying the building from several directions, he entered a nearby building to wait for dark. At 9:00 P.M. he scaled the wall to the balcony near a little-used entrance. Shortly later, a passerby, hearing broken glass and seeing a person (presumably van der Lubbe) fleeing with a flame in his hands, notified the police. An officer went to the scene but watched transfixed while flames began to engulf the internal rooms.

By the time the firemen arrived, the building was already burning down. Ernst "Putzi" Hanfstaengl, an associate of Hitler, saw the fire from his apartment and notified Goebbels, at whose house Hitler was attending a party. Neither Hitler nor Goebbels at first believed Hanfstaengl, who was known for his practical jokes, but as the fire progressed further, even the revelers could see the red sky. One report states that Hitler yelled, "It's the Communists!" Hitler and Goebbels went to the scene. They found Göring, who was distraught over the possible loss of the building's precious Gobelin tapestries. Göring also blamed the Communists. He told Hitler that a number of Communist deputies were in the building shortly before the fire broke out and that one arrest had already been made. Hitler asked about other buildings, and Göring assured him that he had taken precautions to preserve them.

Hitler, Göring, and von Papen then conferred on what action to take. Von Papen went to inform von Hindenburg, and Hitler convoked a meeting of his cabinet and civic and police officials. The police inspector assigned to the case reported that the police had found van der Lubbe, who admitted that he committed the arson as a protest. Göring shouted, "This is the beginning of a Communist uprising," and Hitler added, "Now we'll show them! Anyone who stands in our way will be mown down!" He threatened to hang or shoot Communists, Socialists, and even conservative opponents. When the police inspector revealed that van der Lubbe was not a Communist and had carried out the deed alone, Hitler refused to believe it. "This is a cunning and well-prepared plot," he said. The chancellor then went to the offices of the Nazi Party newspaper, *Voelkischer Beobachter* (People's Observer), and immediately helped compose a version of the story that blamed the Communists for the fire. Göring likewise assisted in changing the report of the official Prussian press service to exaggerate the facts and imply that a conspiracy was involved.

The fire was just the excuse Hitler needed to begin his drive for totalitarian power, to change the Weimar republic into the Third Reich. Hitler argued that a single individual could not have perpetrated the arson. Van der Lubbe, furthermore, had been a member of the International Communist Party and also had been arrested twice in Leiden for setting fires to public buildings. In fact, however, historical research has demonstrated that van der Lubbe did set the fire alone. The International Communist Party to which he belonged was a small splinter group, more anarchist than Marxist in ideology and not part of the Communist International directed by Moscow. Indeed, van der Lubbe and the Communists loyal to Joseph Stalin had little use for each other.

Göring found four Communists to indict in addition to van der Lubbe—Ernst Torgler, a leader of the German Communist Party and a member of the Reichstag, and three Bulgarian agents of the Communist International: Georgi Dimitrov, Vasili Tanev, and Blagoi Popov. In a spectacular trial in which Hitler, Goebbels, and Göring (one of the prosecutors) hoped to prove to the world that a Communist conspiracy actually did exist, the Communist defendants, particularly Georgi Dimitrov, proved their innocence. In fact, Dimitrov went as far as accusing the Nazis of deliberately setting the fire themselves. He humiliated Göring in an unexpected courtroom confrontation which was broadcast and reported around the world. In other countries, Communists and other antifascists organized protests. Nazi opponents convened a countertrial in London with a court of respected international jurists to show that the Nazis did indeed start the fire. Goebbels' propaganda ploy had backfired, causing the government to move the trial from Berlin to Leipzig, where they concluded it with little publicity.

The court acquitted the Communists but found van der Lubbe guilty. The Dutchman was executed shortly thereafter. Dimitrov, Tanev, and Popov were released and were welcomed to the Soviet Union. Some say their acquittal and release came about through pressure from Moscow, which threatened retaliation against German citizens living in the Soviet Union. Furthermore, the court ruled that although the accused Communists were innocent, the fire was part of a Communist conspiracy. The authorities released Torgler several months after the Bulgarians.

Dimitrov in 1935 became the secretary-general of the Communist International and the spokesperson for Moscow's new foreign policy, which was to be implemented by world Communist parties promoting antifascist coalitions even at the expense of delaying the world socialist revolution. In 1948, Dimitrov became prime minister of Communist Bulgaria. Popov also returned to Bulgaria after the war and served in a number of government posts. Tanev was killed in guerrilla warfare during World War II. Torgler, falsely accused of being a Nazi agent, was expelled by the German Communist Party. He settled in Hanover, where he retired from political life.

Impact of Event

Even before Hitler became chancellor, economic crises and flaws in the Weimar Republic's constitutional government subjected Germany to stress and social disorientation. The constitution's provisions allowed President von Hindenburg and Chancellor von Papen legally to act in a high-handed manner. They had no compunctions about doing so, as they had little regard for parliamentary or democratic government in general and the Weimar constitution in particular. The spirit of the law fell victim to this era. The conservative government's favoritism to right-wing nationalists allowed Nazi storm troopers to wreak havoc in the German cities and placed Jews, trade unionists, political moderates, and the political left in a state of jeopardy and fear. These events did not bode well for the promise of civil and political freedom which the drafters of Weimar had hoped to bring to a recovering Germany.

Von Papen and von Hindenburg's political manipulations, in fact, brought Hitler to power. He, too, needed little excuse to begin antidemocratic and anticonstitutional actions, such as the dismissal of state governments and raids on opponents. Nevertheless, the high-handed manner in which the Nazis acted as soon as they gained power could have caused them difficulty in retaining it. After all, they still depended on the barons (von Hindenburg, von Papen, and their associates) for their real authority. These aristocrats disliked the Nazis not so much because of their nationalist and anti-Communist ideology but because of their lower-class origins and "crudeness." Hitler's party may have had the plurality in Parliament, but it did not have the majority and as yet had not demonstrated its ability to win a clear victory at the polls.

Thus, Hitler needed to have extraordinary powers. The Reichstag fire gave him the opportunity to demand the enabling legislation which virtually created a dictatorship for him. Whether he believed that the Communists were conspiring to seize power is immaterial, just as it is immaterial whether, as the Communists then charged, the Nazis deliberately started the fire to get this legislation. Historical opinion considered the latter allegation true until the 1960's, when it was disproved. The fire was an opportune event for Hitler, but if it had not happened, he undoubtedly would have found another route to totalitarian power.

President von Hindenburg enacted the enabling legislation on February 28, 1933, the day after the fire. He cited a constitutional provision permitting the government to rule by decree in times of emergency. The justification was the need for "a defensive measure against Communist acts of violence endangering the state." The decree, in part, read: "Restrictions on personal liberty, on the right of free expression of opinion, including freedom of the press; on the rights of assembly and association; and violations of the privacy of postal, telegraphic and telephonic communications; and warrants for house searchers, orders for confiscations as well as restrictions on property, are also permissible beyond the legal limits otherwise prescribed."

With the enabling legislation, Hitler outlawed the Communist Party and arrested its leadership. He harassed other opposition parties as well, closing their papers and outlawing their meetings. New elections were scheduled for March 5. The government's own actions hindered the opposition campaigns. Despite their efforts, the Nazis could do no better than forty-four percent of the vote. Nevertheless, Hitler held full power. He used the legislation to break down the federal structure of the republic and take over all the state governments. Although originally perceived to be temporary, the decrees enacted under the enabling legislation were permanently applied to the Third Reich. Over the next months, the government banned all political parties except the Nazis. Civil and political guarantees were effectively ended. Discriminatory legislation directed against the Jews was put into effect. Political opponents, some even within the Nazi party, were arrested without cause, forced to emigrate, or even murdered extralegally. The Weimar Republic was dead and the Führer was the dictator of his Third Empire.

Bibliography

Bullock, Alan. *Hitler: A Study in Tyranny.* Rev. ed. New York: Harper & Row, 1962. An older biography of Hitler from a psychological as well as a historical perspective. A good study, but the research is somewhat dated. Follows the Brown Book on the fire. Illustrations, bibliography, index.

Delmer, Sefton. *Trail Sinister: An Autobiography.* Vol. 1. London: Secker & Warburg, 1961. The autobiography of an Australian journalist born in Germany. It contains a very good eyewitness account of the Reichstag fire, the trial, and its consequences. Index.

Fest, Joachim C. *Hitler.* New York: Harcourt Brace Jovanovich, 1974. The best scholarly biography of Hitler, placing him in the context of German history and politics of the twentieth century. Fest tends to follow Tobias on the issue of the Reichstag fire but does not absolutely reject the possibility of a Nazi plot. He believes the actual culprits are irrelevant and argues that the fire provided a convenient excuse to institute totalitarianism. Documented; bibliography, indexed.

Shirer, William L. *The Rise and Fall of the Third Reich: A History of Nazi Germany.*

New York: Simon & Schuster, 1960. A very readable popular history of Nazi Germany by an American journalist who witnessed the early years. Scholarly critics have complained about its lack of rigor and some errors. Written before Tobias's account, it accepts as factual the Brown Book's interpretation of the fire. Documented; bibliography, index.

Tobias, Fritz. *The Reichstag Fire.* Introduction by A. J. P. Taylor. New York: G. P. Putnam's Sons, 1964. This controversial book first revealed the fact that the Nazis did not burn down the Reichstag, but that van der Lubbe did it alone. It is a well-researched refutation of the Brown Book's thesis, although at times it sinks to an anti-Communist polemic. Illustrations, bibliography, index.

Toland, John. *Adolf Hitler.* Garden City, N.Y.: Doubleday, 1976. A biography of Hitler for the general reader. Well researched and readable but lacking the scholarly rigor and insight of Fest. Toland covers the fire and its consequences in great detail, basing his account chiefly on Tobias. Illustrations, bibliography, index.

World Committee for the Victims of German Fascism. *The Reichstag Fire Trial: The Second Brown Book of the Hitler Terror.* 1934. Reprint. New York: Howard Fertig, 1969. A reprint of the 1934 edition published to demonstrate that the Nazis themselves actually burned down the Reichstag. Critics claim that it is Communist propaganda, exaggerating and manufacturing facts and evidence. Presents the case against the Nazis which was believed universally until Fritz Tobias' research. Contains a list of about 750 victims of Nazi atrocities before March, 1934. Illustrations, not indexed.

Frederick B. Chary

Cross-References

Germans Revolt and Form Socialist Government (1918), p. 241; Hitler Writes *Mein Kampf* (1924), p. 389; Mussolini Seizes Dictatorial Powers in Italy (1925), p. 395; Nazi Concentration Camps Go into Operation (1933), p. 491; Citizens Rescue Danish Jews from Germans (1943), p. 641; Nazi War Criminals Are Tried in Nuremberg (1945), p. 667; Barbie Faces Charges for Nazi War Crimes (1983), p. 2193; Israel Convicts Demjanjuk of Nazi War Crimes (1988), p. 2370.

FRANKLIN D. ROOSEVELT APPOINTS PERKINS AS SECRETARY OF LABOR

Categories of event: Women's rights and workers' rights
Time: February 28, 1933
Locale: Washington, D.C.

The appointment of Frances Perkins as the first female secretary of labor showed that women could play a key role in national politics

Principal personages:

FRANCES PERKINS (1882-1965), a social worker with a strong background in industrial and labor relations before her appointment as secretary of labor

FRANKLIN D. ROOSEVELT (1882-1945), the thirty-second president of the United States (1933-1945)

AL SMITH (1873-1944), the "Happy Warrior," who worked with Perkins in New York State politics and gave her her first significant appointive post

MARTIN DIES (1901-1972), the first chair of the House Committee on Un-American Activities

HARRY BRIDGES (1901-1990), a radical leader of the longshoremen and target for deportation

Summary of Event

Franklin Roosevelt appointed Frances Perkins as secretary of labor on February 28, 1933. She took office on March 4, 1933, and served until July 1, 1945. For Perkins, the appointment recognized almost thirty years of distinguished service as a social worker and civil servant with nationally recognized expertise in labor relations. For Roosevelt, this was a practical way to seek the support of female Progressive reformers, who had few visible political achievements to show for the attainment of suffrage in 1920. By appointing Perkins, Roosevelt secured a cabinet member who had recognized national expertise in the area overseen by her department. She provided greater integrity than would have a man recommended by the American Federation of Labor, since she possessed an independent background that allowed critical thinking and did not force allegiance to labor union positions.

Perkins was the daughter of Fred and Susan Perkins, both of colonial stock. They anticipated that their talented daughter's primary career would be as wife and mother, although they were unconventional in encouraging her to graduate from Worcester Classical High School in 1898 and Mount Holyoke College in 1902. The Perkinses provided financial assistance to their daughter in the early stages of her social work career, although they would have been happier if she had remained a volunteer and not become a professional social worker.

Perkins began to form an independent identity as a student at Mount Holyoke, where she did her first research in factory conditions as a class project. More importantly, Perkins demonstrated political ability at Mount Holyoke, where she was elected class president by her classmates. Perkins deserted the conservative Republican politics supported by her parents, who were successful and respected members of the small business class. In becoming Episcopalian as an adult, Perkins also deserted the Congregational faith of her parents. Perkins' intense devotions to her faith contrasted sharply with the haphazard Episcopalianism of Franklin Delano Roosevelt.

After college, Perkins did volunteer work and some teaching. While teaching in Lake Forest, Illinois, Perkins met Graham Taylor, head of the Chicago Commons settlement house. Through Taylor, Perkins met Jane Addams, Ellen Gates Starr, and Grace Abbott, who were social reform leaders. By 1907, Perkins had lived at Hull House, worked at the Chicago Commons, and firmly decided on a career in social work.

In September, 1907, Perkins became general secretary of the Philadelphia Research and Protective Association. She received a nominal salary of fifty dollars per month from this organization, which worked with foreign immigrant girls and black girls who had migrated to Philadelphia from the South. Both groups of vulnerable young women often were forced to work under extremely exploitive conditions or were recruited for brothels. While serving as an advocate for the poor in Philadelphia, Perkins attended classes in economics and sociology at the Wharton School of Finance and Commerce.

After two years in Philadelphia, Perkins moved to New York in 1909 and used a $500 fellowship to attend the New York School of Philanthropy. Living in settlement houses, Perkins qualified for a master's degree in political science at Columbia University on June 10, 1910, with her thesis, "A Study of Malnutrition in 197 Children from Public School 51." Despite the fact that her degree was granted in political science, most of the courses Perkins had taken were in economics and sociology.

In 1910, Perkins became general secretary of the National Consumers' League. Through the Consumers' League, Perkins formed a lasting friendship with its national director, Florence Kelley. Perkins also gained a national reputation for her surveys of industrial conditions. Conditions were unhealthy and dangerous in most occupations, and Perkins saw the Triangle Shirtwaist Fire in March 25, 1911, in which 146 women either burned or jumped to their deaths. Influenced by this fire, Perkins served from 1912 to 1917 as executive secretary of a committee on safety, which was formed to press for better working conditions. As a political result of the Triangle fire, the New York State Factory Commission was created. Perkins served as an investigator on the staff of the commission's director of investigation from 1912 to 1913.

Perkins married Paul C. Wilson, an economist on the staff of New York City reform mayor John Purroy Mitchell. This marriage lasted until Wilson's death in 1951, despite the fact that he was hospitalized for mental illness throughout most of the marriage. Perkins was the breadwinner for Wilson and their daughter Susanna, who was born in 1916. Both Perkins and her husband agreed that Perkins would keep her maiden name for professional purposes.

In 1919, Governor Al Smith, whom Perkins had known since 1911, appointed Perkins to the State Industrial Commission. She served from 1919 to 1920, and Smith reappointed Perkins after he began his second term as governor in 1922. Perkins also served with the Industrial Board of the State Labor Department. In 1926, Smith recognized Perkins' increasing professional credibility as an expert in labor law by naming her chair of the Industrial Board. When Smith lost his presidential race in 1928, Franklin Roosevelt was elected governor of New York. Roosevelt appointed Perkins as industrial commissioner of New York. This state position was a significant first for a woman, and it helped prepare Perkins for her cabinet appointment.

This background of education and study made Perkins a highly qualified cabinet appointee. There was no need or expectation of affirmative action to advance her as a representative woman. She was prepared by experience to reorganize the Labor Department for Roosevelt and to participate in the passage of the Social Security Act of 1935. Despite the fact that the House Un-American Activities Committee introduced impeachment action against her in 1938 at the instigation of Martin Dies, who resented her refusal to deport radical longshoreman Harry Bridges, Perkins was a generally successful cabinet member. Her appointment and service set a precedent that women qualified for such service. Although Perkins did not favor an equal rights amendment, since she viewed it as a threat to protective legislation for women, she must be viewed as a practical advocate of advancement for women in the terms and forms appropriate to her generation.

Impact of Event

Roosevelt's appointment of Perkins had enduring consequences in six diverse areas of human rights concern. Like many successful college-educated women of her day, Perkins broke important ground in proving that women could be competent professionals, and she devoted her career to alleviating the misery created by the excesses of industrial capitalism in diverse areas of public concern. Trained in social work, she sought practical measures to protect the dignity of American workers.

First, Perkins' success established the previously untested competence of women to hold cabinet rank. As the first female cabinet member, she helped make it possible for other women to serve in future cabinets. Women such as Oveta Culp Hobby and Elizabeth Dole, who served in later cabinets, benefited from Perkins' success. Although Perkins supported protective legislation for women and opposed the idea of an equal rights amendment, her contributions greatly furthered women's search for equal participation in American politics.

Second, Perkins was a consistent proponent of emerging unions and organized labor's right to organize and bargain collectively, even though as a social worker she had showed more interest in the rights of nonunion labor than the American Federation of Labor (AFL) would have liked. She supported prounion legislation such as the Wagner Act, and she made impassioned pleas to industrial employers to recognize that their employees could not effectively negotiate with them as individuals. She believed, however, that social legislation needed to address the concerns of nonunion labor in an era when labor union leadership often considered aid to nonunion labor as counterproductive to their organizing efforts.

Third, she was a consistent advocate of the emerging economic, political, and social interest of black labor, to the extent that this was possible in the New Deal era. She insisted that New Deal work relief programs serve African American workers even in the deep South, and she symbolically integrated the Labor Department cafeteria in racially segregated Washington, D.C. She also worked to promote black employees into responsible professional positions in the Department of Labor.

Fourth, Perkins opposed the Federal Bureau of Investigation's desire to fingerprint all American citizens as potentially totalitarian. She defeated J. Edgar Hoover on this issue. This victory extended her influence beyond matters of strictly labor concern.

Fifth, Perkins fought to end the intimidation of resident aliens, such as longshoreman leader Harry Bridges, who were perceived as dangerous radicals. She suffered great political and personal embarrassment over this issue, but she protected the civil rights of alien workers even while losing the Labor Department's traditional control of immigration enforcement to other agencies.

Sixth, she used her maiden name, even though she was Mrs. Paul C. Wilson, and she consistently insisted on being addressed as "Miss Perkins." This decision helped establish the right of women to retain their maiden names.

Taken together, Frances Perkins' concerns for the rights of labor, minorities, and women left a significant legacy to the human rights enjoyed by contemporary America. She passed a torch of reform to the New Frontier and beyond, since she was an active lecturer at Cornell into the era of John F. Kennedy. She was a unique combination of Christian idealist and practical politician who successfully applied the doctrines of the Social Gospel movement in a public context without breaching the separation of church and state.

Bibliography

Cobble, Dorothy Sue. "A Self Possessed Woman: A View of F.D.R.'s Secretary of Labor, Madame Perkins." *Labor History* 29 (February, 1988): 225-229. Cobble reviews the film *You May Call Her Madam Secretary* in this laudatory essay. She views Perkins as a successful pathbreaker for women.

Goldberg, Joseph P. "Frances Perkins, Isador Lubin, and the Bureau of Labor Statistics." *Monthly Labor Review* 103 (April, 1980): 22-27. Goldberg details how Lubin and Perkins modernized the statistical recordkeeping of the Department of Labor. Although the article focuses more on Lubin than on Perkins, it provides useful background to Perkins' career.

Guzda, Henry P. "Frances Perkins's Interest in a New Deal for Blacks." *Monthly Labor Review* 103 (April, 1980): 31-35. Guzda contends that Perkins made the welfare of black labor a priority of the Labor Department in her efforts to include blacks in New Deal programs. Although her actions were minimal by post-Civil Rights era standards, Perkins attempted to see that blacks benefited from New Deal labor relief programs.

Martin, George. *Madam Secretary, Frances Perkins.* Boston: Houghton Mifflin, 1976. Martin provides a comprehensive and definitive scholarly account of Perkins' life. He is clearly an admirer of her and her work in the New Deal. It is notable that he gives fair attention to her religious motivations and to the interaction among Progressive-era women.

Mohr, Lillian Holmen. *Frances Perkins: That Woman in FDR's Cabinet.* Croton-On-Hudson, N.Y.: North River Press, 1979. Mohr provides a competent account of Perkins' life notable for its reticence in describing the nature of Paul C. Wilson's illness. Mohr, a professor at Cornell, knew Perkins during the last years of her life.

Susan A. Stussy

Cross-References

Rankin Becomes the First Woman Elected to Congress (1916), p. 190; Nellie Tayloe Ross of Wyoming Becomes the First Female Governor (1925), p. 412; The Wagner Act Requires Employers to Accept Collective Bargaining (1935), p. 508; Social Security Act Establishes Benefits for Nonworking People (1935), p. 514; Social Security Act Provides Grants for Dependent Children (1935), p. 520; HUAC Begins Investigating Suspected Communists (1938), p. 550; The Equal Rights Amendment Passes Congress but Fails to Be Ratified (1972), p. 1656.

NAZI CONCENTRATION CAMPS GO INTO OPERATION

Category of event: Atrocities and war crimes
Time: March, 1933
Locale: Germany

The opening of Nazi Germany's first concentration camps was an early step in a destruction process that culminated in the Holocaust

Principal personages:

ADOLF HITLER (1889-1945), the Nazi Party leader named German chancellor on January 30, 1933

HEINRICH HIMMLER (1900-1945), the head of the SS and second in power in Nazi Germany; presided over the "final solution"

THEODOR EICKE (1892-1943), the commandant of Dachau beginning in June, 1933; became chief of Nazi concentration camps in July, 1934

HERMANN GÖRING (1893-1946), the Prussian minister of the interior who played a leading role in organizing the Gestapo

RUDOLF HÖSS (1900-1947), an SS officer who became commandant of the death camp at Auschwitz

ERNST RÖHM (1887-1934), the leader of the SA (*Sturmabteilung*), the Nazi storm troopers

PAUL VON HINDENBURG (1847-1934), Germany's president from 1925 to 1934

Summary of Event

Although the Nazis never gained a majority in any freely contested election, their control of Germany began on January 30, 1933, when Adolf Hitler was named chancellor by Paul von Hindenburg, president of the Weimar Republic. Six months later, the Nazis stood as the only legal political party in Germany, Hitler's decrees were as good as law, basic civil rights had been suspended, and thousands of the regime's suspected political opponents had been interned in a growing number of concentration camps. Before the Third Reich fell twelve years later, millions of people— including two-thirds of the European Jews—would perish in the brutal world of concentration camps.

Disregarding the principle that one should not be punished unless found guilty in a fair trial, concentration camps remove from society people who cannot be confined through the normal workings of a state's criminal code. The Nazis did not invent them, nor did they have a systematic design for developing such places as soon as they came to power in Germany. Gradually, however, a deadly camp system did evolve. An early step in that process occurred at Dachau, a town about ten miles northwest of Munich, where one of the first concentration camps was established. The site of a vacated World War I munitions factory provided the needed space for

Dachau's first prisoners, who entered the camp in late March, 1933. Those early inmates were political opponents of the Nazis, mainly Communists and Social Democrats, who were kept under so-called "protective custody."

Heinrich Himmler was the Nazi leader who established Dachau. In 1925, he had joined the SS (*Schutzstaffel*), a small group of dedicated Nazis who served as Adolf Hitler's personal bodyguards. Hitler appointed Himmler head of the SS in 1929. Only about two hundred strong at the time, the SS, under Himmler's direction, eventually numbered in the hundreds of thousands and formed an awesome empire within the Nazi state. Meanwhile, shortly after Hitler became chancellor in 1933, Himmler gained important police powers in Munich and in the entire province of Bavaria. He used his authority to create the Dachau camp.

Bavarian state police guarded the camp at first, but in April, 1933, SS personnel took over. Theodor Eicke became Dachau's commandant in June. As he regulated camp life, including stating rules about work and punishment, Eicke ensured that Dachau's procedures would be systematic and replicable as well as harsh. After Eicke was appointed head of the Nazi network of concentration camps in July, 1934, the system he had developed at Dachau became standard. The SS personnel who trained under him saw to it that his policies were established at other camps as they rose to new positions of leadership in the system. One who did so, for example, was Rudolf Höss, whose Dachau training prepared him to become the commandant of Auschwitz in German-occupied Poland in 1940.

Although the Dachau model fostered by Himmler's SS leadership eventually dominated the Nazi camp system, that outcome was not a foregone conclusion in the early months of the Third Reich. By the end of July, 1933, Nazi Germany held nearly twenty-seven thousand political prisoners in "protective custody." Dachau contained its share, but thousands more prisoners could be found in a variety of other detention centers. These centers lacked overall coordination. They shared only the fact of incarcerating people who predominantly were "guilty" only in the sense that they were judged politically suspect by the Nazis.

An early pretext for arrests of the "politically suspect" was the fire that ravaged the German parliament building on February 27, 1933. Although Nazis may have set the blaze to serve their own purposes, Hitler blamed the Reichstag's destruction on communist arson. The next day, President von Hindenburg signed the emergency decree that the Nazis wanted: By suspending basic rights guaranteed by the Weimar Constitution, and thereby allowing detention for persons suspected of hostility to the state, it opened the door for a policy of *Schutzhaft*, or "protective custody," that would guard the Reich's security by imprisoning those who were suspected of threatening it. Taking advantage of this sweeping decree, the Nazis launched a wave of arrests throughout the country.

Many victims of this campaign were interned in camps quickly set up by the SA (*Sturmabteilung*), the brown-shirted Nazi storm troopers led by Ernst Röhm. Others, especially in Prussia, were imprisoned in detention centers created by Hermann Göring, the chief of the Prussian police, who was also organizing the Gestapo, a secret police force dedicated to maintaining the security of the Nazi state. Precisely how many of these camps existed in 1933 remains unclear, although informed estimates indicate that Prussia alone had twenty of them.

In a regime where terror loomed so large, anyone who could gain control of the Nazi concentration camps would wield immense power; thus, Göring attempted to outdo his rivals, only to be outdone by Himmler. By early July, 1934, Himmler not only had established the SS camp at Dachau but also had gained control of the political police in the Reich's various states—including Göring's Gestapo in Prussia. In addition, he had masterminded a purge of the SA, and appointed Eicke, his SS subordinate, to supervise the concentration camps throughout Germany.

This consolidation of power eliminated most of the small camps that had sprung up wildly in 1933. By September, 1935, the six official concentration camps in the Third Reich were at Dachau, Lichtenburg, Sachsenburg, Esterwegen, Oranienburg, and Columbia Haus (near Berlin). On the eve of World War II, in the late summer of 1939, even those camps—except for Dachau, which was reconstructed in 1937 and 1938—had been eclipsed by newer and larger installations at Sachsenhausen (1936), Buchenwald (1937), Flossenbürg (1938), Mauthausen (in Austria, 1938), and Ravensbrück (a concentration camp for women, 1939).

In the period from 1933 until the outbreak of World War II in 1939, there were changes in the concentration camp population. The number of prisoners fluctuated. Although mostly political prisoners were incarcerated at first, the concentration camps gradually engulfed many other types of people in addition to the communists, social democrats, and trade unionists who had been targeted initially. By 1938, Jehovah's Witnesses, members of the clergy, "asocial elements"—such as homosexuals and those called "habitual criminals"—as well as Gypsies and Jews were among those in the camps. From person to person and place to place, treatment varied to some degree, but exhausting labor, severe punishment, poor food, filth, disease, and execution were all among the possible and persistent threats. Release from a concentration camp was possible, but death while in a camp was likely.

Impact of Event

Nazi concentration camps of the kind that began at Dachau in March, 1933, were only the beginning of an unprecedented twelve-year assault against human rights. What followed from that beginning may be glimpsed by considering further what the term "concentration camp" can mean. Sometimes that category is used to refer collectively to all the camps of detention and death that the Nazis established. The evolution of Nazi policy, however, requires some further distinctions.

Although all the Nazi camps derived partly from impulses and intentions that brought Dachau into existence, not every camp in the Nazi system was simply a holding pen for political detainees. Especially after World War II began with the German invasion of Poland on September 1, 1939, different but related institutions started to appear. There were, for example, labor camps, transit camps, prisoner-of-war camps, and, most destructive of all, extermination or death camps.

The Nazis violated human rights in virtually every possible way, but no group received more inhumane treatment from them than the Jews. In the early years, however, relatively small numbers of Jews were interned in concentration camps such as Dachau and Buchenwald. Not until the summer of 1938, and especially after the *Kristallnacht* pogrom in November, 1938, were large numbers of them imprisoned solely because they were Jews. Even then, most of these Jewish prisoners were eventually released after paying a ransom or proving that they were about to emigrate from Germany. Jewish fate, however, would change catastrophically with the outbreak of World War II.

Nazi ideology held that Jews were the chief obstacle to the racial and cultural purity that Hitler craved for the Third Reich. Political opponents were dealt with ruthlessly to ensure Nazi domination of Germany. Nazi aims soon identified the Jews as an even more virulent threat. Their polluting presence, Hitler believed, would have to be eliminated. For a time, the Nazis relied largely on punitive laws to segregate Jews, expropriate their property, and deprive them of their professions and other rights. The Nazi strategy was to make life so difficult that the German Jews would be forced to leave. This plan did not achieve its goals; thus, Nazi policies aimed at specific population reduction had to change when Hitler went to war to expand geographically the German nation.

Hitler's conquests, especially in Eastern Europe, brought millions of Jews under German domination. What gradually evolved was a policy of mass murder—the "Final Solution" to the Jewish question. From late 1941 until late 1944, the Final Solution was implemented most systematically by the gas chambers that operated at six death camps in occupied Poland: Chelmno, Belzec, Sobibor, Treblinka, Majdanek, and Auschwitz-Birkenau.

Dachau and the other early concentration camps on German soil were never death factories like Treblinka and Auschwitz-Birkenau. The violations of human rights initiated at the first camps, however, were part of wide-ranging aims to stamp out every element of dissent and diversity that stood in the way of Nazi domination. Concentration camps such as Dachau did damage enough to human rights as well as helping to pave the way to other camps. These other camps were even worse because they were specifically designed to remove unwanted lives, especially Jewish ones, by unrelenting mass murder.

Bibliography

Feig, Konnilyn G. *Hitler's Death Camps: The Sanity of Madness*. New York: Holmes & Meier, 1979. This detailed study gives an overview of the Nazi concentration and death camps and, focusing on their structure and function, a camp-by-camp analysis of many of them, including Dachau. Contains helpful maps and photographs.

Gutman, Israel, ed. *Encyclopedia of the Holocaust*. 4 vols. New York: Macmillan, 1990. Contains articles on many concentration camps as well as on the camp system as a whole. Provides surveys of the SS, SA, and Gestapo, as well as essays about individual SS leaders in the camp system. All of the essays in this extensive work have been carefully prepared by highly qualified scholars. Useful maps and illustrations included.

Hilberg, Raul. *The Destruction of the European Jews.* Rev. ed. 3 vols. New York: Holmes & Meier, 1985. An unrivaled study of the bureaucratic process of destruction that the Nazis directed toward the Jews of Europe. Analysis situates the concentration and death camps within that systematic process. Focuses especially on developments that transformed the conventional concentration camps into centers of mass murder such as those at Treblinka and Auschwitz-Birkenau in German-occupied Poland.

Höhne, Heinz. *The Order of the Death's Head: The Story of Hitler's SS.* Translated by Richard Barry. New York: Ballantine Books, 1979. Offers a detailed study of the rise of the SS, its immense power in Nazi Germany, and its central role in administration of the concentration and death camps. Focuses on individual figures as well as on the overall organization of the SS.

Kogon, Eugen. *The Theory and Practice of Hell: The German Concentration Camps and the System Behind Them.* Translated by Heinz Norden. New York: Octagon, 1981. Written by a survivor of Buchenwald, this book was first published shortly after the end of World War II. One of the earliest studies of the Nazi camp system. Kogon sees the SS and its camps as the center of power in Hitler's Germany.

Krausnick, Helmut, Hans Buchheim, Martin Brozat, and Hans-Adolf Jacobsen. *Anatomy of the SS State.* Translated by Richard Barry, Marian Jackson, and Dorothy Long. New York: Walker and Company, 1968. Supports a theory of concentration camp crimes and genocidal treatment of Jews as essential features of Nazism. In particular, Martin Brozat's "The Concentration Camps 1933-45" provides effective documentation.

Rubenstein, Richard L., and John K. Roth. *Approaches to Auschwitz: The Holocaust and Its Legacy.* Atlanta: John Knox Press, 1987. An overview of the Holocaust. Discusses the emergence and development of the concentration and death camps that played a central role in the mass death unleashed by Nazi Germany. Focuses on the victims as well as on the perpetrators.

Wistrich, Robert. *Who's Who in Nazi Germany.* New York: Macmillan, 1982. Incisive biographies give basic information about more than three hundred Nazi leaders. Entries on Himmler, Göring, Eicke, and many others who were involved in the concentration camp system. A helpful reference tool.

John K. Roth

Cross-References

Germans Revolt and Form Socialist Government (1918), p. 241; Hitler Writes *Mein Kampf* (1924), p. 389; Hitler Uses Reichstag Fire to Suspend Civil and Political Liberties (1933), p. 480; Stalin Begins Purging Political Opponents (1934), p. 503; Roosevelt Approves Internment of Japanese Americans (1942), p. 595; Nazi War

THE INDIAN REORGANIZATION ACT OFFERS AUTONOMY TO AMERICAN INDIANS

Category of event: Indigenous peoples' rights
Time: June 18, 1934
Locale: Washington, D.C.

Passage of the Indian Reorganization Act by the United States Congress permitted Native American groups to form self-governing bodies, ending decades of forced assimilation

Principal personages:

JOHN COLLIER (1884-1968), the commissioner of Indian affairs (1933-1945)

FRANKLIN D. ROOSEVELT (1882-1945), the president of the United States (1933-1945)

FELIX COHEN, an expert in Indian law who helped draft the original Wheeler-Howard bill

HAROLD ICKES (1874-1952), the secretary of the interior appointed by Roosevelt

WILLIAM F. ZIMMERMAN, JR., the assistant commissioner of Indian affairs who worked with Collier

CHARLES J. RHOADS, the commissioner of Indian affairs (1929-1933)

Summary of Event

Assimilation of Native Americans into the mainstream Anglo culture was the goal of the United States government from earliest colonial times. Whether government policy called for abrupt, forced acculturation or advocated gradual change, it was understood that ultimately American Indians must adopt the life-style of the whites or perish. The Indian Reorganization Act of 1934 was the first legislation designed to preserve, not to destroy, Native American cultures and to give back some of what had been taken away during the settlement of the United States, including Indian lands.

The greatest loss of Indian lands after the assigning of reservation territories to the various surviving tribes occurred as a result of the Dawes General Allotment Act of 1887. The goal of this legislation was to destroy tribal structure and the communal life-style of Native Americans by encouraging tribal Indians to become individual farmers. Tribal structure and authority were bypassed, as allotments of acreage were made to individuals. A patent in fee, or negotiable title, was issued on this land, which was held in trust by the federal government for twenty-five years and could not be sold until that time expired. Any surplus lands remaining after allotments had been made for a particular reservation were then auctioned off, making possible a massive land grab by eager white settlers. The funds from the sale of these surplus lands were held in a trust fund for the tribes by the federal government. When few Native Americans attempted to farm their allotments, the lands were leased to non-Indians and the meager fees were given to the allottees as rental income.

When this system proved too slow in breaking up the reservations, the Burke Act was passed in 1906. It permitted the secretary of the interior, through a declaration of competence, to release a particular allottee from the twenty-five year restriction of federal supervision. By the 1930's, ninety million acres of reservation lands had been lost through legal means. Unscrupulous, land-hungry settlers often cheated Native Americans out of their allotments, leaving them destitute and no more acculturated than they had been before implementation of the Dawes Act.

Although Native Americans had always had some champions, it was not until the Bursum Bill of 1922 was introduced that the Indian reform movement gathered appreciable force and Indian affairs garnered sustained interest. This bill was designed to permit non-Indians to gain title to lands within the Pueblo Indian land grants. It was defeated by protest of the Pueblo people and their many supporters.

One of the champions of Indian rights was John Collier, who would be appointed commissioner of Indian affairs eleven years later by President Franklin Delano Roosevelt, and would be instrumental in gaining passage of the Indian Reorganization Act. In the meantime, as executive secretary of the Indian Defense Association, he would tirelessly question and protest government policy regarding Native Americans, urging desperately needed reforms.

In 1923, Herbert Work became secretary of the interior. Work commissioned several examinations of the Indian Service, including the Meriam Report of 1928, which served as the blueprint for reforms sought through the Indian Reorganization Act.

Unfortunately, reforms were not attempted until the next administration appointed Ray Lyman Wilbur as secretary of the interior, with Charles J. Rhoads as commissioner of Indian affairs and J. Henry Scattergood as assistant commissioner. Although Wilbur wanted to move quickly with assimilation, Rhoads and Scattergood were cautious. Rhoads's only direct victory was the Leavitt Act of 1932, concerning reimbursable debts, which relieved Native American tribes from millions of dollars in liens placed upon their lands for projects that they had not requested and that gave them little benefit.

Another reform targeted by the Meriam Report was the incorporation of tribes for the purpose of self-government and the management of tribal resources. This issue was basic to the Indian Reorganization Act. The report suggested a special claims commission to hear the claims of individual Indian tribes against the United States. Education and health care were examined and targeted for reforms of often dismal conditions. State employees and agents were permitted to enter reservations to inspect health and educational conditions. Their findings included a higher death rate among Native Americans than in the general population, mainly from diseases such as tuberculosis. Sanitation and quarantine regulations were enforced by the state employees, and efforts were made to improve conditions by teaching personal hygiene and disease prevention. Compulsory school attendance was enforced for Native American children, and some attempt was made to improve the boarding schools. Although the Rhoads administration of the Bureau of Indian Affairs (BIA) improved some conditions, much more was needed.

John Collier was appointed commissioner of Indian affairs in 1933. He set about designing legislation to redress problems made clear by the Meriam Report. Collier's team included assistant commissioner William F. Zimmerman, Jr., and Felix Cohen. The latter became an expert on Indian law and helped to draft the Wheeler-Howard bill, which evolved into the Indian Reorganization Act.

While the act was being assembled into a coherent structure, Collier's administration moved ahead with some reforms. Native American children were transferred from boarding schools to community day schools where possible. The boarding schools that remained in use were developed as special facilities for certain children with needs best met by these institutions. A statement was issued to the effect that BIA employees would no longer interfere with Native American culture, religion, and languages. The bureau itself sought to employ Native Americans in increasing numbers.

President Roosevelt's New Deal reforms were extended to Native Americans through a specially organized branch of the Civilian Conservation Corps (CCC) called Emergency Conservation Work (ECW). This program provided work for Native Americans on the reservations in conservation and improvement projects similar to that offered to other Americans through the CCC. This wage labor caused a temporary increase in money income for many Native Americans but worried Collier, who wondered what would take its place when the relief projects ended.

In 1934, the Indian Reorganization Act was passed by Congress, officially stating the changes that studies such as the Meriam Report had recommended over the previous decade. Congresses were held to permit Native Americans to discuss the act and to vote whether to accept it for their individual tribes.

The Indian Reorganization Act provided for tribes to incorporate and form governing bodies in a democratic fashion. These governing bodies were designed to resemble boards of directors, with an elected chairperson. Individual Native Americans acted as "shareholders," with the right to vote. The act officially ended the allotment process and sought to restore lands lost in the past, or at least to replace them with other lands purchased for the tribes. Native American culture and religions were encouraged, often to the dismay and the protest of Christian missionaries. The boarding school system was further improved, and more community-based day schools were established. A revolving credit system was established, based on the principle of a credit union, whereby Indians could borrow funds to improve their lands or establish businesses. Native American arts and crafts were encouraged as a form of industry and a source of ethnic pride.

Critics would argue that the act's implementation was faulty, specifically, that Native Americans were not fully cognizant of the reorganization process and that the new forms of self-government were alien to the cultural practices of many groups. BIA personnel were not adequately prepared for changes in policy, and the new policy often conflicted with past goals and often with personal philosophies concerning American Indians. Many friends of Native Americans were not sure that the act provided the best means for improving conditions among Indians. At least, under the terms of the Indian Reorganization Act, Native Americans could retain their lands and their culture and still find ways to survive in the modern world.

Impact of Event

A unique procedure was followed in preparing to implement the Indian Reorganization Act—Indians themselves were asked to express their opinions on the legislation affecting them and to vote on whether to accept it on behalf of their tribes. By giving Native Americans a choice, the act implicitly validated them as a people, something that had never before been done by the federal government.

Another reversal of government policy was the encouragement of Native American cultures, including native languages and religious practices. Not all Indians, and certainly not all non-Indians, welcomed this change. Some feared that acculturated Indians would be forced back onto the reservations and into a life-style they had left behind them. This did not occur. Other people were alarmed and offended that the federal government would sponsor officially, and support with public funds, beliefs and practices of cultures deviating from the current ideology of the United States. The communal life-styles of many tribes were suspect.

Others who rejected the Indian Reorganization Act sought to acquire use of, or title to, Indian lands for themselves or as the agents of corporations. They saw these opportunities greatly curtailed and no longer as profitable. The demand for such lands, however, was not great at this time, as the United States was suffering through the Great Depression.

The timing for the Indian Reorganization Act was especially good. Assimilated Indians had suffered more during the Depression than had reservation Indians engaged in subsistence farming. Since there was little demand for land, it was a good time to give back the lands lost through allotment. More than two million acres were purchased and returned to Native American title, including some purchases made for "landless" tribes.

The boarding school system was reformed, radically improving a system that had not provided adequate food or clothing for its charges and had often exploited their labor. Where possible, community-based day schools were established. Indian children were also encouraged to attend public schools where feasible. Educational goals were shifted from irrelevant, elitist training to more practical, agrarian-based learning and technical and professional training. Many graduates chose to return to the reservations and contribute their skills to improving their communities.

One tragic incident involved the BIA's attempt to improve reservation land resources of soil, water, and vegetation. The livestock population had exceeded the carrying capacity of the arid lands on the Navajo reservation. When the Navajo resisted Collier's stock reduction plan, it was forced upon them. Navajos had to watch helplessly as their livestock were sold off or slaughtered. Although the reduction plan allegedly resulted in improved livestock and vegetation, bitter feelings remained among the Navajo, who had voted to reject the Indian Reorganization Act.

The Indian Reorganization Act was the first responsible effort to deal with the problems of a people who the federal government had for years assumed would "vanish" either by assimilation or by extinction. Although BIA personnel failed sometimes in implementing its good designs, it was the first reform meant to give Native Americans a choice in determining their own lives.

Bibliography

Dippie, Brian W. *The Vanishing American.* Middletown, Conn.: Wesleyan University Press, 1982. A comprehensive and sympathetic study of Native American relations with the federal government. Good coverage of the climate of reform leading up to passage of the Indian Reorganization Act. Extensive notes and a good index.

Donns, James F. *The Navajo.* New York: Holt, Rinehart and Winston, 1972. A specific ethnographic study of the Navajo people, this slim volume will acquaint the reader with the culture and life-style of the largest Native American group. Explains the relationship of livestock to Navajo livelihood and culture, a relationship that was disrupted by Collier's stock reduction plan.

Levitan, Sar A., and Barbara Hetrick. *Big Brother's Indian Programs, with Reservations.* New York: McGraw-Hill, 1971. This somewhat dated study explores federal programs that need improvements. Highly critical of government efforts to improve Native American life. Defines Native Americans and briefly discusses the Dawes Act and the Indian Reorganization Act. Covers education, health care, community structure, and the development of economic and natural resources.

Nichols, Roger L., ed. *The American Indian: Past and Present.* New York: John Wiley & Sons, 1971. This text consists of separate articles covering cultural and historical aspects of Native American experience. The reader will find useful further information regarding the Native American and the Civilian Conservation Corps (CCC), federal boarding schools, allotment practice and policy, and the crusade for reform that led up to the Indian Reorganization Act. Includes a bibliography.

Tyler, S. Lyman. *A History of Indian Policy.* Washington, D.C.: U.S. Department of the Interior, Bureau of Indian Affairs, 1973. An extremely well-organized and detailed historical account of United States government policy toward Native Americans. Covers criticism and accomplishments of government programs. A useful guide to the philosophy and expedients behind historical government policy. Highly recommended for the serious student. Includes tables and charts, foldout maps, and black-and-white photographs. Extensive bibliography.

Washburn, Wilcomb E. *The Indian and the White Man.* Garden City, N.Y.: Doubleday, 1964. A collection of documents covering the history of Indian-white relations from first contact through a statement issued by the American Indian Chicago Conference of 1961. Useful only for the opportunity to read statements from individuals such as John Collier and literary excerpts from Ernest Hemingway, William Faulkner, and Herman Melville.

Patricia Alkema

Cross-References

Intellectuals Form the Society of American Indians (1911), p. 121; U.S. Government Encourages Native Americans to Settle in Cities (1950's), p. 820; Government Policies Seek to End the Special Status of Native Americans (1953), p. 897; Congress Ratifies the National Council on Indian Opportunity (1970), p. 1537; The Blue Lake Region in New Mexico Is Returned to the Taos Pueblo (1970), p. 1573; Native Americans Occupy Wounded Knee (1973), p. 1709.

STALIN BEGINS PURGING POLITICAL OPPONENTS

Categories of event: Atrocities and war crimes; political freedom
Time: December, 1934
Locale: Union of Soviet Socialist Republics

Soviet leader Joseph Stalin undertook a brutal four-year campaign of terror against those he believed to be his political enemies in the Communist Party

Principal personages:
>JOSEPH STALIN (1879-1953), general secretary of the Communist Party beginning in 1922
>SERGEI KIROV (1886-1934), the closest aide to Stalin during the late 1920's; led the Party organization in Leningrad
>LEON TROTSKY (1879-1940), a Marxist theorist who played a principal role in orchestrating the 1917 Bolshevik Revolution
>NIKOLAI YEZHOV (1895-1938), the head of the NKVD (secret police) during the most intense period of the purge
>LEV KAMENEV (1883-1936), a close associate of Vladimir Ilich Lenin; became chair of the Moscow Soviet in 1918 and a member of the Politburo in 1919
>GRIGORI ZINOVIEV (1883-1936), the head of the Comintern (Communist International) in 1919 and a collaborator with Lenin

Summary of Event

The murder of Sergei Kirov, the Communist Party leader in Leningrad and a member of the Soviet Politburo (policy-making committee), gave Joseph Stalin an excuse to begin a reign of terror similar to those carried out by earlier Russian leaders Ivan IV and Peter the Great. Scholars have debated for some time over what motivated Stalin to embark on such a destructive course. There are some who have argued that he was disappointed by the failure of his first Five-Year Plan (1928) to achieve all the goals he had set, while others have suggested that his intent was to centralize power in his own hands at the expense of the Communist Party. More than a few have contended that the purging stands as proof of Stalin's unstable and unbalanced state of mind.

Although the "Great Purge" began in December, 1934, there were harbingers of what was to come during the period from 1927 (when Stalin assumed power) to 1934. On several occasions, the Party, at Stalin's urging, had removed hundreds of local Communist leaders from their posts. They were charged with falling under capitalist influence or not pushing hard enough to fulfill Stalin's drive to collectivize the countryside. The areas most affected were Odessa, Kiev, and the Urals. These "preliminary purges," widespread as they were, paled by comparison to what occurred after the murder of Kirov in December, 1934.

Kirov was shot by Leonid Nikolayev, a Communist Party member described by some at the time as disgruntled. Stalin immediately blamed the assassination on his principal political enemies, Leon Trotsky (in exile at the time), Lev Kamenev, and Grigori Zinoviev. It is now generally agreed by scholars that Stalin arranged the murder of Kirov, his friend and ally.

On the day of Kirov's murder, Stalin asked the Party to issue a decree eliminating civil and legal rights for all persons accused of "terroristic acts." This made it possible for the government to arrest, detain (for the purpose of gaining forced "confessions"), or execute anyone it wished. In January, 1935, Kamenev, Zinoviev, and two others were tried, convicted, and sentenced to prison for their alleged roles in the Kirov murder. The length of the sentences was irrelevant, as none of those arrested was ever released. This was the beginning of what became known as the "purification" of the Communist Party. Stalin began with Kamenev and Zinoviev because he perceived them as especially treacherous. They had once worked closely with him in the 1920's but then had turned against him and given their loyalty to Trotsky. After the January convictions, hundreds, perhaps thousands, of Party members came under suspicion. Many were shot, detained, or sent to distant regions of the Soviet Union. Although some in the Politburo were uneasy with this development, Stalin insisted that it was necessary to protect the country from those who wished to "wreck" his great drive for full communization.

The first victims when Stalin began purging the Party were those considered to be "Old Bolsheviks," Party members who had been associated with Lenin and Trotsky during the 1917 Revolution and in the formative days of the Soviet state. Many had been supporters of Lenin's moderate New Economic Policy begun in 1921. The greatest number of those purged in 1935 were individuals who, after Lenin's death in 1924, had supported Trotsky's claim to succeed Lenin as head of the Party and the state. Between 1924 and 1927, Trotsky and Stalin competed for control. Stalin was ultimately successful, and Trotsky went into exile for the remainder of his life. Stalin continued to insist, however, that Trotsky's followers ("Trotskyites"), guided by their leader from abroad, were working to remove him from power. Having been established as his enemies, they became convenient scapegoats to explain every failure that Stalin experienced. He could simply say that the Trotskyites had wrecked his plans.

In 1936, Stalin intensified the purging. Public trials ("show trials") were held in which those accused were expected to confess their misdeeds and to implicate others involved in plots against Stalin. Kamenev and Zinoviev, already in prison, were among sixteen Old Bolsheviks put on public trial in August, 1936. All were charged with conducting a terrorist campaign at Trotsky's bidding, and all were sentenced to death. From that point, the purging began to mushroom. After a second round of show trials in January, 1937, there was no way to brake the terror that Stalin had instigated in 1935. No one except Stalin was insulated from the possibility of being charged as a Trotskyite.

For the first eighteen months after Stalin started the purge, the country at large remained relatively unaffected. That changed in 1937. Nikolai Yezhov, the new chief of the NKVD (secret police), understood that Stalin expected him to dispatch all the Soviet leader's political opponents as quickly as possible. With Yezhov in charge, the purging became much better organized. The NKVD began to arrest thousands of people, usually in the predawn hours, many of whom had no connection with the Communist Party. Anyone accused of disloyalty to Stalin was presumed to be guilty of "wrecking." Desperate to prove their loyalty to the regime, officials and ordinary citizens began to accuse others of treason. Neighbors denounced neighbors, fellow workers denounced each other, subordinates denounced their superiors, and relatives denounced relatives. In each instance, the person denounced to a local official was arrested and charged as an "enemy of the people." Falling victim to the purge was largely chance for those outside the Party, but those most frequently denounced were persons of foreign birth or members of minority groups, especially Ukrainians, Jews, and Armenians. All who were accused were expected to confess (the NKVD used torture when persuasion failed) and to implicate others.

There is evidence that Stalin was aware of the effect on the country of the expanded purge, but by the middle of 1937 even he was powerless to slow it down. The general hysteria in the country made the terror an unstoppable force. Citizens throughout the Soviet Union lived in fear of a late-night or early-morning knock on the door. The terror reached its peak in 1937 and early 1938; thereafter, the NKVD was no longer able to respond to the huge number of accusations. Yezhov, architect of this worst phase of the purging, was himself charged with "Trotskyite" leanings in 1938 and purged. The coming of World War II in the late summer of 1939 finally brought the purging to an end.

Impact of Event

Stalin's purging of political opponents created great problems for the Communist Party and, ultimately, for the country at large. Those officials and Party leaders who were purged had to be replaced, and the replacements were frequently ill-equipped to handle their new responsibilities. The dimensions of the purging serve to illustrate this point. More than one-half of the Communist Party's Central Committee (78 of 139 members) were purged, and more than one-third of those who sat in the Politburo between 1927 and 1938 were expelled. The army and the government suffered more staggering losses: Thirteen of the fifteen commanders of the Soviet Army were purged between 1935 and 1938, as were fourteen of the eighteen ministers of state. Thus, throughout the ordeal the purgers were themselves always subject to being purged.

As the purging expanded beyond the confines of the Party, the effect on the country was devastating. Business and industry came virtually to a standstill, as workers and supervisors were afraid to make an error lest they be charged with "wrecking." In the major cities—Moscow, Leningrad, and Kiev—there was little activity, as residents tried to limit their associations. The Moscow telephone directory was not published in 1938, because most people wanted to keep their telephone numbers and street addresses a secret. Artists, writers, and intellectuals dared not express themselves freely. All were expected to produce works that somehow glorified the Stalinist state and reflected negatively on what had existed before Stalin. Stalin wanted paintings of tanks and factories, not romantic sunsets or anything that might be considered bourgeois. Writers of history were to make it clear that Stalin's regime represented the culmination of all that had gone before in Russia's past.

The most important political consequence of the Great Purge was that Stalin obliterated all political debate and discussion. Members of the Politburo no longer raised questions during their meetings with Stalin. He had succeeded in creating one-person rule, or, as Nikita Khrushchev called it, "the cult of the personality." Although World War II made Stalin a hero in the Soviet Union, the legacy of fear that he instigated was not seriously challenged until three years after his death, when Khrushchev addressed the Communist Party Congress. In that February, 1956, speech, Khrushchev, who had risen to prominence as Stalin's ally during the purge, condemned Stalin as a murderer and Stalinism as a misguided formula for a successful Communist state.

Bibliography

Conquest, Robert. *The Great Terror: Stalin's Purge of the Thirties.* Rev. ed. New York: Macmillan, 1973. This is the most popular, most readable, and perhaps most well-documented account of the Great Purge. Conquest, an English political writer, provides a comprehensive discussion of all aspects of the purge. His epilogue on the "Heritage of the Terror" is especially valuable. Scholars have questioned some of Conquest's conclusions. Appendices, bibliographical note, select bibliography, and index.

Crowley, Joan Frances, and Dan Vaillancourt. *Lenin to Gorbachev: Three Generations of Communists.* Arlington Heights, Ill.: Harlan Davidson, 1989. A very useful introduction to Communist leaders from Karl Marx and Friedrich Engels to Gorbachev. Crowley and Vaillancourt write in a style that is clear and without jargon. The section on Stalin is excellent. Suggestions for further reading and index.

Dmytryshyn, Basil. *USSR: A Concise History.* 2d ed. New York: Charles Scribner's Sons, 1971. A brief but superb general account of Soviet history through the 1960's. The appendices are of great value for students and general readers. Bibliography and index.

Medvedev, Roy. *Let History Judge: The Origins and Consequences of Stalinism.* Edited and translated by George Shriver. Rev. ed. New York: Columbia University Press, 1986. Medvedev, a longtime dissident historian in the Soviet Union, wrote this highly critical history of the Stalinist years in the 1960's. He underscores the human disaster that accompanied Stalin's campaign of terror.

Tucker, Robert C. *Stalin in Power: The Revolution from Above, 1929-1941.* New York: W. W. Norton, 1990. This is the second volume of Tucker's widely acclaimed biography of Stalin. Tucker is concerned with uncovering the personality that craved power so much and used it so ruthlessly. Bibliography and index.

Von Laue, Theodore. *Why Lenin? Why Stalin?* 2d ed. Philadelphia, Pa.: J. B. Lippincott, 1971. This may be the single best essay written about the formative years of the Communist Revolution. Von Laue's grasp of Russian history and its application to early twentieth century events is impressive. Highly recommended for all readers. Suggestions for further reading and index.

Ronald K. Huch

Cross-References

Lenin and the Communists Impose the "Red Terror" (1917), p. 218; Lenin Leads the Russian Revolution (1917), p. 225; Stalin Reduces the Russian Orthodox Church to Virtual Extinction (1939), p. 561; Soviets Take Control of Eastern Europe (1943), p. 612; Khrushchev Implies That Stalinist Excesses Will Cease (1956), p. 952; The U.N. Covenant on Civil and Political Rights Is Adopted (1966), p. 1353; The Moscow Human Rights Committee Is Founded (1970), p. 1549; Amnesty International Adopts a Program for the Prevention of Torture (1983), p. 2204.

THE WAGNER ACT REQUIRES EMPLOYERS TO ACCEPT COLLECTIVE BARGAINING

Category of event: Workers' rights
Time: July 5, 1935
Locale: Washington, D.C.

The Wagner Act secured the rights of workers to establish labor unions and to bargain collectively and also defined unfair labor practices on the part of employers

Principal personages:

ROBERT FERDINAND WAGNER (1877-1953), a U.S. senator from New York

LAWRENCE JOSEPH CONNERY (1895-1941), a congressman from Massachusetts who helped establish labor's legal rights to organize and to bargain collectively

JOHN L. LEWIS (1880-1969), the president of the United Mine Workers of America and founder of the Congress of Industrial Organizations

FRANKLIN D. ROOSEVELT (1882-1945), the president of the United States

FRANCES PERKINS (1882-1965), the first female member of the president's cabinet, secretary of labor from 1933 to 1945

Summary of Event

The right of workers to organize themselves in the pursuit of their interests vis-à-vis employers has not always existed. In 1935, the Wagner Act (formally, the National Labor Relations Act) secured the right of labor (excepting agricultural and domestic labor) to organize and to promote and protect its interests through collective bargaining. The act was the culmination of several decades of labor struggles and industrial strife in the United States. Prior to passage of the Wagner Act, industrialists tended to have a free rein in their struggles with labor, using force, legislation, the courts, and other means to prevent labor from organizing itself. Passage of the Sherman Antitrust Act in 1890 gave industrialists the upper hand in their opposition to "organized labor." That act prohibited contracts that restrained interstate commerce, and industrialists and the courts interpreted it in ways that cast labor organizations as imposing such restraints. The Pullman Strike of 1894 was broken through such an interpretation, and Eugene Debs and other union leaders were imprisoned for their strike activities. The result was the destruction of the American Railway Union, the largest industrial union of the period.

The Clayton Act, passed in 1914, was initially hailed as the Magna Carta of organized labor because its Section 6 declared that antitrust laws should not be construed to forbid the existence of labor organizations instituted for purposes of mutual help. Its Section 20 forbade injunctions in all disputes between labor and capital involving terms and conditions of employment. The Clayton Act was challenged by industrialists under the political climate set by President William Taft, who frequently made public his conservative interpretation of the act. In 1921, the U.S. Supreme Court issued decisions in two labor disputes (*Duplex Printing Press Co. v. Deering* and *American Steel Foundries v. Tri-City Trades Council*) that favored industrialists and rendered the Clayton Act virtually useless in protecting the interests of labor. In effect, labor's Magna Carta simply vanished through the Supreme Court's narrow interpretation of the law.

It was in 1932, with passage of the Norris-LaGuardia Act, that labor again benefited from favorable legislation passed by the U.S. Congress. The act declared that workers shall have full freedom of association, self-organization, and designation of representatives of their own choosing to negotiate terms and conditions of employment free from employer interference. The act also defined and limited the powers of the federal courts to issue injunctions against labor in employment disputes. As they had done with the Clayton Act, employers challenged the Norris-LaGuardia Act in the courts and managed to suspend its application for several years.

Economic recovery during the Great Depression demanded governmental involvement in the resolution of continuing struggles between capital and labor. President Franklin Delano Roosevelt offered Americans a New Deal, and he delivered it in the form of several special governmental measures intended to improve the country's economic conditions. The first major legislation of the New Deal was the National Industrial Recovery Act (NIRA) of 1933. Industrialists and workers alike welcomed passage of the act, which was intended to revive industrial and business activity and to reduce unemployment. Among other things, it was based on the principle of industrial self-regulation, operating under government codes. Industrialists who wanted a code for their industry were required to incorporate Section 7(a) of NIRA, which guaranteed workers' rights to organize and to bargain collectively through representatives of their own choosing.

On August 5, 1933, the president established the National Labor Board to enforce the right of collective bargaining. Robert F. Wagner, the senator from New York, was appointed by President Roosevelt to head the board. The board's effectiveness was limited, however, by a lack of clear jurisdictional and enforcement powers. On June 19, 1934, the Labor Disputes Joint Resolution established the National Labor Relations Board (NLRB) to replace the National Labor Board. The NLRB was to monitor compliance with Section 7(a) of NIRA. Francis Biddle was appointed chair of the NLRB by President Roosevelt.

Industrialists soon began to express discontent with the NIRA and its provision on labor, which they saw as resulting in their "forced marriage" to labor. They claimed that they had never wanted such a relationship and that it had been forced upon them against their better judgment. In 1935, the "forced marriage" ended when the U.S. Supreme Court ruled, in the case of *Schechter Poultry Corp v. United States*, that the NIRA was unconstitutional on several grounds, not the least of which was that it was seen as regulating intrastate commerce, something believed to be within state and not federal power. There no longer was any legal basis for obligating employers to bargain with workers and their representatives. Following the ruling on the NIRA, there came a flood of wage cuts accompanied by increased industrial strife.

The dubious legality of the NIRA and the questionable efficacy of Section 7(a) prompted Senator Robert F. Wagner of New York and Lawrence J. Connery of Massachusetts to introduce a bill early in 1935 that would make collective bargaining the law of the land. The bill became law on July 5, 1935. The framers of this law, the National Labor Relations Act, had been conscious of the fact that it might be attacked on constitutional grounds, so they specifically included a statement declaring that industrial relations may affect interstate commerce, and that the policy of the United States was to eliminate obstructions to the free flow of commerce. The denial by employers of the right of employees to organize and their refusal to accept collective bargaining were seen under this law as having the effect of burdening or obstructing commerce. Section 7 upheld the right of employees to join labor organizations in an attempt to bargain collectively with their employers through representatives of their own choosing. Section 8 of the Wagner Act went on to define unfair labor practices on the part of employers. These included restraining employees in the exercise of their rights, interfering with the formation of a labor organization, discouraging workers from joining labor organizations, and discriminating against employees for having filed charges under the act. Finally, the act created a new National Labor Relations Board, one empowered to enforce the law. In other words, the board was to function as the high court of labor management relations rather than to serve merely as an administrative means for settling conflicts and disputes.

The new law was immediately attacked by various antilabor groups, especially the National Association of Manufacturers (NAM), an umbrella organization promoting business and manufacturing interests. It was predicted by industrial leaders that this law would have the same fate as the NIRA, and employers were openly encouraged to violate it on the grounds that it was unconstitutional. The constitutionality of the Wagner Act was upheld in 1937 by the U.S. Supreme Court in the case of *National Labor Relations Board v. Jones and Laughlin Steel Corporation*. In this case, the steel company maintained its own unions and refused to allow its employees to organize separate unions. The company claimed before the NLRB that it was involved in intrastate, and not interstate, commerce, and that the NLRB did not have jurisdiction in the matter. The board ordered the company to cease and desist from interfering with the right of workers to organize themselves. The company refused to comply with the board's order, so the NLRB petitioned the Federal Circuit Court of Appeals for the Fifth Circuit for enforcement. The court denied the petition, ruling that the board's order was beyond the authority of Congress. The board then took the matter before the U.S. Supreme Court, which ruled the Wagner Act constitutional on April 12, 1937.

Impact of Event

The securing of American labor's rights to organize and to bargain collectively, the establishment of a permanent government agency on labor relations, and the prohibition of unfair labor practices on the part of employers each had a tremendous influence on industrial relations. These provisions of the Wagner Act made its passage an event of historic significance. Workers' rights to organize and to promote their own interests through collective bargaining were secured by this act. Earlier efforts to secure labor's rights had been effectively suppressed by industrialists, often organized by the National Association of Manufacturers. Founded in 1895, NAM promoted the "open shop" and concentrated on opposing and eliminating labor unions.

Establishment of a quasi-independent National Labor Relations Board with clear jurisdictional powers contributed to the formation of strong, independent unions, especially in the years following the act's constitutional affirmation in 1937. The National Labor Relations Board was authorized to determine bargaining unit jurisdictions, hold elections, and certify those unions receiving the majority of votes as the legally binding representatives of the workers. John L. Lewis helped shape important prolabor legislation of the period, served as a member of the National Labor Board (of 1933), and headed the United Mine Workers of America. Under Lewis' leadership, the newly formed Congress of Industrial Organizations (CIO) organized, for the first time ever, hundreds of thousands of mass production workers, including those in the automobile, steel, rubber, packinghouse, and electrical products industries.

The American Federation of Labor (AFL), which was organized along trade lines, had tended to look upon the masses of unskilled workers, many of whom were immigrants, with suspicion and contempt. The rise of industrial unionism, which sought to organize workers along industrial rather than trade lines, including all rather than only skilled workers, was made possible by the Wagner Act, since workers (excepting those in agriculture) could now legally promote their interests collectively with their employers. The AFL, itself spurred on by the successes of the CIO, began to organize unskilled workers in order to protect its own established position among the ranks of labor. As a consequence, relationships on the shop floor began to change. For the first time, hundreds of thousands of unskilled workers had legal union support against the petty dictatorships of shop leaders and managers. A general system of industrial jurisprudence was instituted by the grievance procedures and seniority systems established by the new unions.

In the late 1930's, industrial opposition to the Wagner Act mounted, and President Roosevelt's appointments to the NLRB became more and more conservative, with emphasis on broad mediation experience. As war loomed before America, President Roosevelt emphasized social peace and full production on the home front. Few union leaders dissented from this view, and unions offered no-strike pledges in the aftermath of the Japanese attack on Pearl Harbor. During World War II, a powerful National War Labor Board usurped many of the powers of the NLRB, with the former arbitrating labor disputes and dictating wages while the latter conducted strike votes under the War Labor Disputes Act of 1943. After the war, the Taft-Hartley Act, a piece of proemployer legislation, amended the NLRA and, among other things, killed the NLRB and replaced it with a new, five-member board whose mandate was less important to labor than that of the NLRB.

Bibliography

Boyer, Richard O., and Herbert M. Morais. *Labor's Untold Story*. 3d ed. New York: United Electrical, Radio & Machine Workers of America, 1975. Provides a history of labor's struggles against industrial capitalists from the point of view of labor. It focuses on key events and major personalities between the 1850's and the 1950's. The book also examines conflicts among workers themselves. Includes a good bibliography and an index.

Eby, Herbert O. *The Labor Relations Act in the Courts*. New York: Harper & Brothers, 1943. This text provides a review of court decisions affecting the rights and responsibilities of workers and employers in the years following the enactment of the NLRA. Provides an excellent citation index of legal cases concerning the NLRA and includes the full text of the NLRA and related rules and regulations. No index.

Mathews, Robert E., ed. *Labor Relations and the Law*. Boston: Little, Brown, 1953. This volume contains several excellent articles on various legal and historical dimensions of the relationships between organized labor and employers. Sections of several labor laws, such as the Clayton, Norris-LaGuardia, and Railway Labor Acts, are included in the appendices. Contains an index but not a bibliography.

Millis, Harry A., and Emily Clark Brown. *From the Wagner Act to Taft-Hartley: A Study of National Labor Policy and Labor Relations*. Chicago: University of Chicago Press, 1950. Provides one of the best analyses of the events leading to the passage of the Wagner Act of 1935 and the Taft-Hartley Act of 1947. It examines in detail their provisions, their implementation, and their effects on labor relations. The book contains a useful bibliography and an index.

Sufrin, Sidney C., and Robert C. Sedgwick. *Labor Law: Development, Administration, Cases*. New York: Thomas Y. Crowell, 1954. This text examines the development and application of labor law up to the early period of McCarthyism. It provides detailed information on major legal cases, including text from U.S. Supreme Court decisions. It discusses the importance of the Taft-Hartley Act, which defined unfair labor practices chargeable against labor unions. The book contains an index.

Rubén O. Martinez

Cross-References

"Palmer Raids" Lead to Arrests and Deportations of Immigrants (1919), p. 258; Steel Workers Go on Strike to Demand Improved Working Conditions (1919), p. 293; The Immigration Act of 1921 Imposes a National Quota System (1921), p. 350; Congress Establishes a Border Patrol (1924), p. 377; A U.S. Immigration Act Imposes Quotas Based on National Origins (1924), p. 383; Franklin D. Roosevelt Appoints

Perkins as Secretary of Labor (1933), p. 486; The Congress of Industrial Organizations Is Formed (1938), p. 545; Autoworkers Negotiate a Contract with a Cost-of-Living Provision (1948), p. 766; Chávez Forms Farm Workers' Union and Leads Grape Pickers' Strike (1962), p. 1161; Chávez Is Jailed for Organizing an Illegal Lettuce Boycott (1970), p. 1567; Congress Passes the Equal Employment Opportunity Act (1972), p. 1650; The Supreme Court Upholds an Affirmative-Action Program (1979), p. 2029.

SOCIAL SECURITY ACT ESTABLISHES BENEFITS FOR NONWORKING PEOPLE

Categories of event: Humanitarian relief and workers' rights
Time: August 14, 1935
Locale: Washington, D.C.

With the Social Security Act, the U.S. government assumed responsibility for alleviating the hardships of the elderly, the unemployed, the disabled, and dependent children

Principal personages:

FRANKLIN D. ROOSEVELT (1882-1945), the U.S. president from 1933 to 1945; his New Deal policies tried to promote relief, recovery, and reform

FRANCES PERKINS (1882-1965), the first woman to be a member of a presidential cabinet; served as chair of the Committee on Economic Security

EDWIN WITTE (1887-1960), the executive director of the Perkins Committee

ROBERT WAGNER (1877-1953), a liberal New York senator who introduced an unemployment compensation bill in 1934 and the social security bill in 1935

FRANCIS TOWNSEND (1867-1960), a retired physician who advocated a plan to pay $200 a month to each citizen over age sixty

Summary of Event

In most industrial countries, there were widespread movements during the late nineteenth century to provide governmental guarantees for the fundamental needs of life. Between 1883 and 1887, Germany, under the leadership of Chancellor Otto von Bismarck, was the first country to begin a program of health, old-age, and unemployment insurance. The major European countries followed this example within two decades. In the United States, because of the high values placed on individualism and voluntarism, progress in this area was slow, although in 1890 President Benjamin Harrison signed the Dependent Pension Act, an expensive law which provided benefits to Civil War veterans unable to work.

With the Progressive movement of the early twentieth century, many reformers and organizations called for unemployment and old-age insurance, generally looking to the European models. Two socialist immigrants from Russia, Isaac Rubinow and Abraham Epstein, wrote books and campaigned for a comprehensive system, and the American Association for Labor Legislation, organized by John Commons in 1906, called for the states to establish programs of income maintenance for workers.

In the presidential election of 1912, the Progressive Party, with Theodore Roosevelt as its candidate, advocated a system of social insurance in its platform.

By the end of World War I, the majority of states had limited kinds of social insurance, usually including workers' disability compensation and retirement benefits for public employees. About half the states had public assistance laws which provided older Americans an average of one dollar a day and required beneficiaries to pass a means test. In the private sector, prosperous corporations gradually began to provide pension plans for employees. By 1930, nevertheless, it was estimated that only about 15 percent of the labor force was covered by some kind of retirement plan.

The Great Depression began in 1929. One-fourth of the labor force soon became unemployed. The situation was especially desperate among the 6 percent of Americans who were older than sixty-five. Epstein's organization, the American Association for Old Age Security, clamored for old-age insurance, and Senator Clarence Dill introduced a bill for such a program in 1931. In the presidential election of 1932, the Democratic platform called for unemployment and old-age insurance under state law, but candidate Franklin Delano Roosevelt concentrated instead on the more immediate question of federal relief and public works for the unemployed.

During the first year of the New Deal, Roosevelt and Congress generally avoided the issue of long-term social insurance, but the issue became important in 1934. In February, Senator Robert Wagner of New York and Representative David Lewis of Maryland introduced a bill for unemployment insurance, a proposal influenced by Wisconsin's law of 1932. Later that year, Senator Dill joined with Representative William Connery to propose a federal old-age pension plan. Roosevelt did not choose, however, to give active support to either of these proposals. He decided instead that the time was ripe to work for one omnibus bill. One day, he startled his secretary of labor, Frances Perkins, by stating that there should be social insurance for all citizens "from the cradle to the grave."

In the meantime, pressure from the left encouraged Roosevelt and Congress to proceed with legislation. Dr. Francis Townsend of California popularized a crusade to provide $200 a month to every citizen over age sixty, with the requirement that the money be spent within thirty days. Although authorities agreed that it was prohibitively expensive, the Townsend plan had widespread appeal, with 350,000 citizens joining Townsend clubs and millions signing petitions. Minnesota Congressman Ernest Lundeen introduced a bill that was even more ambitious, designed to provide money to needy people of all ages.

In his speech before Congress on June 8, 1934, Roosevelt declared that the general welfare clause of the Constitution implied that the government should provide "security against several of the great disturbing factors in life—especially those which relate to unemployment and old age." He indicated that he was looking for a sound means to achieve this security, and later that month he issued Executive Order 6757, creating the Committee on Economic Security which was to investigate the issue and make recommendations. Secretary of Labor Frances Perkins was selected as the chair, and Executive Director Edwin Witte, an economist from the University of Wisconsin, was provided with a staff to do most of the research. The committee included a wide diversity of political, academic, and business leaders, but those associated with radical plans, such as Rubinow, Epstein, and Townsend, were excluded.

The committee quickly reached a consensus on the need for a comprehensive system, but members strongly differed on a number of matters. Witte and others favored a decentralized arrangement with federal-state cooperation, while Rexford Tugwell and those in the old-age pension section insisted on a uniform federal framework. A second problem was the question of whether the system should be financed from the general tax or from a special payroll tax on employers and workers. In addition, there was the question of whether all employers would pay the same tax, or whether a merit rating would allow firms with low unemployment to pay a smaller tax. In a special meeting with Secretary Perkins during the night of December 24, the committee arrived at an understanding that most programs would be based on federal-state cooperation. The committee also decided that financing would come from a payroll tax and that all employers would pay the same tax. To the displeasure of liberals, the majority agreed that the report would ignore the controversial question of health insurance and that farmers and many other employee categories would be excluded from the old-age pensions.

The committee presented its official report on January 15, 1935, and two days later Roosevelt forwarded its recommendations to Congress. Within a few days, Senator Wagner and Representative Lewis introduced bills based on the report. Because of widespread support, it was expected that a bill would be passed within two months, but the bills aroused intense congressional debates which lasted seven months. From the left, Louisiana Senator Huey Long, Townsend, and Epstein considered the benefits too stingy, with payroll taxes regressive in their effects. In contrast, conservatives charged that the proposal was un-American and a kind of socialism. When Perkins testified in a congressional hearing, an angry woman interrupted with shouts that the bill was directly copied from the *Communist Manifesto* (1848).

In the House committee, the name of the proposal was changed from the Economic Security Act to the Social Security Act, and it was approved by the House with a vote of 371 to 33 on April 19. The Senate passed a different version on June 19, voting 77 to 6. After a conference committee took two months to reconcile the differences, the final bill was passed by the House on August 8, followed by the Senate the next day. President Roosevelt signed the bill into law on August 14, 1935.

The approved law included four major components: an insurance program of old-age pensions to be operated entirely by the federal government, with payments beginning in 1942; federal funds to go to the states to provide welfare assistance to the elderly poor; federal support for unemployment insurance, to be administered by the states; and federal grants-in-aid to the states for a variety of welfare categories, including programs of public health and assistance to dependent children and the blind.

Impact of Event

The Social Security Act represents a landmark in American history. For the first time, the federal government recognized that it had a responsibility to provide a safety net to protect citizens from hardships. Although controversial, the program always enjoyed public approval, as indicated by the congressional votes in 1935. When presidential candidates criticized social security in the elections of 1936 and 1964, they discovered that this was not a way to win an election. The national pension plan, officially called Old-Age, Survivors, and Disability Insurance (OASDI), has always had the greatest degree of support, and the welfare sections, especially Aid to Families with Dependent Children (AFDC), have been much less popular. In the 1980's, the conservative administration of President Ronald Reagan tried to decrease AFDC payments, but by this time OASDI was widely recognized as a "sacred cow."

In its beginning, social security affected about 60 percent of the labor force, but incrementally the system has been expanded to include more people and to provide additional services. An amendment in 1939 extended benefits to the dependents of retired workers and to their survivors in case of death. In 1951, coverage was expanded to include farm workers and domestic workers. Members of the armed forces were added in 1957. When reforms in 1983 required political leaders and government workers to participate, more than 90 percent of the labor force was under OASDI. In 1965, social security was expanded to include health insurance (Medicare) for those over sixty-five and to provide medical assistance grants (Medicaid) to the states for the poor. An amendment in 1972 provided for the federal government to pay Supplementary Security Income (SSI) directly to the low-income aged, blind, and disabled.

Although modest in comparison with systems in other advanced countries, the social security system in the United States is a very expensive undertaking. By 1990, the payroll taxes to support OASDI were approximately 15 percent, and expenditures of the program composed more than 25 percent of the federal budget. There was much concern about the viability of OASDI after the year 2010, when the "baby-boom" generation would begin to retire. Likewise, with the liberalization of AFDC rules in 1967, more than 90 percent of the poor were soon receiving AFDC assistance, and the growth of single-parent families was dramatically increasing the number of people eligible. The costs of Medicare and Medicaid were especially troublesome. The United States was the only major industrialized country not to have comprehensive medical insurance, and 15 percent of Americans, especially the "working poor," were entirely without medical coverage of any kind.

From a constitutional perspective, the Social Security Act expanded the role of the federal government and had a great impact on the federal-state relationship. In 1935, there was much concern about whether the Supreme Court, based on the Tenth Amendment, would allow the federal government to disperse these large funds for the public welfare. Two years later the majority of the Court upheld the constitutionality of both unemployment insurance and old-age insurance. The majority ac-

cepted the arguments that the meaning of the welfare clause was not static and that
the federal government had the authority to deal with national problems which went
beyond the capacities of the states.

Bibliography

Achenbaum, Andrew. *Social Security: Visions and Revisions.* Cambridge, England:
Cambridge University Press, 1986. An excellent general history of social security
from the early background of the law to the 1980's. The book is especially useful
as a guide to the changes in social security after 1935. The bibliography is very
complete. Achenbaum advocates medical and other benefits for all.

Davis, Kenneth. *FDR: The New Deal Years, 1933-1937.* New York: Random House,
1979. A detailed and scholarly account of the policies and strategies of President
Roosevelt, with a chapter devoted to the passage of the Social Security Act.

Douglas, Paul. *Social Security in the United States: An Analysis and Appraisal of the
Federal Social Security Act.* New York: Whittlesey House, 1936. Written by one of
the important participants on the Perkins Committee, the book gives a detailed
account of the background and the legislative process in the passage of the act.
The book reflects the period, and a complete text of the act is included in the
appendix.

Louchheim, Katie, ed. *The Making of the New Deal: The Insiders Speak.* Cambridge, Mass.: Harvard University Press, 1983. A collection of fascinating essays
by those who participated in the making of the New Deal, with Wilbur Cohen and
Thomas Eliot explaining their roles in the formulation of the Social Security Act.

Lubove, Roy. *The Struggle for Social Security, 1900-1935.* Cambridge, Mass.: Harvard University Press, 1968. An important work in the history of ideas, with a
focus on the clash between the traditions of voluntarism and the goals of social
insurance. The book is especially good in its treatment of the ideas and careers of
Isaac Rubinow and Abraham Epstein.

Nelson, Daniel. *Unemployment Insurance: The American Experiment, 1915-1935.* Madison: University of Wisconsin Press, 1969. A very scholarly and well-researched
study devoted to the single issue of unemployment insurance, emphasizing the
importance of the British model and the passage of Wisconsin's law of 1932. The
book has a great deal of interesting information about individuals such as Commons, Epstein, and Wagner. There is little information about other aspects of the
Social Security Act.

Perkins, Frances. *The Roosevelt I Knew.* New York: Viking Press, 1946. A delightful
personal memoir by the woman who chaired the Committee on Economic Security, including an excellent chapter on the formulation and passage of the Social
Security Act.

Quadagno, Jill. *The Transformation of Old Age Security: Class and Politics in the
American Welfare State.* Chicago: University of Chicago Press, 1988. An interesting study of how the elderly have coped in America from the nineteenth century
to the 1980's. The book compares American traditions with those of Europe and

espouses a sociological theory that the organization of production determines social policy. Despite much useful material, the work is marred by an excessive use of sociological generalization and terminology.

Witte, Edwin. *The Development of the Social Security Act.* Madison: University of Wisconsin Press, 1962. Published posthumously, this is a confidential memorandum which gives an insider's perspective on the work of the Perkins Committee. Witte includes his analysis of the differences between the "Wisconsin plan" and the "Ohio plan." In addition to this essay, Witte wrote other books and many articles devoted to social security, always with an emphasis on the economic perspective.

Thomas T. Lewis

Cross-References

Great Britain Passes Acts to Provide Unemployment Benefits (1920), p. 321; Nevada and Montana Introduce the Old-Age Pension (1923), p. 373; Franklin D. Roosevelt Appoints Perkins as Secretary of Labor (1933), p. 486; The Wagner Act Requires Employers to Accept Collective Bargaining (1935), p. 508; Social Security Act Provides Grants for Dependent Children (1935), p. 520; The First Food Stamp Program Begins in Rochester, New York (1939), p. 555; The World Health Organization Proclaims Health as a Basic Right (1946), p. 678; The United Nations Adopts the Declaration of the Rights of the Child (1959), p. 1038; Congress Responds to Demands of Persons with Disabilities (1973), p. 1731; WHO Sets a Goal of Health for All by the Year 2000 (1977), p. 1893; An International Health Conference Adopts the Declaration of Alma-Ata (1978), p. 1998; The Stewart B. McKinney Homeless Assistance Act Becomes Law (1987), p. 2326; The United Nations Adopts the Convention on the Rights of the Child (1989), p. 2529.

SOCIAL SECURITY ACT PROVIDES GRANTS
FOR DEPENDENT CHILDREN

Category of event: Children's rights
Time: August 14, 1935
Locale: Washington, D.C.

The provision in the Social Security Act of 1935 for federal grants to the states for Aid to Dependent Children established what would become the largest, and most controversial, United States welfare program

Principal personages:
> THEODORE ROOSEVELT (1858-1919), the twenty-sixth president of the United States (1901-1909), who spurred interest in government financial assistance to needy families
> FRANKLIN D. ROOSEVELT (1882-1945), the thirty-second president of the United States (1933-1945)
> GRACE ABBOTT (1878-1939), the head of the United States Children's Bureau (1921-1934)
> JANE M. HOEY (1892-1968), a former social worker who served as head of the Bureau of Public Assistance
> WILBUR J. COHEN (1913-1987), a former staff member of the Committee on Economic Security and then a top administrator with the Social Security Board
> JOHN W. GARDNER (1912-   ), the founder and former chair of the public-interest lobbying organization Common Cause and the secretary of health, education and welfare (1965-1968)
> RICHARD M. NIXON (1913-   ), the thirty-seventh president of the United States (1969-1974); proposed, in 1969, a Family Assistance Plan to overhaul the welfare system

Summary of Event

In June, 1934, President Franklin D. Roosevelt appointed a cabinet-level Committee on Economic Security to draw up plans for national social insurance. The committee's recommendations became the basis for the Social Security Act that Roosevelt signed into law on August 14, 1935. Although the focus of contemporary attention was upon the provisions for old-age and unemployment insurance, the act established so-called "categorical assistance" programs of federal government grants to the states for assistance to the needy over age sixty-five, the blind, and dependent children. The inclusion of the provision for Aid to Dependent Children (ADC) was primarily a result of behind-the-scenes lobbying by reformers associated with the United States Children's Bureau, under the leadership of former bureau head Grace

Abbott, who was a member of the Advisory Council of the Committee on Economic Security. The legislation provided $1 of federal money for every $1 spent by the states for the needy aged and blind, but only $1 for every $2 spent by the states for aid to dependent children. The act provided that the federal government would match a maximum of $15 of state money per month for the needy aged (for a total of $30), and would match a maximum of $12 of state money for the first child (for a total of $18) and $8 of state money for each additional child (for a total of $12). This disparity between the treatment of the needy aged and dependent children was partly a result of the political clout of the old-age lobby and partly a matter of accident. The $1-for-$2 formula for ADC was taken from an existing federal program to aid the widows and dependent children of servicemen who had lost their lives in World War I. That program had included an additional "caretaker" grant for widows. Hasty drafting, however, resulted in the inadvertent omission of such a provision in the Social Security Act.

The ADC provision of the Social Security Act of 1935 grew out of the earlier movement for so-called "mothers' pensions" that had been sparked by President Theodore Roosevelt's 1909 Conference on the Care of Dependent Children. Illinois took the lead in 1911 by adopting a law authorizing local juvenile courts to aid needy children in their own homes. By 1935, only two states—Georgia and South Carolina—had failed to adopt similar legislation. All of the states were permissive, however, simply allowing localities to establish programs. Recipients had to undergo a means test. Most important, the laws restricted assistance to "fit" mothers. Since mothers who had been deserted or divorced or had given birth to illegitimate children were excluded in many places, mothers' pensions were limited almost exclusively to poor widows. Few, even of those, received substantial benefits. In 1931, only 93,620 of the 3.8 million female-headed families in the United States received assistance. The average monthly family grant ranged from $4.33 in Arkansas to $69.31 in Massachusetts. The minimum standards for ADC laid down in the Social Security Act involved an advance over most of the state mothers'-pension plans. The aid had to be given in cash, not in kind or in institutions. State-residency requirements for eligibility were limited to five years, and local-residence requirements were prohibited. The program had to be operated throughout a state, although money grants could vary among localities within a state on the assumption that costs of living varied. Jane M. Hoey, a former social worker who headed the Bureau of Public Assistance within the Social Security Board (later Administration) from its establishment until 1953, was aggressive in demanding state and federal compliance with the federal regulations. She pushed—with some success—for the improved training of case workers, controls upon the size of caseloads, and safeguards against corruption and political manipulation.

Adoption of the new program led to an immediate jump in the number of beneficiaries. In 1935-1936, only three hundred thousand dependent children were receiving assistance. By 1939, ADC was aiding seven hundred thousand. Perhaps most important, the matching-grant approach had the advantage of protecting ADC from yearly battles for congressional appropriations. Liberals still found many shortcomings in the program. States were not required to participate in ADC, and as late as 1938 eight still did not. Even in those states that did participate, many eligible children were left outside the program. An estimated two-thirds or more of the children eligible in 1940 remained uncovered. Benefits varied widely from state to state. As first drafted, the legislation included a requirement that states receiving federal matching grants provide "reasonable subsistence compatible with decency and health." Southern lawmakers alarmed at the threat of federal government intrusion upsetting local racial practices, however, joined with fiscal conservatives worried about the cost to amend the provision to allow the states to fund the categorical assistance programs "as far as practicable under the conditions in such states." ADC payments in 1939 ranged from an average of $8.10 per family a month in Arkansas to a high of $61.07 in Massachusetts. The national average in 1940 was only $32.10 per month for an assisted family. The result was that many mothers were forced to find jobs outside the home. When they did, their earnings were subtracted, dollar for dollar, from their ADC checks.

The years after 1935 saw incremental tinkering with ADC (renamed in the 1960's Aid to Families with Dependent Children, or AFDC). In 1939, Congress extended the $1 of federal money for each $1 of state money formula to ADC. In 1946, the maximum monthly payment subject to federal matching was increased from $18 to $24 for the first child and from $12 to $15 for each additional child. In 1950, the lawmakers voted to give "caretaker" grants to mothers in addition to the grants for their children. In 1958, Congress revised the matching formula by adopting a partial sliding scale that provided for more generous federal contributions to states with low per-capita incomes. In 1961, Congress authorized federal matching grants to states to pay ADC benefits to two-parent families in which the father was either out of work or employed for fewer than one hundred hours a month. (Since this program was not mandatory for states, as of 1988 only twenty-eight states had opted to participate.) The Medicaid legislation of 1965 included a provision for the federal government to pay between 50 and 85 percent (for the poorest states) of the costs for medical care for members of poor families with dependent children. In 1967, Congress approved the Work Incentive Program (WIN) to encourage AFDC mothers to find jobs. The new "thirty plus one-third" rule allowed AFDC recipients to keep without any deduction in their welfare checks the first $30 per month from work plus one-third of any amount above $30. Accompanying rules (called by liberals "workfare") allowed states to drop from the AFDC rolls parents and children over age sixteen who refused "without good cause" to participate in work or training programs.

As the number of persons receiving ADC benefits rose to more than three million by 1960, the growing cost spurred a backlash. The political vulnerability of ADC was heightened when amendments to the Social Security Act from 1939 on placed more and more widows under the Old Age and Survivors Insurance (OASI) program. ADC thus increasingly went to divorced, deserted, and unwed mothers (many of whom were black), spurring loud complaints about subsidizing the undeserving and immoral. Many states took advantage of the local autonomy permitted in the administration of the program to impose stringent income and property qualifications, to establish lengthy residence requirements, to deny aid to families with "employable" mothers, or to restrict ADC to families with a "suitable home" (typically interpreted as a home with no illegitimate children). The most prevalent restriction was the so-called "man-in-the-home" rule barring aid to children whose father (or any other employable male) was living in or visiting the home; many states and localities sent agents out on raids to catch men spending the night in homes receiving aid. What liberals saw as the worst flaw was the low level of benefits. Nearly all the states set their target levels for benefit payments below the official federal poverty line, and approximately two-thirds failed to appropriate sufficient funds even to meet their own standards. In 1966, the average national payment per AFDC recipient was $36 per month, or $1,728 per year for a family of four, compared with the official poverty line for a nonfarm family of four of $3,355.

Impact of Event

The 1960's witnessed a revolution in the American welfare system. Its most striking manifestation was the quantum growth in the number of persons on AFDC—from 3.1 million in 1960 to 10.8 million in 1971. One factor in this jump was the continuing migration out of the rural South to Northern cities, where AFDC payments were more generous and easier to obtain. Another was the acceleration of the worsening instability among lower-class families that had been gaining momentum since the late 1940's. Perhaps the most alarming sign of this larger problem of family breakdown was the sharp jump that took place in the illegitimacy rate.

What appears to have been the most important single factor in the growth of the AFDC rolls, however, was the increase in the percentage of those eligible applying for benefits, from an estimated 33 percent in the early 1960's to 90 percent in 1971. Much of this increase resulted from heightened militancy on the part of the poor, spurred by the new expectations generated by prosperity, the Civil Rights movement, and the rhetoric accompanying President Lyndon B. Johnson's war against poverty. Another contributor was litigation by welfare-rights activists and public-interest lawyers that resulted in Supreme Court decisions striking down state man-in-the-home rules that had effectively denied AFDC benefits to mothers having sexual relationships (*King v. Smith*, 1968), invalidating state-residency requirements (*Shapiro v. Thompson*, 1969), and requiring welfare agencies to give a hearing meeting "minimal due process standards" before stopping benefits (*Goldberg v. Kelly*, 1970). A major role was also played by pressure from the federal welfare bureaucracy for more generous policies. Starting in 1961, the Bureau of Public Assistance (and its successor from 1962 on, the Bureau of Family Services) began cracking down on the rules and restrictions adopted by state and local welfare officials that used such rules as a way of keeping their AFDC costs down. A key figure behind this policy was Wilbur J. Cohen. Cohen became an influential adviser on welfare matters to Presidents John F. Kennedy and Lyndon B. Johnson and served as secretary of the Department of Health, Education and Welfare (HEW). John W. Gardner, the founder and former chair of the public-interest lobbying organization Common Cause and the secretary of HEW from 1965 to 1968, was the second key figure in making the federal welfare bureaucracy an aggressive force for maximizing benefits and coverage.

Conservatives, along with much of the public at large, were upset and alarmed by the rapidly escalating costs of AFDC. Critics were particularly upset by intergenerational poverty, with the daughters and granddaughters of AFDC recipients becoming in turn welfare mothers, and by how many AFDC recipients, when in-kind benefits such as Medicaid and food stamps were taken into account, ended up better off than large numbers of the so-called "working poor." On the other side, liberals continued to complain about the wide variation in benefit payments among the states. In response to this growing chorus of complaints, President Richard M. Nixon proposed in 1969 a Family Assistance Plan (FAP) that represented the most ambitious attempt to overhaul the welfare system since its 1935 establishment. The FAP would have guaranteed all families with children a minimum of $500 per adult and $300 per child a year, or $1,600 for a two-parent family of four. A poor family, as an incentive to work, could keep the first $60 per month of earned income without loss of any government benefits and half the income above that, up to defined maximums. The proposed floor of $1,600 was higher than the AFDC levels in eight Southern states; more important, the plan would have assisted a large number of the working poor with children who were not on AFDC. After a bitter fight, however, the FAP went down to defeat in 1972 in the face of attacks from welfare rights activists who demanded a higher floor, from liberals hostile to the requirement that recipients accept "suitable" work or training, and from conservatives alarmed by the cost.

The defeat of the FAP brought a halt (at least temporarily) to further progress toward a national floor under incomes. The House of Representatives approved in 1979 a measure to set a nationwide minimum for AFDC payments at 65 percent of the official poverty line and to require all states to give AFDC to two-parent families with an unemployed or underemployed father. The bill died in the Senate. The political atmosphere during the presidency of Ronald Reagan (1981-1989) was not favorable to any significant new initiatives or increased spending in the welfare area. By the late 1970's, inflation was beginning to reduce the real value of AFDC benefits. Between 1970 and 1985, the median value of AFDC benefits declined by approximately one-third in real terms. Those years simultaneously witnessed an increasing feminization of poverty. In 1960, women headed 24 percent of all poor households; in 1984 they headed 48 percent of all poor households (including 73 percent of poor black families). The number of poor female-headed families increased over this period from 1.9 million to 3.5 million. There took place an accompanying sharp increase in the proportion of children living in poverty between 1979 and 1982—from 18 to 24 percent of children under age six and from 16 to 21 percent of six- to seventeen-year-olds. The result has been a growing agitation for more federal spending to aid poor children.

Bibliography

Bell, Winifred. *Aid to Dependent Children.* New York: Columbia University Press, 1965. A comprehensive history of assistance to dependent children that examines the mothers'-pension movement, congressional action from 1935 on, and the administration of the ADC program. The work, however, was finished before the tremendous expansion of the AFDC rolls in the later 1960's.

Burke, Vincent J., and Vee Burke. *Nixon's Good Deed: Welfare Reform.* New York: Columbia University Press, 1974. An insightful account of the defeat of President Richard M. Nixon's Family Assistance Plan, the most ambitious proposal to be considered seriously as an overhaul of the existing AFDC system.

Grønbjerg, Kirsten A. *Mass Society and the Extension of Welfare, 1960-1970.* Chicago: University of Chicago Press, 1977. A detailed analysis of the explosive growth during the 1960's of the number of persons on welfare in the United States. The author's explanation emphasizes the importance of the emergence of a broadened conception of citizenship that included a guarantee of a minimum level of subsistence.

Katz, Michael B. *The Undeserving Poor: From the War on Poverty to the War on Welfare.* New York: Pantheon Books, 1989. An exaggerated indictment against what the author sees as a retreat to more niggardly attitudes toward and treatment of the poor since the late 1960's.

Muncy, Robyn. *Creating a Female Dominion in American Reform, 1890-1935.* New York: Oxford University Press, 1991. An excellent study of the network of women reformers, centered around the Children's Bureau, that played a leading role in shaping governmental policy toward children from the turn of the century to the 1930's.

Patterson, James T. *America's Struggle Against Poverty, 1900-1980.* Cambridge, Mass.: Harvard University Press, 1981. A handy, comprehensive survey of the development of the American welfare state focusing on the years since 1930. The major emphasis is on the "changing perspectives, especially of reformers, toward poverty and welfare" and their impact upon "public policy." Like most writers on the topic, Patterson takes a liberal, prowelfare perspective.

Ross, Heather L., and Isabel V. Sawhill. *Time of Transition: The Growth of Families Headed by Women.* Washington, D.C.: Urban Institute, 1975. A landmark study documenting the rapid growth in female-headed households and exploring the reasons for that growth.

Steiner, Gilbert Y., and Pauline H. Milius. *The Children's Cause.* Washington, D.C.: Brookings Institution, 1976. A comprehensive examination of the full range of federal government programs that have been adopted over the years to assist children, especially poor children.

Witte, Edwin E. *The Development of the Social Security Act.* Madison: University of Wisconsin Press, 1962. An invaluable insider's account of the planning for, drafting, and adoption of the Social Security Act of 1935 by the executive director of the Committee on Economic Security.

John Braeman

Cross-References

The Children's Bureau Is Founded (1912), p. 131; Franklin D. Roosevelt Appoints Perkins as Secretary of Labor (1933), p. 486; Social Security Act Establishes Benefits for Nonworking People (1935), p. 514; The United Nations Children's Fund Is Established (1946), p. 689; The United Nations Adopts the Declaration of the Rights of the Child (1959), p. 1038; Head Start Is Established (1965), p. 1284; The United Nations Adopts the Convention on the Rights of the Child (1989), p. 2529.

CONSUMERS UNION OF THE UNITED STATES EMERGES

Category of event: Consumers' rights
Time: January-March, 1936
Locale: New York, New York

After industrialization, buyers and sellers were no longer neighbors or acquaintances; Consumers Union arose to fill the need for tests, standards, and guarantees to protect all consumers

Principal personages:

ARTHUR KALLET (1902-1972), the first director of Consumers Union
COLSTON WARNE (1900-1987), the first president of Consumers Union
DEWEY PALMER (1898-1971), the first technical supervisor of Consumers Union
FREDERICK J. SCHLINK (1891-   ), a coauthor of *Your Money's Worth* (1927), cofounder of Consumers' Research, and unwitting catalyst for the beginning of Consumers Union
STUART CHASE (1888-1985), a coauthor of *Your Money's Worth* and cofounder of Consumers' Research, the predecessor of Consumers Union

Summary of Event

Before the Industrial Revolution, producers and purchasers of food, clothing, and other items were usually neighbors, friends, or even members of the same family. With the rise of factories, however, many common items were no longer produced locally. Instead, they were made by strangers, often in faraway places. The quality of these items varied greatly.

Not only were familiar items such as soap, shirts, and wagon wheels made by machine, but there was also an increasing variety of new products available, with various claims made for them that might or might not prove to be true. The use of electricity brought many electrical appliances onto the market: light bulbs, toasters, hair-curling devices, and more.

There were two ways that consumers could try to judge the quality of a product before purchasing it: by brand name and by advertising. A brand name such as Standard Oil, Armour Meat, or Heinz Soup would be put on many products by companies that made them to try to guide consumers to buy all a company's products if they found that one of them was reliable. Even the most well-known brands, however, often were made under unsanitary conditions or with questionable or inferior ingredients. In many cases, there was no quality control to ensure that the products were not defective.

Advertising became an important tool of producers. Advertisers attempted to create a desire for a product in the public's awareness by promising certain results from using it or by getting endorsements of the products from well-known people—movie stars for beauty products or doctors for medicines. Often these claims either were untrue or were unsupportable by facts. Another problem was the lack of standardization of items. Not only was quality not guaranteed, but sizes, weights, and measures of items also varied, even with products made by the same manufacturer.

The attitude of many businesses about these problems was *caveat emptor*: "Let the buyer beware." The responsibility was left with the buyer to purchase the right product; if a purchaser got a faulty product, it was not considered to be the producer's problem.

In 1927, a book called *Your Money's Worth* became a best-seller within months after it appeared. The authors were Frederick Schlink, an engineer, and Stuart Chase, an economist. The book pointed out serious problems experienced by consumers as they tried to guess their way through the maze of products and advertising. Consumers were "so many Alices in the Wonderland of salesmanship." Shortweighting, quackery, mislabeling, and uselessness were pointed out, with specific products as examples. Scientific testing was proposed by the authors to be the antidote to Wonderland; they noted that the U.S. government had already begun to do testing and to set standards and specifications for products used by the government.

In response to the hundreds of letters they received requesting information about products, Chase and Schlink began Consumers' Research of New York City. Previously a neighborhood consumer club formed by Schlink, it had done its own home testing and produced a mimeographed list of products—"good values" versus products to avoid—called "Consumer's Club Commodity List."

The mimeographed list became *Consumers' Research Bulletin*. It took no financial support of any kind from producers or advertisers and was the first magazine to be established solely to test products for consumers' benefit. Five years after it began, the bulletin had 42,000 subscribers, compared to 565 subscribers in 1927, its first year. Schlink and Chase, with the help of other scientists and writers, published an array of pamphlets, books, and articles in addition to their bulletin. One of these, a book published in 1935 called *100,000,000 Guinea Pigs: Dangers in Everyday Foods, Drugs, and Cosmetics*, was a tremendous success; it inspired a wave of investigative writing about consumer-oriented topics.

100,000,000 Guinea Pigs was written by Schlink with Arthur Kallet, a young engineer who was also on the board of Consumers' Research. Stuart Chase had left Consumers' Research to pursue other interests. Frederick Schlink was at the helm, with a staff of more than fifty as well as a large number of outside consultants. With the growth in size of the staff, there were differences of opinion about the direction the organization should take. This was especially true of decisions about spending. Should resources be used primarily for educating consumers, for political purposes, or for improving the testing program?

In May, 1933, the organization moved into a large stone building in Washington, New Jersey. In Washington, a small town a hundred miles outside New York City, Schlink hoped to be able to expand his testing facilities. He was also drawn to the location because of the lower costs; he believed that people who were seriously interested in the consumer movement would come with him. In fact, however, only six of the seventy employees moved from New York to New Jersey with Schlink, and Schlink, his wife, and close friends became the majority on the board of directors.

Schlink tried to stay in complete control of the organization. He had a difficult time working with anyone who held differing ideas about what Consumers' Research should try to accomplish, and he fired many people who disagreed with him. He also believed that it was a privilege for employees to work for Consumers' Research and so rejected their appeals for higher wages or shorter working hours. When three employees tried to form a labor union in order to improve working conditions, they were fired. Forty other employees then left their jobs in support of them.

Although thousands of workers across the country were also on strike during that time, the strike at Consumers' Research was particularly significant. Consumers' Research had a stated goal of upgrading the lives of consumers; the irony of its own workers having to strike for better conditions was considered humorous by the popular press. Liberal leaders were concerned and offered to help workers and management reach a compromise, but Schlink would accept no such offers. Instead, he used the same strikebreaking tactics as the big corporations—legal injunctions, strikebreakers, and armed detectives. The fifty-five thousand subscribers to the *Consumers' Research Bulletin* were caught in the middle of the ruckus.

Arthur Kallet, who had coauthored *100,000,000 Guinea Pigs* with Schlink, had been a rather inactive member of the Consumers' Research board of directors. When the strike began, however, he resigned from the board and supported the workers. As 1935 wore on with no end to the strike in sight, he helped to keep the strikers together. The idea began growing among them to start a publication of their own, in competition with *Consumers' Research Bulletin*. The group planned to use its many contacts, financial and academic, with unions, researchers, and sympathetic *Bulletin* subscribers to help with its initial efforts. The new publication would support the interests of both consumers and workers. The organization itself would be run collectively, rather than by a management team.

By March, 1936, New York State had given Consumers Union its charter as a nonprofit organization. The first issue of *Consumers Union Reports* magazine was published in May of that year. Three years later, it was known simply as *Consumer Reports* and had gained a larger number of subscribers than *Consumers' Research Bulletin*.

The director of the new organization was Arthur Kallet. Dewey Palmer, formerly technical director of Consumers' Research, became the technical supervisor. Colston Warne, a professor at Amherst College, was made president and served in that role for the next forty-four years.

Impact of Event

When it began, Consumers Union was considered to be a pioneer in the consumer movement. Colston Warne later reported: "The idea of testing and appraising products by name constituted an overdue scientific mechanism designed to restore rationality to the marketplace." This idea, he stated, was "nothing less than a social invention."

To the original four thousand members of Consumers Union, the organization was not only a guide to making better consumer decisions, but also "an *approach* to the choices and problems of our materialistic world," as one charter member wrote fifty years later. Consumers Union's reports helped to bring about improvements in specific products, such as certain electric fans that it reported in 1956 to have dangerously exposed blades. Poor sales of product brands that received bad ratings in *Consumer Reports* caused manufacturers to correct the products' problems. On the other hand, a good product rating in *Consumer Reports* was found by businesspeople to boost sales of an item. Volkswagen cars and Maytag washers both received superior ratings, which spokespeople credited for their tremendous increases in sales.

Consumers Union staff members were at first politically active, doing labor movement picketing, testifying at governmental hearings, and having promotional drives for the poor. Product testing suffered, however, as a result of this focus. Ultimately, it was decided by the board that the testing should not be sacrificed; the scientific rating program was at the foundation of Consumers Union's existence.

Thus, in December, 1939, a joint conference was arranged by Kallet and Warne between the members of Consumers Union and the Cambridge-Boston branch of the American Association of Scientific Workers (AASW) to gain support for Consumers Union among scientists. The conference resulted in AASW's offering to provide advice and assistance not only to Consumers Union but also to consumer organizations in general.

In 1986, its fiftieth anniversary year, Consumers Union reported that it had over the years helped many additional consumer organizations get started. These included the American Council on Consumer Interests, the Emergency Care Research Institute, the Washington Center for the Study of Services, the Consumer Federation of America, the Center for Auto Safety, the International Organization of Consumers Unions, and the British Consumers' Association.

In addition to aiding other consumer groups, Consumers Union directly affected the lives of many Americans by conducting research that led to reforms or legislation in the areas of fallout from nuclear testing, risks of smoking, and automobile safety. It also did pioneering research on air pollution's cost to consumers, unhealthy additives and chemicals in foods, and pesticide dangers in the food chain. During the 1960's and 1970's, these became important issues for reforms.

The original goals of Consumers Union were to provide scientific information about products and to report on the labor conditions under which those products were produced, with the idea of achieving a decent standard of living for all consumers. For the first several years, the labor situation was included in the discussions of products but not in the actual criteria for product ratings. As time went on, the labor analysis was dropped in favor of emphasis on objective scientific testing.

Although the second goal has thus not been pursued as aggressively as the first one, *Consumer Reports* has over the years appealed for food stamps for the poor, demanded fairer tax laws, argued against harsh methods of debt collecting, pushed for national health insurance, and urged provision of "lifeline" banking services and utility rates. Achieving a decent standard of living for all Americans has continued to be a major goal of Consumers Union as it has carried on its strong tradition of providing reliable product information for consumers.

Bibliography

Bishop, James, Jr., and Henry W. Hubbard. *Let the Seller Beware.* Washington, D.C.: National Press, 1969. A lively and informative history of the consumer movement from the 1800's to the 1960's. The book is full of specific examples of consumer problems and the people who attacked them and, in many cases, eventually won legislation to correct them. It is an optimistic look at trends in the consumer movement. Includes an index.

Consumers Union. "50 Years Ago." *Consumer Reports* 51 (January/February, 1986): 8-10, 76-79. On the occasion of its fiftieth anniversary, Consumers Union included this two-part narrative in consecutive issues of *Consumer Reports.* A detailed summary of events leading to, and following, the founding of Consumers Union. Provides a summary of many of its activities and achievements up to 1986.

Nadel, Mark V. *The Politics of Consumer Protection.* Indianapolis: Bobbs-Merrill, 1971. This study looks at governmental policies relating to consumer protection and analyzes the reasons they developed. Includes historical information from the early twentieth century and discussions of Ralph Nader and other consumer advocates of the 1960's. Contains tables, an index, and an extensive list of references.

Olson, Mancur. *The Logic of Collective Action: Public Goods and the Theory of Groups.* Cambridge, Mass.: Harvard University Press, 1965. This scholarly text looks at various types of groups and their interactions. Chapters on labor unions and pressure groups provide an overview of the history and role in society of unions and collective action groups, including the period during which Consumers Union began. Includes an index and footnotes.

Reid, Margaret G. *Consumers and the Market.* New York: F. S. Crofts, 1938. Written at the approximate time of Consumers Union's origin, this book is a fascinating summary of the problems then facing consumers in areas of labeling, quality, advertising, price-setting, and others, with specific examples and historical references. Many tables illustrate clearly the points Reid makes. An appendix and an index are included.

Ryan, Edward W. *In the Words of Adam Smith: The First Consumer Advocate.* Sun Lakes, Ariz.: Thomas Horton and Daughters, 1990. An easily read presentation of the ideas of Adam Smith, the "father of modern economics." Smith's clear prose includes some of the earliest statements of consumer advocacy. The book consists mainly of passages from Smith's nine-hundred-page treatise *An Inquiry into the Nature and Causes of the Wealth of Nations* (1776), with connecting and explanatory comments by Ryan. Includes an index and a bibliography.

Silber, Norman Isaac. *Test and Protest: The Influence of Consumers Union.* New

York: Holmes & Meier, 1983. Silber's work provides the most thorough coverage of the sources listed here. He discusses in detail the origin of Consumers Union and the conditions that led to its formation, in addition to coverage of specific Consumers Union research projects, their impact, and Consumers Union's evolution since its origin. Notes, bibliography, appendix, and an index are included.

Caroline Godwin Larson

Cross-References

The Pure Food and Drug Act and Meat Inspection Act Become Law (1906), p. 64; The International Organization of Consumers Unions Is Founded (1960), p. 1062; Nader Publishes *Unsafe at Any Speed* (1965), p. 1267; The Motor Vehicle Air Pollution Control Act Is Passed by Congress (1965), p. 1310; Congress Passes the Occupational Safety and Health Act (1970), p. 1585; The World Health Organization Adopts a Code on Breast-Milk Substitutes (1981), p. 2130; New York State Imposes the First Mandatory Seat-Belt Law (1984), p. 2220; Manville Offers $2.5 Billion to Victims of Asbestos Dust (1985), p. 2274.

CORPORATISM COMES TO PARAGUAY AND THE AMERICAS

Category of event: Civil rights
Time: February 17, 1936
Locale: Asunción, Paraguay

A regime came to power in Paraguay that offered a program with recognizably corporate elements

Principal personages:

RAFAEL FRANCO (1896-1973), the leader of the Febrerista Party and president in 1936 and 1937

CARLOS ANTONIO LÓPEZ (1792-1862), the president of Paraguay from 1844 to 1862 and father of Francisco Solano López

FRANCISCO SOLANO LÓPEZ (1827-1870), the president of Paraguay from 1862 to 1870

JOSÉ GASPAR RODRÍGUEZ DE FRANCIA (1766-1840), the supreme dictator of Paraguay from 1814 to 1840

JOSÉ FÉLIX ESTIGARRIBIA (1888-1940), a hero of the Chaco War, ambassador to the United States, and president in 1939 and 1940

HIGINIO MORÍNIGO (1897-   ), a Paraguayan military leader and president from 1940 to 1948

JUAN STEFANICH (1889-   ), a politician, journalist, novelist, and essayist whose writings provided the ideological base for the Febrerista Party

BERNARDINO CABALLERO (1839-1912), the founder of the Associación Nacional Repúblicana (Colorado Party) and president from 1880 to 1886

ALFREDO STROESSNER (1912-   ), a hero of the Chaco War and president from 1954 to 1989

Summary of Event

Colonel Rafael Franco's takeover of the Paraguayan government on February 17, 1936, was a response to Paraguay's long history of dictatorial regimes and disregard for the needs of the peasant class. Franco and his Febrerista party represented themselves as nationalist socialists ready to introduce democratic reforms. Franco's military coup can best be understood as a step in the turbulent progression of Paraguayan politics.

Paraguay emerged as an independent nation in 1811 as an isolated buffer state separating Argentina and Brazil. Paraguay at that time was under the despotic control of one man and continued to have essentially one-man rule until the last decade of the twentieth century. José Gaspar Rodríguez de Francia (El Supremo) was not only the author of Paraguayan independence but also the one to establish the parameters of Paraguayan politics. Francia became indispensable to the governing of the state, so that no reasonable alternative to his rule existed. Those few individuals who dared to suggest otherwise found themselves in prison or the cemetery.

Francia focused the nation's resources upon the creation and maintenance of a strong army to defend the borders of his hermit kingdom. The state drafted not only the manpower of the nation but also its economy. The peasants worked as sharecroppers on land leased from the state, state-controlled industries supplied the military and civilian markets, and production and trade were closely regulated. Francia's policies brought a considerable measure of prosperity to Paraguay but also denied the people the most elemental political freedoms.

El Supremo designated no political heir, but ultimately Carlos Antonio López seized control in 1844, after a period of political chaos following Francia's death in 1840. The political autocracy and state socialism initiated by Francia continued, but López did moderate the rigor of the regime. After the death of Carlos Antonio López in 1862, the government of Paraguay was entrusted to his son, Francisco Solano López.

The character and intentions of the younger López remain a subject of historical controversy. He is variously viewed as a barbaric egomaniac who sacrificed his countrymen in pursuit of grandiose schemes and as the quintessential patriot who bravely fell in battle against foreign imperialism. If the true Solano López is obscure, the consequences of the war he presided over, and was killed in, are not subject to dispute. The end of the War of the Triple Alliance (1864-1870) found more than half the population of Paraguay dead and the economy in ruins. The struggle between Brazil and Argentina for regional supremacy that almost destroyed Paraguay also allowed Paraguay to avoid absorption. Moreover, the government imposed by Brazil and Argentina was, within a short time, overthrown by Bernardino Caballero's successful appeal to antiforeign sentiments engendered by the postwar occupation.

Unfortunately, General Caballero inherited an empty treasury from his predecessors. He saw little choice but to continue the sale of the extensive state enterprises begun by the occupation governments. Foreign corporations established feudal enclaves (*latifundios*) throughout the nation and subjected the peasantry to merciless exploitation. Thus, the prospects, albeit tantalizingly brief, of a broadly based representative political system which surfaced at the end of the war vanished without a trace.

The Chaco War, a boundary dispute with Bolivia, lasted three bloody years (1932-1935), diverted enormous amounts of manpower and resources from Paraguay's economy, and caused significant numbers of casualties. Although the peace treaty confirmed Paraguay's control of twenty thousand square miles of the Chaco, the "victory" cost the nation two dead per square mile, a casualty rate that many Paraguayans attributed to the failure of the Paraguayan government to prepare adequately for war.

The government was further indicted for its inability to sponsor meaningful reforms in the structure of Paraguayan society. Land reform was first on the list of demands, followed by improvements in the standard of living, the public welfare services, and working conditions, and the reform of an educational system that was probably the poorest in Latin America. As was the case throughout most of Latin America in the period before World War II, the landowning aristocracy reaped the benefits of governmental power and the middle class was largely nonexistent. Paraguay, in short, was in need of renovation and redemption, if not revolution.

Colonel Rafael Franco, a prominent figure in the Chaco War, led a group within the Paraguayan military in a coup that took place on February 17, 1936. Once in power, the revolutionaries deemed it necessary to present themselves as more than simply another *junta* of discontented officers. Therefore, the nation was informed that Paraguay would return to the nationalistic socialism of the Francia-López era, with democratic overtones added. A serious attempt to encourage the growth of small and medium-sized land holdings was undertaken. In addition, regional agricultural schools, agricultural experiment farms, and a bank for low-cost agricultural loans were proposed. Equally as important, a labor department was created and a moderately progressive labor code was promulgated.

The official goal of the revolution was a "natural democracy" of peasants and workers, a regime that would identify and utilize the best parts of individualistic democracy, corporatism, and socialism so as to provide benefits to the whole of the Paraguayan people. Colonel Franco repeatedly indicated his opposition to the total transplantation of any foreign system to Paraguay. His Mussolini-type speeches from a balcony in Asunción, however, led some to characterize his government as the first manifestation of fascism in Latin America.

The ideological hero of many in the new regime was Juan Stefanich. Stefanich found little appeal in either laissez-faire capitalism or Marxist socialism. He saw the former as at fault for the worldwide depression and the latter as leading inexorably to a totalitarian state along the Soviet model. Thus, in common with others in countries as diverse as Portugal, Ireland, and Italy in the same period, Stefanich sought salvation in what he termed *democracia solidarista*, which may best be described as an attempt to organize the state along corporate models and thereby accord power to professional and occupational groups.

Stefanich espoused corporatism, but the Franco regime remained a mixture of political and ideological opposites. These diverse elements (corporatism, socialism, and traditional political partisanship) struggled for control of a revolution which came to power without a central theme. This internal conflict assisted those who supported a counterrevolution. Therefore, the Febreristas, as supporters of Colonel Franco were later named, were replaced on August 15, 1937, by a group who gave only lip service to the new governmental programs.

The Febreristas were overthrown for several reasons. They promised land and better social conditions but were unable to undertake anything more than symbolic implementation. Labor was "liberated" through the creation of the National Department of Labor, which defined labor's rights and privileges. There was only enough time, however, for strikes and turmoil, not the requisite negotiations between the workers and management. A decree authorizing the expropriation of land was promulgated, but the land reform program was only a beginning and was not continued by the new regime.

Effective land reform, indeed reform of almost any kind, would be difficult as long as the country was dominated by foreign capital in league with an upper class wedded to the status quo. Despite the renewed power of the old order, the promises of the Febreristas continued to attract support, a circumstance which explains the emergence of José Félix Estigarribia. General Estigarribia, a hero of the Chaco War, ran for and won the presidency in 1939. He was a popular candidate whose speeches indicated a decided preference for many of the Febrerista ideas.

Impact of Event

Most Latin Americans insist that unity, not diversity, is key to political success. Latin American governments eschew attempts to balance competing centers of power and attempt to integrate or eliminate them in the name of collective harmony. The idea that two competing ideologies might barter or negotiate for anything less than total victory is anathema.

Paraguay found itself with two vastly different concepts of legitimate government, the Francia-López tradition of autocratic state socialism and the democratic free enterprise liberalism of the postwar decades. Febrerismo attempted to fuse these opposing principles by recourse to corporatism. The objective of the Febreristas was not a totalitarian state but a "perfected" democratic regime. The state was not to serve as a policeman but rather to regulate and defend society. The state must intervene to solve political, social, and economic problems. Moreover, national interests must take precedence over individual interests. Thus, *democracia solidarista* differed from totalitarianism in that the latter places the state first and fits individuals into a pattern that subordinates their liberties and even denies them. The Febreristas, however, recognized individual liberties and tried to reconcile them with collective or group rights.

The Febrerista experiment was cut short, but the pressure for reform remained undiminished. Thus, the new Estigarribia government scrapped the Constitution of 1870 and replaced it with a new instrument approved by plebiscite on August 4, 1940. The new constitution envisaged a powerful chief executive assisted by an advisory council composed of representatives from business, banking, the church, education, the government, agriculture, processing industries, and the military. The council was designed to oversee an "orderly democracy." The government had extensive powers to intervene in the economy. Furthermore, the president might declare a state of siege and thereby acquire virtual dictatorial powers.

Corporatism fell into disrepute at the end of World War II, as it was often confused with fascism. The latter, however, involves a leadership principle, a mass political party, and an aggressive foreign policy that are not characteristic of the former. Colonel Franco and those elected in accord with the Constitution of 1940 might resemble the fascist dictators of the prewar decades, but they owed more to

Francia and the Lópezes than to Hitler or Mussolini.

For the most part, Latin America adheres to a political framework in which ideological accord is revered. Nevertheless, some Latin American governments rule in the name of the whole by integrating diverse interests. Others govern in the name of a privileged part of that whole by excluding or eliminating representatives of the less privileged. The government of Paraguay, despite its corporate pretensions, adhered more to the latter than to the former.

Bibliography

Kolinski, Charles J. *Historical Dictionary of Paraguay.* Metuchen, N.J.: Scarecrow Press, 1973. The only reference work of this type on the subject of Paraguay. It is not encyclopedic in its coverage, but it does contain a useful multilingual bibliography.

—————. *Independence or Death: The Story of the Paraguayan War.* Gainesville: University of Florida Press, 1965. The only work in English on this important event in the history of Paraguay. Essential to any understanding of the country's political history or prospects for the future.

Lewis, Paul. *Paraguay Under Stroessner.* Chapel Hill: University of North Carolina Press, 1980. Although this monograph is primarily concerned with a political analysis of the Stroessner regime, the author is not unmindful of the impressive influence of the past with respect to the conduct of affairs in contemporary Paraguay.

—————. *The Politics of Exile.* Chapel Hill: University of North Carolina Press, 1965. This work attempts a behavioral analysis of the Febrerista party's organization. This work, the only one in English on the topic, analyzes the workings of the party, its ideology, its formal organization, and the pattern of relationships among the leaders.

Rouguié, Alain. *The Military and the State in Latin America.* Berkeley: University of California Press, 1987. This comparative analysis places Paraguay within the context of the entire continent.

Warren, Harris G. *Paraguay: An Informal History.* Norman: University of Oklahoma Press, 1949. The seminal work in English on the subject. The bibliographic essay is basic.

—————. "Political Aspects of the Paraguayan Revolution, 1936-1940." *Hispanic American Historical Review* 30 (February, 1950): 2-25. This is the only historical treatment of this event in English. It is heavily footnoted and invaluable, although dated.

Zook, David H. *The Conduct of the Chaco War.* New York: Bookman Associates, 1960. The definitive English monograph on a conflict that influenced twentieth century Paraguay to the same degree as the War of the Triple Alliance affected the previous century.

J. K. Sweeney

Cross-References

Hitler Writes *Mein Kampf* (1924), p. 389; Mussolini Seizes Dictatorial Powers in Italy (1925), p. 395; Perón Creates a Populist Political Alliance in Argentina (1946), p. 673; Spain Is Denied Entrance into the United Nations (1946), p. 695; A Greek Coup Leads to a Military Dictatorship (1967), p. 1359; Brazil Begins a Period of Intense Repression (1968), p. 1468; An Oppressive Military Rule Comes to Democratic Uruguay (1973), p. 1715; Allende Is Overthrown in a Chilean Military Coup (1973), p. 1725.

GREAT EVENTS
FROM
HISTORY II

CHRONOLOGICAL LIST OF EVENTS

VOLUME I

VOLUME II

VOLUME III

VOLUME IV

VOLUME V